Presidents and the American Presidency

Presidents and the American Presidency

SECOND EDITION

LORI COX HAN
Chapman University

DIANE J. HEITH
St. John's University

New York   Oxford

OXFORD UNIVERSITY PRESS

Oxford University Press is a department of the University of Oxford. It furthers the University's
objective of excellence in research, scholarship, and education by publishing worldwide. Oxford is a
registered trademark of Oxford University Press in the UK and certain other countries.

Published in the United States of America by Oxford University Press
198 Madison Avenue, New York, NY 10016, United States of America.

Library of Congress Cataloging-in-Publication Data
Names: Han, Lori Cox, author. | Heith, Diane J., author.
Title: Presidents and the American presidency / Lori Cox Han, Chapman
   University, Diane J. Heith, St. John's University.
Description: Second edition. | New York, NY : Oxford University Press, 2017.
Identifiers: LCCN 2017009777 | ISBN 9780190611460 (paperback)
Subjects: LCSH: Presidents—United States—History. | Political
   leadership—United States—History. | BISAC: POLITICAL SCIENCE /
   Government / Executive Branch.
Classification: LCC E176.1 .H265 2017 | DDC 973.09/9 [B]—dc23
LC record available at https://lccn.loc.gov/2017009777

9 8 7 6 5 4 3 2 1
Printed by Webcom, Inc. in Canada.

To the memory of our advisors and mentors on the American presidency,
William W. Lammers, University of Southern California,
and
Elmer E. Cornwell Jr., Brown University

BRIEF CONTENTS

CONTENTS

PREFACE

Perhaps the most common debate among presidency scholars centers on the question of how best to study both the presidency as a political institution and those who have held the office. In developing this textbook, we wanted to provide a comprehensive text that combined both approaches by including contemporary issues surrounding presidents as individual leaders as well as the institutional perspectives and evolution of the office. Our goal was to focus on the "real" presidency, that is, to provide a unique perspective and analysis that explains exactly what a president does on a day-to-day basis and how the political and institutional environment affects the daily governing outcome. We also wanted to incorporate what we consider an underutilized resource on the presidency for undergraduate students, which are the millions of archival documents available at presidential libraries. We have both conducted extensive research at presidential libraries across the country (to date, all 13 libraries from Herbert Hoover through George W. Bush) and know firsthand the significance and richness of the many memos, letters, and oral histories available to scholars and journalists alike. These documents add a personal knowledge and perspective of what actually happened behind the scenes in the White House and help to explain the strategic and decision-making processes of presidents during the past century. As a result, we believe that these documents add an important pedagogical tool for an instructor's use at the undergraduate level.

We have also incorporated our own experiences in teaching the presidency into the presentation of the topics throughout the text. We are both faculty members at universities (Chapman University and St. John's University, respectively) that value classroom instruction as much as faculty scholarship. The presidency is, for both of us, not only our major field of expertise, but also a favorite course that we both teach regularly. We have learned over the years what works when attempting to engage students beyond a cursory and fleeting knowledge of the material in an attempt to prepare for an exam. We share a pedagogical approach to teaching this course that provides students with a deeper understanding of the presidency as an institution and its importance within the constitutional framework of the American government. Specifically, we consider the leadership qualities of the men who have held the office and why that matters for their ultimate success or failure, and, from a broader perspective, why it is important to develop critical thinking and analytical skills when studying American government. The former two issues serve to pique many students' interest in the subject, whereas the latter helps students to become more informed citizens.

The plan of the book is straightforward; we cover all of the important subjects necessary to gain a comprehensive understanding of the topic within a semester/ quarter-long course on presidents and the presidency. Chapter 1 provides an introductory discussion on the historical context, theories and methodologies, and sources that are all part of the study of presidents and the presidency. Chapter 2 analyzes the presidency within the framework of the U.S. Constitution and how the various interpretations of presidential powers since the founding era have shaped the office and the decisions made by its occupants. Chapters 3, 4, and 5 consider the public connection of presidents and the presidency to the American electorate—presidential campaigns and elections, presidential communication strategies, the president's relationship with the news media, and public opinion. Chapters 6, 7, and 8 consider the institutional aspects of the office in how presidents interact and manage their relationships with Congress, the federal courts, and the executive branch. Finally, Chapters 9 and 10 cover the important topics of presidential domestic and foreign policymaking and the role that presidents play in the development and implementation of policy outcomes.

Along the way, we also incorporate numerous archival documents to highlight key issues; some show the seriousness and gravity of the decisions that presidents face while in office, while others provide an interesting and sometimes light-hearted view of the real governing process in the White House and how partisan concerns can also play a role. In each chapter, we also provide three features: "Then and Now," "In Their Own Words," and "Researching the Presidency." "Then and Now" takes a specific issue and compares a more historical approach to a more contemporary view to analyze how presidents have dealt with certain challenges while in office. For example, "Then and Now" in Chapter 2 considers the political implications of the presidential power to pardon. "In Their Own Words" highlights one archival document that helps to illustrate a specific topic of each chapter. For example, in Chapter 10, we highlight a letter from General Lauris Norstad to President John F. Kennedy about the global political implications following the Cuban Missile Crisis.

In the second edition we have added a new feature entitled, "Researching the Presidency," which provides a brief look at new and innovative empirical research on the presidency. For example, in Chapter 7 we look at research on how presidents talk publicly about Supreme Court decisions. Also new to the second edition is the "Selected Bibliography," which contains some of the most important works (both historical and contemporary) on the presidency. We have also included an updated list of online resources for each chapter.

We have many people to thank for their contributions to both the first and the second editions of this book. First, we are truly grateful for the guidance and patience of our editor at Oxford University Press, Jennifer Carpenter, who provided encouragement, guidance, and deadlines when needed. The entire editorial team at Oxford University Press remains amazingly helpful. We are indebted to the many reviewers who took time out of their busy schedules to give helpful feedback on individual chapters as well as the manuscript as a whole. Your insight, critiques, and expertise were truly appreciated. We also appreciate all of the help from archivists at each presidential library in the National Archives and Records Administration system; your wealth of knowledge has been invaluable over the years. We are also grateful for the many colleagues we have had the pleasure to work with throughout our careers who share our passion for researching and teaching the presidency. Our involvement in the Presidents and Executive Politics section of the American Political Science Association (formerly the Presidency Research Group) has enriched our professional lives on many levels. We also consider ourselves blessed to have studied with some of the best researchers of the American presidency, who helped to set us on our own paths as presidency scholars. At the undergraduate level, we took courses with Larry Berman at the University of California, Davis, and Theodore Lowi at Cornell University, respectively. And it is to our graduate advisors, the late Bill Lammers at the University of Southern California and the late Elmer Cornwell at Brown University, respectively, that we dedicate this book.

Lori Cox Han also thanks her husband, Tom Han, and children, Taylor NyBlom and Davis Han, for their continued support, inspiration, and unconditional love. In addition, several people at Chapman University deserve recognition, including Gordon Babst, Chuck Hughes, Drew Moshier, Lisa Sparks, John Compton, Jennifer Keene, Greg Daddis, Bob Slayton, and Erin Berthon, all of whom make Chapman a better place to work. Two amazing research assistants and political science majors, Brianna Pressey and Kyle Koeller, provided essential help with updates for this second edition. Finally, a special thanks goes to Patrick Fuery, dean of Wilkinson College, and Daniele Struppa, president of Chapman University, for providing support, financial and otherwise, for this book and many other research endeavors.

Diane Heith also thanks her husband, Stephen Kline, and her son, Owen, for their love and support. Rosalyn and Elliott Heith also provided much needed support and assistance, which were essential components for finishing a project like this one. Several people at St. John's University made it possible to work on this project while also serving as department chair: Laura Schramm, Meg O'Sullivan, and Patricia Bittner. They deserve much gratitude for all their help.

Finally, the many students over the years who have taken our respective presidency courses at Chapman, Austin College, and St. John's (and even the very first courses at the University of California, Los Angeles, and Brown University) deserve thanks for their contributions to this final product.

TABLES AND FIGURES

Presidents and the
American Presidency

CHAPTER 1

Introduction: Studying Presidents and the Presidency

A t 9:45 a.m. on Wednesday, April 27, 2011, Barack Obama entered the White House press room to make a seemingly routine statement to members of the press. Although presidents for decades have made similar announcements on any number of issues to White House reporters, this particular announcement was unique. The purpose of Obama's statement was not to announce a personnel change to his staff, a judicial nomination, or a policy initiative. Instead, Obama announced the release of his "long-form" birth certificate from the state of Hawaii. The release of the much-discussed birth certificate was an attempt by the Obama administration to finally put to rest the rumors, first begun during the 2008 presidential campaign, that Obama had not been born in the United States (a constitutional requirement to hold the office of president). The so-called birther movement, with much help from the press, had continued to demand proof that Obama was a bona fide citizen of the United States and that he had not been born in Kenya, the homeland of his father. The short-form birth certificate from Hawaii (which earned its statehood in 1959, two years prior to Obama's birth in Honolulu), released during Obama's presidential campaign, had not satisfied the small group of conspiracy theorists, headed by then–potential Republican presidential candidate Donald Trump, who were convinced that Obama had something to hide.

In the much-heralded release of the long-form birth certificate, Obama summed up his frustration over what he called a political distraction compared to more serious policy issues, like the economy, that needed his attention:

But we're not going to be able to do it if we are distracted. We're not going to be able to do it if we spend time vilifying each other. We're not going to be able to do it if we just make stuff up and pretend that facts are not facts. We're not going to be able to solve our problems if we get distracted by sideshows and carnival barkers. I know that there's going to be a segment of people for which, no matter what we put out, this issue will not be put to rest. But I'm speaking to the vast majority of the American people, as well as to the press. We do not have time for this kind of silliness. We've got better stuff to do. I've got better stuff to do. We've got big problems to solve. And I'm confident we can solve them, but we're going to have to focus on them—not on this.[1]

However, this story continued to make headlines, off and on, for the next five years, including a reversal in September 2016 by Trump, who went on that same year to become the Republican presidential nominee, that Obama, indeed, had been born in the United States.

Obama's schedule during that week in 2011 shows how the president's job is filled with both policy and political concerns. Obama and his wife Michelle traveled to Chicago after the birth certificate press briefing to tape an episode of the *Oprah Winfrey Show* before ending the day in New York at a Democratic Party fundraiser. The following day, Obama held meetings with his national security team over the ongoing situation in Libya, met with Hispanic leaders from across the nation about immigration reform, and also met and held a joint press conference with Panamanian president Ricardo Martinelli. On Friday, the First Family traveled to Alabama to meet with local officials and to survey the damage from the devastating tornadoes earlier in the week. Then, the Obamas traveled to Cape Canaveral, Florida, to view the launch of the space shuttle *Endeavor*, and Obama ended that day with a commencement address at Miami Dade College before returning to the White House. Then, Saturday evening, Obama appeared at the White House Correspondents' Dinner, an annual event where presidents (and a guest comedian) roast Washington reporters. While at the Correspondents' Dinner, Obama and his advisors knew that a major story was potentially unfolding halfway around the world; the next evening, on Sunday, May 1, Obama announced that Osama bin Laden had been killed in Pakistan by a special-operations team of U.S. Navy Seals.

Although the killing of bin Laden, the al Qaeda leader who planned and orchestrated the 9/11 terrorist attacks, was an extraordinary event for the Obama administration, the other activities during those few days exemplify the complexities of the contemporary presidency. The president must serve as both the head of state and head of government; his public and political activities, as well as his duties as commander in chief of the armed forces, represent only a few of the many responsibilities that go along with the job title "President of the United States." On any given day, a president may order military actions, oversee and direct major policy initiatives implemented by the executive branch, hold a press conference or give interviews to members of the press, hold a state dinner at the White House for a visiting dignitary, veto a congressional bill, nominate a federal judge or ambassador, or make a political appearance on behalf of other members of his party or for his own reelection. Presidents must also contend with political distractions in the media-driven, hyperpartisan environment that is Washington. Whereas members of Congress may have opportunities to develop policy expertise by serving on or chairing particular committees and whereas Supreme Court justices are experts of U.S. constitutional law, the president must be all things to all Americans—politically, constitutionally, and symbolically. As such, presidents and their staffs must be able to multitask while juggling the variety of demands placed on the nation's chief executive. As Obama himself stated to *60 Minutes* in his first interview after the killing of bin Laden, "The presidency requires you to do more than one thing at a time."[2]

The American presidency is a unique political position, both from the institutional nature of the job and from the many ways that an individual president can shape the office itself. This book considers both American presidents and the presidency, that is, those who have held the position and the institutional structure of the office within the executive branch of government. We examine the strengths and weaknesses of both the presidency as a political institution and recent presidents and their leadership skills. However, we seek to examine the "real" presidency, that is, not just the theoretical analysis of the institution or assessments of the individuals who have served as president, but also the day-to-day responsibilities and challenges that go with the job. In the following chapters, we showcase the real aspects of the presidency, as well as the differences between individual and institutional perspectives on decision making. Toward that goal, we incorporate archival documents from multiple administrations to reveal the inner workings of the White House. The documents and oral histories at presidential libraries and other archives around the country represent a virtual treasure trove of detailed analysis and stories of what actually happened, not only publicly but also behind the scenes, in each administration. It is through inter- and intraoffice memos among the president and his closest advisors that governing strategies are developed and policy decisions are made, and it is through oral histories of administration officials that candid assessments are offered regarding the successes and failures of each presidency. We rely on these documents to allow a president and/or members of the administration, through their own words, to animate the discussions in each chapter from the perspective of political actors who were present to understand and appreciate the depth and breadth of presidential power and leadership.

HISTORICAL CONTEXT

The president of the United States is easily the most recognizable political figure to any American citizen and, globally, one of the most powerful leaders in the world. As a political institution, the American presidency has long been a fascinating case study of the powers and intricacies of the office because it defies comparison to anything before or since. To date, 44 individuals have held the office of the presidency, and although each served his country with varying degrees of success, the presidency as an institution remains a focal point of political power, both nationally and internationally. Yet, only minor changes related to the presidency have been adopted in the U.S. Constitution since its ratification in 1789. The essential characteristics of the American presidency are as recognizable today as they were more than 200 years ago. However, the presidency of the eighteenth century outlined by the framers seems weak compared to the powers that emerged by the twenty-first century. The American presidency is one of the most resilient political institutions ever developed, enduring numerous wars (not the least of which was the Civil War from 1861 to 1865), scandals (such as Watergate, which led to Richard Nixon's resignation from office in 1974), economic turbulence (such as the Great Depression following the stock market crash in 1929), and even assassinations (four presidents have been killed by an assassin's bullet, including Abraham Lincoln in 1865, James Garfield in 1881, William McKinley in 1901, and John F. Kennedy in 1963). Still, the powers of the office, along with the governing strategies of each individual president, have varied at different times because of different circumstances (political and otherwise). In general, the history of the presidency can be divided into three principal eras: the traditional presidency, the modern presidency, and the postmodern/contemporary presidency.[3]

The Traditional Presidency

This era includes presidents from the late eighteenth century until the turn of the twentieth century, and with a few notable exceptions, most of these men were not particularly memorable. During this era, the presidency was not the grand political prize that it is considered today, and many early politicians did not aspire to hold the office. The presidency offered modest prestige, narrow authority, and meager resources; in fact, governors of prominent states, such as New York, Massachusetts, and Virginia, wielded more political power. Although presidents during the early years of the republic were honored and respected for their public service and political contributions prior to 1789, they occupied an office that was unassuming and limited with respect to national defense and foreign policy. This is what the framers of the Constitution had intended, which left presidents for the most part passive participants in the policymaking process. As a result, throughout the nineteenth century, most presidents merely carried out the laws passed by Congress, which assumed the role of the dominant policymaking branch.

The four most memorable administrations during the traditional era include George Washington (1789–1797), Thomas Jefferson (1801–1809), Andrew Jackson (1829–1837), and Abraham Lincoln (1861–1865), all of whom are "towering exceptions" during an era when presidential powers remained modest and limited.[4] Washington, as the first to hold the office, set many precedents and shaped the model of presidential leadership for generations to come. Jefferson, as the author of the Declaration of Independence and one of the most prominent among the founding fathers, is remembered for articulating his beliefs in republicanism and a limited national government. Yet, he pushed the constitutional boundaries of presidential powers with his decision to use military force against the Barbary Pirates in 1801 and with his purchase of the Louisiana Territory in 1803 (he did not consult Congress on either decision). Jackson became the first "common man" to hold the presidency and rose to power as both grass-roots politics and political parties became prominent electoral fixtures as voting rights were expanded beyond land-owning elites. Lincoln, considered by some scholars and many Americans the greatest president, held the nation together during the Civil War, yet is also known for expanding presidential powers by relying on extraconstitutional and/or unconstitutional measures in doing so (including the suspension of habeas corpus).

The Modern Presidency

The expansion of presidential powers, particularly in regard to shaping the national agenda, waging wars, and connecting with the American public, did not become

Abraham Lincoln is often considered the greatest U.S. president because of his leadership during the Civil War.

a regular and expected feature of the presidency until the twentieth century. The development of the modern presidency, including the powers of the office and the large bureaucracy of the executive branch, reshaped the office. Of the three branches, the executive branch has moved farthest from its origins and least resembles the intent of its framers. According to presidential scholar Louis Koenig, Theodore Roosevelt (1901–1909) and Woodrow Wilson (1921–1929) were the modern presidency's "architects, as asserters of bold undertakings in domestic and foreign affairs, as gifted mobilizers of public opinion, as inducers of congressional concurrence."[5] Then, with the election of Franklin D. Roosevelt (FDR) in 1932, a new political era began that included a dramatic expansion of the federal government in both size and power. FDR (1933–1945) brought several important changes that solidified the modern presidency: enhanced presidential staff resources, a greater presidential role in policymaking, a stronger relationship with the mass public, and a greater presence in the realm of international relationships. FDR's presidency yielded new understandings of the modern presidency, focusing on increased expectations for presidential action and the increased capacity to pursue presidential leadership.[6]

FDR's New Deal, as well as America's involvement in World War II, began what would be an era of expansive growth in domestic and foreign powers of both the presidency and the executive branch. During this time, the presidency eclipsed Congress and even political parties as the "leading instrument of popular rule."[7] Harry Truman (1945–1953) and Dwight Eisenhower (1953–1961) would also preside over the continued influence of the presidency as the lead actor in domestic and international affairs, in part because of the growth of the U.S. economy and the continuing Cold War. Similarly, the public aspects of the office, along with the public's expectation for strong leadership, continued to expand, particularly with the presidency of John F. Kennedy (1961–1963) and his administration's successful use of television. This era is also marked by the strength and dominance of the United States as a global and economic superpower, which allowed presidents to pursue extensive policy agendas both at home (such as Lyndon Johnson's Great Society and the War on Poverty during the 1960s) and abroad (containing the spread of communism as part of America's Cold War strategy). Yet, the failure of U.S. containment policy during the protracted Vietnam War would call into question the powers of the modern presidency; both Johnson (1963–1969) and Richard Nixon (1969–1974) would be labeled "imperial" presidents for their actions in Vietnam and for Nixon's involvement in and eventual resignation resulting from Watergate.[8]

The Postmodern/Contemporary Presidency

Following the Vietnam War and Watergate, the powers of the modern presidency were diminished as resources necessary for a president to wield power fell "well short of the tasks he is expected to perform and the challenges to be faced."[9] According to some scholars, the American presidency had entered a new, "postmodern" phase.[10] Although differences exist in the exact definition of postmodern as applied to the American presidency, most acknowledge that changes had occurred to create what can be called a more "contemporary" presidency. For example, by the 1980s, presidents were no longer able to pursue big domestic political agendas; divided government became more common (with the White House controlled by one political party and at least one house of Congress controlled by the other), and with a spiraling national debt and increasing budget deficits, the president had much less room to shape the domestic agenda through the creation of new federal programs like those during the New Deal and Great Society. Instead, Ronald Reagan's (1981–1989) electoral success and popularity were based in part on his promise to reduce the size of the federal government. In addition, with the end of the Cold War by the end of the 1980s, presidents had lost power in the international arena. Cooperation in what George H. W. Bush (1989–1993) called "the new world order" became more important than protecting the United States from the spread of communism and the imminent threat of a nuclear war with the Soviet Union. Yet, George W. Bush (2001–2009) reasserted power with military actions in both Afghanistan and Iraq based on the belief that the United States must preempt and prevent potential threats to national security (known as the Bush Doctrine).

Other trends have contributed to this postmodern/contemporary presidency, including the way in which Americans select their presidents; the political skills necessary for a candidate to succeed on the campaign trail are different from those needed to handle the complex domestic, economic, and global demands of the job.[11] The challenges faced by Bill Clinton (1993–2001), George W. Bush, and Barack Obama (2009–2017) represent both the increased powers and the diminished capacities of governing that have evolved in recent decades. In the post-9/11 era, the War on Terror may have helped to expand presidential powers in some areas, yet the Bush and Obama administrations also faced trying economic circumstances that severely limited presidential powers over the policymaking agenda. In addition, presidents must now contend with a political environment dominated by hyperpartisanship and fueled by unyielding yet fragmented news media coverage.

Although the president today may still be the "focal point of public life," the reality is that "presidents are seldom in command and usually must negotiate with others to achieve their goals."[12]

THEORIES AND METHODOLOGIES

Although presidential studies itself is considered a subfield within the discipline of political science, specific areas within presidential studies have also emerged as part of the growing literature on both presidents and the presidency. One way to categorize different theories or methodologies associated with the study of the presidency is to simply ask whether the approach is "president centered" (aspects of the individual holding office at a particular time) or "presidency centered" (the institutional aspects of the office and/or the executive branch). More specifically, the president-centered approach can include exploring the informal power structure within the White House and its impact on presidential leadership, considering the behaviors of presidents through a psychoanalytic approach, or analyzing a president's leadership style through the public aspects of the office. The presidency-centered approach can include studies focusing on the formal powers of the executive office, presidential/congressional relations, or the executive branch as a political institution. In the presidency-centered approach, scholars focus their attention in an effort to better understand (and sometimes predict the actions of) the president, his staff, and other relevant political actors within the executive branch. In addition, interdisciplinary research on the presidency has merged the growing literature in political science with that of psychology, history, communication, economics, and sociology, among others. As a result, both the quality and quantity of research devoted to the presidency continue to grow and evolve.

Classics in Presidential Studies

The first study of the presidency as a social and political institution was the 1825 publication of *The Presidency of the United States* by Augustus B. Woodward, whose work included five categories of study: the man, public politics, Washington politics, executive politics, and didactic reviews (attempts to synthesize the other categories and draw lessons from the presidency).[13] During the twentieth century, as the discipline of political science expanded, so, too, did the study of the presidency. During the 1940s and 1950s, prominent works on the presidency focused mostly on the constitutional powers of the office and other interpretive works that provided descriptive analysis of the White House and its occupants. For example, Edward S. Corwin, in his classic *The President: Office and Powers* (first published in 1940), analyzed the framers' intent regarding presidential powers as an "invitation to struggle" between the presidency and Congress, particularly regarding matters of foreign policy. Perhaps the most quoted line of Corwin's work suggests that the powers of the presidency can be defined by the man who holds the office: "Taken by and large, the history of the presidency is a history of aggrandizement, but the story is a highly discontinuous one. . . . That is to say, what the presidency is at any particular moment depends in important measure on who is President."[14] Similarly, Clinton Rossiter's *The American Presidency*, first published in 1956, explores the evolution of presidential powers and the president's many roles as chief of state, chief executive, commander in chief, and chief diplomat, among others. Through his interpretive and historical analysis, Rossiter concluded, "The President is not one kind of official during one part of the day, another kind during another part—administrator in the morning, legislator at lunch, king in the afternoon, commander before dinner, and politician at odd moments that come his weary way. He is all these things all the time, and any one of his functions feeds upon and into all the others."[15]

In 1960, one of the most quoted books of all time on the presidency was published—*Presidential Power* by Richard Neustadt. A former advisor to President Truman, Neustadt was one of the first political scientists to recognize that personality, character, and political skill were important in the development of presidential leadership. According to Neustadt, power is found in the president's ability to bargain and persuade. Neustadt defined power as personal influence on governmental action, which is separate from the formal powers outlined by the Constitution. He argued that there is great weakness in the presidency, mainly present in the gap between public expectations and the actual capabilities for leadership. Neustadt sought to better understand "personal power and its politics: what it is, how to get it, how to keep it, how to use it." Neustadt had a pessimistic view of the presidency, in that the president must stand alone and rely on his own political skills to get things done. Others within the system have competing agendas, and only the president himself can wield influence to achieve his goals. As such, the theme of Neustadt's work is presidential weakness, since the president needs more than his formal constitutional powers to achieve policy results. The president shares powers, so he must bargain with others within government out of need. Despite his formal powers, real presidential power is the power to persuade, making the president a clerk with five constituencies: executive officials who need guidance, Congress who needs an outside agenda, partisans who need a record to run on in the next election, citizens who need a symbol to complain to or seek aid from, and foreign countries where U.S. policies play a role. In the end, a successful president is one who knows how to harness his power and use it wisely, especially when juggling the responsibilities from these five constituencies. A fine balance must be struck between a man who is hungry enough to seek power, yet not abuse it. In Neustadt's view, FDR represented presidential leadership at its finest.[16]

IN THEIR OWN WORDS

LEADERSHIP

Presidents, like presidency scholars, have long been interested in the notion of "leadership." The following unsigned memorandum from 1928, an attempt to define leadership, is among the personal papers of Franklin D. Roosevelt at his presidential library:

MEMORANDUM

There is no magic in Democracy that does away with the need of leadership.

The danger in our Democracy lies in our tendency to select leaders who are similar to the rank and file of us, whereas the hope of Democracy seems to lie in our selecting leaders who are superior to the rank and file of us.

Should we hunt for leaders who will lead us, or for leaders who will follow us?

Should we look for leaders who will always think like us, or for leaders who will sometimes think for us?

Should we elect men to office because they promise to vote for certain measures, or because we can trust their minds and their morals to guide them alright on measures in general once all the facts are before them?

Shall leaders be human substitutes for their constituents or phonograph records of the fluctuating moods of their constituents?

No man of authentic greatness of mind and character will purchase political position at the price of adjourning his own intelligence and becoming the errand boy of either Main Street or of Wall Street.

We have today side by side an old political order fashioned by a pastoral civilization and a new social order fashioned by a technical civilization. The two are maladjusted. Their creative inter-relation is one of the big tasks ahead of American leadership.[17]

Newer Methodologies Evolve

Political scientists would not significantly expand methodological perspectives in presidency research for another two decades. The shift to bring the subfield more in line with the disciplinary rigor of political science got its start in 1977 when political scientist Hugh Heclo published a report on the state of research devoted to the presidency. Heclo concluded that although the topic itself was "probably already overwritten," there existed "immense gaps and deficiencies" stemming from a lack of empirical research and too much attention paid to topics such as presidential power, personalities, and decision making during a crisis.[18] At the time, many studies were devoted to the more recent presidencies of Eisenhower, Kennedy, Johnson, and Nixon, along with more contemporary political topics such as the Cold War, the Cuban Missile Crisis, the Vietnam War, and Watergate. As a result, Heclo argued that the field of presidential studies needed more reliance on primary documents, a better understanding of how the presidency works day to day (to help it perform better), and a broader, more interdisciplinary approach.[19] Despite several "well-intentioned publications" on the presidency, Heclo concluded, "considering the amount of such writing in relation to the base of original empirical research behind it, the field is as shallow as it is luxuriant. To a great extent, presidential studies have coasted on the reputations of a few rightfully respected classics on the Presidency and on secondary literature and anecdotes produced by former participants. We still have remarkably little substantiated information on how the modern office of the President actually works."[20]

By the early 1980s, presidency scholars began reassessing the trends of their research, and as a result, many began to bemoan the state of their "underdeveloped subfield."[21] Along with the classics on presidential power and personalities, presidential research until that point also tended to focus on a "political-actor perspective" that centered on the question of determining "how presidents differed in their decisions." This president-centered approach often relied on descriptive analyses or anecdotal comparisons between presidents and suffered from what many referred to as the infamous "$n = 1$" syndrome, meaning that presidents provided small data sets from which to conduct studies befitting the methodologically rigorous standards of social science research practices.[22]

In 1983, presidential scholars George C. Edwards III and Stephen J. Wayne published *Studying the Presidency*, in which they argued that more "theoretically sophisticated and empirically relevant" work was necessary to expand the presidency literature to keep pace with the "phenomenal growth of the presidency: the expansion of its powers, the enlargement of its staff, the evolution of its processes."[23] Problems in studying the presidency had traditionally stemmed from the general unavailability of data, the lack of measurable (particularly quantitative) indicators, and the absence of theory, all of which "impede the collection and analysis of data, thereby discouraging empirical research." Specific problems included the fact that operational and institutional aspects of the presidency were usually shrouded in secrecy, presidential documents can remain closed for years if not decades, primary source material is not always readily available, interviews with administration officials can be biased and incomplete, and high-profile journalists are more likely to gain access than most scholars. Given that, little about the presidency had lent itself to quantitative and comparative study, other than public opinion, voting studies, and legislative scorecards.[24] The authors also suggested that presidency scholars should develop newer methodologies more in line with scientific approaches found within social science generally and political science specifically, including legal perspectives (sources and uses of presidential powers); institutional perspectives (analysis of the workings of government); roles and responsibilities (understanding presidential actions within the institutional setting); structure and process (how the president/presidency function, operate, and interact with other political actors/institutions); political perspectives (power orientation and decision making); and psychological perspectives (analyzing personalities of individual presidents).[25]

The President-Centered Approach

Many presidency scholars have maintained an emphasis on presidential leadership and its importance in understanding the role of the president in both policymaking and governing, yet at the same time began to change the direction of research by relying on a broader theoretical perspective and including extensive data for comparative analysis. Many still rely on Neustadt's *Presidential Power* for at least a starting point, while also recognizing the limitations that an individual president can face in effecting political change.[26] Leadership, particularly in the political context, has a variety of definitions and is considered a malleable term, but in general it is defined as a process involving influence that occurs in groups and includes attention to goals; attention is also paid to the individual traits of the leader, his or her behavior, patterns of interacting, and relationships with others.[27] Although no clear standard has yet to emerge, many scholars have provided useful insights as to what makes a president successful as a leader, as well as which presidents have failed and why. As Bert Rockman states, the study of presidential leadership is both fascinating and complex in that presidents may vary in temperaments, but all are confronted with similar pressures while in office—"it is the manipulable factor in a sea of largely nonmanipulable forces."[28]

One of the most widely recognized theories of leadership is the work of James MacGregor Burns, who introduced the idea of transformational leadership in the late 1970s.[29] For Burns, leadership is more than just the act of wielding power; it involves the relationship between leaders and followers. Transactional leadership refers to what most leaders are able to accomplish—the day-to-day exchanges between leaders and followers that have come to be expected. Transformational leadership, in contrast, provides more than just a simple change in the political process. A transformational leader provides broader changes to the entire political system that raise the level of motivation and morality in both the leader and the follower. As Burns states, "transforming leaders define public values that embrace the supreme and enduring principles of a people."[30] Similarly, Bruce Miroff defines five presidents as "icons of democracy" (John Adams, Abraham Lincoln, Theodore Roosevelt, FDR, and John F. Kennedy) as American leaders who fostered the American democratic ideal.[31] Miroff argues that successful democratic leaders respect their followers, are committed to the notion of self-government, and nurture the possibilities of civic engagement through a public dialogue, all of which are necessary for true political leadership.[32]

Although many studies of presidential leadership can still be traced back to Neustadt's view that modern presidential power equates the ability to bargain and persuade,[33] other important works have redefined, modified, and/or expanded the notion of presidential leadership to encompass various views of presidents and the presidency, including the president as a transformational leader as well as the state of the postmodern/contemporary presidency.[34] Other topics contributing to the growing literature on presidential leadership consider changes in the political environment,[35] the institutionalization of and leadership within the executive branch,[36] policymaking and the president's relationship with Congress,[37] and the public presidency and changes in White House communication strategies.[38]

Seeking to better understand the effect of a president's personality on his administration's successes and failures, along with the notion of "presidential greatness," represents another line of inquiry among those scholars interested in the president-centered approach. Americans expect their presidents to be the epitome of political leadership, and several presidents come to mind when thinking about presidential greatness, including George Washington, Thomas Jefferson, Abraham Lincoln, Theodore Roosevelt, FDR, or Ronald Reagan.[39] However, although some presidents have moments of great leadership, few have been great leaders. According to Thomas E. Cronin and Michael A. Genovese, three important aspects of presidential leadership must be understood: political time (different types of leadership are necessary for different circumstances); political vision (a strong presidential vision can energize the nation and achieve political power); and political skill (personality can make a difference in presidential leadership, and under certain circumstances the right individual can make a difference, but not all presidents can succeed in a given situation).[40]

Leadership style and presidential personality can also be determining factors in the success or failure of a president's tenure in office. According to Fred Greenstein, the presidential "difference," that is, determining the effect that a president can have on the many facets of his administration and of the presidency itself, can be best understood by considering the following factors: public communication skills, organizational capacity, political skill, policy vision, cognitive style, and emotional intelligence.[41] James David Barber's work on presidential character is best known for its categorization based on psychology and personality types: levels of activity as either active or passive and affect (or feelings) toward activity as either positive or negative, which point to a president's deeper layers of personality and how that will determine his success or failure.[42] Although other presidency scholars have criticized Barber's approach as being too narrow to offer a consistent analysis across presidencies, given that reducing "personality to a handful of types ignores the complexity of human motivation," the fact that the first edition of Barber's work was published during the Nixon administration gave the work high prominence because Nixon provided a fascinating case study of presidential leadership through a psychological/political lens.[43]

Public leadership—that is, the art and skill of communication on the public stage—has gained increasing significance in terms of understanding the more general notion of presidential leadership. The importance of public leadership to effective governance is perhaps most pronounced when viewing that of a president. In its political context, public leadership can be defined simply as the ability of a public official to use the public component of a political office to accomplish a specific task, goal, or agenda item. As such, the end result of public leadership can be something as specific and tangible as the passage of a new law or the start of a government initiative or something as broad based and intangible as rhetoric that motivates, inspires, or comforts the masses. However, at either extreme, public leadership skills matter and play a large role in allowing a public official to accomplish his or her political goals.[44]

As such, the public presidency and presidential communications have also emerged as important fields of inquiry. According to Jeffrey Tulis, the framers were suspicious of a popular leader and/or demagogue in the office of the presidency, since such a person might rely on tyrannical means of governing.[45] However, the presidency experienced a fundamental transformation by becoming a "rhetorical presidency" during the early part of the twentieth century, causing an institutional dilemma. By fulfilling popular functions and serving the nation through mass appeal, the presidency has now greatly deviated from the original constitutional intentions of the framers, removing the buffer that the framers established between citizens and their representatives.[46] Roderick Hart also argues that the rhetorical presidency is a twentieth-century creation and a constitutional aberration. The president not only is a popular leader vested with unconstitutional powers, but also uses rhetoric as a "tool of barter rather than a means of informing or challenging a citizenry."[47]

According to Samuel Kernell, presidents of the modern era have utilized public support by "going public," a style of presidential leadership where the president sells his programs directly to the American people. Going public is contradictory to some views of democratic theory, but is now practiced by presidents as a result of a weakened party system, split-ticket voting, divided government, increased power of interest groups, and the growth of mass communication systems.[48] More recent scholarship has expanded on and even questioned Kernell's theory of going public. George C. Edwards III argues that presidents are not always successful in changing public opinion on certain issues by simply giving a major speech or engaging in other public activities.[49] And, according to Jeffrey Cohen, the polarization of political parties and the growth and fragmentation of media sources have forced presidents to develop innovative public strategies to target key constituencies, which is a dramatic shift from the more simplified view of going public to a national constituency as first argued by Kernell in the 1980s.[50]

The Presidency-Centered Approach

On the other end of the methodological spectrum are those scholars who support the institutional approach to studying the presidency, arguing that it is the institution itself that shapes both presidential behavior and political outcomes. According to this view, the presidency became greatly institutionalized and politicized during the twentieth century, leaving the president out of the loop, so to speak, and mostly irrelevant as an individual in much of the decision-making processes. As a result, scholars should not waste time on understanding the role of presidential leadership, but should instead rely on a rational choice model of presidential theory building.[51] For example, Terry Moe explains that presidents have considerable resources and strategies at their disposal to meet expectations for leadership. The ambiguity of the Constitution in relation to presidential power offers presidents important structural advantages over Congress and other political actors. Congress, for example, cannot match the resources of the executive branch in terms of expertise, experience, and information. The president can also act unilaterally in some instances, and therefore act more swiftly and decisively, than Congress. To avoid the need for bargaining, presidents can ensure that appointees within the executive branch are loyal to him (similar to political patronage) and can also centralize decision making within the White House to increase his own power (policy decisions and implementation, such as through executive orders).[52] Other studies have offered substantive quantitative approaches to better understand specific aspects of the presidency as an institution, including unilateral actions by presidents,[53] public appeals,[54] presidential control of the bureaucracy,[55] and war powers[56] (to name a few).

A more historical approach known as "new institutionalism" suggests the need to look beyond institutions to also include an analysis of the ideas and people that influence those institutions.[57] In his book *The Politics Presidents Make*, Stephen Skowronek provides a theory of "political time" by offering a cyclical explanation of presidential power, dependent on the political time during which a president serves. When a president takes office, the political environment that he encounters is in part a result of the actions of his predecessors as well as recent national and world events. Therefore, the president's circumstances, or the political time in which he finds himself in office, will determine how much authority he has to achieve political change. According to Skowronek, there are four distinct phases of political time: reconstruction, articulation, disjunction, and preemption. Each phase depends on the status of the ruling political order and the president's relationship to that order. Four presidents who are considered our greatest were reconstruction presidents— Thomas Jefferson, Andrew Jackson, Abraham Lincoln, and FDR—an opponent of the vulnerable ruling political order. Each was elected to office as a result of sweeping political change; that is, their respective elections represented a major political defeat to the opposing political party. Articulation describes a resilient ruling order of which the president is an ally. Lyndon Johnson's election in 1964 is a good example because the Democratic Party held a strong majority in the Congress when Johnson was elected in his own right following his succession to office in 1963 after Kennedy's assassination. Disjunction represents a vulnerable ruling order of which the president is an ally. For example, both Herbert Hoover and Jimmy Carter were elected at a time when their parties controlled Congress, yet each became a one-term president because the policies of their parties became unpopular with voters. Finally, preemption represents a president who is an opponent of a resilient ruling order. Richard Nixon provides a good example because he was elected in 1968 despite Democrats maintaining a strong majority in Congress.[58]

Researching the Presidency

History

The title "presidency scholar" can be somewhat generic because it does not denote the disciplinary expertise of the author. Although scholars in many fields can study aspects of the presidency, most presidency scholars are either political scientists or historians. The basic difference between the two can be found in their methodologies or, more simply, in the questions asked. A recent issue of *Presidential Studies Quarterly* was devoted to historical research on the presidency, highlighting the work of younger scholars "making new inroads into historical understanding of the presidency." According to guest editors Bruce Miroff and Stephen Skowronek, "no group of scholars has exclusive claim to the study of presidential history" because it is "the common reservoir of material used by all."[59] Yet, distinct methodologies have emerged to mark differences between historians and political scientists.

Unlike political science, which defines the properties that make up institutions themselves, presidential history focuses on the development of societies over time. Historians assert that society shapes institutions, and they employ qualitative methods to compose narratives about the evolution of the presidency. Those narratives reflect the belief that society and its institutions are driven by one of five fundamental factors: race, class, gender, culture, and ideology. These factors can be viewed as "windows" through which societal and institutional change are understood and described. To facilitate these descriptions, presidential historians often rely on biographical studies of presidents and their contributions to institutional change.

Within political science, "new institutionalism" involves a revision of established methods of studying the presidency. It is a diverse area of study that comprises everything from qualitative approaches to the presidency to quantitative ones about individual and institutional choices, behaviors, and attitudes. Although the main focus of new-institutionalist research is still the institution of the presidency itself, it includes the relationship between institutions and history. This blended method, which retains the assumption that institutions shape history and not, as historians believe, the other way around, views the choices and decisions presidents make as complex rather than based on simple and predictable quantitative models. Because of its wide scope, new institutionalism can include several disciplines, but describing it as interdisciplinary is somewhat misleading. Instead, it is a group of fields within a revised discipline united by its acceptance that methodological boundaries are fluid and that history is helpful as a tool for understanding the presidency.

In addition, American political development (APD) arose out of the conviction that history and presidential studies are naturally linked. Similar to "historical institutionalism," which relies on the study of institutions to explain historical change, APD examines historical change through the study of institutional transformations. According to APD, institutional transformations influence equally significant historical transformations, which lead to new patterns of American politics and government. Still, distinctions among APD, historical institutionalism, and new institutionalism are often difficult to see, because all examine interactions between institutional and historical development. Distinctions arise out of differences in emphasis instead of real inconsistencies. Having said that, some key distinctions do exist, regardless of the many similarities. Unlike the other two, APD is based on the assumption that historical change is a consequence of institutional transformations, and its approach is essentially qualitative. Like historians, APD scholars rely on narrative descriptions of their subjects and believe that institutional decisions are complex by their very nature.

Other works have also offered important methodologies and/or theories about studying the presidency as an institution. Louis Fisher has written extensively on the legal and constitutional aspects of the presidency, including presidential war powers and the separation of powers between the president and Congress. For example, in *The Politics of Shared Power: Congress and the Executive*, Fisher analyzes the practical implications of this constitutional relationship: "Very few operations of Congress and the presidency are genuinely independent and autonomous. For the most part, an initiative by one branch sets in motion a series of compensatory actions by the other branch—sometimes of a cooperative nature, sometimes antagonistic." Fisher argues that the presidency as an institution, and the powers that belong to individual presidents, are best understood by recognizing that both the presidency and Congress operate within a political environment that also consists of the judiciary, the bureaucracy, independent regulatory commissions, political parties, state and local governments, interest groups, and other nations, since the Constitution "anticipates a government of powers that are largely shared but sometimes exclusive." The practical result of this institutional relationship simply means that a president's power to achieve results can depend on many factors, including cooperation and/or resistance from Congress, the courts, or other political institutions with whom the president and the executive branch must share power.[60]

Finally, Lyn Ragsdale's research relies on three dimensions to describe the parameters of the presidency as an institution: organization, behavior, and structure. She recognizes that presidents can make marginal changes to the organization of the presidency, but the office is not reinvented with each new occupant in the White House. Also, presidents tend to behave in similar ways, since they are faced with a similar political and institutional environment. Her view moves beyond the institutional approach to include structural elements, which "describe the most typical features of a single institution." It is through rigorous data analysis across several presidencies that explanations can be found to define the president's role within the institution of the presidency; ultimately, "the institution of the presidency shapes presidents as much as presidents, during their short tenures, shape the institution."[61]

SOURCES FOR RESEARCHING THE PRESIDENCY

A variety of sources exist for individuals studying the American presidency, whether undergraduate students or senior academic scholars. Primary sources, which include original documents from an administration (such as memos written by members of the Kennedy White House during the Cuban Missile Crisis), the transcript of a presidential speech (such as Barack Obama's State of the Union Address in 2016), or collections of writings from a particular president (such as the writings and correspondence of Thomas Jefferson), can be found at various libraries as well as numerous online databases. Secondary sources, which include oral histories of various administration officials, interviews of presidents and administration officials by the news media, or studies published by academic scholars of the presidency, are also readily available. The presidency, as well as the individuals who have held the office, remains one of the most studied features of American government. As such, the public's interest in the topic has in part encouraged the availability of information and numerous sources for novice and professional observers alike. Two of the most important sources of information on the presidency include the presidential library system, which is under the auspices of the National Archives and Records Administration (NARA), and the *Public Papers of the Presidents of the United States*, published by the federal government.

Presidential Libraries

Although access to presidential documents is only one source of information when studying a particular president or administration, the memos, notes (sometimes handwritten), and other documents from those who worked in the White House provide a unique perspective into the decision-making and thought processes of some of the most powerful figures in American government. Perhaps one of the best examples is Fred Greenstein's work on the Eisenhower presidency. As Greenstein writes in the introduction to his classic book, *The Hidden-Hand Presidency: Eisenhower as Leader*, he thought a visit to the Eisenhower Library in Abilene, Kansas, would confirm the widely held view that Eisenhower was a "pliable puppet of his aides" who was "lacking in political skill and motivation" and merely a "figurehead chief executive." Instead, while going through numerous files, Greenstein discovered a much different presidency:

> I had barely begun examining the recently opened files of Eisenhower's personal secretary, Ann Whitman, which contained Eisenhower's most confidential correspondence, his private diary, notes on his meetings and telephone conversations, and even transcripts of secret recordings of his one-to-one meetings with other high officials, when I experienced a shock of nonrecognition. The Eisenhower revealed in Mrs. Whitman's files could scarcely have been less like the Eisenhower who spawned the pre-Beltway Washington joke that, while it would be terrible if Eisenhower died and Vice-President Nixon became president, it would be worse if White House Chief of Staff Sherman Adams died and *Eisenhower* became president. The Eisenhower of Mrs. Whitman's files *was* president—he, not Sherman Adams, and not Secretary of State John Foster Dulles, was the engine force of the Eisenhower presidency. To my surprise, the Whitman papers and other records of the copiously documented Eisenhower presidency were laden with evidence of an alert, politically astute Eisenhower who engaged in the traditional kinds of persuasion and bargaining which are the standard activities of other presidents but which were believed to have been abjured by the amiable Ike. To my greater wonder, the records also testified to a nonstandard mode of presidential leadership on Eisenhower's part, one in which the president characteristically worked his will by indirection, concealing those of his maneuvers that belied his apolitical exterior.[62]

Greenstein's work on the Eisenhower presidency, as well as countless other projects that stem from research at presidential libraries, serves as a reminder that much insight can be gained by examining the memos, correspondence, diaries, phone and visitor logs, and numerous other documents available at presidential libraries.

According to NARA, presidential libraries are repositories for the papers, records, and historical materials of the presidents, working to ensure that these irreplaceable items are preserved and made available for the widest possible use by researchers. The goal of presidential libraries is to "promote understanding of the presidency and the American experience" as well as to "preserve and provide access to historical materials, support research, and create interactive programs and exhibits that educate and inspire."[63] The working papers for each administration since Herbert Hoover are available in presidential libraries. The Library of Congress houses the papers for most administrations prior to Hoover. NARA's Office of Presidential Libraries administers a nationwide network of 14 presidential libraries, and 6 other libraries not overseen by NARA also exist (see Table 1.1). Presidential libraries are not normal libraries; instead, they are archives and museums that house the documents and artifacts of a president and his administration. Millions of visitors pass through presidential museums each year, and researchers and journalists

Table 1.1 Presidential Libraries

PRESIDENTIAL LIBRARY/ MUSEUM	LOCATION	OPERATED BY
John Quincy Adams	Stone Library, Adams National Historical Park, Quincy, Massachusetts	National Parks Service
Abraham Lincoln	Springfield, Illinois	State of Illinois
Rutherford B. Hayes	Fremont, Ohio	Ohio Historical Society and Hayes Presidential Center, Inc.
William McKinley	Canton, Ohio	Stark County Historical Society
Woodrow Wilson	Staunton, Virginia	Woodrow Wilson Presidential Library Foundation
Calvin Coolidge	Northampton, Massachusetts	State of Massachusetts
Herbert Hoover	West Branch, Iowa	NARA
Franklin D. Roosevelt	Hyde Park, New York	NARA
Harry S. Truman	Independence, Missouri	NARA
Dwight D. Eisenhower	Abilene, Kansas	NARA
John F. Kennedy	Boston, Massachusetts	NARA
Lyndon Baines Johnson	University of Texas Campus, Austin, Texas	NARA
Richard M. Nixon	Yorba Linda, California	NARA
Gerald R. Ford (Library)	University of Michigan Campus, Ann Arbor, Michigan	NARA
Gerald R. Ford (Museum)	Grand Rapids, Michigan	NARA
Jimmy Carter	Atlanta, Georgia	NARA
Ronald Reagan	Simi Valley, California	NARA
George H. W. Bush	Texas A&M University Campus, College Station, Texas	NARA
William J. Clinton	Little Rock, Arkansas	NARA
George W. Bush	Southern Methodist University Campus, Dallas, Texas	NARA
Barack Obama	University of Chicago, Jackson Park, Chicago, Illinois	NARA

can access documents from each administration to aid in their work. Although numerous events, supported by the president's private foundation (to help promote the legacy of each president as well as to provide financial support for educational programs), may be held at each presidential library, the library archives themselves are managed by NARA archivists, which ensures open access with no political or ideological affiliation.

The presidential library system first began in 1939 with FDR, who wanted to preserve the papers and other materials from his time in office. Prior to the precedent set by FDR, papers were often dispersed to family members or administration officials, and many were even destroyed. Following FDR's lead, Harry Truman also decided that he wanted a library to house his presidential papers. Toward the end of Truman's term in 1952, the White House stated publicly the president's intentions regarding his papers: "By tradition, going back to the earliest days of our Nation, papers of every President are regarded as his personal property. However it is the intention of President Truman to donate his papers to the government after the completion of a suitable library to be built from private funds."[64] Then, in 1955, Congress passed the Presidential Libraries Act, which established a system of libraries, which were to be built through private funds and then turned over to the federal government to maintain and oversee. Since that time, when a president leaves office, NARA establishes a Presidential Project until the new presidential library is built and transferred to the federal government.

Subsequent laws have also been passed that have changed the governing structure of presidential libraries. In 1978, Congress passed the Presidential Records Act (PRA), which established that presidential records documenting the constitutional, statutory, and ceremonial duties of the president are the property of the U.S. Government. Although the first presidential libraries built acknowledged the fact that presidential papers were the personal property of the president, NARA had great success in persuading presidents to donate their historical materials to be housed in a NARA-run presidential library. However, Richard Nixon's resignation from office in 1974 brought with it numerous lawsuits over ownership of his presidential papers, which in part encouraged Congress to change the law. In 1974, Congress also passed the Presidential Recordings and Materials Preservation Act, placing Nixon's papers in federal custody to prevent their destruction.[65]

Another provision of the PRA, signed into law by Jimmy Carter, stipulated that each presidential library established after Carter's would be governed by the Freedom of Information Act (FOIA), a law passed in 1966 to ensure public access to government documents of a nonclassified nature. Currently, the Reagan, Clinton, and both Bush libraries operate under the rules of FOIA (as will the future Obama library), which means that a researcher must submit a request to gain access to any documents not already opened and processed by NARA archivists. The process of building a presidential library and providing public access to presidential documents can take several decades: from the initial site selection, funding, and construction of the facility, and especially the review and processing of documents by archivists, to fully opening most collections in a presidential library can take 20–30 years or more.

In 2001, a controversy erupted over the release of documents at the Reagan Library; under the PRA, documents are released 12 years after a president leaves

Harry Truman at the construction site of his presidential library in Independence, Missouri, April 21, 1956.

office. The George W. Bush administration sought to delay the release of the Reagan documents, and on November 1, 2001, Bush issued Executive Order 13233, which limited access to the records of former presidents that reflected "military, diplomatic, or national security secrets, Presidential communications, legal advice, legal work, or the deliberative processes of the President and the President's advisers." In effect, this order provided executive privilege to the family members of former presidents to decide which documents to withhold. Executive privilege, or the government's right to maintain the secrecy of certain documents, is traditionally only given to the president himself and other executive branch officials to keep certain information confidential so as not to interfere with the administration's ability to govern (particularly in regard to national security). The executive order also gave the current White House the right to review any documents prior to their release and to withhold any documents they believed should be kept classified.

Numerous groups, including the Society of American Archivists, the American Library Association, the American Political Science Association (with strong support from the Presidency Research Group, the subsection of the American Political Science Association devoted to the study of the presidency[66]), and several historical organizations, vehemently protested the executive order. A statement by the Society of American Archivists proclaimed, "The archival and public information implications aspects of this order are profound, being contrary to established archival principles and standards, being inconsistent with existing statutory law, and, most important, being at odds with the principles of open access to information upon which our country is founded."[67] Lawsuits were filed, and various members of Congress sought to take action to get around the executive order. Even Gerald Ford weighed in on the controversy, stating, "I firmly believe that after X period of time, presidential papers, except for the most highly sensitive documents involving our national security, should be made available to the public, and the sooner the better."[68] Executive Order 13233 stayed in effect through the rest of Bush's time in office, which meant that it also covered the records to be released in January 2005 from his father's library. On January 21, 2009, during his first full day in office, Barack Obama kept one of his campaign promises by revoking that order and issuing Executive Order 13489, which returned to the NARA archivists, not the White House or former family members of presidents, the ability to release documents in a timely manner. (For more information about conducting research at presidential libraries, see Appendix A).

BUILDING A PRESIDENTIAL LIBRARY

THEN . . .

During his second term of office, Franklin D. Roosevelt began to consider what to do with the numerous documents and other materials from his time in office. Knowing that many previous presidential papers had been lost, destroyed, sold for profit, or ruined in storage, FDR sought to provide a public repository for future study based on his presidency. He sought the advice of Waldo G. Leland, an American historian and archivist, and other notable historians who formed an executive committee to oversee the project (of which Leland served as chair from 1938 to 1941).[69] In accepting the position, Leland wrote in a letter to FDR in December 1938, "I shall consider it as an honor and a privilege to be of service in carrying out your plans for the permanent housing of your records and related historical material. The plan is one which appeals to me very strongly and which will, I am confident, be of great importance for the advancement of historical studies in this country."[70] In 1939, FDR donated his personal and presidential papers to the federal government, pledged a part of his Hyde Park, New York, estate as the site of the eventual library and museum, and asked the National Archives to take custody of his papers and other historical materials and to oversee his library.

Leland served as a strong public advocate for the library project for several years. At a dinner with FDR and other historians serving on the library project's advisory and executive committees, Leland articulated the importance of preserving FDR's papers:

> The proposal by the President to present to the nation his papers, archives, books and other collections, to be housed in a special building on a part of his Hyde Park estate, also to be donated by him, has naturally aroused a great deal of interest among scholars. One cannot fail to be impressed by the magnitude and importance of so generous a gift. Most scholars would argue without difficulty that the quarter of a century through which the United States is passing, from the close of the War into the decade of the 'forties, is one of the most significant periods of American history. It is a period in which great changes that have long been in preparation are manifesting themselves; it is a period in which the ideas of the people of the United States have been

subjected to the most penetrating tests, and there are few citizens who will emerge from this quarter-century with the same ideas, opinions, and points of view that they held at its beginning. Consequently, the proposal of the President to establish, under public control, exercised by the National Archives, at which is undoubtedly the key collection for the study of this most recent period, is particularly welcome to all students of American history. If, as seems likely, the President's collections should attract other related collections, such as the papers of members of his administration, there would soon be accumulated a body of material such as does not exist anywhere else, and the Franklin D. Roosevelt Library would become one of the chief centers of research in contemporary history in the United States.[71]

At the same dinner, FDR himself recalled that while a student at Harvard, he had served as the librarian of the Hasty Pudding Club and had sought advice from an aged book dealer on Cornhill: "One of the first things that old man Chase said to me was 'Never destroy anything.' Well, that has been thrown in my teeth by all the members of my family almost every week that has passed since that time. I have destroyed practically nothing. As a result, we have a mine for which future historians will curse me as well as praise me. It is a mine which will need to have the dross sifted from the gold. I would like to do it, but the historians tell me I am not capable of doing it. . . . It is a very conglomerate, hit-or-miss, all-over-the-place collection on every man, animal, subject of material. . . . But, after all, I believe it is going to form an interesting record of this particular quarter of a century . . . to which we belong."[72]

The FDR Library would set several important precedents as the presidential library system developed and expanded during the next several decades. For example, in 1939, a committee was formed to raise private funds to initiate the project and construction of the building prior to the library being turned over to the federal government and the National Archives and Records Administration for oversight and maintenance. In addition, numerous FDR administration officials would donate their papers to the library, as has become the norm. Although the FDR papers would not open to researchers until 1950, as early as 1943, FDR himself began to give instructions to the director of his library about what should and should not be opened to researchers:

> Before any of my personal or confidential files are transferred to the Library at Hyde Park, I wish to go through them and select those which are never to be made public; those which should be sealed for a prescribed period of time before they are made public; and those which are strictly family matters, to be retained by my family. . . . With respect to the file known as "Famous People's File," the same procedure should be followed. Those which are official letters may be turned over to the Library, but those which are in effect personal such as, for example, the longhand letters between the King of England and myself, or between Cardinal [Archbishop of Chicago George] Mundelein and myself, are to be retained by me or my Estate and should never be made public. . . . With respect to the file called "Family Letters," in the main they are to be retained by me or my Estate. . . . In all of the papers which are to be turned over to the Library from my personal files or from

non-personal, official files, there will be some which should not be published until a lapse of a certain length of time and which, in the meantime, should be put under seal. This is for the reason that they may refer to people who are still alive in a way which would be embarrassing to them. . . . I should judge that the average length of time of sealing should be from ten to fifteen years, but there may be some which should be sealed for as many as fifty years.[73]

. . . AND NOW

Unlike FDR, not every former president has acreage and/or an estate to donate for the location of his presidential library and museum. Some presidential libraries have been built on or near the actual site of the president's birthplace (the Hoover Library in West Branch, Iowa; or the Nixon Library in Yorba Linda, California) or what is considered the president's hometown (the Truman Library in Independence, Missouri; the Eisenhower Library in Abilene, Kansas; the Kennedy Library in Boston, Massachusetts; and the Clinton Library in Little Rock, Arkansas). Other libraries have been built on university campuses (the Johnson Library at the University of Texas at Austin, the Ford Library at the University of Michigan, the George H. W. Bush Library at Texas A&M University, and the George W. Bush Library at Southern Methodist University [SMU]). Still other libraries, such as the Carter Library in Atlanta and the Reagan Library in Simi Valley, California, were built in areas that had regional significance to each president. And in recent years, competition for securing a presidential library has at times been fierce.

Since the George W. Bush Library opened in 2013, the state of Texas can boast more presidential libraries than any other state. The first, the Johnson Library at the University of Texas at Austin was first dedicated in 1971 with former President Johnson and then-current president, Richard Nixon, in attendance. Although Johnson had not attended the University of Texas at Austin (he was a graduate of Southwest Texas State Teachers' College, now Texas State University–San Marcos), he had been born and raised in the Texas hill country just outside of Austin. At the dedication ceremony, Johnson stated, "We are all partners in this hopeful undertaking. The people of Texas built this library. The National Archives will manage the Library. The documents I have saved since the 1930s are being given, along with the documents of many others who served with me. Those documents contain millions and millions of words. But the two that best express my philosophy are the words, 'Man can.' I wish President Truman, the father of the Presidential Library System, could be here. He said he didn't want his library to be a tribute to him. He wanted it to serve as a real center for learning about our government. We are doing that here."[74]

As early as one month after George H. W. Bush took office in January 1989, lobbying of the president and his administration began over where his library would be located. Texas A&M University, located in the central-Texas town of College Station, was in the running from the beginning. In a brief letter to Perry Adkisson, chancellor of the Texas A&M University system, Bush wrote in February 1989, "Just a quick note to say I appreciate your interest. Though I can say I'd like the Presidential papers to land in Texas, it will be some time before options are pursued. Send the proposal . . . but, again, no rush."[75] By October 1989, other sites had already made initial bids for the library, including the University of Houston,[76] Rice University in Houston, Texas Tech University in Lubbock, Yale University (Bush's alma mater), and private groups in Kennebunkport, Maine (where the Bush family had a vacation home) and Houston.[77] By then, not even a year into the Bush presidency, the president seemed to be leaning toward Texas A&M. However, Jim Cicconi, Bush's deputy chief of staff (and the eventual vice president of the George Bush Presidential Library Foundation), advised members of the administration to not let their initial preferences be made public and vetoed the idea of a presidential meeting with Texas A&M's designated library architect:

> A meeting with the President would 'jump the gun.' . . . While well aware of the President's inclination toward locating the library at A&M, the Houston crowd still wants the chance to be heard, and have their proposal considered by the President. This includes many long-time friends of the President who are partial to Houston. . . . If they feel they never had a chance, and that the whole process was an 'inside deal' . . . there would no doubt be hard feelings despite our best efforts. A meeting with an architect, more than anyone else, makes it look like the deal has been cut. This will undoubtedly leak into the Texas papers, and will appear as if the Archives process is a sham . . . I also worry about the perception of reviewing architectural plans for a library before our first year is over. We set up the Archives process to help the President keep this decision away from the Oval Office for a while, and to insulate the President from the type of personal lobbying he has had to undergo. This meeting would bring it right back onto his desk.[78]

On May 3, 1991, Bush informed Texas A&M that they had been chosen for the site of his presidential library. Among the factors Bush cited included the university's commitment to integrate the library into the academic activities of the university; the planned public service school and Center for Presidential Studies; the "ample space for future facilities, impressive setting, and easy access for visitors" found on the campus; and the university's commitment to "provide or secure all funds necessary to construct the library and related University facilities, and to establish separately an operational and program endowment [to] ensure not only that the financial requirements of the Presidential Libraries Act are met fully, but also that the library's ongoing programs will be vigorous and of high academic quality."[79]

The George W. Bush Presidential Library, located on the SMU campus, also faced tough competition from other universities and locations, including Baylor University in Waco (officials began lobbying Bush even before he took the oath of office in 2001), Texas Tech University in Lubbock, the University of Texas system, the Texas A&M system, the University of Dallas, Midland College, and the City of Arlington. Speculation grew by 2007 that SMU (of which First Lady Laura Bush was an alumna) would be the selected location, which also drew protests from some SMU faculty who claimed that the university had bypassed faculty governance in the decision-making process to compete for the library (some faculty members were also opposed to Bush administration policies and did not want SMU forever linked with his presidency).[80] A Methodist group also opposed the library's location at SMU, claiming that it was inappropriate to link Bush's presidency to a university bearing the Methodist name.[81] Nonetheless, the Bush White House announced in 2008 that SMU would house the presidential library.

Dedication of the George Bush Presidential Library and Museum (left to right: Lady Bird Johnson, Jimmy and Rosalynn Carter, George and Barbara Bush, Bill and Hillary Clinton, Gerald and Betty Ford, Nancy Reagan), November 6, 1997.

Similar speculation and lobbying swirled around the location of the future Obama Presidential Library. Early in Obama's first term, the University of Chicago (where Obama once taught at the law school) and the state of Hawaii (where Obama was born) made early bids to secure the project. However, like their immediate predecessors in the Bush White House, Obama advisors stated that a first term was much too early to discuss plans for a presidential library (Bush officials did not officially discuss plans for a library until 2005).[82] Chicago, and specifically land close to the University of Chicago, emerged as the presumptive favorite. Columbia University in New York (where Obama received his bachelor's degree), the University of Illinois at Chicago, and the University of Hawaii were also among the top contenders. However, the specific location was finally announced in July 2016—Jackson Park, a green area of more than 500 acres on Chicago's South Side, east of the University of Chicago. The decision was not surprising given that the Obamas still owned a home on the city's South Side where the campus is located. In addition, Chicago mayor Rahm Emanuel, who served as Obama's first chief of staff, devised a plan for the Chicago Parks District board to transfer 20 acres to the city for the library's use. Emanuel had campaigned aggressively for the library to be located in his city. The issue was especially salient during Emanuel's 2015 reelection campaign (in which Obama campaigned on his behalf), as black voters overwhelming supported bringing the library to Chicago. As a result, the final announcement on the library's location was delayed several months because the Obama Foundation did not want to appear to be giving Emanuel an unfair advantage in the campaign (Emanuel won reelection in a two-person runoff with 56 percent of the vote).

Public Papers

Started in 1957, the *Public Papers of the Presidents of the United States* series is the official annual compilation of presidential papers. It provides a comprehensive public source of data on the American presidency. Because it now spans numerous administrations, this resource has aided scholars interested in a more institutional approach to studying the presidency because it allows researchers to employ a comparative methodological approach. The National Historical Publications Commission originally suggested this endeavor since no uniform compilation of presidential messages and papers existed. The *Public Papers* is now the annual version of the *Weekly Compilation of Presidential Documents*, which began publication in 1965. As of January 2009, the *Weekly Compilation* has been replaced by the *Daily Compilation of Presidential Documents*. Both the *Public Papers* and the *Weekly/Daily Compilation* are published by the Office of the Federal Register, National Archives and Records Service, and are printed by the U.S. Government Printing Office. Administrations included in the series of *Public Papers* include those of Herbert Hoover through Barack Obama, with one exception—the papers of FDR were published privately prior to the creation of the official *Public Papers* series. Other privately published series of presidential papers by scholarly presses include *The Papers of James Madison*, published by the University of Chicago Press; *The Papers of Woodrow Wilson* by Princeton University Press; and *The Papers of Dwight David Eisenhower* by the Johns Hopkins University Press. Other series of presidential papers include *The Adams–Jefferson Letters: The Complete Correspondence between Thomas Jefferson and Abigail and John Adams*, published by the University of North Carolina Press; and *The Writings of George Washington from the Original Manuscript Sources, 1745–1799*, published by the George Washington Bicentennial Commission.

The Government Printing Office currently publishes volumes of the *Public Papers* approximately twice a year, and each volume covers approximately a six-month period. The papers and speeches of the president of the United States that were issued by the Office of the Press Secretary during the specified time are included in each volume of the *Public Papers*. These include press releases, presidential proclamations, executive orders, addresses, remarks, letters, messages, telegrams, memorandums to federal agencies, communications to Congress, bill-signing statements, transcripts from presidential press conferences, and communiqués to foreign heads of state. The *Papers* presented the material in chronological order, and the dates shown in the headings are the dates of the documents or events. Remarks are checked against a tape recording and any signed documents are checked against the original to ensure accuracy. The appendixes in each volume of the *Public Papers* are extensive and include listings of a digest of the president's daily schedule and meetings and other items issued by the White House press secretary; the president's nominations submitted to the Senate; a checklist of materials released by the Office of the Press Secretary that are not printed full-text in the book; and a table of proclamations, executive orders, and other presidential documents released by the Office of the Press Secretary and published in the Federal Register. Each volume also includes a foreword signed by the president, several photographs chosen from White House Photo Office files, a subject and name index, and a document categories list.

Federal Depository Libraries contain hard copies of the *Public Papers*. With more than 1,200 locations throughout the United States and its territories, these libraries, which can include city, county, state, or university libraries, were first established in 1813 to safeguard the public's right to know by collecting, organizing, maintaining, preserving, and assisting users with information from the federal government through no-fee access. Electronic versions of the *Public Papers* can be found at the Government Publishing Office website as well as on individual presidential library websites. In addition, the American Presidency Project (americanpresidency. org), established in 1999 by John Woolley and Gerhard Peters at the University of California, Santa Barbara, is an extensive online archive containing nearly 120,000 documents related to the study of the presidency. The archive includes data consolidated, coded, and organized into a single searchable database for *Messages and Papers of the Presidents: Washington through Taft* (1789–1913); the *Public Papers*; the *Weekly Compilation*; the *Daily Compilation*; and numerous other documents related to party platforms, candidates' remarks, statements of administration policy, documents released by the Office of the Press Secretary, and various election databases. Finally, with its creation during the Clinton administration, the official White House web page (www.whitehouse.gov) has also evolved as an extensive database for presidential speeches and other public remarks, as well as the president's daily schedule and other information about the work of the current administration.

CONCLUSION

Studying the modern presidency, whether from an institutional perspective or by looking at the individuals who have held the office, can be both a fascinating and a complex task. Much has changed about the presidency since the early days of Washington, Jefferson, or Jackson. By the twentieth century, as America gained prominence as an economic global leader and as military and diplomatic relationships grew more complex with the Cold War and its aftermath, the presidencies of Kennedy, Reagan, and Obama appeared different from those of their early predecessors. Yet, it is instructive to remember that although the circumstances in which a president must govern can change drastically, little has changed about the office vis-à-vis the powers and limitations found within the U.S. Constitution. As this discussion shows, scholars relying on a variety of methodological and/or theoretical perspectives have made notable contributions to the presidency literature. In addition, the debate among presidency scholars now has the depth and breadth that was missing several decades ago, and healthy disagreements exist on not only what questions should be asked, but also how they should be answered.

Throughout the chapters that follow, we will explore the many aspects of American presidents and the presidency, providing a thorough examination that considers both a president-centered and an "institutional-based" approach to studying the presidency. In doing so, we provide an effective approach for students of the presidency to understand the complexity of the office, the differences that can occur from the individuals who hold the office, and the uniqueness of perhaps the most fascinating political office ever created. More important, relying on key documents from various presidential libraries will animate various discussions about White House decision making on many topics, which in turn will more accurately describe the real presidency as an institution as well as the actual day-to-day responsibilities of the president.

CHAPTER 2

Presidents and the Constitution

During the first few days of his administration, Donald Trump exercised what is now considered a tradition for new presidents after taking the oath of office—he signed several executive orders overturning actions that had been implemented by his predecessor, Barack Obama. Among them, within hours of being sworn in as president, Trump overturned an executive order freezing the implementation of any new regulations related to the Affordable Care Act, giving federal agencies discretion to delay or change provisions of the law deemed overly costly. In addition, he signed executive orders that withdrew the United States from the Trans-Pacific Partnership (considered Obama's signature trade deal), instituted a hiring freeze within the federal workforce, and reinstituted limits on foreign nongovernmental organizations that receive tax dollars from performing abortions. Trump did not heed Obama's advice from a few weeks earlier, when the outgoing president offered this perspective on unilateral actions: "My suggestion to the president-elect is, you know, going through the legislative process is always better, in part because it's harder to undo."[1]

In most cases, presidents rely on executive orders to manage the day-to-day operations of the many agencies within the executive branch, which is granted through legislation that delegates constitutional authority to the president. Some presidents have used executive orders more than others. FDR averaged 307 executive orders per year during his time in office (a total of 3,721), whereas three presidents issued only one executive order during their tenures (John Adams, James Madison, and James Monroe).[2] More recent presidents have often relied on executive orders to bypass Congress, especially when it is controlled by the opposing party, to implement certain policies. In early

2014, Obama stated that "I've got a pen, and I've got a phone," his message to a deadlocked Congress that he would bypass them through executive orders and "calling people together" to get things done in Washington.[3] Yet, despite his public warning to members of Congress that he was prepared to govern without them, Obama relied less on executive orders than many other presidents. In fact, he averaged 35 executive orders per year, which is the lowest yearly average for any president since Grover Cleveland's second term (1893–1897).

Although they have the full force of law, executive orders are, like any other law or regulation, subject to judicial review and can be struck down by federal courts as unconstitutional. Such was the case for Obama's attempt at unilateral action on immigration reform. In November 2015, the Fifth Circuit Court of Appeals ruled that Obama's use of executive orders to prevent the deportation of roughly 5 million undocumented immigrants was unconstitutional. The case, *Texas v. United States*, upheld a previous ruling by a U.S. District Court that placed an injunction against the implementation of two specific programs: the Deferred Action for Childhood Arrivals and the Deferred Action for Parents of Americans. Under these executive orders, those who qualified would have been given work permits or have deportation blocked because of family ties of those who are U.S. citizens. Obama took this action following both the 2014 midterm elections (when Republicans held control of the House of Representatives and gained a majority in the Senate) and years of congressional inaction on immigration reform. After the ruling, the White House hoped that the U.S. Supreme Court would take the case and reverse the decision. The Supreme Court did take the case, which addressed a basic separation of powers issue—can the president unilaterally make decisions involving implementation of immigration laws or does such action circumvent the will of Congress and its constitutional authority to pass laws? However, Obama did not get the result he had hoped for because the Court handed down a split 4–4 decision (because of the vacancy left by Antonin Scalia's death) in June 2016, which left the Fifth Circuit's previous decision intact.

Despite having some unilateral powers, one of the great ironies of the contemporary American presidency can be found in the fact that although Americans see the office as powerful, presidents enjoy few enumerated powers in the U.S. Constitution. In addition, except for specific unilateral powers like executive orders or pardons, presidents must rely on other political actors for approval and implementation of nearly all their actions. However, because the Constitution is not always clear regarding presidential powers, it has been in the silences of the document that many presidents have expanded the powers of the office. From a constitutional standpoint, the presidency is now far more powerful than the framers could have intended or expected as presidents have seized power to cope with crises while in office. There have been distinct periods when the presidency was considered weaker than it is today and other times when the power and prestige of the office have been damaged. Yet, although it is largely institutionalized, the presidency is still dependent on the performance and character of its occupant. Institutional demands as commander in chief along with public demands regarding the president's role as head of state have often led presidents to stretch constitutional boundaries. Understanding how the framers viewed executive power and how that led to the design of the presidency at the Constitutional Convention, along with how certain presidents have shaped the constitutional parameters of the office beyond the framers' intentions, helps to explain the contemporary role of presidential powers as part of the current governing process.

THE FRAMERS' PLAN AND THE CONSTITUTIONAL CONVENTION

The creation of a head of state at least as powerful as the British king who would also act as the head of government contradicted several decades of colonial history and, to many, ignored the purposes of the American Revolution. Americans had traditionally resisted a centralized executive with authority over colonial/state governments, so the appearance of a comparatively assertive presidency in 1787 was ironic. Indeed, the Confederation government of the 1780s lacked a national executive altogether, reflecting skepticism toward the consolidation of executive authority. The colonies had benefited from a long line of largely powerless and ineffective governors and a correspondingly permissive relationship with the crown during the eighteenth century, so Americans had become accustomed to ostensibly powerless chief executives. After the English revolution of 1688, real political power lay with Parliament, so British monarchs exerted decreasing control over territories in North America, where residents eventually regarded freedom from executive interference as a constitutional precedent. Following independence, political experiments at the state level only confirmed the American preference for weak central government, so all signs pointed toward the opposite of what eventually happened with the design of the American presidency in 1787.

Inherited Practices and Ideas

In the late eighteenth century, when the framers of the Constitution created the presidency, nonhereditary civilian heads of state were uncommon. The world's leading powers almost uniformly opted for hereditary monarchs or emperors, whereas smaller nation-states employed some variation of authoritarian, nonrepresentative rule. Although the idea that a nonhereditary elected official should preside over government was unique for its time, from a historical perspective, it was not unprecedented. Examples of executive leadership could be found in ancient Athens[4] and Rome,[5] as well as during the Renaissance when several Italian city-states appointed nonhereditary princes as their chief executives.[6] Even in England, known for monarchical governance, a nonhereditary commonwealth was briefly established after the execution of Charles I in 1649.[7] Finally, in the American colonies themselves, colonial governors exercised many of the executive functions that the presidency would later assume at the federal level. They were never more than isolated cases, however, and did not constitute a tradition from which the framers could choose a relevant precedent.

Although the framers embraced continuity and incremental change rather than revolution and radical transformation, the presidency was in many ways radical, if not transformative. The framers' overall constitutional design arose from innovation and adaptation as they borrowed, inherited, and assimilated relevant aspects of British political culture. Affirming familiar political ideals as the foundations of republican rule, they nevertheless chose something unfamiliar for the executive branch of the American government. As students of European history and Western political philosophy, the framers combined English commonwealth ideology with classical and Renaissance ideas about leadership into a distinctly American conception of executive authority. In addition to their experiences with colonial governance, the most significant influence over the framers was their English heritage. By the eighteenth century, Great Britain was a constitutional monarchy with a unique respect for political liberty and the rights of citizens. Although it was not progressive by today's standards, it far surpassed its European rivals, most of which practiced some form of nonrepresentative authoritarian rule.[8]

Aside from English political tradition, classical concepts about republican government shaped American political thought during the revolutionary period. The framers of the Constitution regularly consulted the writings of prominent Greek and Roman philosophers and relied on historical accounts of the rise and demise of ancient regimes. James Madison and Alexander Hamilton were greatly impressed by classical philosophy and the many political insights it offered. In addition, the histories of the Athenian and Roman republics were prominent reminders of the potential and promise of human governance. Ironically, classical ideals, which exerted such a powerful influence over American political thought, had only a marginal impact on English politics, but their contribution to the development of an American political tradition is undeniable.[9]

Classical ideas about republics, governance, civic responsibility, and the allocation of power fascinated the framers, as did ancient attempts at democratic rule. They were convinced that an understanding of the rise and subsequent fall of the Roman republic held the key to managing the birth and death of republican government. Many of them viewed the late Roman republic (before the onset of decay in the early first century BC) as the best historical example of effective and legitimate republican governance, so they consciously modeled the American republic on Roman institutions, ideas, and political practices. However, the collapse of republican governance in the first century BC taught the framers compelling lessons about the accumulation of power within a single institution and the threats posed by an unchecked executive, even a nonhereditary one. The demise of the Roman republic and its replacement by an imperial regime demonstrated both the promise and vulnerability of republican governance. To those contemplating the complexion of the emerging American presidency, Roman history illustrated the need not only to separate civilian from military leadership but also to make the military accountable to civilian rule. Last, the history of the Roman consulship showed that executive power must be strictly confined to specific duties and responsibilities and that republican executives should not be given general power or authority.

During the late seventeenth and eighteenth centuries, the Enlightenment transformed Europe's intellectual terrain and, by extension, the political consciousness of the American colonies. Rejecting the divine right of kings as a medieval fiction, Enlightenment thinkers doubted the ideological assumptions on which early-modern ideas of executive authority had been predicated. In so doing, they redefined classical republicanism and simultaneously planted the seeds of what would eventually become the West's dominant political creed—liberalism.[10] In the framers' world, republicanism and liberalism were the cornerstones of political ideology and contemporary practices. Accordingly, American founding fathers believed that some people are better equipped to rule, whereas others are naturally suited for nonpolitical responsibilities. Thus, government should reflect and leverage inherent social hierarchies and should optimize the intrinsic capabilities of its citizens.

Republicanism may have been more relevant to the American political system designed by the framers, so it dominated early in the nation's history, but liberalism eventually prevailed. By the twentieth century, the American political system had become thoroughly liberal, despite the framers' original intentions. Throughout its history, liberalism has upheld four basic principles of government, which are also the key features of modern American politics: individual rights, government by consent, limited government, and legal and constitutional neutrality toward citizens and the impartial protection of individuals and their rights.[11] More than any other aspects of liberalism, individual rights and limited government influenced the framers' plans for an American presidency. The need to protect individuals, their property, and their natural liberties was inextricably linked to the related need to limit the size of government, especially the scope of executive authority. The framers believed that the best way to secure the rights and liberties of the American people was by preventing the accumulation of too much power by any one branch of the government, and they were convinced that an unchecked executive could pose an immediate threat to republican governance. As apparent victims of royal abuses during the 1760s and 1770s, Americans were intimately familiar with potentially tyrannical executive authority and power, so the framers intentionally restricted executive authority in the United States. Given their experiences, they concluded that a nonhereditary civilian executive would be considerably less likely to exceed his authority than a hereditary monarch or a military leader. Thus, the Constitution provides for a civilian chief executive accountable to the very people whose rights he must protect.[12]

By 1775, many colonial leaders had become convinced of an imperial conspiracy to deprive colonists of their rights and property through executive usurpations of power and authority, and they did whatever possible to discredit the actions of the imperial government in London. The resulting friction intensified into a constitutional debate of monumental proportions, as increasing numbers of British Americans dedicated themselves to what they perceived as a struggle against tyranny. The seemingly unconstitutional seizure of power by the British executive triggered a reaction that no one could have foreseen.[13] The exaggerated claims of imperial tyranny in the Declaration of Independence notwithstanding, American colonists suffered more from neglect than from abuse by the British crown. Consequently, their views of executive authority were a reflection less of royal and Parliamentary corruption than of a relatively weak and decentralized imperial executive whose authority over military defense was unchallenged but whose power over internal matters was consistently contested. Constitutionally speaking, this precedent supported the related conviction that executive authority does not legitimately extend beyond certain aspects of foreign policy and international commerce and that the authority to regulate internal affairs had devolved to state governments. All in all, the history of imperial governance in British North America fostered a colonial tradition of weak executive rule, which formed a lasting impression on the men who created a new American presidency in 1787.

The Confederation Executive

With the onset of war in 1775 and then independence, state governors were no more effective than the colonial governors they had replaced. At the national level, the Continental Congress became the reluctant successor to the British crown, assuming a role as the political center of the former empire and makeshift head of state. However, since it lacked formal constitutional authority over the recently independent states, political leaders from across the continent pushed for the creation of a wartime government that could legitimately handle the required tasks. Not surprisingly, diplomatic and military priorities were paramount, so little thought was given to long-term constitutional concerns. Created as an answer to those priorities, the new government operated under the Articles of Confederation, which were adopted in 1778 (although not ratified until 1781, when the revolutionary war was all but over).

Handicapped from the beginning by a lack of constitutional foresight and political efficacy, the Confederation government had to beg, borrow, and steal to meet military necessities and political realities. In its dual role as lawmaker and executive, the Confederation Congress had formidable expectations, but it never became either. A legislature with symbolic powers and doubtful authority, it was restricted to an advisory capacity and was continually unable to enact prospective legislation. Adding insult to injury, the Confederation government did not even have the power to enforce the few laws it enacted. As commander in chief, it was deprived of the resources and institutional legitimacy it required for strategic and operational management, and it could not implement its decisions without prolonged bargaining and haggling. With no formal executive branch, any exercise of executive power was more a function of occasional concession or peculiar circumstance than institutional authority. Real authority lay with the states, and compromise with the central government was difficult at best. The states were clearly more powerful than the central government, and they could, and usually did, undermine the central government's efforts to act decisively.[14]

By 1787, the lack of a constitutional executive with the necessary authority to succeed the crown as head of state made the Confederation government unworkable. The futility of repairing a nonexistent Confederation executive seemed obvious, as did the folly of a unified American government without a head of state. The need for an effective and legitimate executive was not the only reason, or even the primary reason, for the emergence of the Constitution; several other factors also contributed to the decision to abandon the Confederation government. Nonetheless, had the need for a formal and active executive not existed, the outcome could have been very different. Legislative paralysis could have been addressed through reform at the state level, at least in some respects, as could the legal and jurisdictional questions that hampered the proper interpretation and enforcement of the law. However, unlike the legislative and judicial deficiencies plaguing the Confederation government, the absence of a central executive could not be addressed by state and local governments in a practical manner.

Aside from its inability to enforce laws and coordinate national defense, the Confederation government could not adequately handle foreign affairs. Without a unified or duly authorized head of state, the Confederation government could not manage relationships with foreign regimes, nor could it settle the numerous diplomatic issues that confronted it after the war. In addition, it was powerless to regulate or facilitate international trade and interstate commerce, which simply compounded existing economic difficulties. In matters of international trade, the former colonies rarely coordinated or aligned their commercial policies, so they subjected foreign ventures and governments to overlapping and contradictory agreements that undermined continental economic efficiency and overall viability. Lack of cooperation among the states and consistent economic policies made the former colonies unattractive prospects for international trade, which further undermined the stature and credibility of the Confederation government. As such, badly needed financial assistance was slow in coming and ultimately inadequate to alleviate the strain of accumulated foreign debts.[15]

The framers of the Constitution therefore committed themselves to a presidency with sufficient authority to enforce the country's laws, ensure national security, direct foreign policy, and promote international commerce. These powers represented the most deficient aspects of executive authority under the Articles of Confederation. At the same time, the framers, mindful of their experience with the British crown and the lessons of history, assiduously avoided granting the new presidency too much power. Like the rest of the government of which it would be a part, the American presidency would have limited authority, sufficient to redress the executive deficiencies of the Confederation yet not so powerful to pose a threat to the republic or its political institutions. In addition, the constitutional and political crises of the 1780s strengthened the framers' traditional inclination to dilute and filter popular sovereignty in a way that precluded democratic excesses. Their devotion to popular sovereignty never entailed tolerance of unrestrained democracy or the unfiltered exercise of the popular will, so they shrewdly insulated the presidency from base priorities and selfish interests.

Painting by Howard Chandler Christie of George Washington presiding over the second Constitutional Convention in 1787.

Federalism

Since the Constitution's ratification in 1789, federalism has enabled governors and state legislatures to promote state-specific priorities more effectively, such as law enforcement, emergency services, community development, and education, to name a few, and it has preserved a kind of political adaptability not possible in more centralized regimes. At the same time, federalism has allowed American presidents to focus on the issues, like national defense, foreign policy, and international commerce, that the Confederation government had been so powerless to confront. During the past 100 years, executive powers and the scope of federal authority generally have expanded beyond the framers' intentions, but federalism has remained the defining feature of American governance nonetheless. The American presidency has acquired partial or complete authority over tax and monetary policy, health care, education, energy, workplace issues, welfare, communications, and countless other aspects of modern life in the United States, and the growth of federal power has frequently come at the expense of local and regional governance, yet the states still control an overwhelming majority of governmental duties and responsibilities.

The absence of historical or contemporary models on which to base a federal presidency was not the only challenge facing the framers. Some of the delegates to the constitutional convention, as well as those to state ratification conventions, the most prominent of whom was Alexander Hamilton, worried that a two-tier system of politics would promote unhealthy competition and jealousy between state and federal governments and would, thus, undermine federal executive authority and credibility, if not also legitimacy. Even manifestly presidential responsibilities such as national defense and federal law enforcement could overlap with competing gubernatorial powers, especially since any federal defense and security regime would heavily depend on the deployment and cooperation of state-based militias. Also, skeptics were concerned that federalism would impede rather than facilitate the formulation and implementation of national economic policies by ceding too much power over economic and financial issues to state governments, thereby decreasing the effectiveness of the presidency over an area that represented one of the most glaring deficiencies of the outgoing Confederation government. Hamilton and his intellectual brethren may have preferred a unitary national government free of jurisdictional ambiguities, but federalism prevailed, and the presidency created by the framers alleviated most of Hamilton's anxieties. Indeed, as one of the principal authors of the *Federalist Papers*, Hamilton became a staunch supporter of the Constitution and the American presidency.[16]

General versus Limited Authority

Nothing was more critical to the development of an American presidency than the distinction between general and limited executive authority, which arose from contemporary interpretations of sovereignty. On a broader level, no general concept is more important for a proper understanding of executive authority than sovereignty itself.[17] Indeed, it lies at the heart of the framers' conceptions of republican government and political power, so it is the intellectual cornerstone of the presidency. Sovereignty revolves around crucial questions regarding the nature of rule, most significantly those that examine the right to rule. This was a principal concern for the framers, who hoped to identify and delimit the scope of legitimate political authority and to define the determinants of governance in an American republic. In that regard, the relationship between sovereignty and the presidency was a primary focus of constitutional inquiry, as was the viability of prevailing theories of sovereignty. Their ultimate objective was the elucidation and maintenance of the apparently clear boundary separating general and limited authority and the establishment of a limited federal government, but the centrality of sovereignty as an ideological and constitutional context was always evident.[18] Like their contemporaries in other countries, they were aware that sovereignty held the key to the utilization of executive power.

Over the almost two centuries between the English settlement of Virginia and the creation of an American republic in 1787, the principle of representative, accountable executive rule based on consent and limited authority, which was linked to broader theories of popular sovereignty, became one of the cornerstones of American politics.[19] In 1787, despite wishing to replace the feckless Confederation executive with a more vigorous and powerful continental executive, most Americans still supported limitations on executive authority. They had not forgotten the alleged abuses of power by the British crown and Parliament during the years prior to independence, and they knew of too many historical examples of unchecked executive authority to accept any form of general authority. During the early decades of the eighteenth century, ideas of specific governmental powers and limited governmental authority, although unfamiliar or irrelevant to most contemporary societies, made an indispensable contribution to colonial political thought and cemented an American bias against general authority. Such ideas ultimately formed the basis of a liberal-democratic society dedicated to limited government, individual rights and liberties, and rule by consent, and they provided the constitutional logic for a presidency whose authority would be inherently confined to positively identified powers.[20]

The concept of specific powers, or limited authority, was an American political innovation born of unique experience and historical circumstance. Partly an incarnation of colonial restrictions on royal power and gubernatorial authority and mostly a reaction to Parliamentary excesses of the 1760s and 1770s, the idea of limited executive authority reassured the framers, who wished to prevent future tyrannies by creating an American presidency with specific, not general, powers. Without a doubt, general executive authority would have offered American presidents greater adaptability and institutional agility, but the last thing the framers wanted to encourage, even with someone as trusted as George Washington (who most assumed would be the first president), was political adventurism or constitutional experimentation within the presidency. The creation of a new government unleashed tremendous political changes, but most of all, the Constitution represented stability, certitude, and tradition. According to the framers, only limited authority could preserve those qualities. The historical record is unusually compelling and comparatively unambiguous in that regard.[21]

Therefore, presidential powers derive from a limited, not general, grant of authority by the people. Admittedly, interpretation of framers' intent is complicated by what they assumed but did not explicitly state, particularly because most of today's Americans are not familiar with the framers' intellectual context. So, the current lack of familiarity with eighteenth-century constitutional ideologies, even among legal scholars, obscures the political principles that should still animate the implementation of relevant constitutional directives and often prevents the elucidation of framers' intent. The situation has not been helped by the wording of Article II of the Constitution, which can appear confusing and even contradictory, but anyone familiar with the framers' world should nonetheless be aware of their opposition to general executive authority. Neither the Constitution nor its related contemporary literature can be reconciled with open-ended executive power; those documents illustrate that the framers created a presidency with limited authority comprising only specific powers that correspond to the fulfillment of nothing more than essential, or core, duties.[22] The framers perceived those duties as the only legitimate areas of executive authority, since they reflected the few political tasks Americans were incapable of fulfilling without a federal executive. Through limited executive authority, they intended to address the basic deficiencies of power that plagued the Confederation government—nothing more. From the perspective of executive responsibilities, those deficiencies included the inability to protect and preserve individual rights and political liberty; the inability to enforce federal laws; the lack of national-defense capabilities; the inability to manage foreign affairs; and the inability to facilitate interstate or international commerce.[23]

As a direct response to those deficiencies of governance, the framers of the Constitution established the presidency to secure and enforce the rights and political liberty of its citizens; to enforce federal laws; to provide a system of national defense; to conduct and manage foreign relations; and to coordinate interstate commerce and international trade. The Constitution granted the presidency only as much authority as was required to redress previous deficiencies, and the framers painstakingly avoided any implications to the contrary, the ambiguities in Article II notwithstanding. Overall, the framers created a narrowly defined government that would discourage the accumulation of too much power in any single institution and, therefore, minimize the potential for corruption and tyranny. In addition to making the president head of government and not just head of state, precautions included constitutional impediments to the concentration of power, like the separation of powers, checks and balances, the limited scope of federal responsibility, and the establishment of constitutional qualifications and conditions for political service. Perhaps the most significant of those conditions for a government in the late eighteenth century was the subordination of military to civilian leadership. The founding generation of Americans believed that to minimize the potential for tyranny and corruption, the military must be categorically accountable to, and separate from, both the voters and their civilian presidents. History was (and still is) replete with examples of military oppression and abuse of power, and the framers wanted to ensure the military would never be used against the American people.[24]

Another important precaution that reinforced the principle of limited executive authority was the designation of specific terms of office. The Constitution defines a four-year presidential term, so service cannot be extended indefinitely by power-hungry autocrats or demagogues, whereas political tradition quickly placed further constraints on presidential officeholding through the habit of serving no more than two terms (a tradition initiated by Washington). Even prior to the ratification of the Twenty-Second Amendment in 1951, which limited presidents to two terms, no American president except FDR ever held office longer than two terms (he died just months into his fourth term in 1945). In addition, passage of the Twenty-Fifth

Amendment in 1967 dealt with succession to the presidency and provided procedures for filling a vice presidential vacancy as well as responding to a presidential
disability.[25] The credibility and legitimacy of the presidency have depended, at least
in part, on the periodic and voluntary surrender of political authority to the citizens
who possess it, which has distinguished the American system of politics from most
others. A president's willingness to surrender authority based on constitutional criteria and political custom and his implicit assurance that both his service and his
authority are inherently limited are key aspects of a system whose focus is the prevention of tyranny and political corruption.

Separation of Powers/Checks and Balances

The framers created three separate and mostly independent branches of government whose duties and responsibilities, although overlapping in some aspects, are
nonetheless distinct. The need to divide the basic functions of government and keep
them from interfering with one another was driven by the fear of tyranny and corruption, so the Constitution established institutional boundaries that would prevent
the consolidation of too much power and authority within a single branch of government. However, viable governance presupposes coordination and collaboration
among three branches working in concert, since the failure of any one branch would
precipitate the failure of the entire regime. Apart from other concerns, the framers
worried that conflating naturally distinct constitutional roles within single institutions would eventually produce paralytic inefficiency and inefficacy; their government could become a jack of all trades but a master of none, thereby undermining
its ability to respond to evolving circumstances.[26]

Although the framers sought political balance through the distribution of authority among three branches, they also knew that political realities would inevitably
favor one of them more than the others. This may not necessarily be the case today,
especially because of the unforeseen and unprecedented expansion of executive
power and authority over the past 75 years, but Congress was initially the most influential, if not powerful, institution within the U.S. government—which the framers
had predicted. Common sense, recent history, and their constitutional design all
pointed to the emergence of a federal legislature that was the center of political activity in the newly established republic. The federal judiciary, as Alexander Hamilton
observed, had the authority neither to implement nor to enforce its rulings, so its
power would derive almost wholly from moral credibility, and the presidency was
inherently circumscribed by necessity and tradition. Congress, in contrast, was left
to address the overwhelming majority of the duties and responsibilities of governance, as Article I, Section 8, of the Constitution demonstrates.

In light of the federal legislature's political and constitutional prominence, the
framers redoubled their efforts, through the separation of powers and the allocation
of crucial powers to the executive, to counteract the accumulation of potentially
tyrannical power within Congress. The British Parliament had aptly illustrated the
danger and imprudence of permitting a single institution to enact, enforce (through
cabinet ministers), and interpret (through the House of Lords) legislation, so the
framers of the Constitution curbed congressional supremacy through countervailing grants of authority to the presidency, although the creation of an independent
judiciary was also an indispensable measure in that regard. Making the president

both head of state and head of government was one example, as was his designation as commander in chief of U.S. military forces. In addition, providing the presidency with the authority to enforce laws was a key element of an emerging American tradition of rule of law that rested, among other things, on due process and equality before the law. Finally, presidential authority over foreign policy and diplomacy greatly decreased foreign access to the American legislative process and the related collusion between foreign and selfish domestic interests. In all, the presidency, although confined and heavily circumscribed by today's standards, was, aside from its primary purposes, a bulwark against legislative tyranny.[27]

With respect to the executive branch, separation of powers was a two-way street, so its limitations of power and authority addressed not only potential legislative tyranny but also possible presidential abuses of power. Pursuantly, separation of powers meant that, aside from obvious policy responsibilities and a constitutionally designated role at the end of the lawmaking process, unlike heads of government in parliamentary systems, presidents were unable to participate actively as legislators, or superlegislators. As crucial as it was for the framers to deprive Congress of the authority to enforce its own laws, it was just as important for them to prevent the nation's chief law-enforcement officials from shaping legislation to suit executive priorities and interests. In addition, separation of powers entailed the dilution of presidential authority through the existence of an independent judiciary, which deprived the executive branch of potentially coercive powers over the nation's courts.

Historically, interactions between Congress and the presidency have been the most common examples of checks and balances, so the judiciary has not been as susceptible to institutional interference and oversight as the other two, but this is exactly what the framers intended. They assumed that the greatest internal threats to the republic could arise through the abuse of executive or legislative authority, and they conceptualized checks and balances accordingly. Moreover, although they granted the president specific authority over legislative procedures to undermine potential congressional monopolies of legislative power, the framers were evidently more worried about curbing executive power and ensuring that presidential authority would remain inherently limited. As such, the Constitution empowered Congress to supervise executive action in key areas, such as treaty-making, war-making, presidential appointments, the complexion and existence of executive departments, and presidential conduct as it relates to impeachable offenses.

Rule by Elites and the Electoral College

Every four years, tens of millions of Americans go to the polls to elect a president, although it is the Electoral College, not the national popular vote, that determines the outcome. As a matter of constitutional procedure, the popular vote at the state level is converted into an electoral vote, which controls election outcomes. Some critics argue that the Electoral College is a constitutional relic that serves no obvious purpose, yet it is a conspicuous reminder of a time when the popular vote did not determine presidential elections—in fact, of a time when the popular vote was altogether irrelevant. The Electoral College was the linchpin in an electoral system that valued social hierarchy and political elitism, and it was viewed as a necessary precursor for effective executive governance. The framers wanted to legitimize an elective presidency and stabilize a society that had emerged from more than a dozen years of political chaos. Regardless of its current function, the Electoral College played an active and indispensable part in the selection of America's chief executives during the early republic, and it addressed an essential political need.

Today, electors fulfill a ceremonial function that confirms the election result in each of the 50 states and the District of Columbia. Each state's electoral vote is assigned to the candidate who wins the popular vote, and several states have laws that forbid electors from voting against the popular vote winner. However, as has been the case in a handful of elections, and most notably in 2016 (as discussed in Chapter 3), "faithless electors" can cast a vote for someone other than the popular vote winner. In the late eighteenth and early nineteenth centuries, however, the electors' votes were the only ones that mattered. The Electoral College decided presidential elections, and the public accepted those decisions. Like today, the number of electors each state appointed was equal to the sum of its senators and allotted representatives, but, unlike today, electors had full discretion and authority to choose the candidates they, not the public, preferred. So, not surprisingly, as the newly established American republic awaited the outcome of the first presidential election in early 1789, members of the Electoral College met (in their respective states) to elect George Washington.[28] With no primaries, political parties, or formal nominees, to say nothing of a popular vote, the first presidential election was no less legitimate than its more democratic counterpart today.

Having little say in the selection of electors and, therefore, the president himself, the public was not directly involved in the first several presidential elections, which is exactly what the framers of the Constitution intended.[29] Prior to 1828, America's chief executives owed their jobs to a cloistered, if not secretive, system designed to maintain leadership by political elites and minimize democratic influence. Acting in an ex officio capacity, congressmen named candidates with little or no input from ordinary Americans and submitted official lists of nominees to the Electoral College, which then elected the country's presidents. For a generation, the popular will, although politically relevant in other ways, was largely irrelevant during presidential elections. Backed by tradition and a deferential citizenry, America's "natural aristocracy," as Jefferson referred to the nation's elite class, continued to dominate the presidency through the 1824 election.[30]

Wishing to ensure constitutional stability and political legitimacy, the framers limited the scope of popular sovereignty through the Electoral College and thereby hoped to blunt the impact of political ignorance and democratic excess on the political process. As contradictory as it may sound, especially for a government based on popular sovereignty, the Electoral College was established as a counterweight to democracy. Contrary to American lore, the framers never intended to extend political rights to everyone, nor did they equate popular sovereignty with sociopolitical egalitarianism. To them, popular sovereignty did not entail rule by ordinary citizens, direct public participation in politics, or a society of equals, and it certainly did not mean everyone should enjoy the privileges of citizenship. Popular sovereignty implied rule by propertied white men, which did not include unqualified white males, women, minorities, or slaves. As such, popular sovereignty involved the separation of governance from unfiltered public opinion and the existence of an intermediate mechanism or body through which such opinion could be filtered and refined.[31]

Despite the framers' intentions to preserve the Electoral College as the guardian of presidential elections and maintain political control by elites, changing political circumstances ultimately produced significant deviations. The duties and responsibilities of the presidency invariably evolved as a result of social, economic, and diplomatic changes, and the process by which its occupants were chosen evolved accordingly. Starting with the election of Andrew Jackson in 1828, America's presidents gradually became more representative of the public at large, as the public played an increasingly significant role in American politics and the selection of the nation's chief executives.[32] Today, general elections determine the electoral vote, and ordinary citizens, not just political elites, have become presidents, so the public is cognizant of its indispensable role in the presidential election process. Presidents are no longer the hand-picked representatives of a natural aristocracy because they embody the cultural diversity of a nation with more than 300 million people from all walks of life and all backgrounds. Indeed, most of America's modern presidents have been ordinary men whose rise would have been prevented by the hierarchies that characterized the first generation of American politics.

POWERS OF THE OFFICE

Unlike today, the presidency was not a coveted political prize for founding-era public servants, not least because the head of state and commander in chief of the early American republic had few responsibilities—and that is how the framers hoped things would remain. The presidency was, at best, a humble institution, especially compared to its counterparts throughout the Western world, with narrow authority, scarce resources, and, until the political reforms of the 1820s and 1830s, restricted access. Without a doubt, governors in politically prominent states, such as New York, Massachusetts, and Virginia, had more power and prestige than the nation's presidents, and the states' resources and support staffs dwarfed the minimal capabilities of the federal executive branch. In the international arena, foreign diplomats and heads of state, although frequently impressed by the men who occupied the office, had little respect or admiration for the early American presidency itself. Adding insult to injury, most foreign observers expected this relatively unsophisticated republic in the North American wilderness to fail within a generation.[33]

Since 1787, the American presidency has evolved beyond the intentions of the men who designed it. The executive branch and the authority it possesses have far outstripped their deliberately restrained expectations, so today's presidency often appears to share little or nothing with the modest and unassuming prototype of the founding era. Wars, economic progress, and tremendous social transformations have reshaped the function and purpose of the presidency, and related constitutional reinterpretations have enlarged the scope of legitimate executive activity. Of these changes, perhaps none has been as visible or significant as the steady expansion of presidential authority. A response to the economic and diplomatic realities of an industrialized world, the contemporary presidency is an administrative bastion equipped with numerous cabinet departments, regulatory agencies, and advisors that run one of the most formidable bureaucracies on earth. Not surprisingly, the executive branch of the U.S. government has traveled farther from its roots than the two other branches, and its constitutional link to framers' intent has been weakened.

The twenty-first-century presidency may not be the institution the framers envisioned, but the founding-era original is still relevant. Particularly today, awareness of constitutional purposes can illuminate ongoing debates about the legitimate scope of presidential authority. During the George W. Bush presidency, those debates centered on his administration's sweeping claims of executive authority and privilege with respect to the prosecution of the so-called War on Terror and related constitutional justifications based on framers' intent. Many also questioned Barack Obama's expansive use and acquisition of economic powers to substantiate market interventions and implement controversial health-care measures, which have been subject to increasing constitutional scrutiny in terms of their relationship to legitimate constitutional purposes. Unfortunately, in both cases, people on all sides of the issues have relied on framers' intent and historical precedent more as political expedients for rhetorical swordplay than veritable constitutional foundations, but the significance of framers' intent and historical precedent as constitutional anchors was apparent all the same. Such episodes, however cynical, have only confirmed the importance of the intended meaning and purposes of the constitutional provisions that define the presidency.

The Vesting Clause

Since the 1960s, the most pointed controversies regarding the scope of executive authority have, in one way or another, focused on the vesting clause in Article II. It stipulates, in a general manner, that the "executive power shall be vested" in the president of the United States, but lacks the specificity of Congress's enumerated powers as outlined in Article I, Section 8. The constitutional allocation of authority to Congress clearly refers to individual "legislative powers therein granted," whereas Article II has no similar qualifying language. The purpose, meaning and relevance of the vesting clause, although unambiguous to the framers of the Constitution, have become obscured by latter-day interpreters.[34]

Today, experts are frequently unable to determine the powers granted to the presidency through the vesting clause in Article II. Consequently, advocates of the modern presidency and its unabated accumulation of power over the past several decades have taken advantage of the seeming ambiguity in the vesting clause to rationalize an ever-increasing scope of executive authority. Presidential apologists from both political parties have argued that the terseness of the vesting clause reflects the framers' preference for general executive authority. More to the point, they have relied on general-authority criteria to acquire wide-ranging discretionary powers within the national-security, foreign-policy, and, to a lesser although significant extent, law-enforcement arenas.

Admittedly, on the one hand, Article II itself provides few clues to the intent of the vesting clause, but, on the other hand, contemporary political literature does, and it exposes assumptions about natural limits on executive power that cannot be reconciled with theories of general authority. From today's perspective, the framers could be faulted for not articulating those assumptions in supporting constitutional documents or defining the "executive power" explicitly in Article II. Nevertheless, they were convinced that presidential authority was inherently limited regardless of the lack of constitutional specificity in the vesting clause, and, given the prevailing political mindset and contemporary conceptions of political authority, no one would have viewed the vesting clause as a grant of general executive authority. For better or worse, the framers believed the vesting clause required no qualifications or restrictions and was, thus, legally sufficient.

The enumerated powers in Article II reflect the president's pivotal duties and responsibilities, at least as the founding generation envisioned them. Ultimately, the inclusion of enumerated powers alongside the implied powers of the vesting clause, many of which overlap, may undermine the theoretical efficiency and conceptual simplicity the framers endeavored to achieve in the Constitution, but, in another sense, it can only help. The framers prioritized certain aspects of the presidency above others, and they revealed their intentions through this textual redundancy, which, if anything, confirms their allegiance to limited executive authority. Not surprisingly, the powers identified in the latter sections of Article II epitomize a presidency confined largely to its national-security authority, which shows that the framers conceptualized the president mostly as head of state and commander in chief. Aside from the authority to enforce federal laws and make executive and judicial appointments subject to congressional approval, Article II of the Constitution focuses on foreign policy and national defense.

War Powers and Diplomatic Authority

Although the framers of the Constitution may have provided a sparse list of specific presidential powers, perhaps the most notable is the president's role as commander in chief of the military. Specific, yet mostly undefined, this presidential power has been one of the most debated constitutional issues in recent decades. Although the Constitution specifically grants Congress the power to declare war in Article I, Section 8, of the more than ten conflicts in which the United States has participated since 1945, not one was sanctioned by a congressional declaration of war. In other words, although the United States has fought many wars since the end of World War II, the last time Congress invoked its constitutional authority to declare war was in 1941. All subsequent wars have been started by America's presidents. As members of Congress became more concerned with reelection than with making tough decisions over which they could lose votes, they willingly relinquished the legislature's power to declare war. America's commanders in chief, for their part, gladly seized a power not granted to them by the Constitution, thereby enhancing their ability to pursue foreign-policy objectives without political impediments.

This constitutional predicament over war powers escalated with congressional passage of the War Powers Resolution. Passed in 1973 over Richard Nixon's veto, it requires America's commanders in chief to consult with Congress prior to the introduction of troops into any military theater, but it simultaneously recognizes a presidential power to respond to exigent circumstances without notification when such notification would compromise the integrity or effectiveness of military action. The net effect of this concession was an acknowledgment in all but word of a presidential power to declare war through a statutory loophole that to many seems patently unconstitutional. Over the next four decades, Jimmy Carter, Ronald Reagan, George H. W. Bush, Bill Clinton, George W. Bush, and Barack Obama availed themselves of this loophole to begin or augment American military operations all over the globe and secure a presidential power to declare war.

IN THEIR OWN WORDS

THE WAR POWERS RESOLUTION

Although the constitutionality of the War Powers Resolution has never been determined by the Supreme Court, presidents are nonetheless mindful of its provisions because presidents do not want a constitutional showdown with Congress when initiating military action. As a result, preparing a strong case vis-à-vis the War Powers Resolution is often part of the strategic calculation, as this memo from White House Counsel C. Boyden Gray to George H. W. Bush shows as the White House prepared for war in the Persian Gulf in the summer of 1990:

> I believe it probable that you will be asked about application of the War Powers Resolution (WPR) to the Persian Gulf crisis in your meeting tomorrow with congressional leaders. I have prepared this background paper and the attached contingency talking points for your use in connection with the meeting.

BACKGROUND

The WPR contains two basic provisions: (1) a requirement that Congress be notified within 48 hours of significant new deployments of U.S. combat forces into foreign countries, and (2) a 60-day clock that is triggered when such deployments are into hostilities or situations where hostilities are imminent.

When the 60-day clock is triggered, the President must withdraw the forces within 60 days unless Congress has declared war or passed a joint resolution authorizing continued use of the forces.

We do not dispute the constitutionality of the WPR's congressional notification requirement, but every Administration since the WPR was adopted over President Nixon's veto has considered the 60-day clock an unconstitutional infringement of the President's authority as Commander-in-Chief.

Consistent with the congressional notification requirement, you reported the Persian Gulf deployment to Congress on August 9. Your report stated that you were acting "consistent with" rather than "pursuant to" the WPR. The formulation, first used by President Carter in reporting the Desert One operation and continued by the Reagan and Bush Administrations, emphasizes the Executive branch's position that portions of the WPR are unconstitutional.

You further stated in the August 9 report "I do not believe involvement in hostilities is imminent; to the contrary, it is my belief that this deployment will facilitate a peaceful resolution of the crisis."

This sentence had the effect, in our view, of making clear that the 60-day clock had not been triggered, because the clock begins to run only when hostilities are imminent.

Some members of Congress believe that the 60-day clock has been triggered. They note that, under the WPR, the clock begins to run either when the President reports that hostilities are imminent, or when he was required to report that hostilities were imminent but failed to do so.

In other words, the basis of their position is that you were wrong in asserting in the August 9 report that hostilities were not imminent.

Chairmen [Claiborne] Pell has already written you proposing that we negotiate with the Senate Foreign Relations Committee the text of a joint resolution authorizing the deployment.

Chairman [Dante] Fascell reportedly has instructed the House Foreign Affairs Committee staff to begin drafting a similar resolution that would authorize the deployment for 15 months.

There is a precedent for such a resolution. In 1983, Congress passed a joint resolution granting authorization under the WPR for U.S. participation in the Multinational Force in Lebanon—subject to an 18 month limitation—notwithstanding that President Reagan had never reported to Congress that involvement in hostilities was imminent.

President Reagan signed the resolution into law, but issued a signing statement that, while thanking Congress for its support, noted his disagreement with the limitations contained in the resolution and with Congress' premise that the 60-day clock had been triggered by the outbreak of hostilities.

Chairmen Pell and Fascell seem eager to negotiate a similar resolution with us concerning the Persian Gulf. Such a resolution is legally unnecessary, but would have the political advantage of wedding Congress to our policy.

The disadvantage of negotiating such a resolution is that Congress, in its eagerness to prevent "another Viet Nam," may attempt to constrain the size, scope, and duration of the deployment, just as it did in the Lebanon resolution.

I recommend that you tell the congressional leadership you are prepared to work with them, but will not accept a resolution that constrains your freedom of action.[35]

Despite the obvious significance of the president's role as commander in chief and the fact that national-defense authority seems indispensable, for most of the nation's history, both that role and its authority have been inherently restricted by Americans' unwillingness to tolerate the presence of professional armed forces at home or abroad. Opposed to professional armies since at least the late seventeenth century, Americans remained dedicated to founding-era attitudes regarding the size and utilization of federal forces, which endured almost without interruption until the twentieth century.[36] As a result, the early executive branch was considerably smaller than it is today. In addition to the president and vice president, it included the departments of war, state, and treasury, several military regiments, and a few executive support personnel. The reduced military presence was particularly striking, even in an age when armed forces were much smaller than they are today. Whereas most armed forces in the West numbered in the tens of thousands, the early U.S. military was confined to no more than a few thousand.[37]

Founding-era Americans were also strong advocates of neutrality, which, like the aversion to standing armies, became an almost permanent feature of national political culture, at least until the Cold War. Opposed to any type of international adventurism or foreign entanglements, Americans believed that even if the political will for interventionism were to arise, the nation's restricted military capacities would ultimately undermine both the incentive and possibility for such action. The

George W. Bush signs the Patriot Act into law on October 26, 2001.

framers of the Constitution were particularly adamant about avoiding the foreign-policy mistakes that continually embroiled major European powers in geopolitical quagmires, and they hoped to prevent the country's presidents from encouraging, promoting, or participating in international situations that could destabilize the republic.[38] Convinced that international commitments would only drain vital domestic resources and eventually cause internal problems, the framers expected their presidents to promote both neutrality and global isolationism, which is why the Constitution allocated checks-and-balances authority to the Senate over treaties and appointments through its advise-and-consent powers and to both chambers of Congress through the power to declare war and make required appropriations.

Law-Enforcement Authority

Article II, Section 3, of the Constitution instructs the president to "take care that the laws [of the United States] be faithfully executed," but the provision is buried deep within a list of ancillary powers identified by the framers. In fact, the text and its supporting documents depict the president's law-enforcement authority almost as an afterthought, bereft of the constitutional and practical significance present-day Americans associate with it. Yet, the relative insignificance of the president's role as chief law-enforcement officer accurately reflects the framers' intentions and expectations. To an extent, they wanted to deprive the presidency of anything remotely resembling the by-then lapsed prerogative powers and privileges of the British crown, since the prevention of executive tyranny was a priority. As such, the textual construction clearly implies that law-enforcement authority would be neither extensive nor primary.

Over the past century, the executive branch has acquired extensive law-enforcement capabilities, and agencies like the Federal Bureau of Investigation, the Drug Enforcement Administration, and the U.S. Secret Service, among others, dominate national law-enforcement efforts. Such an expansive presence reflects both the ever-growing demand for federal law enforcement throughout the United States and the unprecedentedly wide-ranging scope of federal law-enforcement duties and responsibilities. However, that simply was not the case in the eighteenth and most of the nineteenth century on either front. First, the demand did not exist because policing, criminal law, and law enforcement were only emerging as veritable concerns and, from a national perspective, comparatively few federal laws required actual enforcement resources.[39] Unlike today, the federal government was not a center of national political activity, and the overwhelming bulk of the nation's political business transpired at the state and local levels. Second, the federal government's duties and responsibilities were inherently limited, so the presidency's law-enforcement capabilities and resources were minimal.

The framers did not envision the expansion of federal law-enforcement capacities beyond rudimentary levels, because they could not imagine a juncture at which law enforcement would become a principal objective of the federal government. Consequently, the allocation of anything more than minimal resources to federal law enforcement would have been unwarranted and wasteful. Indeed, the workhorse of modern federal law-enforcement activity, the Department of Justice, was absent from the executive branch until 1870, leaving the attorney general, initially provided with only a clerk and a small staff, to cover federal law-enforcement responsibilities. Congress supplemented the attorney general's office with roughly a dozen federal marshals, whose number rose as a result of steady territorial expansions westward, but their duties were often confined to the facilitation of court proceedings and enforcement of judicial rulings. Contrary to popular lore, the marshals service was poorly trained, understaffed, frequently mismanaged, resolutely unglamorous, and largely without the authority possessed by county sheriffs or even for-hire private law-enforcement organizations.[40]

Aside from supervision of federal territories and enforcement of judicial rulings, the most important federal law-enforcement responsibility was the prevention and prosecution of treasonous acts. Despite the prominence of certain high-profile treason cases during the past 70 years or so, especially those dealing with espionage and the revelation of national-security secrets, treason no longer poses a substantial threat to the stability or survival of the republic. However, the newly established American republic seemed particularly susceptible to plots against the government, not least because of the federal government's limited physical resources and capabilities and the relative instability and turmoil of the two decades prior to 1787. The framers perceived treason as a real and, perhaps, imminent problem that necessitated corresponding vigilance within the presidency.[41] Still, as the prosecution of arguably the two most famous convicted traitors in U.S. history, Julius and Ethel Rosenberg, cogently illustrated in the early 1950s, this is a significant aspect of the executive branch's law-enforcement authority.[42]

In addition to the power to interdict and prosecute treasonous activity, albeit almost entirely unrelated, the president's pardon power was a crucial, although controversial, part of his executive authority and still is today. Because the crown had abused its pardon privileges to protect royalist stalwarts and other political allies, many Americans were worried that any sort of presidential pardon authority, especially the power to grant general pardons, could become a naked political expedient and, thus, an instrument of executive corruption. In addition, because crimes in Great Britain were violations against the monarch, as a matter of law and constitutional principle, pardon privileges were an inherent and natural part of royal authority. However, according to American law and the very logic of republican governance, crimes were violations against the people, which apparently militated against a presidential pardon power and for congressional authority over pardons. Be that as it may, even opponents of presidential authority over pardons acknowledged the political risks and procedural inefficiencies associated with granting such authority to the legislature. Furthermore, as Alexander Hamilton forcefully argued, especially in *Federalist* 74, whose main focus was pardons for treasonous acts, the pardon power would be a necessary and uniquely effective tool for political reconciliation and even the deescalation of insurrections and rebellions.[43]

Over the years, the clemency power has become what many of its original detractors had feared. Clemency includes presidential pardons or the commutation of a sentence for crimes committed against the U.S. government. It has occasionally been used as the framers had intended, as exemplified by Gerald Ford's pardon of Richard Nixon to facilitate national reconciliation following the Watergate scandal or Jimmy Carter's amnesty for Vietnam-era draft evaders. Nonetheless, the pardon power has become a political tool with which outgoing presidential administrations either reward key individuals and their political supporters for personal loyalty, financial contributions, and simple partisanship or indemnify themselves from potentially damaging legal and political scrutiny regarding specific presidential acts. Eleventh-hour pardons have become a standard of sorts, with presidents, aware that accountability and even popularity are largely irrelevant concerns during the dying hours of an outgoing administration, hurriedly issuing dozens of reprieves, commutations, and other orders for executive clemency immediately prior to leaving office.[44] Bill Clinton's pardon of fugitive financier Marc Rich may have been one of the more visible instances of political remuneration through executive clemency, but Clinton was no different in this regard from either his recent predecessors or his successors.[45] On December 19, 2016, Barack Obama broke the record for the largest single-day use of the clemency power, granting 153 commutations and 78 pardons. In total, Obama would grant clemency to 1,927 individuals (1,715 commutations and 212 pardons), surpassing all presidents but three: FDR (3,687), Woodrow Wilson (2,480), and Harry Truman (2,044).[46]

PRESIDENTIAL PARDONS

THEN . . .

Although much of Article II of the Constitution may seem open ended and vague regarding presidential powers, the framers did provide a handful of specific and enumerated powers. One of those is the power to pardon. Article II Section 2 states that the president "shall have Power to grant Reprieves and Pardons for Offences against the United States, except in Cases of Impeachment." There is a distinction between a reprieve and a pardon; the former reduces the severity of a punishment, whereas the latter removes both the punishment and the guilt of the crime. Accepting a pardon, however, is the equivalent of an admission of guilt, although it removes the legal possibility for punishment. Normally, the modern-day process of seeking a presidential pardon begins with an application to the Department of Justice; those attorneys in the Department of Justice who handle such matters consult with other attorneys and judges in seeking recommendations. The Federal Bureau of Investigation also conducts a check on the person applying for the pardon. Department of Justice attorneys then provide a list of those it recommends for a pardon to the White House Counsel; the president ultimately decides for whom to grant a pardon.

Presidents have often used the pardon power to forgive politically motivated actions. For example, George Washington granted pardons to leaders of the Whiskey Rebellion, and Andrew Johnson pardoned Confederate soldiers after the Civil War. Similar pardons were granted during the twentieth century, when Harry Truman pardoned violators of Selective Service laws during World War II and Jimmy Carter pardoned those who fled the country to avoid the draft during the Vietnam War. Perhaps the most famous (or infamous depending on one's viewpoint) of all time came on September 8, 1974, when Gerald Ford pardoned Richard Nixon for any and all crimes that he may have committed against the United States in relation to the Watergate scandal. Nixon, who accepted the pardon, was considered an unindicted co-conspirator in the subsequent cover-up of the burglary of the Democratic National Headquarters at the Watergate complex in Washington, DC, in July 1972. More than two years later, Nixon resigned from office on August 9, 1974, rather than face impeachment by the House of Representatives.

Ford, who only consulted a handful of advisors within the administration prior to granting the pardon, surprised the nation with his decision. In a statement to the American people, Ford argued that the decision was in the best interests of the nation to move past the damage to the nation's psyche from the Watergate scandal:

> [I have] searched my own conscience with special diligence to determine the right thing for me to do with respect to my predecessor in this place, Richard Nixon, and his loyal wife and family. Theirs is an American tragedy in which we all have played a part. It could go on and on and on, or someone must write the end to it. I have concluded that only I can do that, and if I can, I must. There are no historic or legal precedents to which I can turn in this matter, none that precisely fit the circumstances of a private citizen who has resigned the Presidency of the United States. But it is common knowledge that serious allegations and accusations hang like a sword over our former President's head, threatening his health as he tries to reshape his life, a great part of which was spent in the service of this country and by the mandate of its people. After years of bitter controversy and divisive national debate, I have been advised, and I am compelled to conclude that many months and perhaps more years will have to pass before Richard Nixon could obtain a fair trial by jury in any jurisdiction of the United States under governing

decisions of the Supreme Court. . . . The facts, as I see them, are that a former President of the United States, instead of enjoying equal treatment with any other citizen accused of violating the law, would be cruelly and excessively penalized either in preserving the presumption of his innocence or in obtaining a speedy determination of his guilt in order to repay a legal debt to society. During this long period of delay and potential litigation, ugly passions would again be aroused. And our people would again be polarized in their opinions. . . . But it is not the ultimate fate of Richard Nixon that most concerns me, though surely it deeply troubles every decent and every compassionate person. My concern is the immediate future of this great country. In this, I dare not depend upon my personal sympathy as a longtime friend of the former President, nor my professional judgment as a lawyer, and I do not. As President, my primary concern must always be the greatest good of all the people of the United States whose servant I am. . . . My conscience tells me clearly and certainly that I cannot prolong the bad dreams that continue to reopen a chapter that is closed. My conscience tells me that only I, as President, have the constitutional power to firmly shut and seal this book. My conscience tells me it is my duty, not merely to proclaim domestic tranquility but to use every means that I have to insure it. I do believe that the buck stops here, that I cannot rely upon public opinion polls to tell me what is right. . . . Finally, I feel that Richard Nixon and his loved ones have suffered enough and will continue to suffer, no matter what I do, no matter what we, as a great and good nation, can do together to make his goal of peace come true.

Following Ford's announcement, his approval ratings plummeted and talk immediately began about whether Ford had cut a deal with Nixon over the

Gerald Ford signs his pardon of Richard Nixon on September 8, 1974.

pardon; some suggested that Ford had promised to pardon Nixon once he became president following Nixon's resignation from office. Until his death in 2006, Ford vehemently denied that any deal had been made, always claiming that he believed he had done the right thing for the nation to heal the political wounds of Watergate. Regardless, the shock of the Ford pardon caused a stir even among his closest advisors. Ford's first press secretary and long-time friend Jerald terHorst resigned in protest over the Nixon pardon. Ford also appeared before Congress on October 17, 1974, to give sworn testimony about the pardon; he testified that there had been no deal made over the pardon (he was the first president to testify before Congress since Lincoln). Although most scholars agree that the Nixon pardon cost Ford the 1976 presidential election, no one will ever know whether that was foremost in voters' minds when Jimmy Carter was elected. Right or wrong, Ford's decision to grant the pardon remains an enduring symbol of his presidential legacy.

. . . AND NOW

Although no other pardon has caused as much of a political stir since Ford's pardon of Nixon, more recent presidential pardons have been controversial nonetheless. On Christmas Eve 1992, just weeks before he was to leave office, George H. W. Bush pardoned six Reagan administration officials, including secretary of defense Caspar W. Weinberger, for their involvement in the Iran–Contra scandal. Weinberger and others had been indicted, pled guilty, or were already convicted of crimes connected to Iran–Contra. The pardons, which canceled the upcoming trial for Weinberger, ended any further investigation into the matter. Critics of the pardon suggested that Bush was protecting himself as well; independent counsel Lawrence Walsh had been investigating Bush's involvement in Iran–Contra and had learned that Bush had withheld diaries from investigators that would have contradicted his public statements that he had not been "in the loop" as vice president over the Iran–Contra affair.

Whereas Bush chose to grant the Iran–Contra pardons on Christmas Eve, with the news appearing at a time when most Americans would not be paying much attention to politics, Bill Clinton followed a presidential tradition of granting pardons on his last day in office. The most controversial was what many termed his "eleventh-hour" pardons of fugitive financier Marc Rich and his business partner Pincus Green, both of whom had been indicted for tax evasion and illegal oil trading with Iran. In the "Petition for Pardon" received by the Department of Justice, the attorneys representing both Rich and Green argued:

> Mr. Rich and Mr. Green are internationally recognized businessmen and philanthropists who have contributed over $200,000,000 to charity in the past twenty years, and who have donated countless hours to humanitarian causes around the world. . . . [They] seek a pardon even though they have never been convicted of a criminal offense in the United States or any other country. However, they and two of their companies were wrongfully indicted nearly twenty years ago, primarily on tax and energy charges stemming from their participation in oil transactions under then-existing

Department of Energy oil regulations and controls. Those controls, deemed to be unworkable, incomprehensible and counterproductive, were abolished by President Reagan in one of his first official acts in January, 1981, and now are seen as a relic of the era of excessive economic regulation of the oil industry. [They] have complete defenses to the indictment. While the indictment makes many accusations, the prosecution admits that tax-related charges were the cores of the case. Yet two of the country's leading tax professors have analyzed the tax treatment of the transactions at issue, and concluded that they were correctly reported. Nevertheless, Mr. Rich and Mr. Green remain under indictment and in effective exile from the United States. This is so even though their companies have resolved all charges, and all others who engaged in similar transactions were pursued civilly, or not at all. This petition for a pardon on behalf of Mr. Rich and Mr. Green seeks to put an end to that exile by resolving an otherwise intractable situation between Mr. Rich, Mr. Green and the United States government, and by righting an injustice that has persisted for nearly two decades. [They] are now in their late sixties. They have not traveled to the United States in over seventeen years. Without a Presidential Pardon, there is little if any chance that this matter will be resolved. The current situation is the unfortunate result of unfair and unwarranted treatment of two men against whom no criminal charges should have been brought. A Presidential Pardon will promote the interests of justice, will rectify a wrong, and will finally put this matter to rest.[47]

Clinton handed out 140 pardons and several commutations on his last day in office, including one to his half-brother Roger Clinton for drug-related charges a decade earlier and one to Susan MacDougal, who served 18 months in prison for her refusal to testify against Clinton in the Whitewater investigation. Yet, it was the Rich pardon that drew public outrage from both Democrats and Republicans when it was learned that Rich's ex-wife, Denise Rich, had raised and donated more than $1 million to the Democratic Party and provided the Clintons with $10,000 for their legal defense fund and $7,300 worth of furniture and other gifts. Congressional investigations were launched, and the pardons were also investigated by federal prosecutors (who eventually found no wrongdoing on Clinton's part in granting any pardons).

For George W. Bush, the pardon that became the most high profile at the end of his eight years in office is one that never occurred. Much speculation arose over whether Bush would pardon I. Lewis "Scooter" Libby, former chief of staff to vice president Dick Cheney. Libby had been convicted in federal court for obstruction of justice, perjury, and making false statements in connection to the investigation of the leak of the covert identity of the Central Intelligence Agency officer Valerie Plame. Plame's husband, former ambassador Joseph Wilson, had written an op-ed in the *New York Times* in 2002 that contradicted Bush administration claims that Saddam Hussein had weapons of mass destruction; Libby's leak of Plame's identity was seen as political payback. Following the conviction, Libby was sentenced to 30 months in federal prison with a $250,000 fine and two years' probation. On July 2, 2007, Bush commuted Libby's jail sentence, but left the fines and probation terms intact. Bush explained his decision:

> Mr. Libby was sentenced to thirty months of prison, two years of probation, and a $250,000 fine. In making the sentencing decision, the district court rejected the advice of the probation office, which recommended a lesser sentence and the consideration of factors that could have led to a sentence of home confinement or probation. I respect the jury's verdict. But I have concluded that the prison sentence given to Mr. Libby is excessive. Therefore, I am commuting the portion of Mr. Libby's sentence that required him to spend thirty months in prison. My decision to commute his prison sentence leaves in place a harsh punishment for Mr. Libby. The reputation he gained through his years of public service and professional work in the legal community is forever damaged. His wife and young children have also suffered immensely. He will remain on probation. The significant fines imposed by the judge will remain in effect. The consequences of his felony conviction on his former life as a lawyer, public servant, and private citizen will be long-lasting.

Despite heavy lobbying by Cheney, Bush declined to grant Libby a full pardon prior to leaving office. Cheney later stated publicly his disappointment over Bush's decision, and the lack of a pardon for Libby reportedly caused a rift between Bush and Cheney in their post–White House years.

Although the president may be the chief law-enforcement officer of the federal government, presidents are not themselves immune from or above the law. As such, the framers provided for the removal of the chief executive if such a circumstance should arise; the ultimate constitutional sanction against abuse by the president is impeachment and removal from office. The Constitution defines impeachment at the federal level and limits impeachment to "the President, Vice President, and all civil officers of the United States" who may only be impeached and removed for "treason, bribery, or other high crimes and misdemeanors." Although the constitutional provision of "high crimes and misdemeanors" does not have a specific definition, common law tradition suggests that any personal misconduct is an impeachable offense. Others have suggested that Congress alone may decide for itself what constitutes an impeachable offense. Only two presidents to date have been impeached—Andrew Johnson in 1868 and Bill Clinton in 1998—but both were acquitted by the Senate and remained in office.[48] Whether a president can be impeached for strictly political reasons, as opposed to criminal actions that are indictable, is a constitutional issue that has yet to be resolved.

Legislative Authority

The framers strictly limited the president's constitutional role as head of government, which is confined to the approval or rejection of congressional legislation, the assessment and presentation of relevant policy issues through the State of the Union message, the recommendation of potential legislation, and, in certain circumstances, the adjournment of Congress. Compared to the legislative authority of contemporary British prime ministers, the president's authority was modest at best. The framers of the Constitution did not grant American presidents an active role in anything but the final stage of the legislative process, and they did not envision the power to approve or reject legislation as a grant of legislative authority but a check on Congressional authority itself and a constitutional filter that would promote the legitimacy of prospective federal laws.[49]

Without a doubt, the framers did not want an American prime minister, and they expected the president to devote most of his attention to national security, diplomacy, rudimentary economic coordination, and law enforcement. Yet, Article II, Section 3, of the Constitution suggests that the president is also a policymaker, if not the policymaker in chief. His responsibility to keep Congress apprised of administration objectives and to evaluate the nation's political course through the State of the Union message and his authority to present necessary legislation to Congress reveal his inherent role as policymaker. This means that, although the framers certainly did not intend to create an American prime minister, they did anticipate more than passive presidential involvement in the legislative process through, if nothing else, the formulation and coordination of relevant domestic policies and the enactment of laws that do not conflict with those policies. From a modern perspective, and the framers never would have articulated it in this way, they expected the president to have a policy agenda that would provide a political rationale and derivative strategies for prospective legislation.[50]

The framers' apparent expectations regarding presidential policymaking notwithstanding, they lived in a political world that was markedly different from anything today. Therefore, it is imperative to place those expectations in the proper context and remember that the framers of the Constitution envisioned policymaking, and the president's role in it, as something much simpler, considerably less politicized, and substantially more insular than it eventually became. In today's media-driven political environment, the president, his vast support staff, interest groups, and even the public are all active players in the policymaking and legislative processes. The president himself, especially someone as proactive, for instance, as Lyndon Johnson, Bill Clinton, or George W. Bush, has become not only a policymaker in chief but also the legislator in chief, which is not what the framers intended. The Bush administration shepherded targeted legislation through Congress much like a prime-ministerial cabinet and even ignored established legislative protocols whose purpose was to minimize presidential interference in the legislative process. Although Clinton and, especially, Johnson seemed less imperious and dismissive of entrenched traditions, they were no less forceful, but their innate political skill, which Bush lacked, enabled them to persuade opponents and overcome political obstacles with unique efficacy.[51]

In the late eighteenth century, in contrast, the politicization of the legislative and policymaking processes of the kind that characterizes modern governance would have been unthinkable to all but the most corrupt individuals. Indeed, the American republic was born into a world that delegitimized political parties and rejected professional politics, and the framers anticipated presidents would always be part of a largely nonpartisan elitist minority that preserved lawmaking and policymaking as collaborative and deliberative, not competitive, processes. Although some scholars have referred to the Federalists and Jeffersonian Republicans of the early republic as the first political parties, they were really nothing of the sort, lacking the organization, professionalization, funding, and long-term ideological identification that define political parties.[52] The president's role as policymaker was more that of a moderator in a closed debate among intellectual elites than that of a political competitor advocating his own, or his party's, political priorities.

Appointment and Removal Power

The president's power to appoint judges, executive officials, and military officers has long been one of his most potent tools for shaping the long-term political landscape. Through their appointment and removal powers, presidents have been able to influence both contemporary policies and future political developments, thereby securing legacies that have occasionally far outstripped any accomplishments from their actual tenures in office. Despite the numerous constitutional, political, and sociocultural changes that separate twenty-first-century America from the founding-era republic and the many related disparities between framers' intent and current practices, this has been one of the few constants throughout much of American history.

The framers were acutely aware of the significance associated with the constitutional power to appoint judges and subordinate executive officials, such as department heads.[53] Even before the advent of the spoils system, or political patronage, during the Jacksonian era and its proliferation thereafter, Americans recognized the political and constitutional impact of such authority, which is why this topic caused ongoing debates among the delegates to the Constitutional Convention in 1787.[54] Historically, the appointment power had resided with the crown, but as Parliamentary authority increased during the eighteenth century, most of it was appropriated by the legislature. To the dismay of colonial Americans, Parliament used its authority to appoint ministers, judges, and various administrative officials as nothing more than an overtly political instrument to build partisan coalitions and defeat opposing policies, largely ignoring the long-term political consequences of its decisions.[55]

Political experimentation at the state level following independence only confirmed that the appointment power was no safer in the hands of potentially demagogic legislatures catering to base interests than it had been with the erstwhile imperial executive. So, by 1787, the centralizing faction of American political elites, who pushed for a relatively strong national government, was committed to returning all appointment powers to the executive. A substantial contingent of Southerners, supported by some small-state delegates, remained skeptical of plenary executive authority in this area and pushed for congressional control of appointments and even a few more radical, democratically oriented options. The eventual compromise, which emerged in the final days of the convention, produced the by-now familiar power-sharing scenario whereby the president retained the proposed appointment authority with senatorial advice-and-consent powers as part of the upper legislative chamber's checks-and-balances authority. This was not a perfect solution, but even the Anti-Federalists, who had been traditional opponents of centralization and an active presidency, realized that it was far more efficient than placing such a politically charged task in the hands of several dozen legislators.[56]

The removal power was another matter. Federal judges would serve based on good behavior, so their removal by the president, or others, for nonimpeachable factors such as policy differences or ideological incompatibilities was a nonissue. However, that left a sizable number of executive appointees who would serve at the pleasure of the party or parties to whom they were ultimately accountable. Who would have the authority to dismiss them? These days, Americans take it for granted that the president has the authority to remove most executive appointees, some regulatory personnel excepted, with or without cause, since this seems to be an intrinsic and logical extension of his authority to appoint them. Founding-era Americans were not so sure. Many delegates to the Constitutional Convention believed that congressional advice-and-consent powers implied corresponding privileges to participate in the dismissal of presidential appointees. Others argued that to avoid the politicization of the policymaking process and, thus, deny the president any incentives to silence criticism and compel compliance through dismissal, the legislature or a special commission of sorts should have complete authority over removals.[57]

In the end, separation-of-powers criteria trumped worries about the politicization of presidential appointments, and founding-era critics of presidential appointment authority realized that moving the power to dismiss executive personnel outside the executive branch would violate the separation-of-powers doctrine. Nevertheless, because presidential authority to dismiss, not to reappoint, or otherwise remove executive officials is not explicitly granted in Article II, states' rights advocates and other opponents of implied presidential powers continued to question the president's ability to do so for some time. The issue was finally settled by the 1926 Supreme Court case *Myers v. United States*, in which the justices interpreted the power to dismiss executive personnel as a logical element of presidential appointment authority and a necessary part of his constitutional duty to execute the laws of the United States. As clarified by the Court in subsequent rulings, that power is not absolute, however, and does not categorically extend to certain regulatory appointments, whose dismissal standards are neither as lenient nor as deferential to presidential authority.[58]

The appointment and removal powers have become politicized, and many of the framers' fears regarding the use of such powers for the promotion of partisan priorities were, as it turned out, justifiable. But, despite the ongoing use of presidential appointments to reward partisan loyalty and encourage political compliance, comprehensive bureaucratic reforms during the early part of the twentieth century enhanced, if not secured, the long-term legitimacy of the process. The high-water mark of political patronage through executive appointments, as well as the consequent corruption it fostered, came during the middle and late decades of the nineteenth century, as incoming administrations almost summarily replaced outgoing administrations' appointees with their own loyalists, even in the most minor and insignificant posts. Professional incompetence and lack of experience should have been obstacles to appointment, especially for key positions, but the spoils system ushered in by the Andrew Jackson and Martin Van Buren administrations of the 1830s set a dangerous precedent that elevated party loyalty above professionalism and competence.[59] By the late nineteenth century, repeated malfeasance, inefficiency, and inequity finally motivated Congress to act, and, over the following several decades, it spearheaded a series of civil-service reforms that enshrined merit as the key criterion for bureaucratic appointments and promotions.[60]

Executive Privilege and Immunity

Because the Constitution does not explicitly refer to executive privilege or immunity in Article II or elsewhere, their constitutional and legal viability has been questionable, as has their scope. Therefore, constitutional interpretation of executive privilege has been problematic for generations, a situation that has been exacerbated by the lack of founding-era documents regarding the topic. The fact that neither the Constitution nor its supporting material contains much information about executive privilege only confirms the intended modesty of the office, not least since contemporary documents suggest that the duties and responsibilities of the presidency would be sufficiently confined to obviate habitual reliance on executive privilege. In addition, the framers expected America's presidents to remain part of a relatively narrow stratum of sociopolitical elites who rejected professional politics and organized partisanship, which supposedly would have minimized the presidency's exposure to the political liabilities immunity and discretion are necessary to prevent.

As incredible as it may seem today, the framers simply could not foresee the politicization of governance that has occurred in the United States, nor could they envision a time when the president's duties and responsibilities would be so extensive and even so imperial that executive privilege would be more than an isolated concern. However, Article I, Section 6, of the Constitution does identify specific immunities granted to members of Congress to protect them in the fulfillment of their legislative duties, so the omission of similar provisions in Article II could not have been mere oversight or coincidence. To critics of the modern presidency, this has been further proof of the comparative insignificance of executive privilege for the framers, whereas to its advocates, it has been evidence of the framers' presumption of privilege, executive included. As it turns out, both camps are correct, but the interpretive dilemmas and debates regarding executive privilege have continued unabated. Over the years, especially since the 1970s, the Supreme Court has offered some guidance through rulings that have conditionally denied the existence of both absolute immunity and categorical discretion.[61] Most notably, the Supreme Court ruled in *U.S. v. Nixon* (1974) that executive privilege does exist, but no one, not even the president, is completely above the law and the president cannot use executive privilege as an excuse to withhold evidence that is "demonstrably relevant in a criminal trial." The Supreme Court has also recognized broad presidential immunity against civil suits involving claims stemming from their official actions, in *Nixon v. Fitzgerald* (1982). But in *Clinton v. Jones* (1997), the Supreme Court held that presidential immunity does not extend to suits involving the president's private conduct and allowed the sexual harassment lawsuit brought against Clinton by former Arkansas state employee Paula Jones to go forward prior to the end of Clinton's term.

EXPANSION OF PRESIDENTIAL POWERS

History has shown an expansion of presidential powers beyond what the framers originally intended for both the president as an individual actor and the presidency as an institution. The powers of the presidency have been expanded tremendously by certain presidents while in office, which usually coincided with times of crises. Several presidents shaped the office in which they served by adopting broad interpretations of their responsibilities, and many expansions of power have occurred when presidents claimed "the silences of the Constitution." However, presidents themselves have viewed their own powers in office differently, depending on the state of the economy and world affairs. Presidential personalities can also determine much about how presidential power is exercised. For example, FDR was faced with a severe economic crisis when he first took office and exercised many presidential powers. His legacy, and the constitutionality of many of his actions, is still being debated. Yet, FDR's years in the White House reflect an undeniable transformation of presidential powers, and he is one of several presidents who changed the nature of the office forever.

Theories of Presidential Power

The first several men to hold the office of the presidency set important early precedents regarding presidential powers. Many historians argue that one of the motivating factors for the framers in how they designed the office of the president at the Constitutional Convention was a result of the widely shared view among them that George Washington would serve as the nation's first chief executive. As such, the framers placed much trust in Washington to shape the office for future occupants. Indeed, Washington did set an important, albeit informal, precedent of only serving two terms. He also expanded the powers of the office by setting the precedent that department heads should support the president's policies, going beyond the Constitution's suggestion to receive written opinions on policy matters. Washington also set a precedent for presidents, not Congress, to determine which foreign ambassadors to receive or which foreign countries would be granted diplomatic recognition. Similarly, Thomas Jefferson played an important role in the early development of presidential powers. Jefferson often responded to political, rather than legal, considerations, such as the Louisiana Purchase in 1803, considered controversial at the time since the Constitution did not grant specific powers to the president to acquire new territory. Jefferson was also the first president to govern through leadership of what would be considered an early iteration of a political party and dominated the affairs of Congress through the Democratic-Republican caucus. Jefferson never had to veto legislation, because no bill he seriously opposed ever reached his desk for consideration.

Since that time, the actions of subsequent presidents have led to the development of numerous theories to explain the constitutional role of presidential power within the American governing process. Notable among those include the prerogative, the stewardship, and the literalist theories. The prerogative theory of the presidency is most often attributed to Abraham Lincoln, who stretched the emergency powers of the office more than any other president as a result of the Civil War. Lincoln unilaterally authorized many decisions and then called Congress back into session to make them legitimate; he called up the militia and volunteers, blockaded southern ports, expanded the army and navy beyond statute limitations, closed the mails to treasonous correspondence, arrested persons suspected of disloyalty, and suspended the writ of habeas corpus. Lincoln justified his actions both as commander in chief and through the "vesting" and "take-care" (that the laws be faithfully executed) clauses of the Constitution: "I have never understood that the presidency conferred upon me an unrestricted right to act. . . . I did understand, however, that my oath to preserve the Constitution to the best of my ability imposed upon me the duty of preserving, by every indispensable means, that government—that nation, of which the Constitution was the organic law. . . . I felt that measures otherwise unconstitutional might become lawful by becoming indispensable to the preservation of the Constitution through the preservation of the nation."[62]

Theodore Roosevelt argued for the stewardship doctrine, which supports expanding the role and powers of the president, if it is done in the interest of the public and is not unconstitutional. At the turn of the twentieth century, Roosevelt ushered in the era of the rhetorical president and, as such, believed that he was the steward of the people. Accordingly, he effectively used the bully pulpit to link the president with the people. Like Lincoln, he found broad powers within the vesting and take-care clauses and saw the president as an agent of social and economic reform. He called his domestic program the "Square Deal," and it focused on three main issues: conservation of natural resources, control of corporations, and consumer protection. Roosevelt also greatly enhanced the role of the president as a statesman in the international arena. During his presidency, he initiated the building of the Panama Canal, expanded the size and scope of the U.S. Navy, and intervened militarily in several nations (most notably in Latin America). The latter, which began to move the United States away from its traditional isolationist posture, is known as "Roosevelt's Corollary" to the Monroe Doctrine. The Monroe Doctrine, first introduced in 1823 by James Monroe, stated that the United States would view further efforts by European countries to colonize land in the Americas as an act of aggression. Roosevelt expanded that view to justify U.S. power to act as an international police force and proclaimed the Americas independent of European control. In 1913, Roosevelt wrote in his autobiography, "I declined to adopt the view that what was imperatively necessary for the nation could not be done by the President unless he could find some specific authorization for it. My belief was that it was not only his right but his duty to do anything that the needs of the nation demanded unless such action was forbidden by the Constitution or by the laws."[63]

William Howard Taft, Roosevelt's immediate successor, argued for the opposite in terms of presidential power. A supporter of a literalist approach to the presidency, also known as the Whig theory, Taft believed that the president should only have those powers as specifically outlined in the Constitution: "The true view of the Executive functions is, as I conceive it, that the President can exercise no power which cannot be fairly and reasonably traced to some specific grant of power or justly implied and included within such express grant as proper and necessary to its exercise. Such specific grant must be either in the Federal Constitution or in an act of Congress passed in pursuance thereof. There is no undefined residuum of power which he can exercise because it seems to be in the public interest."[64] Taft's view of the presidency and its powers, more in line with James Madison's strict interpretation of the powers of the office, left him in a weaker position vis-à-vis Congress and his attempts to continue Roosevelt's policy agenda. Taft's deference to Congress, his move away from the public connection that Roosevelt had developed, and his perceived ineffective leadership as a result of his inability to wield the available powers of the presidency as Roosevelt had contributed to Taft's failure to win reelection in 1912.[65] Roosevelt's entrance in that year's presidential election as a third-party candidate, challenging his former friend and political ally, also helped open the door to Woodrow Wilson's election.

Wilson, a political scientist and former president of Princeton University, held views of presidential power similar to Roosevelt's; both were more closely aligned with Alexander Hamilton's view of a strong, energetic presidency. Wilson sought to exercise fully the powers of the office (particularly through his unitary approach in leading the nation into World War I), and whereas Roosevelt had sought to link the presidency directly to the people by removing the influence of political parties, Wilson instead wanted to make the president a strong party leader. His view of the Constitution "was based on a notion that government is made to adapt to changing times—with the chief executive leading the way—as opposed to the more restrained notion of governmental power so esteemed by the founders."[66]

The Constitutionality of Expanded Presidential Powers

Between 1860 and 1920, the executive branch experienced significant changes, which were ultimately at odds with the framers' conception of it. Lincoln, Roosevelt, and Wilson led the charge toward a more modern presidency capable of accommodating greater authority and expanded resources. Nevertheless, despite some potentially dangerous precedents that affected the future evolution of the presidency, these changes did not yet represent an irreversible breach of constitutional principles or the framers' vision of republican government. During the late 1940s and into the early 1950s, such a breach started to appear so that, by the 1970s, the American presidency had transcended many of the boundaries of legitimate authority defined by the framers. In particular, Lyndon Johnson and Richard Nixon have been labeled "imperial" presidents, mostly because of the actions of each regarding the use of military force in Vietnam (and, in Nixon's case, surrounding Southeast Asian countries as well) in an attempt to stop the spread of communism. According to Arthur Schlesinger Jr., the use of presidential powers was out of control and had exceeded its constitutional limits during the Johnson and Nixon years.[67]

How did the system of checks and balances fail so miserably to prevent, or at least overturn, these constitutional transgressions? Why have the American people tolerated the aggressive acquisition of power by America's commanders in chief and the abdication of congressional responsibility and oversight with respect to national defense? These questions have no easy answers. They arise from the same dilemma that resulted in questionable constitutional increases of congressional authority over social and economic issues since the 1930s. Just as Congress acquired powers that went beyond any of those granted to it by the framers to confront the social and economic crises unleashed by industrialization (particularly FDR's actions during the Great Depression of the 1930s), the presidency amassed sufficient authority to address the military and diplomatic crises unleashed by the Cold War. In both cases, exigent circumstances required action and not political debate about constitutional amendments, so Americans and their political officials turned a blind eye to what they perceived as the necessary costs of political compromise. The most serious of these costs was what some would argue to be an unconstitutional expansion of governmental authority that equipped federal officials with powers that would have been unthinkable just a century before.

As convincing as such an explanation may be, it only tells half the story. Because the framers of the Constitution were aware of the public's susceptibility to lapses of judgment and they worried that even majority decisions could be illegitimate, they took precautions against exactly these kinds of situations. They made sure that, even in the unlikely event that the regular constitutional checks and balances did not work properly, a remedy of last resort would compensate for their mistakes. That remedy was the federal judiciary, specifically the U.S. Supreme Court. As the institution charged with the interpretation of federal laws and actions and determining the meaning of pertinent constitutional principles, the Supreme Court was established to address constitutional violations and maintain the integrity of the nation's foundational laws. Although some doubts existed during the early republic about the finality of the Court's broader theories, the founding generation had no doubts about the Court's ability to decide the constitutionality of particular acts or the finality of its opinions regarding specific cases.

In general, the Supreme Court has been willing to allow expansion of executive power over constitutional objections (see Table 2.1). Two cases, however, show the Court's willingness to define the issue of inherent powers when dealing with domestic issues. In *Youngstown Sheet & Tube Company v. Sawyer* (1952), the Court struck down Harry Truman's seizure of the nation's steel mills, rejecting Truman's argument

Table 2.1 Key Supreme Court Decisions Defining Presidential Powers

YEAR	CASE	HOLDING
1861	*Ex parte Merryman*	Lincoln's suspension of the writ of habeas corpus unconstitutional
1862	*The Prize Cases*	Lincoln's emergency powers extended to allow military blockade of Southern ports
1866	*Ex parte Milligan*	Use of military tribunals unconstitutional where civil courts remain operational
1926	*Myers v. United States*	Presidents can remove executive officers without advice and consent of Senate
1936	*United States v. Curtiss–Wright Export Corporation*	Presidents, not Congress, have plenary powers over foreign affairs
1944	*Korematsu v. United States*	FDR's executive order to create Japanese American internment camps constitutional
1952	*Youngstown Sheet and Tube v. Sawyer*	Truman's executive order for government seizure and operation of steel mills unconstitutional
1974	*United States v. Nixon*	Executive privilege not absolute and does not apply in a criminal investigation of the executive branch
1982	*Nixon v. Fitzgerald*	Presidents have immunity from liability for damages from official acts
1997	*Clinton v. Jones*	Presidents do not have immunity from civil suits involving unofficial acts
1998	*Clinton v. City of New York*	Line Item Veto Act unconstitutional
2004	*Rasul v. Bush and Hamdi v. Rumsfeld*	Detention of enemy combatants without due process rights unconstitutional
2006	*Hamdan v. Rumsfeld*	Military commissions established by the Bush administration to try foreign terrorism suspects unconstitutional
2008	*Boumediene v. Bush*	Foreign terrorism suspects can challenge their detention in U.S. courts
2014	*National Labor Relations Board v. Noel Canning*	Presidents cannot make recess appointments unless the Senate is in recess and cannot conduct business

for inherent executive power stemming from the domestic economy and the Korean War effort. The Court recognized an inherent executive power transcending enumerations in Article II but nevertheless found Truman's action to be impermissible since Congress had already considered and rejected legislation permitting such an executive order. This case was a reminder that the stewardship theory is neither entirely self-derived nor without limitation and that the president's actions within the domestic sphere are subject to judicial scrutiny.

Similarly, in *New York Times Company v. United States* (1971), the Court declared no threat to national security because of the publication of the Pentagon Papers. Richard Nixon had sent his attorney general, John Mitchell, into federal district court to seek an injunction against the *New York Times* for its series of stories on the Pentagon Papers, leaked classified documents (a 47-volume study) detailing the history of United States involvement in Vietnam. The ruling was a victory for advocates of freedom of the press and a rebuke to Nixon over his claim of national security. A few days after the Supreme Court handed down its ruling, White House aide Patrick J. Buchanan suggested to Nixon how he might make political gains despite the legal defeat, showing that a Supreme Court decision can have both constitutional and political reverberations:

> We are being damaged on three grounds because of these documents: 1. We are being portrayed as "repressive" for attempting to hold up the documents, "political" because we appear to be covering up something, and "ridiculous," in that we have appeared ineffectual and comical with our lack of success. 2. More important, the American support for the war effort is being seriously damaged as the impression is being left to stand that somehow the United States is the guilty party in the entire war. This feeling nationally could affect continued national support for the President's withdrawal program, and for US support in Saigon. 3. The whole question of lack of trust in government which is raised by this matter is being used against us as well as Johnson—and we have to build a firewall between the Administrations. On the necessity side, we have to get clear of the fallout from this entire episode. On the advantage side, the *Times* and *Post* are vulnerable; and there is considerable presidential mileage to be gained from speaking out now.[68]

Regarding foreign policy, as early as 1936, the Supreme Court gave its approval on presidential primacy in *United States v. Curtiss–Wright Export Corporation*. In 1934, Congress had adopted a joint resolution authorizing the president to prohibit U.S. companies from selling munitions to the warring nations of Paraguay and Bolivia. Congress also provided for criminal penalties for those violating presidential prohibitions. Curtiss–Wright brought suit, claiming that Congress had unconstitutionally delegated its lawmaking powers to the president. Despite the Court having ruled against delegation of legislative power in domestic issues in *Schechter Poultry Corporation v. United States* (1935) a year earlier, the Court said that the delegation of power was constitutional when dealing with foreign affairs. The Court referred to the president as the "sole organ of the federal government in the field of international relations." This is based on the belief, first articulated by John Marshall when he was a member of the House of Representatives in 1799 (Marshall would become chief justice of the United States in 1801), that presidents should have independence when acting with regard to foreign policy. This is similar to unitary executive theory, which holds that the president controls the entire executive branch based on the vesting clause in Article II.[69]

Since that time, the Court has often deferred to and recognized congressional acquiescence to grant the president broad powers in the foreign-policy arena. Presidents have authority to make treaties with foreign nations with the advice and consent of the Senate. The broad scope of this power was endorsed by the Supreme Court in *Missouri v. Holland* (1920), which involved a treaty between the United States and Great Britain involving migratory birds from Canada. The Court rejected the claim made by Missouri that Congress did not have the authority to pass regulations against the killing of such birds stemming from the treaty. Presidents also use executive agreements as an alternative to treaties or to implement treaty provisions. Unlike treaties, executive agreements do not require the concurrence of the Senate.

Researching the Presidency

Unilateral Powers

Executive orders are not the only weapon available in a president's unilateral powers arsenal; presidents can also issue proclamations, executive agreements with other nations, administrative and national security directives, military orders, pardons, recess appointments, and signing statements. These unilateral actions do not need legislative coordination or approval, although they can be challenged as unconstitutional. The use of unilateral powers by presidents has emerged in recent years as an intriguing and expanding area of research for presidency scholars, challenging in many ways the more traditional "strategic" view of presidential actions based on Richard Neustadt's seminal work, *Presidential Power*. The research on unilateral powers has expanded the discussion, and it has become "a significant research paradigm in its own right, widely perceived as capturing a significant portion of what presidents actually do."[70]

Two specific works are worth noting for helping to expand this area of inquiry regarding presidential powers. The first, Kenneth R. Mayer's 2001 book *With the Stroke of a Pen: Executive Orders and Presidential Powers*, shows that presidents can and do go beyond merely the power to persuade to implement major policy changes through executive orders. Mayer argues that executive orders "can have profound consequences."[71] Notable examples include Thomas Jefferson's purchase of the Louisiana Territory in 1803, Abraham Lincoln's Emancipation Proclamation in 1863, FDR's creation of the Executive Office of the President in 1939, and, more recently, George W. Bush's creation of military tribunals to try enemy combatants. The second, William G. Howell's 2003 book *Power without Persuasion: The Politics of Direct Presidential Action*, also shows how and when presidents rely on unilateral powers, the extent to which it provides an advantage to presidents over other political actors, and perhaps most important, why this topic is so relevant: "If we want to account for the influence that presidents wield over the construction of public policy, we must begin to pay serious attention to the president's capacity to create law on his own."[72] Presidents continue to expand their use of unilateral powers, and presidency scholars have also continued to expand research on this topic to better understand the constitutional implications of presidential action when they go it alone.

Valid executive agreements are legally equivalent to treaties, but presidents often use them to bypass Congress. Most involve minor matters of international concern, such as specification of the details of postal relations or the use of radio airwaves. The president can also terminate a treaty without Senate approval, as determined by the Court in *Goldwater v. Carter* (1979), which dealt with the termination of a defense treaty with Taiwan.[73]

Presidential power to act in a national emergency and to commit military forces to combat situations has a long heritage. The president is the commander in chief, yet Congress has the power to declare war. The commander in chief may need to "repel sudden attacks," but must share power in this regard with the Congress to protect against the possible abuse of presidential power in waging war. In *Ex parte Merryman* (1861), Chief Justice Roger Taney declared Lincoln's suspension of habeas corpus to be unconstitutional on the grounds that only Congress has the power to suspend the writ "when in Cases of Rebellion or Invasion the public Safety may require it." In *The Prize Cases* (1863), the Court acknowledged the necessity of deferring to the president's decisions in times of crisis. With the absence of a formal declaration of war from the Congress, Lincoln in 1863 ordered the capture of vessels by the Union navy during the blockade of Southern ports. Under the existing law at the time, the vessels would become the property of the Union only with a formal declaration of war. But the Court found the seizures to be legal, stating that "the President is not only authorized, but bound to resist force. He does not initiate the war, but is bound to accept the challenge without waiting for any special legislative authority." Additionally, Justice Robert Grier noted that the "President was bound to meet [the Civil War] in the shape it presented itself, without waiting for the Congress to baptize it with a name."[74]

Another difficult constitutional question involves the extent of presidential power in the domestic sphere during wartime, especially as it relates to the rights of American citizens. The Court has given mixed answers to this question. For example, in *Ex Parte Milligan* (1866), the Court declared that Lincoln's orders for the trial of civilians by military courts were unconstitutional. Yet, in one of its more infamous rulings in *Korematsu v. United States* (1944), the Court declared constitutional the internment of Japanese Americans by the FDR administration during World War II. In 1988, Ronald Reagan signed legislation providing reparations to those same Japanese American families.

These types of issues would again come before the Supreme Court following the 9/11 terrorist attacks and the subsequent application of presidential authority by the George W. Bush administration. The Bush administration argued that as a wartime president, Bush had greatly expanded constitutional authorities to combat terrorism and protect national security. He and his advisors relied on the unitary executive theory regarding many of their actions. For example, Bush claimed that he had the authority to indefinitely detain foreign nationals as well as U.S. citizens determined to be "enemy combatants" at Guantanamo Bay. However, the Supreme Court did not always concur with Bush's interpretation of presidential powers. In *Rasul v. Bush* (2004), the Court rejected the claim that federal courts lacked jurisdiction over foreign nationals held in Cuba and affirmed the right of these individuals to seek judicial review of the basis for their detention. In *Hamdi v. Rumsfeld*

(2004), the Court ruled that the president has a right to detain U.S. citizens as enemy combatants, but that citizens have a right to consult with an attorney and to contest the basis for their detention before an independent tribunal. The right to hold an enemy combatant indefinitely was not granted under the Authorization for Use of Military Force passed by Congress to fight terrorism after 9/11. In *Hamdan v. Rumsfeld* (2006), the Court ruled that military commissions set up by the Bush administration lacked "the power to proceed because its structures and procedures violate both the Uniform Code of Military Justice and the four Geneva Conventions signed in 1949." And in *Boumediene v. Bush* (2008), the Court ruled that foreign terrorist suspects held at Guantanamo Bay have constitutional rights to challenge their detention in U.S. courts.[75]

CONCLUSION

The framers' intent versus contemporary practices can often present an interesting paradox. Although the Constitution has changed little regarding the presidency since 1787, the framers would probably not recognize the office, not only because of the size of the executive branch but also because of the scope of presidential powers. Yet, one can argue that modern presidents have, for the most part, governed within the parameters of the Constitution since the framers left many areas of authority vague and open to interpretation. How presidents and their advisors have interpreted the Constitution, particularly in the areas of the vesting clause and the president's role as commander in chief, is often the most significant determinant of how a president approaches his duties while in office. Whereas some presidents have taken a strict view of the Constitution and have not read any extra powers within the vagueness of the language of Article II, most, if not all, presidents since FDR have taken a more permissive view of the powers of the office. Those who bemoan the expansion of the executive branch and the size of the accompanying bureaucracy, as well as the willingness of so many presidents to commit U.S. military forces without a congressional declaration of war, would argue that the actions of presidents throughout the twentieth century and into the twenty-first are a constitutional aberration. Others, perhaps more realistically, recognize that the dramatic social and economic changes since World War II, not to mention national-security and defense issues, require a strong presidency to react swiftly to changing world events. Regardless of one's viewpoint, there is no denying that the individuals who have held the office of the presidency have played just as important a role in shaping presidential powers as have the changes to the institution itself.

In recent years, neither the Bush nor Obama administrations showed any interest in reversing course regarding an expansive view of presidential powers. If anything, both presidents reignited the debate over the president's role as commander in chief; many considered the Bush years a reemergence of the imperial presidency with his response to terrorism, and Obama also expanded constitutional boundaries in this area (for example, with his use of drone strikes).[76] These debates are not without partisan motivations, however, because many of the arguments depend on whether the president is "doing the right thing" (from those in the president's party) or is engaging in an unconstitutional "power grab" (from those in the opposing party).

The Supreme Court, more so than Congress, has remained at least somewhat responsive in its role to check the powers of the president, whereas Congress has abdicated much of its responsibility (especially regarding war powers). Since precedent can play such an important role in the actions of those in power within the American system of government, it seems unlikely that a course correction regarding the expansion of presidential powers will occur anytime soon. The institutional expansion of the powers of the presidency, as well as the individuals who serve as president, will undoubtedly continue to challenge the framers' intent as well as responses from both Congress and the Supreme Court over the constitutionality of presidential actions.

CHAPTER 3

The Presidential Selection Process

T he 2016 presidential election was unlike any other in recent history. Initially, there did not seem to be anything exceptional or out of the ordinary in the prenomination phase, although it was an open race for both parties with no incumbent president or vice president running. This scenario often leads to a large field of contenders, especially for the party that is out of power. As a result, 17 Republican candidates were seeking their party's nomination. On the Democratic side, many experts predicted that Hillary Clinton would easily win her party's nomination even before she had officially declared her candidacy. Clinton's clear front-runner status, along with the difficulty in a party maintaining control of the White House for three consecutive terms (it had only happened once since the 20-year tenure of FDR and Truman from 1933 to 1953, with George H. W. Bush's election in 1988 to succeed Ronald Reagan), would leave only four other candidates willing to run against the Clinton juggernaut. Yet, despite the presence of Clinton and former Florida governor Jeb Bush in the race, as well as their close ties to the previous four presidencies (the former being Bill Clinton's wife and having served as Barack Obama's secretary of state and the latter being the son of George H. W. Bush and brother of George W. Bush), 2016 became a year dominated by political outsiders and a strong antiestablishment mood among voters as the candidacies of both Donald Trump and Bernie Sanders cracked the foundations of the status quo.

Trump, a real estate mogul and reality television star who won the Republican nomination and the presidency, and Sanders, a self-described Democratic socialist who nearly upended Clinton's inevitable nomination by winning 23 Democratic primary contests, confounded political pundits who routinely wrote off their chances. In contrast to previous elections, Trump and Sanders rewrote the conventional wisdom about presidential campaigns in numerous ways: each demonstrated that raising money from big donors, saturating the airwaves with negative television ads, having extensive government experience, and having party support would not determine the outcome. Ultimately, the 2016 election was a signal of how the process to elect a president has deviated from the original constitutional design. In addition, given Trump's Electoral College victory (304–227) despite Clinton having won the popular vote (48.2 percent to 46.2 percent), it also served as a reminder of how the framers sought to insulate electing a president from the American public and ensure the relevance of small states.

Today's presidential campaigns and elections have become multi-billion-dollar propositions to strategically market candidates to voters while under the constant scrutiny of the news media. Presidential campaigns are increasingly candidate-centered, media- and money-driven, seemingly never-ending affairs that showcase all of the political players that take part—the candidates, their spouses, and/or family members; campaign managers, strategists, fundraisers, spokespeople, and volunteers; party officials at the national, state, and local levels; interest groups; pollsters; and political reporters and pundits in every known medium. And let's not forget the voters, who must attempt to pay attention during a campaign cycle that keeps getting longer and process the information that bombards them, all in an attempt to decide which candidate will receive their vote. This is no longer the simple process that the framers envisioned, one in which a small gathering of political elites would caucus and cast votes to select the president.

How, then, does this complex and chaotic process of presidential elections continue to yield a result every four years that leads to the peaceful transition of leadership without revolution? Americans nominate and then elect presidential candidates through various stages of the campaign process, including the prenomination phase, primaries and caucuses, the national party conventions, and the general election. The process of campaigning for president has a dramatic effect not only on the election outcome but also on setting the stage for the president's future governing prospects. In the end, who chooses to run for president, and who succeeds in winning the election, greatly affects not only the day-to-day governing of the nation, but also the institution of the presidency.

THE NOMINATING PROCESS IN HISTORICAL PERSPECTIVE

The rules of the presidential selection process laid out in the Constitution highlight the framers' preoccupations and predispositions. The framers believed in political elitism and contended that property ownership was evidence of the responsibility necessary to participate in political affairs. During the Constitutional Convention, the framers considered including a property qualification for the presidency, since most states required gubernatorial candidates to own property. The convention even adopted a motion that judges, legislators, and the executive must own property, but ultimately rejected it because they could not agree on an appropriate level to set the qualification.[1] Consequently, the Constitution states that a presidential candidate must only be a natural-born citizen, at least 35 years of age, and have lived in the United States for 14 years.

However, there is no method for nominating elected officials in the Constitution; the framers did not provide for nomination procedures because of their shared belief in an available pool of appropriate candidates. A simple ranking of the field would be sufficient in an environment that did not include firm partisan divisions. In the presence of partisan divisions and the establishment of political parties, the concept of a consensus-created pool of appropriate candidates withered. The two-party system emerged as political elites divided over ideology while recognizing that opportunities to advance that ideology improved with organization outside government. Capturing offices to shape government outcomes became the driving force behind the evolution of political parties.

Between 1800 and 1824, as the party system began to take shape, presidential selection was rooted in the caucus. In use prior to the adoption of the Constitution, the caucus was an informal meeting of political leaders held to answer questions concerning candidates, strategies, and policies. The essence of the caucus, when applied to nominations, was that by weeding out candidates before the election, leaders could assemble substantial support behind a single candidate and decrease the possibility that the votes "will be split among several candidates."[2] The caucus system remained effective while the framers dominated the political class. Time and increased democratization eroded what was known as "King Caucus" as the scope of political participation widened.

As the influence of the Federalists began to wane, the only group closely resembling a political party between 1816 and 1824 fielding a presidential candidate was Thomas Jefferson's Democratic-Republican Party. The absence of a second party did not mean ideological consensus, despite this time being called the "Era of Good Feeling." Political battles arose about leadership, particularly the choice for the presidential nomination. The tension produced by the lack of inclusiveness in the nomination process came to a head in the presidential election of 1824. Democratic-Republicans dissolved as disparate factions nominated four distinct candidates: John Quincy Adams, Andrew Jackson, William Crawford, and Henry Clay. Jackson received the most Electoral College votes, but not enough for a majority, so the election fell to the House of Representatives. The Twelfth Amendment (ratified in 1804) only allows for the top three vote-getters to be considered, so the race then fell to Jackson, Adams, and Crawford. However, Clay was Speaker of the House and as such exercised enormous influence on the outcome. Adams won the election and Clay became his secretary of state. The "corrupt bargain," as it became known, effectively dismantled the Democratic-Republican Party as it dissolved into the Whigs (who supported Adams and Clay) and the Democrats (who supported Jackson). Adams may have won the election but Jackson won the era because, by 1828, he won the presidency and his party controlled Congress.

Disgust with the outcome and the machinations of the 1824 election ushered in change to the nominating process. By 1836, both the Whigs and the Democrats used a national convention that featured state delegates (chosen by state conventions of local party leaders) to nominate their respective presidential candidates. As a result, a party's presidential nominee was connected to a widely dispersed party organization. The power of that political network as a connection to the electorate slowly became a source of power for the president, beginning as early as Jackson's linking of the presidency to the people during his two terms in office (1829–1837).

National party conventions controlled the presidential nomination process for more than 100 years. Although the convention process enabled participation by a larger group of people who were not all of the same financial status or the same region, it was not an open process. First, only party members participated. Second, between 1850 and 1950 there was a consolidation of power under party bosses. The classic picture of presidential nominations consisted of men behind closed doors in smoke-filled rooms determining the outcome, regardless of how many rank-and-file party members filled the convention hall as delegates. Power, not rules, determined the outcome, and the hold over presidential nominations by party leaders made the convention process frustratingly undemocratic for many participants.

To counter the weight and import of party leadership, progressive reformers introduced the primary as a means to influence the choice of the presidential nominee. Prior to the Progressive Era (1890s to 1920s), voters chose sides, not candidates. Individuals voted along party lines, and split-ticket voting was impossible until the adoption of the Australian ballot (allowing for choice in secret) in the late 1890s by the majority of states. Reformers revolted against the control of local and state party leaders making back-room deals with cronies.[3] As a result, the primary system was gradually adopted by some states, whereas other states employed a caucus method for party rank-and-file members to select candidates. These choices by the regular membership of the party influenced the choices of the state delegates to the national convention. Each party determined for itself how influential the choices of the regular membership would be. The creation of the primary system by progressive reformers intended to undermine the power of a narrow group of party leaders. However, party leaders were reluctant to cede all control in selecting party nominees.

The last major reforms to the nominating system came in 1972, following the tumultuous Democratic National Convention in 1968 that included rioting in the streets of Chicago to protest, among other things, the Vietnam War and the selection of Vice President Hubert Humphrey as the presidential nominee. Although Humphrey had the most pledged delegates at the end of the primary process, he had not competed in any state primaries, instead earning his support through state caucuses whose delegates were determined by party leaders. Senators Robert Kennedy (NY) and Eugene McCarthy (MN) had been competing for delegates in the primary contests, but following Kennedy's assassination in June after winning the California primary, his delegates remained uncommitted going into the convention. Party bosses selected Humphrey as the nominee, ignoring the number of delegates that McCarthy had won in the primary process. Following the convention, the McGovern–Fraser Commission was formed to enact changes to the nominating process. The commission recommended a more open and democratic process for selecting delegates, which would result in more rank-and-file party members, as opposed to party bosses, having a say in the selection of the nominee. By 1972, both Democrats and Republicans began to hold primary elections in many more states, which left party bosses with less power. The system in place today reveals how party insiders attempt to retain control of the nominating process while permitting a broader array of voices to participate.

THE PRENOMINATION PERIOD

The adoption of the primary process, as well as the use of caucuses in some states, represents efforts to broaden participation in the selection of nominees for the two major parties. The creation of what in practice amounts to a series of mini-elections summed together to produce the requisite delegate count at the national party convention changed the incentives and behavior for candidates, party elites, and voters. For example, in 2016, there were 75 different state primary races between February 1 and June 14. In some states, like South Carolina and Wyoming, the Democrats and Republicans did not hold their primaries on the same day. Other states, like Louisiana, have Democratic primaries and Republican caucuses. Consequently, candidates for the nomination from either party must make critical strategic decisions regarding the allocation of resources. Beginning with the prenomination period and concluding with the national party's nominating conventions, the process of selecting major party candidates to vie for the presidency in the general election is dominated by money, media, and momentum and represents the American political version of "survival of the fittest."

Deciding to Run

Technically speaking, the constitutional requirements for president are minimal. However, many unofficial requirements influence the viability of a candidate: prior political experience, name recognition, party support, adequate funding and fundraising abilities, strong appeal from the party base (particularly during the primaries), appeal to independent or swing voters (particularly during the general election), and strong leadership and communication skills. Throughout American history, the pool of viable candidates for both president and vice president has been almost exclusively Protestant, white, and male (Barack Obama and Hillary Clinton being obvious exceptions). The character, personality, and style of candidates matter greatly, especially because reporting during presidential campaigns has become increasingly cynical, sensationalized, and hypercritical, leading to an increased focus on the "cult of personality" during presidential campaigns.[4] Although issues and partisan loyalty still matter, presidential campaigns have increasingly become "candidate-centered" contests.[5]

Every campaign cycle, a short list of potential presidential candidates emerges, put together in part by the news media through speculation based on the behavior and travel patterns of notable politicians (for example, who is traveling to Iowa and/or New Hampshire or speaking at high-profile party events). This so-called on-deck circle of potential candidates typically consists of roughly 30 to 40 individuals, usually prominent members of Congress, governors (past and present), former or current vice presidents, and former presidential and vice presidential candidates.[6] The image of "master politician" with political experience and a substantive policy record, once necessary to run for the presidency, has given way to the image of the Washington outsider, requiring strong speaking skills, an emphasis on anti-Washington rhetoric, and broad public appeal outside of Washington. This strategy proved successful for previous governors Jimmy Carter, Ronald Reagan, Bill Clinton, and George W. Bush and even helped Barack Obama, who had only been in the U.S. Senate for four years prior to his election as president.[7] In 2016, the Republican field included two high-profile chief executive officers (Trump and Carly Fiorina, former chief executive officer of Hewlett Packard) and a pediatric neurosurgeon (Ben Carson). Trump would become the first president elected with no previous political or military experience.

All of these "unofficial" requirements for the presidency have contributed to the dearth of women presidential candidates, since so few women have held the appropriate leadership positions within government that allow them access to the on-deck circle.[8] However, in 2016, for the first time, each major party had a woman candidate seeking the presidential nomination. As the only woman in a crowded Republican field, Fiorina focused on her corporate experience and the need to put a noncareer politician in the White House. She gained momentum in the polls following her impressive performance in the first two Republican debates in August and September 2015. Her narrative attracted more media attention in the ensuing weeks, which increased her standing in numerous polls. Yet, her momentum began to stall as her poll numbers plateaued in late October despite another strong performance in the third GOP debate that month. She was often labeled a strong candidate but was never viewed as a favorite to win a particular state on the primary map; she dropped out of the race in February 2016 after a poor showing in both Iowa and New Hampshire. Clinton, in contrast, would make history as the first woman to win a major party nomination. As she stated in her acceptance speech at the 2016 Democratic National Convention, "when there are no ceilings, the sky is the limit." Research has suggested that a critical gender difference exists in the candidate emergence phase because of a substantial winnowing process that yields a smaller ratio of women candidates; women are often less likely to receive encouragement and support from party officials at this crucial stage, and women themselves have been less interested in running for public office; when they do run, they choose lower-level offices instead.[9] The emergence of candidates from professions outside of politics may help weaken these barriers going forward.

The Invisible Primary

First dubbed the "invisible primary" by journalist Arthur Hadley in 1976, the pre-nomination period is between the end of one presidential election and the first primary of the next.[10] Two things seem to matter more than anything else during this time period—money and media—particularly because the invisible primary has grown increasingly longer in recent years with the front-loading of primaries (which means states have moved up their primary election dates in an attempt to have greater influence over the selection of the nominee). Candidates now announce their intentions to run earlier than ever before, sometimes well over a year prior to the Iowa caucuses (which, on January 3, 2008, was the earliest any nominating contest had ever been held; in 2016, the Iowa caucuses were held on February 1). During this phase, candidates attempt to raise large sums of money, hire campaign staffs, shape their ideological and partisan messages, attempt to gain visibility among party elites (and gain high-profile endorsements), and hope to be "taken seriously" by the news media.[11]

As a result, this "primary before the primary" is the early contest to raise both money and support among party elites and potential voters. In recent years, the amount of money a candidate can raise to have on hand for the start of the primary season has become a preliminary mechanism to taper the field of candidates. A two-tier campaign often emerges during the preprimary period; that is, a few candidates are considered viable early on, whereas others never break through to that ranking of "serious contender" (and, as a result, do not receive a tremendous amount of attention from the media or donors). How is this hierarchy determined? Although there is not a specific formula, voters normally take their cues as to which candidate is viable and which is not from news media coverage, so the sheer number of mentions in news stories that a candidate receives can be important. It is during the invisible primary when the often relentless "horse-race" coverage of the campaign begins, when "reporters feel obliged to tell us which candidates are leading or trailing well over a year before any primary election votes are cast."[12] Often, "media buzz" about a candidate can amplify the effects of raising money, hiring staff, and shaping the message of the candidate early in the process.

In the invisible primary for the 2016 race, the two-tier process was not between candidates who were rising to the top, although that separation did occur. Among the Republicans, there were so many candidates vying for a spot in the August debates that using an aggregate of polls to cull the top 10 candidates left enough candidates to create what became known as the "undercard" debate held before the main event. Instead, the separation occurred between traditional and nontraditional candidates. Fundraising for the Clinton and Bush campaigns and their super PACs (separate but aligned organizations) outpaced their competitors. Many political experts expected Bush to be the front runner, especially given the vast resources amassed by the pro-Bush super PAC Right to Rise USA, which raised $103 million during the first six months of 2015 (much more than any other candidate).[13] Yet, throughout the summer and fall of 2015, the top Republican tier included Trump, Fiorina, and Carson, three antiestablishment candidates who had never held political office and

Republican presidential candidates in front of Air Force One at the Ronald Reagan Presidential Library, Simi Valley, California, September 2015.

had raised considerably less money. For the Democrats, only Sanders became a significant challenge to Clinton, especially when he garnered large crowds at his rallies and began competitive fundraising from small donors throughout the fall of 2015.

In the early stages of a campaign, relationships with party insiders can be just as significant as early attention from the press. Although the changes that occurred during the Progressive Movement in the early twentieth century, and after the McGovern–Fraser Commission reforms in the early 1970s, successfully opened the nomination process to more influence by rank-and-file voters, party insiders still seek to control who runs for the presidency. Potential nominees then seek to reassure party insiders of their willingness to support and work for the party as a whole. Governors of states, particularly larger and/or swing states (states that are not solidly Democratic or Republican), are of critical importance, not just for an endorsement but also for their potential assistance since governors control their party's state organization and its roster of volunteers and supporters who can be turned out to help a campaign effort.

Certain groups can also be critical in the preprimary period for endorsements and the promise of support—both volunteers and financial. In 1999, George W. Bush was able to capitalize on Republican groups' distaste for Senator John McCain's (R-AZ) political stances on issues such as campaign finance reform, taxes, and gay marriage.[14] As a result, interest groups lined up to support Bush over McCain and made the next phase of the invisible primary easy for Bush (the eventual Republican nominee).

The trend toward a more dominant candidate-centered campaign process has allowed viable candidates to emerge without the support of party insiders or to lose the nomination even with that same party support. Bill and Hillary Clinton, respectively, provide an excellent example for both situations. In 1991, Bill Clinton was not considered a front runner for the Democratic nomination, and many party officials were not convinced that he was a strong enough contender to challenge incumbent George H. W. Bush in 1992. Clinton's savvy campaign strategy, which included an aggressive response to negative media stories about the candidate's personal life, coupled with the fact that other big-name Democrats (like Mario Cuomo, Richard Gephardt, and Al Gore) were reluctant to get into the race in 1991 while Bush's approval ratings remained high (after the success of the Gulf War), left the Arkansas governor the most viable candidate in a weak field of Democratic contenders by early 1992.

In contrast, Hillary Clinton had been hailed as the early front runner and presumptive Democratic nominee twice: first in 2005 and then in 2013. News media coverage in both periods had all but given the Democratic nomination to Clinton because of her political star power, early fundraising advantage, and support from numerous Democratic Party insiders. Yet, Barack Obama's victory in the Iowa Caucus on January 3, 2008, sent a shock wave through the political establishment that changed what had seemed to be the inevitable—Hillary Clinton as the Democratic presidential nominee. As Obama continued to raise more funds than Clinton and win key primary contests throughout the winter and spring of 2008, Democratic Party faithfuls continued to defect from Team Clinton to Team Obama, proving that early support from party insiders does not always guarantee the nomination.[15] In 2016, although she lost 23 contests to Sanders, Clinton retained the support of the party insiders, particularly superdelegates, which ensured her nomination despite the closeness of the race.

Traditionally, the prenominating phase demonstrates the candidates' "behind the scenes" strength, revealed through their fundraising, endorsements, and name recognition. However, political scientist Thomas Patterson argues,

> Of all the indicators of success in the invisible primary, media exposure is arguably the most important. Media exposure is essential if a candidate is to rise in the polls. Absent a high poll standing, or upward momentum, it's difficult for a candidate to raise money, win endorsements, or even secure a spot in the pre-primary debates. Some political scientists offer a different assessment of the invisible primary, arguing that high-level endorsements are the key to early success. That's been true in some cases, but endorsements tend to be a trailing indicator, the result of a calculated judgment by top party leaders of a candidate's viability. Other analysts have placed money at the top. Money is clearly important but its real value comes later in the process, when the campaign moves to Super Tuesday and the other multi-state contests where ad buys and field organization become critical. In the early going, nothing is closer to pure gold than favorable free media exposure.[16]

Trump received much more of that "pure gold" than any other candidate. In 2015, major news outlets gave Trump a high volume of media coverage that was more positive than negative in tone, which contributed to his eventual rise in the polls. The Democratic race received less than half the coverage of the Republican race during the fall of 2015. Yet, Clinton received more negative coverage than any other candidate, whereas Sanders received the most favorable coverage.[17]

PRIMARIES AND CAUCUSES

Beginning with the prenomination period and continuing throughout the primary and caucus contests, perhaps one thing is more important to a presidential candidate than any other—momentum. Several things work together at various levels to build and create (or for unsuccessful candidates, to destroy) momentum, including name recognition, support from national and state party officials, media attention, public opinion (as calculated by various public opinion polls), and fundraising. During the Republican primary contest of 1980, candidate George H. W. Bush famously quipped that his campaign had "Big Mo" following his defeat of Ronald Reagan in the Iowa caucuses. However, Reagan's campaign regrouped, came back to win the New Hampshire primary, and stole the momentum back from Bush to win an overwhelming majority of the remaining Republican contests (although Bush did secure the vice presidential spot on the Republican ticket). Although one element of momentum (for example, party support) can help to secure other elements (like media attention and fundraising), momentum during the primary season can be fleeting and difficult to build and maintain. All of the elements of momentum must fall into place at just the right time for a candidate to capture his or her party's nomination.

As such, the process of the primary contests themselves, as well as the timing and schedule of the contests, are key to understanding how a candidate moves from announcing a campaign to representing a major party during the general election. Aspirants for the title of presidential nominee must run the gauntlet of the state primaries and caucuses. However, the trek is different depending on whether the candidate seeks the Democratic or Republican nomination. Each national party makes its own rules regarding the criteria needed to achieve the nomination. In addition, the states and state parties also create rules and regulations to follow. Some rules, like New Hampshire's state constitution's requirement to always be the first primary of the season, barely influences candidates; other rules, like the number of delegates needed to achieve the nomination, are significant.

Iowa and New Hampshire

Long recognized as the first presidential contests, the Iowa caucuses and the New Hampshire primary are the first stops for presidential candidates to prove themselves in the electoral arena. As smaller geographic states with much smaller populations and media markets than delegate-rich states like California or Texas, candidates engage in what is often referred to as "retail politics" by getting up close and personal with residents for many months leading up to the actual contests. Although a win in Iowa and/or New Hampshire does not guarantee that a candidate will have what it takes to win his or her party's nomination (as was the case for Bush in 1980 after his win in Iowa), both contests nonetheless receive tremendous attention from candidates during the prenomination period and can help to catapult a campaign into the national spotlight in an attempt to capture momentum. For example, Barack Obama's Iowa victory over rivals Hillary Clinton and John Edwards in 2008 showed that he could compete with the so-called Clinton political machine as well as the impressive Edwards campaign organization that had been left nearly intact since Edwards' 2004 presidential run. In addition, Obama's victory helped to quell fears within the Democratic Party that an African American candidate could not win in a predominantly white state like Iowa.

Some candidates opt out of campaigning in one or even both states in an attempt to wait out the primary calendar for states in which they will have a better chance of picking up a sizable number of delegates. For example, Bill Clinton focused most of his primary resources on New Hampshire in 1992 because Senator Tom Harkin of Iowa was also in the race (Harkin, as the state's favorite-son candidate, easily won the caucus with little campaigning necessary). In 2008, former New York City Mayor Rudy Giuliani believed he would do better in larger states that were later on the primary calendar (such as Florida, California, and New York) and virtually ignored Iowa and never gave his full attention to campaigning in New Hampshire. Despite leading many national polls throughout 2007, Giuliani's strategy of waiting out the primary calendar failed badly; he dropped out of the race by the end of January 2008 with his campaign deeply in debt and having won only one delegate (of 2,380) to the Republican National Convention.

More candidates who have won in New Hampshire have gone on to become president than those who have won in Iowa. Winning both contests did not propel Jimmy Carter or George H. W. Bush to reelection (or Gerald Ford, who was running for the first time after being appointed to the vice presidency and then succeeding Nixon after he resigned), nor did it help Al Gore, John Kerry, or Hillary Clinton win the White House (see Table 3.1). In addition, New Hampshire can provide candidates with an opportunity for an early "comeback" on the campaign trail. Bill Clinton earned his nickname "the Comeback Kid" after his strong second-place finish in New Hampshire in 1992 (amid media reports that his campaign was finished following allegations of womanizing and draft dodging). Hillary Clinton won an important (albeit close) contest over Barack Obama in New Hampshire in 2008 to stem the increasing tide of momentum for Obama's campaign coming out of Iowa. Similarly, Donald Trump's 2016 victory in New Hampshire, when coupled with his second-place finish in Iowa, increased his momentum. However, although the influence of both Iowa and New Hampshire in the nominating process has been diminished in recent elections because of the excessive front-loading of primaries (see below) and although the demographics of each state are hardly representative of the nation at large (in terms of race, ethnicity, and socioeconomic factors), both states and the national parties are committed to maintaining their status as the first presidential contests, thereby allowing Iowa and New Hampshire to narrow the field of presidential contenders.

Super Tuesday

The term "Super Tuesday" has been around since the 1980s and first gained prominence in 1988, when nine southern states decided to hold their Democratic primaries on the same day in early March in an effort to create an unofficial regional primary. Since then, Super Tuesday has picked up many other states and has moved

Table 3.1 Winners in Iowa and New Hampshire since 1976 (Eventual President in Bold)

	IOWA CAUCUS	NEW HAMPSHIRE PRIMARY
1976	Uncommitted*	**Jimmy Carter (D)**
	Gerald Ford (R)	Gerald Ford (R)
1980	Jimmy Carter (D)	Jimmy Carter (D)
	George H. W. Bush (R)	**Ronald Reagan (R)**
1984	Walter Mondale (D)	Gary Hart (D)
	Ronald Reagan (R)	**Ronald Reagan (R)**
1988	Richard Gephardt (D)	Michael Dukakis (D)
	Bob Dole (R)	**George H. W. Bush (R)**
1992	Tom Harkin (D)	Paul Tsongas (D)
	George H. W. Bush (R)	George H. W. Bush (R)
1996	**Bill Clinton (D)**	**Bill Clinton (D)**
	Bob Dole (R)	Pat Buchanan (R)
2000	Al Gore (D)	Al Gore (D)
	George W. Bush (R)	John McCain (R)
2004	John Kerry (D)	John Kerry (D)
	George W. Bush (R)	**George W. Bush (R)**
2008	**Barack Obama (D)**	Hillary Clinton (D)
	Mike Huckabee (R)	John McCain (R)
2012	**Barack Obama (D)**	**Barack Obama (D)**
	Rick Santorum (R)	Mitt Romney (R)
2016	Ted Cruz (R)	**Donald Trump (R)**
	Hillary Clinton (D)	Bernie Sanders (D)

* More Democratic voters chose to remain "uncommitted" at 37 percent than to pledge their support to any candidate; Jimmy Carter received the most of any candidate, at 28 percent.

up on the primary calendar. Although candidates can sometimes wrap up the nomination on Super Tuesday by securing a majority of delegates, they must at least provide a strong enough showing to continue the flow of money into campaign coffers and to be labeled competitive by the press for their campaigns to survive. In 2008, Super Tuesday was held earlier than ever before, on February 5, with 24 states holding primaries or caucuses in which a total of 52 percent of Democratic Party delegates and 41 percent of Republican Party delegates were at stake.

In 2016, so many Southern states signed up for the contests on March 1 that the date was nicknamed the SEC primary since, like the college athletic Southeastern Conference, it included contests in Arkansas, Georgia, Alabama, Kentucky, Louisiana, Tennessee, and Texas. (The Southern states of Virginia and Oklahoma also voted that day, but are not part of the SEC in the world of college athletics). With the Florida primary scheduled for March 15, the South seemed like it was going to have a much louder voice in the outcome of the presidential nomination than in previous years. This could have benefited Republican candidates with southern roots, such as Bush and Senator Marco Rubio, both of Florida, or Senator Ted Cruz of Texas, but it did not.

The 2008 campaign highlighted another calendar issue that has emerged in recent campaigns, which is the front-loading of presidential primaries and caucuses. Front-loading means that states move up the date of their primary contests so that their state will become more relevant in the selection of presidential nominees. For example, in 1992, Californians did not have the chance to cast a ballot for any political candidate in the presidential primary until the first Tuesday in June. However, the contest for the Republican and Democratic nominations (won by George H. W. Bush and Bill Clinton, respectively) had already been decided by early April. That meant voters in the most populous state did not have a real say in either party's nomination. Consequently, in 1996, California, along with other states like New York and Texas, decided to move their primaries to March to play a more influential role in the selection process. This change, in turn, impacted the role of money. To survive the early contests, candidates needed even more money to spend on these big states even earlier in the process. This put more pressure on candidates and their campaigns to raise larger amounts of money and left those candidates without strong financial support and broader national appeal at an even greater disadvantage. During the 1996 Republican primaries, the well-funded campaign of Senate majority leader (and eventual nominee) Bob Dole of Kansas had a much easier time surviving the numerous March primary contests than did some of his challengers, like political commentator Pat Buchanan or former education secretary and Tennessee senator Lamar Alexander. Although money had always been an important determining factor in the selection of presidential nominees, front-loading the primaries placed an even higher fundraising burden on White House hopefuls. In 2008, 71 percent of the primaries and caucuses occurred between January 3 and February 19. Moreover, those races included big states like California and New York, where it is expensive to run because of the cost of advertising in large media markets. Running out of money during the primaries, as well as the inability to raise more, is a loud signal of the death of a campaign. The 2016 calendar was a reversal of the dramatic changes from 2008 and a return to a pre-2000 approach as it ended extreme front-loading with all contests held from February 1 to June 14.

The Delegate Count

Although the goal for all presidential candidates throughout the primary season is to secure enough delegates to capture their party's nomination, the process differs for each major party. In the Republican Party, each state's delegate total is equal to the number of members of Congress in its state delegation, plus their state party representatives, plus the number of presidential electors in the Electoral College (which is the House delegation plus two senators), plus the number of states with Republican governors and a majority in the legislature.[18] In most states, the winning Republican candidate in the state's primary or caucus then receives all the state's delegates, in what is known as a winner-take-all system. Consequently, the front-loading of the primary calendar benefits Republican hopefuls with the greatest name recognition or early momentum.

The Republican calendar in 2016 demonstrated the competing forces within the nomination process. Party insiders want to wrap up the contest early, ensuring the eventual nominee a brief battle, whereas the state parties want to have a significant say in determining the nominee. To accommodate these competing interests in 2016, the Republican Party changed their rules and prevented states from using winner-take-all primaries until after March 15. States could still opt to move up the calendar, but they would not be able to award all their delegates to a single candidate if they chose that route, slowing down the potential for a sweep of a significant number of states. Proportional allocation, depending on the rules of each state, typically matches the popular vote. Winner-take-all typically encourages a quicker outcome because a candidate can build an insurmountable lead, whereas proportional allocation allows for greater shifting of momentum.

The sheer number of Republican candidates in 2016 appeared to make a quick outcome unlikely. If two or more candidates split Iowa, New Hampshire, and South Carolina (all in February), it would be difficult for any candidate to achieve enough momentum to build a bandwagon effect. As many polls predicted, Cruz took Iowa but Trump won the next three Republican contests. March could have been the decisive sweep for Trump. He won 18 contests, whereas Bush and Rubio dropped out, Cruz won 7, and Governor John Kasich took only his home state of Ohio. As Trump racked up victory after victory, the Republican race turned increasingly acrimonious, with more than 36,000 signing a pledge (#NeverTrump) against Trump as the nominee. The contentiousness took such a negative turn in March and April that the prospect that the Republican Party would not have a clear nominee with 1,237 amassed delegates heading into their convention became the dominant political conversation. States with primaries later in the calendar saw an increase in interest and attention as it became clear their participation might actually influence the outcome. However, after victories for Trump in the northeast in April and in Indiana on May 3, both Kasich and Cruz dropped out, leaving Trump with a clear path to the nomination and hopes for a brokered convention dashed.

The Democrats adjust their rules much more frequently than do the Republicans; they seem to do it every four years, whereas the Republicans only do it when deemed necessary. Democrats spend more time on their rules because they are more complicated and more focused on increasing ordinary rank-and-file member participation. The Democrats emphasize participation and population in their formulas, counting the state's Electoral College allocation, plus the state's popular vote in the last three presidential elections.[19] In addition, the Democrats rely on proportional allocation of delegates, rather than a winner-take-all system. However, the Democratic allocation system does not account for 100 percent of the delegate total at the convention because Democrats also rely on what are known as "superdelegates." First created in 1982, superdelegates were a response to the nomination reforms put into place in 1972 to turn over the selection process to the rank-and-file party members. In 1982, following Jimmy Carter's failed bid at reelection in 1980, the Democratic Party decided to take back some of that power from the voters and return it to the party bosses. Superdelegates represented important wings within the party, like those who held political office in Congress or high-profile state politicians (such as governors) and other notables (like a former president or vice president).

Superdelegates played an important role in the 2008 nomination battle between Obama and Clinton. At the start of the primary season, Clinton had a commanding lead among superdelegates who had pledged their support to her candidacy, but after Super Tuesday and the emergence of Obama as the front runner, unpledged superdelegates slowly began to pledge their support to Obama, and others who had already pledged their support to Clinton switched to Obama once it seemed likely that he would win the nomination. In 2016, Bernie Sanders supporters focused on the undemocratic nature of the superdelegates, of which the majority supported Clinton. Prior to the Democratic convention, 540 superdelegates had pledged support to Clinton, whereas only 44 had pledged to support Sanders (of 712 total).

PRESIDENTIAL NOMINATIONS

THEN . . .

In 1974, Gerald Ford became President of the United States without ever running a national campaign either as a presidential or as a vice presidential candidate. On December 6, 1973, then–House Minority Leader Ford took the vice presidential oath of office after both chambers of Congress approved Nixon's appointment of Ford to replace resigning Vice President Spiro Agnew. Ford would become president less than a year later on August 9, 1974, after Nixon resigned in the wake of the Watergate scandal. Thus, Ford became president without a single vote cast, outside of the confirmation votes by Congress. On taking the Oath of Office on August 9, 1974, Ford acknowledged his peculiar path to the presidency:

> I am acutely aware that you have not elected me as your President by your ballots, and so I ask you to confirm me as your President with your prayers. And I hope that such prayers will also be the first of many. If you have not chosen me by secret ballot, neither have I gained office by any secret promises. I have not campaigned either for the Presidency or the Vice Presidency. I have not subscribed to any partisan platform. I am indebted to no man, and only to one woman—my dear wife—as I begin this very difficult job.[20]

In deciding to run for the presidency in 1976 after serving out the remainder of Nixon's term, Ford, despite being the incumbent, needed to create an electoral coalition much in the way any other candidate would, by first running for his party's nomination. Traditionally, a sitting president is not challenged for his party's nomination, but under certain circumstances it can happen, as it did in 1976 when former California governor Ronald Reagan challenged Ford for the Republican nomination. The race for the nomination was close and contentious, and it remains the last nomination battle not settled prior to the start of a national party convention.

Ford, a moderate Republican, did not have the full support of the more conservative members of his party, who were troubled by Ford's inability to counter the liberal policymaking by the Democrats, who controlled Congress. More concerning, however, was the President's foreign policy. Reagan criticized Ford for his Vietnam policy, as well as his negotiation of the Helsinki accords with the Soviet Union. Reagan's challenge initially amounted to nothing because Ford won the first primaries and caucuses with comfortable margins. However, the momentum shifted once Reagan won North Carolina and then followed by winning the key state of Texas. After Texas, the primaries were much closer and more contentious, culminating in no declarable winner prior to the start of the Republican Convention. Ford had the lead with 1,130 delegates, but needed 1,187 to win.

The lack of an outright winner created an environment in which votes were traded and outcomes negotiated. Rumors swirled as advisors negotiated a Ford/Reagan co-presidency, Reagan as vice president, or Reagan as transportation secretary. The tide seemingly turned on Reagan's announcement of Pennsylvania senator Richard Schweiker as the other half of a Reagan ticket. Schweiker, a moderate, was enough of an anathema to conservatives that votes changed sides to give Ford 1,187 votes, enough to win the nomination. The intraparty challenge to Ford revealed the flaws in his efforts to create an electoral coalition. Ford's base Republican coalition was diminished by the reality that half the party voted for someone other than the President to be the party's nominee. Many believed that Ford's loss to Jimmy Carter was virtually inevitable as a result of his pardon of Nixon in 1974 and the dire economy of the 1970s, but also because of this internal party challenge.

. . . AND NOW

The 2008 presidential campaign was unique for many reasons, beginning with the unusual circumstance of a completely open race for the first time since 1952 (meaning that no sitting president or vice president sought the nomination of either party). In addition, the Democratic Party had a strong chance of nominating either the first person of color or the first woman to run for the presidency. For the Democrats, Hillary Clinton had secured the status of front runner as early as 2005. By the end of 2006, most news organizations had all but given the Democratic nomination to Clinton, regularly labeling her as the only candidate capable of winning the nomination. The news media seemed to love the story of Hillary running for president (she was routinely referred to as simply "Hillary" by the news media), and polls at the time began to show that Americans would overwhelmingly support a woman candidate for president.[21]

However, the political landscape by early 2007 presented a different reality for Clinton's candidacy. Still considered the strongest candidate and probable front runner among the Democratic candidates for the upcoming primary season, the door was nonetheless left open for other challengers within the Democratic Party. Although Clinton's name recognition and star power had obvious advantages, the downside came in the political baggage that she brought to the campaign. Nonetheless, Clinton maintained her front-runner status throughout 2007, continually besting her other opponents in public opinion polls, as well as Republican contenders (like John McCain and Rudy Giuliani) in national polling in Democratic/Republican matchups. On January 20, 2007, when Clinton officially declared her candidacy, she told supporters on her web page announcement that "I'm in, and I'm in to win."[22] Clinton's announcement came just days after Barack Obama officially announced his candidacy and also set off the furious race for campaign donors among all the Democratic hopefuls.

Most assumed that no one could match the fundraising prowess of the Clinton machine; Bill Clinton had been perhaps the most successful fundraiser for the Democratic Party, and the Clintons turned to the same donors and fundraising methods to fund Hillary's presidential campaign. Bill Clinton's strategy in 1995 and 1996—raise all of the available Democratic funds early to discourage any challengers in the primary—seemed to be the plan for Hillary's presidential campaign as well. The former president was also still a big draw among Democratic donors, and Clinton's campaign had developed a network of large donors known as Hillraisers, donors who not only contributed the maximum legal contribution directly to the Clinton campaign, but also bundled contributions of $100,000 or more from other donors (in effect serving as fundraisers on behalf of the Clinton campaign). But during the first and second quarters of 2007, the Obama campaign actually outfundraised Clinton; Obama raised $25 million to Clinton's $20 million for the first quarter of 2007 and $31 million to Clinton's $21 million for the second quarter. Not until the third quarter of 2007 did Clinton finally raise more money than Obama—$22 million to $19 million—although that still left her trailing $75 million to $63 million overall going into the last few crucial months before the Iowa caucuses.[23]

The initial primary results quickly matched the excitement gleaned from the dueling fundraising totals (especially among new donors). Unexpectedly, Obama won the Iowa caucus, which immediately changed the script of the campaign. By beating Clinton in a caucus state, he demonstrated superior organization, which challenged the idea that Clinton owned the Democratic machine and insiders. In addition, by winning in a state that was 94 percent white, Obama demonstrated that race alone would not be a determining factor. Although Clinton rebounded in New Hampshire, she did not experience another significant victory until Super Tuesday on February 5 (also called Tsunami Tuesday in 2008 given the increased number of states that held primaries). It was then that Clinton won the big states as expected: California, Massachusetts, New Jersey, and New York, as well as a few others. However, she did not sweep the day; Obama won 12 states and had solid showings in the states that Clinton carried. Thus, because of the proportional allocation of delegates in the Democratic Party, Obama accumulated more delegates from February 5 and marginally took the lead in the race for the nomination.

In the aftermath of Super Tuesday, the narrative of the race changed again. The press began describing the Clinton campaign in disarray. There were numerous negative stories regarding the frivolous spending of campaign money, the tension between her top campaign advisors, the need for the candidate to lend money to the campaign, and the loss of front-runner status. Conversely, the press began marveling at the Obama campaign's fundraising prowess, error-free caucus and primary strategy, and the candidate's star power. In short, in all arenas, momentum shifted to Obama.

Certain miscalculations, involving fundraising and mismanagement of campaign funds, ignoring smaller states (particularly those with caucuses as opposed to primary contests), and the campaign's seeming belief in inevitability that Clinton would win the nomination all played an integral role in the primary contests that Clinton lost. Having spent $100 million through only the first contest in Iowa, in which she came in third, the Clinton campaign was broke at a time when it needed money most, forcing Clinton to loan herself $5 million to stay afloat through Super Tuesday. The lack of funds after Obama's win in Iowa meant that the Clinton campaign could not effectively staff ground operations in states where it needed to compete. In addition, when Clinton revealed that she had lent herself $5 million, this worked counter to the image she was trying to project going into the big primary states of Ohio, Texas, and Pennsylvania as being able to relate to average, working-class Americans. When Clinton conceded to Obama in June 2008, she had raised a total of $223 million, had loaned her campaign a total of $11.4 million, and ended the campaign roughly $22.5 million in debt.

Rivals for the 2008 Democratic nomination, Hillary Rodham Clinton and Barack Obama campaign together in the general election.

Money issues during the campaign were also closely tied to another problem that the Clinton team experienced—the lack of an effective "ground game" that could compete with that of the Obama campaign. During the primary season, grass-roots organizers and local volunteers can make a big difference in voter education, voter registration, and voter turnout. Sufficient campaign funds also help to pay staff members in various field offices across the country. For the Obama campaign, which was also having tremendous success in tapping into the youth vote (particularly on university campuses), the ground game helped to solidify the Obama 50-state strategy—compete in every state and for every delegate. The Clinton campaign, in contrast, had a large-state strategy that assumed that their candidate would wrap up the nomination by Super Tuesday, and with an empty campaign coffer in the weeks after the Iowa caucus, they had an impossible task in readjusting strategy with limited resources. In addition, some of the larger states that Clinton would win later in the spring of 2008, like Ohio, Texas, and Pennsylvania, came too late to alter the outcome because Obama had already built an insurmountable lead in delegates.

Clinton finally suspended her campaign on June 7, 2008, because Obama had more than the simple majority delegate total he needed to claim the nomination. In contrast to how Reagan's challenge of Ford had weakened the incumbent president on the campaign trail, the competitive contest between Obama and Clinton ultimately appeared to strengthen the Obama campaign, which allowed the Democratic nominee to continue his record-breaking fundraising and to appear more comfortable and confident going forward into the general election against John McCain.

FINANCING PRESIDENTIAL CAMPAIGNS

Running for president is not cheap. To run a successful campaign, major expenses include paying consultants and staff, conducting polls, sending direct mail and email, creating a website, creating a social media platform and presence, gaining media exposure through advertisements, and—let's not forget—fundraising itself. Thus, an aspiring presidential candidate, who does not spend his or her own money, must fundraise long before citizens cast any votes in any primary or caucus to reach potential voters. As a result, fundraising becomes its own contest before and during the campaign because it can serve as a signal of viability. The linking of fundraising to attractiveness to voters results from the obvious conclusion that donors give money (large or small amounts) to people they want to see win and not to people they think will lose.

Campaign Finance before *Citizens United*

The influence of money on the American political process is not new. Consider that in the earliest days of the republic, only those who owned land (i.e., had money and wealth) were allowed to vote. One of the best-known stories about George Washington as a politician is about his campaign for the Virginia House of Burgesses in 1758. To entice voters to give Washington their support, his election managers provided a half-gallon of alcoholic beverages per voter on Election Day.[24] Later, in 1777, when James Madison ran unsuccessfully for the Virginia state legislature, he attributed his loss to his failure to provide similar alcoholic refreshments to the voters.[25] From the time of the first presidential elections, many of the candidates, including Washington, John Adams, and Thomas Jefferson, paid for the expenses related to their own campaigns. These were men of means, after all, and the campaigns themselves were not particularly costly. But within a few decades, it took more money to run for the presidency than most aspiring politicians could afford to spend.

During the 1830s and the era of Andrew Jackson's presidency—also known for the birth of the modern political party—presidents found an effective way to reward those who had financially supported their campaign. Under what became known as the "spoils system," winning candidates rewarded their political supporters with government jobs and contracts. The development of national party committees was also an important step in helping candidates raise funds for political campaigns. The Democratic National Committee (DNC) was first established in 1852 to raise funds for the party's presidential candidate, Franklin Pierce. The Republican National Committee (RNC) was first established in 1856. Today, the DNC and RNC serve as the headquarters for coordinating party organization on the national level and as the main fundraising apparatus for their respective party.[26] The influence of corporate money on the political process also dates back to the mid-nineteenth century. After the Civil War, some of America's greatest industrialists and the corporations they built (like Union Pacific, Standard Oil, and New York Life Insurance) became an important source of political financing, particularly to those candidates seeking the White House. Members of the wealthiest families in America, including the Vanderbilt, Astor, and Cooke families, heavily financed the 1868 presidential campaign of Republican Ulysses S. Grant. These influential Americans represented some of America's earliest "fat-cat" donors, a term used to describe wealthy individuals who spent vast amounts of their money in an attempt to influence the outcome of an election.[27]

By the end of the nineteenth century, the Gilded Age (known as a time of dramatic industrial growth as well as high levels of political corruption at all levels of government) was replaced by the Progressive Era, during which various reform movements arose in an attempt to clean up the corruption and influence of money in politics. Those who were supportive of the Progressive movement believed that large corporate contributions to campaigns, particularly at the presidential level, were destroying the American democratic process by giving wealthy business owners too much control over the government. At that time, virtually no laws existed to regulate the flow of money into campaign coffers. Consequently, the influence of corporations in American elections became a major concern among reformers, prompting Theodore Roosevelt to mention the issue in his Annual Message to Congress in 1905:

> In political campaigns in a country as large and populous as ours it is inevitable that there should be much expense of an entirely legitimate kind. This, of course, means that many contributions, and some of them of large size, must be made, and, as a matter of fact, in any big political contest such contributions are always made to both sides. It is entirely proper both to give and receive them, unless there is an improper motive connected with either gift or reception. If they are extorted by any kind of pressure or promise, express or implied, direct or indirect, in the way of favor or immunity, then the giving or receiving becomes not only improper but criminal. It will undoubtedly be difficult, as a matter of practical detail, to shape an act which shall guard with reasonable certainty against such

misconduct; but if it is possible to secure by law the full and verified publication in detail of all the sums contributed to and expended by the candidates or committees of any political parties, the result cannot but be wholesome. All contributions by corporations to any political committee or for any political purpose should be forbidden by law; directors should not be permitted to use stockholders' money for such purposes; and, moreover, a prohibition of this kind would be, as far as it went, an effective method of stopping the evils aimed at in corrupt practices acts.[28]

In 1907, Congress passed the first law to alter the campaign finance landscape, banning corporations and national banks from making contributions to candidates for federal office. Over the next decades, other congressional acts would follow, including passage of the Hatch Act in 1939, which barred federal employees from taking an active role in federal campaigns, with amendments passed in 1940 attempting to limit campaign contributions and expenditures for federal candidates. In 1947, passage of the Taft–Hartley Act banned political contributions by labor unions because of the perceived power and influence of union leaders, like corporate leaders, on election outcomes.[29] However, much to the chagrin of those supporting campaign finance reform during the first half of the twentieth century, Congress had little to no authority to enforce these laws. Even when attempts at enforcement were made, candidates and their campaign managers always seemed to find various loopholes to get around the law and keep the money flowing into presidential (and congressional) campaigns. It would take Richard Nixon's resignation as president in 1974 to make Congress finally get serious about reforming campaign finance laws.

The Federal Election Campaign Acts of 1971 and 1974

To attempt to end the influence of fat-cat donors, Congress enacted the Federal Election Campaign Act (FECA) of 1971 to provide a format for disclosure, which meant that campaigns would have to provide public information about who gave them money and how the money was subsequently spent. The legislation created a comprehensive set of rules by which to regulate money in federal campaigns (including primaries, runoffs, and general elections) and national party conventions. Not only did the law require a "full and timely" disclosure of contributions, but also it set a ceiling on media advertising expenditures, established limits on contributions from candidates and their families, and permitted labor unions and corporations to ask for voluntary contributions from members and employees.

Ironically, it was the FECA with its attempts to regulate presidential campaign contributions that in 1974 helped to bring down Nixon, the same man who had signed the law three years earlier. During the presidential campaign of 1972, when Nixon was running against Democrat George McGovern, the RNC acted in violation of the 1971 FECA by using a secret "slush fund" to finance various illegal activities. One of these activities was a break-in at the DNC headquarters located at the Watergate Complex in Washington, DC (hence the term Watergate, which was used to describe various political scandals associated with Nixon's presidency). Two *Washington Post* reporters, Carl Bernstein and Bob Woodward, were assigned to cover the Watergate break-in and became convinced that the burglars were connected to the Nixon White House. The reporters were instructed by an anonymous source (known only as "Deep Throat" until revealed in 2005 to be former deputy director of the Federal Bureau of Investigation, W. Mark Felt) to "follow the money" to link the break-in to Nixon. They did, and a secret White House tape recording that implicated Nixon in the cover-up of the DNC break-in led to Nixon's resignation from the presidency on August 9, 1974.

In October 1974, just two months after Nixon's resignation, Congress passed several major amendments to the FECA, which were promptly signed into law by Gerald Ford. The legislation became "the most sweeping change imposed upon the relationship between money and politics since the founding of the American republic."[30] Specifically, the 1974 FECA created the Federal Election Commission (FEC), outlined contribution and spending limits at both the presidential and the congressional level, and created a system of public financing for presidential campaigns. One of the most important changes to the campaign finance system from these amendments included the establishment of the FEC, a bipartisan panel that oversees campaign finance regulations. The overriding goal of the FEC is voluntary compliance with federal election campaign laws, and the agency has the authority to enforce federal campaign laws involving money. Federal candidates (those running for the presidency or Congress) must report their contributions and expenditures to the FEC, and in return, the FEC provides public disclosure of that financial information to interested parties like the news media or other watchdog public interest groups (like the Center for Responsive Politics at opensecrets.org).

Other significant changes came through the use of contribution limits, initially established on campaign contributions at $1,000 per candidate per election for individuals and $5,000 per candidate per election for political action committees (PACs) (known as "hard money" contributions). The goal was to diminish political corruption, allow candidates to spend more time campaigning and discussing issues rather than fundraising, and reduce the reliance on and influence from fat-cat donors. In addition, PACs, which are basically the fundraising arm of labor unions, corporations, or other special interest groups, began to emerge more prominently in the early 1970s as a way for unions and corporations to get around the ban on campaign contributions by soliciting voluntary contributions from members and employees to help fund campaign expenditures. By the end of the 1970s, interest group PACs had also taken hold as a way to keep money flowing into the federal electoral process. Along the same lines, the FECA put into place limits on how much candidates could spend during their campaigns (including both primaries and general election campaigns for presidential candidates). The general idea was that if all candidates shared the same spending ceiling on campaign expenditures, then the electoral contest would be more fair and less subject to influence by major monetary contributions to one candidate. However, the Supreme Court, in its landmark decision *Buckley v. Valeo* (1976), criticized this aspect of the law as curtailing freedom of speech unless a candidate was using public funds to pay for his or her campaign.

Despite implementation of these reforms, a major loophole emerged with the use of "soft money" contributions, which were unlimited funds given by individuals directly to the political parties rather than the candidates. Soft money was raised by national party committees and spent on local voter education or get-out-the-vote efforts. Since there were no limits on the amount of money that could be given to the DNC or RNC, either by an individual donor or by a PAC, this was a perfect way to get around the rules set out under the FECA and still donate as much money as possible to influence the outcome of a presidential race. The only rules regulating the use of soft money stated that the funds could not be used for express advocacy for a candidate, but they could be used instead for issue advocacy. Although both the DNC and the RNC spent some of their soft money contributions on state and local party efforts to increase voter registration and to educate voters about party issues, a large part of soft money funds actually ended up being spent on the presidential race in the form of issue advocacy television advertising. This turned out to be a beneficial loophole for both parties, since it allowed presidential candidates to stay within their spending limits during the general election campaign, yet still have their national party committees spend millions of dollars on television ads right up until Election Day. And with the help of Supreme Court rulings during the late 1980s and early 1990s that stated issue advocacy was a protected free-speech right under the First Amendment, soft money contributions to both the Democratic and the Republican parties increased dramatically.[31]

Public Funding of Presidential Campaigns
In presidential politics, being independently wealthy or knowing lots of people who are is not a prerequisite for becoming a presidential candidate. However, without these advantages, the problem then becomes where the money comes from. In response to this issue, the 1974 FECA provided public funding for presidential elections in the form of matching funds during the primary period, a flat grant to major parties to run their nominating conventions, and larger grants for full public financing for major party candidates during the general election. In theory, public funding of any campaign, whether at the national or at the local level, is supposed to encourage more candidates to run for office by leveling the financial playing field.

In 1976, Congress began funding presidential campaigns and conventions through what is known as a tax checkoff. This method allows taxpayers to designate money for the Presidential Election Campaign Fund by checking a box on their federal income tax return. This checkoff instructed the Internal Revenue Service to earmark $1 from federal taxes to be placed in the fund (the amount was increased to $3 in 1993). Although many Americans continue to believe that money corrupts the political process, few choose to participate in the tax checkoff for the Presidential Election Campaign Fund. Participation in the program has declined each year, from a high of 28.7 percent for 1980 returns to 5.4 percent for returns filed in 2015.[32] Many Americans incorrectly assume that checking the box on their federal income tax return increases their tax burden and adds $3 to the amount they owe to the Internal Revenue Service. In reality, it merely earmarks the funds and does not add to an individual's overall tax bill.

The Presidential Election Campaign Fund includes money for the primaries and general election (convention public funding was repealed in 2014). However, not everyone who wants to become president can meet the threshold requirements to receive public financing. Candidates can qualify for matching funds by raising at least $5,000 in each of 20 states. Only contributions from individuals, up to $250, can be matched.[33] If candidates accept matching funds, they must also adhere to spending limits (in 2016, the nomination phase limit was just over $57 million per candidate).

Public funding in the general election comes in the form of a large grant, and by accepting the funds, each major party candidate also agrees that the same amount will serve as a spending limit. However, a major party nominee has not accepted public funding in the general elections since 2008, when John McCain received $84.1 million in public funds to conduct his general election campaign (and was allowed to raise an additional $46.4 million for legal and accounting expenses). Barack Obama refused public financing that year, choosing instead to rely on donations. He raised the record-breaking total of $745.7 million in private funds for his primary nomination and general election campaign. Not surprisingly, by Election Day, the Obama campaign outspent McCain on television ads by a four-to-one margin.[34]

Campaign Finance Reform and *Citizens United*

Despite the major campaign finance reforms enacted by Congress in the 1970s, money continued to be the driving force in presidential campaigns through the 1990s. The loopholes created by the system, along with the political desire among many Americans to enact further reform, reached a boiling point after the 1996 election. Bill Clinton, a prolific fundraiser, along with several savvy advisors, had finally reached parity with Republicans in the area of raising soft money. However, Clinton's success with fundraising in 1996 did not come without a political price tag. In the frenzy to raise as much money as possible, the Clinton campaign was not diligent in screening the sources of some contributions. The Republican-controlled Congress launched an investigation in 1996 and 1997 into alleged illegal fundraising practices by the President's reelection team. The charges levied against Clinton included a long list of supposed transgressions: illegal foreign contributions, including attempts by the Chinese government to influence the outcome of the election; nights in the Lincoln Bedroom at the White House in exchange for large campaign contributions; laundering campaign funds through conduit groups; and large sums of soft money being funneled to the DNC from corporations, labor unions, and wealthy individuals.

Democrats tried to fight back by making their own charges against Republicans, especially with regard to the large sums of soft money from corporations and wealthy individuals, but the public paid little attention to either side. In truth, both parties had abused the campaign finance laws that were in place at the time. Republicans, whose goal had been to expose the Democrats' improprieties, were—in doing so—highlighting the weaknesses of the campaign finance regulations and leading the way to something they never wanted: campaign finance reform. At the same time, despite their newfound success in raising money, Democrats could not back away from the issue of campaign finance reform, which they had long championed and was strongly supported by their key constituents. The Democratic Party and Clinton continued to publicly support the policy reform that they knew would now hurt them financially in the same way that they had hoped it would hurt the Republican Party.

The investigation into alleged campaign finance abuses played strategically into the hands of two senators in particular—McCain and Russ Feingold (D-WI). The McCain–Feingold proposal, first introduced in 1995, addressed the continuing problem of soft money, especially the so-called issue advocacy ads that both parties were spending millions of dollars to air. The ads, whose producers took great pains to avoid the magic words *vote for, vote against, oppose,* or *support,* looked more like regular express advocacy campaign ads, which violated the spirit of the campaign finance laws. As a result, the McCain–Feingold bill sought to prohibit corporations and labor unions from using soft money to pay for any electioneering communications, that is, broadcast ads that mention a federal candidate or officeholder within 30 days of a primary or 60 days of a general election. McCain and Feingold also argued that since contribution limits had never been raised since the initial legislation was passed in 1974, candidates were increasingly beholden to other sources of money. Since the contribution limits had not kept up with the rate of inflation, a $1,000 contribution in 1976 was worth less than $250 by the year 2000.

Finally, after a seven-year struggle, McCain and Feingold, along with their supporters in both the House and the Senate, succeeded in passing their bill, the Bipartisan Campaign Reform Act, which George W. Bush signed into law on March 27, 2002. Once signed, the law doubled the hard money contribution limits for individuals in federal elections (which includes congressional campaigns) to $2,000 per candidate per election in a given campaign cycle (primaries, runoffs, and the general election are still viewed as separate elections for each candidate). Since then, the amount has been adjusted every two years; for the 2015–2016 campaign cycle, the limit was set at $2,700. But perhaps more important, and certainly more controversial, the new law banned soft money, which substantially impacted campaign fundraising strategies for 2004. Immediately after the law went into effect, several groups, including the American Federation of Labor–Congress of Industrial Organizations, the American Civil Liberties Union, and the National Rifle Association, along with the RNC and perhaps the law's most outspoken opponent, Senator Mitch McConnell (R-KY), filed a lawsuit in federal court claiming that various provisions of the Bipartisan Campaign Reform Act were unconstitutional. The legislation was a clear case of an issue that made strange political bedfellows, with "unions, corporations, right-to-lifers, civil libertarians, gun owners, broadcasters, Christians, fat cats, purists who think it doesn't go far enough, Democrats, Republicans, Congress, the White House, and even the regulators who are supposed to enforce it" opposed to some or all of the provisions of the bill.[35]

Initially, in May 2003, a federal court ruled that the ban on soft money was unconstitutional, but on appeal, the U.S. Supreme Court in a December 2003 decision, *McConnell v. FEC,* upheld the ban on soft money contributions. Although it was divided 5–4 in its ruling, the Court was able to save the legislation and uphold its original ruling in *Buckley v. Valeo* by stating that Congress had the right to protect the integrity of the electoral process. McCain, Feingold, and all of the ardent campaign finance supporters (including public interest groups like the Center for Responsive Politics and Public Citizen, long-time advocates of serious campaign finance reform) had achieved a big victory.

Always resourceful, it did not take long for the presidential candidates and political parties to find other ways to raise money. According to the FEC, the financial activity of all presidential candidates in 2004, including the national Democratic and Republican conventions, totaled more than $1 billion, a 56 percent increase over the same campaign activities just four years prior in 2000; by 2008, that figure doubled again, to nearly $2 billion. To replace soft money, politicians discovered another option—527s—to take its place. As tax-exempt groups organized under section 527 of the Internal Revenue Code to raise money for political activities, these nonparty organizations are not required to register with the FEC since their main purpose is not to influence the outcome of federal elections. Most 527s are run by interest groups to raise unlimited soft money, which is then spent on voter mobilization or certain types of issue advocacy activities, just not for efforts that expressly advocate the election or defeat of a federal candidate. These groups, widely viewed as nothing more than shadow committees of the political parties, provided an alternative to soft money by allowing various wealthy individuals to donate large sums of money without technically breaking the new laws that went into effect in 2002.

In 2010, the Supreme Court issued another ruling regarding the regulation of money and behavior of groups during presidential campaigns. In *Citizens United v. Federal Election Commission*, the Court ruled that corporate spending on political advertising, or in this case a political film, entitled *Hillary: The Movie*, could not be limited and was not subject to Bipartisan Campaign Reform Act guidelines. The Court did not strike down the ban on direct corporate contributions but did strike down the prohibition of both nonprofit and for-profit entities broadcasting "electioneering communications." The Court ruled that so long as disclosure of the sponsors occurred, the communication was constitutional. The ruling enraged participants across the system, including Democrats, Republicans, and even Tea Party activists, who condemned the apparent advantage granted to deep-pocketed institutions to influence the political environment of the campaign. The ruling was so controversial that competing institutional views played out on the highest stage during the 2010 State of the Union address, when Obama called out the Supreme Court for its ruling: "With all due deference to separation of powers, last week the Supreme Court reversed a century of law that I believe will open the floodgates for special interests—including foreign corporations—to spend without limit in our elections. I don't think American elections should be bankrolled by America's most powerful interests, or worse, by foreign entities. They should be decided by the American people. And I'd urge Democrats and Republicans to pass a bill that helps to correct some of these problems."[36] Several members of the Court were in attendance for the President's State of the Union, and Associate Justice Samuel Alito visibly frowned and said "not true" in response to Obama's lecture. Six weeks later, Chief Justice John Roberts weighed in during his State of the Judiciary address: "First of all, anybody can criticize the Supreme Court without any qualm . . . some people, I think, have an obligation to criticize what we do, given their office, if they think we've done something wrong. . . . On the other hand, there is the issue of the setting, the circumstances and the decorum. The image of having the members of one branch of government standing up, literally surrounding the Supreme Court, cheering and hollering while the court—according to the requirements of protocol—has to sit there expressionless, I think is very troubling."[37]

Presidential Fundraising after *Citizens United*
The 2012 race was the first presidential election in the aftermath of the Supreme Court landmark ruling. There were significant changes to the process, as predicted by both *Citizens United* supporters and detractors. The 2012 campaign cycle was only the second in which super PACs were the dominant fundraising vehicle. The money raised and spent by each super PAC has no limit, as long as there is no

coordination between the super PAC and a particular campaign. In 2012, the funding spent on behalf of candidates via super PACs, along with the ability for each campaign to raise large sums of money, meant that neither Obama nor Republican nominee Mitt Romney would need the public financing because each easily raised more than the $91 million available from the federal government.[38] Super PAC spending on behalf of Romney totaled more than $400 million, while the total for Obama was $163 million. A majority of that money was used on negative attack ads in opposition to one of the candidates.[39] The ability to target money spent in a particular state allowed the Romney campaign in 2012 to saturate the airwaves at key moments in the primary contest to knock out his Republican rivals (what fellow candidate Newt Gingrich called "carpet bombing" in key primary states such as Florida).[40] The 2012 and 2016 races demonstrate what aspects of the old model of presidential campaign finance survived the *Citizens United* ruling and how technological change can influence the campaign's quest for donors.

Seeking Donors

Candidates and their campaigns put significant time and attention into fundraising, particularly in an era where they will likely need to raise millions without relying on public financing. The old-school model of fundraising relied on traditional methods, beginning with candidates tapping their friends, family, and acquaintances for the hard money individual donations ($2,700 in 2015–2016). The old methods relied on the breadth and depth of a candidate's Rolodex of phone numbers and addresses (today's contact list would add email to that important cache of information). The need to connect with a wide variety of individuals willing to support a bid for office is one of the factors that previously advantaged candidates with political experience because they would have expanded their contacts as they moved into more important positions.

After the inner circle of potential donors is solicited, campaigns must go wider. Telemarketing and direct mail were the mainstays of the pre-Internet world, and even in today's connected society, phone calls and mailers can still work to gain the attention of potential donors. Like with the inner circle, the better the list of names and numbers, the easier it is to fundraise. The campaigns in 2012 and 2016 used sophisticated voter data management tools to individually shape direct mail just as campaigns can shape and tailor email messages.[41]

To broaden their reach further, candidates turn to bundling. An individual or PAC can solicit contributions from individuals on behalf of a candidate and then "bundle" them together to make one large (and legal) contribution to the campaign. Since each of the individual contributions is within the limit for hard money prior to being bundled, this allows an individual or group to give a large contribution to a particular candidate.[42] Although some groups have a policy objective or other goal they hope to achieve by bundling, there are other incentives to bundle thousands of dollars of campaign contributions. Both national parties reward their top contributors with many perks, including private meetings with top policymakers (and even the president), being seated next to a prominent politician at a party event, or an ambassadorship to a prime locale. For example, Barack Obama appointed Colleen Bradley Bell ambassador to Hungary in 2014. She was confirmed 52–42 over the objections of John McCain, who argued, "We're about to vote on a totally unqualified individual to be ambassador to a nation which is very important to our national security interest. Her qualifications are as a producer of the television soap opera 'The Bold and The Beautiful,' contributed $800,000 to Obama in the last election and bundled more than $2.1 million for President Obama's re-election effort. . . . I am not against political appointees . . . I understand how the game is played, but here we are, a nation [Hungary] that is on the verge of ceding its sovereignty to a neo-fascist dictator getting in bed with Vladimir Putin and we're going to send the producer of 'The Bold and The Beautiful' as the ambassador. I urge my colleagues to put a stop to this foolishness. I urge a no vote."[43] In 2016, Hillary Clinton had more than 1,100 individuals bundling for her, raising more than $113 million. The lawmakers, entertainers, and businessmen and -women donating more than $100,000 were called "Hillblazers."[44]

The largest source of money for candidates, however, comes from PACs and super PACs. With the freedoms allowed from the Supreme Court's *Citizens United* ruling and the appeals court ruling in *SpeechNow.Org v. FEC* (2010) to lift the limits on PACs that were not coordinating with campaigns, the flow of money to these unfettered organizations increased, as did their political activity. As a result, in 2016, super PACs supporting Hillary Clinton raised and spent $217.5 million, almost triple the $82.3 million raised and spent by Trump super PACs.[45] In addition, in 2012, a new form of expenditure organization—the 501(c)(4)—began working in concert with super PACs and became the perfect vehicle to hide donor information and create what is called "dark money." A 501(c)(4) can also make unlimited donations, but the advantage is that it is "protected by the principals of both freedom of speech and freedom of association, and as a consequence, its 'membership' or donor list can remain private, while the Super PAC donors must be disclosed."[46]

Despite all the fundraising and spending in the 2016 election, much outsider group money was left on the table because of the preferences and predilections of the top candidates—specifically Sanders and Trump. In opposition to the skewing of power toward the wealthy exacerbated by *Citizens United*, 2016 demonstrated two different approaches to representing the choices and preferences of ordinary citizens. Sanders, drawing on the Obama 2008 model, celebrated small donors and used technology to draw them in. At his campaign rallies, Sanders often asked the crowd, "What's my average contribution?," and the crowd yelled back, "$27." Unlike most campaigns, Sanders did not set up a separate fundraising organization; instead, the digital team managed online and tech-driven solicitations. In addition to the emails and a "donate now" tab that all campaign websites have, Sanders' team was the first to use texting to raise funds. During a Republican primary debate, the campaign "rolled out a text-to-donate tool asking supporters to text the word 'NOW' each time they felt outraged, a command that triggered a $20 campaign donation."[47] Sanders was able to raise more than $200 million in small donations during the Democratic primary. Obama, in 2012, raised a staggering $483 million from donations of $200 or less. Both phenomena suggest the acceptance by American citizens of the principle cemented by *Buckley v Valeo*: money is speech and a way for voices to be heard prior to voting.

Trump raised a phenomenal sum from small donors and rejected the dominance of the wealthy, ironically, by highlighting his own personal wealth. Jeb Bush and his super PAC led all Republican contenders in the summer of 2015 with funds raised. In contrast to some of his rivals, for a political unknown, Trump had phenomenal name recognition among voters. That recognition originated with his real estate properties and his television show, but when coupled with the intense media attention he received, Trump catapulted into the top tier quickly. However, without the enormous sums raised by others, many questioned Trump's ability to succeed. Refusing to rely on donations from wealthy donors during the invisible primary and initial phase of the nomination calendar and even highlighting how he used to donate to candidates, Trump stood proudly on his personal wealth. In his announcement speech on June 16, 2015, Trump said, "I don't need anybody's money. It's nice. I don't need anybody's money. I'm using my own money . . . I'm not using donors. I don't care. I'm really rich."

Self-financing candidates, like Trump, have advantages over challengers, since they can spend lavishly on their campaigns without wasting precious campaign time on fundraising. This can be particularly important since early money is crucial to keep the campaign momentum going. And personal loans from the candidate to his campaign can be repaid through fundraising efforts later. Similar to Trump's desire to "drain the swamp," H. Ross Perot, who ran as an independent candidate in 1992 and 1996, was quoted as saying, "If someone as blessed as I am is not willing to clean out the barn, who will?" Perot spent $63.5 million on his 1992 campaign; however, in 1996, he took public funding and spent only $8 million of his own money.

Despite his rhetoric about not being tied to special interests or other donors, Trump did turn to fundraising for the general election. Trump donated $66 million of his own money and also used his own private jet, which a candidate would normally lease. However, he was able to use his outsider status to raise $280 million from donors of $200 or less. This is more than half of what Obama achieved but is respectable considering Trump did not start fundraising in earnest until after the Republican convention in July 2016.

NATIONAL PARTY CONVENTIONS

The role of the national party convention has changed dramatically in the past century. In the age where party insiders dominated the nominee selection process, the convention was a hotbed of intrigue and activity where rules were created, deals were struck, and favorite candidates were promoted. Today's convention lacks that drama because the primary process predetermines who the party's nominee will be months earlier. The national convention instead serves as the kickoff for the start of the general election season, a gathering for party insiders, and unites party regulars who will then go home and fight for their nominee in their state. The convention also serves as an introduction to the nominee for voters who did not participate in or even pay attention to the primary process and is a signal for those voters that the campaign for the presidency is under way. Consequently, both the Republican and the Democratic conventions are made-for-television events, scripted to showcase the party and the nominee. The nominee's acceptance speech serves as the highlight of the convention because it is the first (and often only) opportunity for each candidate to speak directly to voters with full media coverage and without the usual interpretive filter provided by news reporters, anchors, and other analysts.

The first national conventions to be televised were those of both major parties, both held in Philadelphia, in 1948. For Harry Truman, his televised acceptance speech at the Democratic National Convention represented an important moment of the campaign; lagging in public opinion polls and having governed in the shadow of FDR since succeeding to the presidency in 1945, Truman's speech rallied Democrats with its stinging attack on the Republican Congress. White House advisors had recognized the significance of the speech as it was being developed:

> We would like to make the following recommendations for the President's Acceptance Speech: It should be a fighting talk . . . The President should not just exude confidence, but confidence with reasons. He should give our side some good solid substance upon which to hinge the campaign arguments. Platitudes and truisms should be avoided like the pox. The speech should be short—ten to fifteen minutes maximum. It should be read after thorough study. The words and phrases should be short, homely, and in character. This is no place for Churchillian grandiloquence. Here is the outline of the attached draft: Introduction—The President's confidence and the reasons therefor—His programs are what the people want—Issue for issue, we're right and they're wrong. High Prices—The story of inflation—The choice facing the American people: No action with the Republicans or price control with the Democrats. Housing . . . Do we want Democratic action or Republican promises? Education, health, and other progressive measures—How the 80th Congress killed them all—A brief rundown. Conclusion—What the President expects to do himself—The job of everyone who feels as we do on these great issues is to tell this story.[48]

The national party convention continues to offer the presidential nominee of each party a chance to speak directly to the American public at a time when many voters are just tuning in to the election. The reception of the candidate's speech by

George H. W. Bush gave his famous "read my lips, no new taxes" pledge to delegates at the 1988 Republican National Convention.

the press, pundits, and citizens often determines which side gets the convention "bounce" in the polls. Like Truman, incumbent presidents running for reelection still pay special attention to this momentous speech because it can help to set the tone for the upcoming general election campaign. In August 1992, White House speechwriter Tony Snow provided the strategy behind the convention address by George H. W. Bush:

> The President's acceptance speech, for good or ill, will set the tone for this year's Republican Presidential Campaign. It must be a winner, and should be. . . . A good speech should do two things. It should tell a story and it should make an argument. In this case, we should tell the story of George Bush's life. The President, despite his long tenure in the public eye, remains an enigma to most Americans. We should strip away layers of mystery in ways that fit the man. The argument we seek flows from the biography. Americans should re-elect George Bush because he alone can lead America at this historic juncture. He also has tried to unleash American greatness through a program of continued reform. As the speech tells a story and makes an argument, it should try to achieve several important goals: It must define the President. It must define the opposition. It must draw clear distinctions between the political parties. It must unite the party and the country. And it must create the kind of enthusiasm that will transform viewers into volunteers. . . . If they meet these conditions, they can lift the President to a plane far above where Clinton could possibly stand. They also will provide the Vision Thing by describing in clear and concrete terms what four more years would provide: a more vigorous economy, thriving in the new international marketplace (Olympic analogies might work); an education system in which parents can choose schools for their children, and in which the schools provide the best education in the world; safe streets and neighborhoods where cops and citizens work together to take on criminals, and especially drug kingpins; smaller government and lower taxes, so you keep more of your hard-earned pay; and an America brimming with confidence and ambition—the America we all know and love. When the President steps off the stage in Houston, every listener should be able to answer the question: If we re-elect George Bush, what will our lives be like four years from now? If they cannot answer that question, we're in deep trouble.[49]

Today, other than the candidate's acceptance speech, although much of the rest of the convention itself is often anticlimactic, excitement can emerge out of the choice for the vice presidential running mate. This serves as the first major decision a presidential nominee makes; thus, voters, pundits, and even the opposing campaign scrutinize both the process and the person selected. In the framers' original model, the vice president was the candidate for president who came in second in the balloting. In the modern era, the vice presidential choice is a reflection of the candidate at the top of the ticket and often serves as a statement about what the presidential nominee is lacking from a strategic perspective. Historically, vice presidential candidates have been chosen to promote geographic balance (for example, John F. Kennedy's selection of Lyndon Johnson in 1960, the popular Texan as the running mate for the Massachusetts native) or party unity (for example, Ronald Reagan's selection of George H. W. Bush in 1980 and John Kerry's selection of John Edwards in 2004 both represented the nominee's selection of a close rival during the primary season). Other selections have attempted to shore up a candidate's perceived lack of

Table 3.2 Presidential Running Mates since 1960

	DEMOCRATIC	REPUBLICAN
1960	Sen. Lyndon Johnson (TX)	Henry Cabot Lodge, Jr.
1964	Sen. Hubert Humphrey (MN)	Rep. William Miller (NY)
1968	Sen. Edmund Muskie (ME)	Gov. Spiro Agnew (MD)
1972	Sargent Shriver	VP Spiro Agnew
1976	Sen. Walter Mondale (MN)	Sen. Bob Dole (KS)
1980	VP Walter Mondale	George H.W. Bush
1984	Rep. Geraldine Ferraro (NY)	VP George H.W. Bush
1988	Sen. Lloyd Bentsen (TX)	Sen. Dan Quayle (IN)
1992	Sen. Al Gore (TN)	VP Dan Quayle
1996	VP Al Gore	Jack Kemp
2000	Sen. Joseph Lieberman (CT)	Dick Cheney
2004	Sen. John Edwards (NC)	VP Dick Cheney
2008	Sen. Joe Biden (DE)	Gov. Sarah Palin (AK)
2012	VP Joe Biden (DE)	Rep. Paul Ryan (WI)
2016	Sen. Tim Kaine (VA)	Gov. Mike Pence (IN)

experience in a certain area (for example, Obama's selection of Joe Biden in 2008 brought years of foreign policy experience to the Democratic ticket) or can provide balance to the insider/outsider perspective (for example, as state governors, both Bill Clinton's selection of Al Gore in 1992 and George W. Bush's selection of Dick Cheney in 2000 brought Washington insiders to their tickets). Sometimes running mates are chosen with history in mind, such as Walter Mondale's selection of Geraldine Ferraro as the first women vice presidential nominee in 1984 and Al Gore's selection of Joe Lieberman as the first Jewish nominee in 2000. Even public relations considerations can matter; George H. W. Bush seemed to like the energy and youth that the 41-year-old Dan Quayle brought to the Republican ticket in 1988. In 2016, Clinton's pick of Senator Tim Kaine (D-VA) was perceived as a safe pick from a swing state, and the fact that he was fluent in Spanish was seen as an advantage in appealing to Latino voters. Trump chose Indiana governor Mike Pence, who brought one important thing to the ticket that Trump lacked—years of governing experience. Pence was a Washington insider, well liked by Republicans and an ardent fiscal and social conservative. Pence's calm, unflappable demeanor as well as his experience in the House of Representatives and as a governor reassured many within the Republican establishment about Trump's candidacy (see Table 3.2).

THE GENERAL ELECTION

Although the framers designed an election process removed from direct democracy, which balanced issues of representation and geography, they also rejected the notion of campaigning for the office. An adage of the time claimed, "The office should seek the man, the man should not seek the office."[50] However, the early behavior of the states in Electoral College voting demonstrates how rule design influenced strategy, long before the intentional behavior of campaigning took place.

The Electoral College

The Constitution requires the states to select their electors for the Electoral College, in a manner of their choosing (e.g., by popular vote, by state legislature, or by lottery if they wanted to), so long as it was completed within the 34-day period prior to the first Wednesday of December and voting was completed by that Wednesday. Defining a beginning and ending date naturally introduced strategy to the process. States who voted early could produce a momentum shift toward a candidate; states who voted later could be the deciding vote in a close outcome. In 1845, Congress settled the strategic jockeying and created a uniform date for choosing their electors, which today translates to presidential elections held on the first Tuesday following a Monday in November. The Electoral College vote still does not officially occur until December because this was a statutory law and not a constitutional change.

As discussed in Chapter 2, the Electoral College is an institution created by the Constitution to describe the membership of the body that votes for the president. There is no grand meeting of all the electors, so it is a college in name only. The Electoral College is made up of the electors from all 50 states plus the District of Columbia, which are allocated by each state on the first Tuesday in November. Most states today choose their electors by allocating all electors to the plurality winner of the popular vote; victors do not need 50 percent of the vote, just more than all the other candidates receive. Only Maine and Nebraska do not allocate electors based on the winner-take-call calculation. Instead, the candidate who wins each congressional district wins that electoral vote, whereas the candidate who wins the popular vote in the state wins the two votes represented by the state's two seats in the U.S. Senate. The electors vote in December at their state capital, and more than half the states have laws that require the electors to vote for the party nominee whom they have been chosen to represent. Rarely do "faithless electors" cast their vote for someone other than the candidate on their slate. Given the automatic nature of the Electoral College vote, the position of elector is more of a symbolic reward than an opportunity to influence the presidential outcome. Yet, the Electoral College still influences election strategy and ultimately the outcome of the race.

The Electoral College imposes strategic decision making on candidates based on the allocation of votes. The Electoral College, like so much in the framers' design, is a compromise between population and size. The design combines the population allocation of the House of Representatives with the assignment of two Senate seats, thus granting all states a minimum of three Electoral College votes. The number of votes in the Electoral College expanded over time as the number of seats in the House of Representatives increased because of increased population and because the number of states in the Union expanded. As such, 538 became the magic number in 1964 based on the 435 seats in the House of Representatives, 100 seats in the Senate, and the three votes given to the District of Columbia by the Twenty-Third Amendment. With 538 available Electoral College votes, a candidate needs 270 votes to become president. The pathway to achieving the magic number introduces strategy and "electoral math" to presidential campaigns.

The first calculation that a candidate must consider is the winner-take-all aspect of most states. The disparities in Electoral College vote allocation resulting from population seemingly encourage candidates to allocate time, money, and effort to states with the largest populations. From this perspective, California, Texas, New

York, Florida, Illinois, and Pennsylvania are worth more; for example, California is 8.13 times more "attractive per electoral vote" than Alaska. Not only do populous states have more partisan voters, but also they have more undecided voters to sway. Over time, however, population calculations were not as effective for creating a campaign strategy since they did not account for voting behavior.[51]

Campaign strategists have long been aware that there are both decided and undecided voters and that the battle for victory exists in turning out one's supporters and reaching those who remain uncommitted. As a result, the size of a state's population is no longer the only factor that determines campaign strategy. For example, the three largest states in the nation have consistently voted for one party in recent decades—a Republican candidate has not won California since 1988 or New York since 1984, and a Democratic candidate has not won Texas since 1976. As a result, the opposing party's candidate spends little time campaigning in a state where he or she has little chance of winning the electoral votes (although fundraising still occurs). In effect, consistency of partisan voting led to irrelevance for some of the largest states as campaigns refocused to other states where the outcome was in doubt.

Competitive states, also known as "battleground" or "swing" states, receive massive attention from candidates' campaigns, the parties, interest groups, and the media because the outcome is unknown. Correspondingly, voter participation in these states increases.[52] The more effort and resources political elites put into campaigns, the more people turn out to vote. In states without massive mobilization efforts, turnout remains stable or can decline because uncommitted or inactive citizens are not mobilized. Even among committed partisans turnout can decline when the candidates do not appear in the state, run ads, or otherwise demonstrate that the race matters. The number of competitive states is small and has been for several campaign cycles. A 2015 joint initiative of the American Enterprise Institute, the Brookings Institution, and the Center for American Progress predicted that there would be 11 competitive, or so-called battleground, states in 2016, including Colorado, Florida, Iowa, Michigan, Nevada, New Hampshire, North Carolina, Ohio, Pennsylvania, Virginia, and Wisconsin.[53] Thus, of the 270 Electoral College votes needed to win, the outcomes of 146 are what decided the race. In 2016, Trump won all but Colorado, Nevada, New Hampshire, and Virginia. In effect, the Electoral College system encourages the candidates to reject the notion of running in all 50 states. Candidates also must consider the practicality of allocating a large percentage of resources to states with few Electoral College votes or to states with a large number of Electoral College votes that they have little chance of winning. In the states where the candidates do compete vigorously, appeals to uncommitted voters are critical.

IN THEIR OWN WORDS

THE ELECTORAL COLLEGE STRATEGY

Although George H. W. Bush would lose reelection in 1992, during the summer of 1991, the Bush White House was optimistic about their chances for a second term. White House advisors began discussing strategy based on what they perceived to be the plan of the eventual Democratic nominee for the 1992 campaign based on the Electoral College map. Although Bill Clinton would only win 43 percent of the popular vote compared to 38 percent for Bush and 19 percent for Perot, Clinton won 370 of the Electoral College votes to Bush's 178 (and zero for Perot), despite early projections by Bush's political team:

> The June 15 *Washington Post* carries a remarkable story out of Middleburg, VA on the Democrats' latest strategy huddle for 1992. According to the *Post*, the Democrats have adopted a strategy of political triage that divides the country into "baskets" of winnable and unwinnable states. Democratic strategists go on to identify 13 states as unwinnable—"so firmly Republican in their presidential voting patterns that an investment of cash and staff is a waste of resources." The basket strategy is remarkable in many ways: The Democrats are ready now to **write off** more states in '92 than they **won** in '88. Mike Dukakis won 10 states and 111 electoral votes in 1988. The 13 states written off by the Democrats for 1992 total 106 electoral votes. They represent a population of close to **50 million Americans—a full one-fifth of the country**. The basket strategy suggests the Democrats are no longer a national party. 17 months before the election, they are ready to run up the white flag. We should do everything possible to make certain the public hears more about the Democrats' basket strategy: The President should refer to the basket strategy—contrast it with a Republican approach that is active and aggressive in all 50 states. Our message: **the Democrats may be ready to write off 50 million Americans, but the Republican Party is ready to reach out to every American in every state. The President should drive home this message whenever he visits one of the "forgotten states."** The basket strategy cuts the legs out from under State Democratic campaigns, and creates an opening for Republicans to translate support for the President into support for the Party. In these states, our objective should shift from "state to slate:" we should aim at a Republican sweep to create the coattails we need to make inroads in Congress.[54]

For today's presidential candidates, the Electoral College has become part of a campaign strategy, which differs substantially from what the framers had in mind. Also, as highlighted by the 2000 and 2016 presidential elections, many flaws exist. First, a candidate can win the popular vote yet still lose the election. Although Al Gore beat George W. Bush in the popular vote by roughly 500,000 votes (Gore earned 48.4 percent of the vote to Bush's 47.9 percent), Bush won the Electoral College when he was declared the winner in Florida by the Supreme Court in *Bush v. Gore* (2000). Until 2000, a popular-vote winner had not lost the Electoral College, and thus the presidency, since 1876, when Democrat Samuel Tilden won 51 percent of the popular vote but Republican Rutherford B. Hayes, with only 47.9 percent of the popular vote, won the Electoral College. In 2016, Trump won the Electoral College 304 to 227,[55] whereas Clinton won the popular vote by nearly 3 million.

The contentious legal battle in 2000 over the vote count in Florida also highlighted the deadlines set for casting of electoral votes; the Supreme Court's ruling in effect stopped the recount in Florida to meet the statutory deadlines set for casting the Electoral College votes. The controversy stemmed from the different standards Florida counties used to count ballots during the recount to determine which candidate had won the popular vote in the state (and thus the 25 electoral votes that would decide the presidential contest in the Electoral College). Whether the Supreme Court should have accepted the case on appeal from the Florida State Supreme Court also stirred controversy. Nevertheless, the Supreme Court ruled that the Florida Supreme Court's method of recounting ballots was unconstitutional in that the different standards violated the equal protection clause. However, a 5–4 majority also declared that there was not enough time to conduct a recount of the vote and that no other remedy was available in deciding the election. The decision stopped the recount and allowed Florida secretary of state Katherine Harris to certify Bush as the winner, thus giving Bush Florida's 25 electoral votes, bringing him to a total of 271. The decision was controversial, in part because the justices in both the majority and the minority relied on unprecedented constitutional arguments mostly out of line with their own judicial philosophies. The more conservative justices in the majority had argued against states' rights to end the recount, which gave Bush the victory, whereas the more liberal justices in the minority had argued on behalf of states' rights to have Florida continue the recount.

The existence of the Electoral College itself remains controversial. Advocates for eliminating what is considered by many an "archaic system" argue that it is no longer necessary since voters now have the information they need to make an informed decision. In addition, opponents of the Electoral College argue that the system is dangerous, with the possibility of electing a president who is not the choice of the people, which would cause a constitutional crisis (although the latter did not occur in 2000 or in 2016); that some states benefit unduly from this system; that different states use different methods for selecting electors and there is no guarantee that electors will abide by the popular vote in all states; and because of the winner-take-all system in most states, some popular votes are nullified.

However, the Electoral College also has its defenders, who argue that it recognizes the important role of the states as political units and guarantees that the president will be represented by a geographically broad constituency. In addition, the Electoral College combines the elements of popular democracy with representative democracy; it can expand the sense that the president has the mandate to lead the country (for example, Ronald Reagan won 51 percent of the popular vote in 1980, but 91 percent of the electoral vote); it discourages the influence by extreme minor parties; it enables minority groups to wield power through significant blocs of electoral votes in a state; and it discourages voter fraud.[56] To date, little progress has been made to either eliminate or amend the Electoral College. Several states are considering altering their selection of electors similar to the process used in Maine and Nebraska, thus eliminating the winner-take-all system. In addition, as of January 2017, ten states (California, Hawaii, Illinois, Massachusetts, Maryland, New Jersey, New York, Rhode Island, Vermont, and Washington) plus the District of Columbia have joined the National Popular Vote Interstate Compact, an agreement to award all their respective electoral votes to the popular-vote winner (all were won by Hillary Clinton in 2016).

Appealing to Voters

In the late 1800s and early 1900s, voter turnout was much higher than it is today because of the strength of partisanship and the public nature of voting. The Australian balloting process made voting private and by candidate, rather than individuals placing the entire slate of candidates in a ballot box in full view. The parties knew that victory was a simple matter of mobilizing more supporters than the other side was able to. In the twenty-first century, partisanship and turning out supporters matters, but reaching the uncommitted is often what determines the outcome of a presidential contest.

Candidates know how to reach partisans; the nomination period is when candidates demonstrate why they should be their party's standard-bearer. The task of reaching nonpartisans is much more complicated and requires multiple tools and strategies. Individuals identify with a party because the party's ideals, platform, and candidates correspond well to their own. Few individuals agree with a party 100 percent of the time, but agreement the majority of the time is often acceptable for self-identification. Once individuals self-identify as a party member, by registering or volunteering or any myriad of activities, individuals typically remain a partisan. Strength of identification can change over time, but partisan identification usually remains consistent.[57] Individuals who do not self-identify with a party do so out of lack of knowledge of the similarity between their own views and the view of one of the parties or because not enough of their views match the party ideology. Sometimes individuals simply prefer to consider themselves "independent" rather than affiliated with a partisan entity. Individuals who do not use the party as a cue for a candidate who meets their ideological criteria need other means to decide. Those criteria can be issue based or candidate based.

Because of the variability in their decision making (which is in contrast to partisan voters), independents can either make or break a presidential campaign. The campaign must not only determine what independent voters want from a presidential candidate, but also encourage them to vote. Although candidates appear at rallies, town halls, and other meet-and greet-events, most individuals never meet a presidential candidate. The information exchange between voters and candidates takes place through the media and technology.

Donald Trump addresses his supporters on the night of his election in 2016.

Campaign Communications

Informed citizens are considered a critical component to a functioning democracy, and media have long been influential in presidential campaigns. The expansion of technology has also enhanced the role that the press can play in electing a president, particularly by the start of the television age in the 1950s. Since then, voters have had a growing number of choices in how they receive information about candidates; information during the presidential campaign can come from mediated sources (legacy outlets like newspapers and television or newer venues like blogs), unmediated sources (social media, websites, or candidate advertising), and presidential debates.

Mediated sources

Although Americans over the age of 15 watch more than 2.5 hours of television a day,[58] the time spent watching news, and election news in particular, is changing. In 2010, Americans averaged about 70 minutes a day absorbing news, with 57 of those minutes coming from sources that package the content for the individual (i.e., television, radio, and newspapers).[59] In 2008, television was the most cited source of all political information during the presidential campaign.[60] In 2016, Americans still preferred to get their information from television, but that number has been declining and will continue to do so as the population ages because those individuals who are predominant television users are 50 and older.[61] The campaign information in television news, newspaper articles (whether online or in print), and radio ads comes through a reporter or anchor/host. Therefore, for a candidate, media coverage can be a double-edge sword: the name and issue exposure can be helpful for voter decision making and it is free (unlike running ads), but when candidates appear on television or in news articles, the information is transmitted through an interpretive filter. For partisans, media coverage is unlikely to affect voter choice, although it could influence the decision to participate. For independent voters, the content and quality of information from news sources can have an impact on decision making. Although the coverage was not always positive, the abundance of free press nonetheless aided Trump in seeking the Republican nomination.

Campaigns are now "structured to garner the most favorable media exposure, reaching the largest number of prospective supporters, with the greatest degree of candidate control over the message," as strategies maximize photo opportunities, talk show appearances, or appearing at unique events or locations.[62] Prior to 1992, candidates did not appear on talk shows; those shows were considered "soft" in contrast to the "hard" news shows like *60 Minutes* or other network news programs. After Perot announced his independent run for president in 1992 on CNN's *Larry King Live*, candidates began to gravitate to newer outlets with larger audiences, where questions were less confrontational. By 2008, candidates routinely appeared on daytime talk shows as well as late-night and other comedic/satirical shows. In recent years, several presidential and vice presidential candidates have appeared on *Saturday Night Live*, including Barack Obama, Hillary Clinton, Sarah Palin, and Bernie Sanders. The show is also known for its impersonations of candidates, which can increase ratings but does not always please the candidates themselves. Tina Fey's caricature of Palin in 2008 received so much attention that, to this day, many still believe Palin actually said, "I can see Russia from my house." In 2016, Alec Baldwin's impersonation of Trump received similar ratings, and the clips frequently went viral, even eliciting this tweet from Trump: "Watched *Saturday Night Live* hit job on me. Time to retire the boring and unfunny show. Alec Baldwin portrayal stinks. Media rigging election!" A former *Saturday Night Live* staffer summed up why this content can be so powerful: "Eighty million people watched the debate, 130 million people will vote, 50 million others are still looking for places to get their news, and comedy can fill that gap. . . . Maybe it's going to take comedians to do the job that cable news has relinquished for so much of the campaign."[63]

Soft news or entertainment-based content can shape the narrative of the campaign and define the candidate for voters, but is often at odds with the campaign's preferred narrative. For independent voters, the press serves a critical purpose by providing voting cues, because they reject the party as a shortcut mechanism for choice but still must be able to choose among the candidates. The press provides information that should allow voters to distinguish between the candidates. However, campaigns are often frustrated by having little control over the focus and tone of the coverage that media provide. The type of news coverage provided during the campaign dramatically influences voters beliefs about the candidates, and the weakening of the party–citizen connection has awarded the press a role it was unprepared to assume: that of election mediator.[64] Between 1985 and 2007, the Pew Center for the People and the Press, a nonpartisan organization, found that "the American public continues to fault news organizations for a number of perceived failures, with solid majorities criticizing them for political bias, inaccuracy and failing to acknowledge mistakes." In a Pew Research poll after the 2016 election, 78 percent of those polled rated the press with a grade of C or lower on how they handled the campaign; 38 percent gave the press a failing grade.[65]

The quality and quantity of network news coverage decline relates to "a tendency to emphasize the campaign's horse race over matters of substance, a frequently controversial performance with respect to the core values of accuracy and fairness, a declining amount of attention paid to candidates (as opposed to that lavished on the journalists covering them), and declining volume of coverage of the election overall."[66] More significant for the candidate is the press preference for coverage that focuses on the "horse race" of the campaign, as well as a narrative about the "game" of presidential politics (who is ahead, who is behind, who has raised the most money, whose campaign runs smoothly, etc.). Game coverage challenges a candidate's ability to distinguish himself or herself substantively from opponents. Instead, much like *Baseball Tonight* on ESPN, reporters, pundits, and bloggers analyze "performance" indicators and offer predictions of outcomes based on those measures. In presidential primaries, both opinion poll and primary results work in concert as the press highlights candidates rising in the polls and either focus on the negative aspect of less successful candidates or, worse, provide no coverage of second-tier candidates. The press preference for these "inside baseball" results, which do not relate to policy positions or to analysis of future behavior, creates a "bandwagon effect" because voters tend to want to support a winner; thus, positive numbers lead to positive coverage, which produces better primary results, which in turn produces positive poll numbers.[67] During the general election, public opinion polls are the only measurable performance indicator between September and Election Day (although the press will also convene focus groups and town halls to evaluate performance, in particular during the presidential debates).

Researching the Presidency

Forecasting Elections

There have been election predictions for as long as there have been newspapers. The desire to capture the views of voters as well as the desire to "call it" first drives the media interest in prediction. In contrast, political scientists try to predict outcomes to determine a better understanding of what drives voting behavior. In particular, the focus on short-term voting behavior versus long-term systemic inputs produce reams of scholarship about ideological constraints and the immutable power of economic circumstance to affect voting.

In 2016, the two styles of prediction collided thanks to a popular website, fivethirtyeight.com, and its director, Nate Silver. Silver correctly forecasted 49 of 50 state outcomes in the 2008 presidential election and all 50 in 2012. In 2016, the website's prediction meter was copied and displayed prominently by many media organizations, including the *New York Times*. On Election Day, prior to any states being called, the *New York Times'* prediction meter indicated that Hillary Clinton had an 85 percent chance of winning the presidency. Like the famous "Dewey beats Truman" newspaper headline in 1948, these prediction meters were wrong. In a postelection *mea culpa* article by the *New York Times*, their public editor noted that "the Times isn't the only news organization bewildered and perhaps a bit sheepish about its predictions coverage. The rest of media missed it too, as did the pollsters, the analysts, the Democratic Party and the Clinton campaign itself."[68]

Silver, the *New York Times*, and many other predictions models, including those of some political scientists, turned out to be flawed—the fundamentals that had worked in 2008 and 2012 were not effective in 2016 and all the results were skewed. Moreover, the effects were cumulative, creating an erroneous statistical advantage for Clinton. These models were primarily based on state polling data. As Silver noted, "People mistake having a large volume of polling data for eliminating uncertainty. It doesn't work that way. Yes, having more polls helps to a degree, by reducing sampling error and by providing for a mix of reasonable methodologies. Therefore, it's better to be ahead in two polls than ahead in one poll, and in 10 polls than in two polls. Before long, however, you start to encounter diminishing returns. Polls tend to replicate one another's mistakes: If a particular type of demographic subgroup is hard to reach on the phone, for instance, the polls may try different workarounds but they're all likely to have problems of some kind or another. The cacophony of headlines about how 'CLINTON LEADS IN POLL' neglected the fact that these leads were often quite small and that if one poll missed, the others potentially would also."[69] Thus, the results showed overperforming and underperforming; Clinton overperformed in many blue states, but underperformed in the battleground states, which turned out to be significant for the outcome.

Not all forecasting models were wrong in 2016. With much less fanfare than Silver, political scientist Helmut Norpoth has been correctly predicting presidential elections since 1996. His Primary Vote model relies on the outcome in the New Hampshire and South Carolina primaries, as well as the Democratic vote share in 2008 and 2012 (since they controlled the White House).[70] In March 2016, the Primary Vote model predicted with 87–99 percent certainty that Trump would win. Another political science model, Time for Change from the Center for Politics at the University of Virginia, has successfully predicted outcomes since 1988. Their model is based on the approval rating of the incumbent president and changes in the gross domestic product in the election year. They found in August 2016 "a net approval rating for Barack Obama of +6 in the

Gallup weekly tracking poll for the week of June 27–July 4, an estimated second quarter change in real GDP of 1.2% according to the Bureau of Economic Analysis, and the fact that Hillary Clinton is seeking a third consecutive Democratic term in the White House, the Time for Change Model predicts a narrow victory for Donald Trump—51.4% of the major party vote to 48.6%."[71] However, their Electoral College forecasting had Clinton ahead.

All the incorrect results had one thing in common: reliance on state polling data. For numerous reasons, the data were unreliable. In contrast, the political science modeling relied on fixed outcomes—gross domestic product or voting—and a theoretical understanding of how those figures reflect choices made. Ordinarily, these predictions have a trivial impact on election outcomes. However, the introduction of the prediction meter and the popularity of Silver's fivethirtyeight.com made the flaws in the mathematical model much more significant. The reliance on the prediction meter by the media gave statistics the perception of certainty. Moreover, the meter itself is the worst type of game coverage. Normatively, it begs the question: Do we need this information, and, does it help voters decide?

Unmediated information

Campaigns are about choice: the choice to vote and for which candidate. To make these choices, citizens need information. For partisans, the choice of nominee is often the more significant decision because they are unlikely to vote for the other party. For nonpartisans, or less strongly partisan individuals, the choice to vote and for whom remains throughout the general election. These individuals need information; consequently, the inability of the press to provide distinguishing information potentially undermines citizens' ability to make a choice. Candidates do a far better job providing distinguishing information, which makes sense, because it is their responsibility to articulate why they are the best choice. Moreover, the differences between "the campaigns' messages and the media's messages are immense. . . . the mediated coverage of much campaign news has become so negative and so inaccurate that the unmediated speeches, advertisements, and Internet web pages of the highly self-interested campaigns produce more-substantive, more-useful, and more-accurate forms of campaign discourse."[72] Consequently, campaigns spend millions on outreach via advertising, their websites, email, texting, a presence on YouTube, iTunes, and the numerous social networking sites.

Television ads have long been the gold standard mechanism to reach voters, particularly undecided voters. Ads allow the candidates to reach voters without the filtering provided by the press. In a 30- or 60-second spot, candidates can provide biographical information, set the campaign's issue agenda, cast blame, and manage charges levied by an opponent or the media.[73] Some of the most powerful and memorable advertising primes and defuses; candidates prime voters by setting up a focal point for the campaign, which may or may not have been on the minds of voters. When defusing, candidates use ads to respond to critiques by downplaying or re-framing the charge.

One of the most effective priming ads of all time only ran once. In 1964, during the campaign between Lyndon Johnson and Barry Goldwater, the Johnson campaign ran the now-infamous "Daisy" ad, which shows a young girl in a meadow, picking the petals off of a daisy while counting from one to nine. After she reaches nine, an unseen male voice begins counting down from ten. At zero, a mushroom cloud replaces the picture of the little girl. Johnson then warns, "These are the stakes. To make a world in which all of God's children can love, or go into the dark. We must either love each other or we must die."[74] Although the ad only ran once, all three networks reran the ad in its entirety the next night. Reaction was massive and relatively negative because the ad essentially asserted that a vote for Goldwater was a vote for the use of nuclear annihilation. The ad dramatically primed voters to view Goldwater as a trigger-happy war hawk who would lead the United States into a nuclear showdown with the Soviet Union.

Effective ads do not have to be negative, nor do they even have to mention the opponent. Perhaps the most effective positive ad came from Ronald Reagan's reelection campaign in 1984. The ad opened with the line, "It's morning again in America," and merged a positive narrative about Reagan's performance along with concerns that his opponent, Walter Mondale, would return the United States to the economic and social upheaval of earlier times. With a picturesque montage of America, a narrator intoned,

> It's morning again in America. Today more men and women will go to work than ever before in our country's history. With interest rates at about half the record highs of 1980, nearly 2,000 families today will buy new homes, more than at any time in the past four years. This afternoon 6,500 young men and women will be married, and with inflation at less than half of what it was just four years ago, they can look forward with confidence to the future. It's morning again in America, and under the leadership of President Reagan, our country is prouder and stronger and better. Why would we ever want to return to where we were less than four short years ago?

Campaign ads are rarely as positive as Reagan's, partly because it is hard for most candidates to remain above the fray of the campaign but also because of the power of negative ads, which can effectively define negative attributes of an opponent. Because of the increase in the use of negative ads in the 1980s, media organizations began to run "ad watches" to check the accuracy of the charges leveled by opponents. Ad watches became prominent in 1988 and were relatively effective at distinguishing fact from fiction and dispelling dramatic rhetoric and potentially misleading portrayals.[75] However, the media's interest in and their effectiveness at policing campaign advertising has waned in recent years, in part because of the high volume of ads and the speed with which they are now produced, and thus now provide only a limited check on the unfiltered information put out by each presidential campaign.

Ads are the primary technique used to define an opponent. During the 2016 nominating phase, Democratic candidates spent approximately $136 million running more than 230,000 spots on television (there were even more online). Democratic-leaning outside groups spent only $3 million airing 1,500 ads.[76] In contrast, Republican candidates aired 114,000 ads and Republican-leaning groups aired 138,000 for a combined total spending of $270 million. However, Trump's campaign produced only 19 ads and did not begin running any until November 2015. In contrast, Ted Cruz had 42 different ads running between April 2015 and April 2016. Moreover,

Trump used his own money and had no super PAC support for ads during the primaries.[77] During the general election, the Clinton campaign dramatically outspent the Trump campaign on advertising. In the final weeks, Trump spent $39 million on television ads and $29 million in digital ads. In contrast, Clinton spent $72 million on television ads and $16 million on digital ads.[78] The consequences of the outspent candidate winning will likely have significant repercussions on future elections as candidates and consultants try to determine whether the Trump social media strategy is reproducible.

Beyond digital ads, the Internet and social media are critical tools for candidates to reach out to voters; candidates have been online since 1996.[79] However, the value of the online world was not evident until Howard Dean's 2004 campaign for the Democratic nomination. Despite his poor showing at the polls, Dean demonstrated that candidates could raise money, meet and organize volunteers, and connect with voters online. Even more so, the 2008 campaign demonstrated that candidates who embraced the online world increased opportunities and maximized support. Significantly, the Web enabled candidates (who took advantage of it) to distinguish themselves from their opponents; identify and encourage likely voters; and raise money to support their candidacies without the enormous expense of television advertising.

The Obama campaign's use of the Internet in 2008 to reach voters during the prenomination, primary, and general election periods redefined the unmediated options for candidates. The Obama campaign brought to fruition the enormous potential of the online environment for fundraising, mobilizing supporters, and setting the campaign agenda. Although the entire slate of candidates in 2008 in both parties crafted effective web pages, the Obama campaign's web page and web presence set a new standard. All candidate web pages include the basics: pictures of the candidates, their families, and an American flag from some vantage point. Most sites included video and blogging by the candidate and campaign insiders. Obama's web page, which was much more frequently trafficked, encouraged users to investigate and, more important, to come back. Visitors to Obama's website could form their own "My Barack Obama" page and thus bookmark things that were of interest to them. The Obama site also encouraged registration, providing the campaign with an easy mechanism for continued outreach through email and texting. The massive fundraising effort, which produced $750 million in campaign dollars, took place virtually all online, with a large amount coming from individual donations of less than $100. The Obama campaign successfully combined outreach with fundraising, bringing traditional participants into the process along with new ones, particularly younger voters.

The 2008 campaign also marked a turning point for campaigning online in terms of social networking sites and new media outlets like YouTube and iTunes. All candidates placed linking icons on their web pages to sites like Facebook, encouraging voters to seek out the candidate in places not previously thought of as political. As valuable as the social sites were, the video-sharing site YouTube created a wholly distinct subset of unmediated candidate outreach. YouTube enabled candidates who were not receiving traditional press coverage to connect with interested voters. There are multiple ways to find content on YouTube. An individual can search for content specifically, search for content generally, or view suggested videos (i.e., most popular, watched now, promoted, or featured). During the 2008 primaries, a general search on YouTube for the campaign or campaign names demonstrated the interest in Ron Paul; he was the most widely noted general hit with more than 100,000, with Obama and Clinton trailing with more than 40,000 (as of March 2008). The traditional press coverage of Paul in contrast was miniscule because the press deemed his candidacy not viable.

Thanks to Trump's use of social media, the 2016 campaign was dominated by the presence of Twitter as a medium. The reporting of Trump's late night/early morning tweets was extensive and pervasive, so much so that after the election, the *New York Times* posed the question: "If Trump Tweets It Is It News?"[80] Moreover, a Pew Report found that Clinton and Sanders posted as frequently on Facebook and tweeted as frequently as did Trump, but the public response was far different. In every measurable category of user attention—Facebook shares, comments, and reactions, as well as Twitter retweets—the public responded to Trump's social media updates more frequently on average than to either of the other candidates' posts.[81] Trump's use of social media as a tool to achieve attention was considerably more effective than the usage by either Clinton or Sanders. The 2016 campaign revealed a greater entrenchment in all categories of social media activity when compared to the 2012 campaign, with one exception. In 2012, Romney and Obama updated their Facebook status much more frequently.[82]

Presidential debates

There are typically three presidential debates and one vice presidential debate during the general election phase of the campaign. During the primaries, there are typically more; in 2008, a total of 26 were held for Democratic candidates and 21 for Republican candidates. Similar frequency of debates occurred for Republican primary candidates in 2011–2012 and for both parties in 2015–2016. For the two nominees during the general election campaign, the debates enable direct outreach in a live setting. For partisans, the debates offer an opportunity to see their candidate "win;" for independent voters, the debates are an opportunity for comparison shopping. For citizens, the debates represent the only time both candidates answer the same questions and also address each other directly. Thus, citizens learn about the candidate's issue positions, but also get a feel for whether the candidate is "presidential."

For candidates, the debates are potential minefields. Not only are voters paying attention (80 percent watched at least one debate in 2008), but also the media coverage is intense.[83] Ratings were even higher in 2016: 84 million viewers tuned in to watch the first debate between Clinton and Trump on September 26.[84] Consequently, the campaigns negotiate everything with the Presidential Debate Commission: how many debates, what style (single moderator, multiple questioners, and/or town hall), podium versus table, and even camera angles. The media typically pick a debate winner and loser, and often the title is based on expectations. In 2000, Gore was an experienced debater who knew the issues; thus, for George W. Bush, success was defined more liberally than the norm. In 2016, both campaigns claimed victory after each debate, relying on polling to bolster their claims. However, neither so-called snap polls conducted by news outlets nor online polls immediately after a debate are reliable.

Occasionally, a debate moment becomes the talk of the campaign or defines a candidate. The 1960 debate between John F. Kennedy and Richard Nixon defined not only the campaign but also the potential for television. Live television allowed Kennedy to demonstrate comparably his fitness for the office in terms of knowledge and policy acumen. Moreover, Kennedy famously "won" the debate on television, whereas Nixon fared better with radio listeners. Television was a relatively new medium in 1960; consequently, Nixon did not realize the cost of not wearing makeup and sweating profusely under the hot lights. However, most postdebate winners and losers stem from comments, successful one-liners, or horrendous gaffes, which can define the candidate for independent voters as the line becomes the focus of the postdebate coverage. One of the more damaging debate utterances came from Gerald Ford in 1976:

> MR. FRANKEL (Reporter from the *New York Times*). Mr. President, I'd like to explore a little more deeply our relationship with the Russians. . . . Our allies in France and Italy are now flirting with communism; we've recognized a permanent Communist regime in East Germany; we virtually signed, in Helsinki, an agreement that the Russians have dominance in Eastern Europe; we bailed out Soviet agriculture with our huge grain sales, we've given them large loans, access to our best technology, and if the Senate hadn't interfered with the Jackson Amendment, maybe you would have given them even larger loans. Is that what you call a two-way street of traffic in Europe?
>
> THE PRESIDENT. I believe that we have negotiated with the Soviet Union since I've been President from a position of strength. . . . If we turn to Helsinki—I am glad you raised it, Mr. Frankel—in the case of Helsinki, 35 nations signed an agreement, including the Secretary of State for the Vatican. I can't under any circumstances believe that His Holiness the Pope would agree, by signing that agreement, that the 35 nations have turned over to the Warsaw Pact nations the domination of Eastern Europe. It just isn't true. And if Mr. Carter alleges that His Holiness, by signing that, has done it, he is totally inaccurate. Now, what has been accomplished by the Helsinki agreement? Number one, we have an agreement where they notify us and we notify them of any military maneuvers that are to be undertaken. They have done it in both cases where they've done so. There is no Soviet domination of Eastern Europe, and there never will be under a Ford administration.
>
> MR. FRANKEL. I'm sorry, could I just follow—did I understand you to say, sir, that the Russians are not using Eastern Europe as their own sphere of influence and occupying most of the countries there and making sure with their troops that it's a Communist zone, whereas on our side of the line the Italians and the French are still flirting with the possibility of communism?
>
> THE PRESIDENT. I don't believe, Mr. Frankel, that the Yugoslavians consider themselves dominated by the Soviet Union. I don't believe that the Romanians consider themselves dominated by the Soviet Union. I don't believe that the Poles consider themselves dominated by the Soviet Union. Each of those countries is independent, autonomous; it has its own territorial integrity. And the United States does not concede that those countries are under the domination of the Soviet Union. As a matter of fact, I visited Poland, Yugoslavia, and Romania, to make certain that the people of those countries understood that the President of the United States and the people of the United States are dedicated to their independence, their autonomy, and their freedom.[85]

Whatever the president meant by his response and his follow-up, the press and the Carter campaign pounced on the incredible error. The coverage fundamentally undermined the Ford campaign's ability to define itself as more knowledgeable on foreign policy than Carter, a former governor from Georgia. Consequently, it is not surprising that presidential campaigns infinitely prefer to disseminate their message in controlled settings, without the press to interpret their statements.

THE CONSEQUENCES OF WINNING

Elections have obvious consequences for both the winner and the loser. The process by which we elect presidents can significantly affect the winning candidate long after the voting booths are closed. The campaign for president influences the president's coalition, his mandate for action, and governing itself.

The Coalition

Coalitions (a set of groups who support a campaign) form the basis for electoral support. The winning presidential candidate assembled two overlapping but distinct coalitions—one for the nomination and one for the general election. The coalitions are distinct because they serve separate purposes.[86] The nominating coalition consists of party insiders and elites, relevant interest groups, and voters in the primary, which produces the requisite delegate count to win. The general election coalition consists of the nominating coalition plus the elites, groups, and popular supporters, made up of demographic voting profiles, necessary to win the requisite Electoral College votes.

Candidates assemble an electoral coalition with a distinct goal in mind: winning on Election Day. Once the candidate takes the presidential oath, goals change. Once in office, the president will technically not need an electoral coalition for four years, but cannot abandon the promises made to these groups without jeopardizing reelection because the same groups will form the basis for that coalition. Instead, the president must translate the electoral coalition into a governing coalition. The governing coalition consists of Congress, presidential staff and other appointees, interest groups, the bureaucracy, the media, and the public.[87]

The governing coalition is the assemblage of groups and individuals who will support and work toward the president's legislative and administrative goals. The president is limited in his ability to act unilaterally, particularly in the domestic sphere. Therefore, coalitions of support must exist to advance the presidential agenda; the margin of victory as well as a strong coalition of support is also known as a presidential mandate (that is, the perception that a president, through his electoral success, has been given a mandate by the public to pursue his policy objectives). A president who won with a large, stable, electoral coalition and was able to translate that support to governing support would be fairly confident in the ability to achieve his agenda. A president who won with a narrow coalition and a narrow victory would conceivably have a hard time achieving his agenda. A narrow electoral coalition or an unstable one, defined by transient support from independents, requires a president to search for groups and individuals to create a governing coalition issue by issue. Not only is this an expensive use of presidential capital, but also it is dangerous to the initial electoral coalition. Lacking a large, stable core of support, the president must seek compromises, which elicit the necessary group support without damaging the interests of his electoral coalition.

However, it is important to remember that other factors outside of the president's control can also play a role in whether agenda priorities are achieved and can turn the traditional theory about strong versus weak coalitions on its head. For example, although George W. Bush was elected in 2000 with a narrow coalition and margin of victory and although he was not perceived to have been given a strong mandate from the voters, the terrorist attacks on September 11, 2001, provided a national tragedy that galvanized broad support, even among Democrats, for Bush's actions regarding national-security issues. Similarly, although Obama was elected with a strong coalition and a seemingly strong mandate in 2008 to bring political change to Washington, the economy (labeled the worst recession since the Great Depression of the 1930s) severely handcuffed the Obama administration's ability to easily pass domestic legislation in 2009–2010, even with a strong majority of Democrats in both houses of Congress.

The Message and the Mandate

Not only does the campaign provide the president with a coalition, but also it shapes the presidential agenda. Candidates form their coalition based on individual appeals but also issue appeals. During the nominating phase, the issue differences between candidates within a party can often be so minimal as to be irrelevant or they can matter significantly. For example, the power of social conservatives in the Republican Party's nominating phase in recent years has made it difficult for candidates who are not strongly committed to the social conservative agenda (such as being pro-life, opposed to same-sex marriage, etc.) to be successful. During the general election, however, the issue differences between candidates are typically much more meaningful. Moreover, as noted earlier, candidates are effective at distinguishing themselves from their opponents. The differentiation can take the form of personal characteristics, but more often than not, it occurs over the policy agenda.

The assertions made by a candidate, like Obama's "Change You Can Believe In" in 2008 or Trump's "Make America Great Again" in 2016, shape the campaign battlefield but also determine the presidential agenda. Studies demonstrate that presidents do seek action on their campaign promises and achieve results most of the time, even if the result is a much compromised version of the president's initial plan (for example, Obama's health-care reform in 2010).[88]

The promises made by candidates are a blueprint for their focus once they take office. It makes sense that candidates tell voters what they want to do for them and the country, and voters evaluate their candidate choices based on the congruence between their personal goals and those of the candidates. Consequently, winning candidates often claim to have a mandate for action. In particular, when there is a large disparity in outcome between candidates, the mandate claim is more likely. In 1932, FDR swept to victory with a 472–59 margin in the Electoral College and 22,800,000 votes to Herbert Hoover's 15,750,000. FDR's win was so complete that he carried more counties than a presidential candidate had ever won before, including 282 that had never voted Democratic. The campaign between Hoover and FDR centered on the different view of the role of government for responding to the Great Depression. With the overwhelming victory, FDR could easily claim public support for an activist government.

In 1980, Ronald Reagan beat Jimmy Carter, 489 Electoral College votes to 49 and by a margin of nine percent in the popular vote. Consequently, Reagan argued he had a mandate for advancing his conservative agenda. Public opinion polls throughout the 1980s challenged the notion of a mandate as well as public support for Reagan's programs; Reagan was always personally well liked, but his policies were not always as popular. In fact, mandates are particularly difficult to claim even with the presence of surveys that reveal why people voted for a particular candidate. Although Reagan won a landslide in the Electoral College, his nine percent victory in the popular vote represented just under 51 percent of the popular vote. Moreover, those postelection surveys revealed a public voting against Carter as much as it did voting for Reagan.

Campaigning versus Governing

In running for the office of the presidency, candidates spend at least one year, and sometimes as many as four, campaigning in a single four-year election cycle, and most become effective in the skills of campaigning. Candidates must fundraise from big and small donors; they must speak before crowds and appear in the media and in advertising to get their message out. Candidates must also exercise management skills over an organization facing multistate campaigns. Some of these skills directly relate to the task of governing as president. Presidents must define their goals and their message and be able to deliver that message via speeches to crowds large and small. Presidents must also be effective managers of the White House staff and the bureaucracy.

Yet, on a fundamental level, campaigning differs from governing.[89] Campaigns have a final decision point, because all effort is geared toward achieving results on a given day. Governing is a continuous stream of decision making and decision points; presidents do not go home after losing a vote in Congress on a key agenda item. Campaigning is also by definition adversarial, because a choice for one is a choice against the other. Governing in a system of checks and balances is characterized by compromising. Governing is complicated by a purely adversarial approach. Ultimately, the skills that make someone a great campaigner might not serve the office of the presidency. Moreover, an individual with the skills to be a great president might be stymied by the requirements to be a great campaigner.

CONCLUSION

The campaign and election process has changed significantly since the framers designed the Constitution. The modern process reflects the duality of partisanship for both candidates and voters. Candidates must appeal both to diehard partisan supporters during the nominating campaign and to less partisan and nonpartisan voters during the general election. The distinct messages and approaches required by a candidate, who must be partisan enough to win the nomination but not so partisan as to turn off moderate and independent voters, offer a wealth of challenges for modern presidential candidates. Moreover, modern candidates must be masters of technology to reach voters through both mediated and unmediated systems. In addition, the role of money in the presidential campaign process means that those candidates who are best suited to successful fundraising will most always have more success than those who are not. As a result, the "survival of the fittest" process of electing a president can winnow out any number of potentially great leaders who may not be great campaigners.

For voters, the campaign and elections system is all about choice. Partisan voters now have more choice because they have the opportunity to participate meaningfully in the selection of the party nominee. Voters also have choice in terms of how and where they receive information about the candidates for president. Voters can engage the candidates directly via Facebook, Twitter, or candidate web pages or watch candidate speeches and advertising online. Or, voters can seek out information in traditional mediated sources: newspapers, radio talk shows, and television news programs. It is worth considering whether the constitutional system, unchanged since ratification of the Twelfth Amendment in 1804, still functions effectively in the modern environment. For those who seek further democratization of the process through a more open nominations process or by abolishing the Electoral College in favor of the popular vote, the process appears flawed. Still others contend that the long process, with its emphasis on money and media, produces candidates who are ill-suited for the job of being president even if they can successfully "run" for president.

Despite the efforts to clean up the corruption in politics and stop the flow of money during campaigns, money still plays a determining role not only in who wins an election, but also in who will run in the first place. In addition, thanks to the ever-present and watchful eye of the news media, candidates need a positive image and must perform well on the campaign trail. Even if someone seems destined for greatness as a president, without adequate campaign financing or successful public relations, his or her candidacy does not stand a chance. As a result, a disconnect exists between what the framers had in mind for insulating the presidency, as well as the selection of the president, from the public and today's style of presidential campaigning, where so many relevant aspects of the presidential selection process are played out on center stage. Not only have the men and women who have run for the presidency shaped the presidential selection process, but also the winners of these contests have historically shaped the institution of the presidency. As we will discuss in subsequent chapters, however, what it takes to successfully run for president does not automatically equate to what it takes to be a successful president managing the day-to-day task of governing once in office.

CHAPTER 4

The Public Presidency: Communication and Mass Media

Perhaps one of the greatest legacies of Barack Obama's presidency will involve his use of media to communicate with the American public. Although the Obama communication strategy may not have always helped sell important policy issues on the president's agenda, Obama raised the bar during his eight years in office in his use of social media and other entertainment venues to deliver his message. For example, in July 2010, Obama made history by becoming the first sitting president to appear on a daytime television program with his visit to ABC's *The View*. Although this was not Obama's first appearance on the show (he had appeared twice before, including while he was a presidential candidate in March 2008), he nonetheless broke new ground in the ever-expanding media venues in which presidents now make appearances.[1] But he did not stop there, relying on many other outlets while incorporating popular culture trends, including an appearance on *Between Two Ferns with Zach Galifianakis* to encourage young Americans to sign up for health insurance through the Affordable Care Act. He also "slow jammed" the news with Jimmy Fallon on *The Tonight Show*, filled out his college basketball bracket each March on ESPN, read mean tweets on *Jimmy Kimmel Live*, and ended his last appearance at the White House Correspondents' Association dinner with a mic-drop, saying simply, "Obama out." Some referred to the president as the "pop culture king."[2]

Donald Trump, while offering a stark contrast in style to Obama's method of communication, will no doubt continue to break with many communication precedents during his time in office. His unconventional campaign, during which he relied heavily on Twitter and cable news appearances (many by phone) to communicate with voters, not to mention the lack of political correctness that became a hallmark of his candidacy, suggested that he would redefine traditional expectations for presidential communication as well as the presidential–press relationship. Although many presidents have at times had a combative relationship with the press, Trump's attacks on specific media outlets and individual journalists continued beyond his campaign and into his transition. On January 11, 2017, nine days before he took the oath of office, he held a press conference where he openly sparred with a reporter from CNN, refusing to let the reporter ask a question, responding, "Don't be rude" and "You are fake news." The exchange emanated from CNN's coverage of a story that intelligence agencies had briefed Trump on allegations that Russian operatives claimed to have damaging personal and financial information about Trump. The story originated with BuzzFeed, which also published the alleged 35-page classified dossier, which Trump said was "fake," and he called the online news site a "failing pile of garbage."[3]

Seeing high-profile politicians appear in more diverse and casual media venues is not a new trend, nor is seeing a president engage in a combative exchange with a reporter. The strategy behind these activities is also not difficult to decipher. For Obama, appearing on daytime television or in other untraditional formats allowed him to bypass political reporters in a setting where he excelled, and the media coverage surrounding those appearances kept a mostly positive story line in the news for days. In addition, Obama's relaxed demeanor in a more informal setting reminded many viewers of candidate Obama in 2008 (especially important at times when his approval rating dropped below 50 percent). According to media critic Howard Kurtz regarding Obama's appearance on *The View*, "Anyone who scoffed at the president's decision to hang with Whoopi and the gang was out to lunch. . . . The appearance was good for him, good for *The View* and, incidentally, good for the audience."[4] For Trump, attacking the news media as dishonest (a Gallup survey in September 2016 showed that only 32 percent of Americans trust the news media)[5] energized his supporters and emphasized his message of shaking up the status quo in Washington.

Yet the question remains: Are such appearances or behavior toward the press beneath the dignity of the office, or instead, must presidents continue to shift their communication strategies to keep up with not only changes within the news media industry, but also popular culture trends and public expectations? A clear definition of a president's effectiveness as a communicator requires bringing together a variety of factors, not the least of which is the state of the news industry itself, which is primarily responsible for bringing presidential messages and images to the public. The office of the presidency is the most high profile and public of any position within the federal government, and presidents who are skilled communicators have a distinct advantage in the many public aspects of the job. Not only have the public and ceremonial aspects increased in recent decades, but also the many acts of presidential communication make up a large part of the symbolism attached to the office. In addition, as presidential advisors in recent years have developed more innovative ways for a president to communicate with both the public and the news media, public expectations for effective communications have also increased. The office of the presidency now demands strong communication skills; the president serves as the communicator in chief, the point person for direct interaction with the American people. This public role of the presidency demands the constant development of White House communication strategies, including the public events that are now part of the day-to-day operation of the presidency, as well as management of the presidential–press relationship, which can help determine news media content and tone of coverage.

THE EVOLVING RHETORICAL PRESIDENCY

Whereas most nineteenth-century presidents operated almost exclusively outside of the public's view, by the start of the twentieth century, presidents began to rely on the public aspects of the office to rally support for their policy agendas and to increase their own popularity. The emergence of the rhetorical presidency reflected the president's willingness and ability to engage people directly through substantive dialogue, as opposed to the formal, perfunctory, and strictly limited contact with the public during the nineteenth century. The start of the "rhetorical presidency" can be traced to William McKinley (1897–1901), Theodore Roosevelt (1901–1909), and Woodrow Wilson (1913–1921) because all three relied on public speaking tours and press coverage to garner support for their respective policy agendas.[6] It was Roosevelt's use of the bully pulpit to engage in a public dialogue with American citizens that began to advance the president's role as the national leader of public opinion. Roosevelt used his rhetorical skills to increase the power of the presidency through popular support, which was in alignment with his view of the presidency itself—that he was the steward of the people and that weak presidential leadership during the nineteenth century had left the American system of government open to the harmful influence of special interests. Roosevelt expanded presidential power in many areas by drawing on broad discretionary constitutional powers; his "Stewardship Doctrine" demanded presidential reliance on popular support of the people, increasing the public's expectation of the man and the office. Referring to his speaking tours around the country as "swings around the circle,"[7] Roosevelt often appealed directly to the public through his active use of the bully pulpit to gain support of his legislative agenda to place public pressure on Congress.[8]

As part of what is referred to as a deliberative democracy, some scholars view presidential rhetoric as a positive institutional and constitutional feature, as well as one imagined by the framers as a necessary element of a properly functioning republic that allows presidents to speak directly to the public. Rhetoric also plays an important role in the institutional setting of the presidency by enabling different presidents to shape the presidency in a stable and constant manner.[9] However, other scholars view the rhetorical presidency as a danger to the republic. The framers were suspicious of a popular leader and/or demagogue in the office of the presidency, since such a person might rely on tyrannical means of governing.[10] The presidency experienced a fundamental transformation by becoming a rhetorical presidency during the early part of the twentieth century, causing an institutional dilemma. By fulfilling popular functions and serving the nation through mass appeal, the presidency had deviated from the original constitutional intentions of the framers, removing the buffer that the framers established between citizens and their representatives.[11] In addition, it has been argued that the rhetorical presidency is a twentieth-century

Theodore Roosevelt helped to launch the era of the rhetorical president with his enthusiastic and fiery public speeches.

creation and a constitutional aberration. The president is not merely a popular leader vested with unconstitutional powers, but also uses rhetoric as a "tool of barter rather than a means of informing or challenging a citizenry."[12]

Later presidents, although not all, would follow Roosevelt's strategy, as the spokesperson for the American public, of relying on the bully pulpit to elevate the power of the presidency. Through his public leadership, Wilson, especially during World War I, established the presidency as a strong position of leadership at both the national and international level. He contributed to a more dominant view of the presidency through his use of the bully pulpit and used his rhetorical skills to promote many progressive policy initiatives. For example, Wilson relied on an "ambitious" whistle-stop railroad tour to gain support for U.S. entry into the League of Nations (although he failed to achieve that goal).[13] The emergence of several new communications technologies began to change the rhetorical presidency even more.

The Radio Era

Radio emerged as the first such technology to aid presidents in their public efforts. One of the first known public radio broadcasts came in 1916 with a postelection report on Wilson's reelection campaign delivered from an experimental station in New York. The beginning of commercial radio began with the broadcast of the 1920 presidential election results by KDKA in Pittsburgh. This report of Warren G. Harding's election is the political event "that first brought radio's potential to the attention of politicians."[14] Considered by most media scholars the first "radio president," mostly because of the availability of the new technology during the 1920s, Harding's inauguration was the first to be broadcast by radio and his was the first presidential voice heard by most Americans. He delivered a series of messages to the American public by radio during the summer of 1923, including an address in St. Louis that was carried by special wire to New York City.[15] Later that year, following Harding's death, Calvin Coolidge delivered his first message to the Congress as president, which was broadcast to a national audience. Mostly unknown during his tenure as Harding's vice president, Coolidge effectively used radio to introduce himself to the nation. His performance on radio broadcasts to the American public was considered successful, and this discouraged any serious challenge for the Republican Party's presidential nomination in 1924.[16]

Elected in 1928, Herbert Hoover also had a long-term relationship with radio. He served as secretary of commerce during the Harding and Coolidge administrations from 1921 through 1928, and one of his main duties was to develop and regulate radio. Hoover recognized the use of radio by government officials as an interesting dilemma; radio could be both a "powerful educational force" and a tool for political propaganda. In his memoirs, written in 1952, Hoover wrote, "There is little adequate answer to a lying microphone . . . propaganda is seldom the whole truth [and] the officials currently in office have preponderant time at the microphone, and theirs becomes the dominant voice."[17] During his four years in the White House, Hoover delivered 23 "Radio Addresses to the Nation" on foreign, domestic, and economic policy issues.[18] In one address, he stated, "Of the untold values of the radio, one is the great intimacy it has brought among our people. Through its mysterious channels we come to wider acquaintance with surroundings and men."[19]

FDR relied heavily on the bully pulpit, particularly his use of radio, to gradually persuade the American public to support his New Deal policies during the 1930s and America's involvement in World War II during the early 1940s. To establish "direct contact with the people," FDR delivered the first of his 30 fireside chats at the end of his first week in the Oval Office in March 1933.[20] Considered a success,

Franklin Roosevelt delivers one of his many "fireside chat" radio addresses to the American public.

the speech allowed FDR to reassure the American public that he would guide the Depression economy into recovery. He began the first radio address by saying, "I want to talk for a few minutes with the people of the United States about banking," and continued for 20 minutes explaining in simple language what Americans could do to assist in the recovery. This began an effective trend that FDR would rely on throughout his tenure in office—the use of radio to enter the living rooms of Americans to talk about the problems and challenges facing the country. Although FDR was also successful in his mastery of the press, skillfully managing news out of the White House through his frequent press conferences in the Oval Office, radio was his "most important link with the people."[21] Although he was not remembered as a great orator, FDR's successor, Harry Truman, used radio with even more frequency as the medium and its presence around the globe expanded through the late 1940s and early 1950s. After a radio address on July 20, 1950, the Truman White House reported that the address "was heard by more people throughout the world than any other address ever delivered. . . . Radio representatives say 'everyone with a radio or television set' heard the address. Their figures indicate that nearly 130,000,000 persons in the United States heard the President on radio and television."[22]

The Television Age
The rhetorical aspects of the office, as well as the use of the bully pulpit, took on an even greater importance for presidents with the start of the television age. The rapid expansion of television during the 1950s, often referred to as the "golden age" of television, occurred while Dwight Eisenhower occupied the White House.[23] Eisenhower became the first president to utilize television as a means to more effectively communicate with the American public, and his administration became much more visible than any before it through the use of filmed press conferences for later use by the networks, televised cabinet meetings, and televised fireside chats. Yet, the true potential of television as a governing tool would not be realized until the presidencies of John F. Kennedy in the early 1960s and then Ronald Reagan in the 1980s. Both were known for their frequent use of inspiring and eloquent speeches about public policy and their visions for the country. Kennedy relied on the bully pulpit, aided by television coverage, to talk of a "New Frontier" and motivated many Americans to become active in public service. Reagan saw the bully pulpit as one of the president's most important tools, and reliance on his skills as an actor provided a strong image of moral leadership that helped to restore many Americans' faith in government institutions.

Following Kennedy's election in 1960, the use of television as a means for presidential communication increased dramatically. Where Eisenhower had been somewhat reluctant about his use of television, Kennedy and his advisors saw the expanding medium as an excellent governing tool for the president to expand his influence and power over national politics. By the mid-1960s, the president had become a central focus of news from Washington and began to have more power over shaping the national agenda by rapidly reaching, through both television and print media sources, his national audience. The ability to help shape public opinion, through televised and highly covered speeches and press conferences, began to provide the president an important advantage during the legislative process. As the influence of television increased, presidents worked even harder to keep the initiative and control over the policy agenda coming out of the White House. Presidential leadership in the television age required effective communication skills and the ability to positively shape public opinion in ways that matched the needs of the medium; as such, the presidential image became crucial.[24]

Kennedy's skillful use of television has had a lasting impact on the office of the presidency. His use of live televised press conferences, his eloquent speaking style, and the youthful images of both his family and administration on American television screens set a standard that his predecessors had difficulty matching. Kennedy also had the advantage of the uniqueness of the new medium, and many presidents that followed him have longed for that innocent era during the early 1960s when personal and political scandal did not dominate political reporting from Washington. In addition, most presidents during the television age could not master their use of television; only Kennedy and Reagan were considered strong communicators who used television to their advantage through public leadership efforts. In contrast, as a result of their ineffective use of the bully pulpit, Johnson, Nixon, Ford, Carter, and George H. W. Bush were instead "used by television."[25]

To understand the significant changes that television created in the relationship between American citizens and their presidents in the three decades between 1960 and 1990, think about the many changes that occurred in the television industry alone. In 1960, only three television networks existed—ABC, NBC, and CBS—and the evening newscast on each was a black-and-white 15-minute broadcast. By 1990, the three networks were competing with not only several independent television stations in major media markets like New York and Los Angeles, but also growth among cable and satellite programming options. The nature of news had also been forever changed by CNN, whose success as an all-news cable channel created what is known as the "24-hour news cycle." No longer were Americans limited to news in their daily newspapers and the traditional evening network news broadcasts; breaking news could be accessed at any time during the day through cable television. The expanding technological advancements during this time would contribute to major changes not only within the news industry, but also in the relationship between American citizens and their president, as well as the news media, who were expected to provide the important link of information between them. The up-close-and-personal look at our presidents that television began to provide also altered the political environment in which the president must lead. In addition, the immediacy of television coverage accelerated the decision-making process for presidents. These trends only increased with the rapid expansion of technology beginning in the 1990s.

The Internet Age

Although it is hard to imagine life without email or the Internet, these were still relatively new technologies in the early 1990s. The news media as an industry began to consider the use of both, particularly the Internet, an effective means to communicate with its customers, and government officials and politicians also began to consider use of technology to better communicate with citizens and voters. Clinton, the first president raised during the television age, often relied on alternative television opportunities or "new media" talk shows and live town hall meetings to bypass the traditional Washington press corps and speak directly to the American people. Television events such as those worked well for Clinton by giving him more options in delivering his message unfiltered to the audience, and expanding mediums and technology in a more general sense have also adversely affected the leadership potential for presidents.

Throughout the 1990s, the Internet dramatically changed the nature of political reporting. For example, one of the biggest political stories out of Washington in 1998 was the investigation of Clinton's relationship with White House intern Monica Lewinsky. The first news outlet to break the story was an unlikely one. A website with both political and entertainment news, *The Drudge Report*, maintained by Matt Drudge, first began in 1994. Drudge broke the Clinton/Lewinsky story wide open when he posted a report stating that *Newsweek* had information about an inappropriate relationship between the President and an intern, but that the weekly news magazine was holding the story. Soon after, *Newsweek* ran its story, and this incident became one of the earliest in which the Internet had a major impact on how the traditional news media reported political news.

Throughout the 2000s and beyond, the American political environment continues to be shaped by the increased competition among more and more news outlets, as well as newer and ever-expanding technological advancements. Not only are new mediums emerging, but also new and old mediums continue to merge, which has led to a greater fragmentation of news. This means that Americans no longer have a shared experience of political news from one of a handful of sources (like a daily newspaper or the evening network news). This, in addition to the hyperpartisan content of news, particularly on cable news and on the Internet, poses many challenges for presidents to maintain control over their public image and policy message. What was once referred to as relying on the bully pulpit to speak to the American public is now often viewed as "spinning" the president's message. Because of the "intense focus on marketing" of their presidencies, both Clinton and George W. Bush generated short-term public relations gains but "suffered from severe longer-term political problems as a result of their public relations strategies."[26] In addition, in such a saturated media environment that includes so much political news, presidents can rarely command the attention of the American public through rhetorical means because they are sometimes viewed as just another talking head.

Although all presidents have had to contend with changes in both technology and the news media industry while in office, the Obama administration provides a good case study for its use of new media. During his two terms, both Obama and the White House had a strong presence on social media; Obama had Facebook, Twitter, and Instagram accounts, and the White House had Twitter and Snapchat accounts. In fact, by the time Obama left office in January 2017, Obama had 80.4 million followers on Twitter (@BarackObama), the White House had 13.2 million followers (@WhiteHouse), and @POTUS had 13.4 million followers. In addition, the White House web page continued to expand, and the presidential weekly radio address evolved into a weekly video address that could be easily viewed on the White House web page or on YouTube. Trump entered the White House that same month with more than 22 million followers on Twitter (@realDonaldTrump). As the Obama administration shows, along with the Trump transition, managing the rhetorical aspects of the presidency, as it began at the turn of the twentieth century, continues to be an evolving challenge for presidents and their advisors regarding available technology and the public expectations of the office.

PRESIDENTIAL COMMUNICATION: STRATEGIES AND RESOURCES

Communication strategies have become an important and permanent part of the everyday operation of the White House. A communication strategy consists of various components, including the leadership style of the president, presidential rhetoric and speechwriting, presidential public activities, the presidential policy agenda, and the presidential/press relationship. An effective presidential communication strategy can be a critical factor in developing and implementing the administration's policy goals. To understand how a president communicates is to understand an important base of power for the modern presidency[27] and to recognize "the importance of communications to everything that a president does."[28] The president for some time has been considered the "interpreter in chief" and the "nation's chief storyteller." Presidential rhetoric has changed over time as media technologies have continued to expand, providing citizens with more in-depth coverage of the president. Especially because of visual and online coverage, presidential advisers now develop communication strategies that seek more support for the president as a person or leader and less support for specific policy proposals. This has led to an emphasis on symbolic and ceremonial, rather than deliberative, speech.[29]

In addition, the television age of politics also brought with it the "going public" strategy, which assumes that a president can gain public support for his policy agenda by speaking directly to the American people through national addresses and other high-profile media appearances.[30] However, in recent years, evidence suggests that this strategy is not always effective in shaping and/or moving public opinion in a president's favor. Not only can the president's voice be easily drowned out among the cacophony of other political voices in the various news mediums now available, but also Americans are not as attentive to the national news as they once were.[31] Recent presidents have opted for a strategy that instead focuses more on "going local." As political parties have become more polarized and media sources more fragmented, presidents now choose to go local as opposed to "going national" in their public strategies to gain support from the base of their parties, select interest groups, and voters in key areas since, for example, an address to the nation does not carry the same significance that it once did.[32] Therefore, presidents now seek to gain support among certain constituencies as opposed to the nation at large.

Researching the Presidency

Presidential Travel

Presidency scholars have referenced for years the idea of a "permanent campaign" because presidents rely on campaign-like events as part of their governing routine. In his 2012 book *The Rise of the President's Permanent Campaign*, Brendan J. Doherty provides empirical data and analysis that shows the extent to which recent presidents continue to fundraise, engage in party activities, and use public events to promote the overall political goals of their administration and their political party. One of the questions Doherty addresses is the strategic use of presidential travel, which can allow the president to advance his own reelection effort, raise funds, support other party members, "exert pressure on recalcitrant legislators," promote a policy agenda to those outside of Washington, attend ceremonial events (like a university graduation), respond to natural disasters, and/or influence public opinion. Sometimes, a president wants "simply to get out of Washington."

Travel plans can illustrate their strategic priorities, and a "tremendous amount of effort goes into preparing for a presidential journey."[33] There can be great reward from the effort; some of the most memorable rhetorical images of presidents occurred outside of Washington, including Kennedy's trip to Berlin in 1963, Reagan's 1984 D-Day commemoration speech in Normandy, and George W. Bush at Ground Zero in New York just days after the 9/11 attacks.[34] Doherty finds that clear patterns of electoral incentives have emerged that help to explain presidential travel, particularly during a first term. Advisors look to the same strategies in governing that helped to get them elected based on the primary campaign and Electoral College map. However, as with all other communication strategies, presidents must be mindful that the consequences of presidential travel may go beyond simply the images that American citizens see of their president: "The media's focus on electoral motivations can help to fuel the perception that presidents care more about key electoral states than the other states they lead, and this could be damaging to a president's image as a unifying national leader."[35]

This means that presidents must adapt their public strategies to the ever-changing media environment in which they attempt to govern; frustration often arises from the fact that because of intense media coverage, there is hardly a moment when the president is not on center stage, yet he seems to have less control over how and where he is covered. Regardless of specific strategy, presidents continue to go public more often and in a growing number of venues than their predecessors, so an effective White House communication strategy is a critical component of governing. The president relies on two groups of advisors within the White House to control his public image and that of his administration—the Press Office and the Office of Communications. The press secretary heads the Press Office and is responsible for preparing press releases, coordinating news and holding daily press briefings for the White House press corps, and facilitating the needs of reporters who cover the president. The press secretary also serves as an important public spokesperson for the president and as a liaison between reporters and the White House. The Office of Communications develops a long-term public relations strategy and coordinates presidential coverage in regional and local media outlets.

The Press Office and Press Secretary

In 1983, the Reagan Press Office compiled an extensive report on the role of the office and the responsibilities of the press secretary. More than three decades later, the description still accurately reflects the goal of this important office for the contemporary presidency:

> The Office of the Press Secretary is the window through which the world sees the President. This office sits astride a vast pipeline through which flows virtually every action of the President and his Administration—appointments, proclamations, statements, and most important, the articulation of the President's initiatives and policies. At the end of the pipeline is the ever-watchful, all-too-often cynical White House press corps. Through their eyes—like a telescope in reverse—the world sees the President and the judgments of the press become the public perception. The management and direction of the Office of the Press Secretary becomes an important part of the Administration's success—or its failure. The podium of the White House Press Briefing Room is the pulpit most often used to present the President's viewpoint and the Press Secretary becomes the first voice of the Administration.[36]

As the job has evolved, it has become especially important for press secretaries to accurately reflect the views and policy goals of the administration. However, some press secretaries have been handicapped if the president or other top administration advisors do not give up-to-date or accurate information to be provided to the White House press corps. To effectively perform the duties of the job, a press secretary must maintain credibility with members of the press both in the quality of information provided and in facilitating access to top administration officials. Some press secretaries have had closer working relationships with the presidents they have served than others, and some, but not all, have been considered top advisors to the presidents in setting their media strategies. George Akerson, appointed by Herbert Hoover in 1929, was the first official White House press secretary. Stephen Early, serving during the administration of FDR, and James Hagerty, press secretary to Dwight Eisenhower, were considered two of the most capable of all press secretaries ever to hold the position. Both were former journalists themselves, and both had close working relationships with their respective bosses, which earned each of them the necessary respect and credibility among members of the White House press corps. Hagerty was a close advisor to Eisenhower and played a crucial role in the public relations strategy surrounding the President's heart attack in 1955; his effective crisis management helped to avoid public panic over Eisenhower's condition.

Pierre Salinger, Kennedy's press secretary, was influential in developing the television strategy, including live coverage of press conferences, utilized by Kennedy during the early 1960s as television began to gain more prominence in presidential politics. In early 1961, Salinger declared the live coverage of press conferences "here to stay. I do not see any drastic change in format. Television has not basically altered the character of the Press Conference. And the admittance of television to the press conference on its present basis is only simple justice. To allow other media to use their tools to the fullest extent and to deny this same right to the radio and television industry is in my opinion the grossest of injustice. . . . People have been given a new dimension of the Presidency and the President. The President is no longer a mysterious figure operating behind closed doors. . . . Another great cliché in Washington is the subject of over-exposure. In my opinion you cannot over expose the President."[37]

The difficulties associated with the job of press secretary can become obvious when presidents are not always forthcoming with essential information, as with the growing creditability gap that Lyndon Johnson perpetuated during the Vietnam War or his refusal to provide the press with advance information about his travel plans. Each of Johnson's four press secretaries (Pierre Salinger, George Reedy, Bill Moyers, and George Christian) were, at various times, left at the mercy of the White House press corps over the lack or inaccuracy of information given to them by Johnson or other advisors. Presidential scandals can also provide a difficult situation for press secretaries as the point person for providing information to the press. Notable examples include Ron Ziegler's lack of facts as Nixon's press secretary during Watergate and Mike McCurry's attempts to positively spin the scandal surrounding Clinton's impeachment in 1998. Gerald Ford's press secretary, Ron Nessen, a former journalist, was known for his quick temper with members of the press, which often exacerbated an already hostile situation between the White House and reporters following the Watergate scandal and Nixon's overall inaccessibility. Despite Ford's attempts to provide a more open relationship between himself and reporters, Nessen lost credibility in the eyes of the press in his attempts to overinflate the actions and accomplishments of Ford. Both Jody Powell, Jimmy Carter's press secretary, and Marlin Fitzwater, who served both Reagan and George H. W. Bush, were considered effective in the job as a result of the respect they earned among members of the White House press corps and their attempts to attend to the day-to-day needs of reporters in meeting their deadlines.

Both Clinton and George W. Bush employed four press secretaries each, and Obama three, during their respective eight years in office because the position is now considered one that is stressful, demanding, and more likely to cause burnout than other White House staff positions. Dee Dee Myers, the first of Clinton's press secretaries, had been an advisor during the 1992 campaign and became the first woman to hold the job in 1993 (Dana Perino is the only other woman press secretary to date, holding the job from 2007 to 2009). Tony Snow, Bush's third press secretary (2006–2007), was considered effective because of his extensive experience as a journalist (both print and television) and communications advisor and speechwriter for George H. W. Bush. Snow stepped down from his position in September 2007 because of colon cancer, from which he passed away in July 2008 at the age of 53. Obama's first press secretary, Robert Gibbs, had extensive experience as a communications advisor and spokesperson during Obama's senatorial and presidential campaigns and also served as press secretary for John Kerry's 2004 presidential campaign. Gibbs stepped down in February 2011 and was replaced by Jay Carney, a former journalist with *Time*. Carney stayed until May 2014, when he was replaced by Josh Earnest, who had been deputy press secretary in Obama's press office and a previous communications advisor to several politicians. Trump named Sean Spicer, former communications director for the Republican National Committee, as his first press secretary. As recent presidents have shown, the candidate selection pool for the position of press secretary most often includes former journalists (who understand the needs of reporters; see Table 4.1) and/or former campaign or White House advisors (who understand the communication needs of high-profile politicians).

Table 4.1 Press Secretaries Who Were Former Journalists

PRESS SECRETARY	ADMINISTRATION	YEARS	NEWS ORGANIZATION
Stephen Early	Roosevelt/Truman	1933-1945; 1950	United Press International Associated Press Stars and Stripes Paramount News
Jonathan W. Daniels	Roosevelt/Truman	1945	News & Observer (Raleigh, North Carolina)
Charles Ross	Truman	1945-1950	St. Louis Post-Dispatch
Roger Tubby	Truman	1952-1953	Bennington (VT) Banner
James Hagerty	Eisenhower	1953-1961	New York Times
Pierre Salinger	Kennedy/Johnson	1961-1964	San Francisco Chronicle Collier's
Bill Moyers	Johnson	1965-1966	Marshall (TX) News Messenger The Daily Texan (UT Austin) KTBC Radio and Television Stations (Austin, Texas)
George Christian	Johnson	1966-1969	International News Service
Jerald terHorst	Ford	1974	Grand Rapids (MI) Press Detroit News
Ron Nessen	Ford	1974-1977	NBC News
Larry Speakes*	Reagan	1981-1987	Oxford Eagle (University of Mississippi) Bolivar Commercial (Cleveland, Mississippi) Progress Publishers (Leland, Mississippi)
Marlin Fitzwater*	Reagan/Bush	1987-1993	Various newspapers in Kansas
Tony Snow	Bush	2006-2007	Greensboro (NC) Record Virginian-Pilot (Norfolk) Daily Press (Newport News) Detroit News Washington Times USA Today Fox News
Jay Carney	Obama	2011-present	Miami Herald Time Magazine

*Both Speakes and Fitzwater technically served as "press secretary" for Reagan, but James Brady maintained the official title throughout the Reagan years despite his inability to return to the job after being shot in the assassination attempt against Reagan in March 1981.

The Office of Communications

Created by Nixon in 1969, the White House Office of Communications serves as the public relations apparatus for the president.[38] The impetus for the creation of this addition to the White House staff came mostly from Nixon's desire to maintain better control over his media image during the 1968 presidential campaign. Following Nixon's election, the office was created as an agency to supervise all the information services from the executive branch. Since its creation, the role of the Office of Communications has continued to expand to control both the public agenda and the image of the president in the news media. And although the exact functions of the office can vary depending on the individual director and the needs of the president, general responsibilities have included coordinating local and regional media coverage when a president travels outside of Washington, coordinating White House events for non-Washington journalists, and providing technical expertise in the use of all forms of media for presidential appearances.

The importance of this type of media coordination has increased since the Nixon administration and Watergate because of the increased adversarial relationship between the president and the White House press corps. The news media have become increasingly obsessed with covering conflict, which often results in serious discussions of policy issues within the White House being depicted as dissent among top presidential advisers. The goal of the White House is to stop any news reports of internal conflict and push for positive coverage of the president's policy agenda. The Office of Communications handles this through a long-term public relations strategy. Advisers usually spread the "line-of-the-day" throughout the administration, which then takes it to the press; the office also takes the White House message directly to the people when necessary. The goal is to set the public agenda through focus groups, polls, sound bites, and public appearances by the president. This allows ample opportunities for the president to dodge the hostile White House press corps and to rely on alternative modes of communication. Reagan was the first president to master this strategy; his aides realized that their greatest public relations asset was Reagan himself, and they began using two basic tactics to get their message out to the American people: public appearances would be carefully staged and controlled to emphasize Reagan's personality, and he would be promoted as a can-do leader rather than by placing any emphasis on a particular political philosophy.[39]

Members of the news media have also come to rely on the information provided through the Office of Communications. Staff members work hard to facilitate the needs of journalists and to make their job in covering the president easier in the hopes of gaining more favorable coverage for the White House. For example, the Office of Communications provides press releases, fact sheets and other background information on policies, radio actualities, satellite feeds, and a variety of daily photo opportunities that provide a positive spin on the president's activities. This can be especially helpful to smaller news organizations that, in recent years, have experience diminished operating budgets and increased competition within the industry.

By the time Reagan took office in 1981, the Office of Communications had become an important and permanent institutional aspect of governing. Various departments within the Office of Communications headed up the efforts to cater to the needs of the local news media, which included telephone interviews with the president and other key administration officials for local television and radio stations, news briefings for out-of-town press representatives, and mailing fact sheets about Reagan's policy initiatives to local news editors and publishers. The use of a radio actuality service, similar to ones used by the Nixon and Carter administrations, was also continued. Local radio stations around the country could call in to the White House on a toll-free number and receive a ready-to-use news clip from the "White House Broadcasting Service," as it was called during the Reagan years. Throughout Reagan's eight years in office, the strategy to gain coverage for administration policies in the local press had become much more aggressive than with previous administrations. Realizing the impact and influence that the White House would have on small news operations across the country, efforts were made to contact radio stations directly to promote the actuality service and to contact local newspapers with White House statements for inclusion in their stories. Certain states would also be targeted if news out of Washington was of interest to citizens in the area to increase coverage on the president's policies. This continued during the Bush and Clinton administrations as the Office of Communications maintained its role as a public relations outlet for the White House.[40]

Under Clinton, the Office of Communications devised several new techniques to keep in touch with both the press and the public in the Internet age while attempting to control the message about presidential policies. These included increased access to information through a White House web page, which provided information such as Clinton's public remarks, his daily schedule, transcripts of press briefings, and photos. A White House email address was also set up to respond to questions from citizens about Clinton's policies. Although each administration builds on the techniques used by prior administrations within the Office of Communications, each administration also tends to develop a unique strategy to utilize these resources. For example, the Clinton communications operation was "characterized by its flexibility and adaptability in handling unanticipated events and issues, especially where defending the president was involved. Damage control was their strong suit." For George W. Bush, his communications team did better on planning ahead and developing a long-term strategy that "held presidential information very closely," yet often failed to adapt quickly to changing political circumstances where its message was concerned.[41] For Obama, despite his skill as a communicator and the aggressive approach (particularly through social media) by the White House to reach out to the public and enact broad policy changes, it is "difficult for the president to focus the public's attention" on a wide range of issues and to rally support in a fragmented media environment.[42]

Speech Writing

Speeches are an integral part of modern presidential leadership. As the rhetorical presidency evolved and expanded during the twentieth century, so, too, did the importance of presidential speechwriters. The men and women involved in the research and writing of presidential speeches can play a key role in policymaking because they help to shape the president's policy goals and initiatives. Major public addresses, particularly the State of the Union and major policy speeches, set the president's legislative agenda for both the public and Congress. Major addresses and other public appearances are examples of how a president attempts to sell his agenda or other presidential actions, not only to the public, but also to the news media and other political actors. The technological developments of the mass media in recent years have allowed presidents to go public more often and with much greater ease. As such, presidential speechwriters are now an integral part of the White House staff, and some have been extensively involved in the development of White House communication strategies for presidents.

When considering the history of presidential speeches, some early presidents relied on the help of others to write their speeches, most notably George Washington, Andrew Jackson, and Andrew Johnson, but most wrote their own. Thomas Jefferson, John Adams, James Madison, and Abraham Lincoln were all known for eloquent and effective speeches they authored themselves. By the twentieth century, the public leadership strategies and the increased attention placed on public addresses by Theodore Roosevelt and Wilson gave rise to the need for permanent speechwriters within the White House. Beginning with Harding, ghostwriters were used, since it was unthinkable that a president would deliver someone else's words during a public address. Harding hired the first official White House speechwriter, journalist Judson Welliver, who maintained a low public profile.

When FDR entered the White House, presidential speeches became more of a collaborative effort among the president, his advisors, and his speechwriters. Other presidents, most notably Kennedy, Nixon, Reagan, Clinton, and Obama, were also extensively involved in the writing and phraseology of their major public addresses. For example, Jon Favreau, Obama's director of speechwriting from 2009 until early 2013, was known as a "speech arranger" because of the routine that he and Obama had when writing a speech. Favreau would meet with Obama for roughly 30 minutes and write down everything Obama said. Then, Favreau would write a draft of the speech and get edits from Obama; this process continued until the speech was finished. Obama referred to Favreau as his "mind reader."[43]

Although the organization of key advisors and other staff throughout the White House can differ for each administration, a general practice for most modern presidents when writing an important speech to outline major policy initiatives involves the circulation of a draft for input from various policy experts as well as the speechwriters. Access to the president by speechwriters does not always occur, but is essential for those drafting remarks to clearly understand a president's view of a policy. However, some presidents have struggled with effective coordination between those setting the policy and those in the speechwriting office drafting the remarks about policy. Not everyone within the administration will agree with the content of a speech. For example, in 1987, Reagan gave his famous address at the Brandenburg Gate in West Berlin when he told Soviet president Mikhail Gorbachev to "tear down this wall." However, prior to the address, Colin Powell, who at the time was a member of the National Security Council, suggested numerous changes during the circulation of the speech draft:

> We (and the State Department) continue to have serious problems with this speech. Our proposed changes are attached. Important substantive fixes we have proposed earlier in the sections on arms control and the Berlin initiative still need to be made. We still believe that some important thematic passages are wrong. For example, we do not make arms control or other proposals to show our "goodwill." It is against our interest to legitimize the idea that western goodwill is the

missing ingredient *or* that our goodwill is tested by our arms control proposals. A better theme is to show the President's sensitivity to European anxieties about war and division and to stress that the real source of tension is the denial of freedom. In addition, we continue to be uneasy at the negative undertone of the section near the end that questions why Berliners stay in Berlin.[44]

As this memo shows, even one of the most memorable and most quoted speeches of the Reagan years encountered difficulties during the speechwriting process.

Public Events

Presidents now rely heavily on public events as an essential component of governing in a media-saturated political environment. A steady increase has occurred in the number of public events, particularly the use of major public addresses, since the start of the 1980s. This can be attributed to the influence and expansion of television and online coverage, changes in the political environment that have encouraged presidents to go public more often, and each president's public leadership style. It is not surprising that as expanding technologies allowed an increase in the amount and type of White House coverage, the president's schedule of public events also increased. Major public addresses are defined as rhetorical moments when the president addresses the nation or when his address to a smaller group can expect a larger (and perhaps national or international) audience through mass media dissemination. Although presidents since the start of the television age have relied on various public strategies to publicize their policy agendas and to improve their standing with the American public, there are certain major public addresses that are required and expected and leave no doubt that the president will deliver them (even if he is not a gifted speaker). These include the inaugural address and the annual State of the Union address.

The inaugural address represents the start of a president's time in office, and presidents look to the inauguration, as well as the inaugural address, as an opportunity to set the tone for their tenure in office with the public, other political actors, and even the news media; it is also a time to talk about broader political principles, not specific policies. This is one of the many symbolic acts in which a president engages and is the first time that he can address the American public—the national constituency that he uniquely represents—as president. Some of the most memorable and quoted inaugural addresses have occurred during times of great national crisis, such as Lincoln's address in 1861 (often remembered for the "better nature of our angels" line at the end of the speech) or FDR's first inaugural address in 1933 (when he told Americans "the only thing we have to fear is fear itself"). Other presidents, such as Kennedy in 1961 ("ask not what your country can do for you" and "the torch has been passed to a new generation of Americans") and Reagan in 1981 ("government is not the solution to our problem; government *is* the problem"), were skilled public speakers and used the inaugural address to present a recurring theme for their presidencies. Trump used his inaugural address in 2017 to reiterate his campaign theme of "make America great again."

The president's annual State of the Union address is perhaps the most anticipated and analyzed of all presidential speeches. Article 2, Section 3, of the Constitution requires that the president "shall from time to time give to the Congress information on the state of the Union and recommend to their consideration such measures as he shall judge necessary and expedient," but there is no requirement that the president give this information in an address to a joint session of Congress. For presidents Thomas Jefferson (1801–1809) through William Howard Taft (1909–1913), this constitutional requirement was met by submitting a written report to the Congress on the state of the union. Woodrow Wilson (1913–1921) revived the practice of delivering an address to Congress, which has continued almost every year since.[45]

Traditionally delivered near the start of the calendar year, the State of the Union address is not only a report to Congress on the actual "state" of the union, but also a statement of the president's proposed policy agenda for the upcoming year. This has evolved as a unique opportunity for presidents, in upholding their constitutional duty, to remind both the audience in attendance (Congress) and those watching and listening at home (the public) of the president's role in shaping the national agenda. In recent decades, the State of the Union address has involved an extensive White House communications and media strategy plan for events prior to, on the day of, and after the actual speech. The goal is to try to maximize the president's exposure through an event where he looks and sounds presidential with all the attendant pomp and circumstance that the event brings; this is one of the most ritualistic of presidential public events.

ADDRESSING THE NATION

THEN . . .

When a president decides to deliver an address to a joint session of Congress, he normally does so with the intent to make a major policy announcement or to address a national crisis. Aside from the annual State of the Union address, which is a significant—and expected—event, other presidential visits to Capitol Hill are reserved for significant policy initiatives or items of national significance such as impending military action. Such an address allows the president to capture the attention of both the news media and the American public to make the case for his chosen policy or course of action. For example, FDR was giving an address to a joint session of Congress when he declared, "Yesterday, December 7, 1941—a date which will live in infamy—the United States of America was suddenly and deliberately attacked by naval and air forces of the Empire of Japan."[46] In April 1981, Ronald Reagan gave his second address to a joint session of Congress after just three months in office and weeks after surviving an assassination attempt, stating, "I have come to speak to you tonight about our economic recovery program and why I believe it's essential that the Congress approve this package, which I believe will lift the crushing burden of inflation off of our citizens and restore the vitality to our economy and our industrial machine."[47]

Announcing a major policy initiative was exactly what Bill Clinton planned to do in September 1993 when he delivered an address to a joint session of Congress to promote his health-care reform initiative. As part of his focus on the economy and other domestic issues during the 1992 presidential campaign, Clinton made reforming health care and expanding availability of health insurance a top priority during his first year in office. Seen as a major speech and an early test for the Clinton presidency, the initial rollout of the health-care policy provided

Bill Clinton acknowledges the crowd in the House Gallery prior to delivering his State of the Union address on January 23, 1996, on Capitol Hill. House Speaker Newt Gingrich and Vice President Al Gore appear behind him.

an opportunity for Clinton to convince the American public and members of Congress that the plan should be adopted. The speech itself laid out the specifics of how to expand coverage to more Americans while keeping the quality of medical care up and keeping costs down.

Clinton recalled feeling confident as he walked into the packed House of Representatives chamber. Greeted by members of Congress and of his cabinet, Clinton was fully prepared to deliver his address to a national audience—that is, until he realized that the wrong speech was in the TelePrompTer: "My confidence slipped . . . I was looking at the beginning of the speech to Congress on the economic plan I'd delivered in February. The budget had been enacted more than a month earlier; Congress didn't need to hear that speech again."[48] Clinton turned to Vice President Al Gore, who was sitting behind Clinton and next to the Speaker of the House, to inform him of the problem; Gore then summoned White House communications advisor George Stephanopoulos to fix the problem. It took seven long minutes into Clinton's address to insert the correct speech into the TelePrompTer and catch it up with Clinton's actual words. Despite the flurry of words from an earlier speech passing before his eyes, Clinton—a skilled public speaker who had been working on the draft of the speech right up until the limo ride from the White House to Capitol Hill—relied on his written copy of the speech for those first crucial minutes and no one in the viewing audience was the wiser. Behind the scenes, Stephanopoulos was "sick with worry" over what effect this would have on the president's performance, yet Clinton's speech was considered a "home run," particularly when he pulled out a mock-up of his proposed "Health Care Security Card" for the cameras, which Clinton promised would guarantee health coverage to all Americans if Congress adopted his plan.[49] Although the success of the speech was short lived (health-care reform did not pass during the Clinton presidency), the initial public relations strategy for the plan was a success because the health-care address highlighted one of Clinton's best skills as president—he was an excellent communicator capable of delivering a strong performance even under less than desirable circumstances.

. . . AND NOW

Like his most recent Democratic predecessor, Barack Obama also delivered a prime-time, nationally televised address to a joint session of Congress on the topic of health-care reform, on September 9, 2009. The debate about health-care reform throughout the summer of 2009 had been hyperpartisan and divisive, which left White House advisors questioning their decision not only to let Congress write the bill, but also to not have Obama engage in a more direct public relations campaign to support such a major piece of legislation. As one of his top domestic priorities during his first year in office, the President made a strong pitch for health-care reform in his speech, stating that, "I am not the first President to take up this cause, but I am determined to be the last. It has now been nearly a century since Theodore Roosevelt first called for health care reform, and ever since, nearly every President and Congress, whether Democrat or Republican, has attempted to meet this challenge in some way. . . . Now is when we must bring the best ideas of both parties together and show the American people that we can still do what we were sent here to do."[50] Although Obama had already earned a reputation for being a skilled performer in the venue of such a formal speech, it was a little-known Congressman who would dominate the headlines the next day. Representative Joe Wilson (R-SC) shouted out "You lie!" at Obama after the president stated, "Now, there are also those who claim that our reform efforts would insure illegal immigrants. This too is false. The reforms I'm proposing would not apply to those who are here illegally." Amid a somewhat shocked House chamber, Obama responded to Wilson, stating, "It's not true. And one more misunderstanding I want to clear up, under our plan, no Federal dollars will be used to fund abortions, and Federal conscience laws will remain in place," and then continued on with his prepared remarks.

Called "the outburst heard 'round the world" by Brian Williams on the next night's opening coverage on NBC Nightly News, Wilson received much media attention in the following days, which had the effect of highlighting the contentiousness of the issue of health-care reform as opposed to the substance of the Democratic proposal endorsed by Obama. The White House received no bump in approval ratings for the health-care plan after the speech, not only because of the news media's obsession with Wilson's bad behavior but also because fewer Americans now tune in to watch a presidential address (whether on television or the Internet).[51] Although Obama deserved high marks for not letting Wilson rattle him during the speech, the news media coverage that followed seemed to underlie the fact that presidents, no matter how skilled at communicating, have little control over the environment—both political and media—in which they attempt to govern.

Other major policy addresses are also expected of the president, including televised addresses to the nation in times of crisis or national urgency (usually involving national tragedy, U.S. military action, natural disasters, or economic crises), as well as policy addresses with the expectation of national news coverage, thus effecting the public agenda (usually delivered before a large group such as a national convention for an interest group or a university graduation). Although a major policy address by itself demands much attention from White House staffers in various offices (including speechwriting, press and media affairs), the ancillary events that go along with a major policy address (press conferences, presidential and surrogate interviews, photo ops, speech distribution, and other advance work) also play a large role in the communications strategy for a specific presidential speech.

Since the early 1980s, presidents also began to rely on weekly radio addresses—short talks lasting approximately five minutes about a specific topic—to supplement their public agenda, target specific policies, most often domestic or economic, and reach citizens who may not be watching television. The tradition began with Reagan in 1982 (whose advisors thought the medium was a good fit for Reagan because of his early days in radio during the 1930s and 1940s) and was continued by both Clinton and George W. Bush. George H. W. Bush chose not to follow Reagan's strategy and gave only a handful of radio addresses in 1991 and 1992. Although most Americans never heard the weekly radio address, it served a strategic purpose through additional coverage in the news media of a controlled event, since the presidents' remarks routinely made the weekend television news shows, especially on cable news, as well as the national Sunday newspapers.[52] During the Obama administration, the weekly radio address evolved into a weekly video address that could be viewed on the White House web page or other online locations. Although this communication venue had traditionally been used to generate news about presidential policies, Obama's video version was more accessible to Americans without the filter of press coverage.

THE PRESIDENT AND THE PRESS

The news media have always been among the most influential political actors with which presidents must contend. The relationship is often adversarial since the president and news media need each other, yet have different goals—the president wants positive coverage about the actions and policies of his administration, but "big" stories for the news media (which in turn mean higher ratings and circulations) usually come from negative and scandal-oriented stories about the president and/or his administration. Rarely has a president not complained about the news media, the White House press corps, and the coverage he received.

The relationship between the president and the American press has a long and colorful history. American newspapers during the late eighteenth and early nineteenth centuries were highly partisan in both their political loyalties and coverage of events in Washington. By the mid-nineteenth century, with advanced printing capabilities and a desire to provide more objective news coverage for increasing circulations, newspapers began to cover the White House as a formal beat. News coverage of the presidency dramatically increased during the administration of Theodore Roosevelt, who cultivated positive press coverage to maintain strong ties to the American public. Since then, with the rise of the rhetorical presidency and the continual expansion of media technology, presidents increasingly relied on the press to communicate their vision to both the American public and other important political actors. The White House often struggles to define the political agenda through the news media; however, recent scholarship has shown that presidents can, at times, have indirect influence over some issues by influencing the media's agenda, thereby influencing the overall political/policy agenda.[53]

The White House Press Corps

The White House press corps first received working space within the White House during the administration of Theodore Roosevelt, who included press quarters within the new West Wing built in 1904. The White House Correspondents' Association was formed in 1914, which contributed to the trend of professionalization of reporters within the newspaper industry during the early part of the twentieth century. The White House press corps experienced tremendous growth during the 1930s and 1940s as presidential influence over national politics increased under the New Deal programs.[54] Also, FDR's frequent and informal meetings with the White House press corps in the Oval Office were newsworthy events for reporters. His use of press conferences and effective news management efforts contributed to the need for the White House to be covered in various media outlets, since much of the news in Washington was being generated from the executive branch. During the 1930s, more than 350 reporters covered the Washington beat.

Today, approximately 1,700 people hold White House press credentials, and although all are not considered "regulars" on the White House beat, the sheer size of the press corps has necessitated a more formalized daily press briefing than in years past. The emergence of the television age during the 1950s and its expansive growth during the 1960s and 1970s greatly contributed to the growth in size of the White House press corps. Other contributing factors include the increased importance and size of the federal government and the role it plays in the lives of individuals, which requires reporters from non-Washington media outlets to cover policymaking at the national level. Also, the number of foreign correspondents covering the White House has increased in recent decades as other countries have a greater need to understand the impact of American policies in their own countries.[55]

The prominence of the White House beat has also increased within the journalism industry and is now viewed as one of the premier assignments in most news organizations. The reporters who regularly cover the White House include representatives from a variety of legacy and new media outlets, including the top daily newspapers (*New York Times, Washington Post, Los Angeles Times, Wall Street Journal, USA Today*); the major networks (ABC, CBS, NBC, Fox, CNN, MSNBC); wire services (Associated Press, United Press International, Reuters), and weekly news magazines (*Time, Newsweek, U.S. News and World Report*). In recent years, with the growth of Internet news sources, reporters from online sources like *Politico* and the *Huffington Post*, to name a few, are also regulars within the White House press room. The growth in the size of the White House press corps has also contributed to the expansion of both the White House Press Office and Office of Communications, which must handle the increased demands of Washington reporters.

Press Conferences

Press conferences provide the president with an opportunity to make news by formally interacting with the White House press corps. Press conferences have become an institutionalized tradition in which all presidents are expected to participate. A written transcript is kept of all questions and answers, and most presidents begin the session with a prepared opening statement. Since they were first televised live in the 1960s, press conferences have become less about informing reporters and the public about important issues and more about controlling the president's public image. The number of press conferences held by presidents has varied greatly (see Table 4.2). Theodore Roosevelt held some of the earliest press conferences, which were informal sessions with the press on Sundays to combat the lack of interesting news from Washington in Monday's newspapers. Taft was the first president to hold regular press conferences, which occurred twice a week, until he stopped the practice after what was considered "an unfortunate session" with reporters. Wilson, Harding, Coolidge, and Hoover (until the onset of the Depression) returned to the practice of regular press conferences, usually twice-weekly and formal events. Each also required reporters to submit their questions in advance.

FDR changed that requirement, as well as the formal setting for press conferences. He enjoyed an effective relationship with the press, in part because of his frequent and informal meetings with reporters in the Oval Office. FDR held 881 press conferences, a yearly average of approximately 70. He was famous for his congenial personality toward the press and his "off the record" remarks. Through press conferences, FDR was a master at news management and captured many headlines throughout the nation's newspapers. Following his 12 years in office, no other president came close to matching the number of press conferences held. Truman, who averaged 38 per year, returned press conferences to a more formal event and moved the location in 1950 out of the Oval Office and into the Executive Office Building. Truman and his advisors began to exercise more control over the content and structure of press conferences, relying on preconference briefings and an increased use of prepared opening statements. Truman also earned a reputation for his "shoot from the hip" speaking style that would regularly produce unpredictable yet quotable comments. Eisenhower was the first president to encounter television cameras during a press conference, and he allowed taping for later television release.

Kennedy was innovative with his groundbreaking use of live televised press conferences, which both the press and public found entertaining. Johnson could never match the Kennedy style during press conferences and contributed to the growing credibility gap with inaccurate reports on the Vietnam War. The frequency of press conferences dropped during Nixon's presidency because of a belief that the mystique of the presidency must be maintained through limited public appearances. Nixon was also famous for his great disdain of the press and averaged only seven press conferences per year. Ford, during his brief tenure in office, as well as Carter, both attempted to restore credibility to the White House and its relationship with the press by increasing the number of press conferences after the Nixon years. Both Ford and Carter used these opportunities to speak bluntly to the press about the problems facing the nation in the mid to late 1970s. Although neither received high marks for style during press conferences, both Ford and Carter were known for their substantive knowledge of government policies. Carter's advisors also tried to improve the president's performance:

> I think your answers at press conferences are generally too long. Although your command of the facts is impressive, you often lose your audience. Short, punchy answers allow for more questions. The give-and-take becomes more rapid fire. You appear in command, almost combative. Remember, a half-hour after the press conference is over most viewers probably can't remember a single question or answer. They do have an over-all impression though. That impression should be of you, like a baseball batter, hitting whatever is thrown at you—disposing of pitchers. Occasionally, of course, long answers are required, but these should be the exception not the rule.[56]

Although his public skills earned him the nickname the "Great Communicator," Reagan held fewer press conferences than even Nixon did, averaging just less than six per year. This was a result of his unfavorable performances, since Reagan often made misstatements and verbal gaffes during the give and take of questions from reporters. To better control these events, Reagan's advisors implemented new rules for press conferences, including assigned seats for those in attendance (which provided a seating chart for Reagan to reference when calling on reporters), and insisted that reporters raise their hands before asking a question.

George H. W. Bush held more press conferences than Reagan and also began the practice of holding joint press conferences with foreign leaders. Bush afforded the press extensive access to the entire administration; he hoped to gain favorable coverage by holding many informal discussions with reporters, and he courted the press as members of the political elite. His desire for numerous informal, last-minute press sessions in an attempt to create an open and friendly presidency suggests that Bush's strategy reflected what he considered his greatest asset, face-to-face, personal contact with reporters.[57] As a result, much of Bush's overall communication strategy focused on his use of press conferences, with the goal of meeting the needs of newspapers and not the network news, hence the focus on informal question-and-answer sessions as opposed to prime-time press conferences. Press secretary Marlin Fitzwater recognized Bush's strengths and weaknesses in this area and advised the president accordingly to not "try to compete with former movie star Reagan at prime-time news conferences in the awesome setting of the East Room." Fitzwater's plan included the following recommendations to Bush:

- Press Conferences: We recommend that you hold informal press conferences during the day in Room 405, much as you have done recently in announcing new Cabinet positions. These can be announced the same day they are held, and last for 20 minutes to a half-hour, to get credit for having held a full-scale press conference. A minimum of preparation is required, and you are the focus of the news, rather than the reporters.
- East Room Press Conferences: We recommend holding these dinosauras–showus–maximus extravaganzas only on special occasions—perhaps two or three times a year. The East Room press conference has developed in a way that gives more of a forum to the press than it does to the President. The cutaway cameras focus on the questions, often which are prosecutorial and inflammatory. In terms of viewer impact, the question is just as important as the answer. . . . In addition, we want to

develop press conferences that you will get credit for. It always galled me that the press would not give President Reagan credit for holding a press conference unless it was prime-time, 30 minutes, East Room. We should reverse this so that all forums in which you openly address questions, whether in the briefing room or Room 450, are considered press conferences. The way to do that is to immediately establish the nature of your press conferences.

- Frequent Appearances in the Briefing Room: These could be held for 10–15 minutes duration, on an impromptu, irregular basis. We would recommend doing them without prior notification, so that they are limited to the regular working White House press, and require a minimum of preparation on your part. Again, these have to be frequent enough so that the press views them as routine accessibility, rather than signaling any special announcement.

- Pool Briefings: A new idea would be to establish a rotation among regular White House press corps to form a pool of 3–5 reporters who would be taken into the Oval Office once or twice a week for a 10-minute session with the President. The pool would do a report on the interview, and a transcript could be provided to all members of the press corps.

- Ad Hoc Access: Perhaps the most effective means of establishing your accessibility to the press is through ad hoc visits to the press working area, hallway discussions, motorcade interviews, etc. You have maintained press relationships of this nature throughout the campaign and the transition. These kinds of events are in stark contrast to President Reagan's style, and make a considerable impression on press attitudes. We recommend you maintain these informal contacts.[58]

Clinton continued the practice of holding joint press conferences with foreign leaders (a trend that continued with George W. Bush and Obama), yet he did not hold many formal press conferences, particularly during his second term (in part because of his impeachment in 1998). Since the Reagan years, presidents have held fewer formal press conferences in which they appear alone before the White House press corps, relying more on regional and foreign press conferences as well as joint appearances with foreign dignitaries, since these types of press conferences are easier to control and do not give the press as much of a chance to ask questions that the president may not want to answer. However, Clinton always performed well in these impromptu sessions, deftly fielding questions from seasoned White House correspondents; although Clinton's formal press conferences were infrequent, they nonetheless represented an important element of his overall communication strategy. A presidential press conference has some strategic risk, given that the White House cannot control what questions reporters will ask; as such, advisors work hard to prepare the president for all possible situations. For example, Clinton's plan to hold a prime-time press conference in early August 1994 came at a crucial time; major policy issues on the Clinton agenda, including health-care reform, were pending in Congress, various international issues were dominating headlines, and the congressional midterm elections were just three months away. According to his advisors, the time was right for Clinton to hold a press conference because it gave him

an opportunity to accomplish three major objectives: To give extended remarks on the need for health care reform and the importance of universal coverage; To take credit—if the vote has taken place—for a successful crime bill and pivot off that success to demonstrate that Washington is working for people, that your agenda is moving forward here and to show that health care reform can get done; To reassure the American people about the humanitarian effort in Rwanda, the situation in Haiti and the conflict in Bosnia. The effect of a prime-time news conference will be to increase your stake in the upcoming congressional votes on health care. Obviously, there are several snares to be aware of during the press conference: being drawn into a web of questions on the Whitewater hearings and answering a line of questions about polls and process. Attached is a book with proposed Q & A on a number of topics that may come up during the press conference. We will supplement it on Tuesday and Wednesday.[59]

White House advisors often look to press conferences to gain a strategic edge over public discussions of a particular issue. In September 2006, communication advisors to George W. Bush prepared the President for a joint press conference with President Hamid Karzai of Afghanistan by laying out the key themes and talking points they believed would best benefit Bush's foreign-policy priorities in the War on Terror:

Key Themes: Afghanistan is a valued partner in the War on Terror and continues making steady progress in rebuilding its democratic institutions, its economy, and security forces. While we have seen great progress, challenges remain, and that is why the United States will remain fully engaged in Afghanistan. We thank the sacrifice and contributions made by all our partners in securing Afghanistan. Afghan, Coalition, and NATO forces are engaging militants that want to reverse the progress President Karzai and his people have made. We look forward to progress countering the threat posed by narcotics and illicit activity. We are appreciative of the efforts to date and encourage continued support for expanding the Central Government's resources and ability to provide services and security to the provinces. We want strong relations between Afghanistan and its neighbors, including Pakistan. We welcome the close cooperation between the Afghan and Pakistani Governments to improve security and governance in the border areas. Good regional relations will advance stability, democracy, and prosperity throughout South Asia.[60]

As these memos show, press conferences not only are intended to keep the press informed on important issues, but also serve as one of the many tools presidents have at their disposal to implement their overall communication strategy.

The Media Environment

Presidents attempt to govern in a political environment shaped by news media coverage that breeds mistrust, cynicism, and fierce competition among members of the White House press corps. The president is under constant scrutiny by the press, but must be careful in his criticisms of reporters, who can not only give voice to his opponents but also present the news as unflattering to the president's public image. Much of this current environment got its start in the 1960s because of the growing influence of television, as well as the emergence of the "credibility gap," known as the growing sentiment among many American citizens to distrust the statements of government officials. One of the first events that contributed to the credibility gap occurred in 1960, when an American military U-2 spy plane was shot down over the Soviet Union. The Eisenhower administration initially denied that the plane

Table 4.2 Presidential Press Conferences: Coolidge to Obama

PRESIDENT	TOTAL	MONTHLY AVERAGE	YEARLY AVERAGE
Calvin Coolidge (1923–1929)	407	6.07	72.90
Herbert Hoover (1929–1933)	268	5.58	67.00
Franklin D. Roosevelt (1933–1945)	881	6.05	72.66
Harry Truman (1945–1953)	324	3.48	41.73
Dwight Eisenhower (1953–1961)	193	2.01	24.13
John F. Kennedy (1961–1963)	65	1.91	22.89
Lyndon Johnson (1963–1969)	135	2.18	26.16
Richard Nixon (1969–1974)	39	0.59	7.03
Gerald Ford (1974–1977)	40	1.36	16.32
Jimmy Carter (1977–1981)	59	1.23	14.75
Ronald Reagan (1981–1989)	46	0.48	5.75
George H.W. Bush (1989–1993)	137	2.85	34.25
Bill Clinton (1993–2001)	193	2.01	24.13
George W. Bush (2001–2009)	209	2.18	26.13
Barack Obama (2009–2017)	163	1.70	13.58

Source: Gerhard Peters, "Presidential News Conferences," *The American Presidency Project,* ed. John T. Woolley and Gerhard Peters, University of California Santa Barbara, http://www.presidency.ucsb.edu/data/newsconferences.php.

had been spying on the Soviet Union, but when the Soviets produced the captured pilot, Gary Powers, on television, U.S. government officials were forced to change their story. The Kennedy assassination in 1963, followed by the release of the Warren Commission report in 1964, would also contribute to the growing credibility gap. The commission, chaired by Chief Justice Earl Warren, declared that Lee Harvey Oswald had acted alone in assassinating Kennedy. However, a majority of Americans at the time did not believe the lone-gunman theory and remained skeptical of the findings.[61]

The news media had also begun to distrust the information they were receiving from the government, especially official military reports coming out of Vietnam. By the latter half of the 1960s, both White House and Pentagon officials often insisted to journalists that Americans were winning the war against the communist North

Vietnamese (known as the Viet Cong), yet the pictures being broadcast into Americans' living rooms every night on the evening news told a different story. Daily news briefings by military commanders in Saigon were dubbed "The Five O'Clock Follies" by American reporters because of the lack of accuracy in many of the reports. In the battlefields of Vietnam, the Pentagon put few restrictions on American reporters (a policy that would change drastically in the 1980s and beyond), which allowed them direct access to soldiers who could tell their own stories about what was really happening. Both broadcast and print reporters began filing critical stories about American involvement in Vietnam, which contributed to the growing antiwar movement across the nation. In February 1968, Walter Cronkite gave a rare editorial comment on his nightly newscast on CBS, declaring that the war in Vietnam could not be won by the American military. Johnson reportedly told an aide, "If I've lost Cronkite, I've lost Middle America."[62] Just weeks later, on March 31, 1968, Johnson announced to the nation that he would not seek reelection.

As American involvement in the Vietnam War continued into the 1970s, so, too, did the growing credibility gap among the public, the news media, and government officials. Elected in 1968, Nixon distrusted the American press, deplored leaks from his administration to Washington reporters, and placed the names of countless top journalists who had been critical of his policies on his famous "enemies list." Nixon's vice president, Spiro Agnew, routinely criticized the news media for unfair and biased reporting, particularly for their critical views about Vietnam, claiming that the press wielded too much power over public opinion. Agnew claimed that top news executives were liberal elites who held an "Eastern Establishment bias" that did not reflect the views of average Americans; he once referred to top news executives as "nattering nabobs of negativism."[63] The Nixon administration also attempted but failed to impose prior restraint on the *New York Times* and *Washington Post* in 1971 when both papers began reporting on the Pentagon Papers, a 47-volume study on the "History of the U.S. Decision Making Process on Vietnam Policy" that had been leaked to the press by a former defense department analyst. The Supreme Court ruled against the government in the case, *New York Times v. United States* (1971), but only after the stories had been kept out of the newspapers for approximately two weeks following a restraining order from a federal court judge.

Perhaps the seminal political event that defined the 1970s, Watergate—a series of events that unfolded between July 1972 with a break-in of the Democratic Party office at the Watergate Complex in Washington and August 1974 when Nixon resigned from the presidency—also changed the nature of the presidential–press relationship. Bob Woodward and Carl Bernstein, two *Washington Post* reporters who covered the city beat, eventually won the Pulitzer Prize for their two-year investigation into the links between the Watergate break-in and the Nixon administration. The five burglars arrested in 1972 were part of a political sabotage unit put together by top Nixon aides as part of a larger operation to discredit Democratic candidates and ensure Nixon's reelection that same year. In the first months after the break-in, Woodward and Bernstein were nearly alone in their coverage of the story and their determination to link the break-in to the White House. With the help of their inside source, known only as "Deep Throat," they reported the existence of a Nixon campaign slush fund that had paid the burglars. ("Deep Throat" finally revealed his own identity in 2005 as W. Mark Felt Sr., associate director of the Federal Bureau of

Investigation during the Watergate years). Although the *Post* was not the only news outlet investigating the Watergate story, their early reporting of the break-in helped to lay the groundwork for many other news organizations as the story gripped the nation throughout much of 1973 and 1974 until Nixon finally resigned from office on August 8, 1974.

Major changes continued to occur within the news industry with the start of the 1980s, which meant that presidents needed to continue to update their press strategies. Throughout the decade, the network newscasts remained a staple for American television viewers and continued to have influence as major players within American politics. For example, in November 1979, ABC News began a late-night recap of the continuing story of the American citizens held hostage at the American Embassy in Iran. The show evolved into *Nightline*, hosted by Ted Koppel. Koppel, along with Cronkite on the *CBS Evening News*, provided a daily count to American citizens of the number of days the 66 Americans had been held hostage in Tehran, which served as a daily reminder to American voters in 1980 that Carter, running for reelection that year, had been unable to solve the crisis. The hostages were eventually released on January 20, 1981, just moments after Reagan had taken the oath of office; they had been held for 444 days.

The Reagan administration was especially skilled at controlling the images that came out of the White House to provide a complete media package to sell both the president's image and his agenda. Reagan, nicknamed the "Great Communicator," exhibited a style and ease that was tailor-made for television in the 1980s due to his prior experience as an actor. The "stagecraft" of the Reagan years proved a tough act for his successor, George H. W. Bush, to follow. Bush, who wanted his presidency to be more about substance than style, had a difficult time articulating his vision for the country within a rapidly changing media environment.[64] Since then, presidents have focused more attention on keeping up with changes in the news industry and have tried to alter their strategies accordingly. Clinton, a skilled communicator, was a good fit for new media outlets in the 1990s, but faced challenges as a result of the many personal and political scandals that dominated his time in office.[65] George W. Bush faced increasing partisanship in news coverage and the broader political environment, in part because of his resolute messaging about his decisions involving military intervention in Afghanistan and Iraq[66] (for example, his statement that "either you are with us, or you are with the terrorists" 10 days after the 9/11 attacks). Obama embraced new media technologies as well as popular culture trends to speak directly to citizens, particularly younger Americans.

News Coverage of the President

In the post-Watergate years, press coverage of the president and the White House has become more personal, intrusive, and obsessed with scandal. Not only has coverage of national politics, in particular the presidency, personalized and politicized the functioning of the national government, but also the immediacy of cable news and online coverage has accelerated the decision-making process for presidents. Americans have come to expect that the personal lives of presidents will make news, which has also desensitized the public to tabloid-style reporting about personal indiscretions. Presidents must now pay close attention to their image as it is portrayed in media, but determining what is good for the president in terms of control over the message may not be the same as substantive information about the political process for the American electorate.[67]

Presidential honeymoons with the press have become increasingly shorter; Clinton, Bush, and Obama all had relatively short honeymoon periods in terms of press coverage.[68] In addition, although the president and executive branch may dominate news coverage when compared to the other two branches of government, not all of the coverage is positive. More recent presidents have experienced a growing trend in negative press coverage, even during their first year in office. For example, less than 40 percent of the network news coverage of the first year in office for Reagan, Clinton, and George W. Bush was considered positive. In 2009, Obama fared somewhat better, with 47 percent positive coverage on the network news; that percentage, however, still equates to the majority of the news coverage being negative.[69]

IN THEIR OWN WORDS

MEDIA EXPOSURE

Presidential advisors and political pundits alike have long pondered the question "How much is too much?" when considering a president's public strategy. Although no definitive answer has emerged, it is safe to say that the number of media appearances in which a president engages often corresponds to how skilled he is in public settings. For example, does the president appear comfortable and relaxed on television (like Reagan)? Is he adept at impromptu questions (like Clinton)? Or, is the president likely to commit a verbal gaffe with an incorrect statement (like Reagan) or garbled syntax and prose (like George W. Bush)? One of the most important skills that a presidential advisor can possess is knowing the president's strengths and weaknesses, especially with regard to public strategies. A telling example comes from Patrick J. Buchanan's concerns over a possible televised speech by Richard Nixon in 1971:

> Understand thought is being given to televising national the RN appearance before the Detroit Economic Club. Don't think we should do that—for the following reasons:
>
> 1. An hour's show with Richard Nixon answering the concerns of some Detroit Fat Cats does not seem to me particularly good television; it will lack the adversary setting of a press conference, and the sharpness of questions, RN can expect from editors and writers.
>
> 2. An hour is simply too long—to sustain the interest of Middle America.
>
> 3. We have nothing really new to say, from my knowledge; the President has already covered the "news" in Thursday's [press] conference.
>
> 4. The President's greatest political asset is the Presidency—part of the power of that asset adheres in the *distance* between the Presidency and the people. Harry Truman as Harry Truman is a clown—as President, he fills the shoes of Lincoln, Wilson, etc. The more we show of RN the individual in front of a camera, the more in my judgment we diminish some of the mystery, aloofness

that surrounds the office. We make the President too "familiar" a figure—and not in the best sense of that word.

5. What makes China such an interesting, important country and [French President Charles] De Gaulle such an interesting man—is the aloofness, the distance, from the hoi polloi. Every time we put the President on camera in a conventional setting—answering Q and A—we tend, I think, to bring him down closer to the average man—and I don't believe that is to our political advantage—partly for the next reason.

6. I have never been convinced that Richard Nixon, Good Guy, is our long suit; to me we are simply not going to charm the American people; we are not going to win it on "style" and we ought to forget playing ball in the Kennedy's Court. This new emphasis of running the President on the tube at more and more opportunities is a corollary of the theorem that the more people who see the President, the more who will become enthusiastic about him. We are selling personality; but we know from our experience with television shows, how even the most attractive and energetic and charming personalities don't last very long.

7. As I wrote the President long ago, in 1967, we watched Rocky rise twenty points in the national polls in a year in which he was probably not once on national television. When Rocky took to the airwaves in 1968, running around the country—he dropped in the polls as he did in 1964. In short, what is said and written around Nelson Rockefeller's accomplishments—compared with the accomplishments of others—is invariably better received than the presence of Rocky himself in a competitive situation.

8. The President is going to be on with Phase II in October, and with the Vietnam announcements in November. My judgment is that we ought not to put him on the air, without serious thought, and usually only in context with some significant pronouncement.

9. Finally, am not at all against some of the more imaginative ideas for presenting the President—but they should come out of a Media Strategy, which I don't know we have right now—or I don't see how this fits into it.[70]

White House Press Strategies

The president continues to be the most prominent political figure in news coverage, and his actions can dominate day-to-day storylines. Most press secretaries, during the presidential transition or at the start of the administration, map out a specific press strategy. The ultimate goal is to have the president portrayed in the most favorable light possible; highlighting the stature and dignity of the office is also frequently a strategic goal. For example, in December 1988, just weeks prior to George H. W. Bush's inauguration, Marlin Fitzwater declared the need for a new press strategy (in a discussion paper written for the president-elect) that would "[throw] out all the old ways of doing things, and [suggest] an entirely new scheme of press relations." The major premise of this new press "scheme" placed a much greater emphasis on pulling the president back from time on the national stage and replacing the staged events that had dominated the Reagan years with more informal press access (that is, emphasizing substance over style):

> The press takes the irrational position that the President is a public entity, and that reporters must keep watch over every move and utterance on behalf of the American people. To this end they have constructed elaborate schemes, committed millions of dollars and untold walkie-talkies and helicopters to pursue you to the ends of the earth. Thus, our basic task is to introduce them to a new kind of President—the private man. The lessons of history in this regard regale us with stories of Lyndon Johnson careening through the Texas countryside with madcap reporters giving chase; Jimmy Carter sneaking away from Camp David for an afternoon of fishing in the Shenandoahs; and Ronald Reagan having the quietest of dinners at the Jockey Club. The conclusion one reaches from these episodes is that there is no answer to this problem which will satisfy all parties. Thus, our task should be to satisfy you first, and the press as much as possible. We are therefore considering the following: An edict that says: The President of the United States has a right to an uninterrupted and unintruded visit to the ice cream store. It's not news. It's unpredictable. It's personal. And security is enhanced by its very unpredictability.[71]

Presidents have attempted control over the news with the knowledge of the news media's preference to report on politics, but only the subject matter can be controlled, not the tone of the news. Presidential power can be undermined both by a failure of the administration to effectively manage the news and by newsgathering norms within the journalism industry and the skepticism of the press. Although presidents can usually enjoy deference from the press in terms of coverage during times of crisis or certain ceremonial occasions, usually reporters place presidential actions within a political context that reduces the symbolic nature of the presidency to just another politician seeking to retain political power.

That does not mean, however, that White House advisors do not continue to work at trying to control both the content and tone of presidential press coverage. For example, at the end of Clinton's first year in office, his advisors sought to shift the focus of press stories assessing the president's first-year accomplishments:

> The press has completed the run of Congress and the presidency accomplishment stories; we are now entering a phase of coverage that will focus more exclusively on you, your Administration, and the first year in office. Attached is a list of your accomplishments arranged thematically which I think will be helpful for your interviews in December. You also asked for a better sense of what we hope to get out of the interviews. That follows—along with a few other suggestions. The essence, however, is this: **Your tone should be optimistic and presidential; you should stress big themes and the progress we have made on them.** The year should not be judged in a vacuum; it is the *first* year on a long road. Be optimistic; you should be satisfied with the progress we have made, but aware that millions are still hurting—be determined to push ahead. We need an alternative interpretation to the direction the press is headed in their analysis of the first year. **The press' storyline.** You can use these interviews to blunt the emerging conventional wisdom of the press, which is along these lines: This is a President who gets things done, but he too often stumbles across the finish line with his shirt ends hanging

out. They have a dangerous propensity to do everything at the last minute—and it is bound to catch up with them. . . . **Our Storyline**. I came to this office with two great objectives: To change the system and to make it work for middle class families. . . . That was no small order; we live in a uniquely challenging period of time in our nation's history and the needs of working Americans had been neglected for a long time.[72]

Attempts to control press coverage are not always successful; they are among several factors that can increase the tensions between the president and the press. Presidents have historically viewed the press as a hindrance in achieving the public's support for policies, mostly because of the content of most news originating from the White House. For example, presidents often attempt to use the press to its advantage through leaks. Top aides or even the president himself will leak information as a trial balloon to test public reaction to a proposed policy. In this instance, the press agrees to serve as a communication tool of the government to remain competitive with other news outlets. However, sometimes the press leaks information that the White House does not want made public. Often, this information comes from someone else in the executive branch who leaks information without White House approval. For example, in 1941, Harry L. Hopkins, a close aide to FDR, wrote the following memo to the President about a leak from the Defense Department:

> I am enclosing an article from the New York Times of this morning. This article gives the exact figures of our proposed tank production. As usual they quote a "defense official," . . . I realize that under ordinary circumstances it is supposed to be bad form to find out how a newspaper man gets stories but when vital defense information like this is given out to newspaper men I think the person who gave out this information should be fired. It is inconceivable to me that people can be so naïve as to think that information like this is not helpful to the Germans. Would it not be possible for Steve [Early] to set up a unit—or, if not Steve, the F.B.I.—to find out who in the government is giving out this information and make an example of him? The story in this morning's paper is simply one of many that are constantly being leaked out and I think we have got to put a stop to it.[73]

The Carter administration experienced similar frustrations over stories in the *New York Times* and *Washington Post* in July 1978 that included leaked information about the Strategic Arms Limitation Treaty talks. Press Secretary Jody Powell, who declared the leak an internal attempt to alter Carter's policy in this area, wrote the following to the President:

> From what I know of this issue, this sort of leak should not be allowed to pass. Clearly, it came from those who oppose [your policy]. It was done to influence policy and narrow your options. I recommend that you do one of two things: 1. Call in the principals who attended the SALT meeting where this option was discussed and chew them out good. Let them know that you expect your displeasure to be conveyed to their subordinates. 2. Call [Paul] Warnke (ACDA is the most likely source) and let him know that you are upset and want him and his people to know about it. Only if the bureaucracy begins to feel that there is some penalty for this sort of behavior will we see some restraint on their part. Otherwise, the problem will continue to grow worse. There is no doubt in my mind that this leak came from the same people who leaked the "Freeze on SALT" story to the same two reporters—Pincus and Kaiser.[74]

A more recent example shows how leaks have continued to be a presidential frustration. In July 2010, *WikiLeaks* posted 92,000 documents related to the war in Afghanistan. Although Obama responded that the leak raised no fundamentally new issues about the conflict, he nonetheless chastised the move by stating the leak "could potentially jeopardize individuals or operations," and the Pentagon initiated a criminal probe to find out where the leak occurred.[75] Other investigations into leaks were also initiated by the Obama White House (including the high-profile leak of classified National Security Agency materials by Edward Snowden), which prompted many in the press to proclaim that Obama was "at war" with journalists.[76]

In addition to leaks, whether intentional or not from the White House, other issues create tension between the president and the press. Many stories on the president tend to have a superficial or trivial quality. Stories focusing on the personal aspects of the president's life often gain more prominent coverage than stories analyzing policies. Again, competition among reporters, as well as a lack of expertise on many national political issues, fuels this type of coverage. Finally, although most studies on media coverage of news show no systematic bias along partisan or ideological lines, distortion still occurs in coverage of the president. The presentation of news contains a structural bias in how stories are selected, since all issues do not receive coverage. Because of deadlines and limited time and/or space for stories, important issues are often oversimplified.[77]

Presidents and their advisors have also long been concerned about, and in some cases obsessed with, how the White House is covered in the press. Presidents, as well as their advisors, have at times directly criticized reporters, editors, and/or publishers for coverage they do not like. For example, Herbert Hoover sent the following message via telegram to Roy Howard of Scripps–Howard Newspapers in 1931 to complain about coverage of Hoover's actions regarding the Great Depression:

> The country deserves an apology from the Washington Bureau of the United Press for an attempt this morning to ascribe personal and partisan politics to the proposal of the United States Govt. of constructive action to this depression and to reestablish social and economic order in the world. I am confident that you as head of that service do not yourself approve such activities by your agents. The day has not yet come when Americans do not arise above partisan and personal politics in the conduct of their national affairs. Every person in the nation has a right to his own views upon the merit of any action of the Government but has no right to imply that the President lacks true patriotism. As you are aware I have sought and received the support equally of leading men of the Democratic and Republican parties who have given their support with no partisan interest but with solely the patriotic interest of the nation and the world as a whole. This support has been given generously and genuinely by every individual on both sides with whom I have been able to come into personal contact. The attempts to defeat an action by the nation by creation of distrust or to arouse factional conflicts behind its government when engaged in an earnest effort to secure cooperation of other nations in a great emergency is not sympathized in by the opposition or any other patriotic group. I hope you will give the matter your own attention and consideration for I am confident of your patriotism and interest.[78]

FDR sent the following memo to his press secretary, Steve Early, about his dismay over a story by United Press International: "This is a UP story. I do not in the least mind the headline but it is interesting to note that the only person quoted (twice) was Senator [Robert] Taft [R-OH]. Loads of other things were said by other Senators and this is therefore a partisan story and not worthy of a press association. It is worthwhile to check up with the UP occasionally in order that they may know they are being watched, if for no other reason."[79] The Truman administration also kept regular track of newspaper columns, editorials, and radio comments about the President and his policies. For example, a January 13, 1947, "Column Summary" compiled by the Executive Office of the President included selected comments from a list of 70 papers "as received" by the White House. The first column summarized came from Walter Winchell of the *New York Mirror*: "Notes statement that Mr. Truman in his radio address had Hooper rating of 20.4 without guest stars, but contends all the President had 'was every front page in the land, every radio column, commentator and White House reporter advertising it and still he couldn't attract as many listeners as other comedians.'"[80]

Monitoring of the press reached an extreme during the Nixon administration. Early in the first term, key White House staffers began work on an extensive system of evaluating the President's coverage. The goal of the "covert" operation was to determine which members of the press were friends of the administration and, more important, which were enemies. Television commentators were always of particular interest to the White House, which wanted to know where coverage fell into one of three categories: "Generally For Us, Generally Objective, or Generally Against Us." Not only was the project high priority and top secret within the White House, but also attempts to gain detailed profiles on television commentators were extensive, including scouring through correspondent's Secret Service files, which were necessary to obtain a White House press pass. As Press Secretary Ronald Ziegler reported to Chief of Staff H. R. Haldeman in November 1969, the project was precarious:

> We have exhaustedly explored ways in which we could obtain this background without the possibility of a leak that we were undertaking such a project. . . . If we were to pursue information such as where these individuals were previously employed, what their general background is, I am very concerned in the light of the Vice President's recent addresses a serious problem could be caused. As we go along we will attempt to compile such information in personal conversations, etc., but this will take some time.[81]

By mid-1970, White House staffers had compiled an extensive list of more than 200 journalists from television, radio, and print and placed each into one of six categories: "Friendly to Administration, Balanced to Favorable, Balanced, Unpredictable, Usually Negative, and Always Hostile." Not surprisingly, those considered leaning more in favor of the administration came from traditionally more conservative publications, such as *U.S. News and World Report, Business Week*, and the *Chicago Tribune*, whereas many of those considered negative or hostile were from traditionally more liberal publications, such as the *New York Times, Washington Post*, and *Boston Globe*.[82] Friendly members of the press, it was often suggested by White House advisors, should be rewarded for their efforts. For example, backgrounders with the President or special invitations or other perks could be given to those reporters providing favorable coverage. According to Haldeman, a good strategy involved attempts "to do more in-depth discussion between friendly members of the press and the President. . . . We need to develop a plan for working with friendly or potentially favorable members of the press, and also for dividing the hostile working press."[83] The monitoring system was even suggested, at one point, to include keeping tabs on television talk shows such as the *Smothers Brothers* on CBS, where Nixon was the frequent butt of jokes, and *The Tonight Show with Johnny Carson* on NBC, since Nixon was often the subject during the opening monologue. The theory was to have supporters write letters to the producers to object to the anti-Nixon comments and to rely on the Federal Communication Commission's Equal Time rule for reply from the White House.[84] According to advisors in the attorney general's office, "If we simply develop an efficient monitoring system, we probably will find something every night that entitles us to time to reply. And soon the negative comments will become rarer and rarer. . . . I would like to see a week's output of anti-administration material—I think it would knock our hats off—and would come from surprising sources, not just from politicians, but entertainment personalities and various kinds of celebrities generally."[85]

In addition, the Nixon administration was the first to institutionalize the use of the daily news summary, which included the "ideas and opinions contained in a cross-section of news reports, editorials, columns, and articles" from more than 50 newspapers, 30 magazines, and the *Associated Press* and *United Press International* wire services.[86] The administration received numerous requests from many sources to receive a copy of the news summary, but all were turned down since the summary was "strictly an internal document prepared for the President and the White House staff."[87] The news summary was described as including a representative sample of columns, editorials, news analyses, and cartoons from newspapers and magazines, all condensed to reflect the "central theme as well as a quote or two to give the flavor of the piece." The goal was to keep Nixon informed of the views and opinions of the nation: "The President is interested not only in comment and reaction to his programs but he also wants to keep abreast of the daily developments which are going on across the nation and affect every citizen—developments which may well be more important to the country than some piece of legislation. By keeping an eye on stories reported in all the media, the President maintains an excellent feel of the nation's pulse."[88]

Since then, the daily news summary has grown into an important informational tool for presidents in the development of their daily communication strategy. A formalized daily news summary has been used in one form or another since the Nixon years, a practice that has been institutionalized within the press and/or communications offices. The news summary circulates among senior staff members so that they can evaluate the president's coverage, both nationally and internationally, and so that the White House can respond accordingly.[89] For example, the George H. W. Bush administration relied on several information sources to keep up with coverage of the President and his policy initiatives, including an extensive daily news summary of major print and broadcast sources, as well as weekly "editorial round-ups" that summarized editorials and op-ed pieces in major newspapers.[90] In addition, coverage of Bush in roughly 30 regional newspapers, including larger regional daily newspapers such as the *Seattle Times, Dallas Morning News, Minneapolis Star Tribune, Phoenix Republic, San Diego Union*, and *Denver Post*, were tracked by staffers in the communications office.[91] By 1991, the Office of Media Relations had developed an extensive tracking system/content analysis of news coverage of presidential events, including which news organizations covered the event, the placement of the story about the event, and whether the coverage was considered favorable or unfavorable.[92]

CONCLUSION

During the 2008 presidential campaign, a common complaint (especially by Republicans) was that the press was "in the tank" for Obama. Yet, Obama had what some called a "surprisingly hostile relationship" with the news media, with little day-to-day interaction with the White House press corps, strong pushback from advisors over certain stories, and Obama himself often making caustic or sarcastic comments about the press.[93] In addition, despite complaints that he was often "overexposed" in media appearances, Obama mostly avoided formal press conferences and provided less access to the press than expected. But, as with some of his predecessors, Obama's communication advisors sought ways for the President to speak more directly with citizens by going around the traditional venue of the White House press corps. For example, during the same week as his appearance on *The View* in 2010, Obama also debuted a video on the new government website healthcare.gov. Often, goodwill with voters is a more important component of the communication strategy than positive press relations: "Mr. Obama got a chance to remind viewers who voted for him why they did so in the first place. A lot of goodwill can be reaped with an appearance on *The View* or ESPN or even WWE Raw."[94]

Because of the current media environment, presidents have an increasingly difficult task in leading the public. Even presidents who are seen as strong communicators, such as Clinton and Obama, have not been immune from the changing media environment and the competitive nature of presidential news coverage. Finding the right balance of major speeches, media appearances, and other public events, as well as crafting an effective press strategy to go along with such events, all while making the president look like a strong and commanding leader, is no easy task for even the most skilled White House communications advisors. Most presidents continue to take advantage of new media technologies and other strategic opportunities to reach out directly to the American public. However, whether presidents are now overexposed in the media-saturated environment in which they attempt to govern remains an ongoing debate, one that is sure to continue throughout the Trump presidency.

CHAPTER 5

The Public Presidency:
Public Opinion

During the 2000 presidential campaign, Texas governor George W. Bush and Vice President Al Gore did not agree on much, but according to their respective acceptance speeches at their party's national conventions, they seemed to be in agreement about one topic: the president and public opinion. Bush told those in attendance at the Republican National Convention on August 3, 2000, "I believe great decisions are made with care, made with conviction, not made with polls. I do not need to take your pulse before I know my own mind." During his address at the Democratic National Convention on August 17, 2000, Gore stated, "But the presidency is more than a popularity contest. It's a day-to-day fight for people. Sometimes you have to choose to do what's difficult or unpopular."

Political scientists have known for decades the importance of public support in the equation of presidential success. Since the late 1980s and early 1990s, in part because of the expansion of news coverage and the creation of the 24-hour news cycle, presidential approval ratings became more volatile through an increasingly critical public as well as divided partisan support within Congress.[1] Many outside factors, including the economy, international events, and the political environment in general, shape how the president's job performance is evaluated. Above-average approval numbers suggest that a president is succeeding in terms of leadership, whereas below-average approval numbers can suggest that the White House is out of step with American voters. A president's approval rating is also one of the best indicators of whether a communication strategy with the American public is working.

Consider Bush, who was elected by the slimmest of margins in the Electoral College and lost the popular vote to Gore in the 2000 election. Bush began his first term with public approval numbers in the mid-50 percent range, mirroring the fact that half the country did not vote for him. Eight months later, following the September 11 terrorist attacks, his public approval reached 90 percent. Those types of approval ratings, which usually occur during times of national crisis, are difficult to maintain. By the time of Bush's reelection in 2004, his approval rating was back to just above 50 percent. His second term, however, eventually saw a dramatic decline in those numbers, as Bush hit a low of 25 percent approval in 2008 (in large part a result of the flagging economy). According to Gallup, Bush enjoyed a first-term approval rating average of 62 percent, yet endured a 37 percent average during his second term. The average approval rating for Bush's entire eight years in office was 49 percent, which is almost the exact percentage of the public who voted for him in 2000.[2] In 2016, Donald Trump, like Bush, won the Electoral College although he lost the popular vote to Hillary Clinton. Whereas Trump enjoyed a larger Electoral College victory margin, he won only 46 percent of the popular vote. However, he did not experience much goodwill from the public (like Bush did in 2001), and his approval rating on taking office in January 2017 sat at a mere 45 percent, the lowest such number for any new president in the history of polling.[3]

Ronald Reagan maintained a strong connection to the American public throughout his eight years in office. Here, he addresses the nation from the Oval Office on the Space Shuttle *Challenger* explosion, January 28, 1986.

Beyond external polling and approval ratings, over which presidents have little control, internal polling has also become an important element of the overall White House governing strategy in an attempt to "lead the public" in support of the president's agenda. Presidents dating back to Richard Nixon have relied on such polls and have been criticized for developing a "permanent campaign" mentality while attempting to govern, with the inference that presidents are too often checking the pulse of the nation through a poll prior to making a policy decision. The attention paid to polling and approval ratings suggests that the president's relationship with the public represents an important element of the contemporary presidency. Although the public does not directly elect the president, the president's relationship with the public emerged almost despite the constitutional design. Without direct representation to dominate the relationship, the president and the public intersect in two distinct mechanisms, not one. The public appears to be a tool for presidential use to pressure Congress to do what the president and the public want. However, through public opinion polls, the public also provides a nearly continuous evaluation of the president's job performance. As a result, the public and public opinion polls are a double-edge sword; they can help the president achieve his goals of legislation and reelection, but can also hurt the president's standing, his opportunities to exercise leadership, his opportunities to carry out his agenda, his goals of reelection, and, ultimately, his legacy.

THE EVOLVING VIEW OF THE PUBLIC

The institution of the presidency has a strange relationship with the public. In the twenty-first century, public commentary on the president seems omnipresent: typing "President Obama" into Google generates roughly 353 million results. Yet, the people do not directly elect the president. The constitution validates the right and relevance of official public commentary, particularly the right to a free press and the right to petition government. Yet, the Constitution intentionally provides no outlet for the masses between elections. In fact, the framers cautioned against attention to public opinion. Alexander Hamilton argued in *Federalist* 71 that "the republican principle demands that the deliberate sense of the community should govern the conduct of those to whom they entrust the management of their affairs; but it does not require an unqualified complaisance to every sudden breeze of passion or to every transient impulse which the people may receive from the arts of men, who flatter their prejudices to betray their interests."[4]

The constitutional design insulates government, in varying degrees, from the public because the framers both granted and checked power. The Constitution grants the public means to demonstrate their views about elected officials and policies but also grants officials the means to ignore the public. Although the framers clearly supported democratic over autocratic principles, they no more trusted the public than they trusted officials with unlimited power. Hamilton, in 1787, claimed, "The voice of the people has been said to be the voice of God. And however generally this maxim has been quoted and believed, it is not true in fact. The people are turbulent and changing; they seldom judge or determine right."[5]

The first two presidents—George Washington and John Adams—were Federalists, and like Hamilton, they were not champions of popular rule or even party rule. The third president, Thomas Jefferson, author of the Declaration of Independence and head of the Democratic-Republicans, appeared to be a supporter of public participation in government decision making. However, Jefferson's writings suggest he did not intend his party to be permanent, but an ad hoc creation to beat back the Federalists' expansive and elitist tendencies.[6] He instead claimed to want to see his party wither in a return to nonpartisan politics. In practice, as president, Jefferson was the first to use the public's support as a rationale for the exercise of presidential power, but he did it through party, rather than mass, politics.

Andrew Jackson forever linked the mass public with the presidency and cemented the justification of presidential behavior in "the will of the people." Jackson's approach, termed by scholars Jacksonian democracy, rests on the idea that the president is the direct representative of the people and the people's "tribune," the only office with a true national identity.[7] Jackson invoked the idea of the presidency as the people's representative first in the statement associated with his unprecedented veto of the 1832 renewal of the Second Bank of the United States. Moreover, the number of people Jackson could claim to serve was larger and more representative of the populace because he was the first president elected under expanded suffrage, which included voting by non–property owners. However, the force of Jackson's popularity and power remained, like Jefferson's, mediated through a political party. It was the party in this era that gained power and spread democracy, not the presidency.[8] The presidents who followed Jackson—Martin Van Buren, William Henry Harrison, John Tyler, James Polk, Zachary Taylor, Millard Fillmore, Franklin Pierce, and James Buchanan—sustained the president as party leader but could not sustain the use of the public as a source of personal presidential power.

Although not typically thought of as advancing democratic principles, Abraham Lincoln's expansion of presidential behavior continued the evolution for the role of the public in the presidency. Lincoln's presidency was consumed by the actions of a wartime president. As a result, most of the discussion of Lincoln's presidential behavior centered on the expansion of unfettered power; however, he rooted his power in the "will of the people." For Lincoln, the expansion of power was only out of necessity, as he argued in a letter to A. G. Hodges, editor of the *Frankfort Commonwealth*, dated April 4, 1864: "I felt that measures otherwise unconstitutional might become lawful by becoming indispensable to the preservation of the Constitution through the preservation of the nation."[9] While asserting the extensive and potentially illegal expansion of presidential authority in times of crisis, Lincoln also recognized the power of the people to control government. In the Gettysburg Address (given at a dedication of the cemetery where 6,000 soldiers were buried), he asserted "that this nation, under God, shall have a new birth freedom—and that government of the people, by the people, for the people, shall not perish from the earth."

By 1860, presidents, newspaper editors, and the people themselves articulated a participatory role for the public in presidential decision making. However, most nineteenth-century presidents were not using the public to justify significant or history-changing decision making like Jefferson, Jackson, and Lincoln. Thus, although the root of the presidency in national representation was growing, few presidents relied on it. By the time expansive-minded presidents returned to the White House in the twentieth century, the public voice in American politics between elections was commonplace. In fact, by 1900, a British journalist claimed, "In no country is public opinion so powerful as in the United States."[10]

EVALUATING THE PRESIDENT

As mass participation grew, so did the view of mass opinion, as opposed to political opinion, which had been elite based. Opinion by the mass public was difficult to quantify, but newspapers tried to do so as part of their political coverage. Initially, newspapers began tracking public views of political figures and events via straw polls (a show of hands or a tally with pen and paper), letters to the editor, and op-ed pieces. The *Harrisburg Pennsylvanian* conducted the first straw poll in 1832 and accurately predicted that Andrew Jackson would claim the presidency over John Quincy Adams and Henry Clay. Straw polls became a regular feature in newspapers' political coverage, not just their election coverage. Straw polls also became an effective circulation gimmick; when people wanted to participate in the mail-in ballots, they also received a special subscription.[11]

Straw polls counted those who participated in the mail-in ballots and thus were not necessarily representative of voting turnout. The 1936 presidential election and the infamous, erroneous prediction of Republican Alf Landon over President Franklin D. Roosevelt by the *Literary Digest* ended the use of straw polls in favor of scientific polling, which accurately predicted the 1936 outcome. The straw polls prior to 1936 had also been off by 10, 12, or as many as 17 points. However, in 1936, they were off by 20 percentage points and, more problematically, they also got

The famous photo of Harry Truman holding the newspaper that incorrectly declared the winner of the 1948 presidential election.

the outcome wrong. Having staked its reputation on the popularity of straw polls, the *Digest* went bankrupt following the debacle. As a result, consistent evaluation and articulation of the mass public's opinion did not occur until the development of the public opinion poll and evidence of its effectiveness. Archibald Crossley, Elmo Roper, and George Gallup were the first pollsters to use the scientific method and sampling to estimate a population to produce more accurate election predictions. Gallup correctly predicted the 1936, 1940, and 1944 presidential races. In the 1948 race, Gallup and the other pollsters incorrectly forecast that Republican Thomas Dewey would beat President Harry Truman, leading to the now infamous newspaper headline in the *Chicago Tribune* on November 2, 1948: "Dewey defeats Truman." After changing its methodology from quota sampling to probability sampling, the commercial polling business became more accurate and gradually became a trusted source for mass opinion information. Roper and Gallup's polling organizations are still in business today and are considered leaders within the industry.

Researching the Presidency

Polling

How accurate are the techniques used to gather our opinions, and can they be trusted? Polling deserves to be looked at critically considering how much meaning it is granted at times. At the mathematical heart of survey analysis is the population versus the sample. A population can be anything: all U.S. adults, Democrats likely to vote in Colorado, female chief executive officers, or juniors at a university. The sample is the subset of the population who are asked the poll questions. Polls use random probability sampling, which means that each person in the population has the same chance of being selected.

Here is a recent example of polling conducted on a policy issue during the 2016 presidential campaign. Start with a typical population such as eligible voters who are 18 and older and ask whether they favor or oppose building a wall between the United States and Mexico. The response includes 38 percent who say yes, 58 percent who say no, and 4 percent who don't know or refused to answer. If there are approximately 250 million eligible voters, then 95 million are in support, although all 250 million people were not asked the question. How, then, does a pollster reach this conclusion? In March 2016, the Pew Research Center used the results from 2,254 sampled eligible voters and inferred results about the population after learning that 857 (38 percent) supported building the wall, whereas 1,307 (58 percent) opposed it.

This inference can be made because of the confidence level and the reliance on the margin of error. The conventional confidence level in most polls is 95 percent, meaning that there is 95 percent confidence that the error, samples, and results are correct. The margin of error is the mathematical amount that may be wrong since a small sample is being used to estimate a preference among a large population. Using 2,254 voters, the margin of error is plus or minus three percent, meaning instead of being certain that exactly 58 percent are against the wall, that number can range between 55 and 61 percent. Using 2,254 people to infer something about millions cannot predict total accuracy, yet there is still high confidence in the accuracy because the separation between 38 and 58 is outside the margin of error. If results fall within the sampling error, then a prediction cannot be made with any certainty. This is what happened in the 2000 presidential race, where neither Bush nor Gore ever led in the polls outside the margin of error. But can we trust that what 1,000–2,500 people say is a reflection of what 250 million eligible voters think?

Conventional wisdom over the years has suggested that polling can be an accurate reflection of political preferences among the American public. In addition, that same conventional wisdom suggests that presidents pursue policy agendas in the interests of the American public. New research, however, suggests that previous research on policy responsiveness among presidents—that presidents, as part of a governing elite, serve the national interests—is perhaps wrong. In their book *Who Governs? Presidents, Public Opinion, and Manipulation*, James N. Druckman and Lawrence R. Jacobs argue that instead of pursing a policy agenda that represents the priorities of the American public, presidents instead prime the public to focus on personality over issues, shaping and often misleading the public to instead pursue a narrow agenda that benefits the president's core supporters: "In reality, the White House employs tactics and broader strategies toward politics and communications that are routinely geared to shaping public opinion to advance its interests and those of its narrow group of supporters."[12] Perhaps the reliability and accuracy of polls is not the biggest concern when considering the roll of public opinion within governing. Instead, the fact that presidents may manipulate public opinion to their own advantage rather than rely on polling to tell them how to govern is more important to consider.

Job Approval

Regular tracking of the public's view of the president and his job performance began with the Truman administration and the Gallup poll organization. On April 12, 1945, 88 percent of those polled approved of the job Truman was doing.[13] The Pew Research Center has been querying the public since 1992 by asking, "Do you approve of how <insert presidential name here> is handling his job of president?"

The public has not been consistently kind to presidents, at least according to their approval ratings. As Figure 5.1 shows, Barack Obama began his presidency with ratings in the high 60s and ended his presidency with 58 percent approval, hitting a low of 41 percent along the way. Truman began his tenure as president and the era of presidential approval watching under less than ideal circumstances; having only been vice president for three months prior to FDR's death in April 1945 left him at a distinct disadvantage regarding his relationship with the American public. As the junior senator from Missouri when selected as FDR's third vice presidential running mate in 1944, Truman had to forge a personal relationship with Americans during the waning months of World War II as they mourned the loss of their longest-serving president. Approval ratings for Truman stayed strong throughout the fall of 1945, as a letter to the President from Frank Stanton, vice president and general manager of CBS, showed:

> Our Surveys Division has today completed a confidential analysis of U.S. public opinion in which I believe you will be interested personally. The findings are based on face-to-face interviews with representative cross sections of the adult population of the country, conducted in early August and mid-September. The

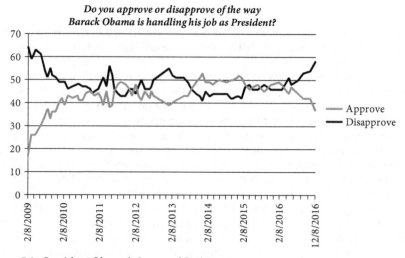

Figure 5.1. President Obama's Approval Rating
Source: Pew Research Center

question asked in both surveys was: "Taking everything into consideration, what sort of job do you feel Truman is doing as President—Excellent, Good, Fair, or Poor?" IN SUMMARY, these two soundings of public opinion indicate: 1. Virtually nine in every ten persons throughout the United States think you are doing an "excellent or good" job as President. 2. Approval of the job you are doing as President has taken a strong upward swing since August. (This continues the trend established by other surveys made in April and August.) 3. What slight criticism exists today seems to be chiefly in terms of anxiety about the future; with the handling of the problems of unemployment and wages constituting the chief worry.[14]

By 1946, the political winds had shifted dramatically for the Truman administration, as this memo among White House advisors shows:

One of my very close friends is the right-hand man of Gallup. I talked to him on the phone this morning because I had heard some disquieting news about Gallup's next report. He checked and called me back to confirm the following: Gallup's report will indicate that never since they have been taking polls has there been such a swing away from the Administration as has been taking place the past six weeks. In their opinion the Senate and House will both go Republican. The questions asked that indicate this trend were regarding housing, Wallace, strikes, government expenses, Russia, and cost of living. I think there is still time to do something dramatic to not only stop the trend but reverse it.[15]

The Truman White House, however, did not have any luck in reversing the trend of public opinion during the fall of 1946, as Republicans won both houses of Congress for the first time since 1928, picking up 55 seats in the House of Representatives and 12 in the Senate.

Maintaining high approval ratings for any president is no easy task. As Figure 5.2 shows, of the 12 presidents Gallup tracked since 1945, only seven averaged approval ratings above 50 percent. Only Dwight Eisenhower, John F. Kennedy, and

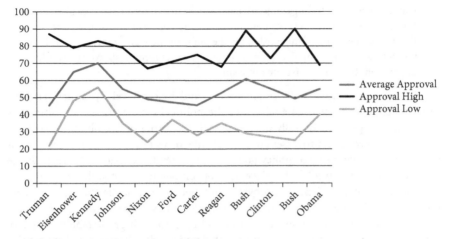

Figure 5.2. Average Presidential Approval
Source: Gallup Presidential Approval Data

George H. W. Bush averaged above 60 percent across their entire time in office. The average high rating was 77.5 percent, although three presidents never made it out of the 60 percent range: Richard Nixon, Ronald Reagan, and Barack Obama. Both wartime presidents, George H. W. Bush, and George W. Bush had very high approval but also very low approval. George H. W. Bush received an 89 percent approval rating and also a 29 percent; his son, George W., received a high of 90 percent and a low of only 25 percent of the nation approving his performance as president.

Where do these fluctuations come from, what produces the approval rating, and what changes attitudes toward the same president? As discussed in Chapter 4, the public learns about the president via mass media. However, individuals filter this information about the president through their own experiences and attitudes. In addition, the environment or the context in which citizens judge a president matters. Presidents are also judged, albeit at times unfairly, on a wide range of issues over which they rarely have control. For example, advisors to Lyndon Johnson became concerned in 1966 that because the president had become so visible to the American public as being in charge of the federal government, his approval ratings were suffering. According to a memo from advisor Tom Johnson to the President,

> It is my view that you have become so closely associated with all the major issues which face this country that you are suffering from it. The people do not hold the Secretary of Commerce or the Budget Director responsible when fiscal policies displease them. They hold you responsible. The people do not condemn the Secretary of the Treasury for tight money and high interest rates. They condemn you. When labor negotiations break down in major industries, the people hold the President responsible; not the Secretary of Labor, not management, not the unions. The same is true on the Defense front. When the war appears to be going badly, it is not the Secretary of Defense or the Joint Chiefs who catch the heat. It is again the President. Much of this is because the President has been encouraged to speak and comment publicly on all these problems. When there are civil riots and civil disobedience, the press expects you to become immediately involved and to produce a satisfactory solution. Often I believe a better course would be to have

your decisions and feelings on particular matters voiced through the Cabinet and through the agency heads who are most directly concerned with the issue. Let them shoulder more of the burden for the faults of their programs. Rather than the President losing popularity for weaknesses, it seems more appropriate for the department head to receive the criticism.[16]

Scholars contend that there are micro- and macro-level dynamics resulting from systemic and personal analyses of the political environment that ultimately drive the willingness of an individual to state they approve of the job the president is doing. The micro-level processes cover what citizens want from the president: "competence in achieving shared policy goals. . . . [and for] the president to be in charge and seem to be in charge."[17] The perception of competence is what they consider the driving factor in presidential approval. Ultimately, "most of the time a president's popularity is the predictable function of some simple variables, time, the economy and important presidential events."[18] Interestingly, no such predictability seems to exist when it comes to approval of presidential policy, what is considered approval at the macro level. In addition, a president's effectiveness at defining his or her "political reality" may be "contingent, at least in part, on structure and timing."[19]

A significant portion of these "important individual events" can include the "rally around the flag effect"; approval ratings increase in response to foreign events or crises. In contrast to the economy or other domestic issues, approval ratings rise in response to the existence of foreign events or crises but not necessarily the president's handling of them; this is termed the "rally around the flag" effect because of the peculiar oddity of signaling approval when a tragedy occurs. On September 14, 2001, 90 percent of the public was not saying "great job handling terrorism, President Bush;" instead, the public signaled its support for the president *to do a great job handling terrorism*. The approval rating then becomes a show of support for the president and the country rather than a true evaluation of prior actions. Not surprisingly, these figures go down precipitously; Bush sustained ratings over 80 percent for only six months.[20] Between March 2002 and March 2003, Bush's ratings continued to decline, to 57 percent approval, in reaction not to crisis but to his crisis response. After the first six months, the approval rating returned to reflect what it normally demonstrates: job performance. Bush's approval rating then predictably jumped from 57 percent at the beginning of March 2003 to 71 percent at the end of March 2003 in response to the beginning of the war in Iraq. However, this rally effect was even shorter as the war in Afghanistan reflected broad-based support among all Americans for both the policy and Bush's handling of it, as support for the war in Iraq quickly defaulted to partisan support as Independents and Democrats significantly declined in support over time as "support for the war and approval of the president declined in tight parallel."[21]

Personal Approval

Instinctively, individuals form judgments about people based on intuitive opinion formation by simply looking at them, whereas deeper determinations are made by listening to them initially and over time. Judgments about the president follow similar patterns; citizens form impressions from their first moment of introduction to the president, from their former public roles, or during the campaign or once the oath of office is taken. Those reactions have nothing to do with the president's performance and everything to do with his likability or his personal, rather than job-related, approval.

Job approval refers to the job of being president; personal approval refers to that hard-to-define "it" factor. The question pollsters ask is, "Do you have a favorable view of President Obama as a person?" By asking the personal question, pollsters try to distinguish views of skill from views of personality. Traditionally, personal views and job performance views were related. If you liked the job the president was doing, you probably liked the president personally and vice versa. Interestingly, Gallup finds that some people can view the president favorably while negatively viewing his performance. Personal favorability ratings are typically higher than approval ratings, although that trend has shifted somewhat in recent years. The eight presidents who served prior to 1992 all averaged favorability ratings above 70 percent while in office. The favorability ratings of the three presidents serving after 1992 look considerably different than that of their predecessors. Their favorability ratings are much lower, and Clinton's and Obama's ratings are almost equivalent to their job approval.

POPULARITY AS A SOURCE OF PRESIDENTIAL POWER

As discussed earlier, the creation of public opinion polls derived from the media desire to predict the outcome of elections. However, the utility of the approval rating quickly moved beyond immediate predicting of elections to long-term forecasting. To use another weather metaphor, the approval-rating question became a barometer for reelection. The presidential approval rating prior to Election Day is considered an excellent predictor of presidential reelection.[22] From this perspective, presidents would work to raise their approval rating to achieve reelection. The ability of the public to evaluate the president between elections can hold the president accountable in the absence of voting. However, the continuous monitoring of presidential job performance injects the public into the political sphere in a manner unintended and unanticipated by the framers' constitutional design. For the framers, the public's opinions mattered only as a single up-or-down vote. In contrast, the modern presidency receives a continuous flow of "votes," producing a tracked measure. The presence of the public's opinions in this constant manner gives power to those opinions in a way that did not previously exist.

Initially, scholars viewed the public as a means to soften up the true avenues to presidential power. In his classic work *Presidential Power*, Richard Neustadt considered the public an indirect resource providing a generic and limited source of power and authority. Neustadt essentially accepted the constitutional role for the public while simultaneously acknowledging the presence of public opinion polling. Mass opinion was important because elites pay attention to it; the public's view of the president matters only because elites anticipate public reaction to the president. It is this anticipation that factors into presidential efforts to persuade elites and, for Neustadt, persuasion *is* presidential power. In contrast, in *Presidential Leadership of Public Opinion*, Elmer Cornwell argued that the presence of public opinion polls as well as a national media intensely interested in the president offers the president a more significant source of presidential power than articulated by Neustadt.[23] Cornwell argued that with few constitutional tools to influence the course of policy and events, "the President can and does and probably should shape popular attitudes, and not just respond to them passively."[24] Cornwell implicitly rejected the idea that approval of the president is an independent evaluation of the president, tangentially related to the system. Thus, Cornwell began the critical analysis for understanding the relationship between the president and the public that emerges from the technological ability to ask the public what they think. Neustadt and Cornwell are not in opposition to each other because Neustadt supports the relevance of the public; they differ over the immediacy of the effect. Put another way, do producers and directors make movies for the critics or for the movie-going public, and does that audience influence the critics and/or the moviemakers? Are presidents simply accepting of the public's perception of their behavior or are they actively courting public support to achieve their goals?

Presidents, as strategic actors, do not accept a passive role in public evaluations of their efforts. In fact, the ability to measure approval ratings produced a dependence on the polls.[25] This dependence is viewed as a follower presidency—presidents respond with action to the fluctuations in their ratings. The preeminent presidential goal then is not reelection, a legacy, or good public policy, but to achieve high approval ratings, because the ratings influence everything else.[26] In particular, presidents choose their leadership strategies focused on policies the public already likes.[27]

The approval rating appeared most significant as a source of power for the president to achieve his legislative program, what Samuel Kernell termed "going public." As discussed in earlier chapters, when going public, presidents present their policy desires to the public to influence Congress.[28] Neustadt claimed public opinion influences the environment for bargaining, since a popular president will have more leverage to bargain with members of Congress. In contrast, Kernell argued that public support preempts bargaining and forces congressional compliance,[29] contending that the need for members of Congress to be reelected forces acceptance of a popular president's desires. Thus, the popularity rating is not simply a barometer for reelection but also a source of significant power, or pressure, to achieve legislative success. A popular president, in Kernell's theory, is usually a legislatively successful president.

As a theory, going public makes great intuitive sense; people like the president and his performance, they want what the president wants, and so Congress responds. Unfortunately, for the president, the process is not that easy. For the president to *use* his approval rating, and not just be victim to its fluctuations, the president must be able to influence the rating. But, to influence presidential approval, the president must communicate and the public must be receptive or at least attentive to the communication. If a tree falls in the forest and no one hears it, did it fall? Similarly, if a president speaks and no one listens, does anything happen?

It was easy to determine how many people heard the president say something when television was in its infancy and there were only three national networks. All researchers had to do was track television usage; if it was on, then people were watching the president. With the introduction of other media outlets, it became harder for the president to capture an audience but also harder for researchers to determine how many people heard what the president said.[30] On June 16, 2010, Obama gave a prime-time address to the nation from the Oval Office (his first in this venue). According to the Nielsen Television Ratings, 32 million people watched it live on television. Looking up the speech on YouTube reveals that 165,000 people watched a replay of the speech. On Twitter, there were 83,000 tweets referencing the speech.[31] Although 32 million viewers may seem like a large number, Obama's 2009 inaugural address better demonstrates how many more people can watch the president: 38 million watched on television and 70 million streamed it live online, meaning that at least 108 million watched Obama's inauguration in comparison to the 32 million who watched his address in response to the Gulf oil spill.

Watching the president, however, is only part of the equation. The president also needs his approval ratings to improve from the attention. Obama's approval rating did improve after his Oval Office address in June 2010, from 40 percent to 44 percent (although a majority still disapproved of his handling of the crisis).[32] If the president must improve his approval rating to achieve success, being unable to improve his rating, either because the nation was not listening or because the people do not agree, is problematic.[33] Even when citizens do not hear the president directly, they still might hear about his job performance from the media. However, the media are unlikely to significantly bolster a president's approval rating. As discussed in Chapter 4, the media no longer serve as a neutral transmitter of presidential performance.[34] In the twenty-first century, media organizations are neither friendly nor dependent, nor do they let the White House dominate news about the president. Instead, "talking heads" or pundits set the tone and tenor of debate, and that tone and tenor rarely improve a president's approval rating.[35]

The more significant component of using the approval rating as a source of power is the part farthest outside the president's control: the actions of Congress. For the approval rating to be a source of presidential power, Congress must be responsive to it. Unfortunately for the president, this rarely occurs, because Congress is only mildly responsive to approval ratings.[36] Research has shown that presidential popularity influences congressional voting only "at the margins," whereas more traditional congressional explanations for voting behavior dominate (e.g., constituency demands, leadership demands, party demands).[37] In addition, high levels of approval reduce the likelihood of a president achieving a particular policy item.[38] Congress is attentive to the president's agenda as a list of priorities but not as specific calls to action.[39] The president's approval rating does have an effect on congressional elections; low ratings of the president generally signal poor reelection rates for members of his party. However, for voting decisions, the threat from the presidential approval rating appears to dissipate. The approval rating is a national measure and, as a result, is of lesser meaning to individual members of Congress.[40]

Even presidents who work with a Congress controlled by his or her own party can suffer in terms of public opinion because both the executive and legislative branches of government, even under united party control, can pursue different policy priorities. A case in point is Jimmy Carter's frustration working with a Democratic Congress during his four years in office, which his advisors claimed hurt his approval rating with the American public. According to Stu Eizenstat, Carter's chief domestic policy advisor, in a memo to the President,

> After conversations with [White House pollster] Pat Caddell and a number of other people, I am convinced that your rating in the public opinion polls is increasingly a function of your relations with Congress and their capacity to pass legislation. While that is to some extent inevitable, your Presidency risks

being measured just by legislative accomplishments. I believe that is dangerous because Congress, in my estimation, has become increasingly unwilling to tackle the tough, substantive issues we have presented and will continue to present throughout your Administration. I think that it is therefore critical that we attempt, to define as much as possible your success as President in non-legislative terms while, of course, continuing to pursue our legislative program with all our resources. (Our legislative record is in fact much better than we have received credit for, and we need to continue to publicize those accomplishments.).[41]

IN THEIR OWN WORDS

PRESIDENTIAL IMAGE AND PUBLIC OPINION

Perhaps no president during the modern era struggled with his public image more than Jimmy Carter. Although his image as an outsider who would clean up the mess in Washington following the Watergate scandal helped propel him to victory in 1976, Carter often struggled with projecting a strong image of leadership once in the White House. Five months prior to his now-famous "malaise" speech, where he spoke to the American public about the "crisis of confidence" in the American government, Carter advisors were hard at work analyzing the president's public image, as well as his prospects for governing and reelection in 1980. In a memo to his White House colleagues, advisor Alan Raymond discussed the "state of the presidency":

Although I am a believer in the cyclical theory of public and media opinion, I also think there's only so far down you can go and still have things swing back your way—or at least swing back far enough. I assume that time and circumstances will lead to a recovery in the second half of this year. My concern is that a large residue of negative feeling and doubt is being built up—around specific issues and around the question of leadership—which may go away temporarily, but which can resurface at the slightest provocation and which is likely, a la Murphy's law, to resurface at the worst possible time.

I don't subscribe to the idea that the President will be judged next year by some vague rating of how well he's done overall. Rather, I think he will be judged in specific areas and on specific issues, and if people think he's not doing *enough*, they'll turn to someone else. People have gotten used to changing Presidents; they have far less respect for the presidency as an institution post-Nixon; and they still see Jimmy Carter as an unknown.

A policy of trying to build support through a general appeal rather than constituency group appeal is risky—because of the lack of excitement in his analytical, rational, structural reform approach to government; and because it guarantees that you'll make some real enemies along the way. We need to be making strong friends—in the media and the electorate—at the same time, and I don't get the feeling we're doing that. With voter apathy and cynicism as high as it is, we have to counter-act "anti-Carter" sentiment *and* give people a reason to *want* to vote our way.

Carving out the middle of the electorate may sound like a fairly safe course for building support, but I don't think it holds up to close scrutiny. I would argue that there are three major categories of voting blocks. First, all voters—the most important group, but one which can't be easily broken down ideologically when it comes to voting. Next, those who consider themselves in constituency groups—including liberal or conservative—and may vote as such. And third, the growing number of people who have intense feelings about a special interest or issue and will vote on the basis of that issue alone. . . .

In the simplest terms, we need to maximize the appeal to all voters, win over some constituency groups, and neutralize the single issue groups. There are areas of weakness, and there are areas that are largely out of our control. But the overriding message to me is that we have to move quickly and dramatically, to reverse the factors we have working against us. I would much rather have the President seen as "fighting for his political life" (which implies that he is facing up to his problems), than have him seen as assuming he will be judged favorably on his overall performance (which implies that he is willing to be the "lesser of two evils").

The overriding problem with the Carter Presidency at this moment is one of leadership, and it is certainly the issue opponents will focus on in the months ahead. It is a volatile issue, one that can seem to change overnight with a single, dramatic event such as Camp David. But I would argue that the public and media perception of leadership is influenced by a variety of factors . . .

While there's no question in my mind that the Washington media elite has overreacted to recent events, there's also no question in my mind that there's little enthusiasm for Jimmy Carter among the public. People don't see him as a strong leader and they don't know what he stands for. Unless we reverse that feeling fairly quickly and dramatically, we'll be going into 1980 with a tremendous handicap; vulnerable not only to true public opinion, but to the "political opinion" that the media will spend all its time writing about as they try to make a race out of it.[42]

PRESIDENTIAL POLLING AS A SOURCE OF POWER

To this point, the public's voice appears to be represented only by the approval rating. Although the approval rating is a virtually continuous measure of the public's opinion of the president, the question itself results in only a limited picture of what the public thinks and does not explain *why* the respondent approves or disapproves. When citizens evaluate the job performance of members of Congress, they first focus on congressional voting. The president does not vote; instead, to quote George W. Bush, the president is the "decider." The approval rating evaluates how well citizens think the president decided, managed, and governed and is almost entirely retrospective, which means that approval rests on the perception of what has already occurred. If presidents want to use public opinion strategically and gain an advantage from public opinion polls, they must know something about it that no one else knows. They also must be able to apply that knowledge to future presidential behavior, such as supporting policy or making a speech.

Since the days of FDR's presidency, presidents and their staffs understood that the ability to ask the public questions privately allows presidents to use the answers to their advantage. FDR was the first president to bring public opinion polling into the White House and he did it for something extremely important—decisions about World War II. He recognized that he needed to know how the public felt about potential choices regarding the war if he wanted to change their minds. Polls became FDR's weapon of choice "to defeat the spreading isolationist sentiment."[43] Choices to counter Americans' desire to stay out of the war, like the "lend–lease" program that lent war materials to Britain, appeared to the press and members of Congress divinely inspired because they were widely supported. In August 1940, FDR's press secretary, Steve Early, was keeping the President informed of public opinion on the issue: "Eugene Meyer of the *Washington Post* just telephoned me from his home in Mt. Kisco, New York, asking that I advise you confidentially. The Gallup Poll to be published next Sunday will show that 62 percent of the voters favor letting Great Britain have American destroyers; that 30 percent are in opposition and 8 percent are indifferent or have no opinion."[44] In fact, by the time FDR went public with lend–lease, he already knew, because of polling data no one else had, that the public supported it.[45] According to a memo from pollster Hadley Cantril,

> Mrs. Anna Rosenberg [FDR's advisor] thought you might like to have on hand some of the findings of my public opinion research . . . I shall be delighted to keep this information up to date for you if you tell Mrs. Rosenberg to whom I should send new material. I shall be glad to make the facilities available to you at any time. We can get confidential information on questions you suggest, follow up any hunch you may care to see tested regarding the determinants of opinion, and provide you with the answers to any questions ever asked by the Gallup or Fortune polls. . . . The Gallup poll particularly has accumulated a vast amount of information that has never been published.[46]

FDR's White House gathered public opinion in secret for two important reasons: first, to minimize "curiosity and preserve the informality of our relationships";[47] and second, they were afraid of appearing to be unable to lead or dependent on public opinion, particularly in times of crisis.

FDR's immediate successor, Harry Truman, was not as enamored of polls; in fact, he questioned their accuracy. Truman, in his memoirs, claimed that polls

> did not represent a true cross section of American opinion . . . I did not believe that the major components of our society, such as agriculture, management and labor, were adequately sampled. I also know that the polls did not represent facts but mere speculation, and I have always placed faith in the known facts. . . . A man who is influenced by the polls or is afraid to make decisions which may make him unpopular is not a man to represent the welfare of the country.[48]

Truman's negative view of polling can be traced to earlier polling debacles, such as the *Literary Digest*'s mistakes in the 1936 presidential race or the inaccurate prediction in Truman's reelection campaign in 1948. Moreover, he was not wrong in his view of sampling problems. In the "Dewey defeats Truman" poll result, the pollsters used the telephone to gather data for the first time. The methodological problem stemmed from the fact that in 1948, few households owned telephones and those that did were three times more likely to vote Republican than Democrat. Non–telephone owners turned out and voted for Truman but were not represented in the sample.

The Eisenhower administration was not antipolling like Truman's, but it is not clear whether Eisenhower himself was interested in or supportive of polling. Like the FDR administration, the Eisenhower White House polled the public about military intervention, particularly on China. The administration wanted to know, for example, whether the public would favor driving the communists out of all of Korea if it meant: (a) a draft, (b) price and wage controls, (c) fighting alone, (d) an increase in killed and wounded, or (e) a full-scale war with China on mainland China.[49] Knowing what option the public would or would not tolerate gives the president boundaries for acceptable action. This is not to say that a president would never recommend a draft because 85 percent of the public disapproved, but rather that it would not be his first, second, or even third choice. Polls used this way are sources of representation and accountability. When the majority does not want something in a representative democracy, it does not mean that it never happens, but it does mean that public officials must weigh the political costs of doing something the public does not like. In some ways, this is exactly what the framers intended.

The Kennedy and Johnson administrations polled more frequently than their predecessors did, primarily for elections, but also for governing and policy decisions.[50] They also followed the trend of their predecessors by monitoring public opinion on key issues. For example, the Kennedy administration began pushing for tax revision legislation as early as 1961. In October 1962, Kennedy signed into law the Revenue Act of 1962, which included various tax reforms, as well as a tax break for businesses; the President had also been considering a personal income tax cut. Mindful of the fact that debt and deficit spending, even with a tax cut, were not popular with the American public, White House advisors kept a close eye on public opinion regarding tax cuts during 1962, as this memo shows:

> We have just learned that the latest Gallup Poll shows heavy popular opposition to tax reduction. The results will appear in tomorrow's newspapers. The question was somewhat loaded, assuming a tax cut meant "the government went further into debt." But the results were lopsided: For tax reduction—19 percent; Against tax reduction—72 percent; No opinion—9 percent. Favoring a tax cut were 15 percent of Republicans, 18 percent of Democrats, and 26 percent of Independents. When asked whether they considered their present income tax payments "about right" or "too high," respondents split about evenly. But only 31 percent of the group that considered their tax burden too large favor tax reduction.[51]

Both the Kennedy and the Johnson administrations also had strong relationships with pollsters, which emerged out of their presidential campaigns. As discussed in Chapter 3, public opinion polling forms the foundation of any presidential campaign effort. Chapter 8 will discuss the influence of campaign staffers in the executive branch, but here it is important to note that campaign pollsters often make the transition from the campaign to governing. Kennedy began this practice by continuing to request information from Lou Harris, his campaign pollster. Lyndon Johnson had a similar relationship with his pollster, Oliver Quayle. Once in office, Harris and Quayle, who also ran commercial polling operations, would piggyback specific presidential questions onto commercial polls, saving the administration money and maintaining secrecy.[52]

As presidents and their staffs sought more public opinion data, the effort to gather the public information specifically about presidential issues lost secrecy, cost more, and became a part of the institution of the presidency. The modern use of presidential polling began in the Nixon administration.[53] In the administrations that followed Nixon (Ford through Obama), all devoted substantial time, money, and attention to building, using, and institutionalizing White House public opinion polling.[54] There is a problem, however, with making polling part of the White House operation: it is illegal. The Hatch Act of 1939 prohibits all federal employees, except the president and the vice president, from engaging in "political activity" on the job. Public opinion polling is clearly a political activity. There is an exception for members of the Executive Office of the President:

> Employees paid from an appropriation for the Executive Office of the President and employees appointed by the President, by and with the advice and consent of the Senate, . . . may engage in political activity while on duty; in any government room or building; while wearing a uniform or official insignia; and while using a government vehicle, if the costs associated with the political activity are not paid for by money derived from the Treasury of the United States.[55]

Therefore, for the White House to consistently and continuously ask the public a range of questions to apply the answers to the presidential goals of reelection and legislation, the president's party pays for it.

Bringing polls publicly into the White House did not change the tightrope presidents walk regarding attention to public opinion. Once presidents began to purchase polls for regular use, fears about discovery concerned the White House, as documents from numerous presidential libraries show. As Nixon's chief of staff H. R. Haldeman once noted, "P [Nixon] called tonight very upset by column quoting [Communications Director Herbert] Klein, that we'll be relying heavily on polls. The problem is always with us. P most anxious to avoid any appearance of being like LBJ."[56] Similarly, a staffer for Gerald Ford wrote, "I think you should not make any direct reference to a private poll (like LBJ) but simply use these things to strengthen your own personal convictions that the American people support you (when they do) in your policy positions."[57] The pollsters were also cagey when trying to describe their influence on the president without challenging his role as a leader. According to Richard Wirthlin, a pollster for Nixon, Reagan, and George H. W. Bush, "The work we do may occasionally focus discussion in the White House on one topic or another. But it wouldn't be fair to typify what I do as getting involved in policy formation."[58] Similarly, Patrick Caddell, Jimmy Carter's pollster, wrote, "I don't think anybody can run a government, particularly the executive branch, by trying to rely on public opinion. That attempts to substitute followership for leadership."[59] George W. Bush's pollsters were even more cryptic regarding what they did for the President because they never said anything publicly. In contrast, Obama, not just his staff, openly acknowledged the importance of opinion polling. In 2013, in an interview with ABC's Diane Sawyer on airstrikes in Syria, the President said,

> Strikes may be less effective if I don't have congressional support and if the American people don't recognize why we're doing this. So I haven't made a final

determination in terms of what next steps would be. My hope would be that I can persuade Congress that this is important. My hope is that I can persuade some of the American people that this is important. But ultimately I understand why a lot of Americans are resistant. I think the polls are clear. I read them. This is not Iraq. This is not Afghanistan. This is not Libya. The goal would be to degrade the capacity of Assad to carry out the specific chemical weapons attacks.[60]

Using White House Polls

Political science analysis of the presidency is often like building a puzzle. The first piece to the puzzle of understanding how presidents use public opinion and for what end is the amount of money spent; presidents spent a lot of money on polling the public, so it must be significant. The second piece is that all administrations, regardless of party or context, were attentive to public opinion. The third piece of the puzzle is how presidents use public opinion. Presidents and their staffs, since 1969, use public opinion polls to help the president do his job and keep his job. Presidents paid for private polls to design the questions asked of the public. Designing the questions enabled the president to test rhetoric, to test policy proposals, and to monitor and track their electoral coalition.[61]

Tracking the Constituency

Presidents enter office having spent the previous year (or longer) campaigning. Most of the campaign polling operation focuses on who is ahead, in which states, and by how much. However, the campaign polling operation also explores *why* a candidate is ahead. A successful candidate must know what drives his supporters, as well as why others are not on board. If the public is a source of strength for the president, then the base of his strength comes from his strongest supporters from the campaign. The president needs those people to support his programs and, ultimately, he needs those people come reelection time. Therefore, the White House needs a mechanism that will reveal whether the president is, at a minimum, keeping his coalition together or, better still, how to expand it. A president whose coalition abandons him is not a second-term president.

At a basic level, a president's electoral coalition consists of members of the president's party, independents, and those few, if any, members of the opposition party who decided to vote for the president. However, individuals are more than simply their party identification; other classifications can be equally meaningful. Traditional descriptors include party, age, region, race, gender, and labor. The beauty of public opinion polling is that you can inquire into all levels of classification to determine who is with you, who is against you, and why. As polling became more sophisticated, so, too, did the ability to get significant results from micro-level analyses. The liberal–conservative spectrum or the urban–suburban–rural divide became frequent assessments. All of these classifications were legitimate groups of people that, if they were all standing in the same place, could be sorted, for example, all people who live in the suburbs over there, urbanites over here.

Identifying patterns in polling data lead pollsters and the White House to create shorthand terminology. For example, the term "Silent Majority" was coined by the Nixon administration to describe those individuals *not* protesting the Vietnam War. The Nixon White House used the polls to classify people by their attitudes about the war. Nixon advisors believed that although the protestors were getting substantial media coverage, in reality there were more people who supported Nixon and his view of how to handle the war. In 1969, a Nixon White House memo described the "Silent Majority" in detail:

> The vast majority of Americans have deep-rooted and sound moral values. They need reassuring that they are not alone and want leaders who also share such values. Of late the emphasis has been so repeatedly placed on other areas that people are questioning the present strength, if not very existence, of this majority. There are thousands of courageous and thoughtful young men in our Armed Forces who dramatically outnumber the draft card burners and flag desecrators. There are thousands of conscientious and dedicated students serving the communities near their campuses who drastically outnumber members of the SDS and others bent on destroying their universities. There have been thousands of young Americans enthusiastically and constructively involved in the mainstream of political life in the past two years who far outnumber the attention-getting and destructive contingent doing so much to provoke present campus turmoil. There are thousands of black Americans working tirelessly and confidently in the private and public sectors throughout the country to accelerate, through legal means, the opportunities black Americans so surely deserve who outnumber the black Americans advocating revolution and destruction. We need to be reminded who, where and how substantial this majority is. Its members constitute the mainstream of American life. Theirs is the spirit and the perspective that continues to attract foreigners to this land. This is the majority that will constructively meet the challenges of today's and tomorrow's problems. It is, as it always has been, the source of our country's greatest hope and pride.[62]

It was not unusual for a White House to consider these individual's views; however, what was unusual was arguing that these attitudes bound these individuals together into a group. Soccer moms or NASCAR dads have also been popular identifiers of invented descriptions to classify attitudes in recent years. The Reagan White House took constituency monitoring further by classifying group identifiers by strength of commitment to the President. Strong supporters, mixed supporters, and low support defined the "core and periphery" of both American society and Reagan's reliable base of support.[63] George H. W. Bush's White House focused on what they termed "base groups" and "target groups," meaning the ones the President had in his corner and the ones that he wanted to add. According to a memo sent between senior staffers, Bush's political base groups were Republican conservatives, Republican officeholders, and Bush supporters, whereas the target groups were conservative Democrats.[64] Similar base versus target comparisons were made for "ethnic and demographic, geographic, and issue oriented" groups.

The rationale for the constituency tracking is to tie current political decisions to reelection. Two recent presidents' problematic electoral constituencies reveal the strategic component of constituency tracking. Nixon appointed Gerald Ford to the vice presidency after his first vice president, Spiro Agnew, resigned because of scandal. When Nixon resigned as a result of the Watergate scandal less than a year later, on August 8, 1974, Ford became the nation's 38th president. Ford took office without ever running on a presidential ticket and, as a result, he had no independent electoral constituency that was based on support for him and/or his policies. Hence, the Ford White House polled incessantly as staffers tried the unenviable task of constructing a Ford constituency without losing whatever was left of Nixon's. To have something to track, the pollsters created a baseline of what they thought the constituency should be and tracked from there.[65] Without an election, the pollsters found that there was no Ford constituency; there was only a generic Republican president constituency. Because of that, Ford also suffered in the ability to present a vision or philosophy of governing to the American public, as advisors lamented during the 1976 campaign: "The basic problem with the Ford Administration, the reason I think the President has such a weak base of support, is that people do not perceive him as having a sense of purpose, a vision for the future of the United States. Although we frequently have the pieces right, there is no sense of an overall whole, no umbrella under which those pieces fit, no 'New Deal,' 'New Frontier,' 'Great Society.' It is essential that we have such a philosophy. It need not be the overblown rhetoric of a 'Great Society,' but it ought to be clear and easily understood."[66]

George W. Bush had a different situation that was similarly problematic. Unlike Ford, Bush ran for office in 2000 but lost the popular vote to his opponent, Al Gore. Bush had an electoral constituency, but simply maintaining it would not be enough for a reelection bid. Bush's constituency reflected the partisan and group divides in the nation in 2000: "White men and married white women supported Bush, while African Americans, Jews, most Hispanics, Asians, union members, and unmarried women voted for Gore."[67] Immediately on entering office, the Bush White House recognized the need to "enlarge his fragile electoral base."[68] As a result, the White House developed a program designed to woo independent and minority voters, realizing that if the same percentage of minorities went for the Democratic candidate in 2004, Bush would be a one-term president. The tragic events of September 11, 2001, temporarily muted the constituency problem created by the divisive 2000 election, as the country united in reaction. Bush maintained enough of that unification, which the Iraq war initially buoyed and then challenged, to win reelection. Barack Obama, in a town hall question-and-answer session with the citizens of Elkhart, Indiana, seven years after his first Town Hall as president in the same location, inadvertently summed up how the polls are tied to presidential term limits:

> Q. And despite the polls, there's a lot of love for you here in Elkhart. [Laughter]
>
> The President. Oh, I appreciate that. You know, I actually—[applause]—one thing is, after 7½ years, you don't worry about the polls no more. [Laughter] You really don't.[69]

Rhetorical Design

The advent of continuous White House polling allows the president and his staff to use polls the way companies do when selling a product. Ignoring whether the product is good or bad or whether it serves humanity, marketers and public relations firms use product testers and public opinion polls to determine the packaging, the name, the logo, and the advertising strategy for any product to sell it. If the product does not sell, then it does not matter that it might have, for example, solved the world's energy problem. Presidents and their staffs confront a similar scenario—they clearly believe in their policies, but recognize that without public support, the policy is unlikely to move forward. So, presidents and their staffs turn to polling data to design what they are going to say to the nation. Presidents can test speeches, phrases, and presentation by asking about it in a poll. Efforts to design rhetoric have been labeled "crafted talk," which means that presidents are not altering their policies, just the policies' presentation.[70] For example, the efforts by Obama's team to use the word "recovery" instead of recession and "investment" instead of infrastructure are strategies determined by presidential polling.[71] The polling data revealed a negative reaction to questions and information with the term "recession." which was absent when using the word recovery. The public did not respond to the President's ideas when the negative term was used, since recovery is more positive and upbeat.

POLLING TO SAVE A PRESIDENCY

THEN . . .

In June 1972, five men broke into the headquarters of the Democratic National Committee at the Watergate Hotel and Office complex in Washington, DC. They were caught trying to wiretap and photograph sensitive material; they were arrested and then indicted along with two others for conspiracy, burglary, and violation of federal wiretapping laws. Although it was considered a minor crime, the grand jury judge John J. Sirica suspected something else: "There were still simply too many unanswered questions in the case. By that time, thinking about the break-in and reading about it, I'd have had to be some kind of moron to believe that no other people were involved. No political campaign committee would turn over so much money to a man like Gordon Liddy without someone higher up in the organization approving the transaction. How could I not see that?"[72] It turned out that the leader of the group, James McCord, was security coordinator for the Committee to Re-Elect the President. At his trial, McCord implicated top officials, including Attorney General John Mitchell. One by one, President Nixon's top staffers were drawn into covering up the involvement of the Committee to Re-Elect the President in the crime. Instead of distancing themselves immediately, they chose to try to hide it and thus were further entangled.

As history shows, the Watergate scandal had huge implications for the presidency. The scandal also demonstrates how public opinion can be both a check on power and a tool in service to power. Nixon argued in his memoirs that his fight against impeachment was "a race for public support" and his "last campaign . . . not for political office but for . . . political life."[73] Although the break-in occurred in June 1972, Nixon was reelected in a landslide in November 1972. Watergate was a maelstrom of intrigue inside the beltway of Washington, DC, but not outside it among most of the electorate. As a result, the Nixon White House was not concerned about the mass public response to Watergate until almost a year later. Nixon and his advisors grew more attentive to poll results as the media coverage of the story escalated. According to Chief of Staff H. R. Haldeman, Nixon "went into the Watergate question . . . [and] wanted to know if we had any polls on apparent reaction to whom it affects, analyzed by voter breakdowns and all."[74] Haldeman responded that "Oliver Quayle [the pollster] says nobody gives a damn about the Watergate. Sindlinger [another pollster] says where it used to be during the election only about ten percent was the highest it ever got that said Watergate was a big issue, now it's two or three percent. He said we just can't find anybody who is interested."[75]

By April 1973, Haldeman wrote that "because of the weight of public opinion, a voluntary departure is necessary" and so he and John Ehrlichman, assistant to the President for domestic affairs, resigned.[76] In just three months, public opinion had turned against the Nixon White House. The public believed that the President's trusted advisors knew about the break-in and therefore had to be removed from their positions. By May 1973, Nixon's pollsters were asking questions about the President's behavior. Nixon told his new chief of staff, Alexander Haig, "By a vote of 59 to 31, they thought the President should be given the benefit of the doubt on this matter and should be allowed to finish his term. You know, the next three and a half years. But the other interesting thing is by a vote of 77 to 13 they opposed suggestions that the President resign."[77]

Nixon believed that the public was behind him; he also believed that public support would protect him from the press feeding frenzy over the congressional investigation into the scandal. On May 8, 1973, Nixon told Haig, "I didn't have to see a Harris poll to realize it, I mean apart from anything else the country doesn't want the Presidency to be destroyed."[78] The next day, Nixon was so interested in the polling data, he interrupted press secretary Ron Ziegler's account of a tough press briefing: "Nixon: Did the Harris poll get any play, the one you mentioned? Ziegler: Yes it did. Oh, yes, sir. It got play on TV last night, got good play. Nixon: Of course they had some negative, but did they get across that point that they didn't want the President to resign? Ziegler: Yes, sir. Absolutely, yes, sir. Nixon: And that 59 to 31 thought that he ought to continue the work? Ziegler: Right. Nixon: Okay. Ziegler: We survived, and we're going to continue to. Nixon: Damn right. Okay."[79]

On May 11, 1973, Nixon informed Secretary of State Henry Kissinger, "Hell, I'll stay here till the last Gallup polls. . . . Goddamn it. We're here to do a job and we're doing the right thing. You know it and I know it."[80] Nixon meant it—and that is exactly what happened. Between May 1973 and August 1974, a flood of damaging information changed public opinion and challenged Nixon's ability to survive the scandal. The television coverage of the Watergate congressional hearings, of which 85 percent of the nation claimed to have watched at least a portion, diminished the President's approval rating. But it was the revelation that the President had a recording system in his office, as well as the release of the tapes after the Supreme Court ruled in *United States v Nixon* (1974) that he had to turn them over to the special prosecutor, that destroyed any public support Nixon had left. "Until the revelation of the taping system, the polls revealed that the public believed Democrats and Republicans were equally guilty of 'campaign tricks' but that the Nixon campaign 'got caught at it.'"[81] After the release of the tapes, public approval of the President dropped to 20 percent and Nixon resigned, before he could be impeached by the House of Representatives, on August 8, 1974.

Richard Nixon gestures toward transcripts of White House tapes after announcing he would turn them over to House impeachment investigators and make them public in April 1974.

. . . AND NOW

For Nixon, the polling apparatus allowed his White House to monitor how important Watergate was to the public. The polls indicated what items produced a negative response from the public and thus needed a public relations counterstrategy. The polls for Nixon were a sophisticated communications advance-warning system. In contrast, Bill Clinton used his polling apparatus to design the public relations counterstrategy and not just to signal the need for such a strategy. The Clinton/Lewinsky sex scandal became international news on January 21, 1998, when news organizations revealed a sexual relationship between the president and a young White House intern. An inappropriate sexual relationship would create a feeding frenzy under any circumstances, but this was an exceptionally explosive scandal because of the charge that Clinton perjured himself and suborned perjury in the federal grand jury investigating him on another matter, Whitewater, a failed Arkansas land deal, from when Clinton was governor of Arkansas.

Whereas the Watergate story was a dramatic whodunit (what did the President know and when did he know it?) revealed piece by tantalizing piece in newspaper accounts and then in the Watergate hearings, the Lewinsky scandal was neither dramatic nor complicated. Yet the media attention dwarfed that of Watergate. The *New York Times* and the three television networks (ABC, NBC, and CBS) alone combined to provide more than 1,300 stories in a little more than a year. And the public was paying attention: approximately 60.3 million viewers watched Clinton's State of the Union speech in January 1998 and his televised apology for the relationship in August 1998. Yet, his approval rating reached its highest point in the month following the revelations, with 69 percent of Americans approving of the job the president was doing after finding out about the scandal. Throughout 1998, Clinton averaged a 65 percent approval rating.

Since scandal usually depresses a president's approval rating, political scientists investigated alternative explanations for Clinton's high rating. What they found was that the public supported the President professionally, but not personally.[82] The economy was good, so the scandal seemed extraneous. Interestingly, the public opinion apparatus itself turned out to be a component of Clinton's survival. According to Clinton's senior advisor George Stephanopoulos, the President received two competing recommendations and he chose to heed the advice that rested on the polling apparatus. Advisors to the President inside and outside the White House, like Erskine Bowles, friend and chief of staff, and Leon Panetta, former chief of staff, recommended coming clean with the country in January 1998. According to Stephanopoulos, "at his moment of maximum peril, the president chose to follow the pattern of his past. He called [former pollster] Dick Morris. Dick took a poll. The poll said lie."[83]

The poll conducted privately for the President tested what knowledge would lead the public to support resignation or impeachment. According to the grand jury investigation led by Independent Counsel Kenneth Starr, "Morris told the grand jury, he did some polling and learned that the public was most concerned about obstruction of justice and subornation of perjury, and not whether Clinton had simply engaged in a sexual affair outside his marriage." The public said, as interpreted by the polls, it would not tolerate a President who committed a crime but would tolerate a president who lied to his wife about an affair. In the polls, a distinction emerged—lying personally versus lying legally. The public rightly rejected lying legally.

This seems to be what Nixon did, polling to find out what the public thought about a presidential scandal. The difference, and it was significant, is that Morris polled the public after the President testified but prior to the scandal becoming public. Clinton insisted throughout the course of the scandal that he never committed perjury or obstructed justice. His efforts seemed laughable as he debated the definition of the word "is." According to Footnote 1,128 in the Starr Report, Clinton told the grand jury, "It depends on what the meaning of the word 'is' is. If the—if he—if 'is' means is and never has been, that is not—that is one thing. If it means there is none, that was a completely true statement. . . . Now, if someone had asked me on that day, are you having any kind of sexual relations with Ms. Lewinsky, that is, asked me a question in the present tense, I would have said no. And it would have been completely true." Yet, in the context of Morris's polling it makes perfect sense. If Clinton wanted to remain president, he needed to stick to the public's script—lying personally is tolerable. All along, the President owned lying personally but never, to this day, acknowledged lying legally.

Presidents used the ability to ask the public their response to anything privately to shape the most frequent thing presidents do: speak about policy. Some presidential rhetoric receives a firestorm of media and public attention, like a State of the Union address, whereas other speeches are heard by just a few and remarked on by even fewer. As discussed in Chapter 4, presidents and their staffs spend a considerable amount of time determining their communication strategies because of the perceived benefit. If presidents could improve their odds of receiving positive feedback for a speech and for the policy the speech is about, would they? The answer is a resounding yes. Unfortunately for the White House, despite this effort, evidence does not support the power of presidential speech to move public opinion significantly. Presidents have the ability to move public opinion and thus influence the environment for policy action, provisionally, because "presidents are successful at leading opinion when they continually push the issue in public, when their approval rating is higher, . . . while delivering speeches on television . . . and when the public is persuadable."[84]

OTHER WAYS TO GATHER OPINION

Polling has dominated the ways in which presidents collected information from the public because it was the best method technology had to offer for more than 50 years. Presidents and their staffs continue to use polls and their counterpart—focus groups—alongside the twenty-first-century additions of Internet polling and the opportunities offered by social media.

Focus Groups

Focus groups are assemblies of 10–20 citizens who are paid a nominal fee to discuss politics. Pollsters and political consultants run the sessions and record them. They use the information to determine what resonates with people. Public opinion polls ask respondents to choose answer A, B, C, or D; thus, the interviewer determines the range of possible answers. Some poll questions allow the public to lead, such as, What do you think is the most important problem facing the country? The fill-in-the-blank response generates a top-ten list that drives the political agenda. Beyond the most important problem, pollsters and presidents use focus groups to flesh out the data obtained from public opinion polls using a group setting to explore responses. Focus groups allow for following up on unusual responses or clarifying reactions.

As discussed earlier, the public typically rallies around the president in response to military exercises or hostilities. Nevertheless, war is fraught with political danger for the president, in addition to the reality of the danger from placing the nation's troops in harm's way. An episode in the George H. W. Bush administration reveals how polls and politics combine, even in the rhetoric for war. In August 1990, Saddam Hussein, President of Iraq, invaded Kuwait. The international community responded first by levying sanctions and then with an international coalition of forces led by the United States. Operation Desert Shield sent troops to Saudi Arabia as protection for that country, and Operation Desert Storm was the operational name for the military invasion of Iraq, which lasted just under two months, January 16 to February 28, 1991.

In preparing the nation for war, Bush did what all presidents do—he spoke to the nation. Bush first gave a radio address on January 5, 1991, and then he gave a televised address to the nation 11 days later. Between August 1990 and January 1991, the Bush White House conducted extensive public opinion polls determining public reaction to Bush's response to the invasion. However, between the President's two speeches in January, the White House also convened focus groups. The White House's political consultants used the focus group sessions to test presidential rhetoric. In a memo to Bush, his consultant, Roger Ailes, noted six bulleted points that arose out of the focus group discussions convened *after* the President's January 5 radio address. Consider these points in comparison to what Bush said in his public address before and after the focus group:

- Point One: The focus group did not buy the argument that "we are there for the human rights of smaller nations."[85] (In the January 5 radio address, Bush said, "Saddam already poses a strategic threat to the capital cities of Egypt, Saudi Arabia, Turkey, Israel, and Syria, as well as our own men and women in the Gulf region. In fact, Saddam has used chemical weapons of mass destruction against innocent villagers, his own people."[86] In the January 16 address to the nation, that argument is no longer used.)
- Point Two: The focus group supported linking oil to freedom but was vehemently against trading "blood for oil."[87] (In the January 5 radio address, Bush said, "The struggling newborn democracies of Eastern Europe and Latin America already face a staggering challenge in making the transition to a free market. But the added weight of higher oil prices is a crushing burden they cannot afford. And our own economy is suffering, suffering the effects of higher oil prices and lower growth stemming from Saddam's aggression." In the January 16 address to the nation, the oil argument is absent with the exception of a quote from Master Sergeant J. P. Kendall of the 82nd Airborne, who addresses the issues raised by the focus group claiming, "We're here for more than just the price of a gallon of gas. What we're doing is going to chart the future of the world for the next 100 years. It's better to deal with the guy now than 5 years from now.")[88]
- Point Three: The American focus group responded positively and supportively when reminded that "Saddam started it."[89] (In the January 5 radio address, Bush does not clearly say "Saddam started it." In the January 16 address to the nation, Bush states, "This conflict started August 2nd when the dictator of Iraq invaded a small and helpless neighbor. Kuwait—a member of the Arab League and a member of the United Nations—was crushed; its people, brutalized. Five months ago, Saddam Hussein started this cruel war against Kuwait. Tonight, the battle has been joined.")[90]
- Point Four: The focus group really liked hearing "all the steps taken by the President to resolve this peacefully."[91] (In the January 5 radio address, Bush devotes 11 lines to explaining the diplomatic steps, including the last effort to have the secretary of state, James Baker, meet with Iraqi foreign minister, Tariq Aziz. In the January 16 Address to the Nation, Bush outlines these steps again, more forcefully, in two paragraphs containing 18 lines.)[92]
- Points Five and Six: The focus group wanted reassurance that "we are showing restraint" and "the U.S. is not the aggressor." (In the January 5 radio address, Bush makes neither point. In the January 16 address to the nation, Bush addresses both points. In particular, Bush poses the aggression issue in the form of a question and provides the answer: "Some may ask: Why act now? Why not wait? The answer is clear: The world could wait no longer. Sanctions, although they had some effect, showed no signs of accomplishing their objective. Sanctions were tried for well over 5 months, and we and our allies concluded that sanctions alone would not force Saddam from Kuwait.")[93]

The changes between the two speeches are not simple edits. The response of the focus group, as representative of segments of the population, mattered enough to the White House to induce change in terms of content and approach to this effort to sell going to war. There is a direct link between the focus group responses to the first speech and the language of the second. The focus group reactions did not produce change in policy or even in any of the facts; instead, the focus group helped the Bush team decide what to emphasize and how to say it. The focus group supported and improved on the primary usage of the poll apparatus to design "crafted talk."[94] The value of focus groups for designing language is in the feedback mechanism. The discussion format allowed for the evolution of hearing the first speech and debating the substance of the first speech. It is in that discussion that the Bush team found commentary about what influenced the respondent attitudes. More important, it taught the White House what the nation would want to hear from the President to produce support for the President and his choices.

Meeting the Public Online

The transfer on January 20, 2009, from the Bush White House web page to the Obama web page not only redefined how the president can set the agenda and communicate with the press; it also redefined how the president could engage with the public and gather public opinion. From his first to his last days in office, the Obama website was a coordinated part of White House efforts to lead with and through the public. In 2009, building on the innovation from Obama's 2008 online campaign successes, the White House website offered what was at the time state-of-the-art means to connect, from email to rich site summary feeds. They created regular features on the page and on YouTube and invited feedback.[95]

By 2016, whitehouse.gov continued to urge visitors to "Get Plugged In," offering opportunities to see Obama's daily schedule, the photo of the day, and ways to get in touch with the President and the White House via email. In addition, a page entitled "Engage and Connect" offered a social hub replete with social media links to Twitter, Facebook, YouTube, Scribd, Flickr, Slideshare, Google+, GitHub, LinkedIn, and Foursquare. The First Lady, Michelle Obama, also had her own Snapchat account "so users can see a behind-the-scenes look at her life in the White House." She used the app to showcase her trips abroad, acknowledging "that more than half of 13- to 34-years-old smartphone users are on Snapchat, which definitely seems like it would make it a great medium . . . to communicate her message to the younger generation."[96] The Engage section of the website offered all the ways in which a citizen could share as well as receive information—including participation in White House petitions—only 12,000 in 2016 wanted the recipe for White House beer, but more than 32,000 wanted action on student loan debt.

In August 2016, Obama took his link to the public out of the mail bag, or email inbox, and created a Messenger link on Facebook. Jason Goldman, the chief digital officer of the White House, explained why in a press release (fittingly posted on the website):

- For the greater part of our nation's history, the only way to get a message to the President and the White House was to send it by mail. Technology made new ways of communicating possible. In the 1880s, the White House began receiving phone calls. In 1994, WhiteHouse.gov introduced a way for the public to submit messages online.
- Today, there are more ways than ever for us to communicate. No matter where you are or what time of day it is, it's possible to connect instantaneously, in real time, to people all over the world. One of our jobs at the White House is to keep up.

- . . . Getting a word in with the President has always been one of the White House's most popular citizen services. . . . Face-to-face time is a little harder to come by these days, but technology makes it possible for anyone with an Internet connection to send a message to the President and his Administration. The White House's Messenger bot, a first of its kind for any government the world over, will make it as easy as messaging your closest friends.
- While we're excited about the technology, what this comes back to is the importance President Obama attaches to hearing from you:
- *"To make sure that in all the hustle and bustle that's taken place here, we don't lose sight of why we're here—which is a bunch of citizens all across the country, needing our help, seeking advice, more than occasionally being angry, wanting to be heard. And what's interesting is not only do these letters help me to stay in touch with the people who sent me here, or the people who voted against me, but a lot of times they identify problems that might not have percolated up through the various agencies and bureaucracies. And more than once there have been occasions where these letters inspired action on real problems that are out there."*
- So, head on over to the White House's Facebook page to send the President a message.

The creation of a Facebook Messenger account is recognition of how differently we now communicate. In many ways, the social media environment can be considered a hybrid of the poll and the focus group. The power of polling is the ability to use the answers of 1,500–2,000 citizens to understand the attitudes of the nation through the power of statistics. However, you can only ask these people simple multiple-choice questions or open-ended questions like the most important problem. Focus groups, in contrast, trade large-scale predictive ability for depth and breadth because the experience allows for follow-up questions, for individuals to expand on their opinions, and, significantly, to move understanding beyond the narrowness of the public opinion poll.

On social media, the White House gets feedback from millions and can get more detailed opinions than multiple-choice answers provide. Thus, between 140-character tweets and the much longer Messenger texts, plus email, posts on YouTube, Facebook, or the other White House sites, ordinary citizens can get their opinions to the White House quickly and easily. Moreover, the White House can ask questions to gather information, as media entities frequently do.

All technology has its drawbacks and its limitations, but as tech becomes more commonplace, issues of access become less of a problem. The overreliance on telephone owners in an era where few had phones led to the erroneous headline proclaiming Dewey's victory over Truman. Today, more than 92 percent of American adults own a cell phone, and 67 percent of those cells are "smart."[97] In addition, 72 percent of all Internet users are on Facebook, which is 67 percent of all adults,[98] meaning that same 67 percent of all adults have the capability to connect with the White House. When letter writing was the norm, one needed to write the letter, address the letter, stamp the letter, and then put it in the mailbox. This process did not require much effort in the pre-Internet world, but it was much more effort than scrolling through apps, finding Messenger, typing or talking a message, and hitting send. It remains to be seen, however, whether this increased connectivity results in increased influence over presidential decisions and goals.

CONCLUSION

For the framers, a voting public represented an important check on power, since voting prevents tyranny by creating the ability to remove an autocratic leader. However, voting did not necessarily give the public a role between elections. Instead, technology created a role for the public between elections through the determination of public opinion. Since the time of Washington's presidency, presidents have given speeches and spoken to the press. However, it was not until the advent of public opinion polls that the public gained a voice and a measure of power between elections. With public opinion polls, the media, pundits, politicians, citizens, and presidents themselves all know where the president stands with the nation at large. The continuous nature of the approval rating, more than 65 years of asking the public whether they approve or disapprove, provides an opportunity to assess presidents while in office and to compare them to other presidents. Public opinion polling on policy issues also allows presidents to design a public relations campaign to support their preferred course of action.

More significant, polling the public creates an artificial measure of accountability because the public pressure revealed by polls would seemingly force presidential compliance. The presence of the polls then exists in tension with the distanced relationship between the public and the president envisioned by the framers. The idea of forcing compliance to polls also challenges modern ideas of leadership. Presidents must now constantly balance whether too much attention to public opinion creates followership and also how too little attention can create indifference. Regardless, the presence of so many polls with so much approval rating data covered by the news media make polling a day-to-day reality for presidents in their attempts to govern.

CHAPTER 6

Presidents and the Legislative Branch

By both constitutional design and political reality, many presidents have had a combative and contentious relationship with Congress. Although at times the president and Congress have worked harmoniously in passing legislation, such as the support that FDR received from a Democratic Congress when passing much of the early New Deal legislation beginning in 1933 or passage of Lyndon Johnson's Great Society legislation in 1965, often the White House and its policy agenda are slowed or even halted by Congress's refusal to support or even compromise with the president.

In keeping with that tradition, Barack Obama's relationship with Congress did not go smoothly. First elected in 2008 with a Democratic majority in both houses of Congress and facing a severe economic crisis, many assumed that Obama would enjoy the type of deference given to FDR in the face of national adversity in passing his legislative agenda. During his first two years in office, Obama achieved legislative success in the areas of health-care reform, reforms to the financial industry, credit card reform, and a major stimulus package, among other items, but none without a serious political fight (often coming from members of his own party) that, in many cases, resulted in major compromises to the initial legislation he had sought. After the Tea Party victories in the 2010 midterm elections, the President's relationship with Congress turned significantly more contentious. In eight years, Obama signed into law more than 1,200 bills, which seems like an impressive legislative legacy. However, that number represents three percent of all bills introduced in Congress.

For myriad reasons, including the tensions between a Democratic president and a Republican Congress, most bills fail before ever reaching the White House for a signature. Obama only vetoed 12 bills in eight years, but ten of those vetoes occurred in the 114th Congress, the final two years of his second term. Congress managed to override an Obama veto only once, but in startling fashion. On September 28, 2016, the House of Representatives voted 348–77 and the Senate voted 97–1 to override the President and pass into law permission for the 9/11 families to sue Saudi Arabia regarding any role in the 2001 terrorist plot. Overrides are not common, but the strength of the Obama override was significant, reflecting the persistence and power of the 9/11 families but also the reluctance of the Republican Congress to follow the White House, even on foreign policy–related legislation. Just one day later, almost 30 senators signed a letter urging Congress to revisit and/or weaken the legislation they just overrode the President to pass. Majority Leader Mitch McConnell (R-KY) blamed the White House for the congressional second thoughts. He charged the President with not sufficiently communicating the international ramifications of passing the Justice against Sponsors of Terrorism Act. Absolving the Congress of their responsibilities for understanding their own votes, McConnell, with no irony, claimed, "I told the president the other day that this is an example of an issue that we should have talked about much earlier. It appears as if there may be some unintended ramifications of that and I do think it's worth further discussing."[1]

All presidents learn quickly once they take office that the gap between expectations, promises, and legislative outcome is enormous. Presidents and their advisors also discover that the skills that helped to win the election, like the ability to raise money, project an attractive image, and put together a successful campaign organization, are much different from the skills required to govern, especially when it comes to dealing with Congress. The job of legislating and administering requires talents that can move a cumbersome and complex government to get things done, such as persuasion, personal and organizational leadership, and managerial skills. Presidents have made campaign promises, which in turn set expectations, regarding a legislative agenda. Yet, the president has not been granted any additions to the limited set of powers provided for by the Constitution in the domestic legislative arena. Consequently, the president's ability to achieve his agenda is conditional. Individual skill, political context, and system design vary across time and presidents. Legislative success is critical to a president's reelection and legacy, but is difficult to achieve because so much is beyond the president's ability to influence, particularly members of Congress, as well as the political environment in which he attempts to govern on a day-to-day basis.

THE PRESIDENT'S FORMAL ROLE IN THE LEGISLATIVE PROCESS

A recurring theme for the presidency is the lack of specific constitutional direction regarding its function. As discussed in Chapter 2, in comparison to Article I of the Constitution, which is devoted to the legislative branch, Article II is brief and open to interpretation as to the extent of presidential powers. Article I provides Congress specific (enumerated) tasks in the domestic arena (e.g., creating a post office, coining money) as well as generic (implied) grants of power (e.g., the necessary and proper clause). Article I, Section 8, gives Congress "all the legislative powers herein granted." The framers expected Congress to have primary responsibility for legislative action. Articles I and II grant the president a role in the creation of legislation and public policy, but it is time and precedent that grant power to those assignments. The president's formal legislative powers only include the power to call Congress into special session (which is much less important now since Congress stays in session most of the year), the power to sign bills into law or to veto bills, the choice to recommend legislation to Congress, and the requirement to provide the State of the Union message, along with the budget message and the economic report to Congress.

The Pathway to Legislation

The president's power to sign or veto bills is the first mention of the president in the Constitution in an active capacity in Article 1, Section 7:

> Every Bill which shall have passed the House of Representatives and the Senate, shall, before it become a Law, be presented to the President of the United States; If he approve he shall sign it, but if not he shall return it, with his Objections to that House in which it shall have originated, who shall enter the Objections at large on their Journal, and proceed to reconsider it. If after such Reconsideration two thirds of that House shall agree to pass the Bill, it shall be sent, together with the Objections, to the other House, by which it shall likewise be reconsidered, and if approved by two thirds of that House, it shall become a Law. . . . If any Bill shall not be returned by the President within ten Days (Sundays excepted) after it shall have been presented to him, the Same shall be a Law, in like Manner as if he had signed it, unless the Congress by their Adjournment prevent its Return, in which Case it shall not be a Law.

Thus, every law of the land emerges out of the same process. Each chamber of Congress votes on the same bill, which then goes to the president for his signature. If the president does not sign the bill, it is returned to Congress, at which point they can change it and send it back or override his refusal to sign it. Congress can override a presidential veto by a vote of two-thirds in each house. Note that the Constitution does not provide a rationale by which the president determines to approve or object to a bill, just a method.

During the Constitutional Convention, the original Virginia Plan (also known as the large state plan) included the right to return or "veto" acts of Congress. At the time, most governors could override the legislature, although some needed the support of a council to do it. Thus, the debate at the time centered on the power of the veto—could the president use it alone and could Congress override it? However, there was no discussion of why the president would veto legislation. Alexander Hamilton raised the issue of why a president would veto legislation during the ratification process, arguing in *Federalist* 73 that the "power to return all bills with objections to the legislature" would grant energy and strength to the presidency. However, he also argued that the "power in question has a further use. It not only serves as a shield to the executive, but it furnishes an additional security against the enaction of improper laws."[2]

The president has ten days (Sundays excluded) to sign or veto a bill. If the president does not sign it or return it while the legislature is in session, the bill automatically becomes law. However, if Congress is adjourned, then the bill is effectively vetoed. This "pocket veto" forces Congress to restart the legislative process and the bill must again pass both chambers and is again subject to presidential veto. Beyond these specifics, the lack of constitutional clarity on the use of the veto elevated early presidential choices in this regard to precedent-setting behavior. George Washington, as the first president, established many precedents long adhered to by his successors. Washington used the veto twice in eight years and made his case based only on Constitutional grounds:

> United States [Philadelphia] April 5 1792.
> Gentlemen of the House of Representatives
> I have maturely considered the Act passed by the two Houses, intitled, "An Act for an apportionment of Representatives among the several States according to the first enumeration," and I return it to your House, wherein it originated, with the following objections.
> First—The Constitution has prescribed that representatives shall be apportioned among the several States according to their respective numbers: and there is no one proportion or divisor which, applied to the respective numbers of the States will yield the number and allotment of representatives proposed by the Bill.
> Second—The Constitution has also provided that the number of Representatives shall not exceed one for every thirty thousand; which restriction is, by the context, and by fair and obvious construction, to be applied to the separate and respective numbers of the States: and the bill has allotted to eight of the States, more than one for thirty thousand.
> George Washington.[3]

The veto rested on constitutional grounds until Andrew Jackson's administration. When Jackson famously vetoed the bill to recharter the national bank in 1832, he, too, cloaked his veto in constitutionality but also asserted political rationales. Jackson claimed in his veto message: "I sincerely regret that in the act before me I can perceive none of those modifications of the bank charter which are necessary, in my opinion, to make it compatible with justice, with sound policy, or with the Constitution of our country (July 1832)."[4] Jackson contended that the states, and not Congress, retained the power to charter, regulate, and tax corporations. This was also Jefferson's original position rejected by Chief Justice John Marshall in *McCulloch v. Maryland* in 1819, the case in which the Supreme Court declared the constitutionality of Congress to establish a national bank based on both the supremacy clause and the implied powers of Congress as found in the necessary and proper clause. The crux of the political argument Jackson was making was based on "exclusivity and favoritism." By "sounding the loaded words 'monopoly' and 'privilege' over and over . . . Jackson laid out his core theme: The Bank's charter gave its stockholders a promise of pelf and power not accessible to other citizens. It made them 'a privileged order, clothed both with great political power and enjoying immense pecuniary advantages from their connection with the Government.'"[5] Once Jackson enabled the political nature of the veto, presidents were less circumscribed by constitutionality in rejecting acts of Congress. Congress rarely overrides a presidential veto; between 1945 and 2016, of the 492 presidential vetoes handed down, Congress only successfully overrode the president's veto 49 times.

Andrew Jackson used vetoes for political, as opposed to purely constitutional, purposes.

The Legislative Veto

As constitutionally mandated, the separated system that requires participation by both Congress and the president in the legislative process has mostly remained unchanged, in part because the Supreme Court has rejected any attempts to alter the process. However, the so-called legislative veto, first used in the 1930s, is a device where one or both houses of Congress pass a resolution to veto certain decisions made in the executive branch. This usually occurs to change a policy or spending by an executive agency. A legislative veto, then, is a statutory act that allows a president or an executive branch agency to take certain actions that will be subjected to a later approval or disapproval by one or both houses of Congress. Legislative vetoes are considered an "arrangement of convenience" for both Congress and the executive branch, since "executives gain decision-making authority they might not have otherwise, and Congress retains a second chance to examine the decisions."[6] In 1932, in response to Congress's authorization of the reorganization of the executive departments, Herbert Hoover submitted his proposal subject to the approval or disapproval of one chamber. The logic stemmed from the fact that, like the use of simple or concurrent resolutions for internal housekeeping in Congress, the reorganization was internal to the executive branch and did not really need the involvement of Congress.[7] Between 1932 and 1983, the legislative veto was used for reorganizational purposes hundreds of times.

However, in 1983, in the case *INS v. Chadha*, the Supreme Court invalidated a legislative veto used to alter a decision by Immigration and Naturalization Services (an executive agency created by Congress) partly on the grounds that it violated the presentment requirement of Article I (which simply means that once Congress approves a bill, it must be presented to the president for approval) and partly on the grounds of separation of powers (that Congress had no right to interfere by vetoing the action of the agency). However, more than 400 legislative vetoes have been included in legislation since 1983, often in the form of what are known as "report-and-wait" provisions that Congress will add to a bill to require congressional consultation by an executive agency before specific actions can be taken.

The Line-Item Veto

In 1995, Congress tried again to change a part of the lawmaking process. Following the Republican victory in the 1994 midterm elections, which saw the party take control of both houses of Congress for the first time in 40 years, the new majority sought to enact their campaign promises that had been labeled the GOP's "Contract with America." One of those promises, championed by the new Speaker of the House Newt Gingrich (R-GA), was to create a "line-item veto" to grant the president the ability to eliminate "pork-barrel" spending by Congress line by line without having to scrap an entire omnibus spending bill. This is a power that nearly all state governors have at their disposal, as well as a power that many presidents have argued that they needed. For example, in 1986, Ronald Reagan urged Congress to give him a line-item veto during his State of the Union address, arguing "we cannot win the race to the future shackled to a system that can't even pass a Federal budget." Reagan's insistence on the line-item veto came from the inability of both Congress and the White House to bring down the budget deficit and the national debt.

Once the line-item veto became law in 1995 (one of the only campaign pledges in the Contract with America to become law), Bill Clinton became the first to use this new presidential power; he relied on the line-item veto 82 times in just 11 bills. However, in a 7–2 decision, the Supreme Court ruled in *Clinton v. New York* (1998) that the line-item veto, as passed by Congress, was unconstitutional because it interfered with the separation of powers doctrine in the Constitution and that the only way to change the power balance between the president and Congress was through a constitutional amendment. As Justice John Paul Stevens argued,

> Under the Presentment Clause, after a bill has passed both Houses, but "before it become[s] a Law," it must be presented to the President, who "shall sign it" if he approves it, but "return it," *i.e.,* "veto" it, if he does not. . . . The profound importance of these cases makes it appropriate to emphasize [that] the Court expresses no opinion about the wisdom of the Act's procedures and does not lightly conclude that the actions of the Congress that passed it, and the President who signed it into law, were unconstitutional. If this Act were valid, it would authorize the President to create a law whose text was not voted on by either House or presented to the President for signature. That may or may not be desirable, but it is

surely not a document that may "become a law" pursuant to Article I, § 7. If there is to be a new procedure in which the President will play a different role, such change must come through the Article V amendment procedures.[8]

In sum, the legislative process proscribed by the Constitution requires the president to sign or return the bill to both chambers of Congress. The Supreme Court has rejected all attempts to alter the process and grant the president more power over legislative outcomes barring a constitutional amendment.

Recommendations to Congress

With the veto, the framers placed the president at the end of the legislative process, which allowed the president to determine which bills became law. With the recommending provision, the framers placed the president at the beginning of the legislative process. Justice Hugo Black, in *Youngstown Sheet & Tube Co. v. Sawyer* (1952), simplistically summed up the president's engagement as "the recommending of laws he thinks wise and the vetoing of laws he thinks bad."[9] Listing recommending legislation as an enumerated power of the president not only grants the president the power to call attention to issues, but also requires Congress to pay attention to the president's offering since it is mandated by the Constitution.

The State of the Union

The clause in the Constitution focused on recommending also grants the president a third role. In Article II, Section 3, the Constitution asserts that the president "shall from time to time give to the Congress Information of the State of the Union, and recommend to their Consideration such Measures as he shall judge necessary and expedient." It is important to note that "giving information to Congress and recommending measures to Congress are two different things. Both can, however be accomplished at the same time and routinely are."[10] George Washington and Alexander Hamilton both viewed the provisions as separate, but differed; Washington viewed the provisions as duties, whereas Hamilton viewed them as powers. Ultimately, Washington's view prevailed, and the president became obligated to provide information on and recommendations for the state of the union.

Washington and his successor, John Adams, delivered their State of the Union in a way familiar to modern America: an address before Congress on the floor of the House chamber. However, Thomas Jefferson ended that practice and the State of the Union was no longer an address before Congress, but a written document. Until Woodrow Wilson again spoke before Congress in 1913, the clerk of the House read aloud the president's State of the Union document. Once Wilson returned the obligation to a rhetorical opportunity, the State of the Union became a significant tool for the modern president as a source of legislative leadership. Where presidential inaugural addresses focus on the type of presidency or type of leadership a president wishes to exercise, State of the Union addresses are much more specific, functioning as a provider of information, a source for policy prescriptions and also an opportunity to showcase the president as a player in the legislative process.[11] Of course, the speeches also include relevant foreign policy determined by the current political context. For example, George W. Bush first used the term "axis of evil" to describe the triumvirate of Iran, Iraq, and North Korea in his 2002 State of the Union address.

The State of the Union address serves as an agenda-setting tool by focusing Congress, the media, the public, and the bureaucracy on the issues and policy dilemmas the president highlights. Moreover, the address represents an opportunity for presidents to single out issues important to him or to key constituents. Consequently, on the domestic side, the modern State of the Union address typically represents competing laundry lists of what the president has done in office, what else he would like to accomplish, and what Congress must do to accomplish the latter. However, presidents often use the State of the Union address to emphasize urgency, necessity, and the importance of issues. Thus, the modern State of the Union address not only serves to fulfill the president's constitutional responsibilities but also illuminates the president's leadership strategies and skills.

Despite the differences across presidencies in terms of time and political context, presidents universally use the speech as a literal statement of the "state" of the union as well as an opportunity for leadership. Consequently, almost all presidents have uttered a variation on the state of the union being "sound," "strong," "stronger," "never stronger," or "the strongest it has ever been." Gerald Ford, under trying circumstances in 1975 resulting from tough economic conditions and a lack of public trust in the presidency following Richard Nixon's resignation in August 1974, tried a different tack:

> Mr. Speaker, Mr. Vice President, Members of the 94th Congress, and distinguished guests: Twenty-six years ago, a freshman Congressman, a young fellow with lots of idealism who was out to change the world, stood before Sam Rayburn in the well of the House and solemnly swore to the same oath that all of you took yesterday—an unforgettable experience, and I congratulate you all. Two days later, that same freshman stood at the back of this great Chamber—over there someplace—as President Truman, all charged up by his single-handed election victory, reported as the Constitution requires on the state of the Union.
>
> When the bipartisan applause stopped, President Truman said, "I am happy to report to this 81st Congress that the state of the Union is good. Our Nation is better able than ever before to meet the needs of the American people, and to give them their fair chance in the pursuit of happiness. [It] is foremost among the nations of the world in the search for peace." Today, that freshman Member from Michigan stands where Mr. Truman stood, and I must say to you that the state of the Union is not good.[12]

In contrast, and during a much more severe economic downturn, Obama took the more familiar path of most of his predecessors by reminding members of Congress about the resilience of the American government:

> Madam Speaker, Vice President Biden, Members of Congress, distinguished guests, and fellow Americans: Our Constitution declares that from time to time, the President shall give to Congress information about the state of our Union. For 220 years, our leaders have fulfilled this duty. They've done so during periods of prosperity and tranquility, and they've done so in the midst of war and depression, at moments of great strife and great struggle. It's tempting to look back on these moments and assume that our progress was inevitable, that America was always destined to succeed. But when the Union was turned back at Bull Run and the Allies first landed at Omaha Beach, victory was very much in doubt. When

the market crashed on Black Tuesday and civil rights marchers were beaten on Bloody Sunday, the future was anything but certain. These were the times that tested the courage of our convictions and the strength of our Union. And despite all our divisions and disagreements, our hesitations and our fears, America prevailed because we chose to move forward as one Nation, as one people. Again, we are tested. And again, we must answer history's call. One year ago, I took office amid two wars, an economy rocked by a severe recession, a financial system on the verge of collapse, and a Government deeply in debt. Experts from across the political spectrum warned that if we did not act, we might face a second depression. So we acted, immediately and aggressively. And one year later, the worst of the storm has passed. But the devastation remains. . . . So we face big and difficult challenges. And what the American people hope, what they deserve, is for all of us, Democrats and Republicans, to work through our differences, to overcome the numbing weight of our politics. For while the people who sent us here have different backgrounds, different stories, different beliefs, the anxieties they face are the same. The aspirations they hold are shared: a job that pays the bills; a chance to get ahead; most of all, the ability to give their children a better life. And you know what else they share? They share a stubborn resilience in the face of adversity. After one of the most difficult years in our history, they remain busy building cars and teaching kids, starting businesses and going back to school. They're coaching Little League and helping their neighbors. One woman wrote to me and said, "We are strained but hopeful, struggling but encouraged." It's because of this spirit, this great decency and great strength, that I have never been more hopeful about America's future than I am tonight. Despite our hardships, our Union is strong.[13]

Senate Confirmations

In stark contrast to the ease with which recommending to Congress passed the Constitutional Convention, designing the appointment power was extremely contentious. When making legislation, and thus domestic policy, Congress was clearly the dominant force, despite carving out a role for the president. In terms of appointments, the assignment of the task would clarify the degree of presidential autonomy with which the delegates were comfortable. The delegates were split over whether the president should have the sole authority to select his subordinates. The cloud hanging over the debate was King George III and his tendencies toward favoritism and patronage. The delegates went back and forth through the summer of 1787 before ending with another grant of shared power. Rather than grant either the Congress or the president the sole ability to fill the executive branch, the framers split the decision making between the president and the Senate:

> He shall have Power, by and with the Advice and Consent of the Senate, to make Treaties, provided two thirds of the Senators present concur; and he shall nominate, and by and with the Advice and Consent of the Senate, shall appoint Ambassadors, other public Ministers and Consuls, Judges of the supreme Court, and all other Officers of the United States, whose Appointments are not herein otherwise provided for, and which shall be established by Law: but the Congress may by Law vest the Appointment of such inferior Officers, as they think proper, in the President alone, in the Courts of Law, or in the Heads of Departments.

Congress alone creates departments and agencies, whereas the president appoints and the Senate confirms or rejects the president's choice, unless the Senate happens to be in recess.

On paper, the appointments process appears simple; however, as with the power of the presidential veto to halt all Congress' efforts, the Senate confirmation process can stymie the staffing of departments and agencies as well as the courts. Obama experienced this firsthand; after taking office in January 2009, most of his nominees for the Treasury Department did not receive confirmation hearings for months, despite the severity of the economic crisis. In addition, the delays on filling judgeships were so acute in 2010 that Chief Justice John Roberts, in his 2011 annual report on the state of the judiciary, urged the President and Congress to put aside their differences and work together. One week later, Roberts applauded Obama's use of the recess appointment process to avoid the "holds" placed on nominees in the Senate for political reasons. A hold is an informal practice by which a senator can inform the party leadership that he or she does not want a bill to reach the floor of the Senate for consideration and may filibuster the bill if it does.

CREATING THE CHIEF LEGISLATOR

As the first president, Washington had an incredible task as he fought to establish an independent executive within the construct of separate institutions sharing powers. Washington defended the executive branch not only from ideology by rejecting the notion of a strong executive but also from a Congress seeking to micromanage. He sought to establish a separate domain for presidential action.

Staking Out a Role

The effort to establish presidential independence was frequently under attack from the first Congress, despite having a congressional ally like James Madison, who at the time was a member of the House of Representatives from Virginia. As Congress formulated the new government by creating departments, it was Washington's job to staff them. Washington focused primarily on "fitness," "merit," and "neutral competence" rather than patronage in his hiring choices.[14] However, Washington's sterling choices did not prevent the Senate from exercising its right of refusal of nominees. On August 5, 1789, the Senate rejected one of the 102 Washington nominees to various appointments (e.g., collectors, officers, surveyors). The nominee, Benjamin Fisbourn of Georgia, apparently had offended one of Georgia's senators at some point in the past. From this first rejection came the precedent that acknowledged the home-state senator's ability to reject, without explanation, a presidential nominee.[15] The bigger fight, however, was over removing an individual from office, a power that the Constitution did not clearly designate. Washington achieved greater success here as he again wrangled with Congress over whose authority reigned supreme. He was respectful of the authority of the legislative branch while protective of the rights and prerogatives of the executive. Consequently, Washington did not directly insert himself into the policymaking process. Instead, his treasury secretary, Alexander Hamilton, became the administrative figure who urged Congress to adopt the administration's recommendations. It was a fine line, but a significant one. Like Washington, Hamilton was a

Federalist, but as his writings in the *Federalist Papers* reveal, he believed in executive power and an active, assertive presidency, perhaps more so than his boss.

Hamilton pushed the first Congress to adopt a comprehensive economic program that included assuming the state's war debts and creating a national bank. The national bank became one of the more controversial policy recommendations in the early years, as the Jackson veto indicated. The controversy over the administration's program (as well as the activity of the president's subordinate) escalated the divisions between Washington's meritorious cabinet, particularly Hamilton and Jefferson. Even Madison, Hamilton's *Federalist Papers* writing partner, criticized the increased policy role adopted by the executive branch, arguing it might "strengthen the pretext for an hereditary designation of the magistrate."[16] The fears of the slippery slope toward monarchy solidified the factions, leading to Washington's famous farewell warning: "without looking forward to an extremity of this kind (which nevertheless ought not to be entirely out of sight), the common and continual mischiefs of the spirit of party are sufficient to make it the interest and duty of a wise people to discourage and restrain it."[17]

Washington's retirement and lack of heir easily put to rest fears of monarchy, a hereditary monarchy in particular. However, the path to presidential participation in policymaking did not disappear with the end of the Washington administration. Washington's precedents, asserting executive prerogatives, like the use of the veto, hiring and firing, and offering program recommendations, waxed and waned over the next 100 years with the strength and ambition of the officeholder. Some, like Jefferson, Jackson, Abraham Lincoln, Theodore Roosevelt, and Woodrow Wilson, were immensely active and assertive with Congress, whereas others, like Rutherford B. Hayes, Chester Arthur, and Calvin Coolidge, were not. A continuous presence in the legislative arena for the president did not take shape until FDR and the Great Depression remade the political landscape.

From Crisis Comes Power

In 1932, FDR won a landslide election over incumbent Herbert Hoover. FDR's overwhelming 472–59 triumph in the Electoral College stemmed entirely from attitudes regarding Hoover's handling of the Great Depression, which began with the stock market crash of 1929 (just six months after he took office). Hoover, believing in the sanctity of legislative leadership, allowed Congress to dominate efforts to combat the economic crisis. Despite cries in the press for leadership, Hoover resisted the demands of popular government.[18] In contrast, FDR embraced it, approaching leadership as a response to crisis. Unexpectedly, he also fundamentally reshaped the president's legislative role in ordinary times. In his inaugural address on March 4, 1933, FDR's first exercise of leadership targeted the nation's confidence:

> So, first of all, let me assert my firm belief that the only thing we have to fear is fear itself—nameless, unreasoning, unjustified terror which paralyzes needed efforts to convert retreat into advance. In every dark hour of our national life a leadership of frankness and vigor has met with that understanding and support of the people themselves which is essential to victory. I am convinced that you will again give that support to leadership in these critical days.

Second, he offered a way out of the dysfunction that flourished between Hoover and Congress:

> It is to be hoped that the normal balance of executive and legislative authority may be wholly adequate to meet the unprecedented task before us. But it may be that an unprecedented demand and need for undelayed action may call for temporary departure from that normal balance of public procedure. I am prepared under my constitutional duty to recommend the measures that a stricken nation in the midst of a stricken world may require. These measures, or such other measures as the Congress may build out of its experience and wisdom, I shall seek, within my constitutional authority, to bring to speedy adoption. But in the event that the Congress shall fail to take one of these two courses, and in the event that the national emergency is still critical, I shall not evade the clear course of duty that will then confront me. I shall ask the Congress for the one remaining instrument to meet the crisis—broad Executive power to wage a war against the emergency, as great as the power that would be given to me if we were in fact invaded by a foreign foe.

FDR argued that he would pursue the normal presidential role; he would recommend legislation and would seek to work quickly to produce law with Congress. More significant, however, he also contended that if the normal role was not sufficient to the enormity of the crisis, then he would use broad presidential power, as if the country had been invaded by a foreign foe. FDR easily won this ideological shift regarding presidential independence and authority because of his personal political skills, the devastation of the crisis, and the vivid memory of Hoover's chosen ineptitude. Consequently, he authored the largest expansion of the powers of the federal government and did so under the imprint of executive branch leadership. FDR achieved impressive dominance over Congress, without any additional constitutional powers provided. Thus, he not only created a primer for presidential involvement in the legislative branch, but also increased expectations of the presidency, in particular as "problem solver in chief."

How did FDR do this? He set the agenda, crafted legislation, and got Congress to pass his legislation with little debate. For example, he reshaped the federal–state landscape and the concept of interstate commerce in only 100 days. He began with the banks; FDR called Congress into special session and declared a national bank holiday. While the banks were closed, he offered a bill to Congress that extended government assistance to private bankers to reopen their banks (which validated actions the president had already taken because it gave him complete control over gold movements, penalized hoarding, authorized new Federal Reserve bank notes, and arranged for the reopening of liquid banks and reorganized the rest). The House passed the bill sight unseen after 38 minutes of debate. The Senate approved it, slightly amended, 73–7 that same night, and by 8:30 pm the president had signed the bill into law. Three days later, the president gave his first fireside chat to explain to the people that it was now safe to return their savings to the banks. People were then eager to deposit their money rather than withdraw it because the people trusted FDR's leadership.

Fourteen other pieces of legislation similarly passed, not only covering banking, but also putting the unemployed to work, refinancing mortgages, and creating dams as a source of cheap hydroelectric power, to name a few. Industrialists and some members of Congress, who believed the President was going too far, had some impact on the course of the debate, but little on the outcome. When Congress adjourned on June 16, 1933, just 100 days after the special session opened, it had written a series of unprecedented legislation. FDR sent 15 messages to Capitol Hill and 15 measures went through to final passage (including two constitutional amendments).[19] Congress, under FDR's leadership, committed the country to government and industry cooperation, promised to distribute tremendous sums of money to staple farmers, experimented in regional planning, pledged billions to save homeowners from foreclosure, and provided for huge public works spending.

In the 100-day special session of Congress, FDR achieved extraordinary leadership over Congress and over the crisis. He not only calmed a nation, but also restored a nation's trust in government and in core institutions. His success was directly related to his personal persuasive skills (by telling Congress and the nation that "this was the right thing to do"), his party's dominant majority in the House and Senate, and his support from the public. In contrast to other presidents, FDR successfully bequeathed his approach to leading Congress, but also the expectations derived from his success, to his predecessors.

ACHIEVING LEGISLATIVE SUCCESS

It can be argued that the most important legacy of the FDR administration was the creation of the modern presidency. He designed a pathway out of crisis and expanded the scope of the presidency by revealing power in the silences created by the Constitution. Even without an epic crisis like the Great Depression, successive presidents have adopted FDR's tactics: campaign on an agenda that requires an active or assertive president, because no candidate has ever urged voters to support a plan to do nothing or do less; attempt to lead Congress to produce legislation that advances the presidential agenda; employ an expanded institutional structure to provide advantage in the exercise of leadership; and rest his leadership on support from the public.

The subsequent administrations, which followed FDR's prescriptions for presidential power in the legislative arena, could not hope to achieve the same legislative success. Fifteen major bills to 15 laws in 100 days is unparalleled. In the absence of a crisis to produce an acquiescent Congress, legislative success for the president is much less certain; it reflects the institutional differences between the branches and varies with individual skill. The Constitution provides the president the opportunity to participate in the legislative process because both the veto and the recommending provision force Congress to pay attention to the president. Thus, the Constitution mandates that the president and Congress work together because they share legislative power. However, sharing power can be difficult for separate institutions with different demands and skillsets. Moreover, modern presidents are judged based on how effectively they fulfill their campaign policy promises. The president needs congressional action to achieve reelection as well as a legacy of achievement. Success in Congress depends on many aspects outside the president's control, forcing reliance on an informal array of tools and options.

IN THEIR OWN WORDS

CAMPAIGNING AGAINST CONGRESS

Harry Truman's campaign against the "do-nothing" Congress in 1948 is perhaps the most famous example of a president attempting to convince the American public that the legislative branch is not doing its job in representing the needs of average Americans. However, other presidents have used similar strategies at election time, since in recent decades, public approval ratings for Congress are often lower than for even the most unpopular presidents. In 1992, possible talking points circulated among George H. W. Bush's advisors that would have the President "chastise the Congress for taking so long to complete essential work such as nominations and appropriations." In addition, some of Bush's advisors wanted the President to highlight the fact that despite being in session year-round, the Congress was actually "part time" in the actual work accomplished.[20]

Even more to the point is this memo from the Reagan White House in 1988 on the topic of the "Do Awful Congress as a Campaign Theme:"

> The performance thus far of the 100th Congress, capped by the acrimony and delay in enacting the FY 1988 budget, affords us an opportunity to make the performance of this Congress a key issue in the 1988 general election. Despite limited historical precedent, this anti-Congress theme might very well become a winning one for the GOP next year.
>
> The polling evidence is overwhelming that Congress is held in low regard by the voting public. However, *individual* members continue to be popular because of their close attention to the needs of the voters back home. Congressmen are admired less for their legislative acumen than for their casework on behalf of individual constituents. The examples of districts giving Republican presidential candidates hefty majorities while reelecting Democratic incumbents are legion.
>
> The Congress is such an unwieldy institution that it has been difficult to draw a connection between its actions and the overall results of its actions. As such, the Congress is able to take credit for favors targeted to specific audiences without being held politically accountable for the impact on the general population.
>
> Until the advent of C-SPAN television coverage, the Congress was a mysterious institution that only the most sophisticated of insiders understood. So many procedural and substantive votes were taken on the same issue that a congressman could vote different ways and offer at least some satisfaction to diametrically opposed constituents. It has become more and more difficult to get Congress "on the record" because more often than not, the record was not very clear.
>
> Ironically, while TV coverage had the intended effect of raising the visibility of members of Congress (especially the leadership), it has also had the unintended impact of exposing congressional practices to media scrutiny. While real reform will come slowly, the possibility that national politics could be impacted by these practices offers congressional critics an immediate forum for their views. Indeed, to the extent that Congress becomes part of the national debate in 1988, the discussion could very well be a springboard for real reform, thus strengthening the forces for change in the next Congress.

The personal embodiment of abuse of congressional practices is Speaker Wright. He has cultivated a high profile and as such is a very visible target. Observers say he is the most partisan Speaker in a long while. He does not hesitate to bend the rules when it suits his purposes. Charges of personal corruption have been leveled against him. Any anti-Congress theme would rely heavily upon him for personalization and example.

The only specific example in recent American history where Congress became an issue was the 1948 presidential election. President Harry Truman, trailing badly in the polls and widely unpopular, campaigned against the "do nothing" Republican Congress, blaming it for a wide variety of misdeeds. In this larger electoral context, the President enjoyed a distinct advantage over a body that necessarily speaks with many voices and seems disorganized. The result was a debate on issues framed largely by the incumbent President, resulting in an unexpected, albeit narrow, reelection victory for Truman. (As one example, Truman successfully blamed the Republican Congress for falling farm prices throughout 1948. He carried every farm state in the election).

This "do nothing" Congress campaign was all the more remarkable because, in fact, the President and Congress had cooperated on several important ventures the year before. In 1947, for instance, the Republican Congress overwhelmingly approved key Truman foreign policy initiatives such as the Marshall Plan for reconstruction of Western Europe and military assistance to Greece and Turkey, who were then under communist attack. By the time the political season was underway however, this was forgotten as the President launched his successful attack on the "do nothing" Congress. The moral is that there a time for cooperation *and* a time for politics.

I believe the opportunity is there for such a theme against this "do awful" Congress. We can avail ourselves of a number of fruitful themes to highlight the failures of this Congress to address the real needs of the American people.

1) POLICIES

This Congress' priorities and policies are opposite the real beliefs of the American people and are detrimental to the interests of the United States. Specifics include congressional desire for protectionist trade legislation; congressional failure to control spending and budget deficits (Balanced Budget Amendment); Congress' war on small business (mandated benefits legislation); and most importantly, the refusal of Congress to face up to our international obligations by hamstringing the Chief Executive (Persian Gulf, Central America, arms control). The goal is to set our priorities against those of the Congress as a part of the public's choice in 1988.

2) POLITICS

The Congressional art of trading favors, whatever value it once had, has become a drag on the economy and threatens to undermine public support for governmental integrity. Pork barrel pursuit of tax breaks, transition rules, special subsidies for a few communities (note enclosed articles on the recent priority of Senator Inouye), regulatory exemptions, and directed purchase contracts for favored constituents and personal vendettas (enclosures) are doing great harm to the country because the public's confidence in the government is being eroded. The goal is to take the congressman's strong suit of constituent service and turn it into a negative by emphasizing the public interest.

3) PROCESS

The Congressional budget process is in disarray. Rather than offering a serious check in spending, it has become another layer of bureaucracy competing the appropriations and authorization committees. Missed deadlines, special interest pleading, and failure to pass a single appropriations bill have reduced the President's role in the budget process and contributed to the huge annual spending increases since 1974, when the budget act was passed. The goal here is to offer a rational explanation for why the deficit continues to be large despite the President's best efforts and to blame the Congress for the current situation.

4) ETHICS

We now have one dozen incumbent congressmen under investigation or convicted of legal or ethics violations. This is in spite of the fact that the independent counsel law does not apply to Congress. Imagine what the situation would be if Congress were subject to the same scrutiny as the executive branch. The goal here is to launch a preemptive strike against other opponents who will most likely seek to make the sleaze factor an issue this year.

Such a campaign would not lack for themes or new material. The President has credibility to critique an institution he has dealt with for seven years. He would be setting the agenda and defining the differences between the parties, a task that is critical if we are to have any hope of increasing our congressional representation next year. The tone need not be angry, but more in sorrow that things have gone so awry. Finally, of course, the timing is critical. The "do awful" label would appear late, but many of the themes could be developed earlier than that.[21]

Individual Behavior

The institutional differences between the executive and legislative branches are powerful forces, which enhance the constitutional system of checks and balances. Legislation is easiest to pass when all actors are of the same political persuasion, yet even then, the labyrinthine process makes no legislative outcome easy. Moreover, although both branches seek to be representative, the power of their connection to constituents stems from different sources, creating different pressures on officeholders. However, the institutional push and pull of the constitutional design does not entirely explain the president's role in the process. Despite lacking constitutional tools, the president has an array of individual options, opportunities, and choices when engaging in the legislative process.

As noted earlier, the Constitution provides the president with a role in the beginning of the legislative process and at the end. Presidents can recommend or even request legislation they want and they can veto legislation they do not want to become law. If, as the saying goes, "the devil is in the details," then the Constitution formally keeps the president out of the critical period where Congress constructs legislation. Informally, however, the constitutional bookends grant the president a role throughout the process. However, the president's ability to influence the specifics of legislation as well as the outcome relates much more to individual skill than to the institutional capacity of the office.

As discussed in Chapter 1, the view of the president as a strategic actor in the legislative process originates with Richard Neustadt's *Presidential Power*; he argued that the "power to persuade is the power to bargain. Status and authority yield bargaining advantages."[22] The president is the preeminent status holder in the corridors of power in Washington, DC, or around the world, for that matter. However, the Constitution grants Congress more authority than it grants the president in the legislative arena. Thus, Neustadt argued, "in a government of separate institutions sharing powers," Congress, too, has power and an array of counterpressures to what the president brings to the table. Consequently, "command has limited utility; persuasion becomes give-and-take." For Neustadt, the essence of presidential leadership is persuasion, specifically, the convincing of individuals "that what the White House wants of them is what they ought to do for their sake and on their authority."[23]

When creating legislation, presidential persuasion targets members of Congress in multiple ways. First, a member of Congress must be persuaded to sponsor the president's preferred version of the bill on which the president seeks action. Second, the president must persuade individual committee members that the president's preferred language must shape the bill. Here, the president's prestige, to use Neustadt's terms, elevates the president's request, but even so, Congress members routinely receive similar persuasive attempts from constituents as well as from interest groups. The president must then persuade individual committee members to vote for the bill in committee and then persuade a majority of the chamber to vote for the bill as well. Despite framing presidential power in terms of individual interactions, the president is not speaking individually to 535 members of Congress. Nor does the president have to speak with all members of Congress. From the first day of each congressional term, the president knows the level of difficulty he will face when seeking passage of his agenda. The institutional norms of Congress determine the president's strategic actions, and the majority/minority status of his party enormously shapes his opportunities to exercise a Neustadtian style of influence.

Bargaining within

A president facing unified government will likely be negotiating the details with his own party, primarily. Although the president's party shares the president's larger goals, the details can result in painful intraparty battles. In 2002, George W. Bush, buoyed by both a Republican Congress and soaring post-9/11 approval ratings, attempted to tackle an entitlement program, often the most legislatively contentious since programs that offer benefits and services have both vociferous defenders and detractors. Bush wanted to add a prescription drug component to Medicare. Since the 1990s, the rising costs of prescription drugs moved coverage of the drugs for the elderly to the top of the agenda. The issue had supporters on both sides because liberals desired an expansion of Medicare toward more universal coverage and conservatives wanted to control costs.

From the initial proposal in the State of the Union, Congress and the President were at odds, despite Republican control of Congress. The Bush plan, which required seniors to abandon the traditional form of Medicare to receive the new benefit, "raised a storm of protest . . . from Republicans and Democrats."[24] The Bush White House designed its plan behind closed doors, with little input or sharing with congressional Republicans. Republicans went so far as to call Tommy Thompson, secretary of health and human services, to testify about the president's plan. However, the White House still refused to release details. Despite lacking any details beyond the President's initial outline in the State of the Union, more and more individuals, groups, and actors in the system stepped in to pressure Congress to resist the idea of requiring seniors to join a private plan. When the President finally released his plan, the requirement was not part of it because Congress had pressured the President to change his plan. However, the Bush White House still set up a two-tier system where those in a private plan received better benefits than those in traditional Medicare.[25] With the release of the President's proposal, the Republican-led Congress went to work, grumbling about the President's offering, which was likely to cause trouble for members of Congress with their politically active elderly constituents.

Given the close split between the parties in the Senate at the time, the Republicans could not legislate with impunity and were forced to compromise with Senate Democrats. Consequently, they produced a bipartisan solution, which rejected Bush's preferred option regarding the different levels of coverage, but they did allow for private coverage. The White House signaled through the media their willingness to accept the compromised Grassley–Baucus bill. In the House, the wrangling in committee between Republicans and Democrats was more contentious because the Republican plan was more in line with the Bush proposal. The response to the Bush prescription drug proposal in committee and then on the floor of both the House and the Senate demonstrates how the president's goals and agenda only go so far, because individual pressure on members of Congress does not necessarily triumph over congressional pressures. In the Senate, the bill passed 76–21, in true compromise fashion, as 40 Republicans and 35 Democrats joined together. However, Bush lost ten members of his own party on a bill that was important to him and his overall agenda.

Aware that the outcome of the bill was in jeopardy, the White House sent Vice President Dick Cheney to lobby those Republican House members on the fence. In the House, the situation was much more complicated because they must first vote on the rules for debate, generated by the Rules Committee, and then vote on the bill. The committee, governed by the Republican majority, opted for a modified closed rule that would limit the number and type of amendments that could be offered.[26] The division over the rule would signal the division over the bill; it passed, but with four Republican defections. Between the vote on the rule and the vote on the bill, the House leadership (but not the President) leaned on the Republicans who had voted "nay" earlier. The outcome was precarious; the allotted time for the vote had to be extended from 15 minutes to an hour. The result was a vote of 216–215, with 19 Republicans rejecting the House's version of the president's proposal.[27]

The process does not end with the two chamber votes; the bill must be reconciled because the president can only receive one bill to sign. The House and the Senate passed two different bills, so they needed to produce a compromise, which the chambers must also pass. Bush met with the entire conference, made up of selected members of the House and Senate, to encourage a swift resolution. However, during July and August, the conference was driven largely by congressional behavior and activity, particularly lobbying by constituents and large groups hoping to influence the outcome. Months went by and little to no progress was made, primarily in terms of the divisions between Republicans. Finally, they passed a compromise with little White House input, which Democrats and conservative Republicans both despised. Yet, the conference had won the sanction of the American Association of Retired Persons, a critical ally because it is the largest and one of the most influential interest groups in the nation. However, both chambers still needed to pass the conference bill, five months after the passage of the House and Senate versions.

At this stage, Bush weighed in heavily, using all the powers Neustadt articulated in terms of bargaining and persuasion. Bush telephoned many members of the Republican caucus personally. The vote in the House, after pressure from the President and the House leadership, was 220–215. The Senate vote was more contentious the second time because the compromise moved the bill away from the original Senate bill. Moreover, the President had an enormous critic in Senator Ted Kennedy (D-MA), who went so far as to signal a filibuster (the procedure by which one senator can bring legislative action in the Senate to a halt by talking a bill to death). Here, too, a rules debate took place because the Republicans had to scramble to come up with enough votes to bring the bill to the floor. The final Senate vote was 54–44, and nine Republicans voted against the bill, with only 11 Democrats voting for passage.[28]

The bill-signing ceremony reflected the importance the President accorded the passage of the prescription drug program. Two thousand invitees watched the President sign the bill alongside mostly Republican members of Congress. The President did not get exactly what he wanted, namely the private system, but did ultimately achieve more privatization of the Medicare system than had existed before. Bush, at various points in the process, expended significant presidential capital, relying on his prestige and position to induce voting in support of the bill. However, this bill process also demonstrates that even with unified government, the president is limited in terms of how much alteration to the congressional process a president can generate via individual bargaining and persuasion.

Bargaining across and within party

In divided government, the president faces two chambers of Congress controlled entirely or partially by the other party. As a result, from day one, the president faces considerably more difficulty for the passage of his agenda. Under unified government, the president and congressional leaders work in tandem to keep a majority together. However, in divided government, the majority party wants something different from the president even if they share the same desire to tackle the issues on the president's agenda. In divided government, the president must persuade his party to remain united with him, all the while working to compromise to bring the other party closer to his preferred point of view. It is a delicate balancing act fraught with danger because compromise with one side creates contentiousness with the other side.

Even when faced with an aggressive, active Congress, there remains opportunity to engage in Neustadtian leadership—personal leadership of persuasion and bargaining. However, the opportunities of success are much more dependent on the power that comes from actual constitutional tools, like agenda setting via the campaign and bill proposal, as well as with veto threats. Moreover, as both united and divided government reveal, when attempting to employ personal leadership, presidents must accept and work within the limitations imposed by the institutional design and nature of the legislative branch.

One way to see how well the president is working with Congress is to look at the results of concurrence between presidential position taking and roll call votes in the House and Senate. Concurrence is related to the state of the president's party's majority but it is also a measure of how well the president and Congress are getting along, regardless of unified or divided government. When George W. Bush had unified government, he experienced concurrence rates of more than 70 percent, meaning that for seven of every ten bills that came to a vote, the outcome matched the President's stated position. Similarly, when Barack Obama enjoyed unified government in 2009 and 2010, his concurrence rate was more than 85 percent. In contrast, under divided government in 2007 and 2008, Bush reversed his success rate, with only three of ten bills passing that agreed with his stated position. Obama's concurrence rates challenge the conventional wisdom suggesting divided government yields only gridlock, as well as the idea that Obama and the Republican Congress never got along. Unlike Bush, Obama managed concurrence rates above 53 percent when Republicans controlled at least one house of Congress, which indicates some measure of success despite the lack of party unity.

Going public

Since FDR, expectations of the president increased exponentially but without a vast increase in official, constitutional powers. Consequently, presidents are in the awkward position of being judged on outcomes that they are unable to control. Roosevelt altered the dynamic of understanding the presidency by revealing alternate means to influence the outcome via nonconstitutional tools. Central to the extrainstitutional premise is Neustadt's power of persuasion, which is the power to get someone else to do what you want them to do, *on their authority*. A skillful president will succeed by virtue of the bargained outcome. Neustadt's argument only narrowly includes the institutional realities under which members of Congress receive presidential persuasive efforts and thus only explains a narrow portion of presidential behavior or the outcomes of the presidential agenda.

The main institutional feature that is left out of Neustadt's argument is the influence of a member of Congress's constituency. An electoral connection exists between members of Congress and those they represent, with members of Congress and their staffs devoting increased time and energy to serving the needs of their constituents. Congress reallocated their time between Washington and their districts and increased staff in their district as a result of electoral pressures.[29] The need to be reelected drives most members of Congress' decision making; after all, you cannot accomplish anything in Congress if you are not reelected. It is easy to dismiss the attention that members devote to their districts, but this has become a core component of representation. Every decision made by members of Congress must include the electoral reality check—will this help me or hurt me during my next campaign? Senators have the luxury of time; their next campaign could be up to six years away, whereas House members are always thinking about reelection since they serve two-year terms. As a result, although party affiliation, personal ideology, and what is good for the country matter, what matters for their states or districts can be more important to members of Congress.

FDR, however, demonstrated that there is another tool in the extraconstitutional tool box that presidents can employ to affect congressional decision making: the public. A new form of leadership emerged when FDR used his fireside chats to calm fears and encourage the public to put their money back into the banks. The influence stemming from the connection between the president and the public is not individual in the way Neustadtian leadership is. Samuel Kernell argues that using the relationship with the public is a form of leadership itself and identified a pattern: the president influences the public through a televised speech, the public responds, and the public then pressures their congressional member to support the president's preferred option.[30]

"Going public" uses what belongs to the president exclusively (i.e., a national platform) to try to affect congressional decision making by attacking the electoral connection between voters and members of Congress. In 1981, Ronald Reagan certified this new style of leadership. Reagan's personal popularity, coupled with support for his ideals (i.e., increased defense spending, lower taxes, eliminating government waste), created an opportunity and advantage, which the President and his advisors seized. Reagan wanted both a budget reflecting his priorities and tax cuts. He illustrated his plan in several speeches to the nation but initially engaged in traditional Neustadtian bargaining with the opposition party. The Democratic majority wanted numerous changes to the President's budget proposals and tax cuts. Reagan resisted these changes, rejecting congressional options time and time again. The Speaker of the House, Tip O'Neill (D-MA), said in a nationally televised interview, "if the vote were tomorrow we could win it. Right now we have the votes. Can he take them away from us? Let's wait and see."[31]

Reagan rose to O'Neill's challenge in devastating fashion. To change those votes, the President undertook a public strategy. Two days before the crucial floor vote in the House, the President gave a nationally televised speech in which he again argued for his preferred option. However, in this speech, the President used his representative relationship as a lever against Congress's relationship with the public:

> I ask you now to put aside any feelings of frustration or helplessness about our political institutions and join me in this dramatic but responsible plan to reduce the enormous burden of Federal taxation on you and your family. During recent months many of you have asked what can you do to help make America strong again. I urge you again to contact your Senators and Congressmen. Tell them of your support for this bipartisan proposal. Tell them you believe this is an unequalled opportunity to help return America to prosperity and make government again the servant of the people.[32]

The reaction from the public and from lawmakers was swift and certain. Citizens' calls in support of the President's plan inundated members of Congress, who received millions more letters and calls than normal.[33] The President won, not by bargaining and persuasion, but by going over the heads of Congress to force compliance from their own constituents.

The identification of going public as a leadership style highlights multiple changes in presidential behavior since the FDR administration. Kernell drew attention to the abandonment of insider strategies for outsider strategies. The change in tactics directly relates to the changing demands on the individual president as well as the institution of the presidency. With the increasing expectations of FDR-like achievements, the president needed more leverage over Congress. Simultaneously, the president became the focal point of an increasingly news-hungry media, driven by the growth of television news in the twentieth century. Radio, then television, and then the Internet granted the president the tools to reach a national audience, who could in turn influence Congress.

Presidential behavior appeared to anoint going public as the preferred means for achieving legislative success in Congress. Since FDR, the number of speeches given by a president increased exponentially. Whether major or minor policy addresses, interviews, or other public appearances, presidents speak constantly about their issues and their agenda.[34] Yet, the increase of rhetoric in the public sphere did not lead to continuous presidential success in Congress. Several factors influence the power of going public. First, presidents must be able to reach a sizeable enough audience to pressure enough members of Congress to support the president's choice. With the abundance of media outlets, it seems odd that the president might not be able to reach a sizeable audience. In the days of the big three networks, it was easy for a president to be confident a televised speech would reach a large percentage of Americans. However, once cable multiplied the number of channels available to a viewer, the audience watching major presidential addresses declined.[35] The Internet only intensified the fragmentation of the presidential audience.

Not only is it now more difficult for presidents to find an audience, but also presidents are less likely to change a significant portion of the electorate's mind on an issue. The Reagan budget experience, where millions were motivated to contact their Congress member, rarely happens. Interestingly, recent presidents are relatively unlikely even to ask citizens to contact Congress.[36] It is so unlikely that citizens contact government that scholars typically rely on public opinion polls to demonstrate citizen approval and support rather than actual examples of support.

Relying on polls introduces a different dynamic to the going-public style of leadership. It is easy to measure the effect of a presidential speech (simply measure approval before and after the speech) but it is difficult to move public opinion significantly.[37] If the president, through the force of his message or the skill of his rhetoric, manages to shift opinion in his favor, there is still the issue of whether that matters to Congress. Opinion polls are national measures of a national figure. Local voters and local influences determine members of Congress's fortunes; thus, national polls only matter "at the margins."[38] What truly limits the power of going public is the simple fact that a president cannot use it all or even some of the time. Congress deals with too many issues for the president to call on the public every time he wants to effect an outcome. However, when a president does choose to use public leadership for a legislative outcome, he is likely to be successful.[39]

Modern Veto Politics

Because George Washington carefully rested his veto on constitutional grounds, it is fair to say that the framers did not envision the use of the veto as a political weapon. Restraint with the only constitutionally defined weapon a president has was short lived. Many presidents have used the veto not as a defense against Congress from encroaching on their powers of office or even against bad legislation, but as a means to implement their own legislative agendas. For example, the first six presidents vetoed a total of nine bills, and three—Zachary Taylor, Millard Fillmore, and James Garfield—vetoed no bills. In contrast, FDR vetoed 635 bills (and was overridden only nine times), which reflects his vision of presidential power and his role and influence over the policymaking process (see Table 6.1). Presidents also use the threat of a veto as a political weapon, like when Reagan told Congress to "make my day" by raising taxes.

Researching the Presidency

Success in Congress

If presidential success is getting everything a president wants or campaigns on, then no president has ever been successful. Scholars who study the presidency and scholars who study Congress have different perspectives of how successful a president can be in achieving his agenda. Presidency scholars tend to focus on the individual skill of the president to persuade or use the tools of the office. Congressional scholars, however, focus on the presidential effect on congressional outcomes. These congressionally centered models find that the president has only a minor effect because party ideology, or the partisan balance in Congress, primarily determines outcomes. A third perspective explores how the institutions work in tandem, as separate institutions sharing power.

Research by Paul Herrnson, Irwin Morris, and John McTague demonstrates how scholars try to work with and bridge these inherent scholarly divides. Rather than focus entirely on presidential behavior during periods of legislative activity, in *The Impact of Presidential Campaigning for Congress on Presidential Support in the U.S. House of Representatives* they instead explore whether presidential campaigning for a member of Congress influences their voting behavior.[40] Presidential campaigning on behalf of a member of Congress can bring attention, goodwill, and fundraising, assuming that the president is popular enough to help. Looking at Clinton and Bush in the midterm races of 1998 and 2002, Herrnson, Morris, and McTague found that both presidents helped only incumbents and that the help translated into increased support on key votes in the session following the election. In fact, the mean level of support in these key votes increased by four points with as few as two or more campaign visits for both presidents. Thus, as important as individual skill is for presidency scholars and as important as majority makeup is for congressional scholars, other actions can significantly affect the outcome of a key vote, which can be the difference between legislative success and failure for the president.

Table 6.1 Presidential Vetoes

PRESIDENT	VETOES	POCKET VETOES	VETOES OVERRIDDEN
Washington	2	0	0
Adams	0	0	0
Jefferson	0	0	0
Madison	5	2	0
Monroe	1	0	0
J. Q. Adams	0	0	0
Jackson	5	7	0
Van Buren	0	1	0
W. H. Harrison	0	0	0
Tyler	6	4	1
Polk	2	1	0
Taylor	0	0	0
Fillmore	0	0	0
Pierce	9	0	5
Buchanan	4	3	0
Lincoln	2	5	0
A. Johnson	21	8	15
Grant	45	48	4
Hayes	12	1	1
Garfield	0	0	0
Arthur	4	8	1
Cleveland	304	110	2
B. Harrison	19	25	1
Cleveland	42	128	5
McKinley	6	36	0
T. Roosevelt	42	40	1
Taft	30	9	1
Wilson	33	11	6
Harding	5	1	0
Coolidge	20	30	4
Hoover	21	16	3
F. D. Roosevelt	372	263	9
Truman	180	70	12
Eisenhower	73	108	2

Table 6.1 (*continued*)

PRESIDENT	VETOES	POCKET VETOES	VETOES OVERRIDDEN
Kennedy	12	9	0
L. B. Johnson	16	14	0
Nixon	26	17	7
Ford	48	18	12
Carter	13	18	2
Reagan	39	39	9
G. H. W. Bush[1]	29	15	1
Clinton	36	1	2
G. W. Bush	10	0	3
Barack Obama	12	0	1
Total	1,506	1,066	110

Source: Gerhard Peters, "Presidential Vetoes," The American Presidency Project, ed. John T. Woolley and Gerhard Peters (Santa Barbara, CA: University of California, 1999–2012), http://www.presidency.ucsb. edu/data/vetoes.php. and http://www.infoplease.com/ipa/A0801767.html.

Contemporary presidents and their advisors recognize that a political strategy must be developed in support of a presidential veto, as when George H. W. Bush vetoed civil rights legislation in October 1990:

> It is becoming increasingly clear that within the next two weeks the President will be in the position of having to veto the Civil Rights Act of 1990. On Monday September 24, the conference committee on Civil Rights will hold its first meeting to reconcile the House and Senate versions of the bill. Since the two bills are so similar, the reconciled bill could be reported out of conference early next week and sent back to the President for action. . . . The President has a strong record on civil rights and it is important that he is viewed as supportive of civil rights at the time of his veto. He must remain on the offensive about his veto of a quota bill. To accomplish this we propose that he deliver his veto statement before an audience of invited guests (tbd) and that he physically present his own major Civil Rights Bill at that time. We recommend that this event be covered by minority press. The picture should be of the President holding his legislation in hand while challenging Congress to pass a true Civil Rights Bill.[41]

Bush eventually signed into law the Civil Rights Act of 1991, a modified version of the bill that he had vetoed the prior year.

Whether presidents employ bargaining or going public, the veto or the threat of a veto rests at the heart of both leadership strategies. There are two types of public veto threats: the line in the sand and the signal.[42] Reagan, speaking to the American Business Conference, famously issued the line in the sand:

> The scene in the Senate Budget Committee this past week was a disappointing one, I think, for the American people. They seem to be in full-scale retreat from

spending cuts and are talking about raising people's taxes again. When push comes to shove, I guess it's always easier to let the taxpayer take the fall. Well, let them be forewarned: No matter how well intentioned they might be, no matter what their illusions might be, I have my veto pen drawn and ready for any tax increase that Congress might even think of sending up. And I have only one thing to say to the tax increasers: Go ahead, make my day.[43]

Bill Clinton illustrated the other form of veto threat, signaling a willingness to negotiate and avoid a bad outcome:

We should not destroy the foreign aid budget. But, furthermore, we should not handcuff the President. That is not the way to conduct the foreign affairs of this country. You cannot micromanage foreign policy. . . . If this bill passes in its present form, I will veto it.[44]

The line-in-the-sand veto threats do not occur often, but when they do, they usually are dramatic and often remembered. From Reagan's "make my day" comment to George H. W. Bush's promise, "read my lips, no new taxes," explicit veto threats are not the norm. Instead, the signaling type of veto—I will veto it *in the present form*—are used more frequently and often with more success for influencing the passage of legislation.[45] However, vetoes do not always have to be public because private veto threats in the course of bargaining can also be effective for achieving concessions in bargaining with Congress.[46]

To understand the implications for each of these two types of veto rhetoric, rational choice can explain the pathways to decision making for the actors involved.[47] In the case of legislation, the actors are the president and Congress. For the veto

Bill Clinton vetoing legislation in April 2000 that would have allowed thousands of tons of highly radioactive nuclear waste to be shipped to Yucca Mountain in Nevada.

threat, the power of the threat comes from uncertainty; "if the president's veto threat is to have any effect on the legislature, Congress must be somewhat unsure about what policies the president will accept [otherwise] the threat could not possibly work since Congress would know what the president will do."[48] Much of the power of the veto threat comes from the president's reputation, providing the power behind the signaling of a veto threat. Will the president stand by the threat, is the president bluffing, and/or is the president willing to compromise? These are the political calculations that both the president and congressional leadership use in determining how and when to negotiate with each other.

Consider how George H. W. Bush handled legislation on the environment. Bush took the presidential oath in 1989 with a big victory after a negative campaign over Massachusetts governor, Democrat Michael Dukakis. One of the central issues that Bush highlighted during the campaign was the environment; one particular negative ad focused on the need to clean up the Boston Harbor (in Dukakis' hometown). The ad showed Bush standing in a boat in the Boston Harbor declaring, "Two hundred years ago, tea was spilled into this harbor in the name of liberty, now it's something else. We've got to do better." In keeping with the legislative role accepted by both Congress and the president, Bush translated his campaign agenda to his presidential agenda and focused immediately on the environment, specifically air pollution.

The Clean Air Act, originally passed in 1963, was significantly strengthened in 1970. However, during the 1980s, Reagan and House Democrats were gridlocked on opposing sides regarding increased regulation. Moreover, through strategic appointments, the Reagan White House actively worked to undermine the existing legislation. With the election of Bush, whom many called the "environmental president," the Democratic Congress faced a potential ally rather than the veto pen of Reagan, although ideological and institutional differences abounded. Nonetheless, Bush seized the momentum of his election to inform Congress about his plans for the environment:

> If we're to protect our future, we need a new attitude about the environment. We must protect the air we breathe. I will send to you shortly legislation for a new, more effective Clean Air Act. It will include a plan to reduce by date certain the emissions which cause acid rain, because the time for study alone has passed, and the time for action is now. We must make use of clean coal. My budget contains full funding, on schedule, for the clean coal technology agreement that we've made with Canada. We've made that agreement with Canada, and we intend to honor that agreement. We must not neglect our parks. So, I'm asking to fund new acquisitions under the Land and Water Conservation Fund. We must protect our oceans. And I support new penalties against those who would dump medical waste and other trash into our oceans. The age of the needle on the beaches must end. And in some cases, the gulfs and oceans off our shores hold the promise of oil and gas reserves which can make our nation more secure and less dependent on foreign oil. And when those with the most promise can be tapped safely, as with much of the Alaska National Wildlife Refuge, we should proceed. But we must use caution; we must respect the environment. And so, tonight I'm calling for the indefinite postponement of three lease sales which have raised troubling questions, two off the coast of California and one which could threaten the Everglades in Florida. Action on these three lease sales will await the conclusion of a special task force set up to measure the potential for environmental damage.

I'm directing the Attorney General and the Administrator of the Environmental Protection Agency to use every tool at their disposal to speed and toughen the enforcement of our laws against toxic-waste dumpers. I want faster cleanups and tougher enforcement of penalties against polluters.[49]

This was a loud signal that there was a new president in office focused on the environment. Moreover, the Bush White House made a strategic decision to work with the career bureaucrats who staffed the Environmental Protection Agency rather than stifle them, like the Reagan administration. Thus, Bush's sincerity and willingness to produce a good-faith proposal gained credibility with Democrats in Congress. Bush made a second key strategic decision for dealing with Congress by creating a small policy group of White House staffers and members of the Environmental Protection Agency who worked quickly and in secret. Consequently, "the proposal they finally produced . . . packed a wallop. Over time, with secrecy, expertise and wide latitude, the [Bush team] . . . came to write the first draft of the far-reaching and ambitious overhaul of the nation's Clean Air Act."[50]

The Bush team spent its first six months on the environment behind closed doors forging a united front between the White House and the Environmental Protection Agency. Bush released the details of his proposal with a big announcement before a large audience, signaling the importance of the proposal. Reaction to the proposal was mixed given the battle lines drawn down the center of Bush's own party. Not only would Bush need to negotiate with the Democrats, but also many members of Bush's own party patently rejected the increased regulation and enforcement for business, particularly the automakers and energy producers.

Negotiating with Congressional Democrats would prove tough for Bush as he entered office; as the previous vice president, many in Washington believed they were familiar with him and understood who Bush was politically. Unfortunately, most Democrats thought of Bush as a weak leader. Therefore, not only did Bush not have the advantage of being unknown, but also he faced an assertive Democratic Congress. If the Democrats could work together, then Bush was less likely to achieve his version of the legislation. Vetoing a proposal that he initiated and campaigned on would be an enormous failure and thus weakened any potential signal of a veto threat. Thus, the campaign provides a component of what Cameron describes as policy reputation. Moreover, environmental policy was the cornerstone of a limited domestic agenda for the President, who seemed more focused on the international issues such as the collapse of communism in Eastern Europe and the Soviet Union. Interestingly, rivalries and conflicts within the Democratic majority produced a three-way negotiation of equals between the Senate and House Democratic leadership and the White House, adding to the uncertainty of negotiations. Bush had only limited help from the Republicans in the Senate because Minority Leader Robert Dole (R-KS), fresh from his loss to Bush in the Republican nomination of 1988, was not helping the President achieve his top priority.[51] Bush benefitted by adopting an agenda item that dovetailed with the Democrats, particularly Senate Majority Leader George Mitchell (D-ME). On other issues, Bush did not fare as well because Mitchell was "singlehandedly preventing enactment of the presidents' chief economic initiative, a cut in the tax rate on capital gains."[52]

As a result, during the Clean Air vote in the Senate, the veto became a dramatic game of brinkmanship. Senator Robert Byrd (D-WV) offered an important amendment on the Senate floor, in defense of his coal-mining constituency. The White House was leery of Byrd and his ability to kill the Clean Air reforms. One of the senators being pulled in different directions was Joe Biden (D-DE). In the middle of the voice vote, Biden received a call from White House chief of staff John Sununu, "who told Biden point blank that passage of Byrd's amendment would guarantee a Bush veto of the clean-air bill."[53] The issuing of the final line-in-the-sand signal, after all the threats back and forth, ensured the outcome for the President. The final bill passed the Senate 50–49, without the Byrd amendment and with Biden's support.

Ultimately, the politics of the veto can be powerful and dangerous all at the same time.[54] Using a veto threat uses resources, such as presidential image and reputation, and puts congressional allies on notice. It also reduces uncertainty about the president's intentions, which can encourage Congress to send a bill the president would sign or could also encourage obstruction. Using a veto, as Obama's experience demonstrated, can be both baffling and embarrassing and can serve as a signal of leadership weakness. Yet it remains the strongest buttress of leadership in the presidential arsenal.

THE CHALLENGES OF SHARING POWERS

The Constitution, as many scholars note, separates legislative power. The bulk of the legislative authority goes to the deliberative body, which is Congress. The framers were careful to delineate both enumerated and implied powers to the legislative branch, while leaving the day-to-day structure and design to the current Congress. Consequently, the evolution of the House and Senate occurred in expected and unexpected ways, creating institutional norms that influence presidential–congressional relations greatly. Not only do Congress and the president draw power from diverse constituencies, but also they have dissimilar decision-making structures and relate to political parties and ideology differently.

Divergent Constituencies

On the first Tuesday in November, the entire country chooses a president from the same set of individuals. Consequently, the president's electoral constituency consists of voters from around the country. Yet, this electoral constituency is not evenly distributed across the population. The geographic boundaries of the presidential district may be the nation, but not everyone participates. Moreover, population is not evenly distributed, nor are voting patterns. In 2016, Hillary Clinton received more popular votes than Donald Trump by winning population centers like New York City and Los Angeles. Trump won the presidency, however, by winning Electoral College votes in more states, despite those states having smaller populations and thus fewer voters. A president takes office constitutionally mandated to represent the entire nation, but achieves that victory through the votes of between 40 and 65 percent of the eligible voting population.

In contrast, the only thing national in congressional elections is the date. Senators represent their state, whereas House members represent their population-determined districts. Although a percentage of Congress members' districts may vote for the president, the electoral coalitions of Congress members and the president are distinctive. More specifically, the factors that engender voting decisions in congressional races might not produce the same outcome in presidential elections. Moreover, congressional districts are not mini-nations in terms of geography, ethnicity, race, or class. Thus, by definition, presidents and members of Congress represent different constituencies.

When considering representation actively, the president and members of Congress are different in this regard as well. Political scientist Richard Fenno argues that a member of Congress views his or her constituency as a series of concentric circles in which the furthest circle, that being the geographic district encompassed by the broadest view of constituency, comprises the individuals the member is obligated to represent.[55] The smallest circle contains friends, family members, and trusted advisors. As the circles decrease in size, the importance to the member increases. Fenno argues that the relative importance of sectors of the district predictably determined resource allocation, notably the Congress member's time and attention. Congressional constituency behavior creates a chicken-and-egg relationship; members of Congress devote time, attention, and voting choices to constituents who are attentive via time, donations, and activity in the district. Individuals who reside in a district but vote for someone else, or do not vote at all, receive much less targeted attention and representation through congressional behavior.

Unlike the president, Congress reflects and represents the nation through aggregation or accumulation. Each member of Congress represents his or her individual district, yet the institution reflects the totality of all members of Congress representing their districts and states. Thus, the Madisonian design sums individual or district-based representation to produce national outcomes. The two institutions, however, are not entirely dissimilar, despite their different constituencies, because the behavior toward the constituency is more alike than not. Given that in recent elections only slightly more than 50 percent of the voting population participates, a modern president might claim to be actively representing the entirety of the nation but their agenda typically represents the electoral constituency. Analysis of presidential rhetoric indicates that presidents "craft their talk" for their supporters and not for the average, or median, American voter. Presidents can ignore mass preferences in favor of strategies designed to persuade "those near the political center to move toward . . . [the president's] own positions."[56]

Presidents can and often do speak for the nation. However, when pressing their policy agenda in Congress, presidents confront the natural outcome of different institutional design. From multiple perspectives of constituency, presidents and Congress members represent different voices in the political sphere. Thus, the president's ability to influence legislation must account for the interaction between individuals representing different subsets of the national audience.

The Decision-Making Process

As Harry Truman famously said about the decision-making process as president, "the buck stops here." George W. Bush clarified Truman, noting, "I am the decider." What these two presidents asserted, and all presidents know immediately on taking office, is that presidents must make choices and they alone bear the responsibility of those choices. The choices and decisions a president must make range from deploying troops, to issuing an executive order, to making an address to the nation regarding a policy preference. As Chapter 8 explores, an enormous array of people work to advise the president in the White House and in the executive branch. But, the final say always remains the president's.

· Life functions much differently in Congress. Individual members of Congress do not issue orders, speak to the nation, or deploy troops. Collectively, they can declare war, create legislation, allocate money, and even impeach presidents and members of the judicial branch. Individual members of Congress illustrate their decision making through voting; the final outcome on policy stems from the policy preferences expressed via voting by the majority. For any bill to turn into legislation, the bill must maneuver through the modern congressional system, replete with committees and subcommittees, rules, and procedures, some traditional, some unorthodox.[57] From bill introduction, to committee, to subcommittee, back to committee, to the floor of the chamber, to the other chamber, to its committee, to its subcommittee, back to committee, to the floor of the chamber, to conference committee, and finally back to floors of both chambers, there are myriad opportunities for a bill to die. At no point does a single individual control the outcome of anything; even the Speaker of the House, arguably the second most powerful individual in government and second in succession to the presidency, can be stymied by his or her own majority.

BUDGET SHOWDOWNS AND SHUTDOWNS

THEN . . .

The central task of the Congress in the constitutional system is to write laws. Of those laws, the most significant and often contentious are the authorization and appropriation for the budget of the U.S. government. Everything the government does requires money. Congress creates laws to acquire that money via taxes, fees, interest on bonds, etc. In an entirely separate process, which begins with the president's proposed budget, the Congress writes laws to spend federal money. The money the U.S. government collects is spent on everything from its own functioning to esoteric pieces of pork. For example, to run the White House in 2010, Congress authorized "for the care, maintenance, repair and alteration, refurnishing, improvement, heating, and lighting, including electric power and fixtures, of the Executive Residence at the White House and official entertainment expenses of the President, $14,006,000." According to Barack Obama's budget, they spent $13,838,000.[58]

Since lawmaking and appropriating are separate processes and are negotiated under entirely different circumstances, setting the budget for a given fiscal year is often a battle. In times of plenty, when the government runs a budget surplus, as it did from 1998 to 2001, lawmakers luxuriate in the ability to increase budgets or at least not cut them. In these rare periods, the arguments between the president and Congress soften as disagreements focus on choices. In times where the government takes in less money than it needs to pay all its bills, the process of creating a fiscal year budget exposes the different priorities between the president and Congress as well as the differences between the two parties. In down economic years, battles often emerge between those who would run a deficit and those who insist the federal government must balance its books.

Running a deficit is much like having a credit card, since the bills get paid but cost more as government pays interest on the money it borrows. As with any big purchase for an individual, whether a new computer, car, or house, one chooses to save the money first or use credit and pay it back later. Deficit hawks decry the "pay it off later" approach. Consequently, difficult economic times create budget showdowns over whether to fund the programs authorized. Occasionally, these tensions boil over and Congress and the president come to an impasse. When an impasse occurs between the institutions on a regulatory bill or pork-barrel spending, the bill simply dies in Congress. In contrast, without reauthorization, the federal government cannot spend money and noncritical offices close their doors, federal employees do not get paid, and all sorts of government activity ceases. During 1995, the government shut down not once but twice because of the inability of Congress and Bill Clinton to compromise on spending.

That year had ushered in sweeping change as the Republicans captured both the House and the Senate. During the first two years of his first term, Clinton presided over unified government because the Democrats controlled the House, Senate, and White House for the first time since Jimmy Carter's presidency (1977–1981). The loss of both chambers of Congress was a devastating blow to the Democrats and to the President personally, particularly in the House, which had been under Democratic control for 40 years. The Republicans captured the House via a savvy plan designed by Representative Newt Gingrich (R-GA) to aid newcomers vying for the unusually large number of open seats resulting from retirements. Gingrich both unified and nationalized the 1994 campaign through his "Contract with America." Among other planks, the contract specifically called for a balanced budget. As the new Republican Speaker of the House with the support of the new freshman Congress members, Gingrich pressed forward with a vote on a budget resolution in the first 100 days of 1995.

The contract called for a balanced budget without touching the so-called third rail of American politics, Social Security, and without reducing defense spending. The Republicans wanted to balance the budget by cutting numerous programs favored by Democrats, namely Medicare, Medicaid, and other federal welfare programs. The budget process would be the means by which the Republicans would press their agenda forward.[59] However, the Republicans did not have large enough majorities in either chamber to be able to override a presidential veto; thus, Clinton and his agenda remained a political force to be reckoned with, despite the devastating midterm losses.

In both the House and the Senate, the new budget proposals, passed on mostly party-line votes, slashed spending and lowered taxes but to different degrees. The Senate Republicans were not tied to the contract and cared less about adhering to it. However, in conference committee the House essentially won the debate because the negotiations between Gingrich and Majority Leader Bob Dole (R-KS) culminated in a large tax cut and severe cuts in numerous programs and the limiting of the ability to raise the debt ceiling (the amount that the federal government may borrow). The resolution that Congress passed did not require a presidential signature because it was binding only on Congress. The reconciliation bill enacts the necessary policy changes from the resolution into law and does require the president's signature.[60]

The Republicans celebrated what they viewed as the first step in undoing the large welfare state created by the Democrats. Representative Chris Shays (R-CT) termed it a revolution. Chairman of the House Budget Committee, John Kasich (R-OH), set the tone of the upcoming debate with the President, claiming, "We are prepared to shut the government down in order to solve this problem."[61] While the Republicans were working among themselves, shutting out both the President and congressional Democrats, the President abided by federal law and submitted a budget in February. He then submitted a revised budget that balanced the federal budget in 10 years. Republicans ignored both proposals, insisting the budget needed to be balanced in just seven years. Clinton employed all the tactics available to him as president. Initially shut out of bargaining and negotiating by the Republicans in the resolution phase, Clinton went public by repeatedly emphasizing his opposition to the deep cuts, particularly those aimed at the poor.

With the government operating under a continuing resolution since the Republicans had missed the October 1 deadline, on November 1, Clinton and the Republican leadership met at the White House but reached no agreements. Just days later, Republicans passed another continuing resolution and increased the debt ceiling but attached provisions the President had signaled he would veto. On November 13, the President vetoed the bill and triggered a government shutdown. The President sent Chief of Staff Leon Panetta to Capitol Hill seeking to avoid the shutdown, but when they insisted congressional Democrats be present at the negotiations, Republicans refused.[62] On November 14, the federal government ceased all nonessential operations. On November 15, Secretary of the Treasury Robert Rubin undertook "extraordinary actions" to avoid a default by the federal government, which was triggered by the failure to raise the debt ceiling. He used cash on hand at the Federal Reserve to pay without borrowing, he stopped issuing securities to state and local governments, and he even raided pension accounts to keep the government under the limit that enables it to borrow money.

Once the government shut down, Congress went back to conference committee to fix the bill, and after six days, the President and Republican leaders found enough agreement to end the stalemate, but only until December 15. A new round of negotiations would have to ensue to pass a veto-proof reconciliation bill. The White House again insisted that congressional Democrats be included; this time, the Republicans relented, likely after seeing public opinion polls that blamed them and not the President for the shutdown.[63]

The second round of negotiations began November 28 and ended November 30, with each side accusing the other of acting in bad faith. On December 6, Clinton vetoed another reconciliation bill and offered his own seven-year balanced budget plan. The Republicans rejected the proposal and the government shut down again until January 2. All nonessential government services were again closed and, more noteworthy, government workers again endured losing their paychecks, this time in the middle of the holiday season. The government continued to function on continuing resolutions until March 28, 1996. In the final set of negotiations, Clinton successfully avoided some of the more draconian cuts proposed by the Republicans, and House Republicans made serious concessions. Clinton fought for money for the environment and education as well as his

Bill Clinton meets with Republican House Speaker Newt Gingrich of Georgia and Republican Senate Majority Leader Bob Dole of Kansas in an attempt to avert a government shutdown in 1995.

AmeriCorps program and prevented the abortion riders that the House insisted on attaching to the appropriations bills.

The 1995 government shutdowns reveal how much leverage and strategy the combination of formal and informal tools provides the President. The President repeatedly used the going-public strategy to signal displeasure with the Republican budget bill, yet did not alter the trajectory of the majority's plans until he vetoed the reconciliation bill. The Republicans were willing to risk the veto because their large victory in 1994 led them to believe the public wanted what they wanted: smaller government. The Republicans expected the public to blame the President for obstructing the mandate from the midterm election. They also expected the President to cave in to that public pressure, although neither scenario happened. Clinton also banked on the support of the public, believing that the public only supported the Republicans in generalities and not when faced with specific cuts; in doing so, he took an enormous risk with the first veto, but not with the second. By portraying his veto as a heroic stand against attacks on the poor, the elderly, education, and the environment, Clinton successfully shifted the balance of power despite the new Republican majority.

. . . AND NOW

In the fall of 2008, in the midst of the presidential general election, the United States experienced its most severe economic downturn since the Great Depression. Although the housing market began its dramatic decline sometime in 2007, the recognition of a new economic reality occurred abruptly as the investment banking giant Lehman Brothers collapsed under the weight of its debts in September 2008. The economic crisis recalibrated the 2008 presidential campaign and helped propel Barack Obama into office. Once in office, the failing economy dominated the new president's agenda. In two short years, the economy was no longer in freefall, but it was not yet recovered. Working with a Democratic Congress in 2009, the Obama administration attempted to stem the economic tide via an enormous stimulus package of government spending. Obama also used the economic downturn to justify seeking health-care reform. With the increased spending by the government alongside the bailout of several major banks and the auto industry, the economic freefall ceased. Wall Street recovered relatively quickly, as did the auto industry. Although not an initial cause of the economic crisis (economists mostly blamed irresponsible behavior surrounding mortgages and mortgage debts), the number of unemployed individuals increased significantly. The increase in the unemployment rate, the astronomical government debt and deficit as a result of the spending and falling tax revenue changed the political dynamic. In the 2010 midterm elections, Republicans made gains in the Senate and took control of the House of Representatives. As in 1995, divided government changed the debate regarding budgeting, and the debt ceiling once again became a means to advance a political agenda.

In 2011, there were three issues on the table for the President and the new, divided Congress: the 2011 budget, raising the debt ceiling, and the 2012 budget. In late 2010, the lame-duck Congress passed an $858 billion compromise that extended both tax cuts and unemployment benefits. The compromise in effect punted the ball down the field because the increased borrowing without increased revenue would necessitate an increase in the debt ceiling (the amount the U.S. government can borrow under law). Despite the unfinished nature of the 2011 budget, federal law required the President to submit his 2012 budget. Obama traveled to Baltimore to go public with the core components of his proposal. As is typical of public efforts in smaller locales, Obama reminded the audience of his campaign pledges, explained what he had been doing in the past two years, and then offered his plan for the future:[64]

> These investments are an essential part of the budget my administration is sending to Congress, because I'm convinced that if we out-build and out-innovate and out-educate as well as out-hustle the rest of the world, the jobs and industries of our time will take root here in the United States. Our people will prosper, and our country will succeed. But I'm also convinced that the only way we can make these investments in our future is if our Government starts living within its means, if we start taking responsibility for our deficits. And that's why when I was sworn in as President, I pledged to cut the deficit in half by the end of my first term. The budget I'm proposing today meets that pledge and puts us on a path to pay for what we spend by the middle of the decade. We do this in part by eliminating waste and cutting whatever spending we can do without. As I start—as a start, I've called for a freeze on annual domestic spending over the next 5 years. This freeze would cut the deficit by more than $400 billion over the next decade, bringing this kind of spending—domestic discretionary spending—to its

lowest share of our economy since Dwight Eisenhower was President. Let me repeat that: Because of our budget, this share of spending will be at its lowest level since Dwight Eisenhower was President. That level of spending is lower than it was under Ronald Reagan.[65]

Obama called his proposal a "cut-and-invest" plan; however, Republicans argued that the 2010 election created a mandate for smaller government and a rejection of Obama's "big government" programs. Obama's proposal combined with the fervor for cuts resulting from the election spurred House Republicans to offer their own plan for the future. In February, the House passed a budget resolution calling for $60 billion in cuts. Resolving the differences reached critical importance as the lame-duck compromise expiration date loomed in early April.

Reminiscent of 1995, the final hours of "will the government shut down or won't it" rested on the tax cuts but also the policy riders Republicans attempted to attach to the budget reconciliation: specifically ending the Obama health plan and ceasing funding for abortion in Washington, DC, and funding for Planned Parenthood, an organization that provides health care for women, including abortions. The President capitulated on the tax cuts, accepting a general number in keeping with House Speaker John Boehner's (R-OH) January numbers (and not the February resolution numbers), but drew a line in the sand over the specific cuts to Planned Parenthood. Senate Majority Leader Harry Reid (D-NV) took to the Senate floor in support of the President's position and characterized the negotiations as being held hostage to a restrictive social policy agenda.

In the midst of these delicate negotiations focused on the size of tax cuts and abortion, House Budget Chair Paul Ryan (R-WI) dropped a bomb into the debate. He authored the Republican response to Obama's 2012 budget, their vision of the future. In stark contrast to the President's cut-and-invest strategy, the Republican plan proposed reducing the deficit by $5.8 trillion over 10 years, mainly through deep cuts in discretionary spending programs and turning Medicare into a defined benefit giving seniors vouchers to buy private insurance, as well as shrinking Medicaid through state caps, reducing the top corporate and individual tax rates to 25 percent.

As in 1996, the effort to curb popular programs created a media firestorm and political consequences for Republicans. Moreover, as in 1996, the Senate was unlikely to pass as restrictive a plan as what the House passed April 15 along party lines, 235–193. The Ryan proposal changed the tenor of the shutdown debate, giving the President momentum, as the reality of the Republican proposals shrunk its popular support. By the end of April, even Republicans were backing away from the plan, although publicly blaming the Democrats. Obama did not have to veto a Republican reconciliation bill because unlike Clinton, Obama did not face a unified Congress. Although the Democrats lost the House in the midterm elections, they did not lose the Senate. The veto threat gave the President the ability to shut down the government when faced with a budget proposal not to his liking, but the compromise was possible because of Democrats' control of both the executive branch and the Senate to stem the tide of the Republicans.

Political Parties

For the president, the political party is an army. These are the troops employed to get out the vote and get the message out during campaigns. Once in office, party insiders often assist the president by making media appearances, where they argue in support of the president's policies. For the president, the party also represents an ideological connection. Voters, donors, volunteers, and other elites affiliate with a particular party for the advancement of ideological goals. The presidency represents the ultimate megaphone for the party's policies, ideologies, and plans for government and for the country.

The party in Congress is more than an identifying ideology and connection with supporters. The political parties also organize the institution; whichever party wins more individual seats determines the rules and assignments within the chamber because of their superior numbers. If all members of the party with the most members in office vote together, then they determine who is Speaker, who gets committee assignments, who gets committee chairs, and who sits on the Rules Committee in the House. Party discipline and loyalty are especially critical to the functioning of the House as they serve to manage the 435 members. These opportunities emerge from majority voting power created by caucusing outside the chamber.

When the president interacts with Congress, he is in an odd position as both leader of his party and leader of a separate institution with separate institutional demands and goals. This dynamic is most evident when comparing unified and divided government. When one party controls the presidency, the House, and the Senate, a common ideology seemingly unifies policymaking that makes sweeping policy change possible. Incidents of major or "landmark" legislation occur more frequently than when government is divided between the parties because the process is more efficient and responsive.[66] Examples of sweeping legislation during a time of unified government include the passage of FDR's New Deal legislation during his first term and Lyndon Johnson's passage of the Civil Rights Act in 1964, the Voting Rights Act and Medicare in 1965, and other Great Society policy changes. Johnson took great pride in his legislative success; the former Senate majority leader, known as the master of the Senate, often kept a legislative scorecard in his coat pocket to readily quote his successes on Capitol Hill. Johnson was perhaps one of the best contemporary presidents in dealing with Congress because of his vast knowledge of the institution; he had served 12 years in the House of Representatives and 12 years in the Senate before being elected vice president in 1960. The scope of Johnson's legislative agenda and his strategy in achieving it are seen in this memo on the administration's legislative program from 1964:

> The following legislative issues should have priority in immediate preparation of materials to be used to support the successful enactment of Administration-sponsored measures pending before the present Congress.
>
> 1. Poverty 2. Foreign Aid 3. Housing 4. Appalachian Bill 5. Mass Transit 6. Transportation Bill 7. ARA 8. Food Stamp 9. Pay Raise 10. Public Debt 11. Medicare 12. Food for Peace 13. Hill–Burton 14. Wilderness Bill 15. Marketing Committee Investigation 16. Civil Rights
>
> On these, we need to establish (a) the need for the legislation, (b) the history of the issue and the legislation, (c) broad context of relationships of each issue to the

overall Administration program and National need, (d) the pertinent quotations from the President and from both Democratic and Republic leaders, currently and in some instances historically.[67]

However, not everyone views the ability of unified government to pass major changes to public policy as a positive thing. In fact, the framers, who were generally fearful of factions and the ability for popular support to take over public policies, made gridlock a prominent feature of the American government through separation of powers and checks and balances. As a result, the government created by the framers is one of incrementalism, which tends to avoid the type of sweeping reforms to government policies that can be destabilizing to the government itself. Under this view, divided government can be seen as a stabilizing force, since incremental or transactional change is more likely than transformational change because the disparate sides are forced to compromise to get anything done. In theory, the requirement for compromise between the parties makes episodes of gridlock much more likely during times of divided government. For example, one of the most significant pieces of legislation signed into law by Bill Clinton came in 1996; he achieved his promise to reform "welfare as we know it" with passage of the Personal Responsibility and Work Opportunity Reconciliation Act by working with a Republican Congress. Two years earlier, he had failed to pass several key issues of his domestic agenda, including health-care reform, working with a Democratic Congress. It is important to note, however, that Clinton's political skill played a role in passing welfare reform as well. Relying on the now-famous Clinton strategy of "triangulation," Clinton, a moderate Democrat, put together his version of welfare reform by co-opting some of the most popular aspects of both Republican and Democratic plans. By taking a little from the left and a little from the right and bringing it together in the middle (to form the triangle), Clinton's strategy provided just enough incentive for support on both sides of the political aisle to pass the legislation.

However, Clinton's legislative success with the Republican Congress serves as more of an exception than the rule. The individual political skill of the president, as well as factors that contribute to the political environment (such as the economy or the public mood on a particular issue), can determine whether bipartisanship is possible. Gridlock relates significantly to the intensity of partisanship, high intensity or hyperpartisanship, which makes compromise and negotiation much less likely as positions and sides harden. This is an important point since divided government has occurred with regularity since 1832 after reforms to the Electoral College moved the

Table 6.2 Party Government

YEAR	PRESIDENT	HOUSE	SENATE	U/D
1933–1945	F. Roosevelt (D)	D	D	Unified
		D	D	Unified
		D	D	Unified
		D	D	Unified
		D	D	Unified
		D	D	Unified

Table 6.2 (*continued*)

YEAR	PRESIDENT	HOUSE	SENATE	U/D
1945–1953	Truman (D)	D	D	Unified
		R	R	Divided
		D	D	Unified
		D	D	Unified
1953–1961	Eisenhower (R)	R	R	Unified
		D	D	Divided
		D	D	Divided
		D	D	Divided
1961–1963	Kennedy (D)	D	D	Unified
1963–1969	Johnson (D)	D	D	Unified
		D	D	Unified
		D	D	Unified
1969–1974	Nixon (R)	D	D	Divided
		D	D	Divided
1973–1977	Nixon/Ford (R)	D	D	Divided
		D	D	Divided
1977–1981	Carter (D)	D	D	Unified
		D	D	Unified
1981–1989	Reagan (R)	D	R	Divided
		D	R	Divided
		D	R	Divided
		D	D	Divided
1989–1993	Bush (R)	D	D	Divided
		D	D	Divided
1993–2001	Clinton (D)	D	D	Unified
		R	R	Divided
		R	R	Divided
		R	R	Divided
2001–2009	G. W. Bush (R)	R	D	Divided
		R	R	Unified
		R	R	Unified
		D	R	Divided
2009–2017	Obama (D)	D	D	Unified
		D	R	Divided
		D	R	Divided
		R	R	Divided

nomination of presidential candidates from congressional caucuses to party conventions. Since then, through the 2016 election, Americans have elected a divided government more than 40 percent of the time. Since 1932, of the 43 congressional elections held (which also encompass 22 presidential elections), unified government has only occurred 22 times (see Table 6.2).

CONCLUSION

The president's role in the legislative process is both guaranteed and limited by the Constitution. However, the degree to which the president can influence legislative outcomes rests on circumstances that are typically in flux. Moreover, institutional conditions combine with the personal skillset of the president in unexpected ways. Does the president's party control all or part of the Congress? Unified government often makes it easier for a president to accomplish his goals, but not always. Does the president keep his word when he makes deals or draw lines in the sand? Presidential behavior in public and behind the scenes can have powerful effects during negotiations with Congress.

The president's success in achieving his legislative agenda is also influenced by circumstances, events, and individuals outside the legislative process. A large electoral victory can provide the president with momentum and a mandate for his agenda. A popular president has more sway with Congress because it is likely a majority of congressional constituents like the president. Ultimately, the president's role in the legislative process is emblematic of the modern presidency. The president remains limited by narrowly proscribed responsibilities (the veto, the state of the union) yet challenged by increased expectations as problem solver in chief. The ability to meet those expectations rest on factors that can be both opportunities and obstacles and help determine a president's success in the day-to-day governing of the nation.

CHAPTER 7

Presidents and the Judicial Branch

O
n March 16, 2016, Barack Obama exercised one of the most important presidential powers outlined in the U.S. Constitution—he nominated Merrick Garland, chief judge of the U.S. Court of Appeals for the DC Circuit, to fill the Supreme Court vacancy left by the death of Associate Justice Antonin Scalia five weeks earlier. As a Harvard-educated attorney with nearly 20 years of experience serving as a federal appeals court judge, no one doubted Garland's qualifications to serve on the high court. However, the political circumstances surrounding the vacancy doomed Garland's nomination from the start. The leader of the Republican-controlled Senate, Mitch McConnell (R-KY), made it clear within hours of Scalia's death that a lame-duck president in his last year in office should not be allowed to fill the vacancy and that any nominee put forward by Obama would not be considered. Obama would nonetheless nominate Garland, stating that despite McConnell's objection, he would fulfill his constitutional duty regarding judicial nominations. Republicans gambled on the idea that a looming vacancy on the Court would matter more to the conservative base in their party than to Democratic and/or liberal voters during the presidential election. Despite continued urging by Obama and other top Democrats throughout 2016 for the Senate to hold confirmation hearings, McConnell and his Republican colleagues held firm in their decision to block Obama from a third pick to the Court. In the end, the gamble paid off; Garland's nomination effectively died on Election Night when Republican nominee Donald Trump won the presidency. Trump instead nominated Neil Gorsuch, a judge of the U.S. Court of Appeals for the Tenth Circuit, to fill the vacancy.

Donald Trump nominates appeals court judge Neil Gorsuch to the Supreme Court.

A Supreme Court nomination is a significant opportunity for a president to make a lifelong contribution to the Court. On average, presidents usually get to nominate a new justice every two years. However, there are no guarantees on the timeline. Gerald Ford, who served less than 30 months in office, had one appointment, whereas his successor, Jimmy Carter, had none during his four years in office. More recently, Bill Clinton and George W. Bush each had only two vacancies during their respective eight years in office. The 11 years that passed between Clinton's second nomination in 1994 (Stephen Breyer) and Bush's first nomination in 2005 (John Roberts) turned out to be one of the longest droughts of high court vacancies in the nation's history. For Obama, Scalia's death marked the third vacancy on the Court during his eight years in office, although he, too—like Clinton and Bush before him—would be limited to filling only two vacancies. The first occurred in 2009, when David Souter (appointed in 1990 by George H. W. Bush) unexpectedly announced his retirement. He was succeeded by Sonia Sotomayor. The second vacancy occurred in 2010 with the retirement of John Paul Stevens (appointed in 1975 by Gerald Ford), who was succeeded by Elena Kagan.

Normally, the retirement of a Republican appointee during a Democratic administration, or vice versa, represents a potential ideological shift on the Court. But neither Souter nor Stevens was a conservative jurist. In fact, Souter's tenure on the Court had not lived up to the expectation of either the president who had nominated him or conservatives who had been assured in 1990 that Souter would be a reliable conservative vote on key decisions. The Bush White House had promoted Souter as a "believer in judicial restraint, a tough trial court judge with a great legal mind who will interpret the Constitution not legislate from the bench" and a judge who had "fidelity to the Constitution and the rule of law."[1] Instead, Souter was more often a reliable liberal vote during his 19 years on the Court, joining his more liberal colleagues in high-profile decisions in areas such as upholding abortion rights, banning school prayer, and limiting the scope of the death penalty. As such, Souter's retirement presented

Obama with what would be considered a status-quo pick by keeping the seat in the hands of a moderate to liberal justice (as did Kagan's nomination to replace Stevens).

Many assumed that Obama, when faced with his first Supreme Court vacancy, would nominate a woman or that he would make history by nominating the first Hispanic to the Court. Obama opted for both with his nomination of Sotomayor, whose resume included experience on the U.S. District Court for the Southern District of New York (nominated by Bush in 1991) and the U.S. Court of Appeals for the Second Circuit (nominated by Clinton in 1997). Despite her qualifications for the job, which included 18 years of experience as a federal judge, a law degree from Yale, and experience both as a prosecutor and in private practice, Sotomayor's nomination received opposition from conservative Republicans. Several in the Senate, along with conservative interest groups, criticized what they considered Sotomayor's judicial activism (although assessments of her time on the federal bench suggested she was more of a moderate, as opposed to liberal, judge), as well as her now-famous "wise Latina" remark. In 2001, while giving a talk at Berkeley Law School, Sotomayor remarked, "I would hope that a wise Latina woman with the richness of her experiences would more often than not reach a better conclusion than a white male who hasn't lived that life." Although taken somewhat out of context by her critics, Sotomayor answered questions about the remark during her confirmation hearings before the Senate Judiciary Committee, stating that whereas personal experiences help to shape a judge's perspective, ultimately the law is the only guide for constitutional interpretation. Sotomayor was confirmed by the Senate on August 6, 2009, by a vote of 68–31 (all opposition votes came from Republicans).

The Souter retirement, along with the Sotomayor confirmation, highlight two of the most prominent features of contemporary relations between the president and the judicial branch. First, presidents have no control over a justice once he or she is confirmed, and there are no guarantees as to whether the justice's decisions will align with the president's political agenda. Also, since justices serve for life terms and there is no set age for retirement, justices can serve for years, if not decades, well past a president's time in office. Second, the confirmation process for federal judges, and in particular Supreme Court justices, has become highly politicized in recent decades and requires presidents to pay close attention to political considerations in their selections. Third, although the president may enjoy influence over the federal courts through his power to nominate judges, the president must also adhere to rulings by federal courts regarding the nature and scope of presidential powers as outlined in the Constitution, thus affecting his ability to govern on a day-to-day basis.

NOMINATIONS TO THE U.S. SUPREME COURT

As outlined in Article II, Section 2, of the Constitution, the president "shall nominate, and by and with the advice and consent of the Senate, shall appoint . . . judges of the Supreme Court." In addition, Article III, Section I, states that "judges, both of the supreme and inferior courts, shall hold their offices during good behavior." Congress holds the power to set the size of the Supreme Court. With passage of the Judiciary Act of 1789, the initial Supreme Court consisted of six justices—a chief justice and five associate justices. The number of justices reached ten in 1863, but was reduced to nine with passage of the Judiciary Act of 1869—a chief justice and eight associate justices. The size of the Court has not changed since that time.

Franklin D. Roosevelt and the Supreme Court

FDR's attempt to "pack the court" following his reelection in 1936, which would have increased the size from nine to 15 justices, is the most prominent attempt to alter the size of the Court since 1869. FDR faced intense challenges when he took office in 1933 stemming from the Great Depression. Although he had the support of Congress and a majority of the public for his New Deal programs, the Supreme Court did not agree with the President's plan to expand the size and scope of the federal government. The Court, with seven of its nine members having been appointed by previous Republican presidents, struck down major provisions of New Deal legislation in 1935–36. Frustrated by the lack of vacancies on the Court (none had occurred during FDR's first term), yet determined to capitalize on his huge reelection victory in 1936, FDR crafted his "court-packing" plan. In addition, he sought advice from his attorney general about the jurisdiction of the Supreme Court (that is, its ability to hear cases) and whether it could be altered. In a January 14, 1936, memo to Attorney General Homer Cummings, FDR inquired, "What was the McArdle [sic] case (7 Wall 506-year 1869)? I am told that the Congress withdrew some act from the jurisdiction of the Supreme Court."[2] Cummings responded, "The case of exparte McCardle, 7 Wallace 506, decided in December, 1868, to which you refer in your memorandum, is one of the classic cases to which we refer when considering the possibility of limiting the jurisdiction of Federal Courts. This whole matter has been the subject of considerable study in this Department, and, in view of recent developments, is apt to be increasingly important."[3]

By early 1937, the FDR administration began its attempt to persuade the public, as well as members of Congress, that the court-packing plan was needed. Of the nine justices, six were over the age of 70, yet none seemed ready to retire. FDR decided that he should receive one new nomination for each of those justices, which would have allowed him to "pack the court" with six new justices of his choice, bringing the total number of justices to 15. This was part of his proposed reorganization of the judicial branch, which would also add many new judicial posts to lower federal courts to help alleviate the backlog of cases. According to Cummings, who was one of FDR's strongest advocates for increasing the number of federal judges, "Delay in the administration of justice is the outstanding defect of our federal judicial system. It has been a cause of concern to practically every one of my predecessors in office. It has exasperated the bench, the bar, the business community and the public. . . . It is a mockery of justice to say to a person when he files suit, that he may receive a decision years later. . . . The evil is a growing one."[4] And, as FDR himself argued in a message to Congress,

> Modern complexities call also for a constant infusion of new blood in the court. . . . A lowered mental or physical vigor leads men to avoid an examination of complicated and changed conditions. Little by little, new facts become blurred through old glasses fitted, as it were, for the needs of another generation; older men, assuming that the scene is the same as it was in the past, cease to explore or inquire into the present or the future. We have recognized this truth in the civil service of the nation and of many states by compelling retirement on pay at the age of seventy. . . . Life tenure of judges, assured by the Constitution, was designed to place the courts beyond temptations or influences which might impair their judgments: it was not intended to create a static judiciary. A constant and systematic addition of younger blood will vitalize the courts and better equip them to

recognize and apply the essential concepts of justice in the light of the needs and the facts of an ever-changing world. It is obvious, therefore, from both reason and experience, that some provision must be adopted, which will operate automatically to supplement the work of older judges and accelerate the work of the court.[5]

FDR also made his case about the court-packing plan through a fireside chat on March 9, 1937, in which he scolded the Supreme Court for thwarting the will of the American people by striking down New Deal legislation:

> The Court in addition to the proper use of its judicial functions has improperly set itself up as a third House of the Congress—a super-legislature, as one of the justices has called it—reading into the Constitution words and implications which are not there, and which were never intended to be there. We have, therefore, reached the point as a Nation where we must take action to save the Constitution from the Court and the Court from itself. We must find a way to take an appeal from the Supreme Court to the Constitution itself. We want a Supreme Court which will do justice under the Constitution—not over it. In our Courts we want a government of laws and not of men.[6]

However, the court-packing plan was not met with as much support, either congressional or public, as FDR's legislative agenda had been. Congress failed to pass the legislation to reorganize the federal judiciary and to allow FDR to pack the Court; in addition, no legislation passed that would have altered or diminished the Court's jurisdiction. However, just a few weeks after FDR's fireside chat, the Court handed down the first of three 5–4 decisions to uphold New Deal legislation. This move by the Court is known as the famous "switch in time that saved nine." FDR also received his first opportunity to replace a retiring justice in the summer of 1937, the first of a total of nine vacancies on the Court during his 12-plus years in office.

Tenure and Removal

FDR's frustration with the Supreme Court highlights one of its most important structural features—all justices, along with all other federal judges, are appointed to life terms. Although justices and federal judges can be impeached by a majority vote in the House of Representatives and removed by a two-thirds majority vote in the Senate, no Supreme Court justice has ever been removed from office; all have served until retirement or death. The definition of an impeachable offense is not clear, although most would agree that removal should be for a criminal offense or ethical lapse and not purely for partisan and/or political reasons. In 1805, Justice Samuel Chase, who had been appointed by George Washington, was impeached but not removed from the bench because of political opposition to his legal decisions. In the late 1950s and throughout the 1960s, several conservative groups, including the John Birch Society, advocated for the impeachment of Chief Justice Earl Warren, a Dwight Eisenhower appointee, for what were considered the Court's activist and liberal rulings (including the landmark case of *Brown v. Board of Education* in 1954) in the areas of due process rights and civil liberties. Two unsuccessful impeachment attempts were brought against Justice William O. Douglas (an FDR appointee) in the House; the first attempt came in 1953 after Douglas granted a temporary stay of execution to Julius and Ethel Rosenberg, the American couple convicted of selling atomic bomb secrets to the Soviet Union, and the second attempt came in 1970 and was led by the House Minority Leader Gerald Ford (R-MI) over alleged ethical concerns stemming from Douglas's publications and involvement with a private foundation. In a speech on the House floor, Ford famously stated that an "impeachable offense is whatever a majority of the House of Representatives considers to be at a given moment in history."[7] Yet, despite Ford's definition, attempts to impeach any federal judge, let alone a Supreme Court justice, have been rare.

Given that Supreme Court justices serve for life, each justice has the potential to serve for several decades. To date, a total of 17 men have served as chief justice, and a total of 112 men and women have served as associate justices, with an average tenure on the bench of approximately 15 years. However, during the twentieth century, two justices attempted to break longevity records for service on the Court. Hugo Black, appointed by FDR in 1937, served for 34 years and one month prior to his retirement in 1971. Similarly, Douglas, also appointed by FDR (two years later in 1939), had served a total of 36 years and six months when he retired in November 1975. Douglas had surpassed the previous longevity record of Stephen J. Field (appointed by Abraham Lincoln), who had served for 34 years and six months, from 1863 to 1897. Ironically, Douglas's replacement on the Court was named by Gerald Ford, who had led the impeachment proceedings against Douglas in the House five years earlier. Ford's selection, John Paul Stevens, also ranks high on the list of longest-serving justices, beginning his 34th year on the Court at the start of the 2009–2010 Supreme Court term and ending the term with his retirement. The tenure of these justices shows the importance of a presidential nomination to the Court, particularly for a president's legacy.

The Nomination Process

When a vacancy occurs on the Supreme Court, a potential justice is first nominated for the position by the president. Since federal judges are the only public officials to enjoy a lifetime appointment, the nomination and confirmation of a Supreme Court justice represents a significant event during a president's administration. When a president nominates, he does so with the intention of influencing the outcome of future decisions to reflect his own political philosophy and policy agenda. However, there is no guarantee that the confirmation process that follows will go smoothly or that the Senate will automatically approve the president's choice. The White House must be strategic in its selection of Supreme Court nominees and reflective of the political environment in which the president finds himself to maximize the nominee's chance for a successful confirmation.[8] In addition, it is important to remember that not all nominations are equal because some are more "critical" than others, such as that for chief justice or the chance to replace a conservative justice with a liberal one or vice versa.[9] Most presidents, with the help of White House staff, have a "short list" of potential nominees ready for when a vacancy should occur. Often, an initial list of judicial nominees takes shape during the transition period after a president wins election in November and prior to the inauguration in January. However, Trump announced his list of potential justices in May 2016, shortly after wrapping up the Republican nomination contest, to reassure conservatives within his party that he would nominate judges with a strict constructionist view of the Constitution.

Presidents rely on many factors in making their decision about whom to nominate, including objective qualifications, policy preferences, political and personal reward, and building political support.[10] A president wants a nomination that will reflect his policy preferences and please his political supporters. The president's "situation" also affects the confirmation process, including his political strength in the Senate (whether the confirmation will go smoothly), his level of public approval (which can place political pressure on the Senate to confirm the nominee if the president has high approval ratings), mobilization of interest group activity (whether interest groups will support or, more important, oppose the nomination), and the importance of the nomination (will it fill the position of chief justice or perhaps replace a woman or minority on the Court?).[11] A "myth of merit" also exists, since merit (whether one is deserving of the position based on experience and skill) plays little, if any, role in the judicial selection process.[12] Despite attempts to keep the Court an unbiased and independent institution, presidential appointments are nonetheless political. Several highly qualified individuals to both the Supreme Court and lower federal courts have been passed over for appointment or failed to be confirmed because of political considerations. The political climate often plays a larger role than merit in who is selected, as do race, gender, religion, and geography.[13] Finally, presidents must "arbitrate among factions" within their administration because conflicts among high-level advisors can play out during the selection process. This can lead to one advisor winning the battle over others in shaping the president's selection, but may not always serve the broader political interests of the president.[14]

Nominees to the Supreme Court are always lawyers, although this is not a constitutional requirement, and most have attended top law schools (in recent years, nearly all of the justices attended Harvard, Yale, or Stanford). Previous jobs usually include appellate judgeships (state or federal), jobs within the Justice Department or other parts of the executive branch, or elected office. Most nominees are older than 50, and a majority are from upper- or upper-middle-class families. Diversity has not been a prominent feature on the Court, although race, ethnicity, and gender have played a more apparent role in considering nominees in recent years. Still, only four women have ever served on the Court—Sandra Day O'Connor (a Reagan appointee who served from 1981 until 2006), Ginsburg, Sotomayor, and Kagan—and only two African Americans have served on the Court—Thurgood Marshall (nominated by Lyndon Johnson in 1967) and Clarence Thomas (nominated by George H. W. Bush in 1991). In 1986, Antonin Scalia (a Reagan appointee) became the first justice of Italian descent (Samuel Alito, nominated by George W. Bush in 2006, is of Italian descent as well), and Sotomayor is also the first justice of Hispanic descent. Most members of the Court in recent years have been former federal appellate court judges (Kagan is a recent exception, having never been a judge, but she was associate White House Counsel in the Clinton administration, Dean of Harvard Law School, and Solicitor General in the Obama administration), and since historically this is the most common place for presidents to look for high court nominees, placing more women and minorities on lower federal courts will increase their presence within the eligible pool of candidates for the Court in years to come (see Table 7.1).

The Confirmation Process

Once the president makes a nomination, the Senate Judiciary Committee considers it. If the committee approves, the nomination then goes to the entire Senate, with confirmation occurring by a simple majority vote. Since 1790, a total of 161 nominations have been made to the Supreme Court, with only 12 rejected by a

Table 7.1 The U.S. Supreme Court

JUSTICE	YEAR OF BIRTH	LAW SCHOOL	YEAR OF APPOINT-MENT	APPOINT-ING PRESI-DENT	PRIOR POSITION
Anthony Kennedy	1936	Harvard	1988	Reagan	Judge, U.S. Court of Appeals (Ninth Circuit)
Clarence Thomas	1948	Yale	1991	Bush	Judge, U.S. Court of Appeals (DC Circuit)
Ruth Bader Ginsberg	1933	Columbia	1993	Clinton	Judge, U.S. Court of Appeals (DC Circuit)
Stephen Breyer	1938	Harvard	1994	Clinton	Judge, U.S. Court of Appeals (First Circuit)
John Roberts	1955	Harvard	2005	Bush	Judge, U.S. Court of Appeals (DC Circuit)
Samuel Alito	1950	Yale	2005	Bush	Judge, U.S. Court of Appeals (Third Circuit)
Sonia Sotomayor	1954	Yale	2009	Obama	Judge, U.S. Court of Appeals (Second Circuit)
Elena Kagan	1960	Harvard	2010	Obama	U.S. Solicitor General
Neil Gorsuch	1967	Harvard	2017	Trump	Judge, U.S. Court of Appeals (Tenth Circuit)

vote in the Senate. The three most recent Senate rejections included two of Richard Nixon's nominees (G. Harrold Carswell and Clement Haynsworth) and one Reagan nominee (Robert Bork). One of the closest votes ever to occur in the Senate came in 1991, when Clarence Thomas received a vote of 52–48 following the controversy over sexual harassment allegations during his confirmation process (as discussed below). In addition, the Senate has taken no action on six nominations and postponed a vote on three nominations. Seven individuals have declined the nomination (something that has not occurred since 1882), and eight nominations were withdrawn, usually because of impending defeat in the Senate and/or negative public reaction to the nominee.

George W. Bush's nomination of Harriet Miers in 2005 is the most recent example of a nomination to end in withdrawal. Bush nominated Miers, his White House Counsel, to replace Sandra Day O'Connor after her pending retirement. Initially, John Roberts had been nominated to replace O'Connor, but his nomination was elevated to Chief Justice following the death of William Rehnquist in September 2005. On announcing Miers's nomination on October 7, 2005, Bush stated,

> I've given a lot of thought to the kind of people who should serve on the Federal judiciary. I've come to agree with the late Chief Justice William Rehnquist, who wrote about the importance of having judges who are drawn from a wide diversity of professional backgrounds. Justice Rehnquist himself came to the Supreme Court without prior experience on the bench. . . . And I'm proud to nominate an outstanding woman who brings a similar record of achievement in private practice and public service. . . . Harriet Miers will strictly interpret our Constitution and laws. She will not legislate from the bench. I ask the Senate to review her qualifications, thoroughly and fairly, and to vote on her nomination promptly. . . . In selecting

a nominee, I've sought to find an American of grace, judgment, and unwavering devotion to the Constitution and laws of our country. Harriet Miers is just such a person. I've known Harriet for more than a decade. I know her heart; I know her character. I'm confident that Harriet Miers will add to the wisdom and character of our judiciary when she is confirmed as the 110th Justice of the Supreme Court.[15]

Despite assurances by Bush that she was the best candidate for the job, Miers's embattled three-week nomination was withdrawn after she was vilified in the press as being unqualified and lacking sufficient experience in constitutional law. Miers, a corporate attorney from Texas prior to working in the Bush White House, had also been roundly criticized by conservatives who feared that despite Bush's personal guarantees to the contrary, she would not be committed to their conservative agenda once confirmed. She had also been sharply criticized by Senate Republicans, including Senate Judiciary Committee Chairman Arlen Specter (R-PA), for lacking an in-depth understanding of constitutional matters. Samuel Alito, a federal appellate court judge with strong conservative credentials, eventually filled the seat vacated by O'Connor's retirement.

Senators are not the only political actors involved in the confirmation process. Since 1956, Supreme Court nominees have been closely scrutinized by the American Bar Association (ABA). The ABA's 15-member Standing Committee on the Federal Judiciary rates nominees as "well qualified," "qualified," or "not qualified," which can play an influential role in the Senate confirmation hearings. This process became an important political element for a president in his selection of justices, since having a nominee's professional credentials labeled unqualified would make confirmation difficult in the Senate. Not all presidents have submitted names to the ABA when making a nomination to the Supreme Court, and some ratings by the committee were controversial. Nixon's appointees, Haynsworth and Carswell, were both rejected by the Senate (many Senators viewed them as unqualified to serve) although the ABA claimed that both were qualified. Later nominations by Nixon were not submitted to the ABA, although the ABA continued to provide its own rating.

The ABA has never given a not-qualified rating, but a less-than-unanimous vote among the committee members for a qualified rating can cause a public stir during the confirmation hearings and weaken the nominee's chances. Reagan's nomination of Bork in 1987 and Bush's nomination of Thomas in 1991, both federal appellate judges, failed to receive unanimous votes from the ABA committee. Although the votes against the two nominees constituted a small minority of the committee (four voted against Bork and two voted against Thomas), the results gave political opponents ammunition in the confirmation process. Many conservative lawmakers have denounced the ABA in recent years for having a liberal bias in both policy positions (like favoring abortion rights and opposing capital punishment) and its stance on judicial nominees. As a result, many Republicans now give less credence to judicial ratings. In 2001, the George W. Bush administration announced that it would not submit the names of judicial nominees to the ABA, eliminating its official role in the nomination process. However, the ABA continued to assess nominees and send its reports to the Senate Judiciary Committee during the Bush years; both Roberts and Alito in 2005 received well-qualified ratings. And in 2009, the Obama administration reinstated the practice of submitting the names of judicial nominees to the ABA, with both Sotomayor and Kagan receiving a well-qualified rating.

Beyond the ABA, legal scholars and prominent attorneys also weigh in on a nominee's qualifications. In addition, interest groups can influence the president's selection process, as groups publicly and privately fight for or against nominations. This is not surprising given that interest groups have a large stake in who sits on the Supreme Court through the decisions that are handed down, since interest groups often litigate public policies and provide financial support for certain cases to be appealed to the Supreme Court. Those interest groups that are important to the president and support his policy agenda can exert influence in the nomination stage. For example, conservative groups lobbied the Bush administration against the potential nomination of Attorney General Alberto Gonzalez in 2005 because of his perceived moderate stance on issues such as abortion. Following the nomination, many interest groups engage in campaign-like activities to either support or defeat the nominee. Estimates suggest that liberal interest groups opposed to the conservative legal views of Robert Bork spent up to $15 million to fight his nomination in 1987. Since then, interest group activity surrounding a Supreme Court nomination has continued to expand, which includes airing television ads and online efforts to lobby for or against the nominee.[16]

Given the campaign environment once a nomination is announced, it is not surprising that the news media also play a prominent role in the confirmation process. News coverage of Supreme Court nominees since the late 1980s, particularly on cable news, has become "highly acrimonious," with intense scrutiny of the nominee's qualifications and legal views.[17] The tone and content of the coverage during the confirmation process often takes on the feel of horse-race coverage similar to presidential campaigns, focusing on whether the nominee is up or down in terms of both Senate and public support, as well as money being spent by interest groups. The infrequency of nominations also contributes to the "big story" approach by news media outlets when one does occur, as does the chance to provide live coverage of a controversial story (as was the case with the Bork and Thomas nominations). From the time of Sotomayor's nomination in April 2009 to her confirmation in August 2009, news coverage focused on her personal and professional history, her "wise Latina" remark, and whether any Republicans would vote for her. With a strong Democratic majority in the Senate and several Republicans already on record to support her confirmation, the amount of news coverage leading up to the confirmation vote seemed to belie the political reality of an almost certain confirmation. According to the Pew Research Center's Project for Excellence in Journalism, the Sotomayor nomination regularly dominated political news coverage throughout the summer months, although "the lack of news, and the empty ritualistic nature of the event, seemed to dominate a weary media storyline."[18]

The Confirmation Hearings

During the confirmation hearings, nominees are expected to answer questions by the Senate Judiciary Committee. This became an accepted practice in 1955 during the confirmation of Dwight Eisenhower's nominee, John M. Harlan. Most confirmation hearings are routine and draw little public attention. However, in recent years, a few notable exceptions have turned the process into a full-blown media circus. In

1987, Reagan's nomination of Bork, a conservative appeals court judge, faced strong opposition from liberal interest groups around the country. According to Reagan, in announcing the nomination,

> Judge Bork, widely regarded as the most prominent and intellectually powerful advocate of judicial restraint, shares my view that judges' personal preferences and values should not be part of their constitutional interpretations. The guiding principle of judicial restraint recognizes that under the Constitution it is the exclusive province of the legislatures to enact laws and the role of the courts to interpret them. We're fortunate to be able to draw upon such an impressive legal mind, an experienced judge and a man who already has devoted so much of his life to public service. He'll bring credit to the Court and his colleagues, as well as to his country and the Constitution.[19]

Yet, although Bork was a well-known and accomplished legal scholar and jurist, his nomination hearings were contentious and highly political, in part because Bork did not shy away from answering questions from Democratic senators about how he would rule on specific cases. He believed in original intent and a strict constructionist view of the Constitution and that many liberal rulings handed down by the Warren and Burger courts, such as *Roe v. Wade* (1973) and other cases expanding privacy rights, should be overturned.

Sensing that the nomination would not go smoothly, Reagan administration officials developed both public and behind-the-scenes strategies to ensure Bork's Senate confirmation. Senior administration officials were provided with talking points from director of communications, Tom Griscom:

> As the confirmation hearings conclude, we enter a new phase of the debate about Judge Bork. During the next several weeks each of you has an important role to play in building support for this nomination. Attached are materials that should be of assistance to you in framing your prepared remarks and answers to press briefings. I ask that in the weeks ahead each of you notify in advance the White House Office of Public Affairs and the White House Office of Media Relations of any domestic travel plans. Those offices will provide you with up-to-date guidance and schedule interviews with local reporters as appropriate. The President has seen statements many of you have made in support of Judge Bork. Your continued participation is essential.
>
> **Key Points for the Weeks Ahead**
>
> - Support for Judge Bork is a test of support for President Reagan.
> - The American people have consistently stated they believe the President should appoint judges who will be tough on crime. President Reagan has done this. This in part explains why law enforcement groups favor Judge Bork, and the American Civil Liberties Union opposes him.
> - Judge Bork enjoys support from across the political spectrum. His supporters include liberals and conservatives, Democrats and Republicans.
> - The same cannot be said about opposition to Judge Bork, which comes primarily from the special interests—individuals and groups who have long demonstrated they are outside the American political mainstream.

- These opponents have grown increasingly shrill in their attacks on Judge Bork. Many have resorted to distortions and misstatements in their attempts to undermine Judge Bork's impressive record. These tactics make the choice between the special interests and the American people's interest.
- Judge Bork is superbly qualified to be the next Supreme Court Justice. He has been forthcoming with the Senate and with the American people. He believes that a judge should interpret the law, not make the law.[20]

Reagan advisors were also keeping a close watch on key senators and how they might vote on the Bork confirmation. A White House memo showed the attention being paid to moderate senators in both parties: Dennis DeConcini (D-AZ) was listed as "generally satisfied with Bork's answers at hearings despite posturing to the contrary. Feels he may have no political alternative (in light of interest group pressure in Arizona) other than to oppose Bork." Lowell Weicker (R-CT) was listed as "undecided but definitely leaning against Bork. Believes Bork has shifted views to secure confirmation and cannot be trusted." And Lloyd Bentsen (D-TX) was listed as "truly undecided. . . . [Thinks] Bentsen will be okay but won't decide until the last moment. Might be worth a personal visit from [Chief of Staff Howard Baker] down the road."[21]

The strategic efforts by the Reagan White House would end up being for naught because Bork failed in the Senate confirmation. After 12 days of intense questioning by the Senate Judiciary Committee (as part of a Democratic-controlled Senate), intense lobbying by interest groups, and negative press coverage of Bork, the qualified yet controversial jurist lost his confirmation bid by a 58–42 vote in the Senate. Since the failed Bork nomination, nominees have been more circumspect during confirmation hearings and have mostly avoided answering any direct questions from senators about potential cases in the hopes of avoiding similar controversy.

Perhaps no confirmation hearing was as controversial as that of Clarence Thomas in 1991. Thomas was nominated by George H. W. Bush to replace the ailing Thurgood Marshall. Thomas, who would become only the second African American on the high court, brought his conservative legal views as well as controversy to the proceedings. On his nomination, Bush had described Thomas as "a fiercely independent thinker with an excellent legal mind who believes passionately in equal opportunity for all Americans" and a justice who would "approach the cases that come before the Court with a commitment to deciding them fairly, as the facts and the law require."[22] But during the confirmation hearings, accusations of sexual harassment by Thomas were leaked to the press. Oklahoma University Law School Professor Anita Hill claimed that Thomas had sexually harassed her while he was her supervisor at the Equal Employment Opportunity Commission. Both testified before the Senate Judiciary Committee, and Thomas denied the allegations on live television as the nation watched, transfixed by the "he said, she said" dialogue that took over the confirmation hearings. In the end, Thomas was confirmed by a close 52–48 vote. Many credit the intense interest in the Thomas confirmation hearings with elevating the national dialogue about sexual harassment in the workplace, as well as contributing to what would be called the "Year of the Woman" in 1992, in which a record number of women ran for and were elected to public office at the state and federal levels (many women were outraged at the all-male Senate Judiciary Committee's questioning of Hill). Thomas, however, called himself a victim of a "high-tech lynching" as a result of the media scrutiny.

Politicizing the Process

Supreme Court nominations used to occur mostly behind closed doors. In most cases, even the president's political opponents in the Senate would allow the president his constitutional prerogative to shape the nation's highest court (the idea that to the victor of the presidential election go the spoils). Although the judicial branch, whose members are appointed to life terms, is the one branch most removed from the political process, confirmations have nonetheless become a highly politicized process. Since 1968, gone are the days of presidential deference when, barring a major controversy, the confirmation process in the Senate was a quiet vote among Washington insiders where members of both parties gave the president his choice. Starting with the failure of Lyndon Johnson to elevate Abe Fortas to chief justice in 1968, confirmations have made the shift from "the politics of acquiescence to the politics of confrontation."[23] Fortas ended up being the wrong candidate at the wrong time for Johnson, who was just months away from leaving the White House. Fortas's close relationship with Johnson also raised conflict of interest and separation of powers issues, as did his acceptance of perceived improper speaking fees. Several young Senate Republicans decided to defy the old rules of the game and opposed Fortas's nomination, and after a filibuster, Johnson was forced to withdraw his nominee. Party discipline in the Senate had begun to decline, allowing members to act more independently and at times against the wishes of the party leadership.[24]

Lyndon Johnson laughs with close friend and advisor, Associate Justice Abe Fortas. Fortas's nomination for chief justice in 1968 was unsuccessful.

Since the late 1960s, the Senate has become a more open and visible institution, thanks in part to media coverage, as well as to the much larger role that interest groups and lobbyists now play in many aspects of the policymaking process. The judicial confirmation process is no exception because interest groups spend millions of dollars to campaign for or against a nominee. This may make the process more democratic, but it brings confrontational politics into a branch of government regarded as being "above politics." The Senate has clearly moved away from its constitutional mandate of providing "advice and consent" on such matters as judicial confirmations. Many appointments throughout the federal judiciary are now based on the nominee holding a more moderate ideological view to avoid controversy during the confirmation process. For example, after the media feeding frenzy during Thomas's hearings in 1991, both of Clinton's Supreme Court nominees—Ruth Bader Ginsburg in 1993 and Stephen Breyer in 1994—were considered moderates who caused no controversy.

In addition to interest group activity and media coverage, several other factors also contribute to the politicization of a nominee's confirmation vote, like whether the president is from the same party as the Senate majority. Thomas' nomination in 1991 represented the last time that a president's selection faced a Senate controlled by the opposing party until Obama's nomination of Garland in 2016. Both of Clinton's nominations came in 1993 and 1994, respectively, when Democrats controlled the Senate; Bush's nominations of Roberts and Alito in 2005 also occurred with a Republican-controlled Senate (Alito's confirmation vote occurred in early 2006); and Obama had a Senate controlled by Democrats during his nomination of Sotomayor in 2009 and Kagan in 2010. Antipresidential motivations can also exist and influence negative voting, as does the ideological base of a senator's constituents since they must consider their voting record for reelection purposes. The president's popularity can play a role as well, since high or low approval ratings can influence whether some senators might be willing to block the president's choice.

Ideological voting by senators on judicial confirmations is much more common now than in previous years. As discussed earlier, the 31 senators who voted against confirming Sotomayor did so based not on her professional qualifications but on her rulings and the belief that she would be a liberal justice. Consider the change that has occurred just since the 1980s in this regard. Scalia was considered perhaps the strongest conservative voice on the Court, and his rulings were greatly disliked by liberals who did not share his strict constructionist view of the Constitution. Yet, he was confirmed by a 98–0 vote in the Senate in 1986 because of his judicial experience and constitutional expertise. Although no one doubted Scalia's conservative viewpoint on constitutional matters, the Senate was still operating under the assumption that their constitutional duty was to simply determine the qualifications and fitness of a judicial candidate, granting the president the prerogative of making his choice. Twenty years later, in early 2006, that assumption had changed to a political question for many senators, who stood ready to judge whether Alito should be disqualified from serving on the Court because of his legal ideology. After the Miers withdrawal, Alito's resume looked more favorable in terms of experience and matched that of his soon-to-be brethren with 16 years as an appellate judge for the 3rd Circuit and a law degree from Yale. Yet, many Democrats in the Senate spoke out against Alito's conservative voting record and did so while looking ahead to the 2006 and 2008 election cycles. By early 2006,

Bush's approval rating had fallen to just over 40 percent, and congressional Democrats sensed an opportunity to win back control of Congress in the 2006 midterm elections. Other senators were also looking ahead to the 2008 presidential contest. As a result, 42 Democratic senators voted against Alito, knowing that he would be confirmed, yet taking a public stand against Bush and his attempt at placing another conservative jurist in a lifelong position on the Court. One particular Democratic senator—Barack Obama of Illinois—spoke out forcefully against Alito prior to the confirmation vote:

> As we all know, there's been a lot of discussion in the country about how the Senate should approach this confirmation process. There are some who believe that the President, having won the election, should have the complete authority to appoint his nominee, and the Senate should only examine whether or not the Justice is intellectually capable and an all-around nice guy. That once you get beyond intellect and personal character, there should be no further question whether the judge should be confirmed. I disagree with this view. I believe firmly that the Constitution calls for the Senate to advise and consent. I believe that it calls for meaningful advice and consent that includes an examination of a judge's philosophy, ideology, and record. And when I examine the philosophy, ideology, and record of Samuel Alito, I'm deeply troubled. I have no doubt that Judge Alito has the training and qualifications necessary to serve. He's an intelligent man and an accomplished jurist. And there's no indication he's not a man of great character. But when you look at his record—when it comes to his understanding of the Constitution, I have found that in almost every case, he consistently sides on behalf of the powerful against the powerless; on behalf of a strong government or corporation against upholding American's individual rights.

Ironically, less than four years later, Obama's own words were mostly forgotten as he argued for a swift confirmation of his nominee—Sonia Sotomayor—based not on partisanship but on qualifications: "There are, of course, some in Washington who are attempting to draw old battle lines and playing the usual political games . . . I hope the confirmation process will begin without delay. No nominee should be seated without rigorous evaluation and hearing; I expect nothing less. But what I hope is that we can avoid the political posturing and ideological brinksmanship that has bogged down this process, and Congress, in the past."[25] Yet, Sotomayor's confirmation, like Alito's, was another example of ideological voting, with many Republican senators casting their vote more in tune with their own constituents and less concerned about judicial qualifications. Of the ten Republican senators who voted in favor of Sotomayor, all but one came from states that Obama had either won or lost by a slim margin in the 2008 presidential election. In addition, none of the ten senators would seek reelection in 2010, an important fact given that conservative interest groups, including the National Rifle Association, lobbied heavily against Sotomayor and would have likely lobbied against those same senators because of their confirmation vote in the next election cycle.

Presidential Legacies
Historically, presidents have selected a new justice an average of every two years. Since justices serve a life term, this is an important opportunity for presidents to enjoy a lasting political legacy. But the outcome of the nomination, as well as the justice's voting record once confirmed, is ultimately out of the president's hands.

Presidents hope to shape the makeup of the Supreme Court not only in the number of appointments, but also in the quality of the decisions from the men and women who will serve on the bench long after the president has left the White House. George Washington holds the record for the most appointments, since he appointed the six original justices plus four additional justices before the end of his second term in 1797. During his 12-plus years as president, FDR came close to Washington's record, with eight appointments to the Court, as well as elevating Justice Harlan Fiske Stone to chief justice. Not all presidents are happy with their choices to the Court once confirmed, however. In a much-quoted story, prior to leaving office in 1961, Dwight Eisenhower was asked whether he had made any mistakes as president. He responded that yes, he had, and that they were both on the Supreme Court—Chief Justice Earl Warren and Associate Justice William Brennan—who were much more liberal than Eisenhower had anticipated.[26]

Ultimately, as history has shown, each president will nominate an individual to satisfy his own agenda. For example, Ronald Reagan promised voters to nominate the first woman to the Court during the 1980 presidential campaign and kept that promise by nominating Sandra Day O'Connor in 1981. But even such a historic appointment was not without some controversy. First, with so few women holding judicial appointments at the time and even fewer with a conservative background, Reagan did not have a long list of potential women candidates to consider. He would have to look outside of the federal court system to find his nominee; O'Connor was a member of the Arizona State Court of Appeals at the time. Second, on O'Connor's nomination, Reagan was criticized by both liberals and conservatives for his choice. Liberals, on the one hand, were happy to see the first woman join the high court, but feared that O'Connor's positions, particularly on women's issues, would be too conservative. Conservatives, on the other hand, feared that O'Connor lacked adequate federal judicial experience and knowledge of the U.S. Constitution and would also uphold abortion rights (Reagan had campaigned to make abortion illegal). Nearly 25 years later, when she announced her retirement from the Court in 2005, O'Connor had earned a reputation as a pragmatic and often centrist voice as an important swing vote on issues like abortion, affirmative action, and privacy rights.[27] Yet, her positions on key social issues did not live up to the more conservative policy agenda supported by Reagan.

Chief Justice William Rehnquist is an example of positive legacy building for a president. First nominated as an associate justice by Richard Nixon in 1971 and confirmed in early 1972, Rehnquist was a strong advocate for the law-and-order, states' rights approach to the U.S. Constitution that Nixon advocated. Within three years of Rehnquist's confirmation to the Court, Nixon had resigned from office in 1974 because of the Watergate scandal. Nixon died 20 years later in 1994, and Rehnquist, following his elevation to chief justice by Reagan in 1986, still sat on the Court as one of its most influential members. Prior to his death in 2005, more than 33 years after his initial nomination and 31 years following Nixon's resignation, Rehnquist was closing in on the record as the Court's longest-serving member. Nixon had chosen well for the purposes of a long-lasting political legacy, as did Reagan with his elevation of Rehnquist to chief justice. Given how long a justice can serve or how powerful the Court can be in setting certain public policies, that is no small accomplishment.

SELECTING A CHIEF JUSTICE

THEN . . .

Of the 44 men who have held the office of the presidency, all but four (William Henry Harrison, Zachary Taylor, Andrew Johnson, and Jimmy Carter) had the opportunity for at least one appointment to the Supreme Court. Although the president has an opportunity to shape the ideological leaning of the Court for years to come through his selection of a nominee, it is the opportunity to pick a chief justice that is perhaps most significant for the future direction of the Court as well as the evolution of a president's legacy. Throughout the nation's history, only 17 men have served as chief justice, so it is a rare presidential opportunity when such a vacancy occurs. However, not all chief justices have been powerful forces on the Supreme Court. Under the first chief justice, John Jay (1789–1795), the earliest sessions of the Court were devoted to organizational proceedings; the first cases did not reach the Court until 1790 and the justices did not hand down their first opinion until 1792. Between 1790 and 1799, the Court decided only about 50 cases and made few significant decisions.[28] The first justices to serve complained that the Court had a limited stature. Jay, concerned that the Court lacked prestige, resigned in 1795 to become the envoy to England and later the governor of New York.[29] Jay was followed in the chief justiceship by John Rutledge, who served briefly in a recess appointment (but was never confirmed by the Senate), and then Oliver Ellsworth, who stayed in the position for five years. Like Jay, both men had been appointed by George Washington (the only president to experience more than one vacancy for this position), but all three failed to make a grand mark.

Despite the pleading of John Adams, Jay could not be persuaded to accept reappointment as chief justice when the post again became vacant in 1800. Adams, a Federalist, instead appointed John Marshall in the last weeks of his presidency in January 1801 to save the Constitution from the incoming Anti-Federalist Jeffersonian Republicans. Marshall served in this position until his death in 1835, the longest tenure of any chief justice, and he "dominated the Court to a degree that no other justice has matched."[30] With Marshall at the helm, the Supreme Court began to take a much more prominent role in governing. The Marshall Court was aggressive in its assertion of power, granting extensive authority not only to the federal government but also to the Court itself. Without a doubt, the most important decision ever handed down by the Court came in 1803, when in his majority opinion in *Marbury v. Madison*, Marshall established the Supreme Court's power of judicial review. Marshall later used that power in another important case, *McCulloch v. Maryland* (1819), in which the Court upheld both the "supremacy" and "necessary and proper" clauses of the Constitution in ruling that the State of Maryland could not tax a federal bank. Marshall's greatest legacy is not only in shaping the position of chief justice, but also in advancing policies that he favored to strengthen the national government during its earliest days. His decisions "stand as a comprehensive exposition of the Constitution on a par with the Federalist Papers, on which he drew heavily. Unlike those famous essays, however, Marshall's opinions were the law of the land."[31]

Roger B. Taney, appointed by Andrew Jackson to succeed Marshall as chief justice (and who held the position from 1836 until 1864), differed from Marshall in many ways. Whereas Marshall was a supporter of a strong national government, Taney supported states' rights. As a justice, he was also more restrained and redefined Marshall's strong nationalist view to allow dual federalism, with states maintaining rights over many social and economic matters. Taney is best remembered for the infamous decision in the 1857 *Dred Scott v. Sandford* case, in which he proclaimed that states were not required to consider blacks citizens of the United States and that slaves were property, a right protected by the Constitution. The decision enflamed public opinion over the issue of slavery and played a role in the election of Abraham Lincoln as president in 1860, followed by the start of the Civil War in 1861.

Following the Marshall and Taney courts, where each chief justice served many years and left many legal and political legacies, a chief justice of the same significance would not emerge again until the mid-twentieth century. On the death of Chief Justice Fred M. Vinson in 1953, Dwight Eisenhower found himself in the position to make a crucial selection for the Supreme Court. After nominating Earl Warren, the former Republican governor of California, Eisenhower explained his selection to reporters:

> From the very beginning, from the moment of the unfortunate death of my great friend, Mr. Vinson, I have been thinking over this whole thing. I certainly wanted a man whose reputation for integrity, honesty, middle-of-the-road philosophy, experience in Government, experience in the law, were all such as to convince the United States that here was a man who had no ends to serve except the United States, and nothing else. Naturally, I wanted a man who was healthy, strong, who had not had any serious illnesses, and who was relatively young—if you can call a man of approximately my age relatively young—relatively young with respect to some others that I was thinking of. On balance, to my mind he is a man who will make a great Chief Justice; and so I selected him.[32]

In his memoirs, Eisenhower also wrote of the Warren nomination: "Among the factors that guided me in the search, partisan politics had no place. . . . My goal was a United States Supreme Court worthy of the high esteem of the American people."[33] The Warren appointment did indeed become a significant selection to the Supreme Court; the new chief justice barely had time to acclimate himself to his new position before he had to confront one of the most important cases in the Court's history in *Brown v. Board of Education* (1954). Many other significant rulings came from the Warren Court prior to his retirement in 1969. The Warren Court "revolutionized constitutional law and American society" with important rulings on privacy rights, criminal procedures that protected the rights of the accused, equal voting rights, and many other policy areas.[34] Yet, despite Warren's presence on the list of most influential chief justices, Eisenhower was not pleased with the liberal direction in which Warren took the Court.

Replacing Warren as chief justice, however, was not an easy political task. Announcing his retirement in June 1968, the initial nomination to replace

Following his nomination by Dwight Eisenhower, Earl Warren became the 14th Chief Justice of the United States in 1953.

Warren fell to Lyndon Johnson at a time when the President was embattled over the ongoing war in Vietnam and had already announced his intentions not to seek the Democratic presidential nomination. Johnson nominated Associate Justice Abe Fortas, whom he had first appointed to the Supreme Court in 1965. A close friend and advisor to Johnson, Fortas's nomination for the Chief Justice job faced considerable opposition in the Senate, particularly from conservatives (including Southern Democrats) who did not like Fortas's liberal rulings. In his confirmation hearings before the Senate Judiciary Committee, Fortas faced tough questions about his close relationship with Johnson as well as speaking fees received from private business interests to give a series of talks at American University. Senate Republicans decided to filibuster the Fortas nomination, and after Democrats (who were in the majority) failed 45–43 on a vote of cloture, Fortas withdrew his nomination. Critical news media coverage of the Fortas nomination also played a role, as did Johnson's inability to recognize the difficult political environment in which he was attempting to make a "lame-duck" appointment to the Court.[35] As a result, Warren remained on the Court until after the presidential election of 1968. Richard Nixon then had the opportunity to fill the vacancy, which he did with Chief Justice Warren Burger, who served until his retirement in 1986.

. . . AND NOW

The death of William Rehnquist in September 2005 marked the end of yet another era for the Supreme Court. Rehnquist had served more than three decades on the high court, with nearly 20 years as chief justice. Naming his replacement would fall to George W. Bush. During the 2000 presidential election, anticipation had run high that the nation's next chief executive would have several vacancies to fill on the Supreme Court. That anticipation helped to galvanize social conservatives within the Republican Party in its support for then-candidate Bush. Throughout his campaign for the White House, Bush had promised to nominate men and women with conservative legal philosophies who were "strict constructionists" (a legal philosophy that limits interpreting the U.S. Constitution to the actual words and phrases used) to federal judicial openings, particularly those on the Supreme Court. Social conservatives had long opposed the judicial activism of earlier Supreme Courts, most notably during the 1960s and 1970s, for expanding privacy and due process rights through more liberal interpretation of the Constitution. Yet, during Bush's first term, he had no Supreme Court vacancies. In 2004, when Bush was reelected, eight of the nine justices were 65 years or older, including two members of the Court—Rehnquist and John Paul Stevens—who were over the age of 80. In addition, Rehnquist's health had been in decline for some time. Battling thyroid cancer, Rehnquist missed several oral arguments during the 2004–2005 term and was visibly frail in January 2005 when he administered the oath of office to Bush at his second inauguration. Despite that, he had no plans to retire.

Instead, Sandra Day O'Connor announced at the end of the Court's session in June 2005 her intention to retire, finally giving Bush his first opportunity for a Supreme Court appointment. It was also an opportunity for Bush to make good on his promise to the social conservatives within the Republican Party, widely credited with his reelection victory in 2004, who expected a justice that would move the Court in a more conservative direction. Although Samuel Alito eventually replaced O'Connor on the Court, John Roberts was the first nominee (followed by Harriet Miers and then Alito). Roberts represented the ideal choice for Bush and his conservative supporters. After graduating from Harvard Law School, Roberts clerked for then–Associate Justice Rehnquist; he also held positions within both the Justice Department and the White House during the Reagan years and served as a deputy solicitor general from 1989 to 1993 while George H. W. Bush was president. George W. Bush appointed Roberts to the U.S. Court of Appeals for the District of Columbia in 2003. On announcing Roberts's nomination to the Supreme Court, Bush stated that Roberts had "the qualities Americans expect in a judge: experience, wisdom, fairness, and civility. He has profound respect for the rule of law and for the liberties guaranteed to every citizen. He will strictly apply the Constitution and laws, not legislate from the bench."[36]

However, Rehnquist died while Roberts' nomination was still pending before the Senate Judiciary Committee, which then prompted Bush to elevate Roberts' nomination to chief justice. Bush urged the Senate to act quickly on the Roberts nomination with the start of the Supreme Court term near: "The passing of Chief Justice William Rehnquist leaves the center chair empty just four weeks left before the Supreme Court reconvenes. It is in the interest of the Court and the country to have a Chief Justice on the bench on the first full day of the fall term. The Senate is well along in the process of considering Judge Roberts' qualifications. They know his record and his fidelity to the law. I'm confident that the Senate can complete hearings and confirm him as Chief Justice within a month."[37] Roberts was confirmed by the Senate by a 78–22 vote (with all dissenters from the Democratic Party), and although it was considered a narrow vote for a chief justice, the vote margin was wider than that of his predecessor (Rehnquist had been confirmed as chief justice by a vote of 65–33 in 1986). For many Court observers, Roberts is viewed as similar to Rehnquist in his judicial philosophy—a conservative jurist who more often than not believes in judicial restraint, relying on precedent, and protection of states' rights. Whether the Roberts Court is viewed as activist or restrained in its rulings and what impact the Court may have on public policies will in part be determined by future vacancies on the Court. With his confirmation in 2005 as chief justice at the age of 50, John Roberts is expected to guide the nation's highest court for several years, or even decades, to come.

NOMINATIONS TO LOWER FEDERAL COURTS

The U.S. Constitution provides little guidance on development of the federal court system. Article III states that a supreme court will exist, and other federal courts would be established by Congress as needed. From the time Congress passed the Judiciary Act of 1789 establishing the first lower federal courts, Congress has continued to expand the size of the federal judiciary as the nation grew both in size (geographically and population) and in complexity (public policies). Today, more than 100 courts make up the federal judicial branch. The lowest federal courts are the district courts, which serve as trial courts with juries. If a district court case is appealed, the next step is a federal court of appeals. There are 12 federal judicial circuits (or territories), and each has its own court of appeals. Congress has also created other specialty courts over the years: the U.S. Court of Military Appeals, which hears appeals of military courts-martial; the U.S. Court of Federal Claims, where cases in which the U.S. government has been sued for damages are tried; and the U.S. Court of International Trade, which hears cases involving appeals to rulings by the U.S. Customs Office.

As with the Supreme Court, district and appeals court judges serve lifetime terms. When a vacancy occurs, the president nominates individuals who then must be confirmed by a majority vote in the Senate; federal judges can also be removed from the bench through impeachment in the House of Representatives and removal by a trial in the Senate. A total of 13 federal judges (including Supreme Court Justice Samuel Chase) have been impeached, and seven have also been convicted in the Senate and removed from office. The first, U.S. District Court Judge John Pickering, nominated by George Washington, was removed from office in 1804 for mental instability and intoxication on the bench. The two most recent federal judges to be convicted in the Senate and removed from office, both of which occurred within months of each other in 1989, include U.S. District Court judges Alcee Hastings, a

Jimmy Carter appointee who was removed from office for perjury and conspiracy to solicit a bride (in 1992, Hastings was elected to the House of Representatives from Florida, where he continues to serve), and Walter L. Nixon, a Lyndon Johnson appointee who was removed from office for committing perjury before a federal grand jury (no relation to Richard Nixon, who escaped impeachment by the full House by resigning from office in 1974).

Nominating and Confirming Federal Judges

Given the number of federal judgeships and the fact that they are for lifetime appointments, presidents can have significant influence over the makeup of the judicial branch by nominating judges who are sympathetic to their policy agendas. Although presidents may not get the opportunity to nominate individuals to the Supreme Court often, they do make more frequent selections for lower court judgeships (about 200 per four-year term). As such, this is an important opportunity for a president to leave his mark on the judicial branch for many years to come. Although lower court appointments are not as high profile as those to the Supreme Court, they are still important decisions made by the White House with the potential for a long-lasting effect on the policy agenda. Judicial selection is influenced by a combination of the president's own policy agenda (the substantive policy goals of the administration), his partisan agenda (using the selection process for political gain for himself or other members of his party), and his personal agenda (the use of the president's decision-making authority to favor a friend or colleague). Judicial selection by the president is "an exercise of policymaking furthering a presidential agenda." For example, the Reagan administration, which considered the federal courts "so activist as to have created an imbalance in the federal system that threatened state powers and expanded federal judicial policymaking beyond the competence and capacity of the courts," viewed judicial appointments as having a direct effect on the success of the president's domestic agenda.[38] Conflict occurs within the process in part because of partisan polarization and because of deterioration of the practice of advice and consent within the Senate.[39]

As of 2017, there are more than 850 federal judgeships throughout the lower courts of the judicial branch, with the number of district and appellate judges more than doubling since 1950. This number often fluctuates, as Congress either increases or decreases the number of judicial positions (the latter rarely occurs) or as judges retire or die and the vacancy remains pending the confirmation process. Some presidents have greatly benefitted from the addition of several lower court judgeships while in office, since having more vacancies provides a greater opportunity to reshape the federal bench to reflect the president's governing philosophy (see Table 7.2). The Constitution set forth no specific requirements for qualifications for these positions. However, being qualified for the position (in nearly all cases, holding a law degree and having some professional experience in the legal field) and being sympathetic to the president's political views are important factors in the selection process.

Because of the volume of appointments, the president does not usually play a direct role in nominating individuals to lower court positions. The Department of Justice, usually through the deputy attorney general, helps to screen potential nominees, along with other White House staff members. For these appointments, members of Congress also typically recommend potential nominees. Members of the U.S.

Table 7.2 Total Appointments to the Federal Bench, Franklin D. Roosevelt through Obama

PRESIDENT	U.S. DISTRICT COURT	U.S. COURT OF APPEALS	U.S. SUPREME COURT
Roosevelt	134	51	9
Truman	101	27	4
Eisenhower	129	45	5
Kennedy	102	21	2
Johnson	126	40	2
Nixon	181	46	4
Ford	50	11	1
Carter	203	56	0
Reagan	290	83	4
Bush	148	42	2
Clinton	305	66	2
Bush	261	61	2
Obama	268	55	2

Source: Biographical Directory of Federal Judges, Federal Judicial Center, www. fjc.gov

Senate rely on what is known as senatorial courtesy in the selection and nomination process, most notably for district court nominations. In a tradition involving federal appointments that dates back to the early days of the republic, senators from the state where a vacancy has occurred are given the opportunity to have a say in the president's nomination. This is done by the so-called blue-slip procedure, where the senators from the home state of the judicial nominee receive notification by letter from the chair of the Senate Judiciary Committee, along with a blue sheet of paper on which the senator can comment on the nominee. If the senator does not return the blue slip, it is understood to mean that the senator does not approve. In addition, if the senator is not consulted, then he or she has the right to request that the confirmation be denied. Because of the traditions and usual collegiality in the Senate, other senators will normally grant this "courtesy" to their colleague. Often, the failure to return the blue slip equals a one-person veto to block a nomination. Knowing this, presidents usually listen to what senators say about filling lower court vacancies. Depending on who is chairing the Senate Judiciary Committee, there have been times when only those senators from the president's party have been allowed to use the practice of senatorial courtesy. For example, during the last six years of the Clinton administration and during which time Republicans controlled the Senate, Judiciary Committee Chairman Orrin Hatch (R-UT) allowed Republican senators to veto Clinton nominees through the blue-slip procedure. But, when fellow Republican George W. Bush entered the White House in 2001, Hatch attempted to weaken the blue-slip procedure to deny home-state Democrats the same opportunity.

Normally, presidents have greater control over the selection of appellate court judges than district court judges, since appellate districts encompass several states, which can serve to weaken the influence of individual senators in the selection process. Since the Reagan administration, presidents have also made a greater effort to select appellate court judges who are closely aligned with their own political ideology. The President's Committee on Judicial Selection, which is made up of White House and Justice Department staffers, was created during the Reagan years to help screen potential judicial appointees based on their previous rulings, speeches, writings, and other types of work to determine their judicial philosophy and political ideology. The Reagan administration, as well as both Bush administrations, was committed to appointing conservative judges to the federal bench (meaning that judges would adhere to judicial restraint and use a narrower—and literal—view to interpret the Constitution). However, neither Clinton nor Obama used a similar strategy to appoint liberal judges (those who are considered activist and rely on a more fluid interpretation of the Constitution to match the political and social times); both focused more on qualifications and an emphasis to appoint more women and minorities to the federal bench.

The increased emphasis by presidents in recent years to shape the federal court system to better match their policy agendas and political philosophies has also increased the contentiousness over nominations in the Senate confirmation process. This was a significant issue during the George W. Bush presidency, as Senate Democrats attempted to block several of Bush's judicial appointments (particularly those at the appellate court level). Prior to 2001, senators had rarely relied on the filibuster to derail a judicial nomination. But when Bush first became president, Democrats in the Senate began relying on the filibuster to successfully block several of his judicial nominations to lower federal courts that they believed were too extreme in their conservative views—a clear example of divisive and partisan politics playing a much larger role in the process. A filibuster is often used by the minority party in the Senate to kill legislation; a filibuster represents unlimited Senate debate, which can allow a senator to literally talk a bill to death. To end a filibuster, a vote of cloture must be taken, which requires 60 votes for success. Democrats successfully blocked several of Bush's nominees during his first four years in office. In response, Senate Republicans threatened to use the "nuclear option" to bypass the opposition by Democrats, a plan proposed to change the Senate rules to allow a vote of cloture with only a simple majority (51 votes) as opposed to 60, thereby taking away the Democrats' power to block a judicial nominee. In 2005, a bipartisan compromise brokered by 14 senators from both parties (nicknamed the "Gang of 14") resulted in an agreement by Democrats to stop filibusters of Bush's judicial nominees except in "extraordinary circumstances." However, during Obama's presidency, Senate Majority Leader Harry Reid (D-NV) and fellow Democrats pushed through the nuclear option to change filibuster rules on all confirmations except those to the Supreme Court in response to Republican efforts to block several of Obama's judicial nominations. After Donald Trump's election in 2016, some Democrats (although not Reid) stated they regretted doing so, as Republicans controlled the Senate and any Trump cabinet or judicial nomination would need only 51 votes to confirm. Senate Republicans would eliminate the filibuster for Supreme Court nominations during the Gorsuch confirmation in April 2017.

The Candidate Pool

As with Supreme Court nominees, those nominated to the lower federal courts are lawyers, although this is not a constitutional requirement. In addition, many federal judges served previously as a state or local judge and/or have worked as a prosecutor. Most nominees also share the partisan affiliation of the president, and many have been involved in partisan politics at some level (which is how many nominees come to light). Historically, few women have been appointed to federal judicial positions. The main reason for the small number of women being appointed stems from the fact that up until the 1970s, few women were entering the legal profession, so a limited pool of qualified women existed for presidential consideration. As a result, the "integration of women into the federal judiciary has been achingly slow."[40] The same has been true of minority candidates for the federal bench.

Carter was the first president to seriously increase the number of women and minorities serving in the judiciary, and as president, he had "both the interest and the opportunity to diversify the federal courts" in terms of gender, race, and ethnicity.[41] Carter's immediate successors, Reagan and George H. W. Bush, appointed fewer women and minorities to the federal bench; Reagan disapproved of using affirmative action policies in judicial appointments. Since then, Clinton, George W. Bush, and Obama made progress in nominating more women and minority-group judges to federal district and appellate courts during their administrations.

THE PRESIDENT'S RELATIONSHIP WITH THE JUDICIAL BRANCH

Although the nomination of federal judges is perhaps the most obvious aspect of the presidential–courts relationship, there are many other ways in which the president interacts with the judicial branch. The political give-and-take among the branches comes through the system of checks and balances within the Constitution. In addition to shaping the personnel of the judicial branch through the nomination process, the president also has some influence over proceedings within the Supreme Court through his selection of the solicitor general, who serves as the attorney representing the federal government when cases are brought challenging the constitutionality of federal laws. Also, the Supreme Court is reliant on other political actors at all levels of government to implement the rulings that it hands down when it decides a case. Since the executive branch is responsible for the implementation of federal laws, the president can play a significant role in the adherence by other federal officials to a Supreme Court ruling. When looking at this relationship from the Supreme Court's perspective, it has often made decisions that define the parameters of presidential powers. As discussed in Chapter 2, the Constitution provides few enumerated powers to the office of the presidency, but the expansion of implied and/or inherent powers has often come through Supreme Court decisions as it "constrains and sustains presidential power" and "has generally upheld presidents when they exceeded strict constitutional limits."[42]

The Role of the Solicitor General

Although the debate over whether the Supreme Court should be involved in policy-making can be contentious, at various times in the nation's history, the Court *has* played a role in shaping public policy. One needs look no further than the landmark decision of *Brown v. Board of Education* (1954) to see a striking example of the judicial branch acting first, with subsequent actions by the president and Congress, to end segregation in public schools and provide a significant and early political victory for the Civil Rights Movement. In addition, the Supreme Court's agenda has, at times, been primarily focused on one specific policy area. From the turn of the twentieth century until the late 1930s, economic issues dominated the cases heard by the Court. Then, civil rights issues, as well as issues involving due process, dominated through the late 1960s and into the early 1970s. During the Rehnquist Court era (1986–2005), issues of federalism and states' rights reemerged, while the Court also kept a strong focus on civil rights and due process issues.[43] A president's selection for a Supreme Court justice can alter the output from the Court in terms of its decisions, but other actors within the executive branch play a role as well. As political scientist Robert Dahl observed, "By itself, the Court is almost powerless to affect the course of national policy."[44]

Perhaps the most important position within the executive branch regarding the Supreme Court and its agenda is the U.S. solicitor general. As the third-ranking official in the Department of Justice, behind the attorney general and the deputy attorney general, the solicitor general holds one of the most important legal positions within government; it is also the only high-level position within the federal government that requires, through statute, that the person holding the position be "learned in the law." The solicitor general is nominated by the president and confirmed by the Senate. The Office of Solicitor General was created in 1870; the size of the office is small, with 25 to 30 attorneys and administrative support. The office is responsible for directly arguing cases before the Court when the federal government is a party to a case. In addition, the solicitor general decides which cases among those lost by the federal government should be appealed to a higher federal court, which makes it the gatekeeper for all appellate litigation involving the federal government. As such, the solicitor general, or his or her deputies, is the legal advocate for all cases where officers or agencies of the federal government are parties before the Supreme Court. To exemplify the significance that the solicitor general can have in the selection of cases and/or their outcomes, the position is often referred to as the tenth Supreme Court justice.[45]

Since the solicitor general's office usually shares political and legal viewpoints with the president, the president's policy views will be reflected in the overall pattern of positions that the solicitor general's office takes in litigation.[46] Despite that fact, the Court gives significant deference to the solicitor general regarding cases, which makes it a unique position working with both branches of government. The solicitor general is expected to formulate consistent legal positions despite the views of the president for whom he or she works and must pursue a changing agenda within the executive branch while assisting the Court in imposing "doctrinal equilibrium." As a result, "politics and law are at the intersection of the solicitor general's responsibilities. . . . The solicitor general operates in a dynamic political environment, but is charged with imposing stability upon the law and legal positions."[47]

Researching the Presidency:

Presidential Statements on Supreme Court Decisions

Supreme Court justices serve for life terms—"holding their offices during good behavior," as stated in Article III—which helps to isolate the Court from many of the same political pressures faced by elected officials. The Court must maintain its legitimacy with other public officials at the federal, state, and local levels to gain compliance with its rulings, but beyond that, justices do not necessarily worry about public opinion or having a productive working relationship with the legislative and executive branches. When a vacancy occurs, the president nominates and the Senate confirms or rejects the newest justice. It is also the job of the Court, in interpreting the Constitution, to hold the other two branches constitutionally accountable.

An interesting angle to consider about the president's relationship with the Court comes in how the two branches communicate with each other. Some presidents infringed on the idea of separation of powers by communicating privately with individual justices to seek advice and/or share their perspective about matters involving the Court (Lyndon Johnson's personal relationship with Abe Fortas and Richard Nixon's regular phone calls with Warren Burger are two such examples). Publicly, the Court, through its rulings, can either restrict or expand presidential powers or can rebuke the actions of an individual president over a specific matter (again, Nixon comes to mind over his initial refusal to turn over the full Watergate tapes). But beyond announcing a nomination to the Court, when and how do presidents speak publicly about the actions of the Court?

New research has emerged to consider this question.[48] Matthew Eshbaugh-Soha and Paul M. Collins Jr. find that when it comes to discussing Supreme Court decisions, presidents more often discuss cases that have been decided as opposed to pending cases. Although it might be assumed that presidents would seek, through public statements, to influence the Court's decision on a pending case that might benefit his legislative or partisan agenda, presidents instead speak out about cases that have already been decided to pursue the primary goals of reelection, good public policy, and historical achievement. In addition, presidents speak publicly about decided cases more often in their second terms to further their historical legacy, and they provide written statements more often to shape implementation of the decision during times of divided government. Eshbaugh-Soha and Collins conclude that more research in the area is needed, particularly in the rare cases where a president does speak out about a pending case, which represents "an intriguing strategy, particularly as it appears to violate the norm of decisional independence."

Implementing Supreme Court Decisions

As Alexander Hamilton explained in *Federalist* 78, the Supreme Court "has neither force nor will, but merely judgment." The cooperation of many other political actors at the federal, state, and local levels is necessary to successfully implement decisions by the Court. Chief among those actors is the president, who, along with the rest of the executive branch, is responsible for the implementation of federal laws. Although decisions by the Court may affect all Americans, those who most immediately respond to actions by the Court include the solicitor general, the attorney general, cabinet heads, and legal counsel for executive branch agencies. Since decisions handed down by the Court are not self-executing, these executive branch officials play an important role by interpreting judicial rulings and advising the president and others within the executive branch on how to implement the ruling through advisory opinions and the creation of agency policies. State attorneys general play a similar role in advising state and local officials on implementation strategies of Supreme Court decisions. Often, the Court is at the mercy of these other political actors to make sure that the ruling goes into effect. The struggle to implement the *Brown* ruling, particularly in southern states, provides an important example. In 1957, Dwight Eisenhower sent National Guard troops into Little Rock, Arkansas, to end racial segregation at the all-white Little Rock Central High and to quell the violence over the enrollment of nine African American students. John F. Kennedy took similar action in 1962 to force integration at the University of Mississippi to allow enrollment by James Meredith, the first African American student to attend "Ole Miss."

However, it is important to note that presidents can also ignore rulings by the Supreme Court, block attempts at implementation, or attempt to strike back at the Court for rulings that the president does not like. Since the earliest days of the republic, presidents have at times found themselves frustrated by the Supreme Court's power of judicial review. Considered the cornerstone of American constitutional law, judicial review denotes the power of a court to review a policy of government and to invalidate that policy if it is contrary to constitutional principles. However, the Constitution remains silent on the issue of judicial review. The Supreme Court assumed the power to review legislation as early as 1796, when it upheld a federal tax on carriages as valid. Judicial review is also implied, according to some interpretations, through the Supremacy Clause in Article VI and in Article III, which establishes the power of the Court to decide cases. However, the framers were never fully committed to the concept of judicial review; it had not been discussed at the Convention, but many delegates assumed that courts would have the final power of interpretation. Many at the time were critical; Alexander Hamilton attempted to allay the fears in *Federalist* 78 by declaring the judiciary to be "the least dangerous branch."

The main power of judicial review comes from the Court's ability to strike down legislation, which did not happen until 1803 in *Marbury v. Madison* (1803). The origin of the case has a direct link to the presidency. The Federalists and John Adams lost the presidency and both houses of Congress to the Jeffersonian Republicans in 1800, but sought to preserve their influence over the national government through the courts. The lame-duck Congress quickly passed the Judiciary Act of 1801, which created several additional federal judgeships for Adams to fill. William Marbury was a Federalist politician appointed to fill a newly created position as a justice of the peace for the District of Columbia. The Senate confirmed Marbury's commission on March 3, 1801, Adams' last day in office. John Marshall, who was the secretary of state, placed the seal of the United States on the letter of commission, which was ready to be delivered. Marshall's brother James was to deliver the commission, but it went undelivered and was eventually lost. Thomas Jefferson became president the next day and ordered his new secretary of state, James Madison, to not deliver copies of the commission to Marbury and other Federalists who failed to get their judgeships. Jefferson then mounted an effort to repeal the Judiciary Act of 1801. Congress, now controlled by Jeffersonian Republicans, obliged and even abolished the Supreme Court term of 1802.

The following year, Marbury filed suit against Madison in the Supreme Court, asking the Court, under its original jurisdiction, to issue a writ of mandamus, an order directing Madison to deliver the disputed judicial commission. By then, Marshall was the new chief justice (appointed by Adams and confirmed in the last weeks of his administration), but despite the conflict of interest, he did not recuse himself. The Court ruled that Marbury had a legal right to his commission and that the Jefferson administration was wrong to deny him. However, the Court would not issue the writ of mandamus because it had no authority to do so. The Court's presumed authority to issue the writ was based on Section 13 of the Judiciary Act of 1789, which granted the Court authority to issue writs of mandamus "in cases warranted by the principles and usages of law." But in Marshall's opinion, the Court could not do that since the relevant provision of Section 13 was unconstitutional because it expanded the Court's original jurisdiction. Article III, Section 2, expressly provides that Congress has the authority to regulate the appellate jurisdiction of the Court, which also implies that Congress has no such authority to regulate or change original jurisdiction. Therefore, Section 13 was invalid since it permitted the Court to issue a writ of mandamus in a case under the Court's original jurisdiction. This is the first time that the Court held an act of Congress to be null and void.[49]

Beyond the legendary dispute between Jefferson and Marshall, Andrew Jackson also provides an early example of a president's attempt to challenge the authority of the Supreme Court, particularly its power of judicial review. When Congress passed a bill in 1832 to recharter the Second Bank of the United States, Jackson vetoed the bill and declared in his lengthy veto message that the Supreme Court alone did not have the power to determine the constitutionality of laws. Jackson wrote,

> The Congress, the Executive, and the Court must each for itself be guided by its own opinion of the Constitution. Each public officer who takes an oath to support the Constitution swears that he will support it as he understands it, and not as it is understood by others. It is as much the duty of the House of Representatives, of the Senate, and of the President to decide upon the constitutionality of any bill or resolution which may be presented to them for passage or approval as it is of the supreme judges when it may be brought before them for judicial decision. The opinion of the judges has no more authority over Congress than the opinion of Congress has over the judges, and on that point the President is independent of both. The authority of the Supreme Court must not, therefore, be permitted to control the Congress or the Executive when acting in their legislative capacities, but to have only such influence as the force of their reasoning may deserve.[50]

Jackson, the popular war hero considered the first "people's president" and a strong states' rights advocate, often challenged the rulings of the renowned Federalist, Chief Justice Marshall. Also in 1832, Jackson famously, and allegedly, declared, "Well, John Marshall has made his decision, now let him enforce it," after the Court ruled to protect Indian tribal sovereignty against encroachment by state laws.[51]

Presidents can take other actions against the Supreme Court. For example, a president can initiate a congressional attack on the Court, as FDR attempted to do with his court-packing plan in 1937. Presidents can also initiate changes in policies or even a constitutional amendment. George H. W. Bush sought a constitutional amendment to ban flag burning after the Court ruled in *Texas v. Johnson* (1989) that the burning of an American flag was an act of free speech protected by the First Amendment. In response, Congress passed H.R. 2978, a bill that provided for a prison term of up to one year for anyone who "knowingly mutilates, defaces, physically defiles, burns, maintains on the floor or ground, or tramples upon" any U.S. flag.

Instead of signing the bill, which he believed would not withstand the Court's scrutiny after the *Texas v. Johnson* ruling, Bush instead urged Congress to pass a constitutional amendment to override the Court's decision.[52] As Bush stated in a written message to Congress,

> After a careful study of the Court's opinion, the Department of Justice concluded that the only way to ensure protection of the flag is through a constitutional amendment. Pursuant to that advice, I urged the adoption of such an amendment. . . . While I commend the intentions of those who voted for this bill, I have serious doubts that it can withstand Supreme Court review. The Supreme Court has held that the Government's interest in preserving the flag as a symbol can never be compelling enough to justify prohibiting flag desecration that is intended to express a message. Since that is precisely the target of this bill's prohibition, I suspect that any subsequent court challenge will reach a similar conclusion. Nevertheless, because this bill is intended to achieve our mutual goal of protecting our Nation's greatest symbol, and its constitutionality must ultimately be decided by the courts, I have decided to allow it to become law without my signature. I remain convinced, however, that a constitutional amendment is the only way to ensure that our flag is protected from desecration.[53]

Since 1989, despite such a constitutional amendment being introduced year after year in Congress, the amendment has never received the necessary two-thirds vote in both the House of Representatives and the Senate to send it to the states for ratification.

Defining Presidential Powers

Through its power of judicial review, the Supreme Court has often found itself able to determine the scope and legitimacy of presidential powers. As discussed in Chapter 2, most often, the Supreme Court approves, expands, or legitimizes presidential powers. One of the most often-cited examples of a Supreme Court ruling that expanded presidential power came in *United States v. Curtiss–Wright Export Corp.* (1936). FDR had placed an arms embargo on countries at war in South America, and the Curtiss–Wright Export Corporation was indicted for ignoring the embargo. The Court ruled that the embargo was constitutional and that the president could be empowered to act alone involving foreign affairs. This ruling has stood as an important precedent in the expansion of presidential powers, suggesting that the president has more powers in the arena of foreign as opposed to domestic affairs. Other notable expansions of presidential powers include *The Prize Cases* (1863), in which the Court ruled that Abraham Lincoln's blockade of southern ports during the Civil War was indeed constitutional, although it was considered an act of war against the Confederate army, and Congress, which has the sole authority to declare war, had not taken action. Also, in one of the Court's most infamous rulings in 1944 (*Korematsu v. United States*), it declared constitutional FDR's decision to relocate and place Japanese Americans in internment camps during World War II. These cases illustrate the Court's willingness to support an expansive view of presidential powers.

However, the Court can also restrict presidential powers, avoid particular issues regarding presidential actions, or give a two-sided opinion in which it rules against a particular president's actions yet expands presidential authority. The latter occurred in two prominent decisions. In 1952, the Court both restricted and expanded presidential powers in *Youngstown Sheet and Tube Co. v. Sawyer*. Harry Truman wanted to seize the nation's steel mills to prevent a strike, and he issued an executive order to have the secretary of commerce seize and operate the mills based on the military needs stemming from America's ongoing involvement in the Korean War. Truman argued that as commander in chief, he had constitutional authority to take action. Congress had deliberated the issue in 1947 when it passed the Taft–Hartley Act (which limited strikes by labor unions), but had voted down the provision to give the president the type of power that Truman was claiming. In its decision, the Court ruled that the president could not take such action without the approval of Congress. Yet, the Court also recognized that the president does have certain inherent powers to take actions not specified by the Constitution. Similarly, in *United States v. Nixon* (1974), Richard Nixon challenged the special prosecutor's subpoena for White House tapes during the Watergate investigation. Although the Court ruled against Nixon and made him turn over the tapes (which implicated him in the cover-up of the Watergate scandal and led to his resignation from office), the Court also claimed for the first time that executive privilege does exist (which means that a president can have private conversations with advisors). However, the Court did not support unlimited executive privilege, which Nixon had sought.

More recently, the Court ruled unanimously in *NLRB v. Noel Canning* (2014) that the president cannot use his authority under the Constitution's recess appointment clause to appoint public officials unless the Senate is in recess and thus cannot conduct Senate business. The ruling invalidated four appointments by Barack Obama—three to the National Labor Relations Board and one the director of the Consumer Financial Protection Bureau—during what the White House considered a recess. However, the Court ruled that despite a break in the Senate's work every three days in short pro forma sessions in which no business was conducted, that could not be considered a recess and thus the appointments were unconstitutional.[54]

IN THEIR OWN WORDS

SEEKING JUSTICE

In 1945, Harry Truman appointed Supreme Court Associate Justice Robert H. Jackson to serve as the U.S. chief of counsel for the prosecution of Nazi war criminals at the Nuremburg Trials, a series of military tribunals held from November 20, 1945, to October 1, 1946. Jackson, a former U.S. attorney general and a member of the Supreme Court since 1941, took a leave of absence from his duties on the Court to represent the United States (one of the four allied countries, along with Britain, France, and the Soviet Union, conducting the trial). Jackson also helped to draft the London Charter of the International Military Tribunal, which created the legal basis for the Nuremberg Trials. Another former U.S. attorney general, Francis Biddle, served as a judge at the Nuremburg Trials. Biddle had succeeded Jackson as attorney general after FDR nominated Jackson to the Supreme Court in 1941. Biddle resigned from the attorney general post after FDR's death in 1945 at Truman's request. According to many historical accounts, this was one of the first resignations of an

FDR appointee that Truman sought, and shortly thereafter, Truman appointed Biddle to the Nuremburg post in an attempt to make up for requesting his resignation as attorney general. The following correspondence between Jackson and Truman highlights the political considerations both in the United States and globally surrounding the trials during the spring of 1946.

In a letter dated April 2, 1946, Truman wrote to Jackson: I appreciated very much your letter of March twenty-fifth, which I just received along with enclosed correspondence with the Chief Justice. I think you have arrived at the right decision. It is vitally important now particularly that this program, on which you are working, be brought to a successful conclusion, no matter how long it takes and, while I regret exceedingly that it is necessary for you to be away from the Court so long, I don't think it would be in the public interest now to break the continuity of your program. I think you have done a remarkable job and I know you want to see it to a conclusion. The arrangements which you have made with the Chief Justice, I think, are entirely satisfactory to all concerned. Best of luck to you and give them everything that is coming to them. I would appreciate it very much if you would elaborate a little bit in your next letter on Mr. Biddle.[55]

Jackson responded on April 24, 1946: Your request that I elaborate concerning Mr. Biddle's attitude toward our case can be answered briefly. Our case has two aspects. One is purely legal—conviction of these particular defendants. The other may be called political. It is the effect of the trial on the future attitude of the German people and other people towards Nazism.

The difficulty is that there seems to be insufficient appreciation on the bench of the international and German aspects of the case. The British judge is an admiralty and equity judge accustomed to handling purely private litigation, but he has seemed unaware of the political implications of this case. I had hoped that Mr. Biddle, in view of his experience in Government, would sense this situation and assert his influence in the direction of a strong control by the Tribunal of such witnesses as Goering and Rosenberg. In this I have been disappointed. Early in my cross-examination, when I tried to get from Goering a "yes" or "no" answer, the Lord Justice, at Biddle's prompting and without any objection by Goering's counsel, informed him that he could make any explanation he desired in connection with his answer. The result was a series of irrelevant speeches full of professions of patriotism and martyrdom which the Allied Control Council fear aroused sympathy for him, and he generally ran over us in a way that gave a bad impression of our own capacity to deal with him. As the *New York Times* said, our appeals for support from the Tribunal were little heeded. I am sure that the ruling proceeded from a zeal to be fair to Goering, coupled with the failure to sense his belligerent determination to revive Nazism and menace to the future peace thereby.

But so far as the strictly legal case is concerned, it has not been harmed. In fact, by their long harangues Goering, Ribbentrop and Rosenberg have been compelled to admit the authenticity of every single document which incriminates them. The defendants themselves have come to a pretty firm conviction that they are licked and have got to the stage of accusing each other and making professions of penitence.

One of the objections to the course the Tribunal has adopted is that it prolongs the case. Five years from now, no doubt, no one will ask whether the case ran a few months more or less. But for today there is a good deal of feeling that it is taking too long. I myself feel that it is, but there are several things to be borne in mind about its duration. In the first place, it is not yet a year from the surrender of Germany and we all know how rare it is that any case in the United States even gets to trial at all within a year after it is commenced. In the second place, we have found much more evidence than we ever expected to get. We now have over 4,000 documents of importance to the case embracing the minutes of secret conferences, speeches, orders, and reports. There never has been a war whose origins have been so carefully documented, and the defense does not impeach them in the least. . . .

The plain fact is there are a good many people (I do not say this includes the judges) who do not want the Nuremburg trail to end in a hurry for they are better billeted and better provided for here than they would be any place else in the world, and at the expense of the United States. This must be borne in mind in deciding whether there should be any future international trials.

I was also disturbed to learn that the British Lord Justice the other night in discussing the delay of the trial remarked that of course I was in a hurry to get the trial over as he understood I desired to get back to the States to run for Governor of New York. Unfortunately, that sort of story has been going around. I have been reluctant to get into the business of answering their rumors, but I shall take pains to let the Lord Justice know and I think you should know that under no circumstances would I consider leaving the bench to run for Governor of New York or any other political office. I am sure that you understand that I am not using this task for political purposes, and the rumor that it has that purpose has, or course, tended to stimulate people to make attacks upon it that would not otherwise do so.

I suppose I am unduly sensitive about these delays because I have been away from home nearly a year and my absence from the Court causes criticism of you as well as of me. Now you have additional complications due to the death of the Chief Justice which leaves only a seven-man Court and may disable it from deciding some further cases. As you know, I should have been back for the sitting of the Court if the Chief Justice had not written me as he did. And if the situation becomes embarrassing to you in any way that could be relieved by my returning for an argument session, I will be ready to do it. My impression is, however, that it will be better as Chief Justice Stone thought to let any undecided cases go over to fall when there will doubtless be a full bench to decide them. But I want to make clear that I am ready to do whatever you think best, having in mind both the domestic and foreign situation.[56]

Truman responded on May 1, 1946: I appreciated very much your good letter of the twenty-fourth and I am more than happy to have the analysis of the approach of the court in this case. I think you are entirely right that they have overlooked the tremendous political implications of this trial, especially as it will affect future aggressions and psychological attitude of Germany and Japan. As I have said before, I think you have done an outstanding job and I can't tell you how much I appreciate your willingness to undergo the hardship of carrying on the trial. I'll talk with you further about the situation when I see you.[57]

CONCLUSION

Although Alexander Hamilton may have declared the Supreme Court to be "the least dangerous branch" in *Federalist* 78, the life tenure of federal judges, along with the difficulty in overturning a Supreme Court decision (which can occur only through a constitutional amendment or the Court overturning its own decision), has at times posed a significant challenge to a president's attempts at and ability to govern. Yet, although the president may have no control over the Supreme Court's power to interpret the constitutionality of federal laws and actions by federal officials, the president does play a significant role in the selection of federal judges and can, through the U.S. solicitor general, help to influence the docket of cases pending in federal courts, including the Supreme Court. There has long been a relationship between the president and the federal judiciary that is based on the give-and-take of shared yet separate powers. Not all presidents have been given carte blanche by the courts in their attempts to expand presidential powers, and not all presidents have been successful in their attempts to reshape the federal judiciary to reflect their ideological perspective and political agenda. Yet, history has shown that certain presidents have, at times, had success in shaping the focus of the Supreme Court through key appointments and have had their actions (particularly those not explicitly outlined in the Constitution) legitimized by the Court. As this chapter illustrates, the relationship between the president and the federal judiciary represents the challenging task of each trying to balance its constitutional functions against the backdrop of the current political environment. However, the evolution of this relationship has played, and continues to play, a vital role in maintaining the checks and balances as set out by the framers of the Constitution.

CHAPTER 8

Presidents and the Executive Branch

A
lthough all presidents serve as the top-ranking official of the executive branch, past presidents have held diverse views regarding the appropriate size of the federal government and the role of the executive branch in the day-to-day lives of Americans. For example, on March 4, 1933, facing the Great Depression, FDR laid out a mandate for a strong federal government to get the country back on track in his first inaugural address: "It is to be hoped that the normal balance of executive and legislative authority may be wholly adequate to meet the unprecedented task before us. But it may be that an unprecedented demand and need for undelayed action may call for temporary departure from that normal balance of public procedure. . . . I shall ask the Congress for the one remaining instrument to meet the crisis—broad executive power to wage a war against the emergency, as great as the power that would be given to me if we were in fact invaded by a foreign foe." During his 12-plus years in office, FDR oversaw a tremendous expansion of the federal government in terms of its size and power with the implementation of his New Deal initiatives. Within a few months of taking office, with Congress's approval, he secured a package of measures covering a broad array of social services and expanding the regulatory authority of the executive branch over workers, employers, farmers, utilities, banks, consumer prices, wages, natural resources, and much more.

Ronald Reagan's view of the role of the federal government, as articulated during his first inaugural address in 1981, stood in stark contrast to FDR's view from 48 years earlier. A one-time New Deal Democrat turned conservative

Republican, Reagan sought to usher in a new era of government with one of the more memorable lines of his presidency: "In this present crisis, government is not the solution to our problem; government *is* the problem." Reagan's belief in the need for smaller government and his campaign promises to get "Washington off the backs of average Americans" helped him defeat incumbent Jimmy Carter at a time when Americans were feeling the economic pain from a recession that included high unemployment and inflation. Since the Reagan years, all presidents have felt public pressure to at least talk about the need to decrease and streamline the size of the federal government. For example, during his State of the Union address in 1996, Bill Clinton proclaimed, "the era of big government is over." Yet, shrinking the size of the federal government, whether through the size of the federal budget, the number of federal agencies, or the number of federal employees, has been elusive. Reagan achieved nominal reductions in a few areas, but did not have consistent results throughout his administration and left office in 1989 with a larger executive branch than when he entered office in 1981.[1]

The enduring question over big versus small government highlights the essence of the debate about the role of government in American's lives: Just how active and (in the views of many) intrusive should the federal government be? The question first emerged during the constitutional debates, and the discussion continues to this day. Reagan's inaugural address linked the economic woes of the 1970s and early 1980s to big and overly intrusive government. The so-called Reagan Revolution refers directly to efforts to dismantle what FDR built—a big government designed to provide a social safety net and regulation of economic behavior. Specifically, the Reagan Revolution objected to the excessive regulation of business, yet Reagan did not explicitly reject FDR's view regarding the active role of the presidency to manage and lead the bureaucracy. Like all modern presidents since FDR, Reagan accepted the role of chief executive to "faithfully" execute the laws of the land and to manage the bureaucracy, but also to "encourage" the bureaucracy to execute his political agenda. Yet, managing the bureaucracy is one of the areas where the institutional aspects of the presidency can greatly outweigh the ability of an individual president to govern on a day-to-day basis and leave a lasting political legacy.

THE JOB OF THE CHIEF EXECUTIVE

The president's relationship to the executive branch comes from three distinct clauses in Article II of the Constitution:

- The executive Power shall be vested in a President of the United States of America.
- He shall nominate, and by and with the Advice and Consent of the Senate, shall appoint Ambassadors, other public Ministers and Consuls, . . . and all other Officers of the United States, whose Appointments are not herein otherwise provided for, and which shall be established by Law: but the Congress may by Law vest the Appointment of such inferior Officers, as they think proper, in the President alone, in the Courts of Law, or in the Heads of Departments.
- He may require the Opinion, in writing, of the principal Officer in each of the executive Departments, upon any subject relating to the Duties of their respective Offices.

As with most aspects of the Constitution, the document is underdefined or silent on critical components of the presidency. For example, what does it mean to "execute?"

And what are the departments? The president receives reports from all departments, but beyond the Army, Navy, and militia, none is specified. The president can hire or "appoint" individuals to serve in the government, but the Constitution makes no mention of firing these individuals. That is the limit to what the Constitution says about the president's preeminent day-to-day job of running the government.

As discussed in Chapter 2, part of the reason for the silence is the desire for a limited presidency. The framers recognized the need for a single individual able to act in a crisis, but they were adamantly opposed to creating an executive with wide-ranging power over a bloated bureaucracy. Moreover, much of the opposition to the Constitution following the Convention in 1787 centered on this new office, which to Anti-Federalists looked suspiciously like a concealed monarchy. Alexander Hamilton, in *Federalist* 69–77, attempted to distance the presidency from the monarchy, specifically by diminishing the powers of the office. In terms of the executive branch, Hamilton noted that a king could appoint and remove whomever he wanted, for whatever position he wanted, whenever he wanted. The president, as defined by the Constitution, could not create offices and could only appoint individuals to those offices with the consent of the Senate. Hamilton contended, "Hence it appears that, except as to the concurrent authority of the President in the article of treaties, it would be difficult to determine whether that magistrate would, in the aggregate, possess more or less power than the Governor of New York."[2] The *Federalist Papers* were written to be political persuasive propaganda; critics could and did take issue with the powers of the presidency. However, Hamilton was correct in that of all the components of the presidency, the executive powers were not controversial. Hamilton argued that unlike everything else, faithfully executing and requiring reports, "no objection has been made to this class of authorities; nor could they possibly admit of any."[3]

The Bureaucracy Evolves

For the first 100 years of the nation, the federal bureaucracy was relatively small. In 1816, U.S. Census data showed 6,327 paid employees in the executive branch, not including military personnel.[4] In contrast, in 2010, there were 2,841,000, nonmilitary, federal employees, who were paid a total of $150,321,000.[5] The first Congress created the first four departments in the executive branch: Treasury, state, and war, plus an attorney general for legal advice. These same departments existed in the government under the Articles of Confederation. The departments contained few employees beyond the secretary and minimal staff. For example, the Department of State initially consisted of two diplomats and ten consular posts abroad, as well as four clerks and a messenger domestically. The total expenditures for state were a mere $56,600. Almost immediately, however, like single-cell organisms whose sole purpose is division, the departments enlarged and specialized. In just 11 years, the Treasury Department had enough distinguishable work to add a commissioner of revenue (tax collector), an auditor, and a general land office.[6] The biggest problem with administration for the early presidents was staffing and corruption—after all, most federal employees were not in Washington, DC. The early federal jobs were collecting duties and taxes and delivering the mail. To manage corruption, the Washington administration relied on appointments of "men of good character," that is, men who were respected in their communities. However, financial incentives existed as well—customs agents received a share of the profits from capturing and selling seized contraband.[7]

Washington could focus on character because of his nonpartisan approach to the office. Immersed in a more partisan atmosphere, his successor, John Adams, tried to use government employment as a political tool. After Adams lost his bid for reelection to Thomas Jefferson in 1800, but before Jefferson took office, Adams appointed numerous loyal Federalists to government positions. As discussed in Chapter 7, he appointed William Marbury Justice of the Peace for Washington, DC. The Senate approved the position but the commission was never delivered, so Marbury sued James Madison (Jefferson's secretary of state) by writ of mandamus, which was an order to an official to do his duty. John Marshall, chief justice of the United States and an ardent Federalist, ruled against Marbury, but in the process, established the power of judicial review. In the aftermath, interparty battles disappeared as the Federalist Party imploded and Jefferson's Democratic-Republican party dominated politics. Appointments to the bureaucracy followed Washington's approach until Andrew Jackson became president.

Attitudes toward the bureaucracy, as well as management of it, changed with Jackson's election in 1828. In keeping with his views of democratizing the federal government, Jackson opened government jobs to men outside the elite, upper classes; instead of relying on "character" to select individuals, Jackson relied on politics and partisanship. After the split in the Jeffersonian Democratic-Republicans, which occurred after the 1824 election, Jackson became the leader of half of the party and took the name with him. The remaining members, followers of John Quincy Adams, named themselves the Whigs, beginning the two-party system. With the return of full-scale political party warfare, the rotation of people in office based on political party victory became the "spoils system," named after New York senator William Marcy's famous quote from 1832, "to the victor belong the spoils of the enemy."[8] However, Jackson's intention was not only patronage or rewarding one's supporters, but also shortened service. By 1832, long tenure in office, in the bureaucracy as well as among elected officials, became the norm. Ironically, Jackson's efforts to democratize the administration made it more formal, routinized, and bureaucratic because more procedures and more positions were needed to help novices do their new jobs.[9]

The spoils system continued until corruption, incompetence, and the assassination of James Garfield in 1881 forced civil service reform. Views about the inability to get a government job without being a party insider came to a head as Charles Guiteau stalked several members of Garfield's administration in hope of receiving a consulship to Paris. After failing to secure a position and being told by Secretary of State William Blaine never to return, Guiteau decided to kill the President. The firestorm after the assassination led to the Pendleton Civil Service Reform Act of 1881. The act applied only to federal employees (so in effect did not completely challenge the political patronage system still in place at the state level) and made merit the criteria for hiring and firing in all but cabinet-level jobs. By 1933, when FDR took office, 80 percent of federal workers were included in the merit system.[10]

The Bureaucracy Today

The twenty-first-century bureaucracy seems enormous because it is more than 400 times the size of the U.S. government in the early years. Today, the executive branch consists of 15 separate departments tasked with overseeing the implementation and administration of the laws and programs created by Congress (see Table 8.1). The departments promote, among other things, the farm economy, the business economy, and energy; they protect citizens from illness and provide standards of manufacturing; they provide services to homeowners and renters, senior citizens, veterans, students, and travelers; and they protect citizens at home and abroad. The executive branch of the United States does not make anything per se, but few aspects of "life, liberty, or the pursuit of happiness" remain untouched by federal government rules and regulations.

For the modern president, the size of government is moot; as Alexander Hamilton noted, the president can neither create nor remove a department, agency, or bureau. The power to reshape the government belongs to Congress and can only be accomplished by legislation. However, contemporary presidents have attempted to shape that legislation by offering proposals to Congress. George W. Bush undertook the most recent reshaping of the federal government in 2002 with the addition of a new cabinet-level agency. After the terror attacks on September 11, 2001, Congress and the president agreed that poor coordination between federal law enforcement agencies hampered the ability to catch the perpetrators prior to the attacks. Bush

Table 8.1 The Cabinet

OFFICE	DATE CREATED
Department of State	1789
Department of Treasury	1789
Department of Defense	1949
(Replaced the Department of War, created in 1789, and the Department of Navy, created in 1798)	
Department of Justice	1870
(The position of Attorney General was originally created by the Judiciary Act of 1789)	
Department of the Interior	1849
Department of Agriculture	1862
(Not given cabinet status until 1889)	
Department of Commerce	1903
Department of Labor	1913
Department of Health and Human Services	1980
(Replaced the Department of Health, Education and Welfare, created in 1953)	
Department of Housing and Urban Development	1965
Department of Transportation	1967
Department of Energy	1977
Department of Education	1979
Department of Veterans Affairs	1989
Department of Homeland Security	2002

(Cabinet offices are listed in order of presidential succession, which by statute, is based on the date the agency was originally created)

charged five White House aides with creating a blueprint to submit to Congress for a new department devoted to homeland security. Although the Senate had its own proposal, the White House's view dominated the outcome. Bush signed a bill into law just five months later, on November 25, 2002, which established the Department of Homeland Security (DHS). Rather than create new agencies and bureaus redesigned to meet the new goals and eliminate old, obsolete agencies, the new DHS, like the creation of the Department of Education in 1979, was a patchwork department created by grabbing assorted agencies out of their old hierarchy and placing them under DHS control. Not only did the swift cobbling together miss important, necessary components to any department, like a "high-level policy planning unit" or a chief intelligence officer, but also it created inevitable turf wars over budget, staffing, and the mission of the agency.[11]

The organizational charts of the executive branch departments also highlight the inefficiencies in department design. For example, DHS (see Figure 8.1) is the third largest of the 15 cabinet-level departments, behind the Department of Defense and the Department of Veterans Affairs, employing more than 200,000 individuals. In contrast, the Department of Education, the smallest department, employs just 4,200 people, but has the same number of subunits as DHS (see Figure 8.2). There are also 13 other departments with as many or more units, subunits, and employees.

The fact that it is Congress that designs the departments, even with presidential input, creates significant duality in the executive branch. Congress is accountable to the people for the laws they create as well as the implementation and administration of those laws through oversight. However, the president's responsibility is to carry out what Congress designs and to hold the bureaucracy accountable to Congress' intentions through execution. Yet, the Constitution "creates a political dynamic in which presidents feel compelled to manage the executive branch, but lack the means to completely do so."[12]

Modern presidents, then, inherit a system separated from electoral politics; the change of party in power in Congress or in the presidency does not remove most civil service employees. Turnover based on partisanship short-circuited the opportunity for employees to develop expertise as the merit system enabled the development of expertise over time. Eliminating partisan turnover purposefully distanced the bureaucracy from politics and the political sphere. The distance produces a beneficial continuity, where not everything changes in the aftermath of an election. However, when large-scale electoral change occurs, like in 2010 when the House of Representatives switched from Democratic to Republican control, then continuity creates a negative distance between the bureaucracy and the nation. Elections reflect changing attitudes or views about issues of the day. With civil service reform, the bureaucracy is immune to these forces, unless the presidency through management and appointments can challenge that immunity and hold the departments accountable.

Part of the problem for the president in controlling the bureaucracy is the fact that Congress's approach to creating departments, agencies, or even programs emerges from its own institutional perspective, not the president's. Congress works collectively; individuals act (vote, write legislation, form coalitions), but the institution, without most individuals standing together, accomplishes nothing. Also, members of Congress do not work in a vacuum; they work in a political arena filled with individuals and groups who want to influence them to influence political outcomes.

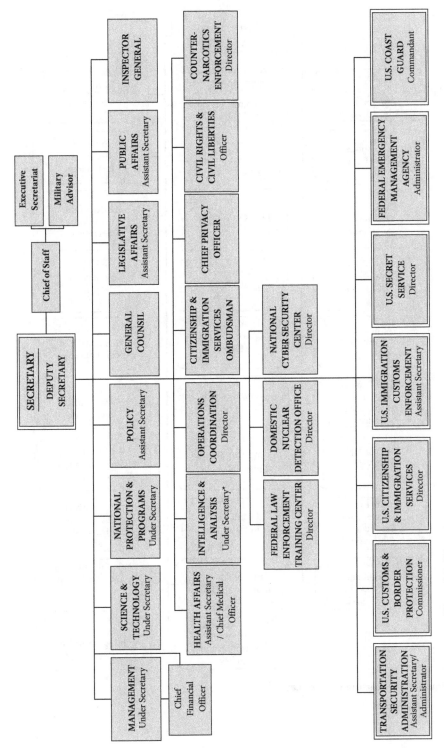

Figure 8.1 Department of Homeland Security.

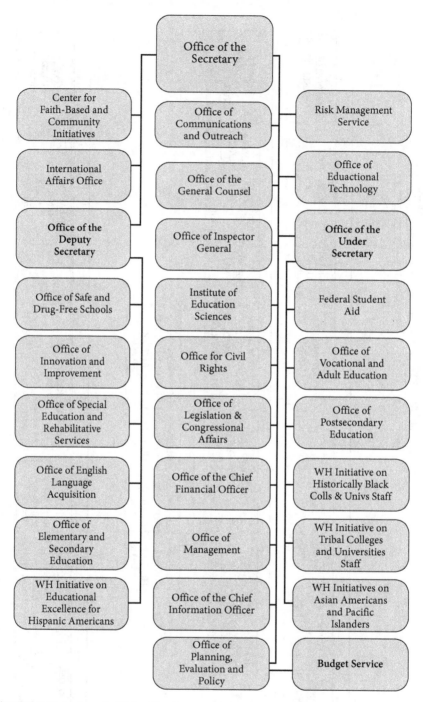

Figure 8.2 Department of Education.

Consequently, departments, agencies, and programs reflect the attitudes and behaviors of politicians and interest groups: "For both interest groups and legislators, politics is not about the system. It is about the pieces of the system, and about ensuring the flow of benefits to constituents and special interests."[13]

To ensure the flow of benefits and maintain the focus that the winning legislative coalition wanted from the department, agency, or program in question, specificity is the weapon. When designing departments, agencies, or programs, winning legislative coalitions seek to specify exactly what the departments, agencies, or programs must accomplish, "what to do and how to do it."[14] The goal is insulation and protection. The winning legislative coalitions are wary of presidents, even of the same party, because the president is institutionally opposed to the way Congress organizes the government. The president is national in executive focus, whereas legislative coalitions are specialized, either regionally or by issue. Even when Congress does not intentionally seek to protect their outcomes from presidential interference, they do not design with presidential control and organization in mind. Virtually everything Congress creates is created incrementally—a piece at a time, "agency by agency, program by program, unit by unit, procedure by procedure—with little overarching concern for the whole."[15] With DHS, the missing key features, like the national intelligence officer, were added later in 2005 after all involved recognized that it was necessary. As a result, the bureaucracy is not set up for presidential control.

The Cabinet

The managerial difficulties for the presidency arise not only from the separation with Congress, but also from the separation within the executive branch. The Constitution grants the president the power to hire and (from key Supreme Court cases) fire political appointees, which also suggests presidential control. However, after the introduction of the merit system, the president can only easily hire and fire approximately 20 percent of the executive branch workforce. These individuals are the top tiers of each department, creating the impression that the president has "his people" in place to execute his agenda.

The department secretaries collectively make up what is referred to as the cabinet. Initially, George Washington met individually with his secretaries, but quickly realized the benefit of collective meetings. There is no provision in the Constitution for a cabinet of advisors; newspaper reporters coined the term during Washington's administration to refer to his four department heads. Today the cabinet officially encompasses the 15 executive branch department heads and several other important positions. Cabinet rank is typically accorded to the vice president and the U.S. representative to the United Nations so they can attend cabinet meetings. Presidents can accord cabinet rank and the privileges that go with it to whatever agency director they like; presidents have awarded cabinet status to the director of the Central Intelligence Agency and the director of the Office of Management and Budget (OMB).

One would expect the cabinet to be a highly useful body of advisors for the president. However, rarely has that happened. Andrew Jackson hated his cabinet and instead turned to an informal body of friends who newspapers dubbed the "Kitchen Cabinet." Abraham Lincoln, right before he issued his Emancipation Proclamation in 1863, convened his cabinet and said, "I have gathered you together to hear what I have written down. I do not wish your advice about the main matter. That, I have

Barack Obama meets with members of his cabinet.

determined by myself."[16] Although they choose and appoint their cabinet secretaries, presidents rarely trust them. Consider how a president chooses a department secretary. Did the appointee have skill in the policy area of the department? Was the appointee helpful in the campaign? Did the president-elect owe the appointee a favor? Was the president looking for an overall *type* of cabinet, such as the "best and the brightest" (like John F. Kennedy) or a cabinet that "looks like America" (like Bill Clinton)? Whatever the rationale, trustworthiness, loyalty, and good advising are not the only or even primary requirements when choosing a department secretary.

Donald Trump did not mine his nomination opponents for cabinet positions, as Barack Obama did when he chose Hillary Clinton to be his secretary of state. Trump faced a different scenario than Obama because the 2016 campaign pitted party insiders against each other as well as against the opposing party. Despite the rejection from many party insiders and his stated desire to "drain the swamp," Trump nominated more Republican insiders with government experience than outsiders (although the "outsiders" were for high-level and high-profile positions, like Exxon's chief executive officer Rex Tillerson for secretary of state). Few nominees appeared to have close personal ties to the incoming president, himself a government outsider, which could present challenges in developing a deeper working relationship.

In addition, many institutional reasons exist for the lack of trust between the president and cabinet secretaries. Once approved by the Senate, a secretary will run an enormous organization (even the smallest department has more than 4,000 people employed). Although it is not always clear what drives the choice for secretary, once appointed, the secretary works for the president and his agenda. Except for the secretary of state, who spends the bulk of his or her time traveling to other countries, most secretaries spend their time within their department. Remember, 80 percent of that department is made up of career civil servants who are experts in their policy areas. The continued service allows for the development of that expertise as well as the development of opinions about the needs and direction of the department. A new president's agenda represents one of two possible paths—in line with the career civil servants or out of line. Even when in line, trade-offs in terms of money and time, as well as between policies, must often be made by a president who approaches the bureaucracy from a national perspective. Individual civil servants bring their local, narrowed policy views to bear on the political appointees. Top officials and even the department secretary can become captured by special interests, termed by some as "going native." Rather than enforcing the president's policies down the organizational chart, the department secretary becomes the voice of his or her people to the president. The focus of the secretary becomes advancing the department goals rather than those of the president. The worst-case scenario occurs when the cabinet becomes a political landmine for the president, a table full of separate goals and requests rather than a group united by the president's agenda.

Cabinet members can also become trusted members of the president's inner circle. If the relationship began during the appointment process, then it is much harder, although not impossible. To turn a casual work relationship into a trusted advisory relationship requires the cabinet member to show the president loyalty, ability, and personality that mesh with the president's needs. Ultimately, the secretary must show he or she is a team player, but this can often be difficult for people who were political stars in their own right. In the executive branch, however, there is only one "star," so to speak, and that title belongs to the president.

CRISIS MANAGEMENT

THEN . . .

In addition to the leadership of the executive branch, a central aspect of the presidency for the framers was crisis management. Shays' Rebellion in 1786 awoke the new nation to the pace of legislative reaction. Despite fears of tyranny, the framers recognized that during a crisis a singular individual often can respond with speed and efficiency where a legislature cannot. Crisis is thrust on most presidents at some point during their tenure in office. However, FDR ran his triumphant campaign in 1932 in response to crisis. He knew that from the first day in office he would be dealing with a vast economic crisis, which by that point had stymied both Congress and Herbert Hoover. FDR asked for broad executive power to wage war against the crisis; however, a president cannot wage war alone. Like any good general going to war, the incoming President had a plan, created by a group of advisors chosen specifically to create it. The press nicknamed FDR's campaign advisors the "brain trust," and the team that developed and executed his New Deal equally fit that bill.

FDR was elected in November 1932; his inauguration was March 4, 1933, as delineated by the Constitution. During this time frame, two important factors occurred: (1) FDR gathered advisors to assist in formulating what became known as the "New Deal" and (2) the Great Depression worsened significantly. Hoover, after losing his bid for reelection, served out the remainder of his term while the country spiraled further downward: "By the end of Hoover's reign, more than fifteen million workers had lost their jobs"; across the nation people were hungry and cold.[17] In contrast, the five months were a boon to the President-Elect.

FDR used his five-month time in waiting to determine a course of action. His choice of advisors was critical to designing and ultimately pursuing his New Deal. FDR chose his advisors from outside the political world, which was not unusual, but certainly not the norm. As governor of New York, he often turned to academia for guidance and continued this practice as president-elect. Raymond Moley, a Barnard College professor, led the campaign brain trust and after FDR's victory continued to serve as he "interviewed experts, assigned men to draft bills, and hammered out the legislation of the Hundred Days."[18]

As the forerunner to his competitive management approach, FDR was not wedded to any one economic doctrine. Most likely, in response to the Republican's rigid adherence to balancing the budget and maintaining sound currency, which was not working, FDR flung ideology out the window. Led by Moley and other academics, this new brain trust "attempted to weave together" conflicting policies and ideologies.[19] The New Deal was the combination of populism (suspicion of Wall Street and regulating agriculture), directing the economy (mobilization from World War I), urban social reformers (concern for the elderly and impoverished), and new nationalism (a rejection of natural law, free competition, and the idolization of small business owners). Throughout the White House, "the New Dealers shared . . . [the] conviction that organized social intelligence could shape society" toward a form of balance.[20] By bringing together a group of disparate people with different perspectives on how to attack the Great Depression, FDR forged a new approach and a new ideology. He shaped his government and his government's policies around the information and advice received from his advisors.

. . . AND NOW

Obama, like FDR, entered office knowing his administration faced a crisis of monumental proportions. Whereas FDR's entire campaign centered on the Great Depression, the economy collapsed just two months prior to Election Day in 2008. Like FDR, President-Elect Obama knew his priorities would be the economy. Unlike FDR, because of the Twentieth Amendment, which changed Inauguration Day to January 20, Obama became president just two and a half months after his election. FDR had time to debate, discuss, consider, and design his advisory team; he also had time to plan with them prior to Inauguration Day. The famed Hundred Days in which the FDR administration sent 15 pieces of legislation to Congress and all 15 passed with minimal changes or debate directly resulted from the five-month time prior to FDR taking office. The speed with which Obama needed to form an advisory circle, however, was not the only difference between his choices of advisors and FDR's.

Typically, presidential candidates begin planning their "transition" from president-elect to president well before they gain the title. The bulk of this planning for the modern presidency is devoted to staffing. As the eventual creator of the modern presidency, at least in terms of the size and scope of the executive branch, FDR's postelection transition not only benefitted from five months, but also, because he lacked an enormous apparatus to staff, his advisors could focus almost entirely on the crisis in their planning. By virtue of FDR's creation of the EOP, as well as the expansion in the number of cabinet positions, Obama needed to fill White House staff positions, as well as the political positions in the bureaucracy. Obama's brain trust, in acknowledgment of the crisis, subdivided the transition along two critical tasks: policy and personnel.

Obama and his transition team assembled a White House staff and a roster of cabinet nominees who met the recent criteria used by administrations not facing crisis. His predecessors, who were not functioning in times of great crisis, focused on creating a "cabinet which looks like America." Clinton and George W. Bush surrounded themselves with more women and people of color than prior administrations. Obama made no overt discussion of race and gender, although he employed a significant number who met those criteria. Not only did he seek the best and the brightest who were representative of America, but also Obama made ending the revolving door between the executive branch and the lobbying industry a key factor in his staffing decisions. The crisis did not shake the President-Elect off the path of ethical reform.

The desire to promote distance between those who worked in the executive branch and the lobbying industry resulted in a massive inquiry into nominees and potential staff members' lives via a 63-item questionnaire and background checks by the Federal Bureau of Investigation. Despite the existence of the most invasive questioning of potential executive branch employees, several of Obama's nominations had ethical problems. Tim Geithner became secretary of the Treasury despite some unpaid taxes; however, New Mexico governor Bill Richardson and former Senate majority leader Tom Daschle withdrew their nominations to become secretary of commerce and secretary of health and human services, respectively.[21]

While the effort to fill these numerous positions continued, another group focused on the President's policy priorities. John Podesta, a former Clinton chief of staff, led the Obama transition during the campaign and after the election. Podesta, who ran a Washington think tank, gave the Obama team an unprecedented policy resource: "No pre-election effort in the past has had a director who could so easily and directly tap into such a policy and planning resource."[22] However, the teams assembling the President's advisors were kept separate from those focused on policy. They created the "virtual firewall," again following Obama's ethical strictures: "Departmental and policy team members would not have favored access to executive branch positions."[23]

Although Obama's team did set records in terms of its White House staff appointments, they were not as effective at filling the departments' subcabinet levels. The effect was most notable in Treasury, where media reports and even former Federal Reserve chair Paul Volcker noted how alone Tim Geithner was: "The Secretary of the Treasury is sitting there without a deputy, without any undersecretaries, without any, as far as I know, assistant secretaries responsible in substantive areas at a time of very severe crisis. He shouldn't be sitting there alone."[24] More interesting, in comparison to FDR, was the separation between campaign policy formation and White House policy formation. FDR hit the ground running, literally acting on day one to close the banks and call Congress into session, at which time they voted on his first bill, just five days later. The first 11 Obama executive orders were items high on the president's to do list, but were not specifically related to the crisis, except symbolically (he froze pay on the top White House staffers making more than $100,000). Congress had been in session since early January and it still took the Obama administration nine days to get a stimulus package through Congress. The plans for the banking industry and the auto industry took longer; without help, Secretary Geithner took until March 23 to bail out the banks.

THE EXECUTIVE OFFICE OF THE PRESIDENT

The president is faced with competing interests and the gargantuan task of managing and leading an enormous group of people who may or may not agree with his direction for the nation. How can the president ensure that the bureaucracy is executing the will of Congress, let alone try to shape it to support his goals? Initially, the president received little assistance. For the first 80 years, presidents employed a secretary or two. However, both Congress and the president viewed these individuals as personal aides rather than governmental employees. In fact, Congress did not even allocate money ($2,500) for an office worker until 1857.[25] Sixty-seven years passed with the president employing his son, son-in-law, or nephew and paying him out of his own pocket. After 1857, Congress slowly appropriated more money and the president hired more secretaries, clerks, stenographers, and messengers. Yet, as recently as the Calvin Coolidge administration (1923–1929), the entire budget for the White House staff, including office expenses, was less than $80,000.[26]

Creating the Executive Office of the President

As with most developments in the modern presidency, the size of the White House staff changed dramatically with FDR. FDR entered office aware that the demands on his executive branch from the Great Depression would require greater administration and coordination from the White House. However, the White House did not have the capacity to create the recommendations for Congress and the bureaucracy that the economic crisis required. FDR began his tenure trying to use the cabinet to enforce his agenda on the departments. However, his department secretaries "went native" and, worse, leaked information to the media.[27] FDR then tried creating "coordinating bodies" separate from the cabinet, made up of cabinet secretaries and the heads of the new agencies he created. He also tried "borrowing" staff from the departments and agencies; individuals were assigned to the White House but their home agencies paid their salaries. None of these techniques was particularly effective. Consequently, FDR pressed ahead with his challenge to Congress in his inaugural address; he wanted "broad Executive power to wage a war against the emergency, as great as the power that would be given to me if we were in fact invaded by a foreign foe." He formally requested that power in 1937 and received it in 1939, well into his second term.[28]

To determine what the management problems were and how to fix them, FDR created the Committee on Administrative Management, headed by Louis Brownlow. The Brownlow Committee produced a report with significant institutional recommendations in 1937. Famously concluding "the President needs help," the committee produced a five-point plan:

- Modernize the White House business and management organization by giving the President six high-grade executive assistants to aid him in dealing with the regular departments and agencies.
- Strengthen the budget and efficiency research, the planning, and the personnel services of the Government, so that these may be effective managerial arms for the President, with which he may better coordinate, direct and manage all of the work of the Executive Branch for which he is responsible under the Constitution.
- Place the whole governmental administrative service on a career basis and under the merit system by extending the civil service upward, outward and downward to include all non-policy-determining positions and jobs.
- Overhaul the more than 100 separate departments, boards, commissions, administrations, authorities, corporations, committees, agencies and activities which are now parts of the Executive Branch, and theoretically under the President, and consolidate them within twelve regular departments, which would include the existing ten departments and two new departments, a Department of Social Welfare, and a Department of Public Works. Change the name of the Department of Interior to Department of Conservation.
- Make the Executive Branch accountable to the Congress by creating a true post-audit of financial transactions by an independent Auditor General who would report illegal and wasteful expenditures to Congress without himself becoming involved in the management of departmental policy, and transfer the duties of the present Comptroller in part to the Auditor, to the Treasury, and to the Attorney General.[29]

Congress did not universally approve of the reorganization plan and, in fact, rejected the initial proposal. Congress correctly surmised that granting the president institutional capacity also granted the president increased power, potentially at their expense. However, there was no denying the need for assistance; thus, the bill passed and FDR signed it into law on April 3, 1939. Reorganization plan number one created the Executive Office of the President (EOP) and the capacity to pursue the presidential agenda.

The Brownlow Report recommended and Congress granted assistance to the president in the form of two offices: the White House Office and the Bureau of the Budget (BOB, which already existed within the Treasury Department). Over time, the EOP expanded by adding offices with increasingly specialized policy expertise and coordination capacity. Some of these offices were created by Congress via statute. However, in some cases the president bypassed Congress and created units by executive order. All offices provide coordination and advice, but the most important initially were the ones created first—the White House Office, BOB (today known as the OMB), the Council of Economic Advisers (created in 1946), and the National Security Council (NSC), with its advisor and staff (created in 1947).

As Table 8.2 shows, today the EOP contains numerous offices. The offices created by Congress by statute continue from administration to administration. The offices created by executive order often continue from administration to administration also, as presidents realize that they share the same institutional needs regardless of political point of view. For example, as discussed in Chapter 4, all modern presidents must deal with the media, so all maintain an Office of Communications.

Table 8.2 The Executive Office of the President (2016)

Council of Economic Advisors
Council on Environmental Quality
Executive Residence
National Security Staff
Office of Administration
Office of Management and Budget
Office of National Drug Control Policy
Office of Science and Technology Policy
Office of the United States Trade Representative
Office of the Vice President
White House Office (which includes the following):
   Domestic Policy Council
   Office of National AIDS Policy
   Office of Faith-based and Neighborhood Partnerships
   Office of Social Innovation and Civic Participation
   National Security Advisor
   National Economic Council
   Office of Cabinet Affairs
   Office of the Chief of Staff
   Office of Communications
   Office of the Press Secretary
   Media Affairs
   Research
   Speechwriting
   Office of Digital Strategy
   Office of the First Lady
   Office of the Social Secretary
   Office of Legislative Affairs
   Office of Management and Administration
   White House Personnel
   White House Operations
   Telephone Office
   Visitors Office
   Oval Office Operations
   Office of Presidential Personnel
   Office of Public Engagement and Intergovernmental Affairs
   Office of Public Engagement
   Council on Women and Girls
   Office of Intergovernmental Affairs
   Office of Urban Affairs
   Office of Scheduling and Advance
   Office of the Staff Secretary
   Presidential Correspondence
   Executive Clerk
   Records Management
   Office of the White House Counsel

Source: http://www.whitehouse.gov/administration/eop/.

However, the EOP also comes to represent the current president's policy agenda. For example, Obama's administration had an office of Energy and Climate Change. His predecessor, George W. Bush, did not have that office but did have an Office of Faith-based and Community Initiatives, which was not part of the Obama EOP.

White House Staff

Technically speaking, the White House staff can range from high-level policy advisors to the White House chef and custodial staff. Politically speaking, the White House staff is connected to the concept of power: "To be a member of the White House staff is to be a presidential employee directly involved in the business of politics, policy making, or some hybrid of both."[30] For the most part, these individuals work in virtual obscurity; few members of the public, generally only the politically attentive, can identify even the president's chief of staff, arguably the most trusted presidential advisor. Yet, they are extremely important to the president. White House staff are not approved by anyone since they serve at the desire and discretion of the president. Their importance stems from immediate and direct access to the president and presidential decisions, and generally they are long-time associates of the president, often having participated in his election campaign. Beyond the chief of staff (see below), other high-profile White House staff members can include the press secretary (as discussed in Chapter 4), the staff secretary (in charge of handling the communication of messages and the circulation of memos/documents between the president and his senior staff), czars (an assistant chosen to focus on a specific policy area), the White House counsel (the president's top advisor on legal issues), the director of the Office of Personnel Management (who is in charge of seeking out individuals to serve in the administration), and the national security advisor (as discussed in Chapter 10).[31]

The EOP includes, on average, 475 to 500 staff members. Interestingly, working in the White House, the center of power in the United States, is often less lucrative than the private sector, but for some the opportunity to influence policy is more important. In 2016, Obama's 472 staff members had salaries ranging from a low of $42,000 to 16 individuals who made the maximum salary of $176,461. Top-level senior staffers are given the job title of assistant to the president, second-tier staffers are called deputy assistant to the president, third-tier staffers are called special assistant to the president, and still others are called either counselors or aides. Most of these individuals serve "at the pleasure of the president," meaning only the president can hire or fire staffers. The director of the OMB and the chair and members of the Council of Economic Advisors and the U.S. trade representative, however, are subject to confirmation by the Senate like the cabinet secretaries. The more important members of the EOP are the national security advisor, domestic policy advisor, counsel (the president's lawyer), director of legislative affairs, the press secretary, and the chief of staff.

Key members of the White House staff often end up doing what the cabinet could or should do, which is monitor the activities of the various departments and agencies to execute the will of Congress from the president's perspective. Remember, the reason the cabinet is not always effective in pursuing the president's broad policy agenda is that they do not entirely share the president's national perspective. In contrast, the EOP and the White House staff are designed specifically to reflect the president's focus.

George W. Bush famously articulated the president's central executive task. In response to calls for the President to fire his secretary of defense, Donald Rumsfeld, Bush said,

> I listen to all voices, but mine is the final decision. . . . And Don Rumsfeld is doing a fine job. He's not only transforming the military, he's fighting a war on terror. He's helping us fight a war on terror. I have strong confidence in Don Rumsfeld. . . . I hear the voices, and I read the front page, and I know the speculation. But I'm the decider, and I decide what is best. And what's best is for Don Rumsfeld to remain as the secretary of defense.[32]

It is important to remember, however, that "deciders" need information and advice. A president cannot know on his own, or spend the time to find out, all he needs to know about extremely important issues. Instead, the president's staff are the experts on any given subject, a policy, or politics. In addition, the White House staff provides coordination between the president and the bureaucracy to impose the president's preferred policies on the bureaucracy. By effectively staffing the political positions and using the White House staff to supervise and put pressure on the civil servants, a president can go a long way toward imposing his views on how policies are implemented. For example, with regulation of deep-sea drilling, it makes a difference if an oilman or an environmentalist is in charge at the Minerals and Mining Agency in terms of their policy perspective and how hard they may fight for certain environmental restrictions and standards. In effect, one can tell a lot about a president's goals by his executive branch appointments.

Organizing the White House Staff

If the greatest threat to presidential decision making is isolation, or not receiving the advice necessary, then organizing the White House staff as well as managing the flow of information becomes a critical task. Interestingly, when choosing among presidential candidates, management skills rarely enter voters' selection factors. The media evaluates a candidate's management skills obliquely, often using previous job experience as shorthand. For example, a former governor or mayor has executive leadership experience, whereas a former legislator does not. Trump benefitted from the equating of business success with managerial leadership during the 2016 campaign, although running a corporation, even a successful one, differs from running a branch of government. However, the most important management skill that a president must have is often the ability to choose the right individuals to successfully manage and utilize the institutional structure of the EOP to the president's political advantage.

Since FDR and the creation of the modern White House, there have been only four models of organization: competitive, hierarchical, collegial, and modified. A competitive system is one in which the advisors do not have set roles. Figure 8.3 diagrams how the staff members relate to the president based on assignments. It appears chaotic to the outside world because advisors receive the same task instead of delegating one task to one individual. FDR used to do this to avoid presidential isolation so that he could receive information from a variety of sources. It takes a keen intellect to balance the competing egos and ideas because staff members have unfettered access to the president. To avoid hostility in the White House, FDR juggled the individuals working on assignments so that staff members were not always in

Figure 8.3 Competitive Model: Franklin D. Roosevelt

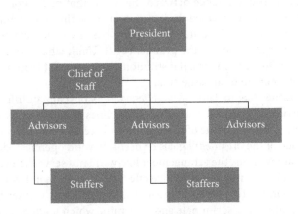

Figure 8.4 Hierarchical Model: Eisenhower and Nixon

opposition with the same individuals. As a management technique, the competitive style is difficult to maintain because it requires excessive presidential participation; no president other than FDR employed a competitive staffing system.

Both Dwight Eisenhower and Richard Nixon employed hierarchical arrangements. Figure 8.4 demonstrates how strict lines of control and command characterize hierarchical staff arrangements. The chief of staff is the key gatekeeping mechanism, which controls and coordinates the flow of paper as well as access to the president. As a former five-star general in the U.S. Army, Eisenhower preferred this method because of his familiarity with it; it was similar to the military, with strict lines of authority and clear delegations of responsibility. Sherman Adams was his chief of staff and was virtually the second most powerful man in Washington. Adams was so powerful that he ran the country while Eisenhower recovered from a mild stroke in 1957, unbeknownst to the public and most of Washington.

Gerald Ford and Jimmy Carter designed their staffing arrangements in response to Nixon's model and the perceived relationship between the staff organization and Watergate. Watergate is the term used to collectively describe the crimes perpetrated by the Nixon reelection committee and the cover-up of that behavior by the White House staff. In the aftermath of the Watergate scandal, critics cited the tendency of Nixon to use his gatekeeper to hide away from staff and issues. Ford and Carter both pledged openness to wash away the Watergate taint on the presidency.

The collegial system is the epitome of the open-door policy; the system is also known as the spokes of the wheel because of how it looks when diagrammed (see Figure 8.5). The collegial model has no hierarchy; all staff members are equal before the president. In contrast to the competitive system, where staffers are equal but tasks are assigned, and the hierarchical system, where access and assignments are rigidly controlled, all ideas and interests funnel to and from the president with no regard to restricting access. Watergate appeared to demonstrate that restricting access to the president led to bad advice and, in turn, bad decision making. The collegial system does open the president to a wider net of ideas and interests, but also provides no mechanism for prioritizing. In the competitive system, staffers fought to have their option chosen. In the collegial system, staffers also fought to have their ideas chosen by the president. The difference between the two is that in the competitive system the president has already decided the issue is worth the time and competition. In the collegial system, every staffer thinks his or her job is of vital importance but it might only be second or third tier on the president's list. Unlike the competitive and hierarchical systems, there is no formal institutional arrangement to indicate the relative importance of a person or an issue area.

Instead, rather like in *Lord of the Flies*, staffers develop an informal hierarchy based on personality or social status. No official lines of authority exist, but it is still clear who is in charge by virtue of personality and access to the president. The problem is that none of the president's goals or needs, beyond openness, determined this informal hierarchy. Thus, the arrangement likely will not serve the president; he will not be isolated, but he might not receive effective advice either. For example, under this arrangement, Carter was so inundated with detail that neither he nor anyone else made any effort to discriminate and determine which matters could be handled at a level below the president. In early 1978, Press Secretary Jody Powell articulated the problems with the lack of organization among the White House staff in a memo to Carter:

> Although some of the criticism of your staff is overdone, one valid criticism is the lack of coordination among key senior staff. This is generally agreed, but no one is in a position to really do anything on it since we are "all equals." At present there is no effective, daily coordination procedure. This is unprecedented in a White House so far as I have been able to tell. I suggest that you *direct* [White

Figure 8.5 Collegial Model: Ford and Carter

House Advisor] Hamilton [Jordon] to convene and chair an early morning meeting composed of himself, [National Security Advisor] Zbig [Brzezinski], [Chief Domestic Policy Advisor] Stu [Eizenstat], [congressional liaison] Frank [Moore], [Chief of Staff to Vice President Walter Mondale] Dick Moe and myself to deal ostensibly with legislative matters. (This will justify the smaller group.) It may be that we will want to have [White House Advisor] Tim [Kraft] or [Appointments Secretary] Phil [Wise] sit in regularly or that we will want [DNC Chairman] John White to come in a couple of times each week, but that can be worked out later. The main point is that there is a great need for more coordination and that *you* must insist that these meetings be held and be religiously attended. (You can enforce your order by requesting minutes of each meeting and list of attendees.) If you will reflect upon my personal distaste for staff meetings, particularly early morning meetings, and my spotty record of attendance at some stretching over the past 6–7 years, you should be convinced that this is an earnest and selfless suggestion on my part.[33]

The management mess created by the collegial system in the Carter White House was highlighted by the media fascination in 1978 and 1979 with the rumor that the President himself kept the schedule of the White House tennis courts. This became a media story partially because it was part of a tell-all article by a former staffer, James Fallows. However, the story gained traction because of the implicit understanding that the President had better things to do with his time than decide who was using the tennis courts. The story represents the clearest example of a president who needed a chief of staff to coordinate and prioritize. Hamilton Jordan became Carter's chief of staff in the summer of 1979, a few months after Carter publicly addressed the tennis court question.

The Reagan White House sought the best of both worlds: the ability to prioritize and control without a loss of access and spontaneity. They created a modified collegial system and set up a hierarchy for prioritizing coupled with collegiality for widespread access to ideas. During his first term, Reagan had three top advisors: Chief of Staff James Baker, Counselor Ed Meese, and Deputy Chief of Staff Michael Deaver (often referred to as the "triumvirate" or "troika"). Baker ran the operations, Meese was a close friend to Reagan and represented his ideals, and Deaver was Baker's top aide. Only four individuals, those three and National Security Advisor William Clark, had direct access to the President. The top of the Reagan hierarchy was narrow but the second level was wider, with more access. At the start of the second term, and with the appointment of a new chief of staff, former treasury secretary Donald Regan, the Reagan White House sought to refine the organizational system it had in place, as outlined in a memo about meetings to Regan from director of policy development, Roger Porter:

Structuring the various offices within the White House and delineating their responsibilities is important. Also important is how they relate to one another. Perhaps nothing in this respect is more crucial than the pattern of meetings that are held. Anyone who has worked at the White House cannot help but be impressed by the number of meetings that take place. One sometimes looks forward to the regular day ending (no one has adequately defined for me what close of business means, although we all use the phrase), which normally means the stream of meetings finally stops, so that you can get some work done. Of course, meetings are essential. And many meetings are scheduled on short notice to address some urgent problem or to organize the work flowing from an assignment that has just been issued. Typically there is a White House senior staff meeting each morning in the Roosevelt Room at 8:00 a.m. This is a tradition that extends back at least through the last four administrations, and likely before then. There are also cabinet council meetings, legislative strategy group meetings, and issue luncheons that I have discussed elsewhere. The purpose of this memorandum is to suggest three meetings that could prove helpful in building a united White House team if they were held regularly with adequate advance preparation.

1. *Policy Management Group*: However many entities comprise the policy development and coordination part of the White House, there will inevitably be a need to do three important things: Clarify who has responsibility for what issues (put less diplomatically, resolving jurisdictional disputes); Inform one another of the current work in progress to avoid duplication and overlap; and Insure that issues are not falling between the cracks because one office believes that another has the lead on addressing the problem. A regular weekly meeting of the responsible officials could help to fulfill these functions as well as build a sense among them that collectively they have responsibility for coordinating policy within the Administration. . . .

2. *Policy Implementation Group*: There is also a need to coordinate the activities of the constituency oriented offices in the White House—legislative affairs, public liaison, intergovernmental affairs, communications and press. All these offices are central to the task of building and mobilizing support for the policies the President has approved. All these offices run the danger that they will become captive of their constituency; that is, that they will come to increasingly represent the interests of their constituency to the White House rather than represent the White House to their constituency. A regular meeting, chaired by the Chief of Staff, involving the heads of these four offices dealing with the Congress, the press, public interest groups, and State and local governments, could go a long way to achieving two objectives: Reinforcing their central mission of mobilizing support for the President's programs rather than meeting the needs (if nothing more than keeping calm) of their constituency; and Coordinating their efforts so that they are all pushing on the same issues and rowing in the same direction. . . .

3. *Overall Strategy Group*: There is also a need to consciously devote time and attention to considering overall strategy—what should the Administration try to accomplish over the next six months, or over the next year? The press of day-to-day activities is almost overwhelming, and it is easy to allow the urgent to drive out the important. Many have suggested creating offices within the White House or within the Executive Office of the President to think about the long term and to consider overall strategy. The impulse is correct, but the mechanism misses the mark. One can never expect a group of people who are divorced from the day-to-day flow of activities to dominate or control the agenda. It is crucial that the key figures in any White House form the nucleus of any such effort. But these are busy people and they don't have lots of spare time to sit and think grand thoughts or ponder elaborate long-term strategies. If they get together, however, perhaps once a month or once every other month, to discuss long-term strategy, it could make a contribution.[34]

Since Reagan, the hierarchical management structure has emerged as the dominant mechanism because most presidents cannot handle the competition or the inevitable power struggle that emerges with the collegial or competitive systems. By default, the chief of staff position has become the most effective mechanism for keeping presidents organized and in control. Unfortunately, the extent to which the Oval Office is open and receptive to advice and information also rests on the chief of staff's relationship with the president.

IN THEIR OWN WORDS

MANAGING THE WHITE HOUSE

One of the most important functions of the White House staff is to not only keep the president informed of important events and issues, but also to organize the massive flow of information that works its way through various White House and executive branch offices on a daily basis. When Bill Clinton first took office in 1993, many of his young White House staffers earned a reputation for being disorganized and lacking the discipline needed to run the White House, as well as manage Clinton's schedule, in an efficient manner. However, John Podesta, assistant to the president and staff secretary in January 1993 (he became Clinton's fourth and final chief of staff in 1998), laid out the elaborate plan for managing "paperflow" in the early days of the Clinton administration:

> This memo sets forth the procedure for all White House staff to follow in sending paper to the President for signature or review. It is an initial cut at establishing a smoothly working paper flow system and I expect that it will require some refinement.
>
> At the outset, it is important to emphasize that *all* paper going to the President should come through the Staff Secretary (with certain exceptions for NSC). All paper leaving the President's office should go *back* to the Staff Secretary to ensure that decisions will be implemented, the appropriate people notified, and good records maintained.

DAILY BRIEFING BOOK

> Marcia Hale will be responsible for putting together the President's schedule and informing the appropriate offices what their responsibilities are for producing background memos, talking points, etc. (Full speeches are discussed below.) Marcia will distribute a draft of the next day's schedule at noon. All offices will be responsible for forwarding briefing book materials to my office not later than 4:30 pm the night before the day in question.
>
> My office will review such materials for quality, completeness, etc. and produce the President's book. Briefing books will be distributed by 8:00 pm.

DECISION MEMO CLEARANCE

> Perhaps the most important function of the Staff Secretary's office is to ensure that decision memoranda are properly staffed before reaching the President. That will require cooperation of all staff. The following procedures should be followed:
>
> Unless a real emergency exists, decision memos must be forwarded to the Staff Secretary at least 48 hours in advance of presenting the document to the President.

I will route the memo to relevant White House staff for comment. The Chief of Staff and Vice President will receive all draft decision documents for comment. I will also route such drafts to Bernie Nussbaum and to Maggie Williams. Other offices will be routed as appropriate. Routing will be Assistants to the President. It will be up to each Assistant to decide proper routing procedures within his or her own office.

Generally, staffing to Cabinet agencies will be done through the Councils. If comment from Cabinet officers is required that cannot be handled through the regular Council process, paper will be routed through the Cabinet Secretary, who will also serve as a collection point for comments coming back from the Cabinet in those circumstances.

My office will serve as a collection point for all comments from the White House Staff and in the circumstances described in the above bullet from the Cabinet (via the Cabinet Secretary) and will attempt to facilitate consensus, prior to presentation of the matter to the President. Where no consensus can be formed, I will ensure that individual views are noted and accurately presented.

BACKGROUND MEMOS

Briefing papers, where no formal action is requested, will be handled in the same general manner as decision memos. My office will be responsible for preparing or editing summaries of all general briefing papers.

SPEECHES

Different administrations have handled the speech clearance process differently, with some vesting principal clearance responsibility in the Staff Secretary, and others in the speech writers themselves. We are going to try out a process under which the Communications staff will have primary responsibility for clearing all speeches and statements of the President released to the press, provided that these procedures are followed:

My office must be on and see the original distribution list of draft speeches to ensure that all offices with a need to review have received a copy.

Comments to speech writers should be cc'd to me, to ensure that those views have been appropriately considered before forwarding a draft to the President.

Drafts of speeches to be presented to the President should flow to and from the President through my office, so that they can be properly handled and archived.

REPORT TO CONGRESS

The Administration prepares over 300 reports to Congress each year, as a result of statutory requirements. Many are submitted under the President's signature. They are frequently thick documents and often come to us with short deadlines. We will try to ensure that agencies submit reports in a timely fashion to give White House staff a meaningful chance to review these reports. We will route them for clearance to the appropriate people.

LEGISLATION

Enrolled legislation (passed by both houses) is received and time stamped by the Executive Clerk. OMB has responsibility for interagency review of the legislation. The Staff Secretary's office will handle clearance of the legislation, signing statements and veto measures amongst the White House staff. The same procedures outlined for clearance of decision memos should be followed.

CORRESPONDENCE

Congressional correspondence as a rule will be reviewed, personally, by the President. Staffing of letters to the Hill will follow the same procedures as outlined for clearance of decision memos. Other correspondence will be routed initially through Marcia Scott, the Acting Director of Messages and Correspondence who is working furiously to bring up our system for answering mail, whether for the President's or First Lady's signature, or for staff signature. A memo laying out the correspondence system will follow shortly.

SEQUENCING AND TIMING

It can be anticipated that staff sending paper to my office will frequently feel that the President must see it in the next 10 minutes. Barring real emergencies, that will generally not be possible. I will be working with Nancy Hernreich to develop a system that will make the President's day work for him.

Morning. With regard to paper, my expectation is that the President will have a short time in the morning to review his briefing book and paperwork, including (i) papers and letters he must review and sign; (ii) decision memos, briefing memos and other matters which he can review that morning or hold for evening review; (iii) a summary of documents and important correspondence received, which he can review in more detail if he wishes.

Daytime Period. The President wants to limit review of paper during daytime working hours. Only essential items which must be signed or reviewed will be brought to his attention during those hours. I will forward essential items to the President through Nancy Hernreich who will be responsible for fitting review of essential items into the day's schedule.

Evening. After the President's morning work period all *non-essential* paperwork will be held until the evening. In the evening, we will give the President a manageable amount of time—no more than 45 minutes to an hour's worth. We will include in these materials all important decision memos which will be discussed the next day.

Weekend. Longer policy papers and think pieces will be held for weekend review, where possible. That will give the President more time to reflect and comment.

FOLLOWING WEEK

By the close of business each Friday, senior staff—and especially the councils—should forward to me a list of any important decision memos that they expect to have presented to the President the next week so that we can build adequate time into the schedule for review at the staff level and by the President.

STYLE

Some changes may be made to the current style of documents intended for the President, but, for now, please use current style forms.

In closing, let me say that my office has a straightforward goal—to protect the President and his decision-making process. Paper coming to him must meet the highest standards of excellence. Papers must be well written. Options must be clearly stated. Those who need to see it must have seen it. Views of advisors must be accurately reflected. Summaries must be brief and accurate. We cannot let the pressure of time compromise those standards.[35]

The Chief of Staff

A president is constantly besieged, both by people who want to see him and by events or crises. There are not enough hours in the day for the president to handle everything, so it falls to the staff to determine which people and material are important enough for presidential attention. As the gatekeeper for the president's time and attention, the chief of staff is the most critical component in determining whether the White House staff effectively serves the needs of the president and the country. The chief of staff as an institutional feature determines the quality of information and advice the president sees and influences the overall management structure of the White House. The chief of staff is also an individual whose personal skills influence the effectiveness of the office.[36]

An effective chief of staff can positively influence presidential decision making in several ways. Since the chief of staff and his aides determine what flows into the president's in-box, how the president and the chief of staff view information is important: What issues are worthy of presidential attention? How does the president like to receive information? Who has unfettered access to the president? How many individuals attend meetings? When are meetings scheduled, and how long should they be? These issues are critical to a successful presidency, yet are never debated during a presidential campaign when considering qualifications for the office.

Issue focus and meeting length seem a trivial factor in organization and decision making, yet the impact can be dramatic. Early in his presidency, Nixon limited his access not only to individuals but also to issues. He informed his top policy aide John Ehrlichman and his chief of staff H. R. Haldeman that he would see information on only three issues: inflation, busing, and Vietnam. Although they were top issues at the time, it was a blanket directive that probably aided his isolation. Clinton's administration initially suffered, not from Clinton's choices but from his organizational flaws. Clinton's chief of staff, his childhood friend Thomas "Mack" McLarty, was unable to counter the president's bad organizational habits. Clinton delighted in all things policy and famously wanted to rehash every nugget of information. At meetings, staffers were alternately delighted by the President's focus, depth of knowledge, and attention and horrified by the inability to disengage and move on to the next meeting or event. Clinton was notoriously late for everything, keeping everyone from assistants to world leaders waiting. Despite providing trusted advice and being a longtime friend, McLarty was replaced as chief of staff by organizationally minded, bureaucratically skilled Leon Panetta in 1994 (Panetta was a former member of the

House of Representatives). The results were significant because "disorganized" and "unfocused" ceased to be common descriptions of the Clinton administration.

The mechanism for good information and advice is management—as in the business world. How the White House is set up often determines the flow of information and the quality of decision making, and the chief of staff, or even the choice to have one, is critical. Ideally, the chief of staff should be an honest broker for ideas. James Baker, Reagan's first chief of staff, believed "the worst chief of staff I think would be a yes man who was never willing to tell the president what his views were or what he thought."[37] The chief of staff also becomes a guardian of the president's time and reputation, both personally and politically, but not all candidates do that well. Ultimately, George H. W. Bush's first chief of staff articulated the truth of the position; John Sununu, a former governor from New Hampshire, understandably said, "the role of the chief of staff is whatever the president wants that role to be."[38]

The need for a chief of staff arises from the task charged to the EOP: manage the bureaucracy from the president's perspective. As such, a chief of staff must have political skills as well as management and organizational skills. Not surprisingly, few chiefs of staff are equally good at both roles, which is why there have often been multiple people doing the "chief" job even when one is appointed, like Reagan's troika of Baker, Deaver, and Meese or George W. Bush's use of Chief of Staff Andrew Card along with close political advisors Karl Rove and Karen Hughes. The complexity and stress of the job also explain why most presidents have multiple chiefs of staff. Not only is the job extremely demanding with little to no time off, but also presidents often realize they need better managers when they have a politico or better politics from a good manager. Typically, management trumps politics because numerous political advisors are available to the president, but the gatekeeper skill is harder to find.

Presidents naturally seek trusted advisors in the chief of staff role; however, recent presidents learned from Clinton's mistake and reserved the role for those individuals with skills, relegating his closest advisors to the number two or three roles in the White House. Obama's first chief of staff, Rahm Emanuel, was the first to relinquish a seat in Congress for the position. Like Bush, and like Clinton after McLarty, Obama hired a skilled outsider to be his chief of staff and kept his close confidants in the nonmanagement roles. Prior to his job as Obama's chief of staff, Emanuel had served as a senior advisor in the Clinton White House and then served six years in the House of Representatives (including a stint as the chairman of the Democratic Congressional Campaign Committee in 2006 when his party won back control of the House). Emanuel left the chief of staff position to run for mayor of Chicago, winning the office in November 2010.

Trump chose Reince Priebus to be his chief of staff. Priebus served as the chairman of the Republican National Committee from 2011 through the 2016 campaign. He also appointed Steve Bannon, the former head of Breitbart News, his chief strategist. In his statement regarding their appointments, Trump noted they would work "as equal partners to transform the federal government."[39] With the addition of his son-in-law, Jared Kushner, as a senior White House advisor, Trump appears to be aiming for a Reagan troika model, with each appointment bringing different skill sets and relationships to the White House. Priebus is the manager and insider, Bannon represents the voice of the core of the Trump constituency, and Kushner is the trusted Trump insider. However, only Priebus has Washington experience; this could be a political advantage but does not reflect management skills.

Concerns with the EOP

The changes in size and responsibility of the White House staff evoke some serious trepidations for people inside and outside government. A staff too large is difficult to supervise; in the worst-case scenario, unsupervised staff members are running around Washington demanding action in the name of the president without the president's knowledge or approval. Both the Watergate and Iran–Contra scandals developed because of a lack of supervision.

The Watergate scandal began June 18, 1972, when five men were caught breaking into the headquarters of the Democratic National Committee trying to wiretap and photograph sensitive material. The lead burglar, James McCord, was the security coordinator for the Committee to Reelect the President. Even worse, all five were paid by the Committee's secret slush fund. All of this information came out during the campaign season, but Nixon still won reelection. Between June 1972 and April 1973, the White House attempted to cover up the crimes and the connections between the activities and the President's men. Investigations by the media, particularly Bob Woodward and Carl Bernstein of the *Washington Post*, along with an investigation by Congress, eventually revealed that an even wider net of crimes occurred and were covered up. Seven of Nixon's staffers were eventually indicted. As discussed in Chapter 5, the public lost faith in the President and in the office as a result of Watergate. In terms of staffing and management, many argue the scandal occurred because of the "we are not above the law, we are the law" atmosphere from the White House. Well into the scandal, the infamous tape recordings of Oval Office conversations reveal that the President knew of the obstruction of justice and even authorized payment after one of his lower-level staffers decided to blackmail the higher-ups. Nixon set that tone with his staff and furthered it by distancing himself from day-to-day operations on most subjects.

The Iran–Contra scandal similarly resulted from a lack of presidential oversight of the Reagan White House staff, and the lack of management seriously influenced American foreign policy. The scandal was nicknamed the arms-for-hostages deal, because Israel would ship weapons to Iran provided by the United States. The Iranian moderates were supposed to get Hezbollah to release six American hostages. The plan changed as the NSC's Lt. Colonel Oliver North diverted some of the money received from Israel to fund anticommunist rebels in Nicaragua, known as the Contras.

The actions of Reagan's NSC staff were controversial on multiple fronts. First, the sales violated the Boland Amendment, passed by Congress, which expressly limited assistance to the Contras. Second, the decision to trade arms for hostages violated the stated position of Reagan and the United States to not negotiate with terrorists. In terms of staffing and management, like Watergate, Iran–Contra revealed the dangers of setting forth zealous staff members with little oversight. Reagan knew and approved of the original effort to work with the moderate Iranians to attempt to secure the release of the hostages. He also knew and approved of the decision to negotiate not just with Iranians but also with the government of Iran. However, he did not know that the NSC changed the plan and diverted money to fund the Contras.

After the scandal became public in 1986, Reagan created the Tower Commission to investigate what went wrong; Reagan himself testified before the commission. The panel asserted that the President should have had better control of his NSC, and, as such, they recommended putting more authority in the hands of the national security advisor. Ultimately, the Tower Commission argued that the illegal, covert activities occurred because established procedures were ignored and senior staff did not review their subordinates frequently enough. In short, bad management can lead to a White House run amok.

In addition to the dangers of lack of supervision, the sheer existence of a White House staff transfers policymaking and implementation away from the experts in the departments to individuals whose skills and expertise might not be equivalent. Hurricane Katrina in August 2005 starkly revealed this to the nation. Katrina was one of the costliest and deadliest hurricanes to hit the United States, and parts of Louisiana, Mississippi, and Alabama would never be the same because millions of individuals lost homes and jobs. For the George W. Bush administration, the hurricane revealed layer after layer of poor management and judgment. In terms of staff management, Katrina demonstrated how narrowing the number of individuals who encounter the president can be dangerous. Hurricane Katrina took place while the President was on vacation at his Crawford, Texas, ranch. Given the state-of-the-art technology at the President's home, his vacation was not necessarily the issue. However, Vice President Dick Cheney and Chief of Staff Andrew Card and other top staff took advantage of the President's vacation to take their own. None of the staff in Texas made sure that the President understood the catastrophic nature of the storm. The advisors with Bush who had his ear (including Deputy Chief of Staff Joe Hagin and advisors Karl Rove and Dan Bartlett) gave communications and tactical advice, but themselves "lacked alternative channels of information and expertise to fill the 'communication void' that debilitated the White House's decision making."[40]

The 9/11 commission inadvertently revealed to the public how the lack of congressional oversight of the White House staff creates a problematic tradition of accountability only to the president. Since Congress does not oversee the EOP, the advisors are not typically called before committees to explain their decision making or their behavior, as are cabinet members. The rationale for the lack of oversight is that the president requires advice protected by executive privilege. Executive privilege allows for conversations and advice to remain private because it protects staffers from subpoena from the legislative or judicial branches. The president could not get unbiased views of events or policies if the staff member had to fear subpoenas and public scrutiny. In the aftermath of 9/11, there was a bitter fight over whether National Security Advisor Condoleezza Rice would testify under oath and about the Bush White House response to terrorism prior to the events of 9/11. The Bush administration eventually caved to public pressure and allowed Rice to testify. Under any other circumstances, it would have probably been preferable for the Bush White House to press the tradition of noncompliance. However, the pressure put forth by the 9/11 widows and the commission (made up of an even number of Republicans and Democrats) made participation unavoidable. The Bush White House "saved face" by contending that since she was appearing before a unique commission and not a committee of Congress, no undermining of executive privilege occurred. Rice was the first and, as of early 2017, the only national security advisor to testify under oath before Congress or any other body.

The most important problem, beyond accountability and staff management, when considering the president's capacity to make decisions and manage the bureaucracy is isolation. Is the president getting enough advice to decide? Is he surrounded by yes-men or by competing ideas and interpretation? It is impossible to make a good decision if no one will tell you what you do not want to hear. The controversy surrounding the decision by George W. Bush to go to war in Iraq features the role of staff in presidential decision making. Per the account of journalist Bob Woodward, in the decisive months of late 2002 and early 2003, the president did not ask anyone other than Rice whether they should go to war. Bush told Woodward he knew what Cheney thought, "and he decided not to ask Powell or Rumsfeld."[41] In what is often considered one of the most important decisions a president makes—sending troops into combat—Bush chose not to ask the opinions of his secretaries of defense and state because he believed he knew what they would say. More significant, Bush felt that the staff and cabinet members did not truly understand, remarking, "If you were sitting where I sit, you would be pretty clear."[42] The President chose not to hear divergent opinions; by January of 2003 he had decided to go to war in Iraq. More concerning than not being asked, Powell chose not to press his divergent point of view. When speaking to Woodward in 2002, Powell articulated an "uncertainty that the president fully grasped the potential consequences" of war in Iraq—what became known as the Pottery Barn Doctrine—"you break it, you buy it"—and that the United States would be responsible for nation-building. If a staff member believes that the president lacks full understanding of the situation but backs down in the face of others' certainty, then ultimately the president does not receive the appropriate advice to decide. In terms of any issue, but especially war, problematic or just unproductive staff relationships can be costly.

PRESIDENTIAL CONTROL OF THE BUREAUCRACY

The EOP with its White House Staff and executive councils gives the president managerial capacity. Since the creation of the EOP in 1939, presidents have expanded techniques that enable some level of control over the political side of the bureaucracy as well as the civil service side. To varying degrees, presidents use the appointment process, the budgetary process, executive orders, the regulatory review process, and signing statements.

Appointments

The expansion of government under FDR and the New Deal enlarged the civil service and the bulk of the initial hires were Democrats. When Eisenhower took office in 1953 as the first Republican president in 20 years, he faced an enormous, largely Democratic bureaucracy. Eisenhower issued an executive order that created 800 to 1,000 appointed positions designed to add Republicans.[43] Prior to the executive order, top-level jobs, below secretary and under secretary, were filled by the promotion of career civil servants.[44] After Eisenhower, career civil servants had to compete with the president's appointments.

The relationship with Congress significantly influences the ease of the president's appointment process. As discussed in Chapter 6, whether Congress and the president are of the same party (unified government) or not (divided government) greatly affects the relationship between the branches. Not only is it easier for a president to see his appointments confirmed under unified government, but also the number of overall appointees expands.[45]

The creation of numerous positions returns the bureaucracy to a facsimile of the patronage era of Andrew Jackson, which can have serious pitfalls for the president. As noted, Hurricane Katrina revealed numerous problems in the management of the Bush executive branch. Not only was the President ill-served by his closed circle of advisors, but also the preference for filling appointments using loyalty over experience exacerbated the consequences of Katrina. Bush's two appointments to the position of director of the Federal Emergency Management Agency (FEMA) loudly signaled his approach to appointments and his view of the agency. In 2001, Bush appointed his former chief of staff from his tenure as governor of Texas, Joe Allbaugh, the director of FEMA. In his testimony before Congress in 2001, Allbaugh asserted a perspective that reflected the Bush view of the agency: federal disaster assistance had become "an oversized entitlement program." Allbaugh stated that his goal and that of the administration would be to "restore the predominant role of state and local response to most disasters."[46] Bush's top disaster official's plan for his new agency was for it to do less.

Allbaugh made the other ill-fated hire for FEMA: Michael D. Brown. Brown moved up the ranks quickly. He started as general counsel and was promoted to deputy director in 2002 and director in 2003, despite no emergency management experience. He was, however, Allbaugh's college roommate and a Republican lawyer who worked as a stewards and judges commission for the International Arabian Horse Association.[47] Brown became the face of mismanagement as Bush famously claimed, "Brownie, you're doing a heck of a job," four days after the hurricane hit. Unfortunately, the complement came a day after Brown told an incredulous CNN anchor that, in contrast to anyone with a television set, he and the government did not know that the New Orleans Superdome housed thousands of displaced individuals who lacked food and water. Brown was relieved of his duties on September 9, 2005, by DHS secretary Michael Chertoff (and officially resigned three days later), just two weeks after Hurricane Katrina made landfall.

Budgeting as Management

Congress created the BOB, as part of the Treasury Department, in 1921, to prevent future fiscal crises like the one that occurred after World War I. The central task of the BOB was to gather all the department and agency budget estimates into a single federal budget. However, the BOB "soon became a foundation for the expansion of presidential power. . . . [as] presidents gradually began to use the budget as a policy tool by adjusting budget estimates to promote their own legislative goals."[48] Nixon expanded the number of political appointees in the agency and renamed it the OMB in 1973. The new name signaled its new focus and responsibilities; the agency would coordinate and prioritize, not just budget.

Budgeting is a powerful presidential tool because the size of the budget determines how much an agency can accomplish. Presidents cannot abolish programs, agencies, or departments regardless of what they think of them. Instead, presidents promote programs by adding to their budgets and isolate or downgrade programs by starving them of needed funds. In the scenario of agency starvation, directors become tools of the administration against the agency, a reverse of going native. As noted in the case of FEMA, but as also occurred in the Bush Consumer Product Safety Commission, the Bush administration's desire to reduce the activism of the federal government often occurred in budgetary fighting with Congress. After a rash of recalls caused by the presence of lead paint in children's toys, the Democratic Congress attempted to enable the Consumer Product Safety Commission to better serve its constituency: consumers. Bush's acting chairwoman, Nancy Nord, assumed the unusual position of advocating *against* more agency funding. Speaker of the House Nancy Pelosi (D-CA) lambasted Nord, arguing, "Any commission chair who (says) . . . we don't need any more authority or any more resources to do our job, does not understand the gravity of the situation." Nord argued in response that "I want to be hiring more safety inspectors and scientists and compliance officers, I don't want to be hiring lawyers. . . . [the bill] could have the unintended consequence of hampering, rather than furthering, consumer product safety."[49]

Executive Orders

Although Congress tasks the departments and agencies to implement and administer the vague, compromised legislation they produce, as the chief executive, the president is ultimately responsible for the implementation of legislation. Consequently, the president has considerable leeway to interpret the implementation, as does the bureaucracy. To ensure the civil service interprets the legislation toward the president's agenda, goals, and ideology, presidents issue directives to the bureaucracy. These directives, proclamations, and presidential decision memoranda all seek to mold the output of the executive branch in that the "legal authority of an executive order must derive from either the law or the Constitution."[50]

As discussed in Chapter 2, the use of executive orders began with George Washington; the Louisiana Purchase (Thomas Jefferson) and the Emancipation Proclamation (Abraham Lincoln) were early examples of how far-ranging and controversial the unilateral behavior could be. However, the orders are not absolute; "they have the force of law, [but] they can be overturned by subsequent administrations, . . . [and] also by congressional action or court ruling."[51] As Chapter 6 demonstrates, Congress limits the president's ability to enact his agenda by legislation. Executive orders, in contrast, enable the president to do administrative and/or symbolic tasks, but also advance his agenda without encountering the complexities of the legislative process.

The increase in the number of executive orders issued by presidents since FDR directly relates to the president's desire to maximize their authority and goals.[52] Executive orders are efficient; presidents need only a pen rather than a majority in Congress. Moreover, executive orders are direct because they are not the results of compromise. They tend to receive less public and media scrutiny (although some, like the treatment of detainees at Guantanamo Bay or the "Don't Ask, Don't Tell" rule about homosexuals serving in the military, can become controversial).[53] As the next tool demonstrates, presidents also like using executive orders to quickly undo their predecessor's work.

Researching the Presidency

Executive Orders and the Public

The unilateral presidency is the term used by scholars to encapsulate the activities presidents undertake without congressional input, in many cases to thwart congressional action or inaction on issues important to the president. Executive orders allow the president to direct the executive branch to do something, generally something Congress has not specifically authorized. This stretching of presidential power and authority has become the norm in an era of polarized party politics. Typically, scholars investigate the unilateral presidency in terms of policymaking—the use of executive orders, proclamations, and signing statements to create policy change toward the president's preferred position. However, Brandon Rottinghaus and Adam Warber argue that the unilateral presidency is using the bureaucracy not only for policy purposes but also for constituency purposes. In short, the unilateral presidency is also part of public leadership.

In *Unilateral Orders as Constituency Outreach: Executive Orders, Proclamations, and the Public Presidency*, Rottinghaus and Warber want to understand whether and when the need for public leadership influences unilateral action. Does the president undertake unilateral actions on agenda items to serve political as well as policy goals? To investigate the connections between unilateral and public behavior, Rottinghaus and Warber explore how "presidents may appeal to constituencies to issue a unilateral order that is of importance to specific constituency groups that comprise presidential coalitions. In this context, presidents often use executive orders and proclamations to celebrate the history, accomplishments, or actions of groups or individuals, or to develop public policies that are of interest to certain segments of society."[54] The use of unilateral orders can provide benefits in both directions because while the group or constituencies benefit from the direct action of the president, the president benefits by being able to time the action. Unlike legislative components of the agenda where the president is at the mercy of the congressional calendar and compromises with the institution, unilateral action is entirely under the president's control. Consequently, actions could be timed to improve approval ratings or distract from undesirable media attention.

Using a data set of executive orders and proclamations directed toward constituencies from Eisenhower to George W. Bush (1953 to 2009), Rottinghaus and Warber determined that Democratic presidents are more likely to use executive orders and proclamations than Republican presidents to appeal to groups. This makes sense given the more diverse nature of the Democratic Party. More important, they find that presidents use the unilateral presidency based on institutional incentives with Congress rather than political advantage with the public. There is more constituency-based unilateral action when Congress is stronger, when there is divided government, when Congress' majority is large, or when avenues toward legislative success are closed. The president is less likely to use constituency-based unilateral action during an election year or when popularity ratings are fluctuating. Rottinghaus and Warber make an important contribution to scholarly understandings of unilateral behavior, reminding us that political calculations are never far removed from presidential policymaking.

Regulatory Review

The regulatory review process is in some ways similar to the budgetary process as a presidential tool. In budgeting, departments and agencies submit their budgets to the OMB, which folds each agency budget into the whole federal budget. In regulatory review, the OMB or any other presidential agencies that are tasked to review perform analyses of the rules created to implement congressional legislation. For example, Reagan created Executive Order (EO) 12291, which required not only the submission of proposed rules but also cost–benefit analyses and evaluations of alternative approaches.[55] Presidents since Reagan have all employed some form of EO to govern regulatory review. Clinton repealed EO 12291 and replaced it with EO 12866, which altered the review process only by making it more favorable to his agenda. George W. Bush retained Clinton's EO but targeted it back toward Reagan's EO and a conservative agenda. On January 30, 2009, Obama revoked Bush's 2007 EO 13422, unentangling the review process from a market-oriented agenda.

Signing Statements

When a president receives a piece of legislation from Congress, he has two options: sign it and make it law or veto it. Since James Monroe, presidents have not simply signed or not signed the bill; they have also issued commentary on the legislation with their understanding of how the law should be implemented. These comments are collectively known as "signing statements" and do not have the force of law that EOs implicitly contain. Instead, signing statements provide symbolic statements as well as guidance for agencies in their rule making and an opportunity to influence future judicial interpretation.

A signing statement from Andrew Jackson in 1830 illustrates how the early presidents used signing statements:

> To the Senate and House of Representatives of the United States.
>
> GENTLEMEN: I have approved and signed the bill entitled "An act making appropriations for examinations and surveys, and also for certain works of internal improvement," but as the phraseology of the section which appropriates the sum of $8,000 for the road from Detroit to Chicago may be construed to authorize the application of the appropriation for the continuance of the road beyond the limits of the Territory of Michigan, I desire to be understood as having approved this bill with the understanding that the road authorized by this section An active role for the vice the limits of the said Territory.
>
> ANDREW JACKSON[56]

Modern presidents, particularly those faced with divided government, have used signing statements "as a means for the president to object to congressional incursions across the border between Articles I and II."[57] George W. Bush used signing statements to assert the power and prerogatives of the institution of the presidency. Bush asserted in 76 distinct signing statements a phrase that encapsulated the president's position: "supervise the unitary executive branch." Here is an example of a Bush signing statement; the highlighted phrases are the ones Bush used to assert presidential authority:

> **Statement on Signing the Palestinian Anti-Terrorism Act of 2006:**
> Today I have signed into law S. 2370, the "Palestinian Anti-Terrorism Act of 2006." The Act is designed to promote the development of democratic institutions in areas under the administrative control of the Palestinian Authority.
>
> Section 2 of the Act purports to establish U.S. policy with respect to various international affairs matters. **My approval of the Act does not constitute my adoption of the statements of policy as U.S. foreign policy.** Given the Constitution's commitment to the presidency of the authority to conduct the Nation's foreign affairs, **the executive branch shall construe such policy statements as advisory**. The executive branch will give section 2 the due weight that comity between the legislative and executive branches should require, to the extent consistent with U.S. foreign policy.

The executive branch shall construe section 3(b) of the Act, which relates to access to certain information by a legislative agent, and section 11 of the Act, which relates to a report on certain assistance by foreign countries, international organizations, or multilateral development banks, **in a manner consistent with the President's constitutional authority to withhold information that could impair foreign relations, national security, the deliberative processes of the Executive, or the performance of the Executive's constitutional duties.**

Section 620K(e)(2)(A) and 620L(b)(4)(B)(i) of the Foreign Assistance Act of 1961, as enacted by sections 2(b)(2) and 3(a) of the Act, purport to require the President to consult with committees of the Congress prior to exercising certain authority granted to the President by sections 620K and 620L. **Because the constitutional authority of the President to supervise the unitary executive branch and take care that the laws be faithfully executed cannot be made by law subject to a requirement to consult with congressional committees or to involve them in executive decisionmaking, the executive branch shall construe the references in the provisions to consulting to require only notification.**

The executive branch shall construe section 7 of the Act, which relates to establishing or maintaining certain facilities or establishments within the jurisdiction of the United States, in a manner consistent with the President's constitutional authority to conduct the Nation's foreign affairs, including the authority to receive ambassadors and other public ministers.

The executive branch shall construe as **advisory the provisions of the Act**, including section 9, that purport to direct or burden the conduct of negotiations by the executive branch with entities abroad. Such provisions, if construed as mandatory rather than advisory, **would impermissibly interfere with the President's constitutional authorities to conduct the Nation's foreign affairs, including protection of American citizens and American military and other Government personnel abroad, and to supervise the unitary executive branch.** George W. Bush, The White House, December 21, 2006.[58]

However, even Republicans in Congress at times objected to Bush's use of signing statements. In March 2006, a bipartisan group of 22 House members and senators wrote the following in a letter to Bush:

We are writing to express our concern with your signing statement of November 22, 2005 for H.R. 2862, the Science, State, Justice, Commerce, and Related Agencies Appropriations Act, 2006. In this statement, five provisions of this law passed by the Congress of the United States are identified, which you say the Executive Branch will "construe as advisory." This statement is disconcerting because it seems to potentially overstep the constitutional power granted the Executive Branch and because these provisions named are undoubtedly important. We are specifically concerned that you identified Section 631 as one of those provisions that you would "construe as advisory." To the contrary, the intent and meaning of Section 631 is clear. This provision prevents the United States Trade Representative (USTR) from inserting language in future trade agreements blocking pharmaceutical imports, even if Congress passes a drug importation law down the road. . . . While this provision does *not* permit prescription drug importation, it does ensure that the pharmaceutical industry, through USTR, cannot take advantage of the President's trade promotion authority to input language that goes against the wishes of Congress. . . . It is in Congress's hands to decide whether the law will be changed to allow drug importation—not the pharmaceutical industry through USTR's trade negotiating authority. Congress sent you a good bill in H.R. 2862 which, among other things, prevents pharmaceutical companies and USTR from evading the legislative branch on the issue of trade in pharmaceuticals. Additionally, both chambers of Congress have shown their strong support to allow the safe, legal importation of patented pharmaceuticals. In conclusion, we would like to reiterate our support and the support of the American people and Congress on this issue. Furthermore, we expect the Executive Branch to perform its constitutional duty and abide by and enforce all the provisions of H.R. 2862.[59]

Taken together, budgeting, issuing EOs and signing statements, and conducting regulatory review now offers presidents an array of tools to attempt to manage the seemingly unmanageable. Functionality is not the president's only goal in employing these tactics. Asserting an ideology, accomplishing an agenda, and leaving a legacy are additional goals. Successful management of the executive branch aids in each aspect of those goals.

VICE PRESIDENTS

If the framers of the Constitution had anything but minor interest in the vice presidency, the historical record seems to provide no evidence. Of the many pamphlets, essays, and correspondences generated by American writers about the Constitution, not one focuses on the vice presidency itself. Alexander Hamilton devoted two paragraphs to it in *Federalist* 68, but his comments offer no insight about the primary purposes of the office. Although other documents reflect Anti-Federalist concerns over the vice president's role in the Senate, they reveal nothing about the nature of the office, nor do they shed any light on its theoretical foundations. Historically speaking, the vice presidency is unusual. Established to meet the unique demands of a presidential system of government, it was without precedent in the late eighteenth century. Yet, from a modern perspective, despite long periods of inactivity or comparative obscurity, the vice presidency has become one of the more essential political positions.

The History of the Office

The first vice president, John Adams, claimed, "My country has in its wisdom contrived for me the most insignificant office that ever the invention of man contrived or his imagination conceived."[60] More than 150 years later, FDR's first vice president, John Nance Garner, colorfully informed Lyndon Johnson, who was considering becoming John F. Kennedy's running mate in 1960, that the office was "hardly worth a pitcher of spit."[61] The position, as many vice presidents have noted, has two functions, both of which involve lots of waiting. In the event of a tie in the Senate, the vice president casts the deciding vote. In the event of the death, incapacitation, resignation, or impeachment of the president, the vice president assumes the job of president. Thus, on a day-to-day basis, there is no constitutionally defined role. The vice presidency lacks both the prestige and power of the presidency, and it may not be the post to which most politicians aspire. However, it is important to remember that nine vice presidents have succeeded to the office of the presidency (as a result of four presidential deaths in office, four assassinations, and one resignation), so the office does have more significance than its detractors commonly assert.

The Constitution, as ratified in 1789, mentions the vice presidency four specific times; there are three additional amendments that deal with the position. The four initial references sum up the job description as designed by the framers:

> The Vice President of the United States shall be President of the Senate, but shall have no Vote, unless they be equally divided. (Article II, Section 3)
>
> The executive Power shall be vested in a President of the United States of America. He shall hold his Office during the Term of four Years, and, together with the Vice-President chosen for the same Term, be elected, as follows . . . (Article II, Section 1)
>
> In Case of the Removal of the President from Office, or of his Death, Resignation, or Inability to discharge the Powers and Duties of the said Office, the same shall devolve on the Vice President, and the Congress may by Law provide for the Case of Removal, Death, Resignation or Inability, both of the President and Vice President, declaring what Officer shall then act as President, and such Officer shall act accordingly, until the Disability be removed, or a President shall be elected. (Article II, Section I, modified by the 20th and 25th amendments)
>
> The President, Vice President and all civil Officers of the United States, shall be removed from Office on Impeachment for, and Conviction of, Treason, Bribery, or other high Crimes and Misdemeanors. (Article II, Section 4).

In addition, per the framers' intentions, the Constitution required electors to vote for two undifferentiated candidates during presidential elections, which was supposed to produce a president and his presumed successor and, in so doing, preserve stability and the unified and steady progress of the presidency. As such, the framers hoped vice presidents would be among their presidents' closest advisors, supporting presidential policymaking and getting on-the-job training for the nation's highest office. Unfortunately, the framers' plans never materialized because personal incompatibilities soon undermined original intent, relegating the vice presidency to a back seat in executive politics. The Twelfth Amendment (which required each elector to cast distinct votes for the president and the vice president, instead of two votes for the president) formally acknowledged the inferiority of the vice presidency and subordinated it to the presidency in a way the framers never intended.

Aside from their constitutional role as presiding officers of the Senate, nineteenth-century vice presidents had no real power or authority. John Tyler, Millard Fillmore, Andrew Johnson, and Chester Arthur ascended to the presidency on the deaths of William Henry Harrison, Zachary Taylor, Abraham Lincoln, and James Garfield, respectively, but their contributions as presidents did nothing to enhance the reputation of the vice presidency. None of the four distinguished himself in the White House, at least not in a positive way; Tyler and Johnson each had a special talent for making political enemies (and Johnson became the first president to be impeached in 1868). The assassination of William McKinley and the succession of Vice President Theodore Roosevelt to the presidency in 1901 began a slow but intermittent rehabilitation of the vice presidency. Roosevelt was a vocal and comparatively assertive vice president and became one of America's most admired chief executives, whose effectiveness in the presidency finally alerted Americans to the potential importance of a historically neglected office.

Yet, in the four decades following Roosevelt's presidency, the vice presidency again largely languished. The death of yet another president, Warren Harding, did not prove as fortuitous for his successor, not least because Calvin Coolidge was no Teddy Roosevelt. However, in 1945, the death of FDR would again catapult a vice president into the political spotlight. At the time, no one could have predicted that Harry Truman, the former junior senator from Missouri and FDR's third vice president (elected to the job in 1944), would become the architect of America's national security state and one of its most formidable commanders in chief. Compared unfavorably to his former boss in almost every possible way by the public, Truman was expected to fade into anonymity with the rest of America's vice presidents. FDR's death in April 1945 shattered those expectations and served as the springboard for an exceptionally effective tenure, especially with respect to foreign policy.

The Contemporary Vice Presidency

Vice presidents today play a more significant role in the day-to-day operation of the White House. For example, Joe Biden's job during the Obama administration was detailed on the White House web page:

> The Vice President has been tasked with implementing the American Recovery and Reinvestment Act, helping to rebuild our economy and lay the foundation for a sustainable economic future. He is also the chair of the administration's Middle Class Task Force, a major White House initiative targeted at raising the living standards of middle class families in America. In addition, he is providing sustained, high level focus for the administration on Iraq policy and has traveled to the country multiple times since being elected as Vice President. Vice President Biden continues to draw on his vast foreign policy experience, advising the President on a multitude of international issues and representing our country to many regions of the world, including travel to Germany, Belgium, Chile, Costa Rica, Bosnia and Herzegovina, Serbia, Kosovo, Lebanon, Georgia, Ukraine, Iraq, Poland, Romania, the Czech Republic, Israel, the Palestinian Territories, Jordan, Spain, Egypt, Kenya and South Africa.[62]

The growth in the responsibilities of the vice presidency arose from extraconstitutional sources, namely presidential discretion. The vice presidency did not expand in tandem with the growth of the EOP and White House staff. Instead, the vice presidency was slow to evolve as an institutional source of administration and management because, like the cabinet, vice presidents are chosen for a variety of reasons. As discussed in Chapter 3, candidates choose running mates for geographic and/or ideological balance and/or for party unity. Like the cabinet, those reasons do not often support governing and management. However, over time, delegation and management did factor into presidential choice and the expansion of the vice president's role in the executive branch.

An early example is Dwight Eisenhower allowing his vice president, Richard Nixon, to attend cabinet, NSC, and other legislative meetings. When Eisenhower was ill, Nixon presided over the meetings as well. Nixon was also the first vice president to have an office inside the White House. Most of Nixon's authority comprised foreign-policy responsibilities because Eisenhower relied on Nixon's expertise on international matters. Nixon even represented the administration on several foreign trips (including his famous "kitchen debates" with Soviet premier Nikita Khrushchev at the American National Exhibition in Moscow in 1959), increasing the visibility of an institution that had been relatively anonymous throughout the previous 150 years. This strongly contrasted with the FDR model; for example, Truman was not exposed to sensitive information. In fact, Truman did not find out that the country had nuclear capabilities until after becoming president in April 1945. Lyndon Johnson (who took the job despite Garner's opinion of it) participated more frequently in legislative efforts, in keeping with the skill set of a former Senate majority leader, yet was still not considered among the inner circle of advisors within the Kennedy administration.

Walter Mondale was the first vice president to achieve institutional power for the office. As noted in the staffing and cabinet discussions, access to the president is perhaps the most significant sign of power. Staff members who see the president frequently are more able to influence issues as well as the President, compared with those who do not. Mondale had a large staff, he saw the president frequently, and, in Jimmy Carter, he had a willing partner for expanding the role of the office.[63] Thus, he was an active participant in many issues. He took the office well beyond "the job's traditional responsibilities to lobby Congress on the administration's behalf, serve as spokesman to the general public and politically important interest groups, attend ceremonial functions in the president's stead, and assist the party's candidates for office."[64] An active role for the vice president still ultimately depends on the choice of the president to allow it; however, Mondale seems to have permanently expanded the institutional capacity of the office. Although not all subsequent presidential–vice presidential relationships were as close, the trend has been for increased activism, capacity, and management.

Recent vice presidents have all received extensive staff, continuous access to the president, and a president willing to rely on the vice president's skill and expertise in specific areas. Al Gore (1993–2001) was intimately involved in policymaking, much more so than his predecessors. He took a special interest in environmental issues, bureaucratic reform, and information technology, and Gore was a trusted advisor to Clinton and an integral part of the administration.

Dick Cheney (2001–2009), a seasoned veteran of two previous administrations with a take-no-prisoners mentality, was Bush's point person on national-security issues. Viewed as the leading advocate of war in the Middle East, Cheney had unprecedented authority over strategic planning and military operations, as well as substantial responsibility over diplomatic issues. However, many considered Cheney's expansive exercise of power a worrisome precedent because Cheney took the office well beyond the activities of his predecessors. His role, particularly in the early years of the Bush administration, has been described as a "surrogate chief of staff," "co-president," and "deputy president."[65] Not only did Cheney manage the response to terror on the morning of 9/11 (Bush was at an education event in Florida), but also he and his office were involved in some of the most controversial decisions and events during the Bush administration. Cheney's vice presidential office has been

Vice President Dick Cheney expanded the powers of his office during the George W. Bush administration.

linked to creating a domestic surveillance program; creating policies for detained suspected terrorists; outing a Central Intelligence Agency agent; and linking Saddam Hussein to al Qaeda (proven false) and to weapons of mass destruction (also proven false), which led, in part, to the invasion of Iraq in 2003.

Joe Biden (2009–2017) chose a less confrontational path, modeled after the Gore–Clinton relationship. As an experienced legislator with impressive foreign-policy credentials, Biden set a new standard for the vice presidency. On January 12, 2016, Obama awarded Biden the Medal of Freedom, with distinction, an honor previously awarded to few individuals. In his remarks, Obama highlighted how the twenty-first-century vice presidency remains an expanded, influential part of the institution of the presidency:

> And for the past eight years, he could not have been a more devoted or effec-
> tive partner in the progress that we've made. He fought to make college more af-
> fordable and revitalize American manufacturing as the head of our Middle Class
> Task Force. He suited up for our Cancer Moonshot, giving hope to millions of
> Americans touched by this disease.
>
> He led our efforts to combat gun violence, and he rooted out any possible mis-
> appropriations that might have occurred. And as a consequence, the Recovery
> Act worked as well as just about any largescale stimulus project has ever worked
> in this country. He visited college after college—and made friends with Lady

Gaga (laughter)—for our "It's On Us" campaign against campus sexual assault. And when the Pope visited, Joe was even kind enough to let me talk to His Holiness, as well.

Behind the scenes, Joe's candid, honest counsel has made me a better President and a better Commander-in-Chief. From the Situation Room to our weekly lunches, to our huddles after everybody else has cleared out of the room, he's been unafraid to give it to me straight, even if we disagree—in fact, especially if we disagree. And all of this makes him, I believe, the finest Vice President we have ever seen.

Mike Pence (2017–present), a seasoned politician who served 12 years in the House of Representatives and one term as governor of Indiana, is viewed as a good counterbalance to Trump, who has no political experience. He is expected to play an important role in presidential–congressional relations in a similar way to his immediate predecessors.

FIRST LADIES

There is no constitutional role for the president's family, yet there is no avoiding the public role that comes from marriage to the president. For most of the country's history, the president's wife has served as hostess in chief. In the modern era, the duties of the first lady include some or all of the following: wife and mother, public figure and celebrity, the nation's social hostess, a symbol of U.S. womanhood, White House manager and preservationist, campaigner, champion of social causes, presidential spokesperson, presidential and political party booster, diplomat, and political and presidential partner.[66] As with the vice president, the extent to which the first lady adopts any, or all, of these roles depends on private negotiations with the president and to some extent public negotiations with the country. The Office of the First Lady has become, in recent years, part of the official organizational structure of the EOP. One of the main responsibilities of the first lady's staff is in the day-to-day dealings with the news media. In addition to a press secretary, most first ladies have also employed a chief of staff, a social secretary, a projects director (for causes that a first lady may adopt), and several other special assistants. Since the 1970s, first ladies have employed anywhere between 12 and 28 full-time employees for their staffs.[67] First ladies also have an office in the White House; to date, only one—Hillary Clinton—chose to have her office in the West Wing, as opposed to the East Wing, of the White House, which was a clear indication of the advisory role that she played within her husband's administration. Regardless of the role that they play, first ladies are "complicated women" who are "called upon to clarify and calm, or to inspire and motivate, projecting a voicing of confidence, reason, and balance."[68]

First Ladies in Historical Perspective

Given the prevailing attitudes toward women during most of the nation's history, the political assertiveness of its first ladies has been a comparatively recent phenomenon, yet there were two early exceptions to the rule. Abigail Adams, wife of the second president, although observant of contemporary social graces, was opinionated and firm, offering advice and counsel to her husband throughout his political career. Likewise, James Madison considered his wife Dolley an invaluable aide while he was president, relinquishing control over the presidential residence to her and relying on her to coordinate the evacuation of the White House during the War of 1812. However, the first presidential spouse to truly break the mold was Edith Wilson, who, for all intents and purposes, ran the presidency following Woodrow Wilson's stroke in 1919.

Like Edith Wilson, FDR's wife Eleanor was pushed into service by unusual circumstances. FDR contracted polio in 1921 and depended on his wife for his political survival thereafter. Eleanor Roosevelt campaigned vigorously for her husband, managed his schedule, acted as his closest advisor, and did as much as anyone to sustain the myth of a vigorous and healthy president. During FDR's presidency, she spoke out against sexism and discrimination, worked hard for the realization of life-long progressive political goals, and transformed the purely ceremonial role of the first lady into a substantive presence within the White House. From both a political and a social perspective, Eleanor Roosevelt's accomplishments were formidable. As first lady, her power rivaled that of her husband's key aides and cabinet secretaries, demonstrating an influence over the president that was rare for anyone, especially the president's wife.

Contemporary First Ladies

The public role for first ladies has mostly been a social one, yet several first ladies since Eleanor Roosevelt's tenure provide distinct examples of the power and influence that can come with being the first spouse. Both Rosalynn Carter and Hillary Clinton opted for active involvement in policy decisions and publicly acknowledged their political role within the administration. Carter became an advocate for numerous causes, most notably research on mental health issues. As the request of her husband, she also sat in on cabinet and other policy meetings, acted as one of his closest advisors, and even served as an envoy abroad in Latin America and other areas. Clinton, perhaps rivaling only Eleanor Roosevelt in the politically significant role that she would play in her husband's administration, was a successful attorney and long-time advocate for children's issues before moving into the White House. As first lady, she acted as one of Bill Clinton's top policy advisors (hence the office in the West Wing) and most notably headed up the Clinton administration's health-care reform policy initiative (first introduced in 1993, but which failed to achieve congressional approval in 1994). After the failure with health-care reform, Clinton lowered her political profile and embraced more traditional activities for a first lady, as well as focusing on social issues, particularly those dealing with women and children.[69] After the Clintons left the White House, Hillary Clinton pursued an active, high-profile political career, serving eight years as a senator from New York and four years as secretary of state (2009–2013), and she ran for the presidency in 2008 and again in 2016 (when she won the Democratic nomination).

Other first ladies, like Mamie Eisenhower, Lady Bird Johnson, Barbara Bush, and Laura Bush, opted for a more traditional, nonpublic role in their husbands' White House. Regardless of the public versus private role of the first lady, several have played unique roles in their husbands' administrations. Jackie Kennedy, a former debutante, is remembered for her trend-setting fashions, redecorating the aging White House, bringing art and culture into Washington political circles, and providing glamor to the Kennedy administration at the start of the television age of politics.

First Lady Michelle Obama meets with soon-to-be First Lady Melania Trump during the presidential transition.

Betty Ford was an outspoken advocate for women's rights and is also remembered for raising public consciousness about addiction by publicly acknowledging her own problems with alcohol. Although she was mostly a traditional first lady while in the public eye, Nancy Reagan was a formidable presence in the Reagan White House in protecting her husband's best interests. Reagan trusted her judgment supremely and even consulted her regarding staffing decisions in the White House and major policy objectives. Michelle Obama, a Princeton and Harvard–educated attorney who put her career on hold during her husband's presidential campaign in 2008, chose the more traditional role of first lady by supporting nonpolitical causes such as support for military families and fighting childhood obesity. And, like several of her predecessors, she also raised two young daughters while living in the White House. In the 2016 presidential campaign, she stepped out of her nonpartisan role, campaigning extensively for Hillary Clinton. Her 2016 convention speech in support of Clinton's nomination was widely acclaimed. Melania Trump is also raising a young son in the White House and has indicated that one issue on which she will focus while first lady is to combat the rise in cyberbullying.

CONCLUSION

The executive branch of the U.S. government is a complex institution; it has multiple missions and an enormous workforce, and its divisions are not all centrally located. Coordinating and controlling this massive organization falls on the president. The president has an array of tools, with ranging degrees of effectiveness, to ensure that the branch does what presidents swear an oath to do, which is to faithfully execute as well as preserve, protect, and defend the Constitution of the United States.

The defining dividing line between the traditional and the modern presidency emerges out of the Brownlow Committee's famous line: "the president needs help." The president needed help because the breadth and depth of the job increased over time. Hand in hand with the increased responsibility is the president's increased desire to control the output of the bureaucracy, in effect, to make it more presidential. To gain control and to benefit from the increased workload, presidents developed the EOP to manage, coordinate, and control the bureaucracy. The degree to which presidents manage, coordinate, and control, however, is considerably influenced by Congress, as well as the bureaucracy itself, the president's cabinet, and even the federal courts. Presidents must deal with the scrutiny of their decisions, the tensions between the political arms and the civil service arms of the bureaucracy, and the compromised legislation emerging out of Congress, as well as the redefinition of legislation by the Court. It is perhaps the president's most difficult assignment, for which he receives the least public payoff.

CHAPTER 9

Presidents and Domestic/
Economic Policy

I n 1973, an issue previously not on the agenda and a group unknown to most Americans dramatically influenced a key area of public policy for Richard Nixon and every president who would succeed him when the Organization of the Petroleum Exporting Countries stopped selling oil to the United States. The initial embargo lasted through 1974 and a second began in 1979. However, the energy crisis precipitated by the embargo lasted through the 1970s and the consequences of the crisis linger today. High energy costs and low energy supply were major issues for each president during the 1970s—Nixon, Gerald Ford, and Jimmy Carter. When he took office in 1977, Carter made energy a cornerstone of his policy agenda although it had not been a priority during the 1976 presidential campaign. Carter's response to the energy crisis was a comprehensive policy response that involved all aspects of the institution of the presidency. The following excerpts from memos and public statements from the Carter White House demonstrate the multidimensional process presidents engage in when trying to "solve" a policy problem:

- White House memo regarding legislative action: "Just over a year ago, the President sent to the Congress a comprehensive national energy plan. As of last week, four of the five parts of that plan had been approved by the Conference Committee. Those four bills will probably be voted on by the full Congress in late July or early August. . . . The purpose of this plan is to hold Congress' collective feet to the fire. Every member who is up for re-election (and even those who aren't) should have to answer to his constituents for Congress' failure to pass an energy plan. We should make no apology for taking them on. . . . However, we should avoid being unnecessarily antagonistic, strident or personal."[1]

- Summary of polling data regarding bureaucratic action: "Recently the numerous energy programs and agencies scattered throughout the government were organized together by President Carter into a new Department of Energy. Some people say that energy programs and policies will now be run much better in this new department. Others say not much will happen, except one more large bureaucracy will have been created. Which view is closer to your opinion?"[2]
- Carter's remarks to state governors regarding intergovernmental action: "My Administration has given energy policy a very high priority during the few months we have been in office. Energy policy is not just a Federal activity. It requires a constructive partnership between the states, local governments and Federal Government. This conference marks the beginning of a continuing relationship and dialogue."[3]
- White House memo regarding public relations action: "The following is a plan for developing public support for the President's energy program. . . . [create a] citizen's committee . . . identify and discuss program with influential columnists, editorial writers, and television types . . . generate public support and statements among influential interest groups . . . [create a] speakers bureau."[4]

Unlike the campaign, or even a legislative battle with Congress, policymaking for the president has no specific beginning or end. Exploring the comprehensive leadership presidential policymaking requires highlights the inherent limitations of the presidency because policymaking in Washington results from the efforts of multiple actors, across the jurisdictions of multiple agencies, and must survive the activities of multiple agendas. As noted in previous chapters, much of the key policymaking activity exists outside the president's control. In domestic and economic policymaking, the president can significantly influence the Washington agenda, but

Jimmy Carter addresses the nation on the energy crisis in 1977.

can rarely exercise much control over the central actors or the context of the policy environment.

The previous chapters have focused on the institution of the presidency by exploring how the office evolved over time in response to changing demands and expectations, as well as the challenges presidents face as they attempt to govern on a day-to-day basis. Intentionally, we have isolated each aspect of interaction the president experiences, with individuals and with other institutions. We defined those relationships and explored whether the tools the president has are sufficient to achieve his goals. The president's agenda was present in each of those chapters as something he needed to accomplish. The president's policy agenda was not the focus but rather the evidence of success. Thus, while evaluating the president's place in the legislative process or discussing how presidents interact with the media to sell their agenda, we have treated policy as an independent variable that allowed the exploration of those institutional dependent variables. Here and in Chapter 10, we explore the policy-making process to determine where and how the president participates by considering the political system as a whole.

THE POLITICAL ENVIRONMENT

Presidential election cycles leave the impression that work in Washington begins anew every four years. However, campaigns and elections are only one factor, albeit influential, affecting the policy environment. Throughout the campaign, presidents reveal their priorities, and with the election results, incoming presidents learn the depth of support behind those policies. However, policy priorities also emerge from environmental pressures, such as the state of the economy and the ebb and flow of public expectations.

Electoral Promises and Mandates

Presidential hopefuls utter a massive amount of campaign rhetoric designed to impart to voters their values, beliefs, and promises of how they will influence the course of the country. Candidates often try to distinguish themselves from their opponents by illustrating the difference in issue positions and by articulating their policy proscriptions for the nation. George H. W. Bush offered his now-infamous campaign promise about taxes at the 1988 Republican National Convention in his nomination acceptance speech:

> Should public school teachers be required to lead our children in the pledge of allegiance? My opponent says no—and I say yes. Should society be allowed to impose the death penalty on those who commit crimes of extraordinary cruelty and violence? My opponent says no—but I say yes. . . . I'm, I'm the one who believes it is a scandal to give a weekend furlough to a hardened first degree killer who hasn't even served enough time to be eligible for parole. . . . And I'm the one who will not raise taxes. My opponent, my opponent now says, my opponent now says, he'll raise them as a last resort, or a third resort. But when a politician talks like that, you know that's one resort he'll be checking into. My opponent won't rule out raising taxes. But I will. And the Congress will push me to raise taxes, and I'll say no, and they'll push, and I'll say no, and they'll push again, and I'll say, to them, "Read my lips: no new taxes."[5]

The phrase "no new taxes" ultimately came back to haunt Bush because he compromised with Congress and did not veto the 1990 budget agreement, which raised taxes. Voters often engage in retrospective voting when they consider whether presidents running for reelection adequately upheld their promises. In the case of Bush, he faced a challenge in the primaries from Patrick J. Buchanan in 1992 based, in part, on the breaking of that promise, weakening him in the general election (which he lost to Bill Clinton).

Campaign promises, however, are more than simple measures to hold a candidate accountable; these policy statements are the goals of the incoming president and his administration. The presidency as an institution has evolved past its smaller, caretaker role, so individuals run for office because they want to do something, change something, or restore something. In the policymaking arena, the institutional development of the office and the personal goals of individuals who run for the office combine to encourage policy activism. Presidents run for office wanting to influence policy and quickly learn they will be judged on their effect on policy outcomes. Both factors encourage presidents to seek a comprehensive policy approach so as not to be dependent on situations or institutions they cannot control.

The election itself sometimes offers victorious presidents a specific tool for influencing policy: a presidential mandate. In the political arena, a mandate refers to the so-called "meaning of the election." The bigger the victory, the more journalists and politicians are willing to label an election outcome a mandate for action. Ronald Reagan claimed his 1980 victory was a mandate for action on his electoral policies that included major changes regarding numerous domestic and economic policies, noting that "it is what the American people told us with their votes they wanted."[6] Many news sources claimed that Barack Obama's election in 2008 constituted "a mandate for change."[7] Declaring the election a mandate grants the president extra leverage to use as pressure on individuals outside the president's control. However, as Obama's mandate illustrates, the details of a mandate can mean different things to different people. In the cases of both Reagan and Obama, however, an argument can also be made that the mandate was partially a vote against their predecessors (Carter and George W. Bush, respectively). Donald Trump's 2016 campaign promises reflect his stated goals of upsetting the status quo and "draining the swamp" of Washington. With Republicans controlling both houses of Congress, Trump's path to accomplishing his goals (like building a wall on the Mexican border, tax reform, and eliminating regulations) seems to be relatively straightforward. However, as Obama learned in 2009 and 2010, unified government may make the process somewhat easier, but major policy changes are still difficult to implement.

The Presidential Transition

With ratification of the Twentieth Amendment in 1933, which moved up the date when a new president takes office from March to January, the long transition from campaign to president evaporated. As a result, presidents lost the opportunity for grand planning, as FDR experienced between November 1932 and March 1933. Consequently, presidents must "hit the ground running" with their policy agenda.[8] Although planning does occur while the candidate is running and after winning the election, and although many of the White House staff come from the campaign, most of the players in the policymaking positions within the executive branch, as well as various departments and agencies, are new to the president and his closest advisors. During this period, the president is not only getting to meet his new employees but also urging them to move forward on his policy agenda.

With the advantage of a longer transition to plan a response to the Great Depression, FDR's administration sent 15 bills to Congress for their consideration in the spring of 1933. As detailed in Chapter 6, Congress passed all 15 in just 100 days. Accordingly, the 100-day mark of a new administration is now considered a critical benchmark. The media use the date to evaluate the performance of the new president. However, presidents also use the date to plan. The time frame of 100 days (approximately the first three months of the administration) coincides with another oft-cited phrase: the presidential honeymoon. The perception is that the press will go easier on a new president for the first few months and the public will be supportive because they want the new president to succeed. However, the president is not starting off new because behavior and patterns established in the campaign carry over to the presidency. In early 2017, Trump's honeymoon seemed nonexistent as he and his staff engaged in a war of words with the press and political opponents via tweets, conference calls, press briefings, and interviews.

Typically, the combination of a less critical audience and the first-100-days benchmark combine to make the first three months of any administration a hotbed of policy activity. In the first 100 days, presidents will often roll back prior administrations' executive orders and issue new ones. They also staff the White House and the executive branch departments with political appointees. Appointments are often signals of policy intent or signs of appeasing players in the policy process. For example, to follow up on his inaugural address statement that "government is not the solution to our problem, government *is* the problem," Reagan filled his policy offices with individuals willing to cut social programs and cut government spending, including Murray Weidenbaum at the Council of Economic Advisers and David Stockman as director of the Office of Management and Budget (OMB).[9]

The Public Agenda

Although presidents would prefer it, the political environment does not get wiped clean after an election. Presidents take office amid wars, recessions, and public frustration with one or more policy areas. Typically, what is awaiting the president on January 20 is present in the campaign, but not always. The environment can be considered a challenge or an opportunity, although often the label is decided after evaluating how well the president performed. As discussed in Chapter 5, public attitudes, as reflected in public opinion polling data, can provide the president with a basis for action or a signal to proceed cautiously. A president who ignores the public mood can find the political costs to be high. Alternatively, an energized electoral base within the president's party unified around a key policy can provide a galvanizing support with a fractious Congress.[10]

In addition to the short-term measurements of mood that public opinion polls provide, presidents also must deal with long-term changes in expectations. One of the most enduring legacies from the FDR administration is the increased reliance on the government and the president. In 1933, as FDR took office, Congress and Herbert Hoover had already been grappling unsuccessfully with the Great Depression. Much of the problem in the late 1920s and early 1930s was reluctance on the part of legislators and the president to use the power of government to interfere in the economic sphere. The doctrine of laissez-faire dominated the thinking of economists and politicians of the time. In this approach, government allows market forces to determine economic behavior. In normal times, supply and demand drive hiring and firing as well as the production of goods and services. The severity of the fluctuation in hiring, firing, and production in the Great Depression challenged acceptance of the normal ebb and flow of the economic cycle. A change in attitude emerged in the 1932 campaign, as FDR articulated a new relationship between government and the economy, where government protects the weakest citizens from economic downturns. The presidency became the focal point of these changed attitudes. As FDR committed the federal government to solving more and more of what had been viewed as normal economic behavior, public expectations of the president grew tremendously. Not only was the president considered "problem solver in chief," but also the state of the economy became a measure of presidential success.

The State of the Economy

The state of the economy is perhaps the most significant contextual situation facing a president, exacerbated by the complexity of economic forces. Since 1940, there have been only 12 years in which the government operated with a budget surplus. When the government takes in less money than it spends, the government is not balancing its books and runs a deficit. Deficits typically hinder a president's ability to create new programs, hire more federal employees, and service more constituencies, but they do offer the opportunity to sell deficit-reduction policies.[11] Generally, presidents operating with budget surpluses seemingly have greater opportunity to expand governmental activity and programs. In addition to the state of the government's bank account, the state of the economy also affects the willingness to add new government programs or cut existing ones; recession, depression, inflation, deflation, or an expanding or contracting economy can all influence presidential policymaking in two ways. First, an economic downturn influences the availability of money because government collects less money via taxes. Second, because government is viewed as a solver of problems, the state of the economy is often viewed as a top policy priority.

The state of the economy and potential solutions to economic problems became a standard measurement for presidents after encapsulation by Reagan's evocative campaign question, "Are you better off today then you were four years ago?" Typically, financial and economic concerns rank at the top of voters' list of most important problems facing the country. Consequently, presidential candidates' abilities and willingness to tackle nagging economic questions dominate their agendas. Voters may or may not always vote with their pocketbooks, but the economy is undoubtedly a primary concern, so presidential agendas reflect that reality. Inaugural addresses are littered with references to improving the country and individuals' economic circumstances.[12] Trump's 2017 inaugural message was blunt on the topic of the economy:

> The oath of office I take today is an oath of allegiance to all Americans. For many decades, we've enriched foreign industry at the expense of American industry; subsidized the armies of other countries while allowing for the very sad depletion

of our military; we've defended other nation's borders while refusing to defend our own; and spent trillions of dollars overseas while America's infrastructure has fallen into disrepair and decay. We've made other countries rich while the wealth, strength, and confidence of our country has disappeared over the horizon. One by one, the factories shuttered and left our shores, with not even a thought about the millions upon millions of American workers left behind. The wealth of our middle class has been ripped from their homes and then redistributed across the entire world. But that is the past. And now we are looking only to the future. We assembled here today are issuing a new decree to be heard in every city, in every foreign capital, and in every hall of power. From this day forward, a new vision will govern our land. From this moment on, it's going to be America First.[13]

Moreover, even presidential popularity, as discussed in Chapter 5, correlates with the state of the economy. Research has shown that since the 1970s, a strong relationship has existed between national economic performance and presidential approval. Generally, these "popularity models rely on macroeconomic conditions; however . . . [presidential] approval is [also] highly sensitive to the stock market's acceleration or deceleration."[14]

DOMESTIC AND ECONOMIC POLICYMAKING

Categorized by type and grouped together according to various individual and institutional preferences, policies determine the direction, scope, and effectiveness of government. These groups of policies generated by presidents and their administrations are called policy agendas and they comprise a coherent and comprehensive blueprint for governance, both in the short and in the long terms. An agenda is a policymaking playbook, reflecting ideological preferences, partisan loyalties, and personal experiences combined with a corresponding constitutional vision or theory. Agendas inherently reflect ideology and partisan allegiance, and for the president, they originate with their campaign promises and party platform. Policy agendas encompass the necessary aspects for planning, packaging, and implementing presidential political priorities.[15]

Regardless of which type of issue is on the president's agenda, there is a standard process each issue goes through, whether the issue is found at the federal, state, or local level. As Figure 9.1 demonstrates, there are six stages to any policy. For the process to begin, there must be an identified problem that becomes an agenda item. In the first stage, problems are defined, actors organize around the issue, and the desire to solve the problem increases. It is not enough for one of these facets to occur; they all need to occur for a "nuisance" to become an "issue." In this first stage, how problems are defined, who is organizing, and the importance of the issue are the critical questions. The second stage focuses on legitimation, communication, and formulation of the problem and its solution. Here, the specificity when delineating and legitimizing the solution(s) is key for moving the process along. The third phase is where decisions are made and funds are appropriated; this stage is defined by bargaining and compromise and typically takes place within legislative bodies. The fourth stage specifies how the decision is delineated or implemented by the bureaucracy and identifies who gets what. The fifth stage involves implementation and focuses on the processes that must occur to carry out the decision. This stage

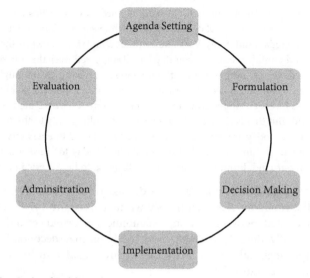

Figure 9.1 **The Cycle of Public Policy**

can encompass, for example, military campaigns; a provision of health, welfare, or educational services; federal law enforcement; improvements in transportation and communication networks; scientific research and exploration; and many other types of services.[16] The final stage—evaluation—considers how effectively the outcome of decision, implementation, and administration solved the original problem. These stages of public policy represent a cycle because the process starts all over again based on what the evaluation phase identifies as new problems.

Modern presidents, unlike their eighteenth- and early-nineteenth-century predecessors, spend the bulk of their time working within the cycle of public policy shepherding domestic priorities and administering the vast bureaucratic apparatus that fulfills domestic duties and responsibilities. Whether those duties and responsibilities address the economy, sociocultural priorities, social services, natural resources and conservation, or law enforcement, they represent the overwhelming majority of the modern presidency's day-to-day business. That business can be difficult, especially as far as the eventual acceptance and implementation of the president's domestic agenda is concerned. The risks and uncertainties inherent in the domestic and economic policymaking processes can be prohibitive because domestic policy requires the participation and cooperation of numerous people and institutions not under the president's direct control. As Chapter 10 will demonstrate, the foreign-policy command structure is more streamlined and unified and can respond quickly to presidential authority when necessary, whereas the domestic-policy establishment is a sprawl that depends on input and agreement from not only the administration but also Congress, the federal bureaucracy, interest groups, and the 50 states, not to mention the various municipal and county governments affected by domestic policy.[17]

The president is involved in all six stages of the policy cycle; however, the influence of the president sits primarily with the ability to set the agenda and the extent to which he can influence through management the capacity of the government to affect policy.

Agenda Setting

Agenda setting is the ability to focus attention on an issue. Media outlets play an important role; it has long been recognized that the press "may not be successful much of the time in telling people what to think, but it is stunningly successful in telling its readers what to think about."[18] However, agendas are not only set; they are also built. The differences between agenda setting and agenda building stem from the differences in the roles played by the media, the public, and policymakers in the political process. For an issue to be significant and successful in the political arena, decision makers must support the issue. There is also a difference between a public agenda (what the public wants) and the formal agenda (what government acts on).[19]

Through both enumerated and implied constitutional powers, the president is uniquely positioned to set both the public agenda (through the media) and the government's agenda (by recommending legislation to Congress). There is no denying the centrifugal role the president occupies in terms of media and public attention. As such, the president can easily draw attention to any issue or policy, first via the presidential campaign and then through major addresses (like the State of the Union). To influence the public and other policy actors, presidents rely on many tools and techniques, including communications strategies, public opinion polling, knowledge and skills among key White House staffers, and the president's formal and informal legislative roles.

Agenda Responsiveness

The centrality of presidential domestic and economic policymaking is reflected in the idea of presidential agenda setting. By exploring presidential agenda setting from the president toward the media, the public, and Congress, the position of each actor implies whether they are leading or following. However, the president does not act alone regarding policymaking; other actors, the policy environment, and events all serve to influence and constrain the president. Research also suggests that presidents now have less control over domestic policy, because "ideas appear to be growing more polarized, opportunities for action more constrained, problems more intractable, assumptions more politicized, research more ideological, solutions more varied, and implementation agents more beleaguered and inflexible. . . . it is not clear that presidents could shape domestic policy even if they had the institutional capacity to do so. They may have little choice but to ride the rapids as best they can, using the increasingly bureaucratized paddles at their disposal."[20]

As discussed in Chapter 8, presidents seek institutional capacity and levers of management control over the civil service in the bureaucracy as mechanisms to shift the implementation and administration of congressional policy. The president does this by inserting policy and staffing expertise into the White House and using the unilateral powers of executive orders and signing statements. The bureaucracy, however, serves two masters, not one. Consequently, during the time of expansive executive branch management and capacity, Congress, too, was seeking to expand its levers of control over policy beyond the legislative process. To expand its own institutional capacity, the staff with policy expertise serving in congressional offices and congressional committees grew exponentially, as has the Congressional Research Service (a nonpartisan congressional think tank).[21] Congress has also developed its institutional relationships and responsibilities, with constituents and with the bureaucracy via oversight. As such, not only does the president get pushback from Congress and the bureaucracy, but also outside actors have strong motivations to seek concessions and responsiveness. For example, interest groups increasingly lobby the administration for support for their preferred policy position, while also lobbying Congress.

Researching the Presidency

Succeeding with the Agenda

The president is in a unique position for agenda setting as the center of media and public attention; a gaggle of White House reporters eagerly awaits presidential news from the president personally, the press secretary, or any aides willing to talk on or off the record. The 535 members of Congress do not gain the media and public's attention as easily. Does the glare of the spotlight serve the president's policy interests? There is an enormous volume of scholarly literature focused on the effectiveness of agenda setting and agenda building. The emphasis on agenda setting mainly explores the ability of the president to influence media coverage. With few exceptions, most studies find that the president can shape and influence the volume of presidential policy coverage and the tone. In *Presidential Framing in the 21st Century News Media: The Politics of the Affordable Care Act*, Jennifer Hopper focuses on how key elements of Obamacare were framed to determine the conditions under which the president can effectively shape public debates. She finds that despite the difficult political and communications environment, the president retains substantial advantages in framing major controversial issues for the media and the public.[22]

Similarly, when exploring agenda building in Congress, Paul Rutledge and Heather Larsen Price find the advantage for the president. Unlike Hopper's focus on a single issue, in "The President as Agenda Setter-in-Chief: The Dynamics of Congressional and Presidential Agenda Setting," Rutledge and Price do a large-scale time-series analysis of 50 years of legislative efforts in the areas of defense, the environment, health care, international affairs, law and crime, and macroeconomics.[23] To determine how influential the president's policy desires are for Congress, Rutledge and Larsen Price tracked the policy messages submitted to Congress. They then evaluate how many of the president's policies received congressional committee hearings. Using sophisticated statistical techniques, it is possible to test for a causal relationship despite the fact that "influence could potentially be exerted on the other by either or both." In fact, they find that in all policy areas the president exerts influence on Congress, in terms of directing congressional attention by submitting policy for their consideration; that is, the congressional agenda is reactive and responsive to the presidential agenda. Interestingly, in the areas of health care, macroeconomics, and defense they find that "as Congress increases attention, the president responds by decreasing attention to each issue area," a somewhat confounding result that suggests the importance of continued research in this area to better understand the presidential–congressional relationship in domestic and economic policymaking.

ACTORS IN THE POLICYMAKING PROCESS

Since the policymaking environment straddles the executive, legislative, and judicial branches, as well as state and local government and the private sector, the primary goal for the president is coordination across issues, actors, and institutions. The secondary goal for the president is obtaining expertise. Presidents are rarely experts in multiple policy areas. Most presidents are elected with government or military experience; Trump is the first president with neither, having spent his entire professional life in business as a real estate entrepreneur. The president's domestic and economic policy experts serve in the EOP; however, there are also individuals outside the administration who influence policy outcomes as well as the president's ability to get things done on his policy agenda.

Inside the White House

The president's primary advisors typically emerge from the presidential campaign. Campaign advisors fall into two types, which can overlap: individuals who are longstanding members of the candidates' inner circle of advisors and experts in campaigning. The experience of a campaign can often turn the so-called hired guns into loyal friends and then members of the president's inner circle. Political strategist Kellyanne Conway is a good example; she first served as a senior advisor and then as campaign manager for Trump (having previously worked for a Ted Cruz Super PAC before he dropped out of the 2016 presidential campaign) and then became a top advisor in the Trump White House. Thus, policy expertise or policy experience is not necessarily what determines who becomes a key advisor to a president. As a result, presidents and their political advisors need policy experts.

On the domestic side, White House policy experts come from universities, think tanks, or policymaking positions in other levels of government or in earlier administrations. On the economic side, experts also emerge from finance, industry, and small-business success. Roger Porter was typical of policy staffers in leadership positions in the White House. Porter served three Republican presidents: as Ford's special assistant to the president and executive secretary of the president's Economic Policy Board; as Reagan's executive secretary of the Cabinet Council on Economic Affairs and director of the White House Office of Policy Development; and as George H. W. Bush's assistant to the president for economic and domestic policy. As the head of economic and domestic policy, Porter's job entailed receiving and channeling multiple policy inputs from inside and outside the administration. In a memo to Chief of Staff John Sununu, Porter illustrated why presidents create these councils and how they are used:

> One of our principal domestic policy objectives is to establish both the reality and the perception of George Bush as the Education President.... Reinforcing [our] themes remains a persistent challenge for us ... [I recommend] establishing a presidential advisory committee on education policy.... Such a committee would ... be patterned after the Economic Policy Advisory Board from the previous administration [and would] include representatives from a wide variety of organizations.[24]

The policy experts in the White House primarily work in the policy councils. They are the real workhorses behind presidential domestic policy, and their contribution enables the transition from political goals and adoption strategies to actionable programs based on actual circumstances. They compile data, perform analyses, prepare strategy, provide expertise, and fulfill any number of other jobs assigned to them by the president or his staff.

The primary offices for domestic and economic policy in the White House are the Domestic Policy Council (DPC), the National Economic Council (NEC), the Council of Economic Advisors (CEA), and the OMB. The DPC handles most areas of domestic policy except law enforcement, drug interdiction, and scientific research. Both Clinton and Obama relied on the DPC considerably, whereas George W. Bush was never as fond of policy councils.[25] However, Bush did establish a separate office under the DPC, the Office of Faith-Based and Community Initiatives, and used it extensively to secure a strategic beachhead for the expansion of federally based religious programs, one of his personal priorities. Later renamed the Office of Faith-Based and Neighborhood Partnerships, Bush envisioned it as a command center to coordinate certain federally subsidized social services and administer church-based community initiatives.[26]

The NEC concentrates on providing the president with economic and financial advice regarding fiscal, business, labor, consumer, and related policy, and it leverages its expertise to outline and explain the technical requirements of specific presidential policies. The CEA, created in 1946, provides the president and his key advisors with macroeconomic and financial research and analysis to enable the preparation and development of potential and current economic policies. Whereas the NEC's role is mostly advisory and political, collaborating with the president and his inner circle on the formulation of political objectives and strategies, the CEA, although secondarily used as an advisory body, exists to compile and evaluate necessary data and provide objective subject-matter expertise. In that regard, the CEA is important, but its significance is dwarfed by that of the OMB, which has become one of the most essential parts of the executive branch. Prior to the establishment of the OMB's predecessor, the Bureau of the Budget, in 1921, budgeting was a congressional responsibility over which the president had little control.[27]

Retooled as the OMB to meet the needs of the modern presidency during related EOP reforms by the Nixon administration, the OMB provides the technical expertise needed by the president during his annual preparation of the fiscal-year budget. Handling the bulk of the effort required by this mammoth task, the OMB works within the broad political framework set by the president and other policymakers and provides requisite financial analysis and evaluation. In so doing, it also ensures that budgetary fiscal requirements match revenue and deficit projections and that the various institutional components of the president's budget are reconcilable. In a related capacity, the OMB oversees executive expenditures, guaranteeing that actual expenses align with budgetary stipulations and that executive agencies comply with federal financial laws. Aside from its budgetary and other financial responsibilities, the OMB has supervisory authority over the executive branch's many regulatory agencies, which means that it plays an important role during the operational stage of the policymaking process. In exercising this oversight authority, the OMB scrutinizes regulatory rule making to ensure it follows overriding policy objectives, relevant federal laws, and procedural guidelines.[28]

Other policymaking organs within the EOP include the Office of National Drug Control Policy, created in 1988 under Reagan, and the Office of Science and Technology Policy, established during the Ford administration. The creation of the Office of National Drug Control Policy was highly politicized, especially after two terms of emphatic antidrug rhetoric by the Reagan administration, and its first director, William Bennett, former education secretary under Reagan, courted considerable controversy through his outspoken views on drug use. The drug czar, as the director was known initially, was an important participant in presidential policymaking during the George H. W. Bush years, but the visibility and influence of the position have declined since the mid-1990s. Another high-profile council, the Office of National AIDS Policy, was created by Clinton in 1993, also within the DPC, but it is funded by the Department of Health and Human Services. The Office of National AIDS Policy arose from campaign promises made by Clinton to AIDS activists and the LGBTQ community and addresses a range of issues, including prevention, treatment, education, and research. Although not as active during the George W. Bush presidency, it was revived by Obama, who made a new national commitment to fighting AIDS both at home and abroad.[29]

Outside the White House

Although the president is most apt to trust and rely on the information presented by his aides and advisors, the policymaking arena is so large that numerous individuals, organizations, and institutions influence the ability of the president to shape public policy. Within government, Congress dominates policymaking, but governors and other governmental entities can have influence. Beyond government, interest groups and members of the private sector also play an influential role in the process.

Congress

Leading the policymaking environment by virtue of its constitutional mandate, Congress influences public policy tremendously by legislating and exercising oversight of the bureaucracy through hearings, reports, and reviews. Members of Congress are like the president in that they are often expected to be knowledgeable about multiple policy areas. However, because of committee assignments, members of Congress are more likely to specialize and become experts in the policy area of the committee to which they are assigned. Congressional staffers to both members and standing (permanent) congressional committees are also policy experts who have considerable input into the policymaking process; they "draft compromise amendments, negotiate agreements, provide advice to members, and prepare . . . reports."[30] In fact, the increased expertise of senators is directly related to the increase in the number of staffers senators now employ.[31]

Other governmental actors

Although Congress dominates federal lawmaking, agenda setting and information regarding policy activities come from those also tasked with creating and carrying out policy below the federal level: governors and state legislators. State governors have long recognized the need to influence Washington policymakers and policymaking. In 1908 they created the National Governors Association to coordinate discussions about policy, what was working, what was not, and what federal legislation might be needed. Their voice is so significant that presidents and their cabinets routinely participate in these annual meetings; the National Governors Association "promotes visionary state leadership, shares best practices and speaks with a collective voice on national policy."[32]

Outside the White House, the Federal Reserve provides the president and Congress a different perspective on financial and monetary policy. The Federal Reserve is a pivotal and extremely powerful policymaker that has a substantial impact on the country's economic and financial objectives. The Fed (as it is colloquially known) includes the Board of Governors and the Federal Open Market Committee (FOMC). Through the Federal Open Market Committee, the Fed's chief target is U.S. monetary policy; secondarily, it addresses unemployment and consumer prices. It was created in 1913 to stabilize the banking system and national currency because the absence of centralized monetary management had contributed to several financial panics and recessions during the preceding several decades. Institutionally and politically independent, neither the board nor the FOMC is accountable to the president in a political sense, so he has little influence over its decisions. Not obliged to follow presidential economic or financial directives, both nonetheless realize the need to reconcile its monetary goals with the president's fiscal policies. The president does have an indirect ability to shape Federal Reserve policy through appointments to the Board of Governors and the FOMC. He appoints the chair, the vice chair, and the remaining governors, who serve on the 12-member FOMC, which controls interest rates and the nation's money supply. Federal Reserve governors serve staggered 14-year terms to minimize the effects of turnover, whereas the chair, who is selected by the president from among the governors, serves a renewable four-year term.[33]

In short, the president's influence over monetary policy extends no further than his powers of persuasion, his appointment authority, and the manifestations of his economic and financial policies. As a semi-independent body, the Fed can serve as a backstop when "the President and Congress [are] deadlocked."[34] The Fed occupies a unique position for assistance with both monetary policy (its traditional role) and fiscal policy (the role assumed during crisis). During the recent crises in the 2000s and 2010s, the Fed has taken the lead "in the absence of, and occasionally even in opposition to, the publicly announced positions of elected politicians."[35] However, given the stalemate in fiscal policy resulting from political party polarization, in times of economic downturn or crisis, coordination among the president, the Treasury Secretary, and the Fed Chair can be critical to weathering the storm.

SAVING THE BIG THREE AUTOMAKERS

THEN . . .

Throughout the 1970s, increasingly stringent emissions and safety regulations forced U.S. automakers to make changes for which they were not prepared. In addition, the ongoing energy crises that produced sharply higher fuel costs and warnings about the depletion of world oil reserves put pressure on the Big Three to design smaller, more efficient vehicles to replace the huge gas-guzzlers to which Americans had become accustomed. Because of its size, market share, and product line, Chrysler was at a distinct disadvantage compared to Ford and General Motors (GM), and its efforts to meet shifting consumer demand and address both regulatory necessities and a restricted supply of oil were largely ineffective. To make matters worse, massive recalls of two of the automaker's leading models only compounded mounting financial difficulties, and a lack of fuel-efficient smaller vehicles to replace its fleet of larger cars depressed sales. Even the appointment of former Ford president Lee Iacocca as chief executive officer in 1978 did not immediately change the troubled auto manufacturer's fate.[36]

Faced with bankruptcy and possibly the total collapse of Chrysler Corporation, Iacocca asked Congress in mid-1979 for more than $1 billion in loan guarantees to save the company. Jimmy Carter instructed his treasury secretary and former Fed chairman G. William Miller to formulate a bailout package, provided it came with necessary concessions from unions, dealers, and stockholders. Unlike many Democrats at the time, Carter was no fan of government interventions or increased executive regulatory authority, as his deregulation of the transportation industry demonstrated, yet he also realized that the financial crisis at Chrysler left him with few alternatives. Allowing Chrysler to collapse was not a feasible solution for several reasons, among which were catastrophic job losses at a time of rising unemployment, the broader economic reverberations of Chrysler's prospective demise during a decade of recurring recessions, pressure from automobile dealers, and a prohibitively high political cost. That does not mean that the political or even financial cost of a bailout would be trivial, especially for an embattled presidency and Congress whose public approval had been undermined by several years of political scandals and mismanagement. Nevertheless, Carter felt compelled to act, although he made sure that any bailout package would incorporate clear criteria for accountability and key benchmarks for the automaker's recovery.[37]

Within a few months, under the direction of Secretary Miller and key congressional leaders, Congress produced the Chrysler Corporation Loan Guarantee Act, which Carter signed in January 1980. The law created the Chrysler Loan Guarantee Board, whose responsibility was to manage the loans and supervise repayment. Under the provisions of the bill, the federal government would not directly lend money to Chrysler but would guarantee $1.5 billion of private financing, and Chrysler's workers, shareholders, and dealers would agree to a further $2 billion of mandated concessions. Widely seen as an ineffective Treasury chief unable to manage critical aspects of economic policy, Miller was praised for what was arguably the only tangible achievement during his tenure. Like Miller, Carter had few domestic-policy successes during his time in office, and his legacy has not improved considerably over the years, but this was ultimately a success. By 1983, Chrysler had repaid all its loans, and the federal government had profited $350 million from its involvement.[38]

In the short term, the Chrysler bailout was effective and justifiable. Under Iacocca's leadership and aggressive new marketing, design, and production strategies, the company rebounded and met all congressional and presidential expectations, even fulfilling its financial obligations to the federal government ahead of schedule. Nevertheless, all was not well. Neither Chrysler nor the other major U.S. car manufacturers had a sustainable long-term business model that was responsive to global economic, demographic, and regulatory trends, to say nothing of changing energy needs. By the 1990s, all three manufacturers were heavily reliant on the production of sport utility vehicles (SUVs) and pickup trucks, from which they made most of their profits. Despite improvements in fuel efficiency, trucks and SUVs were relatively fuel intensive, which made them increasingly expensive to own as oil prices rose. At the same time, because of their dependence on trucks and SUVs, U.S. automakers devoted few research dollars to the development of marketable smaller vehicles or those based on alternative fuels.[39]

Over the same period, competition from abroad intensified, and U.S. consumers increasingly turned to foreign manufacturers for vehicles that were more durable, more efficient, and less expensive than those offered by the Big Three. Growing foreign car sales decreased both market share and profitability for U.S. auto manufacturers, eventually leading to some layoffs and plant closures. But, in the long run, a few layoffs and plant closures could not compensate for ongoing union intransigence, poor planning, and less than competent management, so bloated factories continued to operate at much less than optimum capacity. The Big Three faced escalating production costs because of unsustainable United Auto Worker contracts that secured the highest wages in the industry, and they became financially overextended through elaborate pension obligations that far exceeded industry standards. Foreign automakers, in contrast, were opening plants in the United States, mostly in the nonunionized South, where labor costs were substantially lower and production processes more efficient. Adding insult to injury, foreign car makers were preparing for the future by building vehicles that reflected a gradually but inexorably changing consumer demand. By the start of the twenty-first century, the stage was set for another crisis, but the next one would involve not just one but all of the Big Three.[40]

... AND NOW

By the beginning of the new millennium, things did not look promising for U.S. auto manufacturers, particularly for GM and Chrysler. Yet, as hobbled as they had become as the result of a series of management and production blunders and the inability to adapt to evolving market realities, they might have limped along with some hope of a turnaround had circumstances not intervened and accelerated their decline. The first of these was the 9/11 terrorist attack, which prompted the wars in Afghanistan and Iraq. The resulting regional political instability coupled with a disruption in oil production led to record fuel prices in the United States and elsewhere. In addition, because the major domestic oil companies had not adequately invested in the expansion of production and refining capabilities, their ability to confront rising oil prices through increased production was limited, which constricted supply and destabilized commodities markets even more. Neither the cost of crude oil nor the price of fuel at the pump declined significantly, compelling consumers to buy less expensive, more efficient foreign cars instead of the big SUVs and trucks that had generated the Big Three's profits. Within a few years, their domestic market share dipped below 50 percent, a significant decline from the almost 80 percent during the troubled 1970s.[41]

The second event accelerating the decline of U.S. automakers was the sub-prime mortgage crisis of 2008, which precipitated a banking collapse that crippled many of the nation's leading investment banks and insurance companies. The lending crisis deepened an economic recession that had begun at the end of 2007, further shrinking consumer confidence and purchasing power and severely restricting the availability of investment capital. Meanwhile, as the health of the U.S. auto industry declined, the Big Three secured minor concessions from auto workers and make some retrenchments through asset divestitures, but it was all too little too late. In the autumn of 2008, U.S. automakers asked Congress for help, claiming they needed cash immediately to meet benefit costs and pension liabilities and to avoid financial collapse altogether. In testimony before congressional committees, company representatives warned that failure to act could lead to the loss of as many as three million jobs over the ensuing 12 months. Congress, in turn, requested sustainable restructuring plans from all three automakers, which they submitted, but the legislature was not convinced that auto executives were truly committed to change and viable restructuring.[42]

Having failed to obtain what they needed from Congress, auto executives then turned directly to the George W. Bush administration and Treasury Secretary Henry Paulson, who had been a corporate executive himself. Before the end of the year, the Bush team formulated a plan to save the auto industry with almost $25 billion of government loans for GM and Chrysler and a temporary line of credit for Ford, whose position was not as dire as those of the other two. Contrary to what had been the case with Chrysler in 1979, these were not loan guarantees, whereby the government was just a cosigner for privately obtained financing, but direct loans from federal coffers. To avoid congressional battles over funding and a prolonged legislative process, the Bush administration decided to use funds from the already created Troubled Asset Relief Program (TARP), which had been established to rescue the banking and insurance industries. Authorized to spend up to $700 billion, TARP faced a much broader problem than just the failure of U.S. auto manufacturers, so it could more than adequately cover the auto bailout. As a result, the federal government became a

Executives from the "Big Three" automakers testify before Congress in 2009.

substantial shareholder in GM and Chrysler, which was an equity stake it would relinquish as the companies repaid their loans.[43]

The short-term infusion of cash proved inadequate to the task for both GM and Chrysler, as original congressional skepticism regarding the automakers' plans for restructuring was vindicated. Obama, who had taken office after the initial bailout agreement had been finalized, refused requests for additional funds unless the two companies provided him and the administration's experts with a viable strategy for long-term sustainability and a restructuring plan that addressed prevailing market realities. In the end, neither company avoided continuing financial problems, declining sales, prohibitive labor costs, and mounting pension obligations, but Chrysler was faced with the prospect of absolute collapse. Finally, it sought protection under a bankruptcy filing in May 2009 and GM followed only a month later. Since then, all three automakers have implemented significant strategic and operational reforms, while the bankruptcy courts enforced mandated concessions from the unions, shareholders, and member dealers.[44] As Obama reported in his 2012 State of the Union address,

> On the day I took office, our auto industry was on the verge of collapse. Some even said we should let it die. With a million jobs at stake, I refused to let that happen. In exchange for help, we demanded responsibility. We got workers and automakers to settle their differences. We got the industry to retool and restructure. Today, General Motors is back on top as the world's number-one automaker. Chrysler has grown faster in the U.S. than any major car company. Ford is investing billions in U.S. plants and factories. And together, the entire industry added nearly a hundred and sixty thousand jobs. We bet on American workers. We bet on American ingenuity. And tonight, the American auto industry is back.[45]

Interest groups

As a representative democracy, the American system of government rests on the notion that government serves the people. In addition to the electoral connection between citizens and government, the Constitution guarantees the right to participate between elections to "petition the government for a redress of grievances." Lobbying is the current shorthand for petitioning the government for redress; political lore claims the term lobbying arose to describe the hanging around of petitioners in the lobbies of various legislatures as they waited for an opportunity to speak with politicians. In the 1980s, the lobby of the House of Representatives was nicknamed "Gucci Gulch" because of the high-priced shoes worn by lobbyists.[46] Lobbyists represent organizations seeking to influence the policymaking process by asking for a policy to be created, asking for policy change, or seeking to block policy creation or policy change. As Table 9.1 shows, there are a multiplicity of ways in which issues and groups are represented.

Interest groups participate in the policymaking process in multiple ways, targeting government actors in all levels and sectors of government, including the president, members of Congress, the bureaucracy, state governors, state legislators, mayors, and city and county legislators. Interest groups used to focus their national lobbying efforts on Congress and the bureaucracy, strategically allocating their

Table 9.1 Issue Types and Interest Groups

ISSUE TYPE	EXAMPLE
Single issue	National Rifle Association
Generic business	Chamber of Commerce
Specific industry	Air Transport Association
Union	United Auto Workers
Government	National Governors Association
Public interest	Center for Science in the Public Interest
Professional	American Political Science Association

resources to the prime decision makers. However, as the presidency has increased its presence in the policymaking process, presidents have increasingly become the focus of interest groups. As far back as the FDR administration, staffers in the White House were responsible for maintaining connections with key groups and individuals. However, the Ford White House was the first to create a formal office dedicated to maintaining a relationship with outside organizations within the EOP.[47] The Office of Public Liaison is the contact point for interest groups and the place where "reverse lobbying" (where the White House works to get interest groups on board its agenda) occurs. Groups also attempt to lobby other executive offices like the Office of Intergovernmental Affairs, the Office of Legislative Affairs, the Office of Political Affairs, and various constituency-based units.[48] The Obama administration centralized and expanded the office that deals with outside groups, renaming it the Office of Public Engagement and Intergovernmental Affairs, indicating its wider focus on informing the American people about how decisions are made in addition to focusing on organized interest groups.

Lobbyists and interest groups do not seek to influence the executive branch to the same degree that they lobby Congress. From trade associations to public interest groups, on average, 95 percent of the lobbying contacts are with Congress.[49] Moreover, most of the lobbying efforts remain outside public knowledge until something triggers media coverage. Industry spending in elections is newsworthy; however, what draws greater attention is when the linkage between donations and policy outcomes becomes overt. In 2001, much attention was paid to the Bush administration's strong links to the energy industry, oil companies in particular. Both Bush and his vice president, Dick Cheney, had worked in the oil industry, as did Commerce Secretary Don Evans. The $32 million donated in the 2000 campaign by the energy industry served them well as like-minded individuals took office and advanced policy from that shared perspective. Two specific events emphasized an arguably unfair attentiveness: the policy recommendations of the Vice President's Energy Task Force and the Enron scandal. The Report from the Energy Task Force, which was guiding Bush energy policy, was initially secret. Two public interest groups, the Sierra Club and Judicial Watch, filed a lawsuit under the Freedom of Information Act to identify publicly who participated in the formulation of energy policy. The Government Accountability Office initially sought to sue as well, but dropped the case, contending it could not determine whether industry executives improperly influenced policy.

The focus on energy executives' participation and environmentalists' exclusion intensified when the energy company, Enron, collapsed. The chief executive officer of Enron, Kenneth Lay, was a close friend of Bush, who reached out for help amid the crisis. The perception gleaned from these revelations is that money buys access and opportunity to influence policy outcomes.

ECONOMIC POLICY

Aside from management of the public debt, improvement of transportation networks, some oversight of interstate commerce, and a few other regular duties, the federal government did not interfere in the economy, which is what the framers of the Constitution intended.[50] Because the Constitution did not authorize presidents or the rest of the federal government to manage or regulate socioeconomic activity, the president had little to do with the remarkable physical and economic growth witnessed during the nineteenth century. By the end of the century, however, the hands-off approach, although constitutionally warranted, was becoming problematic, because the framers' rural and agrarian republic was being transformed into an industrial and urbanized giant. Initially, the states and then Congress intervened to help those dislocated by the processes of industrialization and urbanization, but a combination of oppositional court rulings wedded to the notion of governmental noninterference as well as a lack of institutional resources undermined those early efforts. By the Great Depression, the need for an active federal role was obvious to most, and both Congress and presidents committed themselves to providing the necessary federal resources and capabilities for the task at hand.[51]

Economic Growth

For the first half of the United States' history, government action in the economic area focused on facilitating the growth of the economy. Some of the features guaranteed in the Constitution reflect the necessities to fostering a vibrant industrial economy, such as creating a post office, the means to patent (and then profit) from innovations, or creating or easing interstate travel and transport of goods. The early congresses created reams of legislation to facilitate the building of roads, dams, and canals and enabled the creation of an elaborate transcontinental rail system. Tariffs, as well as taxes on imports and exports, were a hotly debated topic and even played a role in the Civil War. Yet although the government was pro-business, it pursued the laissez-faire strategy, where government did not manipulate the economy. There were slow inroads made against this strategy regarding regulation. The presidency had little to do with any of this policymaking because Congress served as the dominant policymaker during the nineteenth century. The fundamental shift occurred after the 1929 stock market crash and brought the president and the executive branch to the center of economic policymaking. After the Great Depression, the laissez-faire strategy gave way to an activist government focused on mitigating the economic extremes, which had caused suffering among the citizenry.

There are two general strategies for easing the consequences of economic fluctuations: attempts to make the fluctuations less severe and providing a social safety net to mitigate the fallout from natural economic corrections. Although public expectations changed to make the president more responsible for the state of the economy, the president has few tools to affect the economy on his own and thus must find power to leverage in other areas. The larger continuous effect that the president has on government economic policy comes from the budgeting process. The president must submit to Congress a budget for the executive branch, including its myriad departments and agencies. Through the budgeting process, the president can put his stamp on policies he would like to see expanded as well as those he would like to see cut. Although Congress ultimately must create the budget via legislation, the president's budget sets the tone and agenda for the debate and markup of the bill.

Fiscal Policy

There are several types of economic policymaking that address the large-scale forces, or macro effects, in the economy as well as the small, micro, effects on behavior. The federal government (as well as state and local governments) can distribute benefits to individuals and can redistribute benefits from individuals or groups to other individuals or groups based on certain criteria. The federal government alone can regulate interstate commerce, promote growth, and stabilize the economy. Yet, the government's ability to do anything depends on the money it takes in. The U.S. government, with its large citizen base and industrial economy, takes in a lot of money, which is used to perpetuate its functioning, provide for the safety and common defense, and do all things Congress has legislated into existence. In the twenty-first century, most of the money the government takes in is spent on the same policy priorities identified in the 1930s: a strong global presence and an economic and social safety net.

The president and the administration have become the central figures in the development of fiscal policies. Fiscal policy refers to those issues associated with governmental revenues and expenditures or, in lay terms, taxes and spending. During the past 90 years, presidents have taken control of fiscal policy, not only because of increasing budgetary responsibilities but also as a result of greater public awareness of the impact of fiscal policies. Consequently, with a billowing public debt and regular annual budget deficits, the public holds presidents accountable for addressing the nation's fiscal problems. Presidents cannot afford to ignore or minimize the significance of either taxes or spending, and they have been compelled to consider both short-term and long-term solutions to structural and cyclical fiscal deficiencies.

Tax policy did not become a presidential focal point until the 1960s as John F. Kennedy's administration began to tackle what it perceived as prohibitively high marginal tax rates among certain socioeconomic groups. Kennedy was the first presidential proponent of supply-side policies, which were based on the belief that minimizing the tax burden of producers and those with potential investment capital would eventually benefit consumers and cause per capita income growth at all levels. In October 1962, Kennedy signed into law the Revenue Act of 1962, which included various tax reforms as well as a tax break for businesses intended to promote industrial investment. Kennedy also pursued a personal income tax cut that would encompass "permanent and basic reform and reduction."[52] During the summer of 1962, White House advisors were busy devising a strategy for how and when Kennedy would pursue the tax cut policy. In an address at Yale University in June 1962, Kennedy spoke extensively on fiscal policy in the United States, but declined to offer much specific detail about any forthcoming plans. According to Ted Sorensen, one of Kennedy's closest advisors, the speech was not a trial balloon about an upcoming policy proposal, but "an academic exercise before an academic audience." However, the reaction to the speech by the business community and conservatives showed the administration that "debt and deficit spending were as unpopular as ever."[53]

In July, Sorensen warned Kennedy about the crucial political timing involved with the issue: "A tax cut is a massive economic weapon. It can only be used once. It has not been used in any previous recession in my memory. . . . You did not want us to over-react in Berlin with a national emergency—I do not want us to over-react now." Sorensen urged Kennedy to only seek a tax cut if both the economic and the political timing were right, that is, if employment and production continued to decline, if the cut would not result in too high of a deficit, and if both Congress and the business community seemed receptive to the move: "Once you are able to go to the Congress and country with positive answers to these items, such a move will be both right and successful. Until then, it is likely to be neither."[54] Kennedy continued to push for tax cut legislation throughout 1963, but congressional support and action were slow in coming. Congress did not pass such a bill until early 1964, just weeks after Kennedy's assassination; Lyndon Johnson signed the Revenue Act of 1964 into law on February 26, 1964, an $11.5 billion omnibus tax reduction and reform bill intended to promote economic growth.[55]

The import of fiscal policy also reflects the activism of the modern presidency. Since FDR, presidents have accepted the mantle of problem solver in chief, resulting in the need to spend federal dollars to fix the problems the president campaigned on during the election. The need to spend more to solve problems competes with the state of the federal budget; with the exception of a few years in the late 1990s and early 2000s, the United States has operated a larger federal deficit and paid interest on a large federal debt. As a result, one of the problems the president now must solve is balancing the creation of new programs to solve new problems with the burden of paying for the past. The problem is that nondiscretionary, or mandatory, spending accounts for roughly two-thirds of all federal expenditures. Nondiscretionary spending includes entitlements, federal pensions, related fixed obligations, and debt service.[56] Discretionary spending includes the defense budget, which ballooned in the aftermath of 9/11 as the United States fought in both Afghanistan and Iraq. Neither Republican nor Democratic presidents are willing to do anything that would either weaken U.S. military capabilities or, more important, create the impression internationally of military decline and retrenchment.[57]

The rest of the discretionary budget contains "sacred cows" that seem impervious to negotiation and compromise. Aside from constituency-based commitments, like industrial or farm subsidies, infrastructure projects and other government contracts, and various state and local programs, to name a few examples, this includes funding for the various federal departments and agencies whose institutional inertia prevents serious spending cuts. In the end, with so much of the federal budget dependent on mandatory or politically sensitive obligations, presidents have little short-term control over federal spending.

Business, Labor, and Consumer Policies
Other aspects of economic policymaking include business, labor, and consumer policies, which target three major market participants and equally important political

constituencies. Balancing the needs and priorities of these three groups can be tricky, especially since business policies can adversely affect both labor and consumer policies. Policies intended to aid or support certain industries or corporations are often perceived as antilabor or anticonsumer. On other occasions, such as the 2009 bailouts of the auto industry by the Obama administration, business-friendly policy works to the advantage of workers by preserving jobs and perhaps even to the advantage of consumers by forcing technological and design changes that make products better. Likewise, protectionist policies, such as George W. Bush's steel tariffs, although highly unpopular with much of his party and free-market advocates generally, were designed to help both the steel manufacturers and their workers.[58] Industry-specific aid, despite the benefits to associated workers, has been perceived by a skeptical public as corporate welfare, and its long-term economic effects can be debilitating and inconsistent with the nation's global market objectives. Although industrial assistance has definite advantages in the short term, it tends to compound existing problems of efficiency and productivity by artificially supporting unhealthy companies or ailing industries.[59] Finally, industrial assistance such as farm subsidies, although they can result in lower retail prices on agricultural products, have come under fire from ordinary Americans who believe their taxes are being used to benefit the rich. Moreover, subsidies of this kind and other forms of corporate aid provide a competitive advantage to industrial giants over family-owned farms and small businesses.[60]

Like business policy, labor policy comes with its own set of problems and concerns, but it is a crucial part of presidential agendas, especially during economically challenging times such as the recession that began at the end of George W. Bush's second term and lasted through Obama's first term in the White House. Labor policy is one of the oldest areas of domestic policymaking in the modern era, with roots that stretch back to the initial waves of industrial unionization and worker politicization during the late nineteenth and early twentieth centuries. Organizations like the American Federation of Labor were instrumental in putting labor policy on the political map and legitimizing it as a principal area of presidential policymaking. Under Clinton and especially Obama, who was confronted with one of the highest unemployment rates in recent history, both unionized and nonunionized workers received greater attention from White House policymakers.[61] Still, the effective power of the presidency in this area, as with other components of economic policy, is comparatively limited.

Finally, consumer policy, which is wholly a twentieth-century phenomenon, is largely within the purview of the executive branch's regulatory agencies, which the president can influence through his appointment authority and powers of persuasion. Although presidents customarily devote some attention in their campaign platforms and policy agendas to timely consumer issues, consumer policies are managed through the rule-making authority of regulators such as the Federal Trade Commission, the Consumer Financial Protection Bureau, the Consumer Product Safety Commission, and the Food and Drug Administration. As the names of these regulatory agencies imply, the focus of consumer policy is the safety and protection of American consumers by establishing and maintaining appropriate quality standards that minimize potential physical harm or danger, curb fraudulent products and services, and expose offenders.[62]

DOMESTIC POLICY

Since FDR's burgeoning involvement in all aspects of the domestic arena, domestic policy agendas ballooned, and the presidency has become involved in many aspects of citizens' lives. The expansive executive machinery that plans and administers essential and nonessential federal programs is so pervasive that it demands continuous attention from the administration and its institutional infrastructure. People have become dependent on the executive assistance, regulation, and enforcement activities within the executive branch, and they expect their presidents to maintain and ultimately improve these services. Consequently, presidential administrations are motivated and compelled to devote considerable attention to the numerous domestic policy areas that reflect public demand, which include social services, sociocultural policies, law enforcement, and energy and the environment.

Social Services

In terms of influence over the day-to-day aspects of Americans' lives, the most important category within the domestic-policy arena is social services. It is also the most resource intensive because it accounts for the bulk of domestic federal spending and the plurality of the domestic federal work force. Covering assistance for the socioeconomically dislocated, social security, health care, education, and many other areas, this part of the president's domestic-policy agenda has grown consistently and almost uncontrollably since its appearance approximately one century ago. It encompasses central programs like Social Security, Medicare, Medicaid, health-care coverage, services for the disabled, America's veterans, dependent children, and students.[63]

Social services constitute the biggest single policy area for presidential administrations, at least from a resource and capabilities perspective, but that has been a historically recent development. The executive capability and willingness to remedy these problems, particularly the structural socioeconomic deficiencies, did not emerge until the 1930s and FDR's attempts to ameliorate living conditions during the Great Depression.[64] Faced with a national emergency on a scale previously unimaginable, FDR pushed Congress to enact appropriate remedial legislation. Within a few months, he secured a package of social-service and regulatory measures targeting workers, employers, farmers, utilities, banks, consumer prices, wages, natural resources, and much more.

The Second New Deal (policies enacted 1935–1938) more aggressively confronted the demand-side manifestations of the depression by increasing consumer purchasing power and capabilities through programs for dislocated minorities, industrial workers, retired persons, and others disproportionately affected by the economic crisis. The presidency and the federal government thus became committed to the redistribution of wealth and income to secure not only social and economic equity but also sustainable per capita income growth. Early in 1935, FDR's administration launched the Works Progress Administration, one of the nation's largest relief agencies and a lasting symbol of New Deal activism. With more than 30 percent of the nation's unemployed among its ranks, it coordinated public-works projects throughout the United States and distributed various kinds of assistance to families hit hardest by the depression. Having a profound impact on rural America and Western states, the Works Progress Administration built schools, libraries, roads, and bridges while providing food, clothing, and shelter in resource-starved communities.[65]

As significant as most New Deal programs were, no single initiative has been as closely associated with the New Deal as the Social Security Act. All subsequent welfare-state enhancements and reforms were inspired and empowered by the Social Security Act, and most ensuing attempts to increase domestic executive authority used it as a political and legal precedent. The law, enacted in 1935 as the core of the Second New Deal, created a guaranteed federal pension for the elderly, unemployment compensation, aid for dependent children, support for unwed mothers, and related services.[66] Further substantial gains in executive social-services capability came with the Johnson administration, whose accomplishments in that regard exceeded those of FDR. Johnson's Great Society covered the poor, the elderly, the young, political and social minorities, mothers, the workplace, schools, housing, the nation's cities, and more. One of the most prominent parts of the Great Society was the War on Poverty, which sought to mitigate poverty by addressing long-term structural deficiencies that depressed the dislocated. As Johnson declared in his 1964 State of the Union address,

> This administration today, here and now, declares unconditional war on poverty in America. I urge this Congress and all Americans to join with me in that effort. It will not be a short or easy struggle, no single weapon or strategy will suffice, but we shall not rest until that war is won. The richest Nation on earth can afford to win it. We cannot afford to lose it. One thousand dollars invested in salvaging an unemployable youth today can return $40,000 or more in his lifetime. Poverty is a national problem, requiring improved national organization and support. But this attack, to be effective, must also be organized at the State and the local level and must be supported and directed by State and local efforts. For the war against poverty will not be won here in Washington. It must be won in the field, in every private home, in every public office, from the courthouse to the White House.[67]

Johnson's Office of Economic Opportunity (OEO), modeled on New Deal precedents, was charged with the development of relevant economic and social-services policies. OEO and its agencies provided job training, housing assistance, educational enrichment, food and clothing subsidies, basic health care, resources for neighborhood improvement, and other services.[68]

The War on Poverty was supplemented by educational reforms that increased federal funding for states and local communities and provided billions of dollars for facilities, teachers, supplies, training, and students. In addition, the newly created Department of Housing and Urban Development (HUD) focused on the revitalization of America's cities through building projects, renovations, and improvements in public infrastructure. HUD, the OEO, and other Great Society institutions were social-services landmarks, but Johnson's signal achievements with respect to the expansion of welfare-state capabilities were Medicare and Medicaid. Medicare looked to the nation's retired persons, with health-care benefits that included hospital treatment, nursing-home subsidies, and physician care, whereas Medicaid, which was to be a joint program with the states, would service the poor, disabled, elderly not eligible for Medicare, dependent children and unwed mothers, and others identified as needy by federal or state governments.[69]

The presidents who followed Johnson were mostly unable to replicate his success creating new, large entitlement programs, although only Democratic presidents attempted it. Therefore, as a domestic policymaker, George W. Bush was an anomaly, because he seemed to abandon the Republican Party's commitment to small government by presiding over the largest increase in nondiscretionary domestic spending since Johnson. Compassionate conservatism, Bush's self-described policy characterization since his days as Texas governor, necessitated greater attention to domestic services than his Republican predecessors had countenanced, but Bush's religious impulses also pushed government further into the provision of social services.[70] In 2010, Obama pushed through the single largest entitlement program since the New Deal—the Affordable Care Act (also known as Obamacare), the culmination of a 70-year effort to create a national health-care policy (as discussed below).

Sociocultural Policies

Sociocultural issues were a significant concern for the framers of the Constitution; however, they left to the states the right to interfere in private and personal matters. Eventually, the emergence of social movements dedicated to moral and ethical reform, such the early temperance efforts, became amalgamated with contemporary political and economic reform efforts, which provided them political credibility.[71] Culminating in the politicization of a full spectrum of sociocultural issues previously considered off limits to the federal government, the American political system has incorporated sociocultural issues as well as strictly political ideals within its ideological foundation. This means that the presidency, even more so than other parts of the federal government, is viewed as a sociocultural policymaker. Americans expect their presidents to have clear positions on topics like abortion, stem-cell research, same-sex marriage, and religion and prayer.

Arguably the most enduring and divisive of these sociocultural issues is abortion. The issue is so divisive that Congress rarely produces reproductive legislation, typically in times of unified government. Instead, legal precedent made policy, as with *Roe v. Wade* (1973). Presidents seeking to influence reproductive policy used unilateral action and stayed out of the legislative sphere, for the most part. On abortion education abroad, there has been a revolving door of executive action. Reagan issued a presidential memorandum to prevent U.S. funding from being used in education about reproductive options (funding abortion procedures was already illegal). Clinton overturned the memorandum with one of his own. George W. Bush issued a new memorandum known as the Mexico City Policy or "global gag rule" to prevent nongovernment organizations from using U.S. funds "to pay for the performance of abortions as a method of family planning, or to motivate or coerce any person to practice abortions." Obama then reversed that memorandum with his own and lifted the ban. In 2017, Donald Trump issued his own memoranda to reverse Obama's and return to the Bush approach: "I hereby revoke the Presidential Memorandum of January 23, 2009, for the Secretary of State and the Administrator of the United States Agency for International Development (Mexico City Policy and Assistance for Voluntary Population Planning), and reinstate the Presidential Memorandum of January 22, 2001, for the Administrator of the United States Agency for International Development."[72]

Law Enforcement

Another major domestic-policy concern for presidents involves law enforcement, which encompasses federal anticrime initiatives, border security and immigration, homeland security and domestic counterterrorism, civil rights protection, and various associated activities. During much of the antebellum period, presidential law-enforcement policy was conspicuous by its absence, and it did not become a substantial concern until the twentieth century. The early presidency was not equipped to deal with such issues mostly because the framers of the Constitution did not authorize it to do so, but most of the needs and circumstances for federal law enforcement that exist today were not present at that time. Even when needs and circumstances initially arose, almost all law-enforcement responsibilities were met by state and especially local governments, whereas other areas of law enforcement that are now under federal jurisdiction, such as civil rights and border security, were largely irrelevant or ignored.[73] As the complexities of industrialization and urbanization coupled with continued population growth created a demand for a more active federal law-enforcement role and a burgeoning federal government issued scores of new federal laws that required enforcement, the executive branch acquired increasing duties and responsibilities. Most important, evolving public awareness and sociocultural attitudes concerning issues such as civil rights enabled and eventually motivated federal administration of matters that had previously been ignored.

Today, presidents and presidential candidates ignore law enforcement at their own peril, since issues like immigration, border security, drug interdiction, and civil rights protection have become among the most important priorities for Americans. These hot-button topics are sure to spark some of the most spirited, and frequently vitriolic, debates in politics, so a presidential candidate's position on any one of them can make a crucial difference in battleground states. Presidential policies on gun ownership and the death penalty, for example, have become political litmus tests for certain voters, and although they represent an admittedly narrow portion of a president's overall domestic agenda, they are pivotal issues.[74] For example, the Clinton administration sought and won passage of the Violent Crime Control and Law Enforcement Act in 1994, the largest crime bill in American history that provided for 100,000 new police officers, billions of dollars in funding for prisons and crime prevention programs, an expanded federal death penalty, and a federal ban on assault weapons. Nearly all aspects of the bill became intense political debating points, particularly the assault weapons ban, because many members of Congress, particularly Republicans, were the targets of intense lobbying by the National Rifle Association to defeat the bill. The Clinton administration's strategy in passing the bill focused on partisan tactics, as explained in this memo from policy advisor Rahm Emanuel to Chief of Staff Leon Panetta:

> We must implement a dual strategy to pass the Crime Bill. This two tiered approach requires that (1) The President set an appropriate tone and tenor; and (2) We organize local officials, cabinet members, and candidates to apply pressure to targeted Republicans. . . . The message that we must send is simple: members of Congress abandoned their constituents. The President's role in the next four days is to make clear that by voting against the Crime Bill members of Congress championed their own political safety, over the people's safety. He must reiterate that they voted against 100,000 police officers; against three strikes and you're out;

against tougher sentencing; against the assault weapons ban; against the death penalty. They abdicated their responsibility to their constituents, showing political cowardice when political courage was needed.[75]

The most obvious aspect of law-enforcement policy is crime prevention, which became a high-profile issue during the 1980s and 1990s, particularly among law-and-order Reagan Republicans. Agencies such as the Justice Department's Federal Bureau of Investigation (FBI) and the Drug Enforcement Administration (DEA), the Department of Homeland Security's (DHS) Bureau of Alcohol, Tobacco, Firearms, and Explosives, and the Secret Service provide essential crime-prevention services, yet the bulk of the nation's crime prevention is handled by state, county, and municipal agencies. Federal crime-prevention policies affect local law-enforcement efforts through various kinds of federal funding for state and community governments, although some measures like federal gun-ownership regulations cannot always be reconciled with local crime-prevention priorities. Still, the primary aim of federal crime-prevention policy is the enforcement of federal laws and the apprehension of those who commit federal crimes. Specialized agencies such as the Secret Service, which investigates counterfeiting of U.S. currency and Treasury bonds, fulfill roles that are unique to the federal government or the states are incapable of handling, such as the prevention of interstate criminal activity.[76]

Since 2001, DHS has become a major part of federal law-enforcement policy, although many of its responsibilities had already been fulfilled by agencies that were incorporated into the department at its creation. The establishment of DHS involved an intensification and redirection of focus rather than the initiation of new policies, but it did result in some pronounced political changes. A reinvigorated counter-terrorism effort through the FBI, the National Security Agency (NSA), and other investigative and intelligence-gathering organizations became a top priority beginning with George W. Bush's presidency, and a more restrictive immigration policy and border-control regime also emerged. Unfortunately, a greater concentration on the prevention of terrorism also meant a corresponding contraction of civil liberties, as intrusions by agencies like the NSA came under fire from various political circles and eventually the public as well. Nevertheless, especially during the Bush years, federal counterterrorist activities proliferated without serious concerns over countervailing constitutional and political implications.[77]

Law-enforcement policy also includes immigration, which is under the supervision of DHS. One of the most divisive issues of the past 30 years, immigration is not confined to worries about terrorist and criminal infiltration into the United States. The real issue has been illegal immigration, which many Americans blame for high crime rates and runaway social-services expenditures, to say nothing of the popular impression that it causes higher unemployment among citizens and legal residents. Like abortion or the death penalty, this has become a volatile topic that requires a long-term solution. Unexpectedly, George W. Bush offered a compromise solution that was not much different from what Obama would propose a few years later, but it was neither stringent enough for mainstream Republicans nor sufficiently welcoming for Democrats.[78] Trump promised throughout the 2016 presidential campaign to "build a wall" to crack down on illegal immigration, linking the issue to both crime and terrorism. He signed several executive orders within his first weeks in office related to this issue.

Crime prevention, immigration, and border security are top priorities, but federal civil rights protection has been just as important, if not more so from a symbolic standpoint. Because of the slow pace of political reform following the Civil War, civil rights enforcement was not a notable federal concern until the late 1950s, but even then, federal efforts were clearly deficient. However, by the 1960s, sociopolitical mobilization among African Americans and a critical mass of progressive white activists and politicians began to turn the tide against continued institutionalized discrimination and the deprivation of minority civil rights. Once again, the Johnson administration was a pivotal innovator, and its legacy includes pivotal civil rights reforms and a considerable expansion of federal authority over civil rights enforcement. Shepherding the Civil Rights Act of 1964 and the Voting Rights Act of 1965 through Congress, Johnson spearheaded a radical reorientation of executive law-enforcement resources. These crucial pieces of legislation extended civil rights protections to minorities, women, the elderly, the poor, and other disaffected groups marginalized by political discrimination.[79]

Presidential authority to eradicate discrimination under the Civil Rights Act was nonetheless limited, because the legislation targeted public establishments and federal contracts, but Johnson used his powers liberally. Through the Office of Federal Contract Compliance, created to prevent discrimination among government contractors, Johnson instituted affirmative-action policies that set a broader political precedent. Convinced that a level playing field for the nation's African American community could only be secured through a system of racial preferences, Johnson relied on his authority and political credibility to implement a wide array of affirmative-action

Lyndon Johnson signs the Civil Rights Act of 1964 into law.

programs.[80] Despite partisan and ideological differences, his immediate successors did not renounce affirmative action programs, especially after the Supreme Court provided its imprimatur through key rulings in the late 1960s and early 1970s. Until Reagan's election in 1980, Republicans did not seriously challenge the viability of affirmative action, preferring to save their political capital for less contentious issues. By the 1990s, even many Democrats had backed away from affirmative action, but a strong commitment to civil rights enforcement remained.[81]

Clinton's Justice Department, under the guidance of Attorney General Janet Reno, made civil rights protection a priority, but its civil rights policies attracted undue criticism from Clinton's political opponents mostly because of a few controversial nominees for top posts at the Justice Department. Perhaps the most problematic of these was Lani Guinier, who was labeled by Republicans the "Quota Queen" and whose unsuccessful nomination cost Clinton considerable political capital; however, the civil rights division at the Justice Department was nevertheless vigilant during Clinton's eight years in office.[82] Obama' first attorney general, Eric Holder, also made civil rights enforcement a principal concern. Both Holder and his successor Loretta Lynch (who replaced Holder in 2015) also focused on police brutality because there were several high-profile police shootings and beatings during Obama's second term, including those in Chicago, New York City, Baltimore, and Ferguson, Missouri. The fact that videos of several of the incidents were shared on social media sharpened the political debate and the desire by many in the African American community to see Obama and his administration take more significant steps. Under Obama, the Department of Justice launched probes and investigations into several police departments, forcing the reevaluation of procedures and behavior.

Energy and the Environment

The environment and climate change, energy, and federal land use of drilling for natural gas and oil have long been polarizing issues, which seem to breed controversy instead of compromise. Most policy and regulation on these issues has a more direct effect on producers than on consumers and on employers than on employees, so consumers and employees feel the effects further downstream. Periodically, however, disasters or events like the 1989 Exxon Valdez oil spill in Alaska, the Deepwater Horizon oil spill in 2010, or the debate over building the Keystone Pipeline and Native American protests over the Dakota Pipeline thrust energy and environmental policy into the spotlight.

Environmental policy is a comparatively recent phenomenon, since awareness of environmental problems such as pollution and resource contamination did not arise until the 1960s. Even so, mainly experts and academics initially paid attention to emerging environmental questions, whereas politicians and the public remained largely apathetic until at least the 1970s. Widespread air and water pollution along with pesticide contamination had become so obvious that they could not be ignored any longer, and medical research was exposing the health risks associated with further inaction. The Nixon administration responded with the creation of the Environmental Protection Agency, while a new generation of environmental activists agitated for appropriate reforms and regulations at all levels.[83]

Despite these gains, environmental protection took a back seat to economic expansion and industrial productivity during the Reagan years, and environmental regulation was increasingly seen as the enemy of economic progress and free enterprise. Gradually, however, both the American public and the broader global community became aware of large-scale problems such as climate change and the degradation of the earth's atmosphere, which ensured that past environmental gains would not be completely lost. Clinton's vice president, Al Gore, made environmental reform and education a personal mission during his two terms, and Clinton's Environmental Protection Agency chief Carol Browner was a tireless advocate of stricter environmental controls. Still, environmental reforms were not helped by a few distracting controversies over the protection of natural habitats at the expense of jobs in vital resource-rich areas.[84] One such incident involved a debate over the spotted owl in the Pacific Northwest and the impact of logging on its habitat and eventually even pitted federal agencies against each other in the process. Although the case was ultimately settled in favor of the logging industry, to critics of federal environmental regulation it was a lasting symbol of governmental intrusion and reformist excess.

During the George W. Bush years, environmental policy was once again surpassed by economic priorities, and many Republicans even began to question scientific conclusions about global warming. Accordingly, the Bush administration refused to sign the international Kyoto Protocol concerning climate change, a decision that was widely attacked by environmental activists and the President's Democratic opponents. As with many other policy issues, the Obama administration reversed course and recommitted the United States to international cooperation on climate change and other environmental problems, while it rededicated itself to more progressive environmental standards at home. The President's cap-and-trade proposal in 2009 was a step in that direction, but, after approval in the House of Representative, the bill languished in the Senate, where it was eventually killed. In the end, however, because of the ongoing war in Afghanistan and the nation's pervasive economic difficulties, Obama was not able to devote as much attention to reformulating environmental policy as he had hoped; this is just one reason why the cap-and-trade legislation failed.[85]

In addition to environmental policy, energy policy has been a prominent, albeit intermittent, aspect of domestic agendas for a few decades. During the 1970s, the Arab oil embargo and the by-now discredited calculations that the global supply of fossil fuels could be depleted in as little as 100 years caused widespread worries, if not outright panic, among policymakers and the public. As discussed at the start of the chapter, Carter was the first president to devote considerable attention to the future development of alternative fuels, and he also decried the country's dependence on foreign oil. No other issue on Carter's domestic agenda received as much attention from the White House as the president's national energy plan. As Carter recalled in his memoirs, "Throughout my entire term, Congress and I struggled with energy legislation. Despite my frustration, there was never a moment when I did not consider the creation of a national energy policy equal in importance to any other goal we had."[86]

By the 1980s, an economic recovery, substantial gains in fuel efficiency, and more realistic estimates about the world's energy supplies eased the country's anxiety about fossil fuels. Although the Clinton administration devoted more attention to energy policy than its immediate predecessors and sponsored research on alternative fuels, national awareness of these issues was relatively low. Not until the war in Iraq and the associated rise in oil prices did the American people and its public officials realize that the situation required a change in energy policies and a serious consideration of long-term alternatives. Energy policy had become a matter of economic sustainability and national security, and the country's dependence on foreign sources of oil was just exacerbating existing economic and strategic vulnerabilities.[87]

HEALTH CARE: A CASE STUDY

The policy environment is a crowded place, with numerous issues and agendas competing for attention. Issues come and go on the president's and the public's agenda based on an issue's relative importance to key constituencies. However, one issue has remained on nearly everyone's agenda for more than 70 years: health care.

The drive for comprehensive health-care coverage for all Americans began as a component of the social safety net created by FDR and the New Deal. In response to the social catastrophes created by the Great Depression, the New Deal promised to provide certainty against the uncertainty provided by a capitalist economic system. Unlike the rising communist and socialist views of welfare, the New Deal did not propose the creation of government ownership within the economic sphere to protect citizens from uncertainty. Instead, the New Deal accepted the inherent fluctuations of hiring and firing produced by supply and demand. Consequently, the New Deal social policies attempted to counter the extreme effects produced by a downturn in the economy, like homelessness, starvation, freezing resulting from the inability to afford heat, the deterioration of health, and even death. The New Deal programs focused on the hardest hit communities—the elderly and widows and orphans—by providing Social Security, a guaranteed monthly income determined by payroll taxes. All workers paid in as insurance and protection for old age. Health-care insurance was initially part of the New Deal but did not survive; national health care for all Americans failed over and over, through seven different administrations, until Obama and the 107th Congress achieved the seemingly impossible with passage of the Patient Protection and Affordable Care Act in 2010. Based on the 2016 presidential campaign and Trump's stated desire to undo "Obamacare" (as it has also come to be known), health care remains a fierce public policy battle. Documents from presidential libraries and elsewhere reveal the vast complexities that emerge when attempting to make health-care policy.

The Issue and the Environment

From the early attempts in the FDR administration, it was clear that health care was not a traditional domestic issue. In fact, FDR viewed health care "as part of the economic challenge that confronted workers."[88] He was not the only one who viewed health care from an economic lens; for the doctors, nurses, hospitals, and later, health insurance companies, health care was a profitable business. However, it is difficult to view health care solely from the business perspective because it is also considered by many a right or a privilege, or a combination of both. As a comparison, K–12 public education is now seen as a basic right although it is not guaranteed by the Constitution; it evolved into a right through policy precedent. In contrast, the policy record from both the federal government and the states is mixed concerning the right to health care. Emergency rooms cannot turn away patients seeking treatment; however, doctors, even those who treat patients with government coverage, like Medicare, can turn patients away. There is no universal agreement that all citizens are entitled to health care. Since the issue first arrived on the national agenda, there were two fundamental questions for policymakers to consider: Will the United States provide care to people who cannot afford market prices of coverage and, if yes, how will the country pay for it?

IN THEIR OWN WORDS

REFORMING HEALTH CARE

The importance of Congress as a key player in policymaking is evident in this memo from House majority leader Dick Gephardt (D-MO) to Ira Magaziner, senior advisor to Bill Clinton for policy development, and Hillary Clinton, first lady and chair of the task force on health care. Titled "Consultation with Congress," Gephardt instructs Magaziner and Clinton on how to handle their dealings with Congress.

> The time and effort you have expended in reaching out to Congress on health care reform have been greatly appreciated. However, to ensure the most positive reception of the health care reform bill in Congress, and the smoothest most rapid legislative process, it is imperative that you begin consultation in earnest with two critical Congressional groups: the Committee Chairs and CBO [Congressional Budget Office].[89]

While Gephardt is arguing for consultation with the knowledgeable members of Congress, a memo two months later from a staffer to Hillary Clinton argued that, "it is best to have a team of Administration lobbyists whose sole task is to pass the President's health care reform bill."[90] Subsequent memos focus on creating "a kind of 'health care university' for Members of Congress . . . if done well, it would: Reinvigorate the 'need for action' mentality that, until very recently had been effectively fanning the flames of desire for comprehensive health reform in Congress; Ease Congressional concerns about, and raise Member comfort levels with, the President's proposal to address the problems; Better enable perspective Congressional supporters to explain, defend, and sell the President's proposal; and Be utilized to help educate surrogates in home Congressional districts."[91]

While the task force is preparing to "educate" members of Congress, members of Congress are sending the President letters regarding what should and should not be in the health care bill. Here are two excerpts:

> Letter from Senator Hank Brown (cosigned by 3 Representatives): "Dear Mr. President: There continue to be rumors regarding the possibility of substantially raising the excise tax on beer as one source for funding government-sponsored health care. We urge you to reject this approach."
>
> Letter from Senator Max Baucus (cosigned by 6 other Senators) "Dear Mr. President: As you finalize your national health reform plan, we would like to again express our serious concern with how the plan would determine state global budgets and offer an alternative proposal. . . . national health reform legislation must require the National Health Care Board to determine how the

national per capita average should be adjusted to reflect the appropriate needs of a state. The legislation should also mandate that the Board develop and implement a transition to the national average so that within six years after enactment state budgets would be based completely on an adjusted national average."[92]

The conflicting view of what health care is and the power behind those who work in the health-care industry yielded difficulties for presidents who wished to advance a health policy agenda. The forces lined up in opposition to providing a universal health-care program equivalent to the universal income program, known as Social Security, were numerous. First, the medical professionals lobbied the executive and legislative branches intensely in opposition to creating universal health care. FDR's own doctor and his son's father-in-law (a famous neurosurgeon) reiterated the American Medical Association's (AMA) intense antagonism to any type of government health insurance. The press for health insurance from FDR and then Harry Truman galvanized the AMA and turned it into a premier interest group and effective lobbyist. The AMA learned and showcased effective group strategies; it organized its own members and also organized other organizations "to echo their indignation over socialized medicine." They also perfected their message: against FDR, the AMA fought to prevent the establishment of national health insurance but did not offer another option. By the Truman administration, the AMA realized it needed an alternative, and so by 1949, the organization pressed for private health insurance plans rather than government-sponsored health insurance.[93]

The AMA continued to fight vigorously any role for the government in health care. By the 1960s, however, momentum gathered to push for health care for seniors and the poor, Medicare and Medicaid. The AMA expanded its approach, recruiting popular individuals and politicians to speak out against "socialized medicine." Perhaps the most famous effort came with a speech made by Ronald Reagan, on behalf of 1964 Republican presidential candidate Barry Goldwater.[94] The AMA recorded Reagan's speech and distributed it to the Women's Auxiliary of the AMA. Dubbed "Operation Coffee Cup," the AMA distributed 3,000 records to doctor's wives and encouraged them to host "recording parties" where they "spontaneously" shared Reagan's opposition to the plans that ultimately become Medicare. In classic grassroots strategy, Reagan urged his listeners to make their views known:

> What can we do about this? . . . We can write to our congressmen and to our senators. . . . And at the moment the key issue is: We do not want socialized medicine. . . . In Washington today 40,000 letters, less than 100 per congressman, are evidence of a trend in public thinking. . . . Representative Halleck of Indiana has said, "When the American people want something from Congress . . . if they make their wants known, Congress does what the people want." So write. . . . that you demand the continuation of our traditional free enterprise system. . . . You and I can do this. The only way we can do it is by writing to our congressman even if we believe he's on our side to begin with. Write to strengthen his hand. Give him the ability to stand before his colleagues in Congress and say, I heard from my constituents and this is what they want. . . . And if you don't do this and if I don't do it, one of these days you and I are going to spend our sunset years telling our children, and our children's children, what it once was like in America when men were free.[95]

There was no more powerful group in the health-care arena between the 1930s and the 1980s. However, the power of the AMA waned because of the lack of congruity among its membership. Doctors split along issues lines relating to managed care, group and single practice, and the values associated with covering the nation. As a result, the AMA no longer spoke with a unified voice. In the multiplicity of voices, a new voice began to dominate, reflecting the change in the economic environment of health care: the Health Insurance Association of America.

Taking a page from the AMA, the Health Insurance Association of America (HIAA) also used technology and media to shape the political agenda and environment. As the Clinton administration, under the leadership of First Lady Hillary Clinton, became the sixth administration to focus on national health care, the association used television advertising to replicate the efforts of Operation Coffee Cup. HIAA created the "Harry and Louise" ads, advertisements featuring a 40-something couple discussing the Clinton health-care proposal in their kitchen:

> Harry [looking at a newspaper]: I'm glad the President's doing something about health care reform.
> Louise [reading the President's plan]: He's right, we need it.
> Harry: Some of these details.
> Louise: Like a national limit on health care?
> Harry: Really.
> Louise: The Government caps how much the country can spend on all health care and says, "That's it."
> Harry: So what if our health plan runs out of money?
> Louise: There's got to be a better way![96]

Thirty years after Reagan's impassioned plea, the argument against government involvement as "socialized medicine" continued to resonate. In the 1960s, medical professionals sought to influence politicians directly via their own participation and that of their friends and families. In the 1990s, the insurers also wanted to influence politicians but attempted to do so by influencing the public rather than their own insular sector. HIAA employed traditional radio, television and newspaper ads and even used half-hour-long infomercials to sway citizens to their point of view, that the government plan will deny choice.[97] This advertising powerfully shaped the political debate because it allowed moneyed insiders to portray their views to ordinary citizens. The Harry and Louise ads received extensive coverage by the press because it was the first time that an interest group ran a policy ad campaign for a national policy debate. Interestingly, the coverage of the ads forced responsiveness from the White House, which in turn generated more attention. Public opinion polls revealed a greater influence from media coverage (which included coverage of the ads) than of the actual advertising because the ads did not get wide airplay.[98]

Almost 20 years after Clinton's failed attempt, the Obama administration faced a different political environment. However, all the players involved took to the airways to try to influence the tenor of the debate. Harry and Louise even made a comeback, now in support of a public option for insurance rather than the private insurance system that existed for individuals who are not eligible for Medicare, Medicaid, and Veterans' Benefits.

Organizing the Policy Process

Since the issue of health care crosscuts so many different sectors of the economy and society, presidents had to be strategic in how they approached policymaking. The presidents seeking to design health policy took three approaches to organizing their policymaking: using an economic committee, using a domestic policy committee, or using a special health-focused committee.

FDR, based on his belief that health care was but one component of economic security, created a committee designed to provide solutions to all threats to economic security. In a speech to that committee, FDR explained what he wanted them to do:

> I am glad to welcome you to the White House and to tell you that I am happy that there is so much interest in the problem of economic security. . . . Many details are still to be settled. The Committee on Economic Security was created to advise me on this matter. It will bring to me, not any preconceived views, but a mature judgment after careful study of the problem and after consultation with the Advisory Conference and the cooperating committees. On some points it is possible to be definite. Unemployment insurance will be in the program. . . . We must not allow this type of insurance to become a dole through the mingling of insurance and relief. It is not charity. It must be financed by contributions, not taxes. . . . There are other matters with which we must deal before we shall give adequate protection to the individual against the many economic hazards. Old age is at once the most certain, and for many people the most tragic of all hazards. There is no tragedy in growing old, but there is tragedy in growing old without means of support. . . . There is also the problem of economic loss due to sickness—a very serious matter for many families with and without incomes, and therefore, an unfair burden upon the medical profession. Whether we come to this form of insurance soon or later on, I am confident that we can devise a system which will enhance and not hinder the remarkable progress which has been made and is being made in the practice of the professions of medicine and surgery in the United States. . . . We are developing a plan of administration into which can be fitted the various parts of the security program when it is timely to do so. We cannot work miracles or solve all our problems at once. What we can do is to lay a sound foundation on which we can build a structure to give a greater measure of safety and happiness to the individual than any we have ever known. In this task you can greatly help.[99]

George H. W. Bush dealt with the issue of health care, not to create a new entitlement program but to stymie the Democratic-controlled Congress's efforts to do so. Bush's goal was to limit government interference by taking a limited regulatory role that would "preserve the private health care system with government and individual choice playing a role to increase that system's efficiency." His DPC handled health care along with other issues higher on the president's domestic agenda.

Clinton and Obama created new structures specifically assigned to designing health policy. By creating separate entities, like FDR, these administrations signaled a high level of interest and attention to this issue. The new organizations also served to funnel all inputs from groups and other officials to one focus. Moreover, by creating new organizations, these administrations could go over or around entrenched attitudes or behavior patterns in the bureaucracy.

Clinton's focus on health care began immediately in November 1992 because he had promised a health-care plan in his first 100 days in office. To meet this ambitious deadline, two separate task forces, unbeknownst to each other, began work on a Clinton plan.[100] Ira Magaziner won the battle between the dueling task forces, because Clinton tapped him to run health policy development for the administration. Clinton created a unique task force, run jointly by Magaziner and Hillary Clinton; her co-chairmanship of the task force was unprecedented because no first lady had previously been responsible for a policy task of such magnitude. Giving a task force the job of policy design and development was an attempt by the Clinton administration to shake up the traditional Washington policy process, particularly by giving leadership to two individuals with "no Washington experience and no official governmental roles." The task force itself was enormous, with "over 600 health care experts, congressional staff, and stakeholder representatives."[101]

In contrast to and perhaps learning from Clinton's experience, Obama created an Office of Health Reform in the EOP, giving it equal status with other offices like the Council of Economic Advisers and the Office of Homeland and National Security. After health-care reform became law in 2010, the office ceased to exist at that level, and health reform issues became the purview of the DPC.

Fighting for Policy

Prior to Obama's success in 2010, the most successful president on health care was Lyndon Johnson, with his landmark achievement of Medicare, health care for the elderly. Much of the success of the Great Society, the nickname for Medicare, Medicaid, civil rights, and other social programs, stemmed from the changed appetite for these policies from the overwhelmingly Democratic Congress elected in the wake of the Kennedy assassination. However, the skill demonstrated by Johnson in managing the Congress and the competing interests arrayed against his programs illustrates the importance of good management for policy success.

There are eight essential lessons for presidential policymaking illustrated by health care, particularly by Obama's successful achievement of landmark health-care reform in 2010. First, presidential policy success depends on a president caring about the issue. Presidents unsuccessful in their effort to achieve health care were passionate about the issue, but it is virtually impossible to achieve success for a presidential policy when the president is not actively engaged. Johnson and Obama cared passionately about passage of their programs. Obama noted, "I did this for my mother," who had died of cancer and faced many obstacles with insurance companies. Johnson fought for Kennedy's legacy as well as his own desires. FDR cared about economic stability, but health care was but one plank and not the most important.

Second, speed matters. Although the policy process seems interminably slow to ordinary citizens, Obama managed to get health-care reform passed with amazing speed. In contrast to the Clinton White House, which used the first nine months in office to simply submit their plan to Congress, the Obama health-care reform passed out of the Senate at the end of the first nine months of his term. Part of the reason for the speed was the third key to policy success: Obama had a plan from day one. In fact, much of the failure of the Clinton plan stemmed from the inability to take advantage of the window of opportunity provided by the presidential honeymoon and the opening the campaign produced.[102]

Fourth, Obama won over the economists in his White House and the economically minded on Capitol Hill. This is more difficult than it sounds and more important than it seems. As Chapter 10 will show, on foreign policy, the president has an advantage over Congress and other groups and organizations because of the dominance of the information provided by the national security advisor, the Homeland and National Security Council, the State Department, the Pentagon, and the Central Intelligence Agency all reporting directly to the president. Congressional committees and interest groups do not have comparable sources of information. In domestic policy, Congress and competing interests do have comparable levels of expertise, specifically within the economic sphere, because both Congress and the president increasingly have highly technical advisors who provide sophisticated advice.

Fifth and sixth, Obama applied his own extraordinary public skills and effectively used the tools of his office to appeal to the public and manage the Congress. Seventh, Obama took the high road and did not get bogged down in the technical debates or the minutia. The devil may be in the details, and the legislative process may be complicated and messy, but Obama remained above that. Finally, Obama focused more intensely when the outcome was balanced precariously, and a single mistake could tip the outcome toward failure.[103] In his 2010 State of the Union address, Obama urged Congress, 'Don't walk away from reform.... Not now. Not when we are so close. Let us find a way to come together and finish the job for the American people. Let's get it done."[104]

CONCLUSION

Undoubtedly, the presidency is the focal point of media attention, public attention, and many other political actors. Nevertheless, the president is not the central actor in policymaking; he is but one player in domestic and economic policymaking. Grand policy change with the president leading the charge is possible, as evidenced by the successes of FDR, Johnson, and Obama. Typically, however, most policy change is smaller and incremental in nature. As a result, policy influence from the president relates not only to the president's skill in pursuit of his goal, but also to the goals of the myriad other players in the process. The president's domestic and economic policymaking process has an inherent logic that underscores a distinctive set of institutional practices. As such, although particular presidents inevitably put their stamp on policymaking through tactical and even strategic procedural changes, the process ultimately transcends those individuals by shaping the presidency itself.

The agendas the president faces and those the president brings to the White House are a function of partisan priorities, ideological preferences, and experiences. Without a doubt, the president is the most important domestic and economic policymaker, but the president is supported by a vast network of individuals and organizations within and outside the White House. From an inner circle of presidential advisors to the various policy councils, agencies, and cabinet departments whose expertise is essential to the formulation of feasible and effective policies, this network eventually involves Congress, interest groups, political contributors, the news media, and countless state, county, and municipal governments. These policymakers may not always work as a team, and the results usually do not match original expectations, but they all contribute in some way to the definition and implementation of presidential domestic and economic policies, which touch most aspects of people's lives.

CHAPTER 10

Presidents and Foreign Policy

Although it is still too early to assess accurately George W. Bush's place in American political history, one of the most notable and enduring debates will center on Bush's expansion of presidential powers related to national security and the War on Terror. Following the terrorist attacks of 9/11, the Bush administration claimed broad presidential powers under Bush's role as commander in chief, not only in the capture, imprisonment, and interrogation tactics used against suspected terrorists, but also in the U.S. invasion of Afghanistan in December 2001 and Iraq in March 2003. While Bush's supporters championed his interpretation of broad constitutional powers during a time of crisis, his political opponents railed against him for his abuse and misinterpretation of presidential powers as outlined in Article II of the Constitution. On Barack Obama's election in 2008, many of Obama's supporters believed, falsely as it turned out, that the renewed "imperial presidency" of the Bush years would fade quickly. However, the Obama administration was not without controversy in this regard, because Obama was also challenged, at least politically, over his use of military intervention as commander in chief.

In February 2011, Obama committed U.S. troops to Libya as part of an international coalition to oust Col. Muammar Gaddafi from power. Gaddafi had begun a campaign to put down civil unrest and protests in Libya, which included killing thousands of innocent civilians. Long considered a pariah state by most other nations because of its state-sponsored terrorist activities, Libya had been under United Nations sanctions since 1993; prior to that, Ronald Reagan had ordered military airstrikes against Libya in 1986 in response to a terrorist bombing of a Berlin nightclub where Americans had been killed. Given the long history of animosity toward Gaddafi's regime, Obama's decision to aid the international military effort to remove Gaddafi from power was not surprising. By March 2011, as the international coalition continued to fight Gaddafi troops in support of those protesting his government, Obama sent a letter to Congress informing members about the military action in compliance with the War Powers Resolution:

> [Gaddafi's] illegitimate use of force not only is causing the deaths of substantial numbers of civilians among his own people, but also is forcing many others to flee to neighboring countries, thereby destabilizing the peace and security of the region. Left unaddressed, the growing instability in Libya could ignite wider instability in the Middle East, with dangerous consequences to the national security interests of the United States. . . . The United States has not deployed ground forces into Libya. United States forces are conducting a limited and well-defined mission in support of international efforts to protect civilians and prevent a humanitarian disaster. . . . I have directed these actions, which are in the national security and foreign policy interests of the United States, pursuant to my constitutional authority to conduct U.S. foreign relations and as Commander in Chief and Chief Executive. I am providing this report as part of my efforts to keep the Congress fully informed, consistent with the War Powers Resolution.[1]

A few days later, Obama addressed the nation about the importance of the mission in Libya:

> The United States and the world faced a choice. Gaddafi declared he would show "no mercy" to his own people. He compared them to rats, and threatened to go door to door to inflict punishment. In the past, we have seen him hang civilians in the streets, and kill over a thousand people in a single day. . . . We knew that if we waited one more day, Benghazi, a city nearly the size of Charlotte, could suffer a massacre that would have reverberated across the region and stained the conscience of the world. It was not in our national interest to let that happen. I refused to let that happen. And so nine days ago, after consulting the bipartisan leadership of Congress, I authorized military action to stop the killing and enforce U.N. Security Council Resolution 1973. . . . Moreover, we've accomplished these objectives consistent with the pledge that I made to the American people at the outset of our military operations. I said that America's role would be limited; that we would not put ground troops into Libya; that we would focus our unique capabilities on the front end of the operation and that we would transfer responsibility to our allies and partners. Tonight, we are fulfilling that pledge.[2]

Although many Americans supported the idea of removing Gaddafi from power, Obama faced criticism from both sides of the political aisle; Democrats worried that the United States would engage in yet another war in the Middle East (with troops still in both Afghanistan and Iraq), and Republicans complained that Obama was acting beyond his constitutional powers by committing U.S. troops (although many had not complained about Bush's actions just a few years earlier). Some on Capitol Hill began to talk about violations of the War Powers Resolution, and in response, Obama sent another letter to Congress in June 2011 stating that the War Powers Resolution did not apply after all to his actions regarding Libya since American military involvement fell short of "full-blown hostilities," asserting that "U.S. operations do not involve sustained fighting or active exchanges of fire with hostile forces, nor do they involve

U.S. ground troops."[3] Whether Obama correctly asserted his powers as commander in chief and whether he was right to claim that the War Powers Resolution did not apply are still open to political and constitutional interpretation.

As political scientist Aaron Wildavsky famously argued, there are "two presidencies"—one dealing with domestic policy and the other dealing with foreign policy. Wildavsky's "Dual Presidency Theory," which he articulated to explain the presidency during the first two decades of the Cold War, suggests that presidents prefer to focus on foreign over domestic policy because they have more constitutional and statutory authority and can act more decisively without much congressional interference. Although the theory is not as accurate today, as Congress has become more involved in the development of foreign policy, Wildavsky's observation is nonetheless instructive when considering the expansion of presidential powers in the foreign-policy arena.[4] Governed by a group of actors that includes the president, his staff and advisors, legislators, lobbyists, international organizations, and foreign governments, all reflecting national strategic priorities and political ideals, foreign policymaking is an essential part of presidential politics.

FOREIGN POLICY DEFINED

Every country has both internal and external priorities, which are addressed through their leaders' political agendas. In the United States, these agendas are realized through separate yet overlapping domestic and foreign-policy establishments that intersect at the White House and are unified through executive leadership and an underlying national interest. Domestic policy (like taxes, jobs, or health care) is often more relevant to the everyday existence of Americans, and presidential candidates often prioritize domestic over international policies in their campaigns. In addition, because of most candidates' lack of foreign-policy experience, all but a few focus on the domestic-policy topics with which they are most familiar. Still, regardless of their campaign platforms and political leanings, presidents frequently become preoccupied with foreign policy to the exclusion, or detriment, of the domestic agendas that got them elected. Yet, presidents cannot afford to ignore, minimize, or defer the vital military and diplomatic concerns that define national security and international survival.

One of the principal reasons the federal government and particularly the presidency exist is to conduct foreign policy. In 1787, the framers of the Constitution created a limited government with comparatively few duties and responsibilities, but foremost among them was foreign policy, which the Articles of Confederation had been unable to address. Foreign policy is arguably more essential than its domestic counterpart, not least because this was one task the states were incapable of fulfilling individually. Foreign policy addresses America's relationship with other countries and its role in the international arena. Viewed another way, it acknowledges the fact that individual countries do not exist in a vacuum and, for better or worse, are shaped by the influences and interactions among them. In the United States, as a manifestation of popular will, foreign policy not only animates core constitutional principles and political ideals but also promotes national interests through resources and capabilities whose aim is the protection of American assets and the advancement of American strategic priorities throughout the world. Whether through the realization of geopolitical objectives that secure the country's international footprint or through the pursuit of economic goals that support American growth and prosperity, foreign policy is an outgrowth and function of domestic priorities that define national interest. Without this connection, foreign policy would be meaningless and irrelevant, the mere manifestation of naked political will.[5]

Foreign policy connects constitutional politics with ordinary politics and, in so doing, transforms ideals into realities. History has also shown that viable foreign policies must be achievable or, as the Vietnam experience proves, they will lose public support and the much-needed consent of the electorate. If American policymaking during the Vietnam War illustrated anything, it was that unachievable foreign policies are politically and constitutionally harmful, because they foster strategic and tactical failures and breed the kind of mistrust that can paralyze the political process. Both Lyndon Johnson and Richard Nixon dealt with extensive protests of their administrations' policies in Vietnam; Johnson often endured chants of "Hey, Hey, LBJ, How many kids did you kill today?" from protesters outside the gates of the White House. Vietnam also played a crucial role in Johnson's decision to withdraw from the Democratic primaries in 1968, as he told a stunned nation on March 31, 1968:

> Believing this as I do, I have concluded that I should not permit the Presidency to become involved in the partisan divisions that are developing in this political year. With America's sons in the fields far away, with America's future under challenge right here at home, with our hopes and the world's hopes for peace in the balance every day, I do not believe that I should devote an hour or a day of my time to any personal partisan causes or to any duties other than the awesome duties of this office—the Presidency of your country. Accordingly, I shall not seek, and I will not accept, the nomination of my party for another term as your President. But let men everywhere know, however, that a strong, a confident, and a vigilant America stands ready tonight to seek an honorable peace—and stands ready tonight to defend an honored cause—whatever the price, whatever the burden, whatever the sacrifice that duty may require.[6]

Finally, foreign policy must promote real national interests whose value is not solely determined by partisan priorities. Agenda setting may be intrinsically partisan, but policies whose partisan interest outweighs national interest are patently invalid.[7]

The creation of foreign policy, or nondomestic political objectives, also involves the formulation of strategy, which is an overall plan for the realization of corresponding policy goals and includes a justification of proposed methods and expected resources. Whereas policy is largely determined by the nation's top political leaders and their advisors, such as the president, key Pentagon and State Department officials, and other national-security and intelligence principals, strategic planning primarily involves high-level support personnel who have responsibilities for the implementation of presidential policies. Their work is augmented through the operational and tactical activities of the men and women who execute specific strategies through corresponding military and diplomatic operations. It turns policy and strategy into reality by allocating required resources and authority for actual programs, whose existence is merely hypothetical until then. Focusing on performance, execution, and service as opposed to mere concepts and ideas, operational activities enhance national-security capabilities and build infrastructural support through military campaigns, diplomatic initiatives, and the enabling congressional legislation that authorizes the mobilization of allocated resources toward the realization of foreign-policy objectives.[8]

However, it is important to remember that the political aspect of foreign policy, and the effect that it may have on public opinion among the American electorate or other nations around the globe, cannot be ignored. For example, five months into the Korean War in November 1950, the political implications of U.S. involvement were a key element in military strategy for the Truman administration, as shown in this summary of a meeting of the National Security Council (NSC), which is a key advisory group for presidents regarding foreign policy:

> Secretary [of State Dean] Acheson said there were three elements involved: (1) political; (2) intelligence; (3) military. Politically we have tried to keep the military conquest of all Korea from being a war aim. In the UN we have never allowed any resolution to require expelling the Communists from all of Korea. We also have not said that we would stay there until that objective has been achieved. Therefore, politically we are not committed to the conquest of all Korea if something short of that can be worked out which is satisfactory. . . . The Soviets would presumably like to have the U.S. involved in a general war with Communist China, which would mean that our European commitments would have to go by the board. This raises the question as to what point the U.S. will be driven to, to attack the problem at its heart, namely, Moscow, instead of handling it on the periphery as at present. General [Oliver P.] Smith pointed out that the Soviets take no risk, since they are perfectly willing to pull the rug out from under their satellite at any time and start talking peace. General Smith, however, felt that the Soviets could hardly contemplate giving up Korea and suffering a major defeat there. General Smith said that we are at the point of facing the question of either going forward or back. He suggested, however, that the political consequences of either standing pat or drawing back would be tremendous. He saw no real reason to change the previous estimate that the Soviets are not prepared themselves to bring on a general war. They would, however, like us involved in a general war in Asia.[9]

Diplomacy versus National Security

A president's foreign-policy objectives necessarily reflect two complementary but distinct concerns, diplomacy and national security, whose goals and priorities should be unified but are not always reconcilable. Ideally, one is an extension of the other, and they work together toward underlying political objectives. Whether through failure or success, diplomacy should in some way set the stage for the execution of national-security policies that follow. The negotiation, deliberation, and debate that characterize diplomacy should animate and support the strategic and tactical activities national security demands. However, despite the unification of diplomatic and national-security interests under a common foreign policy, presidents do not always successfully align those interests. Indeed, the Departments of State and Defense have frequently been at odds over the resolution of important geopolitical questions and the prioritization of specific national interests. For example, Secretary of State Colin Powell and Secretary of Defense Donald Rumsfeld did not always agree on the foreign-policy strategy of the George W. Bush administration following the

9/11 terrorist attacks in 2001, particularly the invasion of Iraq in 2003.[10] Much of his time in office, Obama fared no better in his efforts to align the policies and objectives of the Departments of State and Defense. His State Department's desire for comparatively rapid deescalation of U.S. involvement in the Middle East and Afghan conflicts and frequent sympathy for Palestinian over Israeli interests clashed with the defense establishment's advocacy of a more robust presence in both theaters and its traditional support for Israel.[11]

A prominent cause of the institutional inconsistency between diplomacy and national security is their frequently divergent goals. Theoretically, they promote unified political objectives and, therefore, support complementary policies, but one rejects war whereas the other depends on it. Diplomacy focuses on the peaceful resolution of strategic questions and the prevention of conflict, whereas national security accepts the possibility, if not the probability, of conflict and the use of military force to secure political objectives. Cold War containment policy provides a fitting example of this practical inconsistency. Although both the diplomatic and the defense establishments were committed to containment until at least Reagan's presidency, they often worked at cross purposes. For instance, during the 1970s, diplomats promoted détente, or a cooling of tensions between the United States and the Soviet Union, but the military simultaneously pursued its strategy of mutually assured destruction. Mutually assured destruction, although hardly something defense leaders wanted or anticipated, called for the total deployment of the nation's nuclear arsenal against the Soviets. Although mutually assured destruction was a deterrent, its implementation was not merely hypothetical. Another inconsistency between diplomatic and national-security objectives arises from institutional territoriality. The Departments of State and Defense may answer to the same commander in chief, but they have developed different cultures and different priorities, which has often led to friction between the two. In the context of international politics, this has manifested itself in some unusual and perhaps unexpected ways, as American presidents' diplomatic and defense teams have developed divergent goals and allegiances.[12]

PRESIDENTS AND FOREIGN POLICYMAKING

Foreign policymaking is complicated, and it involves hundreds of individuals and several institutions. At its best, it is a collaborative process that leverages the combined expertise of its participants toward effective results. At its worst, it can be a chaotic sprawl captured by petty jealousies and political hypercompetitiveness. Reality usually lies somewhere between these two extremes. Ideally, policymaking is approximated by the former, not the latter. Envisioned as a collaborative process based on the consideration of viable alternatives, its intentions are best conveyed through the so-called rational-actor model of executive decision making.

Foreign Policy and Decision Making

In a seminal study of the Kennedy administration's handling of the Cuban Missile Crisis of 1962, political scientist Graham Allison sought to create a model that could explain the nature of presidential decision making. Allison hoped not only to describe how decisions are made but also how they should be made. He argued the key to viable policymaking is rationality, which enhances both the legitimacy and the effectiveness of the process. Decisions without reflection, representative participation, or awareness of valid options are inherently flawed, as are those that arise from coercion, manipulation, or dishonesty. A mock collaboration intended to bias the process toward predetermined outcomes is irrational and, therefore, lacks merit. The identification of policy and the formulation of strategy must be a function of true collaboration and an earnest consideration of alternatives, and the final decision must optimize the public interest and support the constitutional principles at stake. Above all, the process, although headed by a president who has the ultimate power and authority to make decisions, must be sufficiently democratic to permit free competition among ideas and, thus, enable the survival of the most viable options. The president may have the constitutional right to make decisions without consultation, but the need for rationality contradicts such an approach.[13]

Despite their significance, presidents' contributions to policymaking do not necessarily arise from the kinds of circumstances Allison predicted. Far from being uniformly rational, presidential policymaking can deviate from the norm considerably. It is not always collaborative, nor is it predominantly deliberative. Presidents frequently steer toward predetermined political objectives and their decision making can be more idiosyncratic than logical, all of which precludes free choice and competition. Connection to overriding constitutional principles, although necessary in theory, is often tenuous at best, and national interest habitually takes a back seat to selfish interest. The president's personal ambitions, as well as those of his advisors, his party, influential legislators, and powerful interest groups, more than occasionally occupy center stage, while the news media exploit political differences among policymakers to feed consumer demand for conflictual stories. The result, although far from disastrous, is also far from the ideal represented by the rational-actor model.

Indeed, Allison's own research ultimately demonstrated that, under extraordinary circumstances, foreign policymaking is anything but rational. In crisis situations, pivotal decisions are usually dominated by the president or a few key advisors, and they customarily produce predetermined outcomes. An apparently collaborative effort is used to steer policymakers toward the president's favored options, and alternative choices are seldom considered seriously. During the Cuban Missile Crisis, for example, Kennedy crafted a response to Soviet deployment of nuclear weapons in Cuba through the so-called Executive Committee, through which he and his brother, Attorney General Robert Kennedy, advanced their own strategic and tactical priorities. The consensus among Kennedy's top advisors pointed in a direction the President refused to follow until he persuaded most of his detractors to change their minds. The American response to the Soviet action was ultimately successful and probably averted a nuclear war, but it was hardly rational.[14]

IN THEIR OWN WORDS

THE AFTERMATH OF THE CUBAN MISSILE CRISIS

The Cuban Missile Crisis in October 1962 is remembered as bringing the United States and the Soviet Union to the brink of nuclear war. Kennedy's determination to stand firm with Soviet premier Nikita Khrushchev about the removal of Soviet missiles from Cuba, accomplished in part through a naval blockade of any additional Soviet ships attempting to arrive in Cuba, is also remembered as a great foreign-policy accomplishment. Although Kennedy had solidified his reputation, both at home and abroad, as the "cold warrior" who would fight the spread of global communism, the actions during the Cuban Missile Crisis also had reverberating effects on other areas of U.S. foreign policy, as this November 1, 1962, memo to Kennedy from General Lauris Norstad, Supreme Allied Commander in Europe (NATO), shows:

Dear Mr. President:

The outcome of the Cuban crisis is being hailed with great enthusiasm by almost everyone over here, as you know. It is regarded as a great achievement for the West, particularly for the United States, and is considered a great success for you personally. Regardless of what it may mean in terms of the over-all interests and activities of the Soviet Union—and I have Berlin particularly in mind—you have averted an armed clash which could have grown to serious proportions, you have greatly enhanced the authority of the United States in world affairs, and you have established yourself with friend and foe alike as a strong leader at a time when strong leadership is sorely needed.

I am sure that the "tough-line" people, not recognizing that toughness is a means to an end and not an end or a policy in itself, will be saying "I told you so." It is my own firm conviction that your action in Cuba was successful because it was taken against an established background of calm firmness, moderation and restraint. With this background, your words and actions of last week stood out in such bold relief that they were thoroughly convincing.

I share the hope that this success can be exploited to achieve a lessening of tension, and believe that an early initiative along these lines could be most useful. It is on this subject that I would like to send you a few personal observations.

To permit the question of missiles in Turkey to be raised again would seem to deny the soundness of your position on the Soviet missiles in Cuba. Further, any official discussion of this subject would, in my judgment, have a serious morale effect in certain vital areas and would prove to be a most divisive issue at a time when we have achieved great unity within the Alliance. I am confident that there would be the strongest opposition, particularly on the part of the Greeks and the Turks to any consideration of the withdrawal of missiles from Turkey as a return gesture for Soviet action in Cuba.

You must have already been pressed to consider various force reduction, disengagement and denuclearization schemes, most of which have already been studied and have failed to stand up to searching analysis. As seen from here, a numerical reduction in Europe, if meaningful at all, would be disadvantageous to us because of the better geographical position of the USSR. The West would be weakened and tensions would thereby increase. Similarly, the events of the last year have served to emphasize the dangers of disengagement and of denuclearized zones, such as called for in the Rapacki Plan.

Any actions or gestures which do not have a sound military basis, or which are based upon trust rather than control, would cause great concern. Surely there can be no reductions in our military effectiveness without guarantees that at least equivalent security can be achieved by others means. In this connection,

John F. Kennedy sits at his desk in the White House on October 23, 1962, shortly after signing a presidential proclamation concerning the Cuban Missile Crisis.

you may recall that on 17 November 1961 I addressed a letter to you which outlined broadly a control and inspection plan. This plan has been discussed off and on over the last five years and I believe it has some support among our European allies. Perhaps France would continue to be cool to the proposition, and I have no basis for believing that [West German] Chancellor [Konrad] Adenauer would look more favorably to the idea today than he did in the spring of 1960. However, I believe that a strong position on the part of the United States at that time might well have persuaded the Chancellor. In the present circumstances, the weight of your judgment might be decisive. I realize that this control and inspection plan is not as comprehensive as some of the broad package proposals that have been considered in the past. However, it is simple enough to be workable and clear enough to have an impact on the public. Since there has been a certain amount of NATO support for this idea in the past, perhaps it could be introduced into the North Atlantic Council as a starting point for discussion, or as one of several ideas to be considered by that body.

Faithfully yours,
LAURIS NORSTAD
General USAF[15]

Similarly, George W. Bush's Middle East policy after 9/11 was anything but rational. The available evidence indicates that Bush came to Washington with the desire to reshape geopolitical dynamics in the Middle East and, if possible, to complete the destruction of the Iraqi regime begun by his father ten years earlier. After the terrorist acts of 9/11, Bush, Vice President Dick Cheney, and Rumsfeld advocated a strategy that called for the democratization of rogue states through the invasion of Iraq and the pursuit of terrorist networks throughout the region. The administration short-circuited serious deliberations and scuttled the consideration of alternatives so it could press for the adoption of its foreign-policy goals, which were eventually accepted by a Congress reluctant to make difficult decisions and more than willing to pass them on to the President. In addition, the public, smarting from the first attacks on American soil since 1941 and eager for revenge, posed few obstacles to the realization of Bush's objectives.[16]

Obama, although seemingly cool-headed and deliberative, was no more successful than his predecessor in making decisions. With considerable pushback from a Republican Congress at odds with his policy priorities and a belief among Republicans that Obama was soft on rogue regimes and America's adversaries, Obama was loath to discuss his policies with all but a few of his most trusted advisors. Unfortunately, problems were exacerbated by a lack of coordination between the State Department and the White House. To his credit, Obama entered office with ambitious goals, which included disarmament, resolution of key geopolitical conflicts, and the reduction of America's military footprint. He was awarded the Nobel Peace Prize early in his presidency for these considerable goals and for his rejection of Bush administration policies that rubbed many the wrong way. In the end, however, reality proved less kind, which increasingly compelled the president and his closest advisors to bypass customary channels and procedures of foreign policymaking. Obama was successful in achieving some of his policy goals, but this happened despite the lack of "rationality," deliberation, and consideration of all but a handful of alternatives.[17]

The Political Agenda

Whether presidents ultimately uphold the principles and ideas touted during their campaigns, they are nonetheless guided by an overriding and evolving set of priorities that reflect their beliefs and interests as well as those of their key supporters and advisors. Unique geopolitical circumstances or inherited foreign-policy dilemmas can cause presidents to abandon specific parts of their agendas (such as the closing of Guantanamo Bay), at least temporarily, for example, Obama, in his handling of the War on Terror, but presidential policy agendas militate against the kind of rationality scholars would like to see. This does not make the policymaking process illegitimate simply because it is structurally skewed toward political and partisan interests that prevent the complete and open consideration of all ideas. It merely confirms that, in the real world, limits to strict rationality of decision making do and must exist.

Yet, history has also demonstrated that even in emergencies, executive policymaking is not unilateral. For many reasons, among them efficiency and efficacy, decision-making processes during crises are abbreviated and confined, but presidents still rely on the advice and input of key advisors. George W. Bush may have isolated himself from normal decision-making channels during the aftermath of 9/11, but he continued to depend on deliberation among his principal foreign-policy officials, whose contribution was essential. Although critics and skeptics often had limited access to the President and the policymaking process, decisions neverthe-less reflected a consensus among those advisors closest to Bush. Admittedly, some presidents have viewed policymaking, even in national-security matters, as a more collaborative process, as was the case with Jimmy Carter and Ronald Reagan, but ultimately presidents have borne the responsibility for the nation's foreign policies and particularly for decisions made during crisis situations.[18]

Foreign policymaking in the United States, whether rational or not, is con-strained by standards of accountability that do not exist in authoritarian regimes or even many other democratic governments, for that matter. American presidents and their foreign-policy teams are accountable to the public, and their decisions must be defensible and at least seemingly rational to maintain public approval. However, foreign-policy issues are often complex and not easily summarized by the news media, which is the prime source of information on which American citizens form their opin-ions on the job the president is doing. The frustration that presidents often experience with news media coverage of foreign-policy matters, as articulated to Kennedy by a top advisor in 1962, has been a recurring theme in most administrations:

> One of the most critical problems facing this Administration in the field of foreign policy is the great and growing gap between the harsh, complex realities with which Washington policymakers must grapple and the generally limited understanding of these realities by most Americans, including the press and Congress. This gap is already dangerous. Unless it can be narrowed you may find it increasingly dif-ficult to take many actions in the conduct of foreign policy that are essential to our national security. Our media of mass communication carry a large measure of responsibility for this situation. Many reporters and editorial writers fail to do their homework and are therefore unable to place the news in perspective or in balance. Many radio and television announcers treat even the most sober world events as "flashes" to be presented in the excited tones of the latest sports bulletin. However, it is not enough for us in government to blame the least responsible of our TV and newsmen or even to point to the failure of our educational system to give even "well educated" Americans an adequate grounding in history and economics. A major share of the responsibility for the information gap lies, in my opinion, in our failure to explain the basis for our policies and to broaden public understanding of the forces with which we must cope. Although more television presentations by you could be helpful, the principal burden rests on our ability to improve and expand our own informational and educational work and to per-suade private institutions and foundations to greatly increase their assistance.[19]

Frustration with the news media notwithstanding, first-term presidents always make decisions, even those made in crisis situations, with an eye to the electorate, and they cannot afford to pursue policies that will consistently alienate potential voters. Some unpopular decisions can be explained as manifestations of urgent na-tional interest, but first-term presidents are not able to ignore or deemphasize public opinion too often if they wish to be reelected. Second-term presidents, in contrast, al-though ostensibly freed from a direct dependence on voter approval, are customarily too worried about their legacies or the needs of their party to depart radically from campaign promises and public expectations, so the likelihood of consistent unilateral action that contravenes public approval is extremely unlikely. In the end, although the public may not always be rational in the casual sense of the word, its input guarantees the ultimate rationality of the policymaking process in the United States.

Furthermore, the formulation and implementation of foreign policy is collaborative—not unilateral. The president's constitutional roles as commander in chief and chief executive officer confer ultimate responsibility for policymaking on him, and he has the authority and power to curtail deliberation and make final decisions. Yet, even in the extreme, those decisions reflect the input and influence of numerous advisors and other officials, as well as those outside government. Unlike heads of state in many other countries, especially authoritarian regimes, presidents are not insular because the presidency is not insular. The presidency functions effectively only if the bureaucracy within which it is embedded works to support it; American presidents are accountable and beholden to too many people, constituents and advisors alike, and their duties are far too complex to be able to make unilateral decisions without a collaborative and cooperative network of key institutions and personnel.[20]

Domestic Actors

In one way or another, foreign policy always begins and ends with the president, even if his ideas do not always initiate the process, but the nuts and bolts of policymaking are in the hands of a small group of trusted aides who act as both advisors and gatekeepers, managing access to key personnel, acting as liaisons between the White House and other participants, and delegating various tasks. Department heads, such as the secretaries of state and defense, plus the national security advisor, the Central Intelligence Agency (CIA) director, and other key agency leaders, are crucial participants, but they are not always part of the president's inner circle. George W. Bush's administration was unusual in this regard, as Rumsfeld, Cheney, and National Security Advisor Condoleezza Rice had prominent roles during the first term as primary policymakers and had the ear of the President. Yet, most presidents, like Reagan and Clinton, have relied on a cadre of trusted aides, if not personal friends, for ideas and advice about key foreign-policy objectives. Obama, who did not have a personal relationship with some of his principal cabinet secretaries, also turned to close friends and colleagues for advice and counsel. Valerie Jarrett, a friend from his days in Chicago and a special assistant to the president, was perhaps the most important of these. Aside from the obvious players, various groups and individuals within the Executive Office of the President and support staffs from relevant departments and agencies are critical for the formulation of foreign policy. They often serve as the real workhorses, doing the heavy lifting during policymaking by compiling data, performing analyses, preparing strategy, providing expertise, and fulfilling any number of related jobs assigned to them by the president or his staff.[21]

The significance of foreign-policy issues, as well as the importance of having staff in place to aid the president in the decision-making process, becomes apparent to every president as soon as he takes office, if not before. For example, in December 1960, Kennedy met with Dwight Eisenhower to discuss the responsibilities of the job, as summarized in a memo by Eisenhower's press secretary, James Hagerty:

> The President started the conversation by saying that one of the by-products of the meeting was that he finally could understand why the Senator had won the election.... Once they were alone in the President's office they discussed at length the problems confronting the President now and in the future. These included

specifically—Berlin, Cuba and the Communist activities in South America emanating from Cuba; the Far East, particularly the problems created in that area by Communist China and Formosa; African problems, particularly the Congo; the problem [French President Charles] De Gaulle has with Algeria; disarmament and nuclear test negotiations with the USSR; and the balance of payments problem and the need to maintain confidence in the United States dollar. In connection with this last point, the question of redeployment of United States troops in Europe was also raised by the President. . . . He said that he went over with Senator Kennedy in great detail the workings of the National Security Council and the Operations Coordinating Board. He said that at first Senator Kennedy did not seem to understand the set-up and seemed to think that the National Security Council made final recommendations in the Security field. The President, however, explained that the Council acts only in an advisory position and that while they can present position papers and give suggestions, they are only an advisory group to the President and that the President, and only the President, has to make the ultimate decision. The President explained to Senator Kennedy that many times these National Security Council recommendations did not involve matters where the President had to make an immediate decision and that the President therefore would have some time to mull over the recommendations, study their effects on our allies, the neutral world, and the Communist world before taking the final step. . . . The President said he had a feeling as he was explaining these matters that the Senator began to realize the magnitude of the responsibility that would rest on his shoulders after January 20th.[22]

Presidential leadership

Without a doubt, the president is the central figure in the policymaking process, but his involvement will vary based on circumstance and leadership style. Crisis situations require a more hands-on approach than would otherwise be necessary, as do certain issues that are of interest to the president, but leadership style is the determining factor with respect to his level of participation and, when it comes to military action, in the decision to intervene.[23] Some presidents, such as Eisenhower, Reagan, and perhaps George W. Bush, were relatively uninvolved in the policy formulation process itself, concentrating on the broadest strokes by identifying the fundamental ideals of foreign policy but delegating practically all subsequent tasks to others. Many have debated whether Reagan's hands-off management style was a result of a growing lack of interest in the nuts and bolts of politics, although he displayed a consistent approach throughout his political career. Bush, in contrast, was accused of surrendering too much power to Cheney and thereby losing rather than actively delegating authority; the evidence suggests that Bush maintained broad control over foreign policy but remained aloof from its day-to-day management because of a lack of interest in the procedural aspects of policymaking. This type of approach has both advantages and disadvantages: it increases efficiency and promotes a division and specialization of labor within bureaucratic environments, but it can also undermine accountability and institutional cohesion, as evidenced by the Iran–Contra scandal during the late 1980s.

On the other end of the spectrum, presidents as different as Carter, George H. W. Bush, and Clinton were intimately involved at almost every level of policymaking, exerting much tighter control and influence over foreign policy, especially from a day-to-day perspective. In Carter's case, this often produced institutional paralysis because the President's micromanagement of even the most insignificant matters inhibited productivity and efficiency and created bureaucratic gridlock that undermined the resolution of key issues. Clinton frequently suffered from the same problem, but his administration was nonetheless much more effective than Carter's. A big part of the reason for this was that, despite Clinton's reluctance to delegate and his unwillingness to distance himself from any aspect of policymaking, he was one of the most gifted and capable politicians ever to occupy the White House and was surrounded by a relatively skilled and informed cadre of advisors. In addition, because Clinton was inherently more interested in domestic policy, he was not nearly as involved in, or preoccupied with, foreign policy, so his participation in the formulation of many foreign policies was limited to the role of architect. Clinton came to the White House with an ambitious domestic-policy agenda, and at times, he viewed foreign policy as a distraction from his more essential domestic priorities. Per White House staffers, Clinton knew "domestic policy, the fine print and the philosophy better than anyone. He has spent his public life not only thinking about domestic policy, but thinking about how best to express it. He has fewer preconceived notions about foreign policy."[24]

Categorization of Obama's foreign-policy decision making per the above alternatives is more complicated because his management style was a unique combination of both, at times aloof and at others involved to the point of being unable, or unwilling, to delegate authority. With issues that attracted his attention more than

Israeli Prime Minister Yitzhak Rabin and Palestine Liberation Organization leader Yasser Arafat shake hands on the "Declaration of Principles" for peace between the Arabs and Israelis brokered by Bill Clinton in 1993.

others, particularly those about which he was passionate, Obama led from the bully pulpit and set the agenda for his diplomatic team. Nuclear disarmament, the environment, climate change, free trade, negotiations with Iran, and relations with Cuba are just a few examples. Even in these areas, however, success could be limited because of a lack of coordination between the White House and Obama's secretaries of state and defense.[25]

National Security Council

The NSC includes the president's senior national security advisors and cabinet officials. Created during the Truman administration with passage of the National Security Act of 1947 (and placed in the Executive Office of the President in 1949), the NSC's primary responsibility is to advise and assist the president on national-security and foreign-policy matters. The NSC is chaired by the president, and meetings are regularly attended by the vice president, the secretary of state, the secretary of the Treasury, the secretary of defense, the assistant to the president for national-security affairs, the chairman of the Joint Chiefs of Staff, and the director of national intelligence. Other White House officials, such as the chief of staff, counsel to the president, the assistant to the president for economic policy, the attorney general, the director of the Office of Management and Budget, or other cabinet secretaries, may also attend. From its inception during the Truman administration, the NSC has served as an important venue for the development of a president's foreign-policy objectives. For example, on June 29, 1950, just four days after North Korea had invaded the Republic of South Korea, the NSC held a meeting at which the following issues were discussed:

- Reviewed the situation in Korea.
- Noted the President's directive that the Council resurvey all policies affecting the entire perimeter of the USSR.
- Agreed that the Council should prepare for consideration by the President recommendations as to the courses of action to be followed in the event that Soviet forces enter Korean hostilities.
- Noted the President's agreement with a suggestion by the Secretary of State that the Department of Defense should prepare for the information of the Council a review of our military capabilities in order to indicate the extent of our freedom of choice.
- Noted Mr. [Averell] Harriman's remarks that the Europeans, though they had grave concern prior to the President's announcement that the United States would not meet the challenge, felt great relief afterwards although they were fully aware of the implications of the statement.
- Noted the President's desire that the British offer of naval assistance, when officially received, be accepted; and that the Vice President, when advised by the Secretary of State of the exact nature of the offer, should inform the appropriate Senators.
- Noted the remarks by the Secretary of the Treasury that a reappraisal of the Treasury situation had been underway since January and was ready, subject to sharpening up, for specific application; and that the Treasury Department had been working closely with the National Security Board in this connection.

- Noted the President's view that the sources of supply in North Korea should be kept under consideration, but that no U.S. attacks should be made across the 38th parallel under current orders.
- Noted that special attention will be devoted to obtaining intelligence concerning clear evidence of Soviet participation in Korean hostilities, and concerning Soviet activities in the vicinity of Yugoslavia and Northern Iran.[26]

Advisors

After the president and the NSC, the most significant players in the policymaking process are a handful of close aides, or confidants, whose role as advisors and gatekeepers is critical for the successful formulation of foreign policy. The president customarily consults them first regarding relevant issues and relies on them to manage and coordinate the information and organizational dynamics within his foreign-policy team. Their input is crucial, and their contributions can often exceed their nominal authority because they are among the most trusted of the president's staff. Frequently, this inner circle of advisors does not include top cabinet officers or agency officials, but individuals who have developed close personal ties to the president himself. Probably the best recent example of this was Reagan, whose reliance, particularly with respect to domestic policy, on a core group of informal advisors and political supporters was considerable. In addition, Reagan moved trusted allies such as Caspar Weinberger and William Casey into key high-level positions (secretary of defense and CIA director, respectively) based more on loyalty and service to him and the Republican Party than on specific subject-matter expertise, which ensured that, beyond his inner circle, the President would be surrounded by a dependable and trustworthy foreign-policy team. Unlike Reagan and Clinton, George W. Bush relied primarily on his principal cabinet officers for primary input regarding foreign policy, and he was unusually close to Cheney, Rumsfeld, and Rice, who eclipsed all but Rove, the president's political strategist, in terms of political clout in the White House.[27] Like Reagan, Obama had a close circle of advisors that he trusted implicitly, to the point that he even elicited foreign-policy advice from those whose specialty was domestic issues.[28]

The Cabinet

The president and his inner circle of advisors are crucial to the policymaking process, but the institutional infrastructure beyond them is essential, and the pursuit of America's foreign policies would be impossible without it. Aside from the presidency itself, the most critical foreign-policy institutions are the Departments of State and Defense, which are primarily responsible for diplomacy and national security, respectively. The State Department is one of the three original cabinet offices and, under the authority of the president, it plans, coordinates, and mobilizes practically all diplomatic activity within and without the United States. Through a vast staff that includes the secretary of state, undersecretaries, numerous ambassadors, teams of emissaries and other diplomats, and thousands of support personnel, the State Department manages a complex array of international relationships and promotes U.S. strategic, political, and economic interests throughout the globe. Its activities, especially in the economic realm, are occasionally supplemented through related efforts by, for example, the Departments of Commerce and Energy or the Office of the U.S. Trade Representative, but it is the principal organ responsible for U.S. diplomatic initiatives.[29]

The other key foreign-policy institution is the Department of Defense, which, unlike the Department of State, is one of the newer members of the president's cabinet. Created shortly after the end of World War II through the National Security Act of 1947, it is the national-security arm of the U.S. government. Headed by the secretary of defense, it comprises civilian leadership such as the secretaries of the Navy, Army, and Air Force, the military's top brass, including the joint chiefs of staff, intelligence officials, tens of thousands of support personnel, and the nation's armed forces. The Department of Defense is responsible for the planning and execution of operational strategies intended to secure American diplomatic objectives. As such, its role as a policymaker is, at least theoretically, subordinate to that of the State Department, since its task is the realization, and not the formulation, of political objectives, but its influence over certain administrations, especially during the Cold War, was at times pervasive.[30]

In addition, the Department of Homeland Security (DHS) coordinates efforts against internal threats to Americans, whether from domestic or foreign sources. In some ways, it can be envisioned as the domestic counterpart to the Defense Department, but its actual authority and resources are limited, and its ability to implement policy is heavily dependent on other institutions. Viewed by many as a superfluous part of a bloated national-security infrastructure, it was founded in the wake of the 9/11 attacks, when the country's civilian leadership faced tremendous pressure to indemnify the nation from future terrorist incursions, but its boundaries have never been properly defined, nor have its resources and capabilities. Aside from its primary duties to prevent (if possible), prepare for, and respond to attacks against the United States and its protectorates, DHS is charged with addressing natural disasters and manmade emergencies, such as oil spills, nuclear contamination, and other domestic accidents. Beyond that, its responsibilities include customs and immigration, air safety through agencies such as the Transportation Security Administration, maritime security, and the protection of natural resources.[31]

Intelligence agencies

America's national-security and diplomatic capabilities also depend on a network of intelligence resources whose duties include the accumulation and analysis of relevant information and knowledge regarding foreign governments, organizations, and individuals. The most visible is the CIA, which is an independent agency that reports directly to the president and his staff through the director of national intelligence. Like the Department of Defense, the CIA was established through the National Security Act of 1947 as an acknowledgment of America's changing national-security needs and priorities during the early stages of the Cold War. Envisioned as a clearinghouse of information on American diplomatic targets and concerns throughout the world that would provide actionable analysis of data gathered through a variety of sources, including espionage, the CIA has supported the country's diplomatic and military efforts during the past several decades. Like the Departments of State and Defense, it has developed its own priorities and allegiances over the years and has never been a mere conduit of information or unbiased participant. Its tendency to view intelligence as a precursor to enforcement or military activity has often created friction with the State Department and promotes alliances with key defense personnel, but it has also pushed its own geopolitical agendas.

The CIA exists alongside other intelligence agencies, both within and without specific executive departments, and perhaps the most notable of these is the National Security Agency (NSA), which is part of the Department of Defense. The NSA is a product of the Cold War, created by Truman on the recommendation of the CIA in 1951 to improve eavesdropping capabilities and protect the transmission of intelligence among American assets. Leveraging some of the most sophisticated technology on the planet, the NSA coordinates the nation's electronic espionage, decryption, and encryption efforts. Because of its vast resources and capabilities, it has been a constant target of antigovernment criticism by both civil libertarians and various reactionary organizations, such as the many independent militias that have arisen in recent decades. Nonetheless, presidents have depended on its capabilities to maintain U.S. security.[32]

Congress

The previously mentioned institutions are indispensable players in foreign policymaking, and at some point, legislators also become involved in the process. In most cases, presidents or their aides consult selected congressional leaders, which can include the Speaker of the House, majority or minority leaders of either chamber, heads or ranking members of pertinent committees, and other prominent representatives or senators. Congressional support for presidential policies is indispensable, because lawmakers can stall, derail, or alter intended legislation and undermine presidential agendas altogether. The president's duties as commander in chief under the vesting clause in Article II and his emergency powers, to say nothing of his authority to make war under the War Powers Resolution, have offered recent administrations ample opportunities to delay or even prevent congressional involvement, but Congress eventually does become involved.

Researching the Presidency

Presidential Accountability

Although Congress has the constitutional authority to declare war, presidents, in their role as commander in chief, can make war. This was a basic distinction that generated much debate among the framers at the Constitutional Convention, and it is an area of research that continues to generate much attention from those who study the presidency. Of interest in recent years has been the role of Congress as a constitutional check against presidents in "wars of choice." Per Bruce Buchanan, a war of choice is a conflict "initiated by presidents against nations that had not attacked the United States but conflicts that were portrayed as both necessary and urgent nonetheless."[33] Specifically, the Korean, Vietnam, and Iraq wars are examples where presidents needed more constitutional accountability. Congress, which provides minimal vetting and oversight as presidents make the decision to initiate war, contributes to a "tradition of failure" because presidents are left "unsupervised at the moment of choice."[34] Douglas L. Kriner's research looks beyond the initial decision by a president to go to war and considers the political conflict between the president and Congress as military action continues. Congress can play a role through indirect influence, whether shaping public opinion or sending a signal about disunity if Congress is not completely on board with the president's plan of action. For example, regarding the Iraq War, George W. Bush took issue with Congress in 2007 for playing any role other than funding the troops. According to Kriner, "Bush's protestations remind us that sometimes the legislature does rise up, engage the military policymaking process, and attempt to reassert its constitutional prerogatives in deciding whether a military venture is 'continued' or 'concluded.'"[35] Although congressional influence over war-making may be limited and situational (depending on factors such as the president's approval rating or the state of the economy, etc.), Kriner concludes that this area of inquiry deserves much greater attention from presidency scholars to develop a clearer picture of the presidential decision—and whether Congress has any say—in the use of military force.

Interest groups

Beyond the executive and legislative branches, various interest groups and campaign contributors can have a disproportionate effect on national politics. Interest groups represent virtually every cause and idea and seem to include anyone with a political agenda, which includes the numerous groups that have a stake in the various American diplomatic and military initiatives. Lobbies are a political conduit for everyone with an axe to grind, enabling certain constituencies to exert political pressure that far outweighs their number. Perhaps the most visible and influential among foreign-policy groups is the American Israel Public Affairs Committee, but countless other interests are represented among foreign-policy lobbyists. These groups comprise virtually everyone and everything that relies on the promotion of American diplomatic and strategic priorities, such as oil and gas, mining, weapons manufacturing, agriculture, and labor unions.[36]

International Actors

Although American foreign policy is a function of national priorities identified and pursued by U.S. policymakers, it is also a product of various exogenous factors that transcend national interests and domestic political institutions. Prominent among these is the geopolitical development of relevant global theaters and the international political environments in which American diplomatic and military personnel pursue the nation's foreign-policy objectives. Those environments are shaped by many influences, not the least of which are the regional and global alliances to which the United States belongs. U.S. foreign policy may be an extension of national ideals and political objectives, but it necessarily reflects the needs and desires of the country's strategic and economic partners as well. Most important, American foreign policy must address the unified international objectives identified through its treaty obligations around the globe.

North Atlantic Treaty Organization

The preeminent alliance, military or otherwise, to which the United States belongs is the North Atlantic Treaty Organization (NATO), which has been the core of anticommunist and, more generally, antiauthoritarian defense efforts among the United States and its Western allies for decades. A product of the Cold War, its original purpose was aptly summarized by a British official who claimed that NATO existed to keep the United States in, the Soviet Union out, and Germany down. Such a characterization may be an anachronism in a post-Soviet world no longer animated by customary East–West polarities, but NATO was indeed established as a bulwark against Soviet expansionism in Europe and a guarantee against German military resurgence. Since the fall of the Soviet Union and its communist satellite states, NATO's mission and direction have been thrown into question, and its role in the geopolitical evolution of twenty-first-century Europe is not clear, nor is its ultimate relevance in a global diplomatic theater that has transcended and redefined traditional relationships.[37]

Following the last round of enlargements in 2009, NATO now comprises 28 states from Europe and North America. Its headquarters is in Brussels, Belgium, and its membership has grown considerably over the past decade. Contrary to what had been the case for most of its history, NATO now includes members from eastern and central Europe and is no longer an exclusive club for the United States, Canada, and their Western European allies. Principal political authority lies with the North Atlantic Council, which is a deliberative decision-making body that acts through consensus instead of voting, thereby ensuring unity of purpose and strategic coordination for NATO initiatives. NATO is led by the secretary general, who, as the head of the North Atlantic Council, represents NATO in dealings with states and other international organizations. The alliance's political structure is complemented by a unified military command, which is controlled by American military personnel but supported by a staff that represents all member countries.

Despite NATO's obvious political role, it is first a military alliance. NATO exists to protect its members from attack by common enemies and to ensure the physical integrity of its territories. It has maintained its Atlantic focus by preserving a fundamental tie between North America and Europe, but the European part of the alliance has shifted its locus of activity eastward. By admitting former Warsaw Pact countries and Soviet republics to its ranks, NATO has undermined some of the cultural and geographic solidarity that characterized the pre-1999 alliance, but that has allowed the alliance to expand beyond the strategic limits imposed on it by the Cold War. Moreover, NATO has become involved in non-European military theaters, such as Afghanistan, that are nonetheless central to European and American strategic interests, and the organization has developed a greater appreciation for diplomacy and predeployment capabilities. Some believe that NATO's continued viability lies in its readiness, willingness, and ability to morph from a military alliance into a largely diplomatic one.[38]

During the Cold War, NATO policy was driven by U.S. foreign policy, and aside from occasional resistance from the French government and other left-leaning regimes, NATO's geopolitical agenda was a function of American diplomatic and military objectives. NATO's needs and priorities influenced U.S. foreign policy, yet mostly to the extent that American political and military leaders recognized the alliance's value as an instrument of Cold War anticommunist policies and strategic initiatives. Since 1991, neither the relationship between NATO and the United States nor the geopolitical dominance of the United States has been as clear, so NATO has gradually exerted a more independent influence over American foreign policy. Furthermore, as the political and economic integration of Europe has grown through the European Union, the European Union has increasingly served as both a counterweight and an alternative to NATO, which has translated into greater pressure on U.S. policymakers to acknowledge European priorities.[39]

Other international organizations

NATO is not the only international organization that plays a role in the formulation of U.S. foreign policy, but it is by far the most significant. As a member of the United Nations and, for example, the Organization of American States, the United States must honor certain commitments that inevitably shape its interaction with participating states, but these other organizations lack NATO's targeted purpose and specific utility. The Organization of American States is essentially a toothless body that represents a historically recurring, yet continuously failed, attempt to unify the nations of South and North America, and it has never been able to bridge the ideological and constitutional differences within its diverse membership. Latin American countries have frequently viewed the United States not as a partner but as a rival, if not an enemy, and their ability and willingness to cooperate have been undermined by socialist and interventionist policies that contradict U.S. values and political ideals. The United Nations, in contrast, although it is broader and more powerful than the Organization of American States, suffers from many of the same problems, and its role as a unified and purposeful policymaker has been limited to no more than a handful of universally acknowledged global crises. The Security Council, its main policy-setting body, often acts to address major geopolitical problems, but it nonetheless lacks the resolve, enforcement capabilities, and practical resources to make a sustained impact on U.S. foreign policy.[40]

U.S. allies

Arguably the most influential international players in U.S. foreign policy, even more so than NATO, are the country's closest allies, such as Great Britain, Canada, Israel, and, to a lesser extent, Germany, Japan, and South Korea. The U.S. relationship with Britain stands out and historically has been the most significant, the American Revolution and War of 1812 notwithstanding. It has been characterized as "the special relationship," not only because of the obvious cultural and historical ties that bind the two countries but also because of the close alignment between U.S. and British foreign-policy objectives. Within NATO itself, the British have been staunchly Atlantic, resisting the growing continentalist pull and occasional anti-Americanism of its European neighbors across the channel, and have been the most consistent defenders of U.S. priorities among American allies. Therefore, British wishes and needs have always had a strong impact on the formulation of U.S. foreign policy, and British leaders are regularly consulted on key strategic decisions, although Obama's foreign-policy team was not as close to its British counterparts as its predecessors had been.[41]

Like Britain, Israel has been an extremely important ally for the United States, and its significance has at times even eclipsed that of Great Britain, but, once again, the relationship with Israel was under strain during the Obama years. Despite the ideological and cultural affinities between the United States and Great Britain,

Israel's strategic value, especially during the Cold War, has been unsurpassed. Since the late 1940s, Israeli stability and strategic integrity have been key objectives of U.S. foreign policy in the Middle East, yet Obama's greater accommodation of Palestinian priorities and decreased tolerance of Israel's assertive self-defense posture produced tension between two allies. Admittedly, Obama is not the first U.S. president to question the wisdom of Israeli defense and negotiating strategies with respect to the Palestinians, as evidenced by Clinton and, even more so, Carter. Because of unrest and uncertainty in the broader Middle East, particularly the Arab revolts that began in 2011, tensions continued between Israel and the United States throughout Obama's time in office, although Donald Trump promised to reaffirm U.S. commitment to Israel even before he took the oath of office in January 2017.[42]

Another important ally is Canada, a founding member of NATO and part of the North American Aerospace Command, which is a joint organization responsible for air defense in Canada and the United States. Its security is closely linked to that of the United States, and the territorial integrity of the North American continent depends on continued cooperation between the two countries. Their mutual affinities are occasionally overshadowed by other issues, such as differences regarding environmental policy, but the U.S. relationship with Canada is likely its most important strategic asset. With a military strength of only 65,000 troops and a population roughly equal to that of California, Canada may not be a geopolitical juggernaut, but its support is indispensable to the United States, particularly because of the political instability that has plagued Latin America. In addition, the obvious cultural ties and similarities, along with historical links and geographical proximity, make Canada a more natural strategic partner than any other country. Just as important, after some friction between Obama and former Canadian prime minister Stephen Harper, the election of the Liberal Party's Justin Trudeau in 2015 brought renewed trust and vigor to the relationship between the United States and Canada.[43]

Whereas the partnerships with Canada, Britain, and Israel arose out of cooperation and mutual interest, those with Germany and Japan were consequences of conquest, which makes them fundamentally different. In both countries, U.S. occupation and temporary military administration evolved into caretaker relationships driven by American strategic interests, although not as much today. The purpose of the initial U.S. involvement was to prevent the remilitarization of Germany and Japan following World War II and thereby promote peace, democratic governance, and geopolitical stability in their respective regions. For the bulk of the postwar period, the United States, supplemented by NATO in Germany's case, provided military defense for both countries and, thus, maintained a substantial troop presence. During the past two decades, both relationships have become strained, as domestic politics and nationalist sympathies in Germany and Japan have fueled resentment against the United States. Both countries, especially Germany, have also improved their own self-defense capabilities and reassessed postwar constitutional military restrictions, which has further militated against a continuation of the status quo ante concerning their ties with the United States.[44] However, Japan, under the leadership of Prime Minister Shinzo Abe, has gradually improved its diplomatic and military relationship with the United States. As with South Korea, another key U.S. ally in Asia, Japan has sought to protect itself from the geopolitically assertive and apparently expansionary policies of China's Xi Jinping, general secretary of the Communist Party and the country's president. Many view Xi as perhaps the most authoritarian and aggressive leader since Mao Zedong, who poses a tangible long-term danger to peace and stability in the region. North Korea's despotic regime under Kim Jong-un, whose dedication to making the rogue state a global nuclear threat, and the Philippines Rodrigo Duterte's diplomatic and military shift away from the United States and its allies added to Japan's and South Korea's worries. Despite any differences between the United States and its allies in East Asia, both Japan and South Korea realize that close ties with the United States are crucial.

THE EVOLUTION OF U.S. FOREIGN POLICY

The inability to formulate or coordinate foreign policy was one of the main deficiencies of the Confederation government of the 1780s and, thus, a principal reason for the creation of the presidency by the framers of the Constitution. Given the narrow authority of the early presidency, particularly in domestic affairs, foreign policy stood out as one of the key responsibilities of the nation's first several presidents. In addition, although the new nation did not have a large standing army by any means, its defense was a top priority, and security issues were of paramount importance. No American wanted the recently created republic to perish because of an inability to defend itself, so its presidents were immediately aware of the need to craft effective foreign policies that would preserve and adequately protect the United States. Few people questioned the significance of foreign policy and the president's ability to control it, especially after the ineffectiveness of the Confederation government.

The Early Republic through World War I

The newly created republic had a pressing international agenda. Threats to its existence were apparent immediately, and the United States was confronted with a slew of international issues that required appropriate attention. One of the biggest problems was a lack of international credibility of an established player, so rivals were eager to test the young nation's resolve. The major European empires resumed their pursuit of key objectives on the North American continent, hoping to secure long-sought territories that surrounded the United States. Britain, France, and Spain, to say nothing of Mexico and the various Indian tribes, all had good reason to provoke the United States, particularly since American gains on the continent had come at their expense. Troubles with France nearly produced a war during John Adams's presidency, and unresolved disputes with Great Britain led to an actual war in 1812, as did border controversies with Mexico in 1846. Indian tribes were handled with special brutality and determination as American troops drove them beyond the frontier.[45]

Still, during the nineteenth century, U.S. foreign policy looked inward, not outward. For at least the first 100 years, U.S. presidents followed a policy of strict neutrality and isolation from European geopolitical developments. Determined to steer clear of the debilitating international entanglements that plagued European powers, U.S. policymakers focused on the North American continent. Foreign policy was driven by an insatiable craving for land and the desire to secure the country's borders. Nothing stood in the way of a continuous acquisition of territory and the creation of a continental buffer that would protect the United States from potential adversaries. The promise of vast riches through the exploitation of minerals and the control of other natural resources lured thousands across the frontier and justified any means necessary to tame the wilderness and expand America's boundaries. One of the earliest acquisitions was the Louisiana Purchase of 1803, which more than doubled the total square mileage of the United States and stretched its boundary to the Mississippi River. Despite doubts about Thomas Jefferson's constitutional authority to negotiate a deal of this sort, the Senate approved the treaty and endorsed the growth of presidential power in this arena. Although the presidency's constitutional role as the caretaker of American territorial expansion was questionable, U.S. presidents eagerly accepted this responsibility.[46]

In the 1820s, as executive confidence in its powers as head of state seemed to grow, James Monroe extended U.S. foreign policy beyond traditional limits by issuing what has become known as the Monroe Doctrine. As much a warning to European empires to stay out of Latin America as a notice to those south of the border that a new international power had arrived, Monroe's declaration drastically increased the scope of U.S. authority abroad, at least on paper. Monroe's international pretense notwithstanding, the primary focus of American expansionism was not south of the border but west of the Mississippi River, where settlers from all backgrounds looked for opportunity and adventure. Within a few decades, Americans became convinced that the control of all lands as far west as the Pacific Ocean was the country's "manifest destiny," and they pursued this goal with a drive that has rarely been witnessed since. A term coined by a patriotic journalist and appropriated by supporters of James Polk during the 1840s to justify the annexation of Texas, California, and other parts of the continent west of the Mississippi, manifest destiny was the justification for territorial gains at any price. By the 1850s, except for Alaska and Hawaii, the United States had acquired most of the land it now controls.[47]

Following the Civil War, the conquest of the North American continent and fulfillment of its manifest destiny eventually turned the nation's attention outward. Seeking markets abroad and eager to enhance its strategic leverage, America looked to the world stage for opportunities. The latter part of the nineteenth century brought with it a gradual but notable change in presidential authority. Although there were many causes, the two most immediate were the Civil War and the closing of the American frontier. With the creation of a formidable administrative machinery to prosecute the war against the South, the federal executive established constitutional precedents during the Civil War that William McKinley, Theodore Roosevelt, and Woodrow Wilson would later use to justify the promotion of American strategic assets abroad. By the end of the nineteenth century, American presidents wielded more authority as heads of state than any of their early predecessors, and they eagerly promoted American military and diplomatic interests outside the North American continent. The closing of the frontier went together with the nation's new military and diplomatic interests, since America's rapidly industrializing economy needed markets for its products.[48]

In 1898, William McKinley manufactured a war with Spain, which resulted in the American acquisition of Cuba, Puerto Rico, and the Philippines. McKinley used the press to promote the administration's international objectives and to popularize an assertive foreign policy that announced America's arrival as an international power. His vice president, Theodore Roosevelt, who became president in 1901 after McKinley's assassination, was even more enthusiastic about the country's newfound international status. Relying on his clout to act as a power broker in Asia and Latin America, he eagerly pushed America's economic and strategic interests wherever possible. Yet, it was one of the country's most unlikely heroes that secured a permanent role for the United States as a world power. Woodrow Wilson, despite an admitted aversion to imperialism and foreign intervention, laid the groundwork for future American global domination. Military incursions into Latin America to protect local populations and U.S. property interests only led to the replacement of foreign rule by American control, and involvement in World War I, although it was based on Wilson's goal of self-determination for liberated colonies, simply ensured American financial and military ascendancy in the West.[49]

World War II and the Cold War

U.S. domination arose from the aftermath of two world wars that obliterated parts of the civilized world and relegated others to political oblivion. After World War I, the United States retreated into isolationism for almost two decades, not abandoning its recently won international status altogether, but nevertheless distancing itself from further involvement in European problems. The twin pillars of American foreign policy during the early days of the republic, small standing armies and neutrality, resurfaced as Americans became weary of the consequences of foreign entanglements at a time when their future was far from certain. Through the nation's participation in World War I, they witnessed the carnage that results from increased militarism, and they were not yet prepared to accommodate a sizable military presence at home. In addition, the economic catastrophe of the 1930s made the American public more focused on domestic affairs and the necessities of basic survival, so the pursuit of resource-intensive foreign policies became a luxury the country could not afford.[50]

FDR was initially committed to neutrality and, most of all, aloofness from military developments in Europe and Asia. As it turned out, circumstances forced his hand and pushed America ever closer to war. After the Japanese attack on Pearl Harbor on December 7, 1941, he had no alternative, and Congress declared war on Japan and Germany. Recognizing the implications of a global conflict fueled by enemies devoted to the extermination of whole populations, FDR's dedication to victory was total. Through an unprecedented commitment of American resources, the President's expansion of executive authority was quick, decisive, and irreversible. More than 15 million men and women served in the armed forces in one capacity or another, and tens of millions of others held jobs that supported the war effort. The country's manufacturing potential was channeled into the production of arms, supplies, food, medicine, and anything else required by America's military, whereas its cultural output was focused on the maintenance of morale. Hollywood, major publishers, and leading radio producers all contributed to the presidency's propaganda machine, churning out movies, books, newspapers, and radio broadcasts that celebrated the superiority of the Allied cause.[51]

At the conclusion of the war, the United States emerged as one of two principal global military powers. Along with the Soviet Union, it was unchallenged as the arbiter of a new world order. Europe desperately needed international leadership from a country with resources and credentials equal to the task. In 1945, the United States was the only possible choice. Although the desire to avoid another global war was an important aspect of U.S. foreign policy after 1945, the overriding concerns were the rising geopolitical influence of the Soviet Union and the political turmoil in key European states. Teetering on the brink of communism, strategically significant countries such as Italy, Greece, and Turkey could not be allowed to fall under Soviet control and undermine the postwar stability of Europe. Others, like France, Austria, and Germany, were susceptible not only to socialists but also to extremists on the right, which made postwar rebuilding efforts difficult. Even Britain, which had been spared the widespread physical devastation that characterized continental Europe, was seriously weakened and confronted by internal problems that created considerable political vulnerabilities. Europe's political situation was precarious, and its susceptibility to Soviet aggression was substantial.[52]

Western policymakers were aware that the military, political, and economic resources to neutralize Soviet aggression could come only from the United States, so the United States became the political and economic arbiter in Europe. American economic muscle would provide the strength to rebuild the European continent, and American political know-how would drive governmental reform, while its military presence would serve as a deterrent against Soviet expansion. Through the Marshall Plan, Truman and his foreign-policy team ensured the democratic future of Western Europe. The Marshall Plan, named for Secretary of State George Marshall, was a comprehensive aid program that paid for the reconstruction of war-ravaged countries and the resurrection of viable economies. In Germany, Austria, Japan, and other places, the United States remained as an occupying force, dictating the day-to-day governance of their peoples and the political complexion of their regimes, whereas elsewhere the promise of American defense forces and U.S. dollars encouraged friendly governments to adopt compliant policies. American presidents oversaw the deployment of millions of American people all over Europe and other parts of the globe and the implementation of liberal-democratic principles of governance throughout its sphere of influence.[53]

At home, burgeoning military and diplomatic needs fueled the growth of an enhanced national-security bureaucracy capable of securing the country's status as a superpower. This effort revolutionized American politics by linking the nation's domestic policies to a more assertive global presence and an ongoing campaign to shape developments abroad. With the overriding goal of maintaining America's strategic leverage and protecting its diplomatic assets, U.S. foreign policy demanded an unprecedented expansion of military and bureaucratic resources during the Cold War. Within a few decades, the United States became a diplomatic and military juggernaut whose ability to take advantage of its economic might was unrivaled. The diplomatic and military resources at its disposal, which included hundreds of thousands of soldiers, a vastly reconditioned State Department, a new Department of Defense with an army of support personnel, an intelligence apparatus comprising the CIA, the National Security Agency, and other organizations, and a growing complex of military and industrial contractors, were staggering. The discretion of the president and his foreign-policy team to utilize those resources was largely unchallenged, and the willingness of American commanders in chief to exercise ever-greater authority appeared to be unlimited.[54]

The Cold War never produced a physical conflict between the United States and the Soviet Union, but it spawned proxy wars around the globe and a keen political competition that polarized international affairs for more than 40 years. Each superpower was intent on maximizing its sphere of influence through client states and securing the cooperation of nonaligned countries through political and economic incentives. For the United States, this was the central plank in its policy of containment, so named because it sought to contain Soviet expansion, aggression, and influence though a countervailing U.S. military, diplomatic, and economic footprint in contested theaters. Support of politically turbulent client states and military insurgencies created head-to-head conflict with Soviet interests, which produced actual wars in almost every part of the world. The bloodiest and arguably the most prominent were on the Korean peninsula, in Indochina and Central Asia, particularly Afghanistan, and throughout Latin America, but plenty of other incidents between Soviet-sponsored and American-backed forces arose in Europe, the Middle East, and Africa. Permanent military deployment was a function of the nation's postwar security needs, and it reflected the international commitments that defined America's role as a superpower, which represented a resounding rejection of the country's traditional aversion of foreign entanglements and its devotion to neutrality.[55]

The longest and most debilitating physical conflict of the Cold War, in terms of both casualties and international prestige, was in Vietnam. At a cost of almost 60,000 American lives during nearly 30 years of involvement of one kind or another, it was an outgrowth of the so-called Domino Theory among foreign policymakers in the United States. The Domino Theory assumed that, because key geopolitical regions were precariously balanced between communism and anticommunism and, by extension, between Soviet and American spheres of influence, a marginal increase in Soviet influence, or communist penetration, in a particular region would lead to the eventual communist takeover of the whole region. In other words, once a strategically significant state in such a region fell to communism, the rest of the states in that region would follow like dominos. American foreign-policy experts became convinced that Vietnam was the strategic lynchpin in Southeast Asia and that the consolidation of communist power in Vietnam had to be prevented at all costs.[56]

Despite clear American military superiority, the commitment of five presidential administrations, and, at least initially, the requisite political will, the Vietnam War was a failure by almost every measure. Most important, it was the first war the United States had lost and, especially to its critics, it was a conspicuous repudiation of the Domino Theory and much of the rationale for U.S. military intervention during the Cold War. Massively unpopular at home by the late 1960s, it produced unrest and protests in scores of American cities and created mistrust and skepticism regarding federal governance that are still felt today. In terms of foreign policy, Vietnam demonstrated the futility of nation-building, particularly as a military objective, and it ultimately affected American willingness to intervene in foreign conflicts that did not invoke a compelling U.S. interest or present a clear and definite exit strategy.

The Post-Soviet World

Containment, the Cold War policy that dominated U.S. diplomatic and military thinking for much of the postwar period, was abandoned prior to the end of the Cold War. The Reagan administration was convinced that the strategic stalemate promoted through containment was a prohibitive obstacle to the eventual resolution of the Cold War, and it adopted a much more assertive posture concerning its dealings with the Soviets. Reagan and his foreign-policy team committed themselves to reversing Soviet gains in traditionally communist strongholds and exerting pressure on Soviet policymakers through an accelerated buildup of U.S. military capabilities. American diplomatic efforts, not only with the Soviets but also throughout targeted global theaters, complemented Reagan's hardline military posture by rejecting the existing international balance of power between democratic and communist forces and supporting anticommunist constituencies in various parts of the globe. Whether Reagan truly was responsible for ending the Cold War because of his comparatively aggressive anti-Soviet initiatives is a matter of debate, but his foreign policies undeniably contributed to the collapse of the Soviet Union and its satellite regimes throughout Eastern and Central Europe.[57]

A seasoned statesman and a foreign-policy veteran, George H. W. Bush endeavored to maintain American dominance during what he called a "new world order" through American diplomatic and military leadership in key strategic theaters, but that proved increasingly difficult. Heading a multinational coalition, the United States invaded Iraq in January of 1991 to liberate Kuwait, and, although the first Gulf War was brief and limited in scope, continued American involvement in the region was not. Through the United Nations, the United States and its allies became guarantors of Kuwaiti and, to an extent, Iraqi stability, which required an ongoing commitment of American resources for the next several years. Closer to home, Bush ordered the invasion of Panama to capture the military dictator Manuel Noriega, a reputed supporter of regional terrorist organizations and narcotics trafficker who posed a security threat to the United States. In other areas, particularly Somalia, the Bush administration intervened for humanitarian reasons, but regional political and military instability eventually undermined the U.S.-led campaign.[58]

Bush's successor was not as eager to commit American military resources abroad and continued American geopolitical dominance was not always a top priority. The Clinton administration, dominated by baby boomers who witnessed the failures of nation-building and interventionism during their formative years, limited U.S. diplomatic and particularly military engagements to situations that invoked a clear national interest or moral imperative. The Clinton years were noteworthy for reliance on the Powell Doctrine, named after Chairman of the Joint Chiefs of Staff Colin Powell, which advocated American military involvement only in those cases with a compelling national interest at stake, a limited engagement, minimal political entanglements, and a recognizable exit strategy. For example, this policy guided U.S. intervention in the former Yugoslavia and strikes against tactical targets in Iraq.[59]

NATION BUILDING

THEN . . .

The 1970s and early 1980s were precarious times for both the United States and the world generally. On May 1, 1975, the last American personnel were airlifted out of South Vietnam as Saigon, the capital, fell to the North Vietnamese. It was the first U.S. military defeat in history, and its lessons seemed clear; foremost among them was that the United States would never again engage in nation-building. However, as the 1980s arrived, political transformations in regions precariously poised between stability and instability threatened the postwar political and economic progress among Western nations and American control of valuable strategic outposts. As Reagan took office in January 1981, the United States faced not only communist expansion and Soviet aggression but also the proliferation of despotic governments in pivotal strategic theaters. Invariably, communism seemed the greater foe; thus, the United States frequently befriended antidemocratic regimes. Afghanistan and Iraq offer just two such examples.

In early 1978, the communist People's Democratic Party of Afghanistan seized power in Kabul, triggering a long and bloody civil war that eventually involved the Cold War's two superpowers. The Afghan civil war would become for the Soviet Union what Vietnam had been for the United States, a strategic and military miscalculation, depleting its resources, morale, and international stature and even contributing to the demise of the Soviet state itself. The presence of Soviet troops to back the communist government against a coalition of Islamist paramilitary factions known collectively as the mujahedeen drew a response from the Carter and Reagan administrations. Carter authorized covert military aid for the mujahedeen following the Soviet invasion in late 1979, but Reagan escalated U.S. involvement through a continuing commitment of funds and materiel provided via Pakistan during the 1980s. Abandoning the decades-old policy of containment and initiating the "rollback" of Soviet influence throughout Asia, Africa, and Latin America, Reagan and his foreign-policy team were determined to do whatever they could to undermine the communist regime in Afghanistan and Soviet strategic objectives as well.[60]

By the time the Soviets had withdrawn from Afghanistan in 1989, the United States had provided approximately $20 billion or more to the mujahedeen rebels. The money and military supplies were given through proxies in Pakistan, whose government became a significant, although uncertain, partner in U.S. efforts against unfriendly authoritarian regimes in the region.[61] As it turned out, the mujahedeen were no better equipped to rule the country than their communist predecessors. After the fall of the communist government in 1992, the civil war became an internecine conflict among the various ethnic factions that had composed the mujahedeen. Divided by tribal loyalties and complex cultural ties, Afghanistan became a breeding ground for extremism and violence.[62]

During the latter part of the decade, the Taliban, a hard-core fundamentalist political party dedicated to the total Islamification of Afghan society and the rule of a dubious antimodernist form of Muslim law, consolidated power in the south and established an emirate that lasted until the U.S. invasion in 2001. The Taliban government committed countless atrocities against the Afghan people in the name of Islam and provided safe haven to various anti-Western terrorist organizations, including al Qaeda. Staunchly anti-American, the Taliban devoted itself to the elimination of U.S. influence in the region. Its support for al Qaeda and similar terrorist groups became a particular threat to Western security, offering a home base for international terrorist initiatives and the spread of global Islamic terrorist networks. Even before the terrorist attacks against the United States in 2001, the Taliban-based regime in Kabul had become an international pariah and the target of Western counterterrorist efforts.[63]

Afghanistan soon became the first front of George W. Bush's War on Terror and, from a geopolitical and historical standpoint, it shared some striking similarities with the second front, which was Iraq. In 1980, Iraq invaded Iran to curb the supposed threat of Shia expansionism posed by the recently installed revolutionary regime in Tehran. After the fundamentalist revolution of 1979, the new Iranian theocratic leadership repeatedly displayed a desire to unify regional Shia populations into a greater Persia. The Iraqi government of Saddam Hussein feared that Iranian revolutionary rhetoric would galvanize the oppressed Shia majority in Iraq and destabilize the secularist dictatorship in Baghdad. The resulting Iran–Iraq War, which Iraq initiated on the pretext of an alleged Iranian assassination attempt against its foreign minister, lasted for eight years at a cost of hundreds of thousands of lives. As one of the longest conventional wars of the twentieth century, it accomplished little, culminating in a status quo ante and the needless depletion of national resources in both Iran and Iraq. It did, however, enable the further consolidation of power by Saddam Hussein and his Ba'athist regime, and it institutionalized a reign of terror that prompted eventual American intervention.[64]

Because of the disdain most Western countries and even the Soviet Union felt for the fundamentalist government in Tehran, the bulk of the international support benefited Iraq, which received various forms of aid, both covert and overt, from several Western nations. The United States was no different in this regard, and because it was forced to choose between the apparent lesser of two evils, it did reluctantly aid Saddam Hussein. The Reagan administration supplied his government with intelligence, technological expertise, and weapons to discredit and ultimately defeat the theocracy in Iran, which had become a major geopolitical problem for the United States in the late 1970s. The overthrow of the friendly government led by the Shah of Iran and the subsequent abduction of American hostages by Iranian revolutionaries in Tehran sparked an international feud that lasts to this day. In addition, the theocracy's sponsorship of fundamentalist insurgencies and terrorist organizations throughout the Middle East, as well as its commitment to the destruction of Israel, ensured the animosity of the Reagan administration and its own commitment to do whatever it could to undermine the Iranian regime.[65]

Whether Western, and particularly U.S., support of the Iraqi government during the war prevented an Iranian victory is difficult to surmise, but Saddam Hussein emerged emboldened and reassured, despite what was at best a stalemate after eight years of conflict. He either misconstrued Western aid as a validation of his cause or simply used it to justify his geopolitical objectives, but regardless, the result was the same. Furthermore, U.S. attacks against Iranian positions during the late 1980s, although in response to anti-American Iranian aggression in international waters, created the impression of an active collaboration between the Iraqi and U.S. administrations, which only strengthened the illusory legitimacy of Saddam Hussein's government. Leveraging his seemingly increased credibility among Western governments, he used the excuse of war to subdue the Kurdish and Shia populations within Iraq, resorting to whatever means necessary—even the use of chemical weapons against his own people; Saddam Hussein's power was secure and unrivaled.[66]

Saddam Hussein's political control did not translate into improved economic circumstances in Iraq, which had been ravaged by the war with Iran. Unable to repay wartime debts to the Kuwaiti government, which had lent the Iraqi regime considerable sums during its conflict with Iran, and feeling economically threatened by Kuwaiti oil production that exceeded the quotas of the Organization of the Petroleum Exporting Countries, Iraq invaded and quickly overran Kuwait in August 1990. The Iraqi regime installed a puppet government in Kuwait, which it annexed as its 19th province and refused to bow to international pressure for a complete withdrawal. As the autumn unfolded, the George H. W. Bush administration became increasingly involved in the quagmire, eventually issuing an ultimatum to Saddam Hussein and preparing for the military liberation of Kuwait. Unwilling to heed U.S. demands, Iraq faced a U.S.-led invasion in early 1991 that swiftly accomplished its objective of liberating Kuwait. This war, too, like the Iran–Iraq War before it, resulted in a status quo ante, although Iraq was confronted with international sanctions and a military inspection and oversight program administered by the victorious powers.[67]

AND NOW . . .

On September 11, 2001, three U.S. commercial jets commandeered by al Qaeda hijackers deliberately crashed into the World Trade Center in New York and the Pentagon in Washington, DC, while a fourth, which was reportedly targeting the White House, crashed in a field in Pennsylvania after being disarmed by American passengers. The first attack against the United States on its soil since Pearl Harbor, the carefully planned plot by Afghan-based terrorists stunned the nation and the rest of the world but provoked a quick response from the George W. Bush administration. In early October, predicated on intelligence confirmation of al Qaeda's responsibility for the attacks and Taliban complicity with al Qaeda and its leader, Osama bin Laden, the Bush administration launched an invasion of Afghanistan. The immediate purpose was the apprehension of al Qaeda operatives, the capture of bin Laden, and the dismantling of the rogue Taliban regime that had run the country for almost a decade. Unlike the first Gulf War, which drew support from a widespread multinational alliance against Iraq, this operation was limited to the United States, Great Britain, and a handful of other allies, and it did not have the endorsement of the United Nations.[68]

Unfortunately, despite initial military success and the swift ouster of the Taliban regime, the situation in Afghanistan soon became problematic for the Bush administration and its allies. Because of the dispersed and decentralized nature of the al Qaeda terrorist network, the capture or elimination of its leadership proved elusive, as did the actual conquest of the Taliban itself, which fled to safe havens in the south of the country and across the border into Pakistan. Moreover, the Northern Alliance, which was the latter-day successor to the mujahedeen remnants that had continued to fight the Taliban government after 1996, was just as fractured, unorganized, and ineffective in terms of national unity and purposeful governance as it had been during the Afghan civil wars of the 1980s and 1990s. It was neither prepared nor qualified to form a government to replace the ousted Taliban regime, yet it was the only option for the United States and its partners. Under UN auspices, the Afghanis created a government under Hamid Karzai, who as a Pashtun, represented the largest ethnic faction in Afghanistan. His government, although welcomed by most observers initially, gradually lost credibility and did not promote long-term stability (Karzai remained in power until 2014).[69]

Counter to the reformulated foreign-policy objectives in the aftermath of Vietnam, the United States was once again involved in nation-building, a task for which the military was neither trained nor designed. After initial accomplishments by the Karzai government and the reconstitution of Afghan society following the depredations of the Taliban years, factionalism, ethnic rivalry, and graft began to undermine whatever progress had been made. In addition, newly trained Afghan security forces proved unable to pacify the countryside, and they were also unable to maintain law and order in major urban centers without substantial international assistance. Adding insult to injury, a hobbling economy fell prey to a traditional black-market temptation, opium cultivation, which fueled narcotics trafficking and related criminal activities.[70] Making matters worse, a Taliban resurgence starting in 2003 from bases in Pakistan and southern Afghanistan overwhelmed the new government and confronted the U.S.-led forces with a considerable military threat, which is just one of the reasons Obama authorized a military escalation in late 2009. Although the Obama administration could claim a victory of sorts in 2011 through the capture and execution of Osama bin Laden, who had eluded Bush's efforts to apprehend him, it outlasted every American conflict except Vietnam, with U.S. troops withdrawn in 2014.[71]

Regarding the second front of the War on Terror, Bush initiated the Iraq War in March 2003. Convinced that Saddam Hussein's government possessed weapons of mass destruction, such as nuclear, biological, and chemical warheads, and that Iraq was a safe haven for al Qaeda and other Islamist terrorist groups, Bush declared that because diplomacy had failed to resolve the growing threat to the West in Iraq, the United States and its allies would seek a military solution. The objectives were like those in Afghanistan, so, unlike the Gulf War in 1991, this war would aim at the conquest of Iraq and the removal of Saddam Hussein from power. The U.S.-led coalition was not as extensive this time, nor was it backed by the UN, which denounced the invasion as premature, provocative, and unnecessary. With wholehearted support from the British and token help from Australia and Poland, combined with various forms of assistance from other countries, the invasion was surprisingly effective in the short term—just as the Afghan campaign had been. Within three weeks, Iraq had been overrun and the government of Saddam Hussein had been toppled after approximately 25 years in power.[72]

Nevertheless, like Afghanistan, Iraq soon disintegrated into chaos. After a temporary U.S. military administration, the allies prepared Iraq for democratic governance and a transition to multiethnic, multiparty rule, which proved as elusive as it had in Afghanistan. Rabid competition, jealousy, and fighting among and even within opposing Sunni, Shia, and Kurd factions compromised the government of prime minister Nouri al-Maliki, as did the geographic splintering of the country into southern, western, and northern enclaves that frequently left Baghdad isolated. Within a couple of years of the apparent victory against the outgoing Ba'athist regime, Iraq had descended into civil war and widespread sectarian violence. Militant southern-based Shias led by the fundamentalist cleric Muqtada al-Sadr and some of his Iranian-influenced rivals along with the restive western-based minority Sunni clans posed ostensibly insurmountable obstacles to the pacification of the country, whereas Kurdish separatism, motivated by years of alienation and repression at the hand of Saddam Hussein, impeded unified governance and the consolidation of natural resources.[73]

As was also the case in Afghanistan, newly established national-security forces proved themselves utterly unqualified and unprepared to handle either the military threat or the increasing terrorist incursions in Baghdad and other urban centers. Thus, U.S. and British forces were compelled to shoulder most of the responsibility for safety and security, even policing, although Americans and Britons grew weary of the personal and financial costs of the war. The ongoing antigovernment political and military campaigns in Iraq along with the new Iraqi government's military impotence forced an escalation of troops by the Bush administration, known as the "Surge," in 2007, which attracted even more criticism of the U.S.-led war at home and abroad. Despite the criticism and the strong antiwar sentiment in many parts of the United States, the Surge was effective and ultimately enabled the wounded Iraqi government to make sufficient progress to enable U.S. troop reductions and eventual withdrawal.[74] Still, sobered by the loss of lives, materiel, and national credibility, Americans were decreasingly sympathetic, as leading Democrats called for a swift and decisive withdrawal from Iraq. Riding a wave of public discontent regarding the war and other issues, candidate Obama in 2008 promised to end U.S. involvement in Iraq and bring the troops home in his first year as president.[75] Once in the White House, although his campaign promises had been too ambitious and unrealistic, Obama did fulfill his promise and completed the military withdrawal by the end of 2011.

Whether George W. Bush and his foreign-policy advisors came to the White House with the intent to reverse course and reinvent the country's international posture has long been the subject of heated debates. Regardless, the terrorist attacks on 9/11 resulted in a wholesale reformulation of American foreign policy and a dismissal of the Powell Doctrine (although Powell was serving as Bush's secretary of state at the time). The so-called War on Terror, launched shortly after the terrorist attacks, ultimately secured a policy of preemptive action against rogue states and organizations and, per its neoconservative supporters, also justified foreign intervention for the promotion and protection of liberal-democratic principles. Consequently, military intervention in Afghanistan and Iraq and a hawkish posture toward Iran and North Korea, both part of what Bush identified as the "axis of evil," were justified by the need to protect American interests and support the consolidation of liberal democracy abroad. The Bush Doctrine, as some have called it, provided an unabashedly ideological basis for military and diplomatic involvement, and it affirmed preemptive military action as a practical, if not moral, necessity. Some have viewed this as an integral part of a neoconservative agenda embraced by the Bush foreign-policy team, but many of the administration's harshest critics were neoconservatives themselves, and Bush's own allegiance to neoconservatism was questionable at best.[76]

In another reversal, Obama rejected the Bush Doctrine and attempted to distance himself and his administration from what he perceived as the foreign-policy excesses of his predecessor. Unfortunately, like many before him, Obama learned quickly that reversals of foreign policy, although warranted and defensible in many cases, are not always achievable. Prevailing geopolitical realities kept Obama from doing what he had wished and promised. Under Obama, the United States maintained a significant number of troops in Iraq, although he implemented a gradual reduction of forces until the official end of the war in December 2011. Subsequent destabilization in both Afghanistan and Iraq eventually led Obama to once again increase American troop levels in both countries, although, reminiscent of the early stages of the Vietnam war, they were often labeled "advisors" or something similar.

In other areas, Obama was cautious and reluctant to commit U.S. resources unless necessary, but he did approve a U.S.-led military effort to aid Libyan rebels in North Africa. Unlike Reagan and George W. Bush, for example, Obama did not enter the White House with an overriding vision of a new world order, particularly one based on the institutionalization of American political ideals abroad. In foreign policy, Obama, much like George H. W. Bush, was more a pragmatist without a specific ideological agenda than a visionary. He did not promulgate an Obama Doctrine and, unlike most of his predecessors, was not preoccupied with American geopolitical dominance. He often seemed more concerned, especially during his first few years in office, with halting Bush-era policies than with implementing a coherent foreign-policy agenda of his own. He did, however, devote considerable resources to the negotiation of a nuclear deal with Iran and a global climate-change accord.[77] Obama also struggled to respond to a quickly evolving geopolitical dynamic that created threats from rogue regimes, terrorist networks (particularly groups such as the Islamic State of Iraq and Syria, known as ISIS), and anti-American religious fundamentalism.

IMPLEMENTING THE FOREIGN-POLICY AGENDA

Despite the complexity of U.S. foreign policy, most presidential actions in this arena fall into one or more of the following categories—the use of war powers as commander in chief, economic and trade issues, human rights, and/or environmental concerns. In some cases, presidents are simply reactive to world events outside of their control, whereas in others, presidents pursue specific policies on the world stage that, at least in their own view, are in the interest of U.S. national and economic security. The process is not as straightforward as it sounds, because none of these four categories exists in a vacuum or in isolation from one another. A president is usually juggling interests in all four areas, trying to devote as much attention as he can to the priorities at the time but remaining aware of the fact that any one of these areas can be pushed to the top of his agenda depending on global circumstances and national priorities.

Presidents and War Powers

Like it or not, war is an extension of politics, and it is also a fundamental part of foreign policy. Congress has not officially declared war since World War II, although presidents since then have initiated various military engagements. In 1950, under the auspices of the UN, the United States intervened in Korea to repel a communist invasion of the southern peninsula by North Korean forces. Later that year, China, which had fallen to communism just a year prior, joined the North Koreans against the U.S.-led effort to aid South Korea. American fears of Soviet involvement were confirmed in 1951, when Joseph Stalin decided to provide military assistance to North Korea. This was the first major conflict of the Cold War and an important test of Western resolve against the spread of communism. In addition, U.S. policymakers considered stability on the Korean peninsula a key to the preservation of a friendly regime in Japan, so the protection of South Korea became an important part of U.S. foreign-policy objectives. The Korean War, never officially terminated through a peace treaty but merely ending in cease-fire that is still effective today, ultimately produced a stalemate that led to the permanent division of the Korean peninsula into North and South Korea. Because of the hostile geopolitical environment and the lack of a peace treaty, not to mention concerns about the safety of Japan, the United States has maintained a troop presence in South Korea since 1953.[78]

Involvement in Vietnam, which was the next major military campaign for the United States, predated the Korean War, but formal U.S. participation in the region did not begin until after the withdrawal of French forces in 1954. Vietnam had been a French colonial possession, so initial postwar anticommunist initiatives were under French control, but those attempts eventually failed. The United States became committed to the preservation of a noncommunist South Vietnam and, by the early 1960s, active military support of the South Vietnamese administration. Contrary to some reports, Kennedy did not plan to withdraw from Vietnam and had

President-Elect Dwight Eisenhower visits the troops in Korea in December 1952.

already authorized the deployment of more than 16,000 troops by the time he was assassinated in November 1963. His successor, Lyndon Johnson, then transformed a limited engagement of several thousand so-called military advisors into a full-scale military endeavor. By July 1965, armed with the Tonkin Gulf Resolution from the previous summer as a de facto declaration of war, Johnson and the Joint Chiefs of Staff were dedicated to total victory over North Vietnam, not just military and political aid to the South Vietnamese government.[79]

The Tonkin Gulf Resolution, a response to one confirmed and one disputed attack on U.S. naval vessels off the coast of North Vietnam, authorized the president to use whatever means necessary to protect the South Vietnamese from communist aggression. This was not a constitutional declaration of war, but the Johnson and Richard Nixon administrations treated it as such, believing they needed no further congressional sanction to prosecute the war in Vietnam. Just as significant, Congress, despite growing discontent regarding the war over the ensuing years among certain members, did not limit presidential war-making authority in any manner, nor did it ever try to enact a formal declaration of war. Coming on the heels of the Korean War and its lack of a congressional war declaration, Vietnam affirmed a constitutionally dubious precedent and, despite the military failure, empowered presidents in a way the Constitution had never intended. By the 1970s, although the nation was war-weary and mistrust of government was at an all-time high, U.S. presidents were armed with a war-making authority that no one seemed willing to question seriously.[80]

In 1973, perhaps seeking a way to address this unconstitutional acquisition of presidential authority, Congress overrode Nixon's veto and passed the War Powers Resolution, which, as it turns out, only exacerbated the problem. Seen by many as a cynical attempt to codify the status quo and sidestep the congressional responsibility for declaring war, the War Powers Resolution recognized a de facto, if not de jure, presidential authority to initiate a war without prior congressional approval. Although the resolution attempted to limit the escalation of hostilities following initial military intervention, it nonetheless confirmed that presidents had the unilateral power to authorize military action in the first place. Reagan relied on this power to order the invasion of Grenada in 1983 and restore constitutional government to the island nation, as did George H. W. Bush when he initiated the invasion of Panama at the end of his first year in office in 1989 to capture its military dictator and suspected narcotics trafficker Manuel Noriega.[81]

Backed by a congressional resolution that once again avoided a formal declaration of war, the elder Bush authorized the invasion of Iraq in January 1991, which produced the first Gulf War and ended in the liberation of Kuwait, the defeat of Iraqi forces, and the imposition of sanctions and UN-administered security controls on the Iraqi government of Saddam Hussein. Unlike its latter-day counterpart, this first Iraqi war was limited in scope and, thus, left the Iraqi government and much of the Iraqi military intact. Also unlike the Iraq War, the American-led war in 1991 had broad-based international backing, with more than 30 coalition members supporting the United States in one way or another. Still, Saddam Hussein's regime continued to confront the United States and its allies with recurring geopolitical problems, which necessitated a limited military response by the Clinton administration in late 1998. By the beginning of the 2000s, serious questions remained about Iraqi intentions and military capabilities, and many analysts worried that Iraq possessed, or would soon possess, weapons of mass destruction.[82]

Although it now seems doubtful that Iraq ever possessed the kinds of weapons British and American analysts had feared, the terrorist attacks on 9/11 in New York and Washington, DC, ultimately prevented a reasoned and deliberate consideration of diplomatic alternatives as the United States prepared for war in the Middle East. First, George W. Bush ordered the invasion of Afghanistan in late 2001, and backed by congressional resolution, he initiated the Iraq War in March 2003. Neither military engagement was authorized by a formal congressional declaration of war, and despite eventual criticism of the war by numerous members of Congress, presidential war-making authority was not circumscribed in any way. These two invasions, part of Bush's overarching War on Terror, continued a constitutional precedent established shortly after the end of World War II by legitimizing a constitutional transfer of authority from Congress to the presidency.[83] Obama was no different in this regard. Although he could claim that his administration did not start any wars, that rests on a distinction without a difference. Aside from committing more troops to Afghanistan and Iraq than he had wanted, Obama deployed American air power in Libya, Iraq, and Syria and approved dozens of drone strikes, especially in Yemen and Pakistan. Like his predecessors, he continued the post-Vietnam practice of acting without specific congressional authorization.[84]

Trade and Economic Interests

Foreign policy focuses on the security and promotion of national and strategic interests abroad, which includes economic objectives, assets, and opportunities. Economic growth and financial stability depend on the penetration and management of foreign markets, which underpin long-term economic prosperity.[85] Recent presidents have understood this well, and they have devoted considerable attention to international trade and the coordination of multinational economic initiatives. Prior to the Reagan administration, allegiance to free trade and globalization was inconsistent. Although they encouraged the easing of trade barriers in some industries, especially in Western markets, most presidents before the 1980s could not let go of protectionist policies that favored American commodities and manufactured goods in industries believed to be vulnerable to foreign competition. Although some aspects of protectionism have survived, the commitment to free trade is nonetheless undeniable.[86]

These days, the need for unencumbered movement of goods and services in international markets, or free trade, is recognized as an indispensable part of economic well-being. The minimization and abolition of tariffs, subsidies, quotas, dumping, and other practices that distort international markets have been goals of the last several presidents, particularly Reagan, Clinton, and Obama. However, they have at times encountered considerable opposition from lawmakers, blue-collar workers, and antiglobalization advocates. Surprisingly, critics received a sympathetic ear from George W. Bush, whose instinct was to protect the auto, steel, mining, and banking industries, while Obama was a steadier and more enthusiastic supporter of free-trade deals than many Republicans, who have been the traditional advocates of free trade. Despite variable but consistent support since the early 1980s, globalization, a consequence of free trade that includes political, economic, and cultural integration, has been a tough sell. Its detractors have viewed it as the domination and enrichment of multinational firms at the expense of the middle class and American labor.[87]

Some opposition can be taken for granted, but modern presidents have increasingly concentrated on negotiating trade deals and lobbying international trade organizations. The General Agreement on Tariffs and Trade (GATT) and its successor, the World Trade Organization (WTO), devoted to the reduction of tariffs, subsidies, quotas, and other trade barriers, have proven useful to presidential administrations as a forum for the promotion of American goods and services. Still, because of their cumbersome size and limited abilities to produce results, presidents have tended to see these institutions and others like them more as avenues for debate and deliberation than as instruments of tangible change. Clinton was a notable exception. He pressed hard for the creation of the WTO, viewing it as a useful arena for the dissemination of American economic ideas, which, he believed, would facilitate international economic integration and the spread of democratic governance.[88]

On the one hand, institutions like the GATT and the WTO, often lacking any authority to enact rules, such as the Group of Seven richest industrialized economies, the Organisation for Economic Co-operation and Development, the Asia–Pacific Economic Cooperation, and others, have proven marginally effective at advancing concrete goals instead of abstract principles. On the other hand, multilateral and bilateral free-trade pacts have been pursued aggressively by recent American presidents. To negotiate quickly and more effectively, most presidents have asked Congress for so-called fast-track authority, renamed trade promotion authority in 2002, which banned filibusters and amendments to trade deals. Under trade promotion authority, Congress was only given authority for up-or-down votes.[89]

The most visible, and possibly most controversial, free-trade pact has been the North American Free Trade Agreement (NAFTA). George H. W. Bush expended great effort to negotiate the deal in the concluding months of his presidency, although it was not ratified until 1994, nearly two years into the Clinton presidency. The agreement resulted in the immediate elimination of tariffs on half of Mexican exports and more than one-third of U.S. exports. With concerns about its impact on the environment and American workers, NAFTA was not universally supported. The proposed Free Trade Area of the Americas, which was supposed to be an expansion of NAFTA to all North, Central, and South American countries except Cuba, has never materialized, and Donald Trump promised to renegotiate NAFTA throughout the 2016 presidential campaign. For Obama, negotiation of the Pacific Rim–centered Trans-Pacific Partnership and the Transatlantic Trade and Investment Partnership with Europe were primary objectives. However, the future of such agreements is in doubt because of political opposition not only from many members of Congress, but also from Trump. Trump signed an executive order withdrawing the United States from the Trans-Pacific Partnership during his first week in office in January 2017, saying he prefers negotiating trade deals one on one with specific countries.

Some international economic issues confronted by U.S. presidents have been fraught with controversy. The most prominent has been the reduction of America's dependence on foreign oil, especially from members of OPEC, an intergovernmental organization comprising many of the largest producers of crude oil, which includes countries in the Middle East, North Africa, and South America. Forty-five percent of American oil imports come from member countries. Decreasing reliance on foreign oil has been an urgent goal since the Arab oil embargoes of the 1970s, which demonstrated the potentially crippling effect of sizeable fluctuations in the price and availability of oil. The United States finally produces as much oil as it imports, but the acquisition of foreign oil is still a necessity. Fortunately, 35 to 40 percent of U.S. oil imports come from Canada, a reliable trading partner. Unfortunately, the importance of Canadian oil exports to the United States has frequently been overshadowed by arguments over the importation of supposedly "dirty oil" from tar sands and shale. For instance, the approval of the Keystone XL oil pipeline pitted pro-pipeline Republicans against anti-pipeline Democrats, and during his second term, Obama ultimately did not approve the project.[90] Trump reversed that decision in March 2017.

Human Rights

The Cold War inaugurated a complicated era for the defense of human rights. Western Europe, with an inherited sense of democratic rule and enforcement of fundamental rights, was intrinsically receptive to American priorities. Germany, with a recent history of disregarding human rights, was particularly receptive to American demands. However, in other countries, instability and an unwelcome communist presence in the region forced Truman to compromise on this issue. The consolidation of anti-Soviet, pro-Western governments was the top goal, so human rights concerns were secondary. The willingness to look the other way occasionally was the price paid for the defeat of communist opposition and the establishment of pro-Western governments.

For example, Turkey, a NATO member strategically poised between Europe and Asia but undemocratic and frequently authoritarian, has been given a wide berth by almost every president since Truman. Not wanting to compromise regional security in the Balkans, Reagan and George H. W. Bush improved relations with Turkey, which had been chilly after the Turkish invasion of Cyprus in 1974, but Turkey's record on human rights did not improve. George W. Bush and Obama were particularly vexed by the increasing authoritarianism of Recep Tayyip Erdogan, Turkey's prime minister, and his blatant suppression of human rights and free speech. Neither incentives nor threats of sanctions proved effective at forcing Erdogan to make necessary democratic reforms. Since Bush, the United States has become more vocal in voicing its disapproval of Turkish abuses and has backed the European Union's promise of prospective accession talks in exchange for various reforms, including the protection of basic rights and liberties. Administration officials have at times strenuously criticized a regime that has almost no respect for free speech, freedom of assembly, a free press, and human rights.[91]

Compromises between human rights and stability provided a rationale for supporting authoritarian anticommunist governments in Central and South America, the most notorious of which may have been the regime of Augusto Pinochet in Chile, but U.S. policies toward human rights in Argentina, Brazil, El Salvador, Haiti, and pre-Castro Cuba were not much different. In the Middle East, this meant support, at various times, for Iraq, Jordan, Lebanon, Egypt, prerevolutionary Iran, and others. Even Israel, the most democratic country in the region and a staunch U.S. ally, did not have a spotless record on human rights. In Europe, U.S. recognition of the fascist regime of Francisco Franco was tolerated.[92] Compromises over human rights and democratic governance seemed necessary to contain the "communist menace" and prevent the fall of strategically significant regimes.[93]

Clinton was the first president faced with what was expected but failed to be a "new world order" following the end of the Cold War, although he was one of the staunchest and most diligent advocates of human rights to ever occupy the White House. He tried almost everything at his disposal to curtail widespread human rights abuses, including pressing for UN and unilateral U.S. sanctions, leveraging the rhetorical power of the presidency, and withholding aid.[94] Similarly, George W. Bush and Obama were fierce critics of human rights abuses. Aside from using unilateral sanctions, they brought pressure on rogue regimes through the UN General Assembly, the Security Council, and the United Nations Human Rights Council. However, their efforts were only marginally effective. Vetoes by permanent security council members China and Russia upended numerous otherwise promising resolutions and encouraged them to use their veto powers as a bargaining chip against unsympathetic resolutions.[95]

Finally, there is the case of countries such as China, Pakistan, Russia, and, most recently, Iran. These countries, particularly China, are geopolitically significant in some way, and better relations with the West are critical. China, for example, is the second largest economy in the world, the most populous nation on earth, and a growing military and diplomatic power. A certain amount of appeasement is necessary because of its effect on the global economy, its growing militarism and geopolitical assertiveness, and the desire to take advantage of Chinese markets, yet China's human rights record is dismal. During the Cold War, China was also valuable as a regional counterbalance to the Soviet Union. Russia's record is no better, but it, too, has been able to leverage its strategic significance and the regional threat it poses to blunt and deter U.S. criticism. Still, the Obama administration used unilateral sanctions against Russia, Russian companies, oligarchs, and corrupt officials to let Russia's president, Vladimir Putin, know that he cannot continue to operate with impunity.

China and Russia are nuclear powers, which makes the foreign-policy math more complicated. Iran, possibly a few to several years away from having nuclear weapons, has gotten a reprieve of sorts because of the recent nuclear deal, the consequences of which may not be known for several years. At the same time, the United States has used sanctions as a weapon against Iranian human rights abuses and its violations of international law. U.S.–Iranian relations have been adversarial since the 1979 Islamist revolution, but the United States is in an uncomfortable position because of the nuclear agreement. For the time being, Obama's successors have been forced to take a wait-and-see attitude with a country that has been one of the largest supporters of state-sponsored terrorism and has openly called for the destruction of Israel. Pakistan offers the United States no easy choices either. Like China and Russia, it has nuclear weapons and its cooperation with the United States is crucial. Because of Pakistan's proximity to Afghanistan and its influence over the Taliban, as well as its difficult relations with India, a U.S. ally, its leaders have often operated with impunity.[96]

Environmental Protections

Concern for the environment has been a relatively recent phenomenon. Johnson and Nixon were the first presidents to tackle environmental problems directly, but their focus was on domestic rather than international problems. The Nixon and Carter administrations began informal talks with Canada over cross-border issues such as acid rain and Great Lakes pollution. The United States, with a population approximately five times that of Canada, produced a disproportionate amount of cross-border pollution. Reagan, often labeled an anti-environmentalist, made it a point to negotiate a treaty with Canada. His efforts resulted in the U.S.–Canada Air Quality Agreement, which was signed in 1991 by George H. W. Bush. The Reagan administration also pressed hard for the negotiation of the Montreal Protocol on Substances that Deplete the Ozone Layer, which UN Secretary General Kofi Annan, called "perhaps the single most successful international agreement to date."[97]

Clinton made climate control a key policy issue. Often labeled the most environment-friendly president, Clinton frequently made Vice President Al Gore the point person on White House environmental policies. Gore used the bully pulpit to make Americans aware of environmental concerns and to push for environmental standards on issues such as climate change and deforestation. Gore and Clinton used the United Nations Framework Convention on Climate Change, drafted in 1992 at the Earth Summit in Rio de Janeiro, as a forum to lobby for reductions in the production of carbon dioxide (CO_2) and other greenhouse gases, which are believed to be responsible for global climate change over the past 100 years. The convention was toothless, however, with no binding limits or targets, only voluntary pledges and no enforcement mechanism. The Clinton administration advocated for reform of the convention and sought to convince member countries of the need for binding and enforceable targets. Through subsequent conferences intended to produce a more adequate agreement, their efforts paid off with the signing of the Kyoto Protocol in 1997.[98]

The Kyoto Protocol, which was not effective until 2005 because of ratification problems among signatories, created binding targets for industrialized nations and goals for developing countries. It had far fewer signatories than the United Nations Framework Convention on Climate Change, just over 50 percent, not least because of enforceable targets and complaints of inequity from both developing and industrialized countries. Clinton pushed for its ratification, which never happened. George W. Bush withdrew the United States from the Kyoto Protocol because most developing nations did not sign it and those that did were not subject to binding limits, leaving the United States exposed to an inordinate burden and a higher probability of rulings against it. Instead, Bush sponsored the creation of the Asia–Pacific Partnership on Clean Development and Climate, a seven-member voluntary organization composed of six industrialized countries and China whose scope extended to the development of cleaner fossil-fuel technologies, sustainable development, cleaner power generation, alternative energy, and the reduction of CO_2 emissions in polluting industries such as coal.[99]

Bush left the White House with mixed results on the environment, and Obama entered the presidency with ambitious plans for U.S. reengagement in climate negotiations and the reduction of deforestation in South America and Southeast Asia. He devoted some of his time to voluntary bilateral agreements on climate change, especially with China. China and the United States are the top two producers of greenhouse gases in the world, emitting 30 percent and 15 percent of global CO_2, respectively. Pro-environment advocates have claimed that targets established through such talks have not gone far enough, whereas workers, union leaders, large numbers of Republicans, and pro-industry commentators have criticized them for being too aggressive. Regardless, these negotiations have resulted in nothing more than voluntary, unenforceable targets.[100]

Obama met with greater success with his administration's involvement in Paris talks that yielded a successor to the Kyoto Protocol. Composed of 194 nations, the Paris Agreement does not have legally binding targets for the reduction of greenhouse gases and halting the rise of the average global temperature. Signatories provide self-determined targets and are held to those goals through international pressure and advocacy. Nevertheless, because of its broad membership and encouraging commitment among both industrialized and developing nations, the agreement has been hailed by some as a landmark in climate negotiations. Obama's supporters have seen the Paris Agreement and the Iran nuclear deal as two of the greatest achievements of his presidency.

CONCLUSION

Because of the expansion of the modern presidency, as well as the increased role of the United States on the global stage during the past century, the presidential role in foreign policy has expanded tremendously since the founding era. Although the presidency may share policymaking responsibilities with Congress, presidents bear "the primary responsibility for shaping, negotiating, and conveying U.S. priorities abroad." In addition, the "constitutional preeminence" of the president's role in foreign policy has become "more pronounced" in recent decades as the United States has maintained its status as a superpower since the end of World War II.[101] Since that time, national security has been front and center for nearly every president as a rationale for many foreign-policy endeavors, whether to deter the spread of communism during the Cold War (including the Korean and Vietnam wars), to protect economic interests, or for the War on Terror following 9/11. The irony for the contemporary presidency regarding foreign policy can be found in the fact that rarely does a president come to office with any significant foreign-policy experience. Serving as the commander in chief and being a statesman who represents the United States on the world stage are not experiences that can be gained in any job or political position other than being president. Also, as with economic circumstances, presidents must play the hand they are dealt in terms of international situations and crises while they are in office. Often, they must walk a fine line to balance national interests and diplomatic relationships, all within the domestic partisan environment in which they must govern. Success in the foreign-policy arena is not always guaranteed, but a president who utilizes the institutional resources at his disposal and can articulate clear objectives to the American public can often have a distinct political advantage. However, public expectations can often outweigh political realities for presidents regarding foreign policy, since the process is complex and multifaceted, and successful outcomes depend on a diverse and constantly shifting coalition of actors whose contributions, although not always desired, are nonetheless essential.

Conducting Research at Presidential Libraries

The first step for anyone interested in conducting research at a presidential library is to check out the library's web page for instruction, procedures, and, most important, the availability of documents and other materials for the specific research topic. Each library has an extensive web page that details the number and scope of collections, online finding aids, and specific instructions on how to arrange for a research visit. In addition, each library has digitized numerous documents in recent years that are now available directly on the library's web page.

Next, it is always recommended to contact an archivist to talk about specific research topics and the availability of documents before arriving at the library. Archivists at the National Archives and Records Administration (NARA) have extensive knowledge of the collections in their respective library, and they are a crucial resource in guiding even the most experienced researcher through the many files, documents, photos, videos, and oral histories. Knowing which documents are essential to access ahead of time can maximize the time spent at the library.

Although each library sets its own hours and, in some cases, specific procedures for research, general rules apply to all NARA presidential libraries. For example, each researcher must fill out a brief, one-page application that describes the purpose of the research visit. In addition, each researcher is given a brief orientation by one of the archivists prior to the start of research. NARA presidential libraries provide the use of photocopiers at a small fee to researchers, and each library has slightly different, yet specific, rules for how to photocopy documents. Digital cameras are also allowed for those who do not wish to make photocopies. Laptop computers are allowed in the research room, as are any papers needed by the researcher (such as a list of boxes or documents), as long as they are checked and marked in advance by the archivists. The use of pens is not allowed; pencils, paper, and other necessary items are provided by the library.

Most documents at presidential libraries are kept in archival boxes and are numbered and organized by collection. For example, the files of Marlin Fitzwater, press secretary to George H. W. Bush, are found in the White House Press Office collection. There are four series, with subseries, included in the Fitzwater files: Subject File (Alpha File, Boxes 1–31, Bush Alpha File, Boxes 32–34); Correspondence File (Alpha/Chron File, Boxes 35–41, Chron File, Boxes 42–44, Alpha File, Boxes 45–53); Guidance File (Boxes 54–128); and Trip Boards (Boxes 129–147). Researchers interested in Bush's press relations, communication strategies, public opinion, or other public relations activities would also look in the White House Office of Speechwriting collection or the White House Office of Records Management collection under the subject files of public relations, speechwriting, or other specific policy topics.

Researchers then request to look at certain boxes, which are delivered to the research room on a cart (not to exceed 18 boxes at a time). Only one box can be placed on the researcher's table at a time, only one folder can be removed from a box at a time, and a placeholder must be used in the box to mark the location of the folder. All of these rules, as well as others, help to ensure that the collection stays in its proper order for use by future researchers. In addition, video surveillance cameras are used in all presidential libraries to protect against the theft or destruction of any documents. Documents with writings, signatures, or other markings by the president are not open to researchers, but photocopies are available in their place. This is true for many other valuable documents as well that have signatures of certain high-profile officials or dignitaries.

Perhaps the most important things to remember about conducting research at a presidential library is to prepare for the trip ahead of time by accessing online finding aids, being organized about what documents to access, and relying on the help and expertise of the archivists. Although the archivists may work at a specific presidential library, they are employees of NARA and their job is to preserve and organize the massive collection of materials and to provide access to those materials to researchers; they do not represent the president, his administration, his family, or any specific political or partisan objective. Beyond the documents themselves, the archivists represent perhaps the most valuable asset to researchers at each presidential library.

National Archives Presidential Libraries Home Page
https://www.archives.gov/presidential-libraries

Herbert Hoover Presidential Library and Museum
210 Parkside Drive
West Branch, IA 52358
319-643-5301
https://hoover.archives.gov
E-mail: hoover.library@nara.gov

Franklin D. Roosevelt Presidential Library and Museum
4079 Albany Post Road
Hyde Park, NY 12538
845-486-7770
https://fdrlibrary.org
E-mail: roosevelt.library@nara.gov

Harry S. Truman Presidential Library and Museum
500 W. US Highway 24
Independence, MO 64050
816-268-8200
https://trumanlibrary.org
E-mail: truman.library@nara.gov

Dwight D. Eisenhower Presidential Library and Museum
200 S.E. 4th Street
Abilene, KS 67410
785-263-6700
https://www.eisenhower.archives.gov
E-mail: eisenhower.library@nara.gov

John F. Kennedy Presidential Library and Museum
Columbia Point
Boston, MA 02125
617-514-1600
https://www.jfklibrary.org
E-mail: kennedy.library@nara.gov

Lyndon Baines Johnson Presidential Library and Museum
2313 Red River Street
Austin, TX 78705
512-721-0200
https://www.lbjlibrary.org
E-mail: johnson.library@nara.gov

Richard Nixon Presidential Library and Museum
18001 Yorba Linda Blvd.
Yorba Linda, CA 92886
714-983-9120
https://nixonlibrary.gov
E-mail: nixon@nara.gov

Gerald R. Ford Presidential Library and Museum
Library: 1000 Beal Avenue
Ann Arbor, MI 48109
734-205-0555
Museum: 303 Pearl Street NW
Grand Rapids, MI 49504
616-254-0400
https://fordlibrarymuseum.gov
E-mail: ford.library@nara.gov

Jimmy Carter Presidential Library and Museum
441 Freedom Parkway
Atlanta, GA 30307

404-865-7100
https://www.jimmycarterlibrary.gov
E-mail: carter.library@nara.gov

Ronald Reagan Presidential Library and Museum
40 Presidential Drive
Simi Valley, CA 93065
805-577-4000
https://reaganlibrary.gov
E-mail: reagan.library@nara.gov

George Bush Presidential Library and Museum
1000 George Bush Drive West
College Station, TX 77845
979-691-4000
https://bush41.org
E-mail: bush.library@nara.gov

William J. Clinton Presidential Library and Museum
1200 President Clinton Avenue
Little Rock, AR 72201
501-374-4242
https://www.clintonlibrary.gov
E-mail: clinton.library@nara.gov

George W. Bush Presidential Library and Museum
1725 Lakepointe Drive
Lewisville, TX 75057
972-353-0545
https://georgewbushlibrary.smu.edu
E-mail: gwbush.library@nara.gov

Barack Obama Presidential Library
https://www.obamalibrary.gov
2500 W. Golf Road
Hoffman Estates, IL 60169-1114
847-252-5700
E-mail: obama.library@nara.gov

Presidential Election Results, 1789–2016

YEAR	PARTY	PRESIDENTIAL NOMINEE	VP NOMINEE	ELECTORAL VOTE NO.	ELECTORAL VOTE %	POPULAR VOTE NO.	POPULAR VOTE %
1789	Federalist (unofficial)	**George Washington**		69	100		
1792	Federalist (unofficial)	**George Washington**		132	100		
1796	Federalist	**John Adams**		71	51.1		
	Democratic-Republican	Thomas Jefferson		68	48.9		
1800	Democratic-Republican	**Thomas Jefferson**		73	52.9		
	Federalist	John Adams		65	47.1		
1804	Democratic-Republican	**Thomas Jefferson**	George Clinton	162	92.0		
	Federalist	Charles Pinckney	Rufus King	14	8.0		
1808	Democratic-Republican	**James Madison**	George Clinton	122	69.7		
	Federalist	Charles Pinckney	Rufus King	47	26.9		
1812	Democratic-Republican	**James Madison**	Elbridge Gerry	128	58.7		
	Federalist	DeWitt Clinton	Jared Ingersoll	89	40.8		
1816	Democratic-Republican	**James Monroe**	Daniel D. Tompkins	183	83.9		
	Federalist	Rufus King	John Howard	34	15.6		

YEAR	PARTY	PRESIDENTIAL NOMINEE	VP NOMINEE	ELECTORAL VOTE NO.	ELECTORAL VOTE %	POPULAR VOTE NO.	POPULAR VOTE %
1820	Democratic-Republican	**James Monroe**		231	98.3		
	Independent	John Quincy Adams		1	0.4		
1824	Democratic-Republican	**John Quincy Adams**		84	32.2		
	Democratic-Republican	Andrew Jackson		99	37.9		
	Democratic-Republican	William H. Crawford		41	15.7		
	Democratic-Republican	Henry Clay		37	14.2		
1828	Democratic-Republican	**Andrew Jackson**	John C. Calhoun	178	68.2	642,553	56.1
	National Republican	John Quincy Adams	Richard Rush	83	31.8	500,897	43.6
1832	Democratic	**Andrew Jackson**	Martin Van Buren	219	76.0	701,780	54.2
	National Republican	Henry Clay	John Sergeant	49	17.0	484,205	37.4
	Independent	John Floyd	Henry Lee	11	3.8	0	
	Anti-Masonic	William Wirt	Amos Ellmaker	7	2.4	100,715	7.8
1836	Democratic	**Martin Van Buren**	Richard Johnson	170	57.8	764,176	50.8
	Whig	William Henry Harrison	Francis P. Granger	73	24.8	550,816	36.6
	Whig	Hugh Lawson White	John Tyler	26	8.8	146,107	9.7
	Whig	Daniel Webster	Francis P. Granger	14	4.8	41,201	2.7
	Independent	Willie Person Mangum	John Tyler	11	3.7	0	
1840	Democratic	Martin Van Buren	Richard Johnson	60	20.4	1,128,854	46.8
	Whig	**William Henry Harrison**	John Tyler	234	79.6	1,275,390	52.9
1844	Democratic	**James K. Polk**	George M. Dallas	170	61.8	1,339,494	49.5

YEAR	PARTY	PRESIDENTIAL NOMINEE	VP NOMINEE	ELECTORAL VOTE NO.	ELECTORAL VOTE %	POPULAR VOTE NO.	POPULAR VOTE %
	Whig	Henry Clay	Theodore Frelinghuy-sen	105	38.2	1,300,004	48.1
1848	Democratic	Lewis Cass	William Butler	127	43.8	1,223.460	42.5
	Whig	**Zachary Taylor**	Millard Fillmore	163	56.2	1,361,393	47.3
	Free Soil	Martin Van Buren	Charles Adams Sr.	0		291,501	10.1
1852	Democratic	**Franklin Pierce**	William R. King	254	85.8	1,607,510	50.8
	Whig	Winfield Scott	William Graham	42	14.2	1,386,942	43.9
1856	Democratic	**James Buchanan**	John C. Brecken-ridge	174	58.8	1,836,072	45.3
	Republican	John C. Fremont	William L. Dayton	114	38.5	1,342.345	33.1
	Whig-American	Millard Fillmore	Andrew Jackson Donelson	8	2.7	873,053	21.6
1860	Democratic	Stephen Douglas	Herschel Johnson	12	4.0	1,380,202	29.5
	Democratic (Southern)	John Breckenridge	Joseph Lane	72	23.8	848,019	18.1
	Republican	**Abraham Lincoln**	Hannibal Hamlin	180	59.4	1,865,908	39.9
	Constitu-tional Union	John Bell	Edward Everett	39	12.9	590,901	12.6
1864	Democratic	George McClellan	George Pendleton	21	9.0	1,809,445	44.9
	Republican	**Abraham Lincoln**	Andrew Johnson	212	90.6	2,220,846	55.1
1868	Democratic	Horatio Seymour	Francis Blair Jr.	80	27.2	2,708,744	47.3
	Republican	**Ulysses S. Grant**	Schuyler Colfax	214	72.8	3,013,650	52.7
1872	Democratic	Horace Greeley[1]	Benjamin Brown	0		2,835,315	43.8
	Republican	**Ulysses S. Grant**	Henry Wilson	286	81.9	3,598,468	55.6
1876	Democratic	Samuel Tilden	Thomas Hendricks	184	49.9	4,288,191	51.0

YEAR	PARTY	PRESIDENTIAL NOMINEE	VP NOMINEE	ELECTORAL VOTE NO.	ELECTORAL VOTE %	POPULAR VOTE NO.	POPULAR VOTE %
	Republican	**Rutherford B. Hayes**	William Wheeler	185	50.1	4,033,497	48.0
1880	Democratic	Winfield S. Hancock	William English	155	42.0	4,445,256	48.2
	Republican	**James A. Garfield**	Chester A. Arthur	214	58.0	4,453,611	48.3
1884	Democratic	**Grover Cleveland**	Thomas Hendricks	219	54.6	4,915,586	48.9
	Republican	James G. Blane	John Logan	182	45.4	4,852,916	48.2
1888	Democratic	Grover Cleveland	Allen Thurman	168	41.9	5,539,118	48.6
	Republican	**Benjamin Harrison**	Levi Morton	233	58.1	5,449.825	47.8
1892	Democratic	**Grover Cleveland**	Adlai E. Stevenson	277	62.4	5,554,617	46.0
	Republican	Benjamin Harrison	Whitelaw Reid	145	32.7	5,186,793	43.0
	Populist	James Weaver	James Field	22	5.0	1,029,357	8.5
1896	Democratic	William Jennings Bryan	Arthur Sewall	176	39.0	6,370,897	45.8
	Republican	**William McKinley**	Garret Hobart	271	61.0	7.105,076	51.1
1900	Democratic	William Jennings Bryan	Adlai E. Stevenson	155	34.7	6,357,698	45.5
	Republican	**William McKinley**	Theodore Roosevelt	292	65.3	7,219,193	51.7
1904	Democratic	Alton B. Parker	Henry Davis	140	29.4	5,083,501	37.6
	Republican	**Theodore Roosevelt**	Charles Fairbanks	336	70.6	7,625,599	56.4
1908	Democratic	William Jennings Bryan	John Kern	162	33.5	6,406,874	43.0
	Republican	**William Howard Taft**	James S. Sherman	321	66.5	7,676,598	51.6
1912	Democratic	**Woodrow Wilson**	Thomas R. Marshall	435	81.9	6,294,327	41.8
	Republican	William Howard Taft	Nicholas Butler	8	1.5	3,486,343	23.2

YEAR	PARTY	PRESIDENTIAL NOMINEE	VP NOMINEE	ELECTORAL VOTE NO.	ELECTORAL VOTE %	POPULAR VOTE NO.	POPULAR VOTE %
	Progressive	Theodore Roosevelt	Hiram Johnson	88	16.6	4,120,207	27.4
1916	Democratic	**Woodrow Wilson**	Thomas R. Marshall	277	52.2	9.126.063	49.2
	Republican	Charles E. Hughes	Charles W. Fairbanks	254	47.8	8,547,030	46.1
1920	Democratic	James M. Cox	Franklin D. Roosevelt	127	23.9	9,134,074	34.1
	Republican	**Warren G. Harding**	Calvin Coolidge	404	76.1	16,151,916	60.3
1924	Democratic	John W. Davis	Charles W. Bryan	136	25.6	8,386,532	28.8
	Republican	**Calvin Coolidge**	Charles G. Dawes	382	71.9	15,724,310	54.0
	Progressive	Robert La Follette	Burton K. Wheeler	13	2.4	4,827,184	16.6
1928	Democratic	Alfred E. Smith	Joseph Robinson	87	16.4	15,004,336	40.8
	Republican	**Herbert Hoover**	Charles Curtis	444	83.6	21,432,823	58.2
1932	Democratic	**Franklin D. Roosevelt**	John Nance Garner	472	88.9	22,818,740	57.4
	Republican	Herbert Hoover	Charles Curtis	59	11.1	15,760,425	39.6
1936	Democratic	**Franklin D. Roosevelt**	John Nance Garner	523	98.5	27,750,866	60.8
	Republican	Alfred M. Landon	Frank Knox	8	1.5	16,679,683	36.5
1940	Democratic	**Franklin D. Roosevelt**	Henry A. Wallace	449	84.6	27,243,218	54.7
	Republican	Wendell L. Willkie	Charles L. McNary	82	15.4	22,334,940	44.8
1944	Democratic	**Franklin D. Roosevelt**	Harry S. Truman	432	81.4	25,612,610	53.4
	Republican	Thomas Dewey	John W. Bricker	99	18.6	22,014,160	45.9
1948	Democratic	**Harry S. Truman**	Alben W. Barkley	303	57.1	24,105,810	49.5
	Republican	Thomas Dewey	Earl Warren	189	35.6	21,970,064	45.1
	States' Rights	Strom Thurmond	Fielding Wright	39	7.3	1,169,114	2.4

YEAR	PARTY	PRESIDENTIAL NOMINEE	VP NOMINEE	ELECTORAL VOTE NO.	ELECTORAL VOTE %	POPULAR VOTE NO.	POPULAR VOTE %
1952	Democratic	Adlai Stevenson	John Sparkman	89	16.8	27,314,992	44.4
	Republican	**Dwight D. Eisenhower**	Richard M. Nixon	442	83.2	33,777,945	54.9
1956	Democratic	Adlai Stevenson	Estes Kefauver	73	13.7	26,022,752	42.0
	Republican	**Dwight D. Eisenhower**	Richard M. Nixon	457	86.1	35,590,472	57.4
1960	Democratic	**John F. Kennedy**	Lyndon B. Johnson	303	56.4	34,226,731	49.7
	Republican	Richard M. Nixon	Henry Cabot Lodge	219	40.8	34,108,157	49.5
	Democratic	Harry F. Byrd	Strom Thurmond	15	2.8	0	
1964	Democratic	**Lyndon B. Johnson**	Hubert H. Humphrey	486	90.3	43,129,566	61.1
	Republican	Barry Goldwater	William E. Miller	52	9.7	27,178,188	38.5
1968	Democratic	Hubert H. Humphrey	Edmund Muskie	191	35.5	31,275,166	42.7
	Republican	**Richard M. Nixon**	Spiro Agnew	301	55.9	31,785,480	43.4
	American Independent	George Wallace	Curtis LeMay	45	8.4	9,906,473	13.5
1972	Democratic	George McGovern	Sargent Shriver	17	3.2	29,170,383	37.5
	Republican	**Richard M. Nixon**	Spiro Agnew	520	96.7	47,169,911	60.7
1976	Democratic	**Jimmy Carter**	Walter Mondale	297	55.2	40,830,763	50.1
	Republican	Gerald R. Ford	Bob Dole	240	44.6	39,147,793	48.0
1980	Democratic	**Jimmy Carter**	Walter Mondale	49	9.1	35,483,883	41.0
	Republican	**Ronald Reagan**	George Bush	489	90.9	43,904,153	50.7
	National Union	John Anderson	Patrick Lucey	0		5,720,060	6.6
1984	Democratic	Walter Mondale	Geraldine Ferraro	13	2.4	37,577,185	40.6
	Republican	**Ronald Reagan**	George Bush	525	97.6	54,455,075	58.8
1988	Democratic	Michael Dukakis	Lloyd Bentsen	111	20.6	41,809,074	45.6

YEAR	PARTY	PRESIDENTIAL NOMINEE	VP NOMINEE	ELECTORAL VOTE NO.	ELECTORAL VOTE %	POPULAR VOTE NO.	POPULAR VOTE %
	Republican	**George Bush**	Dan Quayle	426	79.2	48,886,097	53.4
1992	Democratic	**William J. Clinton**	Albert Gore Jr.	370	68.8	44,909,326	43.0
	Republican	George Bush	Dan Quayle	168	31.2	39,103,882	37.4
	Independent	H. Ross Perot	James Stockdale	0		19,741,657	18.9
1996	Democratic	**William J. Clinton**	Albert Gore Jr.	379	70.4	47,402,357	49.2
	Republican	Bob Dole	Jack Kemp	159	29.6	39,198,755	40.7
	Reform	H. Ross Perot	Pat Choate	0		8,085,402	8.4
2000	Democratic	Albert Gore Jr.	Joseph Lieberman	266	49.4	50,992,335	48.4
	Republican	**George W. Bush**	Richard Cheney	271	50.4	50,455,156	47.9
	Green	Ralph Nader	Winona LaDuke	0		2,822,738	2.7
2004	Democratic	John F. Kerry	John Edwards	251	46.7	59,028,444	48.3
	Republican	**George W. Bush**	Richard Cheney	286	53.2	62,040,610	50.7
2008	Democratic	**Barack Obama**	Joseph Biden	365	67.8	69,456,897	52.9
	Republican	John McCain	Sarah Palin	173	32.2	59,934,814	45.7
2012	Democratic	**Barack Obama**	Joseph Biden	332	61.7	65,899,660	51.1
	Republican	Mitt Romney	Paul Ryan	206	38.3	60,932,152	47.2
2016[2]	Democratic	Hillary Clinton	Tim Kaine	227	42.2	65,844,610	48.2
	Republican	**Donald Trump**	Mike Pence	304	56.5	62,979,636	46.2
	Libertarian	Gary Johnson	William Weld	0		4,488,912	3.3
	Green	Jill Stein	Ajamu Baraka	0		1,449364	1.1

[1] Horace Greeley died on November 29, 1872, after the popular election, but before the Electoral College met. His electoral votes were split among four individuals, including 18 for Benjamin Brown, Greeley's running mate.

[2] Seven electors were "faithless" and voted for other candidates: In Hawaii, Senator Bernie Sanders (VT-D) received one electoral vote. In Texas, Governor John Kasich (OH-R) received one electoral vote and former representative Ron Paul (TX-R) received one electoral vote. In Washington, former secretary of state Colin Powell received three electoral votes and Faith Spotted Eagle received one electoral vote.

Source: The American Presidency Project, "Presidential Elections Data," available at http://www.presidency .ucsb.edu/elections.php.

NOTES

CHAPTER 1

1. "Remarks by the President," April 27, 2011, http://www.whitehouse.gov/the-press-office/2011/04/27/remarks-president.
2. Barack Obama's interview with Steve Kroft, *60 Minutes*, CBS, May 8, 2011.
3. For example, see Louis W. Koenig, *The Chief Executive*, 6th ed. (New York: Harcourt Brace, 1996), 2–3.
4. Ibid., 2.
5. Ibid., 3.
6. Jeffrey Cohen and David Nice, *The Presidency* (New York: McGraw–Hill, 2003), 53–59; and Sidney M. Milkis and Michael Nelson, *The American Presidency: Origins and Development, 1776–2014*, 7th ed. (Washington, DC: CQ Press, 2016), 301–304.
7. Milkis and Nelson, *The American Presidency*, 302.
8. The term "imperial president" is most often associated with the book of the same title by historian Arthur Schlesinger Jr. in which he discusses the modern presidency. See Schlesinger, *The Imperial Presidency* (Boston: Houghton Mifflin, 1973).
9. Koenig, *The Chief Executive*, 4.
10. For example, see, Ryan Barilleaux, *The Post-Modern Presidency: The Office after Ronald Reagan* (New York: Praeger, 1988); Richard Rose, *The Postmodern President*, 2nd ed. (Chatham, NJ: Chatham House, 1991); and Steven Schier, ed., *The Postmodern Presidency: Bill Clinton's Legacy in U.S. Politics* (Pittsburgh, PA: University of Pittsburgh Press, 2000).
11. Rose, *The Postmodern President*, 2–6.
12. Joseph A. Pika, John Anthony Maltese, and Andrew Rudalevige, *The Politics of the Presidency*, 9th ed. (Washington, DC: CQ Press, 2017), 1.
13. Hugh Heclo, *Studying the Presidency: A Report to the Ford Foundation* (New York: Ford Foundation Press, 1977), 7–8.
14. See Edward S. Corwin, *The President: Office and Powers 1787–1957* (New York: New York University Press, 1957).
15. Clinton Rossiter, *The American Presidency* (New York: Time, 1960), 31.
16. See Richard Neustadt, *Presidential Power* (New York: Wiley, 1960).
17. Unsigned memorandum, July 6, 1928, Files of Franklin D. Roosevelt, Family Business and Personal Papers, Writing and Statement File, Box 42, Franklin D. Roosevelt Presidential Library, Hyde Park, New York.

18. Heclo, *Studying the Presidency*, 5–6.

19. Ibid., 31–45.

20. Ibid., 30.

21. *Researching the Presidency: Vital Questions, New Approaches*, ed. George C. Edwards III, John H. Kessel, and Bert A. Rockman (Pittsburgh, PA: University of Pittsburgh Press, 1993), 3–5.

22. Lyn Ragsdale, *Vital Statistics on the Presidency* (Washington, DC: CQ Press, 2008), 1–3.

23. Stephen J. Wayne, "An Introduction to Research on the Presidency," in *Studying the Presidency*, ed. George C. Edwards III and Stephen J. Wayne (Knoxville, TN: University of Tennessee Press, 1983), 4.

24. Ibid., 5–6.

25. Stephen J. Wayne, "Approaches," in *Studying the Presidency*, ed. George C. Edwards III and Stephen J. Wayne (Knoxville: University of Tennessee Press, 1983), 17–49.

26. Early examples include George C. Edwards III, *At the Margins: Presidential Leadership of Congress* (New Haven, CT: Yale University Press, 1989); Mark A. Peterson, *Legislating Together: The White House and Capitol Hill from Eisenhower to Reagan* (Cambridge, MA: Harvard University Press, 1990); and Samuel Kernell, *Going Public: New Strategies of Presidential Leadership* (Washington, DC: CQ Press, 1986).

27. Peter G. Northouse, *Leadership: Theory and Practice* (Thousand Oaks, CA: Sage, 1997), 3.

28. Bert A. Rockman, "The Leadership Style of George Bush," in *The Bush Presidency: First Appraisals*, ed. Colin Campbell and Bert A. Rockman (Chatham, NJ: Chatham House, 1991), 2.

29. James MacGregor Burns, *Leadership* (New York: Harper & Row, 1978).

30. James MacGregor Burns, *Transforming Leadership* (New York: Atlantic Monthly Press, 2003), 29.

31. See Bruce Miroff, *Icons of Democracy: American Leaders as Heroes, Aristocrats, Dissenters, & Democrats* (Lawrence: University Press of Kansas, 2000).

32. Ibid.

33. See Neustadt, *Presidential Power*.

34. See Stephen Skowronek, *The Politics Presidents Make: Leadership from John Adams to George Bush* (Cambridge, MA: Belknap/Harvard Press, 1993); and Rose, *The Postmodern President*.

35. For example, see John H. Kessel, *Presidents, the Presidency, and the Political Environment* (Washington, DC: CQ Press, 2001); and Thomas E. Cronin and Michael A. Genovese, *The Paradoxes of the American Presidency* (New York: Oxford University Press, 1998).

36. For example, see John Burke, *The Institutional Presidency* (Baltimore: Johns Hopkins University Press, 1992); Thomas J. Weko, *The Politicizing Presidency: The White House Personnel Office, 1948–1994* (Lawrence: University of Kansas Press, 1995), and Shirley Anne Warshaw, *The Keys to Power: Managing the Presidency* (New York: Longman, 2000).

37. For example, see Charles O. Jones, *Separate but Equal Branches: Congress and the Presidency*, 2nd ed. (New York: Chatham House, 1999); Jeffrey E. Cohen, *Presidential Responsiveness and Public Policy-making: The Public and the Policies That Presidents Choose* (Ann Arbor: University of Michigan Press, 1997); and William W. Lammers and Michael A. Genovese, *The Presidency and Domestic Policy: Comparing Leadership Styles, FDR to Clinton* (Washington, DC: CQ Press, 2000).

38. For example, see Samuel Kernell, *Going Public: New Strategies of Presidential Leadership*, 4th ed. (Washington, DC: CQ Press, 2007); Jeffrey K. Tulis, *The Rhetorical*

Presidency (Princeton, NJ: Princeton University Press, 1987); Roderick P. Hart, *The Sound of Leadership: Presidential Communication in the Modern Age* (Chicago: University of Chicago Press, 1987); Mary E. Stuckey, *The President as Interpreter-in-Chief* (Chatham, NJ: Chatham House, 1991), John Anthony Maltese, *Spin Control: The White House Office of Communications and the Management of Presidential News*, 2nd ed., rev. (Chapel Hill: University of North Carolina Press, 1994); and Lori Cox Han, *Governing from Center Stage: White House Communication Strategies during the Television Age of Politics* (Cresskill, NJ: Hampton Press, 2001).

39. For example, see Cronin and Genovese, *The Paradoxes*. See also Robert K. Murray and Tim H. Blessing, *Greatness in the White House: Rating the Presidents from George Washington through Ronald Reagan*, 2nd ed. (University Park: Pennsylvania State University Press, 1994); Arthur M. Schlesinger Jr., "The Ultimate Approval Rating," *New York Times Magazine*, December 15, 1996, 46–51; and Brandon Rottinghaus and Justin S. Vaughn, "Measuring Obama against the Great Presidents," *Brookings*, February 13, 2015, https://www.brookings.edu/blog/fixgov/2015/02/13/measuring-obama-against-the-great-presidents/.

40. See Cronin and Genovese, *The Paradoxes*.

41. See Fred I. Greenstein, *The Presidential Difference: Leadership Style from FDR to Barack Obama*, 3rd ed. (Princeton, NJ: Princeton University Press, 2009).

42. See James David Barber, *The Presidential Character: Predicting Performance in the White House*, rev. 4th ed. (New York: Prentice Hall, 2008).

43. See Greenstein, *The Presidential Difference*, 296.

44. See Lori Cox Han, "Public Leadership in the Political Arena," in *Leadership and Politics*, Vol. 2 of *Leadership at the Crossroads*, ed. Michael A. Genovese and Lori Cox Han (Westport, CT: Praeger, 2008).

45. Tulis, *The Rhetorical Presidency*, 28.

46. Ibid., 4–23.

47. Hart, *The Sound of Leadership*, 212.

48. Kernell, *Going Public*, 10–11.

49. See George C. Edwards III, *On Deaf Ears: The Limits of the Bully Pulpit* (New Haven, CT: Yale University Press, 2003).

50. See Jeffrey E. Cohen, *Going Local: Presidential Leadership in the Post-Broadcast Age* (New York: Cambridge University Press, 2010).

51. Examples of this approach include Terry M. Moe, "The Politicized Presidency," in *The New Direction in American Politics*, ed. John E. Chubb and Paul E. Peterson (Washington, DC: Brookings Institution, 1985); and Terry M. Moe, "Presidents, Institutions, and Theory," in *Researching the Presidency: Vital Questions, New Approaches*, ed. George C. Edwards III, John H. Kessel, and Bert A. Rockman (Pittsburgh, PA: University of Pittsburgh Press, 1993); Burke, *The Institutional Presidency*; and Weko, *The Politicizing Presidency*.

52. For an excellent discussion of Terry Moe's work in this area, see Jeffrey Cohen and David Nice, *The Presidency* (New York: McGraw–Hill, 2003), 57–59.

53. For example, see William G. Howell, *Power without Persuasion: The Politics of Direct Presidential Action* (Princeton, NJ: Princeton University Press, 2003); and Ryan J. Barilleaux and Christopher S. Kelley, eds., *The Unitary Executive and the Modern Presidency* (College Station: Texas A&M University Press, 2010).

54. For example, see Brandice Canes-Wrone, *Who's Leading Whom?* (Chicago: University of Chicago Press, 2006); and B. Dan Wood, *The Politics of Economic Leadership: The Causes and Consequences of Presidential Rhetoric* (Princeton, NJ: Princeton University Press, 2007).

55. For example, see Andrew Rudalevige, *Managing the President's Program: Presidential Leadership and Legislative Policy Formation* (Princeton, NJ: Princeton University Press, 2002); and David E. Lewis, *The Politics of Presidential Appointments: Political Control and Bureaucratic Performance* (Princeton, NJ: Princeton University Press, 2008).

56. For example, see Douglas L. Kriner, *After the Rubicon: Congress, Presidents, and the Politics of Waging War* (Chicago: University of Chicago Press, 2010).

57. See Skowronek, *The Politics Presidents Make*.

58. Ibid.

59. Bruce Miroff and Stephen Skowronek, "Rethinking Presidential Studies through Historical Research," *Presidential Studies Quarterly* 44, no. 1 (March 2014): 1–5.

60. See Louis Fisher, *The Politics of Shared Power: Congress and the Executive*, 4th ed. (College Station: Texas A&M University Press, 1998).

61. See Ragsdale, *Vital Statistics*, 7–13.

62. Fred I. Greenstein, *The Hidden-Hand Presidency: Eisenhower as Leader* (Baltimore: Johns Hopkins University Press, 1994), viii–ix.

63. "Presidential Libraries," National Archives and Records Administration, http://www .archives.gov/presidential-libraries/.

64. Letter from Irving Perimeter to Benson Trimble, November 15, 1952, WHCF Permanent File, Subject File, Box 5, Harry S. Truman Presidential Library, Independence, Missouri.

65. Originally dedicated in 1990, the Nixon Library did not become an official NARA presidential library until 2007. After numerous legal battles between the federal government and the Nixon family, Nixon White House documents held in NARA archives in College Park, Maryland, began to be transferred to the Yorba Linda, California, library in 2004; previously, the Nixon Library was run by the privately funded Nixon Foundation and only housed pre- and post-presidential papers.

66. In 2011, the Presidency Research Group was renamed Presidents and Executive Politics.

67. "Call to Action on Executive Order 13233," Society of American Archivists, http:// www.archivists.org/news/actnow.asp.

68. John Wertman, "Bush's Obstruction of History," *Washington Post*, February 26, 2006, http:// www.washingtonpost.com/wp-dyn/content/article/2006/02/24/AR2006022401805.html.

69. At the time, Dr. Leland was director emeritus of the American Council of Learned Societies. The other members of the executive committee included Dr. Randolph G. Adams, director of the William L. Clements Library for American History, University of Michigan; Judge Charles E. Clark, dean of the Yale Law School; Dr. Robert D. W. Connor, archivist of the United States; Dr. Helen Taft Manning, dean of Bryn Mawr College; professor Samuel Eliot Morison of Harvard University; and Dr. Stuart A. Rice, chairman of the Central Statistical Board, Washington, DC.

70. Letter from Waldo G. Leland to Franklin D. Roosevelt, December 14, 1938, Files of Waldo G. Leland, Correspondence and Memos, Box 1, Franklin D. Roosevelt Presidential Library, Hyde Park, New York.

71. Statement by Waldo G. Leland at a dinner for advisory and executive committee members of the FDR Library project at the Hotel Carlton, Washington, DC, February 4, 1939, Files of Waldo G. Leland, Correspondence and Memos, Box 1, Franklin D. Roosevelt Presidential Library, Hyde Park, New York.

72. "The Story of the Franklin D. Roosevelt Library," Address by Waldo Gifford Leland at the Franklin D. Roosevelt Presidential Library, Hyde Park, New York, March 17, 1950, at the opening of the FDR Papers for research, Papers of Waldo G. Leland, Box 1, Franklin D. Roosevelt Presidential Library, Hyde Park, New York.

73. Memorandum for the Director of the Franklin D. Roosevelt Library from Franklin D. Roosevelt, July 16, 1943, Papers of Waldo G. Leland, Box 1, Franklin D. Roosevelt Presidential Library, Hyde Park, New York.

74. Remarks of President Lyndon Johnson at the LBJ Library Dedication, May 22, 1971, http://www.lbjlibrary.org/collections/selected-speeches/post-presidential/05-22-1971.html.

75. Letter from George Bush to Perry Adkisson, February 28, 1989, White House Office of Records and Management, Federal Government, Box 11, George Bush Presidential Library, College Station, Texas.

76. Bush received a letter from Kenneth Lay, chairman, president, and chief executive officer of ENRON Corporation, on March 21, 1989, urging the president to consider placing his library on the University of Houston campus: "More than any other academic institution in your hometown, we believe the University of Houston reflects the values, vision, scope, quality and dedication that characterizes your city and your career in private enterprise and public service. . . . As our 'education president,' it seems proper that your library should be affiliated with a public university in Houston that addresses the broadest current and future educational interests and needs of our country's people, and that reflects in its objectives and interests those areas of study in energy, economics, international affairs and equality of opportunity that have been the focus of your own life's work." Letter from Kenneth L. Lay to George Bush, March 21, 1989, White House Office of Records and Management, Federal Government, Box 12, George Bush Presidential Library, College Station, Texas.

77. Memorandum for the President from James W. Cicconi, "Presidential Library Correspondence," White House Office of Records and Management, Federal Government, Box 12, George Bush Presidential Library, College Station, Texas.

78. Memorandum for Patty Presock from Jim Cicconi, "Possible Meeting with Presidential Library Architect," White House Office of Records and Management, Federal Government, Box 12, George Bush Presidential Library, College Station, Texas.

79. Letter from George Bush to Ross D. Margraves Jr., May 3, 1991, White House Office of Records and Management, Federal Government, Box 12, George Bush Presidential Library, College Station, Texas.

80. Ralph Blumenthal, "SMU Faculty Complains about Bush Library," New York Times, January 10, 2007, http://www.nytimes.com/2007/01/10/us/politics/10library.html?ex=1326085200&en=3170689537c4434c&ei=5088&partner=rssnyt&emc=rss.

81. Angela K. Brown, "Methodists: No Bush Library at SMU," Washington Post, January 18, 2007, http://www.washingtonpost.com/wp-dyn/content/article/2007/01/18/AR2007011800796.html?nav=hcmodule.

82. See Tim Taliaferro, "Obama Presidential Library: University of Chicago Already Angling for It?" Huffington Post, October 26, 2009, http://www.huffingtonpost.com/2009/10/26/obama-presidential-librar_n_333723.html.

CHAPTER 2

1. Scott Detrow, "Obama Warns Trump against Relying on Executive Power," NPR, December 19, 2016, http://www.npr.org/2016/12/19/505860058/obama-warns-trump-against-relying-on-executive-power.

2. Gerhard Peters and John T. Woolley, "Executive Orders," The American Presidency Project, ed. John T. Woolley and Gerhard Peters, Santa Barbara, CA, 1999–2017, http://www.presidency.ucsb.edu/data/orders.php.

3. Tamara Keith, "Wielding a Pen and a Phone, Obama Goes It Alone," *NPR*, January 20, 2014, http://www.npr.org/2014/01/20/263766043/wielding-a-pen-and-a-phone-obama-goes-it-alone.

4. See Christian Meier, *Athens: A Portrait of the City in Its Golden Age*, trans. Robert and Rita Kimber (New York: Metropolitan Books, 1998); Josiah Ober, *Mass and Elite in Democratic Athens: Rhetoric, Ideology, and the Power of the People* (Princeton, NJ: Princeton University Press, 1989); and Martin Ostwald, *From Popular Sovereignty to the Sovereignty of Law: Law, Society, and Politics in Fifth-Century Athens* (Berkeley: University of California Press, 1986).

5. See Andrew Lintott, *The Constitution of the Roman Republic* (New York: Oxford University Press, 1999); and T. E. J. Wiedemann, *Cicero and the End of the Roman Republic* (New York: Oxford University Press, 1991).

6. See Paul A. Rahe, *Republics Ancient and Modern: New Modes and Orders in Early Modern Political Thought* (Chapel Hill: University of North Carolina Press, 1994).

7. See Christopher Hill, *The Century of Revolution, 1603–1714* (New York: W. W. Norton, 1961); and Derek Hirst, *Authority and Conflict: England, 1603–1658* (Cambridge, MA: Harvard University Press, 1986).

8. See Bernard Bailyn, *The Ideological Origins of the American Revolution* (Cambridge, MA: Harvard University Press, 1967); Jack P. Greene, *Negotiated Authorities: Essays in Colonial Political and Constitutional History* (Charlottesville: University Press of Virginia, 1994); Forrest McDonald, *Novus Ordo Seclorum: The Intellectual Origins of the Constitution* (Lawrence: University Press of Kansas, 1985); and J. G. A. Pocock, *The Machiavellian Moment: Florentine Political Thought and the Atlantic Republican Tradition* (Princeton, NJ: Princeton University Press, 1975).

9. See Thomas Gustafson, *Representative Words: Politics, Literature, and the American Language, 1776–1865* (Cambridge: Cambridge University Press, 1992); Henry F. May, *The Enlightenment in America* (Oxford: Oxford University Press, 1976); Carl J. Richard, *The Founders and the Classics: Greece, Rome, and the American Enlightenment* (Cambridge, MA: Harvard University Press, 1994); and Morton White, *Philosophy, "The Federalist," and the Constitution* (Oxford: Oxford University Press, 1987).

10. See May, *Enlightenment*.

11. See John Patrick Diggins, "Comrades and Citizens: New Mythologies in American Historiography," *American Historical Review* 90 (1985): 614–38; Diggins, *The Lost Soul of American Politics: Virtue, Self-Interest, and the Foundations of Liberalism* (Chicago: University of Chicago Press, 1984); David F. Ericson, *The Shaping of American Liberalism: The Debates over Ratification, Nullification, and Slavery* (Chicago: University of Chicago Press, 1993); David J. Greenstone, *The Lincoln Persuasion: Remaking American Liberalism* (Princeton, NJ: Princeton University Press, 1993); and Thomas L. Pangle, *The Spirit of Modern Republicanism: The Moral Vision of the American Founders and the Philosophy of Locke* (Chicago: University of Chicago Press, 1988).

12. See Bailyn, *Ideological Origins*; McDonald, *Novus Ordo Seclorum*; and Gordon S. Wood, *Creation of the American Republic, 1776–1787* (New York: W. W. Norton, 1969).

13. See the following works by John Phillip Reid: *Constitutional History of the American Revolution: The Authority of Law* (Madison: University of Wisconsin Press, 1993); *Constitutional History of the American Revolution: The Authority to Legislate* (Madison: University of Wisconsin Press, 1991); *Constitutional History of the American Revolution: The Authority of Rights* (Madison: University of Wisconsin Press, 1986); and *Constitutional History of the American Revolution: The Authority to Tax* (Madison: University of Wisconsin Press, 1987).

14. See Merrill Jensen, *The New Nation: A History of the United States during the Confederation, 1781–1789* (New York: Alfred A. Knopf, 1950); Richard B. Morris, *The Forging of the Union, 1781–1789* (New York: Harper & Row, 1987); Jack N. Rakove, *The Beginnings of National Politics: An Interpretive History of the Continental Congress* (Baltimore: Johns Hopkins University Press, 1979); and Wood, *Creation of the American Republic*.

15. See Morris, *Forging of the Union*; and Wood, *Creation of the American Republic*.

16. For a summary of Hamilton's views and political preferences, see Forrest McDonald, *Alexander Hamilton: A Biography* (New York: W. W. Norton, 1979).

17. The earliest philosophical treatment of sovereignty, focusing on what was at that time called "raison d'etat," was Jean Bodin, *The Six Bookes of a Commonweale*, trans. R. Knolles (Cambridge, MA: Harvard University Press, 1962) and originally published in 1576.

18. See Isaac Kramnick, *Republicanism and Bourgeois Radicalism: Political Ideology in Late Eighteenth-Century England and America* (Ithaca, NY: Cornell University Press, 1990); and Reid, *Constitutional History* (4 vols.).

19. See Edmund S. Morgan, *Inventing the People: The Rise of Popular Sovereignty in England and America* (New York: W. W. Norton, 1988).

20. See McDonald, *Novus Ordo Seclorum*; and Wood, *Creation of the American Republic*.

21. Despite some of the disagreements about the specific scope of presidential powers, both supporters and opponents of an active centralized government strongly endorsed limited authority. See Publius, *The Federalist Papers*, ed. Isaac Kramnick (London: Penguin Books, 1987); and Herbert J. Storing, *The Complete Anti-Federalist* (Chicago: University of Chicago Press, 2007).

22. See George W. Carey, *The Federalist: Design for a Constitutional Republic* (Urbana: University of Illinois Press, 1989); Publius [Hamilton], *Federalist* 67–77; and White, *Philosophy, 'The Federalist,' and the Constitution*.

23. For a discussion of the deficiencies and proposed remedies, see Carey, *The Federalist*; Forrest McDonald, *E Pluribus Unum: The Formation of the American Republic, 1776–1790* (Indianapolis: Liberty Press, 1965); Publius [Hamilton], *Federalist* 15–25; and Wood, *Creation of the American Republic*.

24. See Bailyn, *Ideological Origins*; McDonald, *Novus Ordo Seclorum*; Publius [Hamilton], *Federalist* 8; and Wood, *Creation of the American Republic*.

25. The issue of presidential succession had been controversial because of the ambiguous language of Article II, Section 1, Clause 6, since it did not expressly state whether the vice president becomes the president, as opposed to simply an "acting" president, if the president dies, resigns, is removed from office, or is otherwise unable to discharge the duties of the office. The problem first arose in 1841, when President William Henry Harrison died after only a month in office. The immediate question was whether Vice President John Tyler would assume the full duties and powers of the office for the remaining 47 months of Harrison's term. Tyler assumed the full powers of the office, as did the eight other vice presidents who have succeeded to the office of the presidency.

26. See Publius [Madison], *Federalist* 47–51.

27. Hamilton makes numerous references to this in the *Federalist*; see *Federalist* 67–77.

28. See Stanley Elkins and Eric McKitrick, *The Age of Federalism: The Early American Republic, 1788–1800* (New York: Oxford University Press, 1993).

29. See Publius [Hamilton], *Federalist* 68.

30. For information on presidential politics prior to 1828, see Lance Banning, *The Jeffersonian Persuasion: Evolution of a Party Ideology* (Ithaca, NY: Cornell University Press, 1978); Elkins, *Age of Federalism*; and Charles Sellers, *The Market Revolution: Jacksonian America, 1815–1846* (New York: Oxford University Press, 1991).

31. The framers' world was neither egalitarian nor democratic, and their conceptions of equality differed radically from today's interpretations. See Reid, *Constitutional History*.

32. On the electoral reforms that began in the late 1820s, see Jennifer Nedelsky, *Private Property and the Limits of American Constitutionalism: The Madisonian Framework and Its Legacy* (Chicago: University of Chicago Press, 1990); Karen Orren, *Belated Feudalism: Labor, Law, and Liberal Development in the United States* (Cambridge: Cambridge University Press, 1991); Sellers, *Market Revolution*; and Sean Wilentz, *Chants Democratic: New York City and the Rise of the American Working Class, 1788–1850* (Oxford: Oxford University Press, 1984).

33. On the presidency relative to other contemporary chief executives, see Beer, *To Make a Nation*; Elkins and McKitrick, *Age of Federalism*; Forrest McDonald, *The American Presidency: An Intellectual History* (Lawrence: University Press of Kansas, 1995); Publius [Hamilton], *Federalist 67–77*; and R. R. Palmer, *Age of the Democratic Revolution: A Political History of Europe and America, 1760–1800*, Vol. 2 (Princeton, NJ: Princeton University Press, 1970).

34. See David G. Adler and Larry N. George, eds., *The Constitution and the Conduct of American Foreign Policy* (Lawrence: University Press of Kansas, 1996); Joseph Bessette and Jeffrey Tulis, *The Presidency in the Constitutional Order* (Baton Rouge: Louisiana State University Press, 1981); Edward Corwin, *The President: Office and Powers* (New York: New York University Press, 1984); and Gordon Silverstein, *Constitutional Interpretation and the Making of American Foreign Policy* (New York: Oxford University Press, 1996).

35. Memo from C. Boyden Gray to George Bush, "War Powers Issues That May Arise in Your Meeting with Congressional Leaders," August 27, 1990, Formerly Withheld, NLGB Control Number 308, George Bush Presidential Library, College Station, Texas.

36. On the opposition to standing armies, see Walter LaFeber, *The American Age: United States Foreign Policy at Home and Abroad, 1750 to the Present* (New York: W. W. Norton, 1994); and Russell F. Weigley, *The American Way of War: A History of United States Military Strategy and Policy* (Bloomington: Indiana University Press, 1977). On anti-militarist ideology, see Banning, *Jeffersonian Persuasion*; Elkins and McKitrick, *Age of Federalism*; Robert Middlekauf, *The Glorious Cause: The American Revolution, 1763–1789* (New York: Oxford University Press, 2007); Wilentz, *Chants Democratic*; and Gordon S. Wood, *The Radicalism of the American Revolution* (New York: Vintage Books, 1991).

37. See Elkins and McKitrick, *Age of Federalism*; Middlekauf, *Glorious Cause*; and Wood, *Radicalism*.

38. See Banning, *Jeffersonian Persuasion*; Lawrence S. Kaplan, *Entangling Alliances with None: American Foreign Policy in the Age of Jefferson* (Kent, OH: Kent State University Press, 1987); and LaFeber, *American Age*.

39. On this point, especially the infancy of American federal law, see Lawrence M. Friedman, *Crime and Punishment in American History* (New York: Basic Books, 1993); Lawrence M. Friedman, *A History of American Law* (New York: Simon & Schuster, 1985); Morton J. Horwitz, *The Transformation of American Law, 1780–1860* (Cambridge, MA: Harvard University Press, 1977); Sellers, *Market Revolution*; and Christopher L. Tomlins, *Law, Labor, and Ideology in the Early American Republic* (Cambridge: Cambridge University Press, 1993).

40. See Friedman, *Crime and Punishment*; Kermit L. Hall, *The Magic Mirror: Law in American History* (New York: Oxford University Press, 1989); and Horwitz, *Transformation of American Law*, Vol. 1.

41. See Banning, *Jeffersonian Persuasion*; Carey, *Federalist*; Elkins and McKitrick, *Age of Federalism*; McDonald, *Novus Ordo Seclorum*; Middlekauf, *Glorious Cause*; and Wood, *Creation of the American Republic*.

42. See Ronald Radosh, *The Rosenberg File* (New Haven, CT: Yale University Press, 1997).

43. See Carey, *Federalist*; Publius [Hamilton], *Federalist 74*; Reid, *Constitutional History*; Tomlins, *Law, Labor, and Ideology*; and Wood, *Creation of the American Republic*.

44. Since the early 1930s, a majority of presidential grants of clemency have occurred in the month of December. See P. S. Ruckman Jr., "Seasonal Clemency Revisited: An Empirical Analysis," *White House Studies* 11, no. 1 (2011): 21–39.

45. On the Rich pardon, see George Lardner Jr., "A Pardon to Remember," *The New York Times*, November 22, 2008, A21; and House Committee on Government Reform, *Justice Undone: Clemency Decisions in the Clinton White House* (Washington, DC: U.S. Congress, March 14, 2002).

46. See "Clemency Statistics," The U.S. Department of Justice, https://www.justice.gov/pardon/clemency-statistics.

47. "Petition for Pardon," Files of Meredith Cabe, Box 1, Bill Clinton Presidential Library, Little Rock, Arkansas.

48. An article of impeachment needs a majority vote in the House, and then conviction in the Senate needs a two-thirds vote. The Senate trial is presided over by the chief justice of the United States.

49. See Carey, *Federalist*; Publius [Hamilton], *Federalist 73*; and Wood, *Creation of the American Republic*.

50. This is evident by implication throughout contemporary documents. For examples, see Publius [Hamilton]; *Federalist 67–77*.

51. On the legislative roles of recent presidents, see Louis Fisher, *Constitutional Conflicts between Congress and the President* (Lawrence: University Press of Kansas, 2007).

52. See Richard Hofstadter, *The Idea of a Party System: The Rise of Legitimate Opposition in the United States, 1780–1840* (Berkeley: University of California Press, 1970).

53. See Carey, *Federalist*; Publius [Hamilton], *Federalist 76–77*; and Wood, *Creation of the American Republic*.

54. On the emergence of the spoils system, see Arthur M. Schlesinger Jr., *Age of Jackson* (New York: Back Bay Books, 1988); Sellers, *Market Revolution*; and Wilentz, *Chants Democratic*.

55. John Trenchard and Thomas Gordon, *Essays on Liberty, Civil and Religious, and Other Important Subjects*, ed. and annotated by Ronald Hamowy. 2 vols. (Indianapolis: Liberty Fund, 1995), contains some pointed contemporary criticisms of the politicization of the crown's appointment powers.

56. See Carey, *Federalist*; Publius [Hamilton], *Federalist 76–77*; and Wood, *Creation of the American Republic*.

57. See Storing, *Complete Anti-Federalist*.

58. On relevant rulings and the evolution of the removal doctrine, see Fisher, *Constitutional Conflicts*; and G. Galvin McKenzie, *The Politics of Presidential Appointments* (New York: Free Press, 1981).

59. On Gilded-Age political patronage, see Richard F. Welch, *King of the Bowery: Big Tim Sullivan, Tammany Hall and New York City from the Gilded Age to the Progressive Era* (Albany: State University of New York Press, 2009).

60. On civil-service reforms, see Stephen Skowronek, *Building a New American State: The Expansion of National Administrative Capacities, 1877–1920* (New York: Cambridge University Press, 1982).

61. See Raoul Berger, *Executive Privilege* (Cambridge, MA: Harvard University Press, 1974); Raoul Berger, *Impeachment: The Constitutional Problems* (Cambridge, MA: Harvard University Press, 1973); Louis Fisher, *The Politics of Executive Privilege* (Durham, NC: Carolina Academic Press, 2004); and Mark Rozell, *Executive Privilege: The Dilemma of Secrecy and Democratic Accountability* (Lawrence: University Press of Kansas, 2000).

62. Letter from Abraham Lincoln to A. G. Hodges, April 4, 1864.

63. See Theodore Roosevelt, *The Autobiography of Theodore Roosevelt* (New York: Scribner's, 1913).

64. See William Howard Taft, *Our Chief Magistrate and His Powers* (New York: Columbia University Press, 1916).

65. See Francine Sanders Romero, "William Howard Taft," in *The Presidents and the Constitution: A Living History*, ed. Ken Gormley (New York: New York University Press, 2016).

66. Saladin M. Ambar, "Woodrow Wilson," in *The Presidents and the Constitution: A Living History*, ed. Ken Gormley (New York: New York University Press, 2016), 367–68.

67. See Arthur M. Schlesinger Jr., *The Imperial Presidency* (Boston: Houghton Mifflin, 1973).

68. Memo from Patrick J. Buchanan to Richard Nixon, July 1, 1971, Papers of Patrick J. Buchanan, Box 1, Richard Nixon Presidential Library, Yorba Linda, California.

69. For a brief discussion on the unitary executive theory, see Stephen Skowronek, "The Paradigm of Development in Presidential History," in *The Oxford Handbook of the American Presidency*, ed. George C. Edwards III and William G. Howell (New York: Oxford University Press, 2009), 762–65.

70. Kenneth R. Mayer, "Going Alone: The Presidential Power of Unilateral Action," in *The Oxford Handbook of the American Presidency*, ed. George C. Edwards III and William G. Howell (New York: Oxford University Press, 2009), 429.

71. Kenneth R. Mayer, *With the Stroke of a Pen: Executive Orders and Presidential Power* (Princeton, NJ: Princeton University Press, 2001), 5.

72. William G. Howell, *Power without Persuasion: The Politics of Direct Presidential Action* (Princeton, NJ: Princeton University Press, 2003), 8.

73. See David M. O'Brien, *Constitutional Law and Politics: Struggles for Power and Governmental Accountability*, Vol. 1, 9th ed. (New York: W. W. Norton, 2014).

74. Ibid.

75. Ibid.

76. See James P. Pfiffner, "The Constitutional Legacy of George W. Bush," *Presidential Studies Quarterly* 45, no. 4 (December 2015): 727–41.

CHAPTER 3

1. Sidney Milkis and Michael Nelson, *The American Presidency: Origins and Development 1776–2014*, 7th ed. (Washington, DC: CQ Press, 2016), 56.

2. See Marc Hetherington and Bruce Larson, *Parties, Politics and Public Policy in America*, 11th ed. (Washington, DC: CQ Press, 2010).

3. Melissa Anderson and Brendan Doherty, "Parties under Siege or Parties in Control? Gauging Causal Influences on Australian Ballot Reform Laws," paper presented at the annual meeting of the American Political Science Association, Philadelphia, PA, August 27, 2003.

4. For a discussion on this trend in news coverage, see Thomas E. Patterson, *Out of Order* (New York: Vintage Books, 1994); and Larry J. Sabato, *Feeding Frenzy: Attack Journalism and American Politics* (Baltimore: Lanahan, 2000).

5. One of the earliest studies to consider this trend is Martin J. Wattenberg, *The Rise of Candidate-Centered Politics: Presidential Elections of the 1980s* (Cambridge, MA: Harvard University Press, 1991).

6. Thomas E. Cronin and Michael A. Genovese, *The Paradoxes of the American Presidency* (New York: Oxford University Press, 1998), 32–27.

7. Richard W. Waterman, Robert Wright, and Gilbert St. Clair, *The Image-Is-Everything Presidency: Dilemmas in American Leadership* (Boulder, CO: Westview Press, 1999), 39–42.

8. For a discussion of electing the first woman president, see Lori Cox Han, *In It to Win: Electing Madam President* (New York: Bloomsbury, 2015).

9. See Richard L. Fox and Jennifer L. Lawless, "Entering the Arena? Gender and the Decision to Run for Office," *American Journal of Political Science* 48, no. 2 (2004): 264–80; and Richard L. Fox," The Future of Women's Political Leadership: Gender and the Decision to Run for Elective Office," in *Women and Leadership: The State of Play and Strategies for Change*, ed. Barbara Kellerman and Deborah L. Rhode (New York: Wiley, 2007), 251–70.

10. See Arthur T. Hadley, *The Invisible Primary* (Englewood Cliffs, NJ: Prentice Hall, 1976).

11. Nelson W. Polsby and Aaron Wildavsky, *Presidential Elections: Strategies and Structures of American Politics*, 11th ed. (Lanham, MD: Rowman & Littlefield, 2004), 92–93.

12. Christopher Hanson, "The Invisible Primary: Now Is the Time for All-Out Coverage," *Columbia Journalism Review* 41, no. 6 (March/April 2003): 58.

13. Tarini Parti, "Jeb Super PAC Raises $103 Million," *Politico*, July 31, 2015, http://www.politico.com/story/2015/07/jeb-bush-superpac-103-million-2016-120853.

14. Marty Cohen, David Karol, Hans Noel, and John Zaller, "The Invisible Primary in Presidential Nominations, 1980–2004," in *The Making of the Presidential Candidates 2008*, ed. William Mayer (Lanham, MD: Rowman & Littlefield, 2008).

15. For a discussion on why Clinton lost the 2008 Democratic nomination, see Lori Cox Han, "Still Waiting for Madam President: Hillary Rodham Clinton's 2008 Presidential Campaign," *Critical Issues of Our Time*, The Centre for American Studies at the University of Western Ontario, London, Ontario, Vol. 2, Fall 2009.

16. Thomas Patterson, "Pre-Primary News Coverage of the 2016 Presidential Race: Trump's Rise, Sanders' Emergence, Clinton's Struggle," Harvard Kennedy School, Shorenstein Center on Media, Politics and Public Policy, June 13, 2016, https://shorensteincenter.org/pre-primary-news-coverage-2016-trump-clinton-sanders/.

17. Ibid.

18. Stephen J. Wayne, "Why Democracy Works," in *Winning the Presidency: 2008*, ed. William J Crotty (Boulder, CO: Paradigm, 2008), 48–69.

19. Ibid., 55.

20. Gerald Ford, "Remarks on Taking the Oath of Office," August 9, 1974, http://www.presidency.ucsb.edu/ws/index.php?pid=4409&st=&st1=.

21. For example, see CBS News, "Ready for a Woman President?," *CBS News Polls*, February 5, 2006, http://www.cbsnews.com; Stewart M. Powell, "Poll Finds Readiness for Female President," *Houston Chronicle*, February 20, 2006, A1; and Dan Smith, "Voters Think U.S. Ready for Woman as President," *Sacramento Bee*, March 10, 2006, A5. In addition, a February 2005 poll by the Siena College Research Institute found that 6 of 10 voters were ready for a woman president and that 81 percent of those surveyed would vote for a woman president. Potential candidates for 2008 that topped the survey included Clinton, Condoleezza Rice, and Senator Elizabeth Dole (R-NC).

22. Dan Balz, "Hillary Clinton Opens Presidential Bid: The Former First Lady Enters the Race as Front-Runner for the Democratic Nomination," *Washington Post*, January 21, 2007, A1.

23. Patrick Healy, "Clinton Steals Obama's Fundraising Thunder," *New York Times*, October 3, 2007, http://www.nytimes.com/2007/10/03/us/politics/03campaign.html.

24. "Booze on Election Day was an American Tradition," National Constitution Center, November 2, 2012, https://constitutioncenter.org/blog/booze-on-election-day-was-an-american-tradition.

25. "Defeated for Election to Virginia House of Delegates," April 24, 1777, *The Papers of James Madison*, vol. 1, *16 March 1751–16 December 1779*, ed. William T. Hutchinson and William M. E. Rachal (Chicago: The University of Chicago Press, 1962), 192–93.

26. Herbert E. Alexander, *Financing Politics: Money, Elections, and Political Reform* (Washington, DC: CQ Press, 1992), 9–10.

27. Alexander, *Financing Politics*, 10–11.

28. Theodore Roosevelt, "Fifth Annual Message to the Congress," December 5, 1905, The American Presidency Project, http://www.presidency.ucsb.edu/ws/index.php?pid=29546#axzz1duSNChlK.

29. For a discussion of early campaign finance legislation, see Diana Dwyre and Victoria A. Farrar-Myers, *Legislative Labyrinth: Congress and Campaign Finance Reform* (Washington, DC: CQ Press, 2001), 3–7.

30. Alexander, *Financing Politics*, 32.

31. Richard J. Semiatin, *Campaigns in the 21st Century* (New York: McGraw–Hill, 2005), 157–58.

32. "Presidential Election Campaign Fund," Federal Election Commission, May 13, 2016, http://www.fec.gov/press/bkgnd/fund.shtml.

33. Ibid.

34. Jim Rutenberg, "Nearing Record, Obama's Ad Effort Swamps McCain," *New York Times*, October 17, 2008, http://www.nytimes.com/2008/10/18/us/politics/18ads.html.

35. Ibid.

36. Barack Obama, State of the Union Address, January 27, 2010.

37. Robert Barnes and Anne E. Kornblut, "It's Obama vs. the Supreme Court, Round 2, Over Campaign Finance Ruling," *Washington Post*, March 11, 2010, http://www.washingtonpost.com/wp-dyn/content/article/2010/03/09/AR2010030903040_2.html?sid=ST2010031502480.

38. Andrew Dowdle, Randall E. Adkins, Karen Sebold, and Patrick A. Stewart, "Financing the 2012 Presidential Election in a Post–*Citizens United* World," in *Winning the Presidency 2012*, ed. William J. Crotty (Boulder, CO: Paradigm, 2013), 163, 168.

39. Ibid., 169.

40. "Gingrich: Romney 'Carpet Bombing' Rival with Ads," *Associated Press*, January 29, 2012, http://news.yahoo.com/gingrich-romney-carpet-bombing-rival-ads-144744488.html.

41. Michael Turk, "Social and New Media—The Digital Present and Future," in *Campaigns on the Cutting Edge*, ed. Richard Semiatin (Washington, DC: CQ Press, 2017), 43–60.

42. Bundling was first used as a strategy in 1992, pioneered by the group EMILY's List, which supports pro-choice Democratic women candidates.

43. Doug Mataconis, "Is Obama Favoring Donors in Ambassador Appointments? That's Nothing New," *Christian Science Monitor*, December 3, 2014, http://www.csmonitor.com/USA/Politics/Politics-Voices/2014/1203/Is-Obama-favoring-donors-in-ambassador-appointments-That-s-nothing-new.

44. Michael Beckel, "Elite Bundlers Raise More Than $113 Million for Hillary Clinton," *Time*, September 23, 2016, http://time.com/4506275/hillary-clinton-bundlers/?iid=sr-link1.

45. See Conor Dowling and Michael Miller, *Super PAC!: Money, Elections, and Voters after Citizens United* (New York: Routledge, 2014).

46. Nina Kasniunas, Mark Rozell, and Charles Kleckler, "Interest Groups, Super PACs and Independent Expenditures," in *Campaigns on the Cutting Edge*, ed. Richard Semiatin (Washington, DC: CQ Press, 2017), 122.

47. Claire Foran, "Bernie Sanders' Big Money," *The Atlantic*, March 1, 2016, http://www.theatlantic.com/politics/archive/2016/03/bernie-sanders-fundraising/471648/.

48. Memo from William L. Batt Jr. to Clark M. Clifford, "President's Acceptance Speech," July 9, 1948, Files of Charles S. Murphy, Presidential Speech File, Box 1, Harry S. Truman Presidential Library, Independence, Missouri.

49. Memo from Tony Snow to Ray Price, Bob Teeter, Samuel K. Skinner, and Clayton Yeutter, "Convention Speech," August 12, 1992, Tony Snow Files, Formerly Withheld, NLGB Control Number 6534, George Bush Presidential Library, College Station, Texas.

50. See "The Electoral College," *David Leip's Atlas of Presidential Elections*, http://www.uselectionatlas.org/INFORMATION/INFORMATION/electcollege_history.php.

51. Stephen S. Brams and Michael Davis, "The 3/2's Rule in Presidential Campaigning," *American Political Science Review* 68 (March 1974): 113–34.

52. See Steven J. Rosenstone and John Mark, *Mobilization, Participation, and Democracy in America* (New York: Macmillan, 1993).

53. Ruy Teixeira, William H. Frey, and Robert Griffin, "States of Change: The Demographic Evolution of the American Electorate, 1974–2060," American Enterprise Institute/Brookings Institution/Center for American Progress, February 2015, https://cdn.americanprogress.org/wp-content/uploads/2015/02/SOC-report1.pdf.

54. Memo from Dan McGroarty to David Demarest and Tony Snow, "Basket Case—Democrats New '92 Strategy," June 18, 1991, Formerly Withheld, NLGB Control Number 6512, George Bush Presidential Library, College Station, Texas.

55. Seven electors were faithless and voted for other candidates: In Hawaii, Senator Bernie Sanders (VT-D) received one electoral vote. In Texas, Governor John Kasich (OH-R) received one electoral vote and former representative Ron Paul (TX-R) received one electoral vote. In Washington, former secretary of state Colin Powell received three electoral votes and Faith Spotted Eagle received one electoral vote.

56. See Cronin and Genovese, *The Paradoxes*. For a full discussion on the Electoral College, see also George C. Edwards III, *Why the Electoral College Is Bad for America*, 2nd ed. (New Haven, CT: Yale University Press, 2011), and Gary Bugh, ed., *Electoral College Reform: Challenges and Possibilities* (Burlington, VT: Ashgate, 2010).

57. Donald Philip Green and Bradley Palmquist, "How Stable Is Party Identification?" *Political Behavior* 16, no. 4 (1994): 437–66.

58. "American Time Use Survey Summary," U.S. Department of Labor, Bureau of Labor Statistics, June 24, 2016, https://www.bls.gov/news.release/atus.nr0.htm.

59. "Americans Spending More Time Following the News," Pew Research Center, September 12, 2010, http://people-press.org/report/652/.

60. "Internet Overtakes Newspapers as News Outlet," Pew Research Center, December 23, 2008, http://people-press.org/report/479/internet-overtakes-newspapers-as-news-outlet.

61. "The Modern News Consumer," Pew Research Center, July 7, 2016, http://www.journalism.org/2016/07/07/pathways-to-news/.

62. Doris A. Graber and Johanna Dunaway, *Mass Media and American Politics*, 9th ed. (Washington, DC: CQ Press, 2015), 315.

63. Adam Howard, "How Saturday Night Live Has Shaped American Politics," *NBC News*, September 30, 2016, http://www.nbcnews.com/pop-culture/tv/how-saturday-night-live-has-shaped-american-politics-n656716.

64. See Patterson, *Out of Order*.

65. "Low Marks for Major Players in 2016 Election—Including the Winner," Pew Research Center, November 21, 2016, http://www.people-press.org/2016/11/21/voters-evaluations-of-the-campaign/.

66. Stephen J. Farnsworth and S. Robert Lichter, *The Nightly News Nightmare: Media Coverage of U.S. Presidential Elections, 1988–2008*, 3rd ed. (Lanham, MD: Rowman & Littlefield, 2011), 3.

67. See Larry M. Bartels, *Presidential Primaries and the Dynamics of Public Choice* (Princeton, NJ: Princeton University Press, 1988).

68. Liz Spayd, "Want to Know What the Public Is Thinking? Try Asking," *New York Times*, November 9, 2016, https://www.nytimes.com/2016/11/10/public-editor/want-to-know-what-americas-thinking-try-asking.html.

69. Nate Silver, "Why FiveThirtyEight Gave Trump a Better Chance Than Almost Anyone Else," November 11, 2016, http://fivethirtyeight.com/features/why-fivethirtyeight-gave-trump-a-better-chance-than-almost-anyone-else/.

70. Helmut Norpoth, "The Primary Model Predicts Trump Victory," *PS: Political Science & Politics* 49, no. 4 (2016): 655–58.

71. Alan Abromowitz, "Forecasting the 2016 Presidential Election: Will Time For Change Mean Time For Trump?," *Sabato's Crystal Ball*, August 11, 2016, http://www.centerforpolitics.org/crystalball/articles/forecasting-the-2016-presidential-election-will-time-for-change-mean-time-for-trump/.

72. Farnsworth and Lichter, *The Nightly News Nightmare*, 5.

73. See Darrell M. West, *Air Wars: 1952–2008* (Washington, DC: CQ Press, 2010).

74. Quoted in West, *Air Wars*, 82.

75. Joseph N. Cappella and Kathleen Hall Jamieson, "Broadcast Ad-Watch Effects: A Field Experiment," *Communication Research* 21 (1994): 341–65.

76. "Advertising Volume Up 122% over 2012 Levels; Spending in Presidential Race over $400 Million," *Wesleyan Media Project*, May 12, 2016, http://mediaproject.wesleyan.edu/releases/ad-spending-over-400-million/.

77. "Primary Ads," Democracy in Action, http://www.p2016.org/ads1/paidads.html#super.

78. "Here's How Much Less Than Hillary Clinton Donald Trump Spent on the Election," *Associated Press*, December 9, 2016, http://fortune.com/2016/12/09/hillary-clinton-donald-trump-campaign-spending/.

79. See Richard Davis, *The Web of Politics: The Internet's Impact on the American Political System* (New York: Oxford University Press, 1999); and John Tedesco, "Changing the Channel: Use of the Internet for Communication about Politics," in *Handbook of Political Communication Research*, ed. Lynda Lee Kaid (Mahwah, NJ: Lawrence Erlbaum, 2004), 507–32.

80. Michael Grynbaum and Sydney Ember, "If Trump Tweets It, Is It News? A Quandary for the News Media," *New York Times*, November 29, 2016, https://www.nytimes.com/2016/11/29/business/media/if-trump-tweets-it-is-it-news-a-quandary-for-the-news-media.html?_r=0.

81. "Election 2016: Campaigns as a Direct Source of News," Pew Research Center, July 18, 2016, http://www.journalism.org/2016/07/18/election-2016-campaigns-as-a-direct-source-of-news/.

82. Ibid.

83. "Most Voters Say News Media Wants Obama to Win," Pew Research Center, October 22, 2008, http://pewresearch.org/pubs/1003/joe-the-plumber.

84. "First Presidential Debate of 2016 Draws 84 Million Viewers," *Nielson*, September 27, 2016, http://www.nielsen.com/us/en/insights/news/2016/first-presidential-debate-of-2016-draws-84-million-viewers.html.

85. "Presidential Campaign Debate," October 6, 1976, http://www.presidency.ucsb.edu/ws/index.php?pid=6414.

86. See Lester Seligman and Cary Covington, *The Coalitional Presidency* (Chicago: Dorsey, 1989).

87. Ibid.

88. For example, see Jeff Fishel, *Presidents and Promises: From Campaign Pledge to Presidential Performance* (Washington, DC: CQ Press, 1985).

89. Hugh Heclo, "Campaigning and Governing: A Conspectus," in *The Permanent Campaign and Its Future*, eds. Norman Ornstein and Thomas Mann (Washington, DC: Brookings, 2000).

CHAPTER 4

1. See Frazier Moore, "Obama on 'The View' Thursday," *Associated Press*, July 26, 2010, http://www.sandiegouniontribune.com/sdut-obama-to-appear-on-abcs-the-view-on-thursday-2010jul26-story.html.

2. Nancy Benac, "'Obama Out': President Ending Reign as Pop Culture King," *Associated Press*, January 5, 2017, http://www.businessinsider.com/ap-obama-out-president-ending-reign-as-pop-culture-king-2017-1.

3. Mike Snider, "Trump Invokes 'Fake News' at Press Conference," *USA Today*, January 11, 2017, http://www.usatoday.com/story/money/2017/01/11/trump-tackles-fake-news-press-conference/96438764/.

4. Howard Kurtz, "A Good 'View' for Obama," *Washington Post*, July 30, 2010, http://www.washingtonpost.com/wp-dyn/content/linkset/2005/04/11/LI2005041100587.html.

5. Art Swift, "Americans' Trust in Mass Media Sinks to New Low," *Gallup*, September 14, 2016, http://www.gallup.com/poll/195542/americans-trust-mass-media-sinks-new-low.aspx?g_source=media%20approval&g_medium=search&g_campaign=tiles.

6. See Jeffrey K. Tulis, *The Rhetorical Presidency* (Princeton, NJ: Princeton University Press, 1987); and Mel Laracey, *Presidents and the People: The Partisan Story of Going Public* (College Station: Texas A&M University Press, 2002). The public aspects of McKinley's administration have only recently been included as part of the rhetorical presidency literature; in addition to Laracey, see also Robert P. Saldin, "William McKinley and the Rhetorical Presidency," *Presidential Studies Quarterly* 41, no. I (March 2011): 119–34.

7. For example, a headline in the *New York Times* on December 3, 1904 (p. 8), declared "Roosevelt's Visit South: Denies That He Plans Swing around the Circle When He Visits Texas." However, Roosevelt is not the first president to be associated with this phrase. Most notably, the phrase is remembered for what is considered a disastrous speaking tour by President Andrew Johnson in 1866 during which he tried to shore up support for his Reconstruction policies and Democratic candidates prior to the midterm elections. See Eric Foner, *Reconstruction: America's Unfinished Revolution, 1863–1877* (New York: Harper & Row, 1988).

8. For example, see Sidney M. Milkis and Michael Nelson, *The American Presidency: Origins and Development, 1776–2014*, 7th ed. (Washington, DC: CQ Press, 2016), 231–33.

9. Karlyn Kohrs Campbell and Kathleen Hall Jamieson, *Deeds Done in Words: Presidential Rhetoric and the Genres of Governance* (Chicago: University of Chicago Press, 1990), 1, 213–19.

10. Tulis, *The Rhetorical Presidency*, 28.

11. Ibid., 4–23.

12. Roderick P. Hart, *The Sound of Leadership: Presidential Communication in the Modern Age* (Chicago: University of Chicago Press, 1987), 212.

13. Stephen J. Farnsworth, *Spinner in Chief: How Presidents Sell Their Policies and Themselves* (Boulder, CO: Paradigm, 2009), 9–10.

14. Newton N. Minow, John Bartlow Martin, and Lee M. Mitchell, *Presidential Television* (New York: Basic Books, 1973), 26.

15. Gleason L. Archer, *History of Radio to 1926* (New York: Arno Press/New York Times, 1971), 317–18.

16. Ibid., 323–24.

17. Herbert Hoover, *The Memoirs of Herbert Hoover: The Cabinet and the Presidency 1920–1933* (New York: Macmillan, 1952), 146–47.

18. See *The Public Papers of the Presidents, Herbert Hoover, 1929–1933* (Washington, DC: U.S. Government Printing Office, 1976–1977).

19. Herbert Hoover, "Radio Address to the Nation," September 18, 1929.

20. The number of fireside chats given by FDR is somewhat disputed; the total of 30 comes from the FDR Presidential Library and Museum's web page at http://www.fdrlibrary.marist.edu/firesi90.html. Only 21 of these radio addresses are listed as "fireside chats" in the Master Speech File in FDR's presidential papers, but the remaining nine, eight of which were delivered between October 1942 and June 1944, were delivered over the radio in the same format as the earlier addresses and are counted as such in most sources.

21. James MacGregor Burns, *Roosevelt: The Lion and the Fox* (New York: Harcourt, Brace, 1956), 167–68.

22. Memo from Eben Ayers to Harry Truman, July 20, 1950, PSF Speech File, Box 42, Harry S. Truman Presidential Library, Independence, Missouri.

23. For example, see Matthew A. Baum and Samuel Kernell, "Has Cable Ended the Golden Age of Presidential Television?," *American Political Science Review* 93, no. 1 (March 1999): 99–114.

24. See Lori Cox Han, *Governing from Center Stage: White House Communication Strategies during the Television Age of Politics* (Cresskill, NJ: Hampton Press, 2001).

25. See the video documentary "Television and the Presidency," The Freedom Forum First Amendment Center at Vanderbilt University, Nashville, Tennessee, 1994.

26. Farnsworth, *Spinner in Chief*, 6.

27. Han, *Governing from Center Stage*, 2.

28. Martha Joynt Kumar, *Managing the President's Message: The White House Communications Operation* (Baltimore: Johns Hopkins University Press, 2007), xiv.

29. Mary E. Stuckey, *The President as Interpreter-in-Chief* (Chatham, NJ: Chatham House, 1991), 1–3.

30. See Samuel Kernell, *Going Public: New Strategies of Presidential Leadership* (Washington, DC: CQ Press, 1997).

31. See George C. Edwards, *On Deaf Ears: The Limits of the Bully Pulpit* (New Haven, CT: Yale University Press, 2003).

32. See Jeffrey E. Cohen, *Going Local: Presidential Leadership in the Post-Broadcast Age* (New York: Cambridge University Press, 2010); and Diane J. Heith, *The Presidential Road Show: Public Leadership in an Era of Party Polarization and Media Fragmentation* (Boulder, CO: Paradigm, 2013).

33. Brendan J. Doherty, *The Rise of the President's Permanent Campaign* (Lawrence: University Press of Kansas, 2012), 90–91.

34. Ibid., 91–92.

35. Ibid., 121.

36. Report on "The Office of the Press Secretary," February 1983, prepared by the Reagan Press Office, document accessed in the Marlin Fitzwater/Press Office Alpha Files, Box 24, George Bush Presidential Library, College Station, Texas.

37. Memo from Pierre Salinger to Ted Sorensen, "The Relations of the President with the Press," April 17, 1961, Files of Pierre Salinger, John F. Kennedy Presidential Library, Boston, Massachusetts.

38. For in-depth discussions on the Office of Communications, see John Anthony Maltese, *Spin Control: The White House Office of Communications and the Management of Presidential News*, 2nd ed. (Chapel Hill: University of North Carolina Press, 1994); and Kumar, *Managing the President's Message.*

39. Mark Hertsgaard, *On Bended Knee: The Press and the Reagan Presidency* (New York: Farrar, Straus and Giroux, 1988), 33–37, 105–6.

40. See Maltese, *Spin Control*, Chap. 7.

41. Kumar, *Managing the President's Message*, 71–72.

42. George C. Edwards III, *Overreach: Leadership in the Obama Presidency* (Princeton, NJ: Princeton University Press, 2012), 79.

43. John Marchese, "Obama's Ghost," *Boston Magazine*, January 2010, http://www .bostonmagazine.com/2009/12/obama-s-ghost/.

44. Colin L. Powell, memo to Tom Griscom, "Presidential Address: Brandenburg Gate (Revised)," June 1, 1987, White House Office of Records and Management Files, SP1150, Ronald Reagan Presidential Library, Simi Valley, California.

45. Wilson did not address Congress in 1919 and 1920 because of health reasons. Warren Harding's two messages in 1921 and 1922, along with Calvin Coolidge's first in 1923, were in-person addresses to Congress. However, Coolidge's remaining State of the Unions between 1924 and 1928 and all four of Herbert Hoover's (1929–1933) were written messages. FDR delivered an in-person State of the Union with his first address in 1934. Exceptions during the modern era include Harry Truman in 1946 and 1953, Dwight Eisenhower in 1961, Richard Nixon in 1973, and Jimmy Carter in 1981. Also, the first "State of the Union" addresses for Bush in 1989, Clinton in 1993, Bush in 2001, Obama in 2009, and Trump in 2017 were technically *not* State of the Union addresses. Instead, they were addresses to a joint session of Congress to lay out administration goals. However, the attention paid to and impact of these speeches is so similar to that of an actual State of the Union address that they are considered comparable for research classification purposes. See Gerhard Peters, "State of the Union Addresses and Messages," The American Presidency Project, http://www.presidency.ucsb.edu/sou.php.

46. Franklin D. Roosevelt, "Address to Congress Requesting a Declaration of War with Japan," December 8, 1941.

47. Ronald Reagan, "Address before a Joint Session of the Congress on the Program for Economic Recovery," April 28, 1981.

48. Bill Clinton, *My Life* (New York: Alfred A. Knopf, 2004), 548.

49. George Stephanopoulos, *All Too Human: A Political Education* (Boston: Little, Brown, 1999), 201–203.

50. Barack Obama, "Address before a Joint Session of the Congress on Health Care Reform," September 9, 2009.

51. See Matthew Eshbaugh-Soha, "The Public Presidency: Communications and Media," in *New Directions in the American Presidency*, ed. Lori Cox Han (New York: Routledge, 2011), 54–55.

52. See Lori Cox Han, "New Strategies for an Old Medium: The Weekly Radio Addresses of Reagan and Clinton," *Congress and the Presidency* 33, no. 1 (Spring 2006): 25–45.

53. See Matthew Eshbaugh-Soha and Jeffrey S. Peake, *Breaking through the Noise: Presidential Leadership, Public Opinion, and the News Media* (Stanford, CA: Stanford University Press, 2011).

54. See Michael Emery and Edwin Emery, *The Press and America: An Interpretive History of the Mass Media*, 8th ed. (Needham Heights, MA: Simon & Schuster, 1996); and Kernell, *Going Public*, 73–81.

55. John H. Kessel, *Presidents, the Presidency, and the Political Environment* (Washington, DC: Congressional Quarterly Press, 2001), 58–62.

56. Memo from Jerry Rafshoon to Jimmy Carter, "Press Conferences," September 26, 1978, Files of Jerry Rafshoon, Box 28, Jimmy Carter Presidential Library, Atlanta, Georgia.

57. George C. Edwards III, "George Bush and the Public Presidency: The Politics of Inclusion," in *The Bush Presidency: First Appraisals*, ed. Colin Campbell and Bert A. Rockman (Chatham, NJ: Chatham House, 1991), 148–49.

58. Memo from Marlin Fitzwater to George Bush, December 20, 1988, John Sununu Files, Office of the Chief of Staff to the President, Formerly Withheld, NLGB Control Number 11317, George Bush Presidential Library, College Station, Texas.

59. Memo from Mark Gearan to Bill Clinton, "Primetime Press Conference," August 1, 1994, Files of Jonathan Prince, Box 4, Bill Clinton Presidential Library, Little Rock, Arkansas.

60. "Questions and Answers for Joint Press Availability with President Karzai of Afghanistan," September 26, 2006, Files of Tony Snow, Box 3, Subject Files, George W. Bush Presidential Library, Dallas, Texas.

61. For a discussion of the credibility gap, see Emery and Emery, *The Press and America*, 443–52.

62. This statement by Johnson to aide Bill Moyers has been widely quoted throughout the years, including in various interviews with Cronkite himself. However, a recent book questions its accuracy; see Joseph W. Campbell, *Getting It Wrong: Ten of the Greatest Misreported Stories in American Journalism* (Berkeley: University of California Press, 2010).

63. Agnew made his famous remarks about the press in an address to the California Republican State Convention in San Diego on September 11, 1970. In the speech, written by Nixon's speechwriter and eventual *New York Times* columnist William Safire, Agnew also referred to the press as "pusillanimous pussyfooters" and "vicars of vacillation" who "have formed their own 4-H Club—the hopeless, hysterical hypochondriacs of history." See Lance Morrow, "Naysayer to the Nattering Nabobs," *Time*, September 30, 1996, http://content.time.com/time/magazine/article/0,9171,985217,00.html.

64. See Han, *A Presidency Upstaged*.

65. See Lori Cox Han, "The President over the Public: The Plebiscitary Presidency at Center Stage," in *The Presidency and the Challenge of Democracy*, ed. Michael A. Genovese and Lori Cox Han (New York: Palgrave Macmillan, 2006).

66. Fred I. Greenstein, *The Presidential Difference: Leadership Style from FDR to George W. Bush*, 2nd ed. (Princeton, NJ: Princeton University Press, 2004), 207.

67. See Matthew Robert Kerbel, *Remote & Controlled: Media Politics in a Cynical Age*, 2nd ed. (Boulder, CO: Westview Press, 1999); Kernell, *Going Public*; and Kessel, *Presidents, the Presidency, and the Political Environment*.

68. Doris A. Graber and Johanna Dunaway, *Mass Media and American Politics*, 9th ed. (Washington, DC: CQ Press, 2015), 183.

69. See Stephen J. Farnsworth and S. Robert Lichter, *The Mediated Presidency: Television News and Presidential Governance* (Lanham, MD: Rowman & Littlefield, 2006), 41;

and Farnsworth and Lichter, "Network News Coverage of New Presidents, 1981–2009," paper presented at the 2010 American Political Science Association annual meeting, Washington, DC.

70. Memo from Patrick J. Buchanan to Richard Nixon, September 17, 1971, Files of Patrick J. Buchanan, Box 3, Richard Nixon Presidential Library, Yorba Linda, California.

71. Memo from Marlin Fitzwater to George Bush, December 20, 1988, John Sununu Files, Office of the Chief of Staff to the President, Formerly Withheld, NLGB Control Number 11317, George Bush Presidential Library, College Station, Texas.

72. Memo from Mark Gearan to Bill Clinton, "Interviews," December 1, 1993, Files of Jonathan Prince, Box 1, Bill Clinton Presidential Library, Little Rock, Arkansas.

73. Memo from Harry L. Hopkins to Franklin Roosevelt, November 27, 1941, Memoranda, Box 23, Papers of Steve Early, Franklin D. Roosevelt Presidential Library, Hyde Park, New York.

74. Memo from Jody Powell to Jimmy Carter, July 10, 1978, Files of Jody Powell, Box 40, Jimmy Carter Presidential Library, Atlanta, Georgia.

75. Michael D. Shear and Ellen Nakashima, "Obama Says WikiLeaks Disclosure Is Reason for Concern but Doesn't Reveal New Issues," *Washington Post*, July 27, 2010, http://www.washingtonpost.com/wp-dyn/content/article/2010/07/27/AR2010072701758.html.

76. Martha T. Moore and Aamer Madhani, "Is Obama at War with Journalists?" *USA Today*, May 27, 2013, http://www.usatoday.com/story/news/politics/2013/05/27/obama-war-media-leaks/2358059/.

77. For discussions on the presidential/press relationship, see Graber and Dunaway, *Mass Media and American Politics*; W. Lance Bennett, *News: The Politics of Illusion*, 9th ed. (Chicago: University of Chicago Press, 2012); and David L. Paletz, *The Media in American Politics: Contents and Consequences*, 2nd ed. (New York: Longman, 2002).

78. Telegram from Herbert Hoover to Roy Howard, June 22, 1931, Box 188, President's Personal File, Herbert Hoover Presidential Library, West Branch, Iowa.

79. Memo from Franklin Roosevelt to Steve Early, April 30, 1942, Memoranda, Box 24, Papers of Steve Early, Franklin D. Roosevelt Presidential Library, Hyde Park, New York.

80. Column Summaries, January 13, 1947, Papers of George M. Elsey, Harry S. Truman Presidential Library, Independence, Missouri.

81. Memo from Ron Ziegler to H. R. Haldeman, November 25, 1969, in White House Special Files: Staff Member and Office Files of H. R. Haldeman, Box 156, Richard Nixon Presidential Library, Yorba Linda, California.

82. Memo from Mort Allin to H. R. Haldeman, July 22, 1970, in White House Special Files: Staff Member and Office Files of H. R. Haldeman, Box 155, Richard Nixon Presidential Library, Yorba Linda, California. For a discussion of the ideological leanings of major newspapers, see Emery and Emery, *The Press and America*, 537–70.

83. Memo from H. R. Haldeman to Herb Klein and Ron Ziegler, November 30, 1970, in White House Special Files: Staff Member and Office Files of H. R. Haldeman, Box 155, Richard Nixon Presidential Library, Yorba Linda, California.

84. Stanley I. Kutler, *The Wars of Watergate: The Last Crisis of Richard Nixon* (New York: Alfred A. Knopf, 1990), 168.

85. Memo from Richard Moore to H. R. Haldeman, June 24, 1970, in White House Special Files: Staff Member and Office Files of H. R. Haldeman, Box 156, Richard Nixon Presidential Library, Yorba Linda, California.

86. John Tebbel and Sarah Miles Watts, *The Press and the Presidency: From George Washington to Ronald Reagan* (New York: Oxford University Press, 1985), 504.

87. Letter from Mort Allin to Richard Britton, January 8, 1971, in White House Special Files: Staff Member and Office Files of Patrick J. Buchanan, Box 3, Richard Nixon Presidential Library, Yorba Linda, California. Extensive documentation on the daily news summaries can be found in the Buchanan files, Boxes 1–8.

88. Letter from Mort Allin to Alice Plato, January 29, 1971, in White House Special Files: Staff Member and Office Files of Patrick J. Buchanan, Box 3, Richard Nixon Presidential Library, Yorba Linda, California.

89. See Han, *Governing from Center Stage*, 82; and Kumar, *Managing the President's Message*, 28.

90. For example, see Memo from Mary Kate Grant to John Sununu, "Weekly Editorial Round-Up," August 17, 1989, Mary Kate Grant Files, Speech Office, Box 8, George Bush Presidential Library, College Station, Texas.

91. Memo from Mary Kate Grant to John Sununu, "Regional Newspapers," March 12, 1989, Mary Kate Grant Files, Speech Office, Box 8, George Bush Presidential Library, College Station, Texas.

92. Memo from Maria Eitel Sheehan to Dorrance Smith, May 22, 1991, Project Files, White House Office of Media Affairs, Freedom of Information Act Request 2003-1478-F, George Bush Presidential Library, College Station, Texas.

93. Josh Gerstein and Patrick Gavin, "Why Reporters Are Down on Obama," *Politico*, April 28, 2010, http://www.politico.com/story/2010/04/why-reporters-are-down-on-obama-036454.

94. Alessandra Stanley, "The TV Watch: Daytime Diplomacy," *The New York Times*, July 30, 2010, http://www.nytimes.com/2010/07/30/arts/television/30watch.html.

CHAPTER 5

1. Henry C. Kenski, "A Man for All Seasons? The Guardian President and His Public," in *Leadership and the Bush Presidency: Prudence or Drift in an Era of Change?*, ed. Ryan J. Barilleaux and Mary E. Stuckey (Westport, CT: Praeger, 1992), 95.

2. George W. Bush Presidential Job Approval, *Gallup*, http://www.gallup.com/poll/116500/Presidential-Approval-Ratings-George-Bush.aspx.

3. Lydia Saad, "Trump Sets New Low Point for Inaugural Approval Rating," *Gallup*, January 23, 2017, http://www.gallup.com/poll/202811/trump-sets-new-low-point-inaugural-approval-rating.aspx?g_source=POLITICS&g_medium=topic&g_campaign=tiles.

4. James Madison, Alexander Hamilton, and John Jay, "Federalist Number 71: The Same View Continued in Regard to the Duration of the Office," *The Federalist Papers*, ed. Isaac Kramnick (New York: Penguin Books, 1987), 409.

5. Alexander Hamilton, speech given June 18, 1788, in *Selected Writings and Speeches of Alexander Hamilton*, ed. Morton J. Frisch (Washington, DC: American Enterprise Institute, 1985), 108.

6. Thomas Jefferson, "Letter to James Sullivan," February 9, 1797, in *The Writings of Thomas Jefferson*, ed. Paul Leicester Ford (New York: Putnam 1895), 118.

7. Michael Nelson, "Andrew Jackson's Veto of the Bank Bill," in *The Evolving Presidency: Addresses, Cases, Essays, Letters, Reports, Resolutions, Transcripts, and other Landmark Documents, 1787–1998*, ed. Michael Nelson (Washington, DC: CQ Press, 1999), 66.

8. See Richard Rubin, *Press, Party and the President* (New York: W. W. Norton, 1982).

9. Abraham Lincoln, "Letter to Albert G. Hodges," in *The Evolving Presidency: Addresses, Cases, Essays, Letters, Reports, Resolutions, Transcripts, and other Landmark Documents, 1787–1998*, ed. Michael Nelson (Washington, DC: CQ Press, 1999), 73.

10. James Bryce, *The American Commonwealth* (London: Macmillan, 1891), 265.

11. Robert Erickson and Kent Tedin, *American Public Opinion: Its Origins, Content and Impact* (New York: Pearson/Longman, 2009).

12. James N. Druckman and Lawrence R. Jacobs, *Who Governs? Presidents, Public Opinion, and Manipulation* (Chicago: University of Chicago Press, 2015), xix.

13. Historical Presidential Approval Rating, http://www.usatoday.com/news/washington/presidential-approval-tracker.htm.

14. Letter to Harry Truman from Frank Stanton, vice president and general manager of the Columbia Broadcasting System, September 29, 1945, PSF Speech File, Box 42, Harry S. Truman Presidential Library, Independence, Missouri.

15. Memo from David K. Nilesto Matt Connelly, October 8, 1946, PSF Political File, Box 49, Harry S. Truman Presidential Library, Independence, Missouri.

16. Memo from Tom Johnsonto Lyndon Johnson, December 9, 1966, White House Correspondence Files, PR, Box 18, Lyndon Baines Johnson Presidential Library, Austin, Texas.

17. Robert Erikson, Michael MacKuen, and James Stimson, *The Macro Polity* (New York: Cambridge University Press, 2002), 30–31.

18. Ibid., 74.

19. Julia R. Azari, Lara M. Brown, and Zim G. Nwokora, eds., *The Presidential Leadership Dilemma: Between the Constitution and a Political Party* (Albany, NY: SUNY Press, 2013), 12.

20. The Gallup Polling Organization, Presidential Approval, Key Statistics, http://www.gallup.com/poll/124922/Presidential-Job-Approval-Center.aspx.

21. Gary Jacobson, "A Tale of Two Wars: Public Opinion on the U.S. Military Intervention in Afghanistan and Iraq," *Presidential Studies Quarterly* 40, no. 4 (2010): 585–610.

22. Robert S. Erikson, "Economic Conditions and the Presidential Vote," *The American Political Science Review* 83, no. 2 (June 1989): 567–73.

23. Elmer E. Cornwell Jr., *Presidential Leadership of Public Opinion* (Bloomington: Indiana University Press, 1965), 5.

24. Ibid., 6.

25. See Paul Brace and Barbara Hinckley, *Follow the Leader: Opinion Polls and Modern Presidents* (New York: Basic Books, 1992).

26. Ibid.

27. See Brandice Canes-Wrone, *Who Leads Whom? Presidents, Policy, and the Public* (Chicago: University of Chicago Press, 2006).

28. See Samuel Kernell, *Going Public: New Strategies of Presidential Leadership*, 4th ed. (Washington, DC: CQ Press, 2007).

29. Ibid.

30. Mathew Baum and Samuel Kernell, "Has Cable Ended the Golden Age of Presidential Television?," *American Political Science Review* 93 (March 1999): 99–114.

31. Brenna Erlich, "Many Facebook and Twitter Users Unhappy with Obama Speech on BP Oil Spill," *Mashable*, June 16, 2010, http://mashable.com/2010/06/16/obama-speech-facebook-twitter-oil-spill/.

32. Frank Newport, "Obama Receives 44% Approval on Oil Spill while BP Gets 16%," *Gallup*, June 21, 2010, http://www.gallup.com/poll/140957/Obama-Receives-Approval-Oil-Spill-Gets.aspx.

33. See George C. Edwards III, *On Deaf Ears: The Limits of the Bully Pulpit* (New Haven, CT: Yale University Press, 2003).

34. See Jeffrey E. Cohen, *Going Local: Presidential Leadership in the Post-Broadcast Age* (New York: Cambridge University Press, 2010).
35. Ibid.
36. See Jon Bond and Richard Fleisher, *The President in the Legislative Arena* (Chicago: University of Chicago Press, 1990); George C. Edwards III, *At The Margins: Presidential Leadership of Congress* (New Haven, CT: Yale University Press 1989); and George C. Edwards III, "Aligning Tests with Theory: Presidential Influence as a Source of Influence in Congress," *Congress and the Presidency* 24, no. 2 (September 1997): 113–30.
37. See Edwards, *At the Margins*.
38. See Mark Peterson, *Legislating Together: The White House and Capitol Hill from Eisenhower to Reagan* (Cambridge, MA: Harvard University Press, 1990).
39. See Jeffrey E. Cohen, *Presidential Responsiveness and Public-Policy Making* (Ann Arbor: University of Michigan Press, 1997); and Jeffrey E. Cohen, "Presidential Rhetoric and the Public Agenda," *American Journal of Political Science* 39, no. 1 (February 1995): 87–107.
40. Stephen A. Borrelli and Grace L. Simmons, "Congressional Responsiveness to Presidential Popularity: The Electoral Context," *Political Behavior* 15, no. 2 (June 1993): 93–112.
41. Memo from Stu Eizenstatto Jimmy Carter, February 21, 1978, Files of Jody Powell, Box 39, Jimmy Carter Presidential Library, Atlanta, Georgia.
42. Memo from Alan Raymond to Jerry Rafshoon and Greg Schneiders, "State of the Presidency," February 20, 1979, Files of Gerald Rafshoon, Box 27, Jimmy Carter Presidential Library, Atlanta, Georgia.
43. Robert Eisinger, *The Evolution of Presidential Polling* (New York: Cambridge University Press, 2003), 42.
44. Memo from Steve EarlyFranklin Roosevelt, August 16, 1940, Files of Steve Early, Box 24, Franklin Delano Roosevelt Presidential Library, Hyde Park, New York.
45. Ibid.
46. Memo from Hadley Cantrilto Franklin Roosevelt, March 7, 1941, Gallup Polls, Box 857, Franklin Delano Roosevelt Presidential Library, Hyde Park, New York.
47. Hadley Cantril, *Human Dimension Experiences in Policy Research* (Newark, NJ: Rutgers University Press, 1967), 39–40.
48. Harry S. Truman, *Memoirs by Harry Truman, Volume Two: Years of Trial and Hope* (New York: Macmillan 1956), 177, 196.
48. Alfred Politz Research, Box 105, Dwight D. Eisenhower Presidential Library, Abilene, Kansas.
50. Lawrence Jacobs and Robert Shapiro, "The Rise of Presidential Polling: The Nixon White House in Historical Perspective," *Public Opinion Quarterly* 59, no. 2 (June 1995): 163–95.
51. Memo from Walter W. Heller to John F. Kennedy, July 31, 1962, President's Office Files, John F. Kennedy Presidential Library, Boston, Massachusetts.
52. Jacobs and Shapiro, "The Rise of Presidential Polling," 169.
53. See Diane Heith, *Polling to Govern: Public Opinion and Presidential Leadership* (Stanford, CA: Stanford University Press, 2004).
54. See Heith, *Polling to Govern*, and Eisinger, *The Evolution of Presidential Polling*, for a discussion of the evolution of the polling apparatus.
55. "The Hatch Act: Rights of Federal and State Government Employees," https://osc.gov/Pages/HatchAct.aspx.
56. See H. R. Haldeman, *The Haldeman Diaries: Inside the Nixon White House* (Berkeley: Berkeley Publishing, 1994), diary entry dated Monday, February 3, 1969.

57. Anonymous, Memoranda Re: Polling, February 1975, in Robert Hartmann, Box 34, Presidential Survey Research Prop 2, Gerald R. Ford Presidential Library, Ann Arbor, Michigan.

58. See Heith, *Polling to Govern*.

59. Ibid.

60. Barack Obama, interview with Diane Sawyer, ABC News, September 9, 2013, http:// www.presidency.ucsb.edu/ws/index.php?pid=109737&st=polls&st1=.

61. See Heith, *Polling to Govern*.

62. Memo from Gregg Petersmeyer to Dwight L. Chapin, "A proposal that the President give a series of informal television addresses for the purpose of meeting the country's crisis of the spirit," September 15, 1969, Files of Dwight Chapin, Richard Nixon Presidential Library, Yorba Linda, California.

63. Ibid.

64. Memo from David Demarestto John Sununu, December 2, 1990, George Bush Presidential Library, College Station, Texas.

65. See Heith, *Polling to Govern*.

66. Memo from Jim Shuman David Gergen, "Future Agenda," May 18, 1976, Files of Ron Nessen, Box 135, Gerald Ford Presidential Library, Ann Arbor, Michigan.

67. Diane Heith, "The White House Public Opinion Apparatus Meets the Anti-Polling President," in *In the Public Domain: Presidents and the Challenges of Public Leadership*, ed. Lori Cox Han and Diane Heith (Albany: State University of New York, 2005), 77.

68. Ibid., 81.

69. Remarks at the *PBS NewsHour*'s "Questions for President Obama" Town Hall Meeting in Elkhart, Indiana, June 1, 2016, http://www.presidency.ucsb.edu/ws/index.php?pid= 117898&st=polls&st1=.

70. See Jacobs and Shapiro, "The Rise of Presidential Polling".

71. Mark Blumenthal, "New Flash: Obama Using Polling Data," Pollster.com, January 9, 2009, http://www.pollster.com/blogs/news_flash_obama_using_polling.php.

72. John Sirica, *To Set the Record Straight: The Break-in, the Tapes, the Conspirators, the Pardon* (New York: W. W. Norton, 1979), 56.

73. Richard Nixon, *RN: The Memoirs of Richard Nixon* (New York: Grosset & Dunlap, 1978), 971–72.

74. Ibid., 715–16.

75. Stanley Kutler, ed., *Abuse of Power: The New Nixon Tapes* (New York: Simon & Schuster, 1997), 275–76.

76. Haldeman, *The Haldeman Diaries*, 803.

77. Kutler, *Abuse of Power*, 407.

78. Ibid., 409.

79. Ibid., 425–26.

80. Ibid., 460.

81. Heith, *Polling to Govern*, 126.

82. John Zaller, "Monica Lewinsky's Contribution to Political Science," *PS: Political Science and Politics* 31, no. 2 (1998): 182–89; Arthur Miller, "Sex, Politics, and Public Opinion: What Political Scientists Really Learned from the Clinton–Lewinsky Scandal," *PS: Political Science and Politics* 32, no. 4 (December 1999): 721–29; Molly Andolina and Clyde Wilcox, "Public Opinion: The Paradoxes of Clinton's Popularity," in *The Clinton Scandal and the Future of American Government*, ed. Mark Rozell and Clyde Wilcox (Washington, DC: Georgetown University Press, 2000).

83. George Stephanopoulos, *All Too Human: A Political Education* (Boston: Little, Brown, 1999), 412.

84. See Brandon Rottinghaus, *The Provisional Pulpit: Modern Presidential Leadership of Public Opinion* (College Station: Texas A&M University Press, 2010).

85. Memo from Roger Ailes to George Bush and John Sununu, January 9, 1991, in John Sununu Files, Chief of Staff, Polling (1 of 3)—1991 [2 of 4] CF04473 2, George Bush Presidential Library, College Station, Texas.

86. George H. W. Bush, "Radio Address to the Nation on the Persian Gulf Crisis," January 5, 1991, *Public Papers of the Presidents*.

87. Memo from Roger Ailes to George Bush and John Sununu, January 9, 1991, in John Sununu Files, Chief of Staff, Polling (1 of 3)—1991 [2 of 4] CF04473 2, George Bush Presidential Library, College Station, Texas.

88. George H. W. Bush, "Address to the Nation Announcing Allied Military Action in the Persian Gulf," January 16, 1991, *Public Papers of the Presidents*.

89. Memo from Roger Ailes to George Bush and John Sununu, January 9, 1991, in John Sununu Files, Chief of Staff, Polling (1 of 3)—1991 [2 of 4] CF04473 2, George Bush Presidential Library, College Station, Texas.

90. George H. W. Bush, Address to the Nation Announcing Allied Military Action in the Persian Gulf, January 16, 1991, *Public Papers of the Presidents*.

91. Memo from Roger Ailes to George Bush and John Sununu, January 9, 1991, in John Sununu Files, Chief of Staff, Polling (1 of 3)—1991 [2 of 4] CF04473 2, George Bush Presidential Library, College Station, Texas.

92. George H. W. Bush, "Address to the Nation Announcing Allied Military Action in the Persian Gulf," January 16, 1991, *Public Papers of the Presidents*.

93. Ibid.

94. See Lawrence Jacobs and Robert Shapiro, *Politicians Don't Pander: Political Manipulation and the Loss of Democratic Responsiveness* (Chicago: University of Chicago Press, 2000).

95. Diane Heith, "Obama and the Public Presidency: What Got You Here Won't Get You There," in *The Obama Presidency: Appraisals and Prospects*, ed. Bert A. Rockman, Andrew Rudalevige, and Colin Campbell (Washington, DC: CQ Press, 2012).

96. Fitz Tepper, "Michelle Obama Is Now on Snapchat," techcrunch.com, June 22, 2016, https://techcrunch.com/2016/06/22/michelle-obama-is-now-on-snapchat/.

97. Lee Rainie and Kathryn Zickuhr, "Americans' Views on Mobile Etiquette," Pew Research Center, August 26, 2015, http://www.pewinternet.org/2015/08/26/chapter-1-always-on-connectivity/.

98. Maeve Duggan, "The Demographics of Social Media Users," Pew Research Center, August 19, 2015, http://www.pewinternet.org/2015/08/19/the-demographics-of-social-media-users/.

CHAPTER 6

1. Seung Min Kim and Burgess Everett, "McConnell: Saudi 9/11 Law Could Have 'Unintended Ramifications,'" *Politico*, September 29, 2016, http://www.politico.com/story/2016/09/mitch-mcconnell-saudi-9-11-bill-228903.

2. James Madison, Alexander Hamilton, and John Jay, "Federalist Number 73: The Same View Continued in Relation to the Provision Concerning Support and the Power of the Negative," *The Federalist Papers*, ed. Isaac Kramnick (New York: Penguin Books, 1987), 418.

3. Copy, DNA: RG 233, Second Congress, 1791–1793, Records of Legislative Proceedings, Journals; LB, DLC:GW (from Philander Chase et al., eds., *The Papers of George Washington, Presidential Series, Vol. 10: March–August 1792* [Charlottesville, VA, 2002], 213–14).

4. "President Jackson's Veto Message Regarding the Bank of the United States," July 10, 1832, http://avalon.law.yale.edu/19th_century/ajveto01.asp.

5. Daniel Felle, "King Andrew and the Bank," *Humanities*29, no. 1 (January/February 2008), https://www.neh.gov/humanities/2008/januaryfebruary/feature/king-andrew-and-the-bank.

6. Roger H. Davidson, Walter J. Oleszek, and Frances Lee, *Congress and Its Members*, 13th ed. (Washington, DC: CQ Press, 2012), 337.

7. Louis Fisher, "The Legislative Veto: Invalidated, It Survives," *Law and Contemporary Problems* 56, no. 4 (Autumn 1993): 273–92.

8. *Clinton v. City of New York*, 524 U.S. 417 (1998).

9. *Youngstown Sheet & Tube Co. v. Sawyer*, 343 U.S. 579 (1952).

10. Donna Hoffman and Alison Howard, *Addressing the State of the Union: The Evolution and Impact of the President's Big Speech* (Boulder, CO: Lynne Rienner, 2006), 16.

11. Ibid.

12. Gerald Ford, "State of the Union Address," January 15, 1975, http://www.presidency.ucsb.edu/ws/index.php?pid=4938#axzz1ICCYyQgE.

13. Barack Obama, "State of the Union Address," January 27, 2010, http://www.presidency.ucsb.edu/ws/index.php?pid=87433.

14. See Leonard D. White, *The Federalists: A Study in Administrative History 1789–1801* (New York: Macmillan, 1948).

15. "Senate History: Nominations," Senate Historical Office, http://www.senate.gov/artandhistory/history/common/briefing/Nominations.htm.

16. James Madison, "Consolidation," National Gazette, December 3, 1971, National Archives, https://founders.archives.gov/documents/Madison/01-14-02-0122.

17. George Washington, "Farewell Address," September 19, 1796, http://www.presidency.ucsb.edu/ws/index.php?pid=65539.

18. William Leuchtenburg, *Franklin D. Roosevelt and the New Deal: 1932–1940* (New York: Harper & Row, 1963), 13.

19. See Leuchtenburg, *Franklin D. Roosevelt*, for a thorough discussion of FDR's tenure in office.

20. Memo from Clayton Yeutter to Charles E. M. Kolb, "A Part Time Congress," April 1, 1992, Formerly Withheld, NLGB Control Number 6267, George Bush Presidential Library, College Station, Texas.

21. Memo from Frank J. Donatelli to Howard Baker, "'Do Awful Congress as a Campaign Theme," January 7, 1988, Files of Ken Duberstein, Box 3, Ronald Reagan Presidential Library, Simi Valley, California.

22. Richard E. Neustadt, *Presidential Power and the Modern Presidents: The Politics of Leadership from Roosevelt to Reagan* (New York: Free Press, 1990), 32.

23. Ibid., 30.

24. Barbara Sinclair, *Unorthodox Lawmaking: New Legislative Processes in the U.S. Congress* (Washington, DC: CQ Press, 2007), 163.

25. Ibid., 163–64.

26. Ibid., 171.

27. Ibid., 173.

28. Ibid., 180.

29. See David Mayhew, *Congress: The Electoral Connection* (New Haven, CT: Yale University Press, 1974).

30. See Samuel Kernell, *Going Public: New Strategies of Presidential Leadership*, 4th ed. (Washington, DC: CQ Press, 2007).

31. Ibid., 157.

32. Ronald Reagan, "Address to the Nation," July 27, 1981, http://www.presidency.ucsb. edu/ws/?pid=44120.

33. Kernell, *Going Public*, 159.

34. See Lori Cox Han, *Governing from Center Stage: White House Communication Strategies during the Television Age of Politics* (Cresskill, NJ: Hampton Press, 2001); and Lyn Ragsdale, *Vital Statistics on the Presidency*, 3rd ed. (Washington, DC: CQ Press, 2008).

35. Matthew Baum and Samuel Kernell, "Has Cable Ended the Golden Age of Television?" *American Political Science Review* 93, no. 1 (March 1999): 99–114.

36. See Diane J. Heith, *The Presidential Road Show: Public Leadership in a Partisan Era* (Boulder, CO: Paradigm Press, 2013).

37. See Brandon Rottinghaus, *The Provisional Pulpit: Modern Presidential Leadership of Public Opinion* (College Station: Texas A&M Press, 2010).

38. See George C. Edwards III, *At The Margins: Presidential Leadership of Congress* (New Haven, CT: Yale University Press, 1989).

39. Andrew Barrett, "Gone Public: The Impact of Going Public on Presidential Legislative Success," *American Politics Research* 32, no. 3 (May 2004): 338–70.

40. Paul Herrnson, Irwin Morris, and John McTague, "The Impact of Presidential Campaigning for Congress on Presidential Support in the U.S. House of Representatives," *Legislative Studies Quarterly* 36, no. 1 (2011): 99–122.

41. Unsigned and undated White House memo, "Civil Rights Communications Plan for Presidential Veto Scenario," Formerly Withheld, NLGB Control Number 4698, George Bush Presidential Library, College Station, Texas.

42. Charles Cameron, John Lipinski, and Charles Riemann, "Research Notes: Testing Formal Theories of Political Rhetoric," *Journal of Politics* 62, no. 1 (2000):187–205.

43. Ronald Reagan, "Remarks to the American Business Conference," March 13, 1985, https://reaganlibrary.archives.gov/archives/speeches/1985/31385b.htm.

44. Bill Clinton, "Presidential News Conference," May 23, 1995, http://www.presidency. ucsb.edu/ws/index.php?pid=51404.

45. Cameron, Lipinski, and Riemann, "Research Notes," 202.

46. Richard Conley, "George Bush and the 102nd Congress: The Impact of Public and Private Veto Threats on Policy Outcomes," *Presidential Studies Quarterly* 33, no. 4 (2003): 730–50.

47. See Charles Cameron, *Veto Bargaining: Presidents and the Politics of Negative Power* (New York: Cambridge University Press, 2000).

48. Ibid., 181–82.

49. George Bush, "Address on Administration Goals before a Joint Session of Congress," February 9, 1989, http://www.presidency.ucsb.edu/ws/index.php?pid=16660.

50. Richard E. Cohen, *Washington at Work: Back Rooms and Clean Air* (New York: Macmillan, 1992), 56.

51. Ibid., 84.

52. Ibid., 85.

53. Ibid., 97.

54. Rebecca Deen and Laura Arnold, "Veto Threats as a Policy Tool: When to Threaten?," *Presidential Studies Quarterly* 32, no. 1 (2002): 30–45.

55. Richard Fenno, "U.S. House Members in Their Constituencies: An Exploration," *American Political Science Review* 71, no. 3 (September 1977): 883–917.

56. B. Dan Wood, *The Myth of Presidential Representation* (New York: Cambridge University Press, 2009), 118.

57. See Sinclair, *Unorthodox Lawmaking*.

58. Budget 2011, Appendix, Executive Office of the President, https://www.whitehouse.gov/sites/default/files/omb/budget/fy2011/assets/eop.pdf.

59. Sinclair, *Unorthodox Lawmaking*, 216.

60. Ibid., 220.

61. Quoted in Sinclair, *Unorthodox Lawmaking*, 218.

62. Ibid., 223.

63. Ibid., 224.

64. See Heith, *The Presidential Road Show*.

65. Barack Obama, Remarks at Parkville Middle School and Center of Technology in Baltimore, Maryland, February 14, 2011, http://www.presidency.ucsb.edu/ws/index.php?pid=88988.

66. See William W. Lammers and Michael A. Genovese, *The Presidency and Domestic Policy: Comparing Leadership Styles, FDR to Clinton* (Washington DC: CQ Press, 2000).

67. White House Memo, May 19, 1964, "The Administration's Legislative Program," Files of Horace Busby, Box 20, Lyndon Baines Johnson Presidential Library, Austin, Texas.

CHAPTER 7

1. "White House Discussion Points, Supreme Court Nomination of Judge David Souter," undated, Mary Kate Grant Files, White House Office of Speechwriting, Box 8, George Bush Presidential Library, College Station, Texas.

2. Memo from Franklin Roosevelt to Homer Cummings, January 14, 1936, President's Secretary's Files, Box 165, Franklin D. Roosevelt Presidential Library, Hyde Park, New York.

3. Memo from Homer Cummings to Franklin D. Roosevelt, January 16, 1936, President's Secretary's File, Box 165, Franklin D. Roosevelt Presidential Library, Hyde Park, New York.

4. Memo from Homer Cummings to Franklin D. Roosevelt, February 2, 1937, President's Secretary's File, Box 165, Franklin D. Roosevelt Presidential Library, Hyde Park, New York.

5. Franklin D. Roosevelt, "Message to Congress on the Reorganization of the Judicial Branch of the Government," February 5, 1937, http://www.presidency.ucsb.edu/ws/index.php?pid=15360.

6. Franklin D. Roosevelt, "Fireside Chat," March 9, 1937, http://www.presidency.ucsb.edu/ws/index.php?pid=15381.

7. House Floor Speech: Impeach Justice Douglas, Box D29, Gerald R. Ford Congressional Papers, Gerald R. Ford Presidential Library, Ann Arbor, Michigan.

8. Bryon J. Moraski and Charles R. Shipan, "The Politics of Supreme Court Nominations: A Theory of Institutional Constraints and Choices," *American Journal of Political Science* 43, no. 4 (October 1999): 1069–95.

9. P. S. Ruckman, "The Supreme Court, Critical Nominations, and the Senate Confirmation Process," *The Journal of Politics* 55, No. 3 (August 1993): 793–805.

10. Lawrence Baum, *The Supreme Court*, 9th ed. (Washington, DC: CQ Press, 2007), 35–41.

11. Ibid., 44–45.

12. David M. O'Brien, *Storm Center: The Supreme Court in American Politics*, 8th ed. (New York: W. W. Norton, 2008), 34.

13. Ibid., 47–50.

14. David Alistair Yalof, *Pursuit of Justices: Presidential Politics and the Selection of Supreme Court Nominees* (Chicago: University of Chicago Press, 1999), 2–3.

15. George W. Bush, "Remarks Announcing the Nomination of Harriet E. Miers to Be an Associate Justice of the United States Supreme Court," October 7, 2005, http://www.presidency.ucsb.edu/ws/index.php?pid=64708.

16. Baum, *The Supreme Court*, 30–33.

17. Doris Graber, *Mass Media and American Politics*, 8th ed. (Washington, DC: CQ Press, 2010), 260.

18. Mark Jurkowitz, "Sotomayor Hearings Lead the News without Making News," Pew Research Center's Project for Excellence in Journalism, July 21, 2009, http://www.journalism.org/index_report/pej_news_coverage_index_july_13_19_2009.

19. Ronald Reagan, "Remarks Announcing the Nomination of Robert H. Bork to Be an Associate Justice of the Supreme Court of the United States," July 1, 1987, http://www.presidency.ucsb.edu/ws/index.php?pid=34503.

20. Memo from Thomas C. Griscom to Senior Administration Officials, "Judge Robert H. Bork," September 30, 1987, Files of Howard H. Baker, Box 3, Ronald Reagan Presidential Library, Simi Valley, California.

21. Memo from Howard S. Liebengood to Will Ball, "Bork Nomination," September 21, 1987, Files of Howard H. Baker, Box 3, Ronald Reagan Presidential Library, Simi Valley, California.

22. George Bush, "The President's News Conference in Kennebunkport, Maine," July 1, 1991, http://www.presidency.ucsb.edu/ws/?pid=29651.

23. Mark Silverstein, *Judicious Choices: The New Politics of Supreme Court Confirmations* (New York: W. W. Norton, 1994), 4.

24. Ibid., 29.

25. Barack Obama, "Weekly Address," May 30, 2009, "Obama Archive," http://www.whitehouse.gov.

26. Henry J. Abraham, *Justices, Presidents, and Senators: A History of U.S. Supreme Court Appointments from Washington to Bush II*, 5th ed. (Lanham, MD: Rowman & Littlefield, 2008), 4.

27. Biography of Sandra Day O'Connor, Oyez, U.S. Supreme Court Multimedia, https://www.oyez.org/justices/sandra_day_oconnor.

28. Baum, *The Supreme Court*, 20.

29. O'Brien, *Storm Center*, 108–9.

30. Baum, *The Supreme Court*, 20.

31. R. Kent Newmyer, "John Marshall," in *The Oxford Companion to the Supreme Court of the United States*, ed. Kermit L. Hall (New York: Oxford University Press, 1992), 526.

32. Dwight D. Eisenhower, "The President's News Conference," September 30, 1953, *http://www.presidency.ucsb.edu/ws/index.php?pid=9709.*

33. Dwight D. Eisenhower, *The White House Years: Mandate for Change 1953–1956* (Garden City, NY: Doubleday, 1963), 26.

34. O'Brien, *Storm Center*, 68.

35. See Silverstein, *Judicious Choices*.

36. George W. Bush, "Address to the Nation Announcing the Nomination of John G. Roberts, Jr., to Be an Associate Justice of the United States Supreme Court," July 19, 2005, http://www.presidency.ucsb.edu/ws/index.php?pid=65036.

37. George W. Bush, "Remarks Announcing the Nomination of John G. Roberts, Jr., to Be Chief Justice of the United States Supreme Court," September 5, 2005, http://www.presidency.ucsb.edu/ws/index.php?pid=65036.

38. Sheldon Goldman, *Picking Federal Judges: Lower Court Selection from Roosevelt through Reagan* (New Haven, CT: Yale University Press, 1997), 1–2.

39. See Sarah A. Binder and Forrest Maltzman, *Advice and Dissent: The Struggle to Shape the Federal Judiciary* (Washington, DC: Brookings Institution Press, 2009).

40. Barbara Palmer, "Women in the American Judiciary: Their Influence and Impact," *Women & Politics* 23, no. 3 (January 2001): 89–99.

41. Richard L. Pacelle Jr., "A President's Legacy: Gender and Appointment to the Federal Courts," in *The Other Elites: Women, Politics, and Power in the Executive Branch*, ed. MaryAnne Borrelli and Janet M. Martin (Boulder, CO: Lynne Rienner, 1997), 154.

42. Larry Berman, *The New American Presidency* (Boston: Little, Brown, 1987), 53.

43. Kevin T. McGuire, *Understanding the U.S. Supreme Court: Cases and Controversies* (Boston: McGraw–Hill, 2002), 171–73.

44. Robert Dahl, "Decision-Making in a Democracy: The Supreme Court as a National Policy-Maker," *Journal of Public Law* 6 (1957): 279–95.

45. Stephen R. Routh, "U.S. Solicitor General," in *Encyclopedia of American Government and Civics*, Vol. II, ed. Michael A Genovese and Lori Cox Han (New York: Facts on File, 2009), 645–48.

46. Baum, *The Supreme Court*, 85.

47. Richard L. Pacelle Jr., *Between Law & Politics: The Solicitor General and the Structuring of Race, Gender, and Reproductive Rights Litigation* (College Station: Texas A&M University Press, 2003), 10.

48 Matthew Eshbaugh-Soha and Paul M. Collins Jr., "Presidential Rhetoric and Supreme Court Decisions," *Presidential Studies Quarterly* 45, no. 4 (December 2015): 633–52.

49. For brief discussions of judicial review and *Marbury v. Madison*, see David M. O'Brien, *Constitutional Law and Politics*, Vol. 1, 9th ed. (New York: W. W. Norton, 2014); and Lee Epstein and Thomas G. Walker, *Constitutional Law for a Changing America: Institutional Powers and Constraints*, 9th ed. (Washington, DC: CQ Press, 2017). For a more in-depth discussion of judicial review and its history in the United States, see William E. Nelson, *Marbury v. Madison: The Origins and Legacy of Judicial Review* (Lawrence: University Press of Kansas, 2000).

50. Andrew Jackson, "Veto Message," July 10, 1832, in *A Compilation of the Messages and Papers of the Presidents*, Volume II, ed. James D. Richardson (Washington, DC: U.S. Government Printing Office, 1896), 582.

51. As quoted in Abraham, *Justices, Presidents, and Senators*, 77, regarding the case *Worcester v. Georgia*, 31 U.S. 515 (1832).

52. See Lori Cox Han, "George H. W. Bush," in *The Presidents and the Constitution: A Living History*, ed. Ken Gormley (New York: New York University Press, 2016).

53. George Bush, "Statement on the Flag Protection Act of 1989," October 26, 1989, http://www.presidency.ucsb.edu/ws/?pid=17706.

54. Adam Liptak, "Supreme Court Rebukes Obama on Right of Appointment," *New York Times*, June 26, 2014, https://www.nytimes.com/2014/06/27/us/supreme-court-president-recess-appointments.html?_r=1.

55. Letter from Harry S. Truman to Robert H. Jackson, April 2, 1946, President's Secretary's Files, Box 187, Harry S. Truman Presidential Library, Independence, Missouri.

56. Letter from Robert H. Jackson to Harry S. Truman, April 24, 1946, President's Secretary's Files, Box 187, Harry S. Truman Presidential Library, Independence, Missouri.

57. Letter from Harry S. Truman to Robert H. Jackson, May 1, 1946, President's Secretary's Files, Box 187, Harry S. Truman Presidential Library, Independence, Missouri.

CHAPTER 8

1. For a discussion on the current state and size of the executive branch, see Matthew J. Dickinson, "The Presidency and the Executive Branch," in *New Directions in the American Presidency*, ed. Lori Cox Han (New York: Routledge, 2011).

2. James Madison, Alexander Hamilton, and John Jay, "Federalist Number 69: The Same View Continued with a Comparison between the President and the King of Great Britain on the One Hand and the Governor of New York on the Other," *The Federalist Papers*, ed. Isaac Kramnick (New York: Penguin Books, 1987), 401.

3. James Madison, Alexander Hamilton, and John Jay, "Federalist Number 77: The View of the Constitution of the President Concluded," *The Federalist Papers*, ed. Isaac Kramnick (New York: Penguin Books, 1987), 435.

4. Series P 62–68, Government Employment, Federal Government Employment, 1816–1945, Historical Statistics of the United States, 1789–1945.

5. Table 496, Federal Civilian Employment and Annual Payroll by Branch: 1970 to 2010, Statistical Abstracts of the United States.

6. Leonard D. White, *The Jeffersonians: A Study in Administrative History 1801–1829* (New York: Macmillan, 1961), 139–40.

7. Ibid., 427–31.

8. Leonard D. White, *The Jacksonians: A Study in Administrative History 1801–1829* (New York: Macmillan 1961), 320.

9. Samuel Kernell and Gary Jacobson, *The Logic of American Politics*, (Washington, DC: CQ Press, 2010), 369.

10. Ibid., 370.

11. Paul Light, "The Homeland Security Hash," *The Wilson Quarterly* 31, no. 2 (Spring 2007): 36–44.

12. Dickinson, "The Presidency," 139.

13. David Lewis and Terry Moe, "The Presidency and the Bureaucracy," in *The Presidency and the Political System*, 9th ed., ed. Michael Nelson (Washington, DC: CQ Press, 2009), 370.

14. Ibid., 371.

15. Ibid., 372.

16. Theodore Sorenson, *Decision Making in the White House: The Olive Branch or the Arrows* (New York: Columbia University Press, 2005), 82.

17. William Leuchtenburg, *Franklin Roosevelt and the New Deal: 1932–1940* (New York: Harper & Row, 1963), 19.

18. Ibid., 33.

19. Ibid., 33.

20. Ibid., 33.

21. John P. Burke, "The Obama Presidential Transition: An Early Assessment," *Presidential Studies Quarterly* 39, no. 3 (September 2009) : 574–604.

22. Ibid., 577.

23. Ibid., 580.

24. Michael D. Shear and Philip Rucker, "Picks for Key Government Posts Play Long Waiting Game," *Washington Post*, March 4, 2009, http://www.washingtonpost.com/wp-dyn/content/article/2009/03/03/AR2009030303970.html.

25. John Burke, "The Institutional Presidency," in *The Presidency and the Political System*, 9th ed., ed. Michael Nelson (Washington, DC: CQ Press, 2009), 342.

26. Ibid.

27. Ibid., 343.

28. For an excellent discussion of the creation and growth of the Executive Office of the President under FDR, see Matthew J. Dickinson, *Bitter Harvest: FDR, Presidential Power and the Growth of the Presidential Branch* (New York: Cambridge University Press, 1996).

29. Summary of the Report of the Committee on Administrative Management, January 12, 1937, http://www.presidency.ucsb.edu/ws/?pid=15342.

30. Justin S. Vaughn and Jose D. Villalobos, "White House Staff," in *New Directions in the American Presidency*, ed. Lori Cox Han (New York: Routledge, 2011), 121.

31. Ibid., 128–31. See also Bradley H. Patterson Jr., *The White House Staff: Inside the West Wing and Beyond* (Washington, DC: Brookings Institution Press, 2000).

32. George W. Bush, "Remarks on the Nomination of Robert J. Portman to Be Director of the Office of Management and Budget and Susan C. Schwab to Be United States Trade Representative and an Exchange with Reporters," April 18, 2006, https://www.gpo.gov/fdsys/pkg/PPP-2006-book1/html/PPP-2006-book1-doc-pg733.htm.

33. Memo from Jody Powell to Jimmy Carter, January 16, 1978, Files of Jody Powell, Box 39, Jimmy Carter Presidential Library, Atlanta, Georgia.

34. Memo from Roger B. Porter to Donald T. Regan, "White House Organization VII: Meetings," January 26, 1985, Files of Donald T. Regan, Box 11, Ronald Reagan Presidential Library, Simi Valley, California.

35. Memo from John D. Podesta to senior staff, "Paperflow," January 22, 1993, Files of Ira Magaziner, Box 1, William J. Clinton Presidential Library, Little Rock, Arkansas.

36. See David B. Cohen and Charles E. Walcott, "The Office of Chief of Staff," *The White House Transition Project*, Report 2017-21, 2017, http://whitehousetransitionproject.org/wp-content/uploads/2016/03/WHTP2017-21-Chief-of-Staff.pdf.

37. Terry Sullivan, ed., *The Nerve Center: Lessons in Governing from the White House Chiefs of Staff* (College Station: Texas A&M University Press, 2004), 39.

38. Ibid., 24.

39. Michael D. Shear, Maggie Haberman, and Allan Rappeport, "Donald Trump Picks Reince Priebus as Chief of Staff and Stephen Bannon as Strategist," *New York Times*, November 13, 2016, https://www.nytimes.com/2016/11/14/us/politics/reince-priebus-chief-of-staff-donald-trump.html?_r=0.

40. Paul 't Hart, *Karen Tindall*, and *Christer Brown*, "*Crisis Leadership* of the *Bush Presidency: Advisory Capacity* and *Presidential Performance in* the *Acute Stages* of the *9/11* and *Katrina Crises*," *Presidential Studies Quarterly* 39, no. 3 (September 2009): 473–93.

41. Bob Woodward, *Plan of Attack* (New York: Simon & Schuster, 2004), 251.

42. Ibid., 252.

43. Lewis and Moe, "The Presidency," 381.

44. Ibid.

45. Ibid., 382.

46. Eric Lipton and Scott Shane, "Leader of Federal Effort Feels the Heat," *New York Times*, September 3, 2005, http://www.nytimes.com/2005/09/03/national/nationalspecial/03fema.html.

47. Charles Perrow, "Using Organizations: The Case of FEMA," *Homeland Security Affairs* 1, Article 4 (August 2005), https://www.hsaj.org/articles/687.

48. Lewis and Moe, "The Presidency," 386.

49. "Consumer Safety Chief Says She Won't Quit," CBS News, October 31, 2007, http://www.cbsnews.com/stories/2007/10/31/national/main3434914.shtml.

50. Andrew Rudalevige, "The Presidency and Unilateral Power," in *The Presidency and the Political System*, ed. Michael Nelson (Washington, DC: CQ Press, 2009), 473.

51. Ibid., 474.

52. See Adam Warber, *Executive Orders and the Modern Presidency* (Boulder, CO: Lynne Rienner, 2006); and Kenneth Mayer, *With the Stroke of a Pen: Executive Orders and Presidential Power* (Princeton, NJ: Princeton University Press, 2001).

53. See Warber, *Executive Orders*.

54. Lewis and Moe, "The Presidency," 390.

55. Brandon Rottinghaus and Adam Warber, "Unilateral Orders as Constituency Outreach: Executive Orders, Proclamations, and the Public Presidency," *Presidential Studies Quarterly* 45, no. 2 (April 2015): 289–309.

56. Andrew Jackson, "Special Message," May 30, 1830, http://www.presidency.ucsb.edu/ws/index.php?pid=66775.

57. Rudalevige, "The Presidency," 471.

58. George W. Bush, "Statement on Signing the Palestinian Anti-Terrorism Act of 2006," December 21, 2006, http://www.presidency.ucsb.edu/ws/index.php?pid=24395.

59. Letter to George W. Bush, March 17, 2006, White House Office of Records and Management, Box 3, "Speeches," George W. Bush Presidential Library, Dallas, Texas. The list of signers includes senators David Vitter, Debbie Stabenow, Russell Feingold, Richard Durbin, Tom Coburn, Herb Kohl, Charles Schumer, Jim DeMint, Carl Levin, John McCain, and Barbara Mikulski and representatives Anne Northup, Gil Gutknecht, Ron Paul, Rahm Emanuel, Mike Simpson, Tom Allen, Dan Burton, Marion Berry, Jo Ann Emerson, Maurice Hinchey, and Sherrod Brown.

60. John Adams, *The Works of John Adams*, Vol. 1, ed. C. F. Adams (Boston: Little Brown, 1850), 289.

61. Patrick Cox, "Not Worth a Bucket of Warm Spit," *The History News Network*, August 20, 2008, http://hnn.us/articles/53402.html.

62. See the Obama archive at http://www.whitehouse.gov.

63. Joseph Pika, "The Vice Presidency," in *The Presidency and the Political System*, ed. Michael Nelson (Washington, DC: CQ Press, 2009), 512.

64. Ibid., 513.

65. Ibid., 515.

66. Robert P. Watson, *The President's Wives: Reassessing the Office of First Lady* (Boulder, CO: Lynne Rienner, 2000), 72.

66. Ibid., 580.

67. Ibid., 112–13.

68. MaryAnne Borrelli, *The Politics of the President's Wife* (College Station: Texas A&M University Press, 2011), 1.

69. Lori Cox Han, *Women and US Politics: The Spectrum of Political Leadership*, 2nd ed. (Boulder, CO: Lynne Rienner, 2010), 132–34.

CHAPTER 9

1. Memo from Greg Schneiders to Gerald Rafshoon, "Developing Public Support for the President's Energy Program," Files of Gerald Rafshoon, Office of Communication, Box 44, Jimmy Carter Presidential Library, Atlanta, Georgia.

2. "Reorganization," Patrick Caddell Poll, September 1977, Files of Gerald Rafshoon, Office of Communication, Box 68, Jimmy Carter Presidential Library, Atlanta, Georgia.

3. Jimmy Carter, White House Governors Conference, Energy Briefing Book, White House Conference on Energy, July 8–9, 1977, Files of Gerald Rafshoon, Box 43, Jimmy Carter Presidential Library, Atlanta, Georgia.

4. Memo from Gerald Rafshoon to senior staff, "Public Support for the President's Energy Program," Files of Gerald Rafshoon, Office of Communication, Box 44, Jimmy Carter Presidential Library, Atlanta, Georgia.

5. George H. W. Bush, "Address Accepting the Presidential Nomination at the Republican National Convention in New Orleans," *August 18, 1988*, http://www.presidency.ucsb.edu/ws/?pid=25955.

6. Quoted in Patricia Conley, *Presidential Mandates: How Elections Shape the National Agenda* (Chicago: Chicago University Press, 2001).

7. Michael Grunwald, "A Mandate for Change," *Time*, November 4, 2008, http://www.time.com/time/politics/article/0,8599,1856560,00.html.

8. See James P. Pfiffner, *The Strategic Presidency: Hitting the Ground Running, 2nd ed.* (Lawrence: University Press of Kansas, 1996).

9. See Richard Harris and Sidney Milkis, *The Politics of Regulatory Change: A Tale of Two Agencies* (New York: Oxford University Press, 1989).

10. See Michael Nelson and Russell L. Riley, eds., *Governing at Home: The White House and Domestic Policymaking* (Lawrence: University Press of Kansas, 2011); and Martin A. Levin, Daniel DeSalvo, and Martin M. Shapiro, eds., *Building Coalitions, Making Policy: The Politics of the Clinton, Bush, and Obama Presidencies* (Baltimore: Johns Hopkins University Press, 2012).

11. William W. Lammers and Michael A. Genovese, *The Presidency and Domestic Policy: Comparing Leadership Styles, FDR to Clinton* (Washington, DC: CQ Press, 2000), 19.

12. See Donna Hoffman and Alison Howard, *Addressing the State of the Union: The Evolution and Impact of the President's Big Speech* (Boulder, CO: Lynne Rienner, 2006).

13. Donald J. Trump, "Inaugural Address," January 20, 2017, https://www.whitehouse.gov/inaugural-address.

14. Christine Fauvelle-Aymar and Mary Stegmaier, "The Stock Market and U.S. Presidential Approval," *Electoral Studies* 32, no. 3 (September 2013): 411–17.

15. See Nelson and Riley, *Governing at Home*; Levin, DeSalvo, and Shapiro, *Building Coalitions*; and John W. Kingdon, *Agendas, Alternatives, and Public Policies* (New York: Longman Press, 2002).

16. See Kingdon, *Agendas*.

17. See Nelson and Riley, *Governing at Home*; and Levin, DeSalvo, and Shapiro, *Building Coalitions*.

18. See Bernard Cohen, *The Press and Foreign Policy* (Princeton, NJ: Princeton University Press, 1963).

19. See Roger W. Cobb and Charles D. Elder, *Participation in American Politics: The Dynamics of Agenda Building* (Baltimore: Johns Hopkins University Press, 1972).

20. Paul C. Light, "Domestic Policy Making," *Presidential Studies Quarterly* 30, no. 1 (March 2000): 109–32.

21. Roger Porter, "The Three Presidencies: Power and Policy," in *The Presidency and the Political System*, ed. Michael Nelson (Washington, DC: CQ Press, 2014), 502.

22. See Jennifer Hopper, *Presidential Framing in the 21st Century News Media: The Politics of the Affordable Care Act* (New York: Routledge, 2017).

23. See Paul Rutledge and Heather Larsen Price, "The President as Agenda Setter-in-Chief: The Dynamics of Congressional and Presidential Agenda Setting," *Policy Studies Journal* 42, no. 3 (August 2014): 443–64.

24. Memo from Roger Porter to John Sununu, Re: Education Policy Advisory Committee, June 1, 1989, Files of John Sununu, CF #6227, George Bush Presidential Library, College Station, Texas.

25. See Nelson and Riley, *Governing at Home.*

26. See Julian E. Zelizer, ed., *The Presidency of George W. Bush: A First Historical Assessment* (Princeton, NJ: Princeton University Press, 2010); and Robert Draper, *Dead Certain: The Presidency of George W. Bush* (New York: Free Press, 2008).

27. See Chris J. Dolan, John Frendreis, and Raymond Tatalovich, *The Presidency and Economic Policy* (Lanham, MD: Rowman & Littlefied, 2007); Matthew J. Dickinson, "The Presidency and the Executive Branch," in *New Directions in the American Presidency*, ed. Lori Cox Han (New York: Routledge, 2011); and Nelson and Riley, *Governing at Home.*

28. See George P. Shultz and Kenneth W. Dam, *Economic Policy beyond the Headlines* (Chicago: University of Chicago Press, 1998); and Dolan, Frendeis, and Tatolovich, *The Presidency and Economic Policy.*

29. See Dolan, Frendreis, and Tatalovich, *The Presidency and Economic Policy;* Nelson and Riley, *Governing at Home;* and Levin, DeSalvo, and Shapiro, *Building Coalitions.*

30. See Walter Oleszek, *Congressional Procedures and the Policy Process,* 8th ed. (Washington DC: CQ Press, 2011).

31. See Barbara Sinclair, *Unorthodox Lawmaking: New Legislative Processes in the U.S. Congress,* 3rd ed. (Washington DC: CQ Press, 2007).

32. "Frequently Asked Questions," National Governors Association, https://www.nga.org/cms/home/about/faq.html.

33. See Stephen H. Axilrod, *Inside the Fed: Monetary Policy and Its Management, Martin through Greenspan to Bernanke* (Cambridge, MA: MIT Press, 2009).

34. Stephen Weatherford, "The President, the Fed, and the Financial Crisis," *Presidential Studies Quarterly* 43, no. 2 (June 2013): 299–327.

35. Ibid., 323.

36. See Doron P. Levin, *Behind the Wheel at Chrysler: Reassessing the Iacocca Legacy* (New York: Mariner Books, 1996); and Charles K. Hyde, *Riding the Rollercoaster: A History of the Chrysler Corporation* (Detroit, MI: Wayne State University Press, 2003).

37. See Levin, *Behind the Wheel;* Hyde, *Riding the Rollercoaster;* and Berton Ira Kaufman and Scott Kaufman, *The Presidency of James Earl Carter, Jr.* (Lawrence: University Press of Kansas, 2006).

38. See Levin, *Behind the Wheel;* and Hyde, *Riding the Rollercoaster.*

39. See Paul Ingrassia, *Crash Course: The American Auto Industry's Road to Bankruptcy and Bailout—And Beyond* (New York: Random House, 2011).

40. Ibid.

41. See Bill Vlasic, *Once upon a Car: The Fall and Resurrection of America's Big Three Auto Makers—GM, Ford, and Chrysler* (New York: William Morrow, 2011); and Ingrassia, *Crash Course.*

42. Ibid.

43. See Zelizer, *George W. Bush;* Vlasic, *Once upon a Car;* and Ingrassia, *Crash Course.*

44. See Vlasic, *Once upon a Car;* and Ingrassia, *Crash Course.*

45. Barack Obama, "Address before a Joint Session of Congress on the State of the Union," January 24, 2012, American Presidency Project, http://www.presidency.ucsb.edu/ws/index.php?pid=99000#axzz1lLnQcTgf.

46. See Alan Murray and Jeffrey Birnbaum, *Showdown at Gucci Gulch* (New York: Vintage, 1988).

47. See Joseph Pika, "White House Office of Public Liaison," *White House Transition Project 2009-03*; available at http://whitehousetransitionproject.org/resources/briefing/WHTP-2009-03-Public%20Liaison.pdf.

48. Kathryn Dunn Tenpas, "Lobbying the Executive Branch," in *The Interest Group Connection: Electioneering, Lobbying, and Policymaking in Washington*, 2nd ed., ed. Paul S. Herrnson, Ronald G. Shaiko, and Clyde Wilcox (Washington, DC: CQ Press, 2004), 251.

49. Scot Furlong, "Executive Policymaking," in *The Interest Group Connection: Electioneering, Lobbying, and Policymaking in Washington*, 2nd ed., ed. Paul S. Herrnson, Ronald G. Shaiko, and Clyde Wilcox (Washington, DC: CQ Press, 2004), 292.

50. See Stanley Elkins and Erik McKitrick, *The Age of Federalism: The Early American Republic, 1788–1800* (New York: Oxford University Press, 1993); and Gordon W. Wood, *Empire of Liberty: A History of the Early Republic, 1789–1815* (New York: Oxford University Press, 2011).

51. See Howard Gillman, *The Constitution Besieged: The Rise and Demise of Lochner Era Police Powers Jurisprudence* (Durham, NC: Duke University Press, 1993).

52. *Congressional Quarterly Almanac, 1964*, Vol. XX (Washington, DC: Congressional Quarterly Service, 1965), 525.

53. Theodore Sorensen, recorded interview by Carl Kaysen, May 20, 1964, 151, Oral History Program, John F. Kennedy Presidential Library, Boston, Massachusetts.

54. Memo from Ted Sorensen to John F. Kennedy, July 12, 1962, President's Office Files, John F. Kennedy Presidential Library, Boston, Massachusetts.

55. *Congressional Quarterly Almanac*, 1964, 518.

56. See Nelson and Riley, *Governing at Home*; Levin, DeSalvo, and Shapiro, *Building Coalitions*; and Dolan, Frendeis, and Tatolovich, *The Presidency and Economic Policy*.

57. See Walter LaFeber, *America, Russia, and the Cold War, 1945–2002* (Boston: McGraw–Hill, 2002); Melvyn Leffler, *A Preponderance of Power: National Security, the Truman Administration, and the Cold War* (Palo Alto, CA: Stanford University Press, 1993); John Spanier and Steven W. Hook, *American Foreign Policy Since World War II* (Washington, DC: CQ Press, 2009); and Lou Cannon, *President Reagan: The Role of a Lifetime* (New York: Public Affairs Books, 2000).

58. See Nelson and Riley, *Governing at Home*; and Levin, DeSalvo, and Shapiro, *Building Coalitions*.

59. See Douglas A. Irwin, *Free Trade Under Fire* (Princeton, NJ: Princeton University Press, 2009); and Dolan, Frendeis, and Tatolovich, *The Presidency and Economic Policy*.

60. See Dolan, Frendeis, and Tatolovich, *The Presidency and Economic Policy*.

61. See Nelson and Riley, *Governing at Home*; Levin, DeSalvo, and Shapiro, *Building Coalitions*; and Dolan, Frendeis, and Tatolovich, *The Presidency and Economic Policy*.

62. Ibid.

63. Ibid.

64. See Stephen Skowronek, *Building a New American State: The Expansion of American Administrative Capacities, 1877–1920* (London: Cambridge University Press, 1982); Gillman, *The Constitution Besieged*; and William E. Leuchtenburg, *Franklin D. Roosevelt and the New Deal: 1932-1940* (New York: Harper & Row, 1963).

65. See Alan Brinkley, *The End of Reform: New Deal Liberalism in Recession and War* (New York: Vintage, 1996).

66. See Andrew Dobelstein, *Understanding the Social Security Act: The Foundation of Social Welfare in America for the Twenty-First Century* (New York: Oxford University Press, 2009); Daniel Beland, *Social Security: History and Politics from the New Deal to the*

Privatization Debate (Lawrence: University Press of Kansas, 2007); Brinkley, *End of Reform*.

67. Lyndon B. Johnson, "Annual Message to the Congress on the State of the Union," January 8, 1964, American Presidency Project, http://www.presidency.ucsb.edu/ws/index.php?pid=26787&st=war+on+poverty&st1=#axzz1lLnQcTgf.

68. See Sidney M. Milkis and Jerome M. Mileur, eds., *The Great Society and the High Tide of Liberalism* (Amherst: University of Massachusetts Press, 2005); Gareth Davies, *From Opportunity to Entitlement: The Transformation and Decline of Great Society Liberalism* (Lawrence: University Press of Kansas, 1999); and Robert Dallek, *Lyndon B. Johnson: Portrait of a President* (New York: Oxford University Press, 2005).

69. See Milkis and Mileur, *Great Society*; and Dallek, *Lyndon B. Johnson*.

70. See Zelizer, *George W. Bush*; and Draper, *Bush*.

71. See Alan Trachtenberg, *The Incorporation of America: Culture and Society in the Gilded Age* (New York: Hill & Wang, 2007).

72. "Restoration of the Mexico City Policy," January 23, 2017, https://www.whitehouse.gov/the-press-office/2017/01/23/presidential-memorandum-regarding-mexico-city-policy.

73. See Elkins and McKitrick, *Age of Federalism*; and Wood, *Empire of Liberty*.

74. See Zelizer, *George W. Bush*; Draper, *Bush*; Nelson and Riley, *Governing at Home*; and Levin, DeSalvo, and Shapiro, *Building Coalitions*.

75. Memo from Rahm Emanuel to Leon Panetta, "Crime Bill Strategy," August 12, 1994, Files of Jonathan Prince, Box 3, William J. Clinton Presidential Library, Little Rock, Arkansas.

76. See Jeffrey B. Bumgarner, *Federal Agents: The Growth of Federal Law Enforcement in America* (New York: Praeger, 2006); Barbara Stolz, *Criminal Justice Policy Making: Federal Roles and Processes* (New York: Praeger, 2001); and Nancy E. Marion, *Federal Government and Criminal Justice* (New York: Palgrave Macmillan, 2011).

77. See Zelizer, *George W. Bush*; Draper, *Bush*; Bumgarner, *Federal Agents*; and Marion, *Criminal Justice*.

78. See Nicolaus Mills, *Arguing Immigration: The Debate over the Changing Face of America* (New York: Touchstone, 1994); Carol M. Swain, ed., *Debating Immigration* (London: Cambridge University Press, 2007); and Hugh Davis Graham, *Collision Course: The Strange Convergence of Affirmative Action and Immigration Policy in America* (New York: Oxford University Press, 2003).

79. See Milkis, *Great Society*; and Dallek, *Lyndon B. Johnson*.

80. See Dallek, *Lyndon B. Johnson*.

81. See Steven A. Shull, *American Civil Rights Policy from Truman to Clinton: The Role of Presidential Leadership* (Armonk, NY: M. E. Sharpe, 2000).

82. See Shull, *Civil Rights*; and Bob Woodward, *The Agenda: Inside the Clinton White House* (New York: Simon & Schuster, 1994).

83. See Daniel J. Fiorino, *Making Environmental Policy* (Berkeley: University of California Press, 1995); Walter A. Rosenbaum, *Environmental Politics and Policy* (Washington, DC: CQ Press, 2010); and Norman J. Vig and Michael E. Kraft, *Environmental Policy: New Directions for the Twenty-First Century* (Washington, DC: CQ Press, 2009).

84. See Rosenbaum, *Environmental Politics*; Vig and Kraft, *Environmental Policy*; and Woodward, *Agenda*.

85. See Vig and Kraft, *Environmental Policy*.

86. Jimmy Carter, *Keeping Faith: Memoirs of a President* (New York: Bantam Books, 1982), 91.

87. See John M. Deutch, *The Crisis in Energy Policy* (Cambridge, MA: Harvard University Press, 2011); Brenda Shaffer, *Energy Politics* (Philadelphia: University of Pennsylvania Press, 2011); and Carlos Pasqual and Jonathan Elkind, *Energy Security: Economics, Politics, Strategies, and Implications* (Washington, DC: Brookings Institution Press, 2009).

88. David Blumenthal and James Morone, *The Heart of Power: Health and Politics in the Oval Office* (Berkeley: University of California Press, 2010), 32.

89. Memo from Dick Gephardt to Hillary Rodham Clinton and Ira Magaziner, "Consultation with Congress," March 3, 1993, Files of Ira Magaziner, Box 3, William J. Clinton Presidential Library, Little Rock, Arkansas.

90. Memo from Howard Paster to Hillary Rodham Clinton and Mack McLarty, "Lobbying on Health Care Reform," May 9, 1993, Files of Ira Magaziner, Box 3, William J. Clinton Presidential Library, Little Rock, Arkansas.

91. Memo from Chris Jennings to Hillary Rodham Clinton and Jeff Eller, "Health Care University" June 28, 1993, Files of Ira Magaziner, Box 3, William J. Clinton Presidential Library, Little Rock, Arkansas.

92. Assorted letters to Bill Clinton, Health Care, Box 1, FOIA 2006-0225, Clinton Digital Library, https://clinton.presidentiallibraries.us/.

93. Ibid., 91.

94. "Profile: Operation Coffeecup," History Commons, August 25, 2009, http://www.historycommons.org/entity.jsp?entity=operation_coffeecup_1.

95. "Ronald Reagan's Warning about Socialized Medicine," *The Lonely Conservative*, August 15, 2009, http://www.lonelyconservative.com/2009/08/ronald-reagans-warning-about-socialized-medicine-video-and-complete-transcript/.

96. Darrell West, Diane Heith, and Chris Goodwin, "Harry and Louise Go to Washington: Political Advertising and Health Care Reform." *The Journal of Health Politics, Policy and Law* 21, no. 1 (Spring 1996): 35–68.

97. Sara Fritz, "Ads Are Designed to Counter Health Care Proposals," *Los Angeles Times*, May 15 1993, http://articles.latimes.com/1993-05-15/news/mn-35593_1_health-care-reform-plan.

98. West, Heith, and Goodwin, "Harry and Louise," 54.

99. Franklin D. Roosevelt, "Address to Advisory Council of the Committee on Economic Security," November 14, 1934, http://www.presidency.ucsb.edu/ws/index.php?pid=14777.

100. Blumenthal and Morone, *The Heart of Power*, 361.

101. Ibid., 363.

102. Ibid., 411.

103. Ibid., x–xi.

104. Barack Obama, "Address before a Joint Session of the Congress on the State of the Union," January 27, 2010, http://www.presidency.ucsb.edu/ws/index.php?pid=87433.

CHAPTER 10

1. Letter from the president regarding the commencement of operations in Libya, March 21, 2001, http://www.whitehouse.gov/the-press-office/2011/03/21/letter-president-regarding-commencement-operations-libya.

2. Barack Obama, "Remarks by the President in Address to the Nation on Libya," National Defense University, Washington, DC, March 28, 2011, http://www.whitehouse.gov/the-press-office/2011/03/28/remarks-president-address-nation-libya.

3. Charlie Savage and Mark Landler, "White House Defends Continuing U.S. Role in Libya Operation," *New York Times*, June 15, 2011, http://www.nytimes.com/2011/06/16/us/politics/16powers.html.

4. See Aaron Wildavsky, "The Two Presidencies," *Trans-Action* IV (December 1966): 7–14.

5. See Alex Mintz and Karl DeRouen Jr., *Understanding Foreign Policy Decision Making* (Cambridge: Cambridge University Press, 2010).

6. "President Lyndon B. Johnson's Address to the Nation Announcing Steps to Limit the War in Vietnam and Reporting His Decision Not to Seek Reelection," March 31, 1968, http://www.presidency.ucsb.edu/ws/index.php?pid=28772.

7. See John Hart Ely, *War and Responsibility* (Princeton, NJ: Princeton University Press, 1995).

8. See Mintz and DeRouen, *Understanding Foreign Policy*; and Bruce W. Jentleson, *American Foreign Policy: The Dynamics of Choice in the 21st Century* (New York: W. W. Norton, 2010).

9. Memorandum for the president, November 10, 1950, President's Secretary's File, Subject Files, Box 187, Harry S. Truman Presidential Library, Independence, Missouri.

10. For example, see Bob Woodward, *Plan of Attack* (New York: Simon & Schuster, 2004).

11. For some examples, see Bob Woodward, *Obama's Wars* (New York: Simon & Schuster, 2010).

12. On diplomacy and national security, see Melvyn Leffler, *A Preponderance of Power: National Security, the Truman Administration, and the Cold War* (Palo Alto, CA: Stanford University Press, 1993); and John Spanier and Steven W. Hook, *American Foreign Policy since World War II* (Washington, DC: CQ Press, 2009).

13. See Graham Allison and Philip Zelikow, *Essence of Decision: Explaining the Cuban Missile Crisis* (New York: Longman Press, 1999).

14. Ibid.; see also Walter LaFeber, *The American Age: United States Foreign Policy at Home and Abroad, 1750 to the Present* (New York: W. W. Norton, 1994); and Walter LaFeber, *America, Russia, and the Cold War, 1945–2002* (Boston: McGraw–Hill, 2002).

15. Letter from Lauris Norstad to John F. Kennedy, November 1, 1962, Presidential Office Files, Subject File, Box 103, John F. Kennedy Presidential Library, Boston, Massachusetts.

16. See Peter W. Rodman, *Presidential Command: Power, Leadership, and the Making of Foreign Policy from Richard Nixon to George W. Bush* (New York: Alfred A. Knopf, 2009); and Colin Campbell and Bert A. Rockman, eds., *The George W. Bush Presidency: Appraisals and Prospects* (Washington, DC: CQ Press, 2003).

17. See David E. Sanger, *Confront and Conceal: Obama's Secret Wars and Surprising Use of American Power* (New York: Broadway Books, 2012); and Martin S. Indyk et al., *Bending History: Barack Obama's Foreign Policy* (Washington, DC: Brookings Institution Press, 2012).

18. See LaFeber, *American Age*; LaFeber, *Cold War*; Mintz and DeRouen, *Understanding Foreign Policy*; and Spanier and Hook, *American Foreign Policy*.

19. Memo from Chester Bowles to John F. Kennedy, "Need for Improving Public Understanding of American Foreign Policy and World Affairs," January 17, 1962, President's Office File, Staff Memos, Chester Bowles, Box 62, John F. Kennedy Presidential Library, Boston, Massachusetts.

20. See Ely, *War and Responsibility*; and David G. Adler and Larry N. George, eds., *The Constitution and the Conduct of American Foreign Policy* (Lawrence: University Press of Kansas, 1996).

21. See Spanier and Hook, *American Foreign Policy*; LaFeber, *American Age*; LaFeber, *Cold War*; Mintz and DeRouen, *Understanding Foreign Policy*.

22. Summary of James Hagerty's discussion with Dwight Eisenhower regarding the December 6, 1960, meeting between President Eisenhower and President-Elect John F. Kennedy, Files of James Hagerty, Box 3, Dwight D. Eisenhower Presidential Library, Abilene, Kansas.

23. For discussions on presidential leadership during military actions, see Elizabeth N. Saunders, *Leaders at War: How Presidents Shape Military Interventions* (Ithaca, NY: Cornell University Press, 2011); and Andrew J. Polsky, *Elusive Victories: The American Presidency at War* (New York: Oxford University Press, 2012).

24. Memo from David Dreyer to David Gergen, "Speech Writers," September 24, 1993, Files of David Gergen, FOIA 2011-0583-F, William J. Clinton Presidential Library, Little Rock, Arkansas.

25. See Woodward, *Obama's Wars*; Sanger, *Confront and Conceal*; and Indyk et al., *Bending History*.

26. Memorandum for the president, June 29, 1950, President's Secretary's File, Subject Files, Box 187, Harry S. Truman Presidential Library, Independence, Missouri.

27. See John W. Kingdon, *Agendas, Alternatives, and Public Policies* (New York: Longman Press, 2002); Mintz and DeRouen, *Understanding Foreign Policy*; and Spanier and Hook, *American Foreign Policy*.

28. See Woodward, *Obama's Wars*; Sanger, *Confront and Conceal*; Indyk et al., *Bending History*.

29. See LaFeber, *American Age*; Mintz and DeRouen, *Understanding Foreign Policy*; Spanier and Hook, *American Foreign Policy*; and Leffler, *Preponderance of Power*.

30. Ibid.; see also Amos A. Jordan et al., *American National Security* (Baltimore: John Hopkins University Press, 2009).

31. Ibid.; see also Rodman, *Presidential Command*; and Campbell and Rockman, *George W. Bush*.

32. See Mark M. Lowenthal, *Intelligence: From Secrets to Policy* (Washington, DC: CQ Press, 2008); Mintz and DeRouen, *Understanding Foreign Policy*; Spanier and Hook, *American Foreign Policy*; and Leffler, *Preponderance of Power*.

33. Bruce Buchanan, *Presidential Power and Accountability: Toward a Presidential Accountability System* (New York: Routledge, 2013), 59.

34. Ibid., 4.

35. Douglas L. Kriner, *After the Rubicon: Congress, Presidents, and the Politics of Waging War* (Chicago: University of Chicago Press, 2010), 3.

36. See Kingdon, *Agendas*; Mintz and DeRouen, *Understanding Foreign Policy*; and Spanier and Hook, *American Foreign Policy*.

37. See LaFeber, *American Age*; LaFeber, *Cold War*; Spanier and Hook, *American Foreign Policy*; and Leffler, *Preponderance of Power*.

38. On NATO, see Lawrence S. Kaplan, *NATO Divided, NATO United* (Greenwood, CT: Praeger, 2004); and Stanley R. Sloan, *NATO, the European Union, and the Atlantic Community* (New York: Rowman & Littlefield, 2002).

39. Ibid. See also David P. Calleo, *Rethinking Europe's Future* (Princeton, NJ: Princeton University Press, 2003).

40. See Calleo, *Europe's Future*; LaFeber, *American Age*; LaFeber, *Cold War*; and Spanier and Hook, *American Foreign Policy*.

41. Ibid.

42. See John J. Mearsheimer and Stephen M. Walt, *The Israel Lobby and U.S. Foreign Policy* (New York: Farrar, Straus and Giroux, 2007); Calleo, *Europe's Future*; LaFeber, *American Age*; LaFeber, *Cold War*; and Spanier and Hook, *American Foreign Policy*.

43. See LaFeber, *American Age*; LaFeber, *Cold War*; Spanier and Hook, *American Foreign Policy*; Leffler, *Preponderance of Power*.

44. Ibid.

45. See Gordon S. Wood, *Empire of Liberty: A History of the Early Republic, 1789–1815* (New York: Oxford University Press, 2011); and Steven E. Woodworth, *Manifest Destinies: America's Westward Expansion and the Road to the Civil War* (New York: Alfred A. Knopf, 2008).

46. Ibid. See also Charles Sellers, *The Market Revolution: Jacksonian America, 1815–1846* (New York: Oxford University Press, 1994).

47. See George Dangerfield, *The Awakening of American Nationalism: 1815–1828* (Long Grove, IL: Waveland Press, 1994); LaFeber, *American Age*; and Woodworth, *Manifest Destinies*.

48. See Steve Fraser and Gary Gerstle, eds., *Ruling America: A History of Wealth and Power in a Democracy* (Cambridge, MA: Harvard University Press, 2005); and Lewis L. Gould, *The Spanish–American War and President McKinley* (Lawrence: University Press of Kansas, 1982).

49. See Thomas J. Knock, *To End All Wars: Woodrow Wilson and the Quest for a New World Order* (Princeton, NJ: Princeton University Press, 1995); and Edmund Morris, *Theodore Rex* (New York: Random House, 2002).

50. See Robert Dallek, *Franklin D. Roosevelt and America Foreign Policy, 1932–1945* (New York: Oxford University Press, 1995).

51. See Dallek, *Roosevelt*; Fraser and Gerstle, *Ruling America*; and LaFeber, *American Age*.

52. See Fraser and Gerstle, *Ruling America*; LaFeber, *American Age*; LaFeber, *Cold War*; and Leffler, *Preponderance of Power*.

53. See Fraser and Gerstle, *Ruling America*; LaFeber, *Cold War*; and Leffler, *Preponderance of Power*.

54. See LaFeber, *Cold War*; and Leffler, *Preponderance of Power*.

55. See Fraser and Gerstle, *Ruling America*; and LaFeber, *Cold War*.

56. See George C. Herring, *America's Longest War: The United States and Vietnam, 1950–1975* (New York: McGraw–Hill, 2001); and Stanley Karnow, *Vietnam: A History* (New York: Penguin, 1997).

57. See Lou Cannon, *President Reagan: The Role of a Lifetime* (New York: Public Affairs Books, 2000); and Richard Reeves, *President Reagan: The Triumph of Imagination* (New York: Simon & Schuster, 2006).

58. See Bob Woodward, *The Commanders* (New York: Simon & Schuster, 2002); Fraser and Gerstle, *Ruling America*; and Spanier and Hook, *American Foreign Policy*.

59. See John F. Harris, *The Survivor: Bill Clinton in the White House* (New York: Random House, 2006); Bob Woodward, *The Agenda: Inside the Clinton White House* (New York: Simon & Schuster, 1994); Fraser and Gerstle, *Ruling America*; and Spanier and Hook, *American Foreign Policy*.

60. See Cannon, *President Reagan*; and Reeves, *President Reagan*.

61. See Fraser and Gerstle, *Ruling America*; and LaFeber, *Cold War*.

62. See Thomas Barfield, *Afghanistan: A Cultural and Political History* (Princeton, NJ: Princeton University Press, 2010); and Seth G. Jones, *In the Graveyard of Empires: America's War in Afghanistan* (New York: W. W. Norton, 2010).

63. See Barfield, *Afghanistan*; Jones, *America's War*; and Fraser and Gerstle, *Ruling America*.

64. See Dilip Hiro, *The Longest War; The Iran–Iraq Military Conflict* (New York: Routledge Press, 1990); and Peter Mansfield, *A History of the Middle East* (New York: Penguin Books, 2004).

65. See Cannon, *President Reagan*; Reeves, *President Reagan*; Fraser and Gerstle, *Ruling America*; and LaFeber, *Cold War*.

66. See Hiro, *Longest War*; Mansfield, *Middle East*; Woodward, *Commanders*; and Fraser and Gerstle, *Ruling America*.

67. See Woodward, *Commanders*; and Fraser and Gerstle, *Ruling America*.

68. See Bob Woodward, *Bush at War* (New York: Simon & Schuster, 2003); Rodman, *Presidential Command*; and Campbell, *George W. Bush*.

69. See Rodman, *Presidential Command*; and Campbell, *George W. Bush*.

70. See Rodman, *Presidential Command*; Campbell, *George W. Bush*; Barfield, *Afghanistan*; Jones, *America's War*; and Fraser and Gerstle, *Ruling America*.

71. See Bob Woodward, *Obama's Wars*; Indyk et al., *Bending History*; and Skidmore, *Unilateralist Temptation*.

72. See Woodward, *Plan of Attack*; and Rodman, *Presidential Command*.

73. See Bob Woodward, *State of Denial: Bust at War, Part III* (New York: Simon & Schuster, 2007); and Rodman, *Presidential Command*.

74. See Bob Woodward, *The War Within: A Secret White House History 2006–2008* (New York: Simon & Schuster, 2009); Woodward, *State of Denial*; and Rodman, *Presidential Command*.

75. See Woodward, *Obama's Wars*; Indyk et al., *Bending History*; and Skidmore, *Unilateralist Temptation*.

76. See Rodman, *Presidential Command*; and Campbell, *George W. Bush*.

77. See Indyk et al., *Bending History*; and David Skidmore, *The Unilateralist Temptation in American Foreign Policy* (London: Routledge, 2010).

78. See David Halberstam, *The Coldest Winter: America and the Korean War* (New York: Hyperion Books, 2007); and LaFeber, *Cold War*.

79. See Larry Berman, *Planning a Tragedy: The Americanization of the War in Vietnam* (New York: W. W. Norton, 1983); Herring, *Longest War*; Karnow, *Vietnam*; and LaFeber, *Cold War*.

80. See Larry Berman, *No Peace, No Honor: Nixon, Kissinger, and Betrayal in Vietnam* (New York: Touchstone Books, 2002); Berman, *Planning a Tragedy*; Herring, *Longest War*; and LaFeber, *Cold War*.

81. See Ely, *War and Responsibility*; and Adler and George, *The Constitution*.

82. See Harris, *The Survivor*; Fraser and Gerstle, *Ruling America*; Spanier and Hook, *American Foreign Policy*; Woodward, *The Agenda*; and Woodward, *Commanders*.

83. See Rodman, *Presidential Command*; Campbell, *George W. Bush*; Ely, *War and Responsibility*; and Adler and George, *The Constitution*.

84. Woodward, *Obama's Wars*; Sanger, *Confront and Conceal*; Indyk et al., *Bending History*.

85. See Spanier and Hook, *American Foreign Policy*; and LaFeber, *The American Age: United States Foreign Policy at Home and Abroad, 1750 to the Present* (New York: W. W. Norton, 1994).

86. See Nitsan Chorev, *Remaking U.S. Trade Policy: From Protectionism to Globalization* (Ithaca, NY: Cornell University Press, 2007).

87. Ibid. See also John M. Rothgeb Jr., *U.S. Trade Policy: Balancing Economic Dreams and Political Realities* (Washington, DC: CQ Press, 2001).

88. See William Krist, *Globalization and America's Trade Agreements* (Baltimore: Johns Hopkins University Press, 2013).

89. Krist, *Globalization*; Rothgeb, *U.S. Trade Policy*.

90. See John Duffield, *Over a Barrel: The Costs of U.S. Foreign Oil Dependence* (Palo Alto, CA: Stanford Law Books, 2007); David M. Snow, *The Middle East, Oil, and the U.S. National Security Policy: Intractable Conflicts, Impossible Solutions* (New York: Rowman & Littlefield, 2016).

91. LaFeber, *American Age*; Leffler, *Preponderance of Power*; LaFeber, *Cold War*.

92. Ibid.; Rodman, *Presidential Command*.

93. Ibid.

94. Ibid.; Indyk et al., *Bending History*.

95. See Rodman, *Presidential Command*; Indyk et al., *Bending History*.

96. See Woodward, *Obama's Wars*; and Indyk et al., *Bending History*.

97. See Sheldon Kamieniecki and Michael Kraft, *The Oxford Handbook of Environmental Policy* (New York: Oxford University Press, 2015); Kevin Hillstrom, *U.S. Environmental Policy and Politics: A Documentary History* (Washington, DC: CQ Press, 2010).

98. Ibid.; Norman J. Vig and Michael Kraft, *Environmental Policy: New Directions for the Twenty-First Century* (Washington, DC: CQ Press, 2015).

99. Vig and Kraft, *Environmental Policy*; Hillstrom, *Documentary History*.

100. Ibid.; Michael Kraft, *Environmental Policy and Politics* (New York: Routledge, 2014).

101. Meena Bose, "The Presidency and Foreign Policy," in *New Directions in the American Presidency*, ed. Lori Cox Han (New York: Routledge, 2011), 180.

BIBLIOGRAPHY

CHAPTER 1

Selected Bibliography

Barber, James David. 2008. *The Presidential Character: Predicting Performance in the White House*, Rev. 4th ed. New York: Prentice Hall.

Barilleaux, Ryan. 1988. *The Post-Modern Presidency: The Office after Ronald Reagan*. New York: Praeger.

Barilleaux, Ryan J., and Christopher S. Kelley, eds. 2010. *The Unitary Executive and the Modern Presidency*. College Station: Texas A&M University Press.

Burke, John. 1992. *The Institutional Presidency*. Baltimore: Johns Hopkins University Press.

Burns, James MacGregor. 1978. *Leadership*. New York: Harper & Row.

_____. 2003. *Transforming Leadership*. New York: Atlantic Monthly Press.

Canes-Wrone, Brandice. 2006. *Who's Leading Whom?* Chicago: University of Chicago Press.

Cohen, Jeffrey E. 1997. *Presidential Responsiveness and Public Policy-Making: The Public and the Policies That Presidents Choose*. Ann Arbor: University of Michigan Press.

_____. 2010. *Going Local: Presidential Leadership in the Post-Broadcast Age*. New York: Cambridge University Press.Cohen, Jeffrey, and David Nice. 2003. *The Presidency*. New York: McGraw–Hill.

Corwin, Edward S. 1940. *The President: Office and Powers*. New York: New York University Press.

Cronin, Thomas E., and Michael A. Genovese. 1998. *The Paradoxes of the American Presidency*. New York: Oxford University Press.

Edwards, George C., III. 1989. *At the Margins: Presidential Leadership of Congress*. New Haven, CT: Yale University Press.

_____. 2003. *On Deaf Ears: The Limits of the Bully Pulpit*. New Haven, CT: Yale University Press.

Edwards, George C., III, John H. Kessel, and Bert A. Rockman, eds. 1993. *Researching the Presidency: Vital Questions, New Approaches*. Pittsburgh, PA: University of Pittsburgh Press.

Edwards, George C., III, and Stephen J. Wayne, eds. 1983. *Studying the Presidency*. Knoxville: University of Tennessee Press.

Fisher, Louis. 1998. *The Politics of Shared Power: Congress and the Executive*, 4th ed. College Station: Texas A&M University Press.

Greenstein, Fred I. 1994. *The Hidden-Hand Presidency: Eisenhower as Leader*. Baltimore: Johns Hopkins University Press.

_____. 2009. *The Presidential Difference: Leadership Style from FDR to Barack Obama*, 3rd ed. Princeton, NJ: Princeton University Press.

Han, Lori Cox. 2001. *Governing from Center Stage: White House Communication Strategies during the Television Age of Politics*. Cresskill, NJ: Hampton Press.

Hart, Roderick P. 1987. *The Sound of Leadership: Presidential Communication in the Modern Age*. Chicago: University of Chicago Press.

Howell, William G. 2003. *Power without Persuasion: The Politics of Direct Presidential Action*. Princeton, NJ: Princeton University Press.

Heclo, Hugh. 1977. *Studying the Presidency: A Report to the Ford Foundation*. New York: Ford Foundation Press.

Jones, Charles O. 1999. *Separate but Equal Branches: Congress and the Presidency*, 2nd ed. New York: Chatham House.

Kernell, Samuel. 1986. *Going Public: New Strategies of Presidential Leadership*. Washington, DC: CQ Press.

Kessel, John H. 2001. *Presidents, the Presidency, and the Political Environment*. Washington, DC: CQ Press.

Koenig, Louis W. 1996. *The Chief Executive*, 6th ed. New York: Harcourt Brace.

Kriner, Douglas L. 2010. *After the Rubicon: Congress, Presidents, and the Politics of Waging War*. Chicago: University of Chicago Press.

Lammers, William W., and Michael A. Genovese. 2000. *The Presidency and Domestic Policy: Comparing Leadership Styles, FDR to Clinton*. Washington, DC: CQ Press.

Lewis, David E. 2008. *The Politics of Presidential Appointments: Political Control and Bureaucratic Performance*. Princeton, NJ: Princeton University Press.

Maltese, John Anthony. 1994. *Spin Control: The White House Office of Communications and the Management of Presidential News*, 2nd ed., rev. Chapel Hill: University of North Carolina Press.

Milkis, Sidney M., and Michael Nelson. 2016. *The American Presidency: Origins and Development, 1776-2014*, 7th ed. Washington, DC: CQ Press.

Miroff, Bruce. 2000. *Icons of Democracy: American Leaders as Heroes, Aristocrats, Dissenters, & Democrats*. Lawrence: University Press of Kansas.

Moe, Terry M. 1985. "The Politicized Presidency." In *The New Direction in American Politics*, edited by John E. Chubb and Paul E. Peterson. Washington, DC: Brookings Institution.

Murray, Robert K., and Tim H. Blessing. 1994. *Greatness in the White House: Rating the Presidents from George Washington through Ronald Reagan*, 2nd ed. University Park: Pennsylvania State University Press.

Neustadt, Richard. 1960. *Presidential Power: The Politics of Leadership*. New York: Wiley.

Peterson, Mark A. 1990. *Legislating Together: The White House and Capitol Hill from Eisenhower to Reagan*. Cambridge, MA: Harvard University Press.

Pika, Joseph A., John Anthony Maltese, and Andrew Rudalevige. 2017. *The Politics of the Presidency*, 9th ed. Washington, DC: CQ Press.

Ragsdale, Lyn. 2009. *Vital Statistics on the Presidency: George Washington to George W. Bush*, 3rd ed. Washington, DC: CQ Press.

Rose, Richard. 1991. *The Postmodern President*, 2nd ed. Chatham, NJ: Chatham House.

Rossiter, Clinton. 1956. *The American Presidency*. New York, NY: Harcourt, Brace.

Rudalevige, Andrew. 2002. *Managing the President's Program: Presidential Leadership and Legislative Policy Formation*. Princeton, NJ: Princeton University Press.

Schier, Steven, ed. 2000. *The Postmodern Presidency: Bill Clinton's Legacy in U.S. Politics*. Pittsburgh, PA: University of Pittsburgh Press.

Schlesinger, Arthur Jr. 1973. *The Imperial Presidency*. Boston, MA: Houghton Mifflin Company.

Skowronek, Stephen. 1993. *The Politics Presidents Make: Leadership from John Adams to George Bush*. Cambridge, MA: Belknap/Harvard Press.

Stuckey, Mary E. 1991. *The President as Interpreter-in-Chief*. Chatham, NJ: Chatham House.

Tulis, Jeffrey K. 1987. *The Rhetorical Presidency*. Princeton, NJ: Princeton University Press.

Warshaw, Shirley Anne. 2000. *The Keys to Power: Managing the Presidency*. New York, NY: Longman.

Weko, Thomas J. 1995. *The Politicizing Presidency: The White House Personnel Office, 1948–1994*. Lawrence: University of Kansas Press.

Wood, B. Dan. 2007. *The Politics of Economic Leadership: The Causes and Consequences of Presidential Rhetoric*. Princeton, NJ: Princeton University Press.

Online Resources

- http://www.whitehouse.gov. The official White House web page, which includes a comprehensive archive of all presidential speeches, information about the president's daily schedule, and historical information related to the presidency as well as past presidents.
- https://www.gpo.gov/fdsys/browse/collection.action?collectionCode=CPD. Published each Monday by the Office of the Federal Register and the National Archives and Records Administration, the Daily Compilation of Presidential Documents is the official publication of presidential statements, messages, remarks, and other materials released by the White House press secretary.
- http://www.presidency.ucsb.edu/. The American Presidency Project contains the *Public Papers of the Presidents* as well as numerous data sets about presidential activities.

CHAPTER 2

Selected Bibliography

Adler, David G., and Larry N. George, eds. 1996. *The Constitution and the Conduct of American Foreign Policy*. Lawrence: University Press of Kansas.

Adler, David Gray, and Michael A. Genovese, eds. 2002. *The Presidency and the Law: The Clinton Legacy*. Lawrence: University Press of Kansas.

Berger, Raoul. 1973. *Impeachment: The Constitutional Problems*. Cambridge, MA: Harvard University Press.

_____. 1974. *Executive Privilege*. Cambridge, MA: Harvard University Press.

Bailyn, Bernard. 1967. *The Ideological Origins of the American Revolution*. Cambridge, MA: Harvard University Press.

Banning, Lance. 1978. *The Jeffersonian Persuasion: Evolution of a Party Ideology*. Ithaca, NY: Cornell University Press.

Bessette, Joseph, and Jeffrey Tulis. 1981. *The Presidency in the Constitutional Order*. Baton Rouge: Louisiana University Press.

Carey, George W. 1989. *The Federalist: Design for a Constitutional Republic*. Urbana: University of Illinois Press.

Corwin, Edward S. 1940. *The President: Office and Powers*. New York: New York University Press.

Diggins, John Patrick. 1984. *The Lost Soul of American Politics: Virtue, Self-Interest, and the Foundations of Liberalism*. Chicago: University of Chicago Press.

Elkins, Stanley, and Eric McKitrick. 1993. *The Age of Federalism: The Early American Republic, 1788–1800*. New York: Oxford University Press.

Fisher, Louis. 2004. *The Politics of Executive Privilege*. Durham, NC: Carolina Academic Press.

_____.2004. *Presidential War Power*, 2nd ed. Lawrence: University Press of Kansas.

_____. *Constitutional Conflicts between Congress and the President*. Lawrence: University Press of Kansas, 2007.

Gormley, Ken, ed. 2016. *The Presidents and the Constitution: A Living History*. New York: New York University Press.

Greene, Jack P. 1994. *Negotiated Authorities: Essays in Colonial Political and Constitutional History*. Charlottesville: University Press of Virginia.

Greenstone, David J. 1993. *The Lincoln Persuasion: Remaking American Liberalism*. Princeton, NJ: Princeton University Press.

Howell, William G. 2003. *Power without Persuasion: The Politics of Direct Presidential Action*. Princeton, NJ: Princeton University Press.

Mayer, Kenneth R. 2001. *With the Stroke of a Pen: Executive Orders and Presidential Power*. Princeton, NJ: Princeton University Press.

McDonald, Forrest. 1979. *Alexander Hamilton: A Biography*. New York: W. W. Norton.

_____. 1985. *Novus Ordo Seclorum: The Intellectual Origins of the Constitution*. Lawrence: University Press of Kansas.

McKenzie, G. Galvin. 1981. *The Politics of Presidential Appointments*. New York: Free Press.

Morgan, Edmund S. 1988. *Inventing the People: The Rise of Popular Sovereignty in England and America*. New York: W. W. Norton.

Publius. 1987. *The Federalist Papers*, edited by Isaac Kramnick. London: Penguin Books.

Rakove, Jack N. 1979. *The Beginnings of National Politics: An Interpretive History of the Continental Congress*. Baltimore: Johns Hopkins University Press.

Reid, John Phillip. 1993. *Constitutional History of the American Revolution: The Authority of Law*. Madison: University of Wisconsin Press.

Rossiter, Clinton. 1956. *The American Presidency*. New York: Harcourt, Brace.

Rozell, Mark. 2000. *Executive Privilege: The Dilemma of Secrecy and Democratic Accountability*. Lawrence: University Press of Kansas.

Schlesinger, Arthur M., Jr. 1973. *The Imperial Presidency*. Boston: Houghton Mifflin.

_____.*Age of Jackson*. New York: Back Bay Books, 1988.

Sellers, Charles. 1991. *The Market Revolution: Jacksonian America, 1815–1846*. New York: Oxford University Press.

Storing, Herbert J. 2007. *The Complete Anti-Federalist*. Chicago: University of Chicago Press.

Wood, Gordon S. 1969. *Creation of the American Republic, 1776–1787*. New York: W. W. Norton.

Online Resources

- http://www.law.cornell.edu/constitution. Home page of the Legal Information Institute at the Cornell University Law School. The site provides a database for the U.S. Constitution, Supreme Court rulings, and other legal issues. The goal of the site is to "promote open access to law, worldwide."
- http://www.oyez.org. The Oyez Project at the Chicago–Kent College of Law provides an online multimedia archive of the U.S. Supreme Court.

CHAPTER 3

Selected Bibliography

Alexander, Herbert E. 1992. *Financing Politics: Money, Elections, and Political Reform*. Washington, DC: CQ Press.

Bartels, Larry M. 1988. *Presidential Primaries and the Dynamics of Public Choice*. Princeton, NJ: Princeton University Press.

Bugh, Gary, ed. 2010. *Electoral College Reform: Challenges and Possibilities*. Burlington, VT: Ashgate.

Cronin, Thomas E., and Michael A. Genovese. 1998. *The Paradoxes of the American Presidency*. New York: Oxford University Press.

Crotty, William J., ed. 2008. *Winning the Presidency: 2008*. Boulder, CO: Paradigm.

———, ed. 2013. *Winning the Presidency 2012*. Boulder, CO: Paradigm.

Davis, Richard. 1999. *The Web of Politics: The Internet's Impact on the American Political System*. New York: Oxford University Press.

Dowling, Conor, and Michael Miller. 2014. *Super PAC!: Money, Elections, and Voters after Citizens United*. New York: Routledge.

Dwyre, Diana, and Victoria A. Farrar-Myers. 2001. *Legislative Labyrinth: Congress and Campaign Finance Reform*. Washington, DC: CQ Press.

Edwards, George C., III. 2011. *Why the Electoral College Is Bad for America*, 2nd ed. New Haven, CT: Yale University Press.

Farnsworth, Stephen J., and S. Robert Lichter. 2011. *The Nightly News Nightmare: Media Coverage of U.S. Presidential Elections, 1988–2008*, 3rd ed. Lanham, MD: Rowman & Littlefield.

Fishel, Jeff. 1985. *Presidents and Promises: From Campaign Pledge to Presidential Performance*. Washington, DC: CQ Press.

Fox, Richard L., and Jennifer L. Lawless. 2004. "Entering the Arena? Gender and the Decision to Run for Office." *American Journal of Political Science* 48, no. 2: 264–80.

Graber, Doris A., and Johanna Dunaway. 2015. *Mass Media and American Politics*, 9th ed. Washington, DC: CQ Press.

Hadley, Arthur T. 1976. *The Invisible Primary*. Englewood Cliffs, NJ: Prentice Hall.

Han, Lori Cox. 2015. *In It to Win: Electing Madam President*. New York: Bloomsbury.

Hetherington, Marc, and Bruce Larson. 2010. *Parties, Politics and Public Policy in America*, 11th ed. Washington, DC: CQ Press.

Milkis, Sidney, and Michael Nelson. 2016. *The American Presidency: Origins and Development 1776–2014*, 7th ed. Washington, DC: CQ Press.

Norpoth, Helmut. 2016. "The Primary Model Predicts Trump Victory." *PS: Political Science & Politics* 49, no. 4: 655–58.

Ornstein, Norman, and Thomas Mann, eds. 2000. *The Permanent Campaign and Its Future*. Washington, DC: Brookings.

Patterson, Thomas E. 1994. *Out of Order*. New York: Vintage.

Polsby, Nelson W., and Aaron Wildavsky. 2004. *Presidential Elections: Strategies and Structures of American Politics*, 11th ed. Lanham, MD: Rowman & Littlefield.

Rosenstone, Steven J., and John Mark. 1993. *Mobilization, Participation, and Democracy in America*. New York: Macmillan Press.

Sabato, Larry J. 2000. *Feeding Frenzy: Attack Journalism and American Politics*. Baltimore: Lanahan.

Seligman, Lester, and Cary Covington. 1989. *The Coalitional Presidency*. Chicago: Dorsey Press.

Semiatin, Richard J. 2005. *Campaigns in the 21st Century*. New York: McGraw–Hill.

_____, ed. 2017. *Campaigns on the Cutting Edge*. Washington, DC: CQ Press.

Waterman, Richard W., Robert Wright, and Gilbert St. Clair. 1999. *The Image-Is-Everything Presidency: Dilemmas in American Leadership*. Boulder, CO: Westview Press.

Wattenberg, Martin J. 1991. *The Rise of Candidate-Centered Politics: Presidential Elections of the 1980s*. Cambridge, MA: Harvard University Press.

West, Darrell M. 2010. *Air Wars: Television Advertising in Election Campaigns, 1952–2008*. Washington, DC: CQ Press.

Online Resources

• http://www.opensecrets.org. The Center for Responsive Politics is an independent, nonpartisan organization that tabulates the financial information that candidates, campaigns, and organizations are required by law to disclose.

• http://www.fec.gov. The Federal Elections Commission is the nonpartisan government entity that administers and enforces federal campaign law and also serves as a clearing-house for all campaign finance contributions and expenditures for federal elections.

CHAPTER 4

Selected Bibliography

Baum, Matthew A., and Samuel Kernell. 1999. "Has Cable Ended the Golden Age of Presidential Television?" *American Political Science Review* 93, no. 1 (March): 99–114.

Campbell, Karlyn Kohrs, and Kathleen Hall Jamieson. 1990. *Deeds Done in Words: Presidential Rhetoric and the Genres of Governance*. Chicago: University of Chicago Press.

Cohen, Jeffrey E. 2009. *Going Local: Presidential Leadership in the Post-Broadcast Age*. New York: Cambridge University Press.

Edwards, George C., III. 2003. *On Deaf Ears: The Limits of the Bully Pulpit*. New Haven, CT: Yale University Press.

_____. 2012. *Overreach: Leadership in the Obama Presidency*. Princeton, NJ: Princeton University Press.

Emery, Michael, and Edwin Emery. 1996. *The Press and America: An Interpretive History of the Mass Media*, 8th ed. Boston: Allyn & Bacon.

Eshbaugh-Soha, Matthew, and Jeffrey S. Peake. 2011. *Breaking through the Noise: Presidential Leadership, Public Opinion, and the News Media*. Stanford, CA: Stanford University Press.

Farnsworth, Stephen J. 2009. *Spinner in Chief: How Presidents Sell Their Policies and Themselves*. Boulder, CO: Paradigm.

Farnsworth, Stephen J., and S. Robert Lichter. 2006. *The Mediated Presidency: Television News and Presidential Governance*. Lanham, MD: Rowman & Littlefield.

Han, Lori Cox. 2001. *Governing from the Center Stage: White House Communication Strategies During the Television Age of Politics*. Cresskill, NJ: Hampton Press.

_____. 2006. "New Strategies for an Old Medium: The Weekly Radio Addresses of Reagan and Clinton." *Congress and the Presidency* 33, no. 1 (Spring): 25–45.

Hart, Roderick P. 1987. *The Sound of Leadership: Presidential Communication in the Modern Age*. Chicago: University of Chicago Press.

Heith, Diane J. 2013. *The Presidential Road Show: Public Leadership in an Era of Party Polarization and Media Fragmentation*. Boulder, CO: Paradigm.

Hertsgaard, Mark. 1988. *On Bended Knee: The Press and the Reagan Presidency.* New York: Farrar, Straus and Giroux.

Kerbel, Matthew Robert. 1999. *Remote & Controlled: Media Politics in a Cynical Age,* 2nd ed. Boulder, CO: Westview Press.

Kernell, Samuel. 1997. *Going Public: New Strategies of Presidential Leadership,* 4th ed. Washington, DC: CQ Press.

Kessel, John H. 2001. *Presidents, the Presidency, and the Political Environment.* Washington, DC: CQ Press.

Kumar, Martha Joynt. 2007. *Managing the President's Message: The White House Communications Operation.* Baltimore: Johns Hopkins University Press.

Laracey, Mel. 2002. *Presidents and the People: The Partisan Story of Going Public.* College Station: Texas A&M University Press.

Maltese, John Anthony. 1994. *Spin Control: The White House Office of Communications and Management of Presidential News,* 2nd ed. rev. Chapel Hill: University of North Carolina Press.

Minow, Newton N., John Bartlow Martin, and Lee M. Mitchell. 1973. *Presidential Television.* New York: Basic Books.

Stuckey, Mary E. 1991. *The President as Interpreter-in-Chief.* Chatham, NJ: Chatham House.

Tebbel, John, and Sarah Miles Watts. 1985. *The Press and the Presidency: From George Washington to Ronald Reagan.* New York: Oxford University Press.

Tulis, Jeffrey K. 1987. *The Rhetorical Presidency.* Princeton, NJ: Princeton University Press.

Online Resources

- http://people-press.org/. The Pew Research Center for the People & the Press is an independent, nonpartisan public opinion research organization that studies attitudes toward politics, the press, and public policy issues.
- https://shorensteincenter.org/. The Shorenstein Center on Media, Politics and Public Policy, Kennedy School of Government, Harvard University, is a research center dedicated to exploring the intersection of press, politics, and public policy in theory and practice.

CHAPTER 5

Selected Bibliography

Azari, Julia R., Lara M. Brown, and Zim G. Nwokora, eds. 2013. *The Presidential Leadership Dilemma: Between the Constitution and a Political Party.* Albany: State University of New York Press.

Bond, Jon, and Richard Fleisher. 1990. *The President in the Legislative Arena.* Chicago: University of Chicago Press.

Brace, Paul, and Barbara Hinckley. 1992. *Follow the Leader: Opinion Polls and Modern Presidents.* New York: Basic Books.

Canes-Wrone, Brandice. 2006. *Who Leads Whom? Presidents, Policy, and the Public.* Chicago: University of Chicago Press.

Cohen, Jeffrey E. 1997. *Presidential Responsiveness and Public-Policy Making.* Ann Arbor: University of Michigan Press.

_____. 2010. *Going Local: Presidential Leadership in the Post-Broadcast Age.* New York: Cambridge University Press.

Cornwell, Elmer, Jr. 1965. *Presidential Leadership of Public Opinion*. Bloomington: Indiana University Press.

Druckman, James N., and Lawrence R. Jacobs. 2015. *Who Governs? Presidents, Public Opinion, and Manipulation*. Chicago: University of Chicago Press.

Edwards, George C., III. 1989. *At the Margins: Presidential Leadership of Congress*. New Haven, CT: Yale University Press.

_____. 2003. *On Deaf Ears: The Limits of the Bully Pulpit*. New Haven, CT: Yale University Press.

Eisinger, Robert. 2003. *The Evolution of Presidential Polling*. New York: Cambridge University Press.

Erickson, Robert, Michael MacKuen, and James Stimson. 2002. *The Macro Polity*. New York: Cambridge University Press.

Erickson, Robert, and Kent Tedin. 2009. *American Public Opinion: Its Origins, Content and Impact*. New York: Pearson/Longman.

Han, Lori Cox, and Diane J. Heith, eds. 2005. *In the Public Domain: Presidents and the Challenges of Public Leadership*. Albany: State University of New York Press.

Heith, Diane J. 2004. *Polling to Govern: Public Opinion and Presidential Leadership*. Palo Alto, CA: Stanford University Press.

Jacobs, Lawrence, and Robert Shapiro. 2000. *Politicians Don't Pander: Political Manipulation and the Loss of Democratic Responsiveness*. Chicago: University of Chicago Press.

Kernell, Samuel. 2007. *Going Public: New Strategies of Presidential Leadership*, 4th ed. Washington, DC: CQ Press.

Peterson, Mark. 1990. *Legislating Together: The White House and Capitol Hill from Eisenhower to Reagan*. Cambridge, MA: Harvard University Press.

Rottinghaus, Brandon. 2010. *The Provisional Pulpit: Modern Presidential Leadership of Public Opinion*. College Station: Texas A&M University Press.

Rubin, Richard. 1982. *Press, Party and the President*. New York: W. W. Norton.

Online Resources

- http://www.gallup.com. A comprehensive site with public opinion and analysis, including historical and comparative data from the Gallup Polling organization, dating from the Truman administration.
- http://elections.huffingtonpost.com/pollster. Huffpost Pollster provides current public opinion and analysis, including blogs about public opinion by practitioners.
- https://ropercenter.cornell.edu/. Housed at the University of Connecticut, a site containing the public opinion data sets of the Roper Center.
- http://people-press.org/. The home page for the Pew Research Center for the People & the Press, an independent, nonpartisan public opinion research organization, which includes polls and commentaries.

CHAPTER 6

Selected Bibliography

Cameron, Charles. 2000. *Veto Bargaining: Presidents and the Politics of Negative Power*. New York: Cambridge University Press.

Cohen, Richard E. 1992. *Washington at Work: Back Rooms and Clean Air*. New York: Macmillan.

Davidson, Roger H., Walter J. Oleszek, and Frances Lee. 2012. *Congress and Its Members*, 13th ed. Washington, DC: CQ Press.

Deen, Rebecca, and Laura Arnold. 2002. "Veto Threats as a Policy Tool: When to Threaten?" *Presidential Studies Quarterly* 32, no. 1: 30–45.

Edwards, George C., III. 1989. *At The Margins: Presidential Leadership of Congress.* New Haven, CT: Yale University Press.

Fenno, Richard. 1977. "U.S. House Members in Their Constituencies: An Exploration." *American Political Science Review* 71, no. 3: 883–917.

Heith, Diane J. 2013. *The Presidential Road Show: Public Leadership in a Partisan Era.* Boulder, CO: Paradigm Press.

Herrnson, Paul, Irwin Morris, and John McTague. 2011. "The Impact of Presidential Campaigning for Congress on Presidential Support in the U.S. House of Representatives." *Legislative Studies Quarterly* 36, no. 1: 99–122.

Hoffman, Donna, and Alison Howard. 2006. *Addressing the State of the Union: The Evolution and Impact of the President's Big Speech.* Boulder, CO: Lynne Rienner.

Kernell, Samuel. 2007. *Going Public: New Strategies of Presidential Leadership,* 4th ed. Washington, DC: CQ Press.

Lammers, William W., and Michael A. Genovese. 2000. *The Presidency and Domestic Policy: Comparing Leadership Styles, FDR to Clinton.* Washington, DC: CQ Press.

Leuchtenburg, William. 1963. *Franklin D. Roosevelt and the New Deal: 1932–1940.* New York: Harper & Row.

Mayhew, David. 1974. *Congress: The Electoral Connection.* New Haven, CT: Yale University Press.

Neustadt, Richard E. 1990. *Presidential Power and the Modern Presidents: The Politics of Leadership from Roosevelt to Reagan.* New York: Free Press.

Ragsdale, Lyn. 2008. *Vital Statistics on the Presidency,* 3rd ed. Washington, DC: CQ Press.

Rottinghaus, Brandon. 2010. *The Provisional Pulpit: Modern Presidential Leadership of Public Opinion.* College Station: Texas A&M University Press.

Sinclair, Barbara. 2007. *Unorthodox Lawmaking: New Legislative Processes in the U.S. Congress.* Washington, DC: CQ Press.

Wood, B. Dan. 2009. *The Myth of Presidential Representation.* New York: Cambridge University Press.

Online Resources

- http://www.house.gov/ and http://www.senate.gov/. The official websites of the U.S. Congress, with information about current and past members of Congress, current and past legislation, and the history of the institutions.
- http://www.dirksencenter.org/. A nonpartisan, not-for-profit institution that promotes a better understanding of the institution of Congress via archival research.
- http://www.c-span.org/. The website of the congressional television channel, C-SPAN. It is a private, nonpartisan, not-for-profit company that provides coverage of Congress, the president, and the Supreme Court. The website provides current video and is a repository for videos dating back to its origins in 1979.

CHAPTER 7

Selected Bibliography

Abraham, Henry J. 2008. *Justices, Presidents, and Senators: A History of U.S. Supreme Court Appointments from Washington to Bush II,* 5th ed. Lanham, MD: Rowman & Littlefield.

Baum, Lawrence. 2007. *The Supreme Court,* 9th ed., Washington, DC: CQ Press.

Binder, Sarah A., and Forrest Maltzman. 2009. *Advice and Dissent: The Struggle to Shape the Federal Judiciary*. Washington, DC: Brookings Institution Press.

Dahl, Robert. 1957. "Decision-Making in a Democracy: The Supreme Court as a National Policy-Maker." *Journal of Public Law* 6: 279–95.

Eshbaugh-Soha, Matthew, and Paul M. Collins Jr. 2015. "Presidential Rhetoric and Supreme Court Decisions." *Presidential Studies Quarterly* 45, no. 4 (December): 633–52.

Goldman, Sheldon. 1997. *Picking Federal Judges: Lower Court Selection from Roosevelt through Reagan*. New Haven, CT: Yale University Press.

McGuire, Kevin T. 2002. *Understanding the U.S. Supreme Court: Cases and Controversies*. New York: McGraw–Hill.

Moraski, Bryon J., and Charles R. Shipan. 1999. "The Politics of Supreme Court Nominations: A Theory of Institutional Constraints and Choices." *American Journal of Political Science* 43, no. 4 (October): 1069–95.

O'Brien, David M. 2008. *Storm Center: The Supreme Court in American Politics*, 8th ed. New York: W. W. Norton.

Pacelle, Richard L., Jr. 2003. *Between Law and Politics: The Solicitor General and the Structuring of Race, Gender, and Reproductive Rights Litigation*. College Station: Texas A&M University Press.

Palmer, Barbara. 2001. "Women in the American Judiciary: Their Influence and Impact." *Women & Politics* 23, no. 3 (January): 89–99.

Ruckman, P. S. 1993. "The Supreme Court, Critical Nominations, and the Senate Confirmation Process." *The Journal of Politics* 55, no. 3 (August): 793–805.

Silverstein, Mark. 1994. *Judicious Choices: The New Politics of Supreme Court Confirmations*. New York: W. W. Norton.

Yalof, David Alistair. 1999. *Pursuit of Justices: Presidential Politics and the Selection of Supreme Court Nominees*. Chicago: University of Chicago Press.

Online Resources

- http://www.supremecourtus.gov/. The official web page of the U.S. Supreme Court, with information about current cases, biographies of the justices, information about court procedures, and the history of the Court.
- http://lp.findlaw.com/. A comprehensive web page providing information on the Supreme Court and its decisions, as well as state courts and relevant decisions.
- http://www.uscourts.gov/. The official web page for the federal judicial branch.
- http://www.fjc.gov. The Federal Judicial Center, which is the education and research center for the federal courts, including a biographical database of all federal judges, past and present.

CHAPTER 8

Selected Bibliography

Borrelli, MaryAnne. 2011. *The Politics of the President's Wife*. College Station: Texas A&M University Press.

Dickinson, Matthew J. 1996. *Bitter Harvest: FDR, Presidential Power and the Growth of the Presidential Branch*. Cambridge, MA: Cambridge University Press.

Han, Lori Cox, ed. 2011. *New Directions in the American Presidency*. New York: Routledge.

Mayer, Kenneth. 2001. *With the Stroke of a Pen: Executive Orders and Presidential Power*. Princeton, NJ: Princeton University Press.

Patterson, Bradley H., Jr. 2000. *The White House Staff: Inside the West Wing and Beyond.* Washington, DC: Brookings Institution Press.

Rottinghaus, Brandon, and Adam Warber. 2015. "Unilateral Orders as Constituency Outreach: Executive Orders, Proclamations, and the Public Presidency." *Presidential Studies Quarterly* 45, no. 2 (April): 289–309.

Sorenson, Theodore. 2005. *Decision Making in the White House: The Olive Branch or the Arrows.* New York: Columbia University Press.

Sullivan, Terry, ed. 2004. *The Nerve Center: Lessons in Governing from the White House Chiefs of Staff.* College Station: Texas A&M University Press.

Warber, Adam. 2006. *Executive Orders and the Modern Presidency.* Boulder, CO: Lynne Rienner.

Watson, Robert P. 2000. *The President's Wives: Reassessing the Office of First Lady.* Boulder, CO: Lynne Rienner.

Woodward, Bob. 2004. *Plan of Attack.* New York: Simon & Schuster.

Online Resources

• http://www.whitehouse.gov/administration. The official web page of the executive branch, which includes the websites of the cabinet, the White House Staff, the Executive Office of the President, and other advisory boards.

• http://www.gao.gov/. The official website of the Government Accountability Office, the investigative arm of Congress. The office supports congressional oversight and accountability of the bureaucracy.

CHAPTER 9

Selected Bibliography

Axilrod, Stephen H. 2009. *Inside the Fed: Monetary Policy and Its Management, Martin through Greenspan to Bernanke.* Cambridge, MA: MIT Press.

Beland, Daniel. 2007. *Social Security: History and Politics from the New Deal to the Privatization Debate.* Lawrence: University Press of Kansas.

Blumenthal, David, and James Morone. 2010. *The Heart of Power: Health and Politics in the Oval Office.* Berkeley: University of California Press.

Brinkley, Alan. 1996. *The End of Reform: New Deal Liberalism in Recession and War.* New York: Vintage.Bumgarner, Jeffrey B. 2006. *Federal Agents: The Growth of Federal Law Enforcement in America.* New York: Praeger.

Cobb, Roger W., and Charles D. Elder. 1972. *Participation in American Politics: The Dynamics of Agenda Building.* Baltimore: Johns Hopkins University Press.

Conley, Patricia. 2001. *Presidential Mandates: How Elections Shape the National Agenda.* Chicago: Chicago University Press.

Dallek, Robert. 2005. *Lyndon B. Johnson: Portrait of a President.* New York: Oxford University Press.

Davies, Gareth. 1999. *From Opportunity to Entitlement: The Transformation and Decline of Great Society Liberalism.* Lawrence: University Press of Kansas.Deutch, John M. 2011. *The Crisis in Energy Policy.* Cambridge, MA: Harvard University Press.

Dobelstein, Andrew. 2009. *Understanding the Social Security Act: The Foundation of Social Welfare in America for the Twenty-First Century.* New York: Oxford University Press.

Dolan, Chris J., John Frendreis, and Raymond Tatalovich. 2007. *The Presidency and Economic Policy.* New York: Rowman & Littlefield.

Fiorino, Daniel J. 1995. *Making Environmental Policy*. Berkeley: University of California Press.Graham, Hugh Davis. 2003. *Collision Course: The Strange Convergence of Affirmative Action and Immigration Policy in America*. New York: Oxford University Press.

Harris, Richard, and Sidney Milkis. 1989. *The Politics of Regulatory Change: A Tale of Two Agencies*. New York: Oxford University Press.

Herrnson, Paul S., Ronald G. Shaiko, and Clyde Wilcox, eds. 2004. *The Interest Group Connection: Electioneering, Lobbying, and Policymaking in Washington*, 2nd ed. Washington, DC: CQ Press.

Hoffman, Donna, and Alison Howard. 2006. *Addressing the State of the Union: The Evolution and Impact of the President's Big Speech*. Boulder, CO: Lynne Rienner.

Hopper, Jennifer. 2017. *Presidential Framing in the 21st Century News Media: The Politics of the Affordable Care Act*. New York: Routledge.

Kaufman, Berton Ira, and Scott Kaufman. 2006. *The Presidency of James Earl Carter, Jr.* Lawrence: University Press of Kansas.

Kingdon, John W. 2002. *Agendas, Alternatives, and Public Policies*. New York: Longman Press.

Lammers, William W., and Michael A. Genovese. 2000. *The Presidency and Domestic Policy: Comparing Leadership Styles, FDR to Clinton*. Washington, DC: CQ Press.

Levin, Martin A., Daniel DiSalvo, and Martin M. Shapiro, eds. 2012. *Building Coalitions, Making Policy: The Politics of the Clinton, Bush, and Obama Presidencies*. Baltimore: Johns Hopkins University Press.

Light, Paul. 1998. *The President's Agenda: Domestic Policy Choice from Kennedy to Clinton*. Baltimore: Johns Hopkins University Press.

Marion, Nancy E. 2011. *Federal Government and Criminal Justice*. New York: Palgrave Macmillan.

Milkis, Sidney M., and Jerome M. Mileur, eds. 2005. *The Great Society and the High Tide of Liberalism*. Amherst: University of Massachusetts Press.

Mills, Nicolaus. 1994. *Arguing Immigration: The Debate over the Changing Face of America*. New York: Touchstone.

Nelson, Michael, and Russell L. Riley, eds. 2011. *Governing at Home: The White House and Domestic Policymaking*. Lawrence: University Press of Kansas.

Pfiffner, James P. 1996. *The Strategic Presidency: Hitting the Ground Running*, 2nd ed. Lawrence: University Press of Kansas.

Rosenbaum, Walter A. 2010. *Environmental Politics and Policy*. Washington, DC: CQ Press.

Rutledge, Paul, and Heather Larsen Price. 2014. "The President as Agenda Setter-in-Chief: The Dynamics of Congressional and Presidential Agenda Setting." *Policy Studies Journal* 42, no. 3 (August): 443–64.

Shaffer, Brenda. 2011. *Energy Politics*. Philadelphia: University of Pennsylvania Press.

Shull, Steven A. 2000. *American Civil Rights Policy from Truman to Clinton: The Role of Presidential Leadership*. Armonk, NY: M. E. Sharpe.

Shultz, George P., and Kenneth W. Dam. 1998. *Economic Policy Beyond the Headlines*. Chicago: University of Chicago Press.

Sinclair, Barbara. 2007. *Unorthodox Lawmaking: New Legislative Processes in the U.S. Congress*, 3rd ed. Washington, DC: CQ Press.

Skowronek, Stephen. 1982. *Building a New American State: The Expansion of American Administrative Capacities, 1877–1920*. London: Cambridge University Press.

Stolz, Barbara. 2001. *Criminal Justice Policy Making: Federal Roles and Processes*. New York: Praeger.

Swain, Carol M., ed. 2007. *Debating Immigration*. London: Cambridge University Press.

Trachtenberg, Alan. 2007. *The Incorporation of America: Culture and Society in the Gilded Age*. New York: Hill & Wang.

Vig, Norman J., and Michael E. Kraft. 2009. *Environmental Policy: New Directions for the Twenty-First Century*. Washington, DC: CQ Press.

Woodward, Bob. 1994. *The Agenda: Inside the Clinton White House*. New York: Simon & Schuster.

Online Resources

- http://www.cbpp.org/. The Center on Budget and Policy Priorities is a nonprofit organization that develops research and analysis on budgeting and tax policy.
- http://www.federalreserve.gov/. The web page of the Federal Reserve System, which is the central bank of the United States founded by Congress in 1913 to provide the nation with a safer, more flexible, and more stable monetary and financial system.

CHAPTER 10

Selected Bibliography

Adler, David Gray, and Larry N. George, eds. 1996. *The Constitution and the Conduct of American Foreign Policy*. Lawrence: University Press of Kansas.

Allison, Graham, and Philip Zelikow. 1999. *Essence of Decision: Explaining the Cuban Missile Crisis*. New York: Longman Press.

Barfield, Thomas. 2010. *Afghanistan: A Cultural and Political History*. Princeton, NJ: Princeton University Press.Berman, Larry. 1983. *Planning a Tragedy: The Americanization of the War in Vietnam*. New York: W. W. Norton.

_____. 2002. *No Peace, No Honor: Nixon, Kissinger, and Betrayal in Vietnam*. New York: Touchstone Books.

Buchanan, Bruce. 2013. *Presidential Power and Accountability: Toward a Presidential Accountability System*. New York: Routledge.

Calleo, David P. 2003. *Rethinking Europe's Future*. Princeton, NJ: Princeton University Press.

Chorey, Nitsan. 2007. *Remaking U.S. Trade Policy: From Protectionism to Globalization*. Ithaca, NY: Cornell University Press.

Duffield, John. 2007. *Over a Barrel: The Costs of U.S. Foreign Oil Dependence*. Palo Alto, CA: Stanford Law Books.

Ely, John Hart. 1995. *War and Responsibility*. Princeton, NJ: Princeton University Press.

Grow, Michael. 2008. *U.S. Presidents and Latin American Interventions: Pursuing Regime Change in the Cold War*. Lawrence: University Press of Kansas.

Herring, George C. 2001. *America's Longest War: The United States and Vietnam, 1950–1975*. New York: McGraw–Hill.

Hillstrom, Kevin. 2010. *U.S. Environmental Policy and Politics: A Documentary History*. Washington, DC: CQ Press.

Indyk, Martin S., Kenneth G. Lieberthal, and Michael E. O'Hanlon. 2012. *Bending History? Barack Obama's Foreign Policy*. Washington, DC: Brookings Institution Press.

Jentleson, Bruce W. 2010. *American Foreign Policy: The Dynamics of Choice in the 21st Century*. New York: W. W. Norton.

Jones, Seth G. 2010. *In the Graveyard of Empires: America's War in Afghanistan*. New York: W. W. Norton.

Kamieniecki, Sheldon, and Michael Kraft. 2015. *The Oxford Handbook of Environmental Policy*. New York: Oxford University Press.

Kaplan, Lawrence S. 2004. *NATO Divided, NATO United*. Greenwood, CT: Praeger.

Karnow, Stanley. 1997. *Vietnam: A History*. New York: Penguin.

Kriner, Douglas L. 2010. *After the Rubicon: Congress, Presidents, and the Politics of Waging War*. Chicago: University of Chicago Press.

Krist, William. 2013. *Globalization and America's Trade Agreements*. Baltimore: Johns Hopkins University Press.LaFeber, Walter. 1994. *The American Age: United States Foreign Policy at Home and Abroad, 1750 to the Present*. New York: W. W. Norton.

_____. 2002. *America, Russia, and the Cold War, 1945–2002*. Boston: McGraw–Hill.

Leffler, Melvyn. 1993. *A Preponderance of Power: National Security, the Truman Administration, and the Cold War*. Palo Alto, CA: Stanford University Press.

Lowenthal, Mark M. 2008. *Intelligence: From Secrets to Policy*. Washington, DC: CQ Press.

Mearsheimer, John J., and Stephen M. Walt. 2007. *The Israel Lobby and U.S. Foreign Policy*. New York: Farrar, Straus and Giroux.

Mintz, Alex, and Karl DeRouen Jr. 2010. *Understanding Foreign Policy Decision Making*. Cambridge: Cambridge University Press.

Polsky, Andrew J. 2012. *Elusive Victories: The American Presidency at War*. New York: Oxford University Press.

Rodman, Peter W. 2009. *Presidential Command: Power, Leadership, and the Making of Foreign Policy from Richard Nixon to George W. Bush*. New York: Alfred A. Knopf.

Sanger, David E. 2012. *Confront and Conceal: Obama's Secret Wars and Surprising Use of American Power*. New York: Broadway Books.

Saunders, Elizabeth N. 2011. *Leaders at War: How Presidents Shape Military Interventions*. Ithaca, NY: Cornell University Press.

Skidmore, David. 2010. *The Unilateralist Temptation in American Foreign Policy*. New York: Routledge.

Sloan, Stanley R. 2002. *NATO, the European Union, and the Atlantic Community*. New York: Rowman & Littlefield.

Snow, David M. 2016. *The Middle East, Oil, and the U.S. National Security Policy: Intractable Conflicts, Impossible Solutions*. New York: Rowman & Littlefield.

Spanier, John, and Steven W. Hook. 2009. *American Foreign Policy since World War II*. Washington, DC: CQ Press.

Wildavsky, Aaron. 1966. "The Two Presidencies." *Trans-Action* IV (December): 7–14.

Woodworth, Steven E. 2008. *Manifest Destinies: America's Westward Expansion and the Road to the Civil War*. New York: Alfred A. Knopf.

Online Resources

- https://www.cia.gov/library/publications/the-world-factbook/. The World Factbook, located on the Central Intelligence Agency webpage, "provides information on the history, people, government, economy, geography, communications, transportation, military, and transnational issues for 267 world entities."
- http://www.state.gov/. The home page for the U.S. Department of State.

CREDITS

CHAPTER 1

p. 5: Library of Congress Prints and Photographs Division Washington, D.C.; p. 19: Sammie Feeback, Courtesy of Harry S. Truman Library; p. 24: George Bush Presidential Library and Museum

CHAPTER 2

p. 33: Howard Chadler Christy - *The Indian Reporter*; p. 45: AP Photo/Ron Edmonds; p. 49: Gerald R. Ford Presidential Library

CHAPTER 3

p. 72: ASSOCIATED PRESS/Chris Carlson; p. 82: AP Photo/John Raoux; p. 94: George H.W. Bush Presidential Library and Museum; p. 101: Associated Press/Paco Anselmi

CHAPTER 4

p. 117: Library of Congress Prints and Photographs Division Washington, D.C. 20540; p. 118: AP Photo; p. 132: AP Photo/Doug Mills

CHAPTER 5

p. 152: Courtesy Ronald Reagan Library; p. 155: AP Photo/Byron Rollins; p. 174: AP Photo

CHAPTER 6

p. 185: Library of Congress Prints and Photographs Division Washington, D.C. 20540; p. 206: AP Photo/J. Scott Applewhite; p. 214: AP Photo/Wilfredo Lee

CHAPTER 7

p. 222: White House Official Photographer; p. 233: LBJ Library photo by Yoichi Okamoto; p. 239: AP Photo

CHAPTER 8

p. 264: AP Photo/Susan Walsh; p. 294: AP Photo/Evan Vucci, File; p. 297: Official White House Photo by Chuck Kennedy

CHAPTER 9

p. 300: U.S. National Archives and Record Administration; p. 315: AP Photo/Susan Walsh; p. 327: LBJ Library photo by Cecil Stoughton

CHAPTER 10

p. 350: AP Photo/Ron Edmonds; p. 345: AP Photo; p. 371: The U.S. Army; Dwight D. Eisenhower Presidential Library

INDEX

Note: Page references in italics indicate photograph; followed by "*f*" indicate figure; "*t*" indicate table.